Practical Friendship

Christian Langkamp

Current Print Edition v. 0.95 – not for resale

The material in the appendix such as the friendship inventory are also made available on the companion website www.practicalfriendship.com where further links will be collected and provided.

Impressum: Autor: Christian Langkamp
Umschlaggestaltung: Selbst
Lektorat/Korrektorat: Cordula Langkamp
Satz mit LaTeX und BibLaTeX, mikTeX distribution

Aktuell Selbstverlag: Am Bilderstock 10, 41352 Korschenbroich
Version 1.0 wird finalisiert, sobald ein offizieller Verlag gefunden ist.

Contents

Preface

If loneliness is an epidemic or disease, then the antidote is meaningful social connections. Building connection can be achieved in three contexts - family, friends and community. Family and the functionality or dysfunctionality of the core unit - the romantic relationship of usually two people - has been studied extensively by psychologists. The scientific research has been adapted for popular readability by J. Gottman and Silver, 2015 and others, and thus science based advice on how to improve romance and family is available. Community likewise under various headings of civil society is being studied by sociologists, and whilst this is an ongoing effort as society changes, comprehensive books like Putnam, 2000 assess the state of society under social capital, cohesion or happiness perspectives. The theory is sufficiently well developed to be understandably connected right into people's lives. Policy can and is being developed, and while a few setbacks always occur, these efforts to improve society based on scientific research are bearing fruit. When delving into the topic of friendship, what startled me was the lack of a general definition of the object. For years I had the habit of giving away books as presents which I thought had been useful to me for resolving key questions facing me in my life:

- Seligman, 2004 'Authentic Happiness' was great for figuring out one's purpose and strengths coupled with the link to the website for the 240 question VIA Character Strength Survey,
- J. Gottman and Silver, 2015 'Seven principles' for avoiding the main pitfalls in romantic relationships [1],
- MacAskill, 2015 'Doing good better' for a good way to think on the 'what do I do with my life' question with the paradigm of effective altruism,
- I. Yalom, 1980 'Existential psychotherapy' for an in depth self evaluation to the 'Something is wrong with me, what now' assessment[2]
- Dobelli, 2017 'Art of the good life' for general life wisdom from a neo-stoic perspective.

[1] I am not the expert here, unfortunately this aspect has largely evaded me to date, but these books have prevented major emotional clumsiness on my side, and the recipients of the books likewise acknowledged that these books helped them along in their thinking

[2] I find the reduction of humankind's existential problems to just four question a genuine masterpiece of bringing philosophy and psychology together

All these books were highly readable, yet were based on a comprehensive and solid foundation in research and scientific thinking. Between those five books, they seemed to provide an answer to almost any character or relationship development issue I encountered over the years. A bit more precisely, they provided starting points and perspectives how to think about such personal problems. However regarding friendship I have to date simply not found that book yet, at least not in the breadth and depth I was looking for.

At first, not finding an in-depth 'How to do friendship' resource book was a continual annoyance for me. I had little snippets of insight from my own friendships which sufficed for discussions over a bottle of wine, but nothing in proper book strength. By this I mean that it is not an opinion of an elegantly writing author synthesised from a dozen personal friendships, but based on a thorough command of 'what is out there' deducing a reasonably comprehensive and covering a generally acceptable consensus view. There are very well written, easy to read self help books on friendship with some wonderful suggestions. Often however these books propose a conjecture or model only a singular aspect well that seemed important to a specific school of thought (such as virtue to the philosopher or emotional disclosure to the psychologist). Furthermore in the emphasis of such themes, the lack of foundation on broad sociological data and tie-in with philosophical sources did highlight limitations of the claims made. The more I was searching for it, the more I realized the need for such a general investigation. In my own social bubble, most people had well functioning social networks, but reports such as the annual publications of the Campaign to End Loneliness show that for vast swathes of society friendship is an elusive element of reality. In particular, loneliness in old age (conventionally defined by retirement in the sixties) was identified as a problem[3]. Given that most of us are well integrated into some degrees of friendship networks in school and early working life, the bulk of the problem transformed to a 'what do people fail to do in the time of adulthood from loosely 30 to 60, that leaves them lonely after this period'.

And thus I set out to collate what material I could find on what people through the ages thought to be 'the best practices of doing friendship' and the result is this book. While I will tie it together in a general concept in the chapter on process, I am therefore cautious that this analytic exercise will generate anything more than a reasonable conjecture at this point. What I however hope to achieve is to identify the moving parts, the elements of the object of friendship, and what can be deduced as likely candidates for good practices. The goal was to create a basis of further discussion.

The market of shorter self help text books just focusing on practical recommendations is excellently covered by Shumway, 2018, Nelson, 2016, Asatryan, 2016 and Rath, 2006 and Millington, 2019. Doubtlessly other books will be added to this list in the coming years. At the other end of the spectrum are the academic collection books of Hojjat, Moyer, and Halpin, 2017 in psychology and the philosophical but highly readable expositions of Alberoni, 2016 and Nehamas, 2016. This book is trying to cover the middle ground as a resource text book, covering academic theory and tying it to practical recommendations. The book that strikes a similar balance is Degges-White and Borzumato-Gainey, 2011 who provides an excellent

[3]Loneliness research particularly in the context of the pandemic points however to the ubiquity of the problem also within the younger generations.

insight into friendship development of women, combining great overview of sociological research with normative insight on how to strengthen female friendships.

I genuinely passionately care about the issue of loneliness, and I think the material collected may help some people to genuinely improve their general perspective on friendship and find ideas on measures that can reduce loneliness in our society. I received consistent feedback that it is great at triggering thoughts and ideas - both on a personal individual level and thinking about one's social environment, and that is its key purpose. There are several practical goals I want to achieve with this, but long term the key contribution is the collation of themes to help consolidate a friendship oriented extensive loneliness or attachment measure. By this I mean rather than asking 'do you feel lonely' or 'do you have somebody to discuss personal problems with' it would be fantastic to develop a questionnaire that is both robust and points which friendship need specifically is not being met for the person queried. This could then allow for very targeted recommendations and interventions both on an individual level and societal and organizational.

This book has a few sections reflecting on the ongoing pandemic. This of course dates this book as written in 2020/2021 during the various lock downs. As this situation changes and the pandemic ends, those sections will need to be rewritten.

I really hope that by reading the following text, you gain ideas for both yourself (maybe adopt the 5 step program set out in section 12.5) and lonely people around you. Good luck with that !

Christian Langkamp
Oxford, April 8, 2021

A part of a book preface always the argument needs to be made why the author is best qualified to write this book. And here is the disclaimer, I don't think I am a highly qualified singular subject-matter expert. On nearly every field that friendship touches, I know that there are experts who know the matter better than me: I am not a philosopher, but have read my share of philosophical books. I am not a psychologist, but loved various academic books on psychology such as I. Yalom, 1980 or Peterson and Seligman, 2004. I am not a classicist, but I sat through a respectable 8 years of Latin and 3 years of classical Greek in school and kept reading. Thus I kept a reasonable acquaintance with Aristotle, Cicero and awareness of the richness of classical concepts such as virtue and reason. I am not a theologian, but my years at Oxford and friendship with some theologians exposed me to thorough discussions and suitable material. I am not a sociologist, but being a trained mathematician and economist allowed me to reasonably competently read the papers. As my school teachers would assert, my writing skills were substantially below par. All I had in the end was passion for the subject and substantial amounts of time on my hand because of still being single end of my thirties. Additionally, I had the immense luck of meeting again and again people who were prepared to help me with advice, suggestions and introductions, always one step at a time (see the epilogue for a list of thanks). Those were the people with whom I could check my understanding of concepts and interpretations, and thus through their help could ensure accurate representation of the concepts in this book. I had originally budgeted another half year of revisions and research. However in Spring 2021 when giving preliminary copies to some friends and some reviewers the feedback was substantially more positive than expected, and I was encouraged to move towards publication. In particular the rationale was that the goal of providing a thinking help to review and improve friendship development and maintenance had been achieved and was needed at this point in time of the last phase of the COVID-19 pandemic.

This is now a stable version, though I will regularly update the PDF on the website.

Chapter 1

Introduction

> Friendship is unnecessary, like philosophy, like art, like the universe itself (for God did not need to create) . It has no survival value; rather it is one of those things which give value to survival.
>
> C.S. Lewis, The Four Loves

> Loneliness is the leprosy of the West.
>
> Mother Teresa

1.1 Why do we need friendship

The difficult cases

Mary is in an old people's home. She moved there after her partner of many years died and she because of personal frailty could not manage some household chores. As her income was too low to procure outside help such as a live-in helper, her family convinced her to move into an old people's home. Even just moving 15 km down the road, she lost access to the neighbours with whom she had loose friendly relations for years, as the public transport bus connection is not direct. She did not maintain the close friendships from her school years after she married, and none of the new casual friends she met later life developed into a close friendship. The activities in the home do not excite her, and thus she sits in her room most of the days watching TV.

John is a young man of 20 years. Not a stellar performer in school, he cracked under pressure as his parents divorced during his GCSE[1] and got very low marks. He dropped out of school also as financial resources were scarce, and his friendships faded as priorities and common topics between him and his school friends who stayed in school diverged. John pursued vocational training in electronic media and technology, however, as with the start of Covid his employer placed

[1] British High School exams when students are 16, setting the stage for the Pre-University stage of A-levels

John on furlough[2]. John has been living with his mum now in lockdown for a year, with no meaningful contact to suitable peers outside some anonymous online gaming contacts.

Philip and Paula have been married for 25 years and had one son. Despite being good parents, the relationship to their son is distant. Political and social views and interests diverged over time and thus contacts are mostly restricted to semiannual visits for Christmas and Paulas Birthday. Phonecalls are rare and they are even unsure whether these are only initiated by their son out of duty rather than genuine connection. After moving cities for Philip's job and concentrating on family life, they did not make any new friends in the new place whilst the friendships from school and university faded. In his mid-fifties now, Philip has been diagnosed with pancreatic cancer and is - additional to his own worries on dying soon- filled with remorse and dread whether it is his fault that Paula in a few months will face the world without him and any other friends to count on.

There are millions of such cases living in the Western world. The suffering is enormous and ubiquitous, though cannot be seen in everyone's face. And we need to help friendship bloom to prevent such cases as described above. For me there is a simple question whenever I hear such a case of acute loneliness: 'Is this necessary?' or 'Is there really nothing simple that they could have done differently?'. The answer to me was that many of these people could start friendships, but then unnecessarily (!) fail in the development and maintenance phase.

The candidates 'at risk'

Mary is a single professional accountant of 30 years living in London. Her girl gang and her in the past years met up every weekend. However, two of them recently have gotten married, and also the others are in long term committed relationships. Mary suddenly is worried that once family life arrives for them, the gang might break apart. Wondering if there is anything that can be done to maintain the group, albeit in a slightly different form, she also realises that she may need to expand her social circle.

Ulisses is a manager of 45 years living in the suburbs. He is married and has two children. Shortly before Christmas he gets away from his home duties for one evening and meets up with two old friends Steven and Peter from university days. Over dinner it occurs to the three of them that they essentially had not met for an entire year, whereas in their 20ies even during working life hardly a week would pass without them having had a beer. They end up talking about Peter's parents, who live by themselves with hardly any outside social contact, and wonder whether they will be like them twenty years down the road.

These two cases are something many people can relate to. We all know that life is busy and a myriad of other obligations makes sure it stays that way. Yet at various moments throughout our year we wonder whether our priorities are

[2]Temporary redundancy with state support

right, and whether we should not do a little more to give appropriate priority to our friends. It is the key assumption of this book that the **best way** to not become a candidate at risk and the best way to avoid becoming a difficult case is to **keep one's friendships in good repair**. This book is the result of an investigation of how to do this best by building and maintaining good friendships.

1.2 Goal of this book

This book is an academically styled resource book on good friendship. It is tailored to two groups:

- **professionals or lay people** who want to improve friendship building in our society, und thus understand how 'it works' in order to get ideas and suggestions for individuals, organisations and society.
- **researchers** in sociology, psychology, communications and public health, who want to expand their perspective on friendship beyond their own traditional school of thought and find out how to make their research more applicable to the fight against loneliness.

The primary aim of this report is a description of 'good friendship'. Whilst this includes academic analysis, this is not at its core. Several books look at friendship how it should be in an idealised state but with a narrow focus, from Aristotle's friendship of the virtuous to Nelson's friendship of positivity, consistency and vulnerability. I want to answer three questions but in the broadest possible scope[3]:

- **Seeing friendship**: What are people grateful and appreciative for in their friendship looking at the past? What do they enjoy in and love about their friendships and what makes them look forward to seeing their friends again? This goal will be realised by providing comprehensive definitions and illustrations of the key themes synthesized from the various literary sources.
- **Understanding friendship**: What perspective do we get on aspects of friendship once the various statements and assertions are brought together? What themes emerge as essential, what themes are more complementary? This goal will be realised by bringing the various sources together who considered a theme as important, looking at interpretations, overlaps and differences in opinion.
- **Improving friendship**: The purpose is to identify practices that help people improve existing friendships and build new ones more effectively. This goal will be realised by bringing together thought [cues] for self-reflexion or activity proposals for developing and intensifying friendships.

This is the core of the book, a derivation of to what degree a consensus view is possible to be distilled from philosophy, psychology, sociology and general

[3]I will explain the method later , but essentially the basis is an extensive literature review of philosophical, psychological, sociological, self help and new media literature. By new media literature I mean items such as newspaper columns, sermons, Ted talks and podcasts.

sources, and to what degree these schools of thought come to different conclusions. Once the object of friendship is suitably described, captured and understood in its aspects, further analysis becomes more fruitful. This includes the attempt to synthesise a process model for friendship (7) and then analyse the problems of maintaining friendships in current society (8) and managing friendship in old age. Also, it allows to subdivide the relationship into a role-based model (9) expanding on Rath, 2006. Whilst this is based on current academic theory, it is more characterised by identifying the gaps where self help and philosophy conjectures good practices that however have not been validated by sound psychometric and sociological research. The goal is to sketch out a sociological theory of friendship that provides a framework to analyse loneliness and develop and evaluate measures to reduce it. The last part will then collate what can be deduced as potential takeaway suggestions both on an individual and a society level to foster friendship (11) and give an outlook onto possible future research.

In all cases, I assume you are convinced that friendship is good for you or people in general and you think it is a suitable medicine or tool against loneliness. You want to do something against loneliness, whether in your own small private circle or in the grander scheme of things, and look for new ideas on how to go about it. The book operates on two levels. Primarily it tries to present a **description and good practices** of friendship. These are to trigger thought and interventions with oneself. They might also serve as suggestions for topics in casual conversation. It is conceivable to build a podcast from it, use the material to develop a social skills course for lonely people, potentially even derive some measures of public policy or public health from it. But at the current stage it is merely a structured collection of material to better enable interdisciplinary debate and understanding of friendship and why it is the ideal tool to combat loneliness.

On a supportive level is the attempt via a data driven meta study to see how much of the conjectured insights can be corroborated by **academic discourse**. As the latter however will only address a subset of specialised readers, I will separate these parts out into comments sections which can be skipped without loss of general content or enjoyment of the exposition of friendship. The core goal is to identify potential candidates for a future friendship attachment scale and providing the links to how existing research can help support our understanding of friendship.

Whilst books in general are written to be read cover to cover, this is by far not the only way nor the most fruitful way to read this book. For full exposition of material passages of the appendix can be jumped to for full exposition of methodology and context. However, they are rather dry and only interesting for the researcher crowd, and thus were relegated to the appendix.

As written in the preface, I hope that lay people will read it, and have included signposts for a casual reading path that skips elements of methodology and academic discussion. It thus focuses solely on the individual and societal improvement material. The fastest way to read the book is to skim - reading only the 'suggestions for thought' in chapters 3, 4 and 5. If one of these suggestions triggers your thoughts, you can just stop and read the relevant background of the section.

1.3 The problem of loneliness

Loneliness is bad for people afflicted by it, and a general rough comparison of the physical health impact of loneliness is the equivalence to smoking 15 cigarettes a day. Additionally loneliness can be even seen as similar to acute hunger (see

Tomova et al., 2020). If you decided to read this book, I assume I will not need to make to you a lengthy argument for the value of connection through friendship and the problem of loneliness - if interested, a substantial review of the medical impact is given Xia and Li, 2018. The bottom line on loneliness is that it is bad and undesirable. Thus the attempt to reduce it should be both a personal and societal goal[4]. The resulting question of course is, why are people lonely. As with any big question, the answer is complex. Indeed, a comprehensive 'solving the problem' answer would and should be on the short list for several prizes, maybe even the Nobel prize for medicine or peace. This book will not achieve that. It does however aim to describe comprehensively the age-old institution of friendship and how it can improve the condition of some people suffering from loneliness.

People feel lonely in part because they do not have any **close** (!) friends[5]. Loneliness can thus in part also be labelled friendlessness. The reason that someone you are concerned for does not have any close friends can be attributed to four sub-statements, at least one of which must hold. At some point it occurred to me that the (adjusted biblical) parable of sowing seeds to plant a forest was also useful to illustrate this point.

1. They bought no seeds: They didn't meet people who they recognised a sufficient friendship potential with.

2. They bought the seeds and planted them, but did not water them: They met people, got to know them and recognized the potential, but didn't develop the friendship.

3. They planted and initially watered them, but then weed came in and suffocated the plants: They didn't maintain the friendships over time.

4. Someone burned the tree down: throughout our life course people expectedly and sometimes unexpectedly die.

The focus of this book is on the good habits that are helpful in developing and maintaining a friendship. However, it is important to be aware of the other obstacles to establishing a friendship that lonely people may have. An extended list of the four themes of the parable is provided in D. It is intended not as an exhaustive checklist, but people unhappy about not having any (close) friends usually admitted two or three of the subthemes as potential causes. Thus with it you are likely to identify potential first steps to take to overcome initial obstacles. My focus for this book however is (1) primarily on **appreciating and maintaining friendships** that are great already, and (2) additionally on **recognizing** the ones with **greater potential** and developing them.

[4]There is a concept called solitude, which is being by oneself by choice. Loneliness is unchosen alone-ness

[5]The **close** is the important part and I will come back to it in the good practice and policy section

Chapter 2

Definition of friendship

If your interest is only casual reading,
please skip ahead to the section 2.4

To be friends, then, they must be mutually recognized as bearing goodwill and wishing well to each other for one of the aforesaid reasons.

Aristotle, Nicomachean Ethics

Voluntary interdependence between two persons over time, that is intended to facilitate social-emotional goals of the participants, and may involve varying types and degrees of companionship, intimacy, affection, and mutual assistance.

Hays, 1988, p.395

2.1 Challenges for a definition

Before we can continue with describing how friendship works, we need to address on what concept of friendship we mean. The question of 'how does a person A know or decide that a person B is a friend' has grappled humankind for at least four thousand years with themes of friendships elaborated upon already in the Gilgamesh epic. The transformation of the concept of friendship throughout the times has been explored in manifold fashion in books such as Mark Vernon, 2010 or Grayling, 2013 and shall not be repeated here[1]. While these mostly focused on male friendships, since the start of a scholarly female perspective on friendship established by Gilligan, 1982 research has caught up with works such as M. Yalom, 2015. Often these stay in a tradition such as the classical philosophical school, a feminist school or an extended enlightenment/early modern time focus, but rarely seriously expand into the insights of modern psychological and sociological research. Likewise, modern surveys of friendship such as the recent one

[1] I collected a short introduction of the key sources in the appendix - E on page 375.

edited by Hojjat, Moyer, and Halpin, 2017 provide a full coverage of the sociological and psychological research, but are essentially oblivious of most classical and philosophical writing on the matter[2].

In the 20th century sociologists and psychologists such as Simmel and Heider started studying the concept of friendship, whether more its nature and effects within the pair or dyad, or what impact it has on networks and how people move within society and networks. Theories on Social Penetration theory and Social Exchange theory have been conjectured, elaborated upon and tested. Sociologists and psychologists are unsettled about the loss of meaning of 'friend' given today's superficiality. It is thus Facebook kidnapping the term as a label for connection on their platform. Equally, the supposedly more meaningful term 'friendship' classifying the relationship that two 'true' friends have towards each other is not even close to uniformly agreed upon. Indeed, even linguistically classical philosophers, psychologists and sociologists can be shown to occupy different spheres even when addressing an identical theme[3]. In 2020 the criticism of Fischer, 1982 on the inadequacy of the various definitions of friendship available holds more than ever. Fischer, 1982, p.288 defines the task at hand thus: "These observations lead to the conclusion that "friend" is probably too vague a concept to be used in scientific research. We cannot, however, abandon it. It is too important a "folk concept", an idea that people use to order their worlds. And, it is too much a part of our own intellectual apparatus. But we should at least have a systematic, empirical understanding of what Americans seem to mean when they call someone a friend." Matthews, 1986 likewise criticises the inadequacy and partiality of focus of various friendship definitions in sociological and psychological literature prior to her exploration of friendship in old age.

It is almost like the two disciplines of both classical & modern philosophy and sociology & psychology coexist on different planets, in different ivory towers, with Chinese walls in perfect working order. But which discipline's insights should now the interested lay person turn to in order to find out about good or true friendship? What properties or descriptors can distinguish a good friend and differentiate her or him from a mere acquaintance or temporary friendly relation? Which author or works should they turn to in order to find out not just to recognize, but actually how to improve or spice up their existing friendships?

2.2 Building bottom up

It is not surprising that books or texts coming from different disciplines or schools of thought emphasise different things, even when looking at the common object. Historians and philosophers usually trace the subject by school of thought. This is often then ordered by evolution through time. Psychology usually separate out by focus group, e.g. children, adults or gender. Sociologists generally look

[2]While Aristotle is cited, Cicero (or Laelius), Epicurus, Seneca, Olyan, biblical references to Jonathan and David or Jesus and his Disciples, or Augustine are all absent. Likewise, modern philosophers like Nehamas, Alberoni, Grayling are nowhere to be found. A singular quote of C. S. Lewis is used out of context to corroborate the view of friendship having a powerful influence on health. Given that a core statement in Lewis, 1960 is 'friendship having no survival value' this shows the disconnect between the image of friendship purported in the psycho-sociological school and the classical thought (of which Lewis is a rather peculiar instance).

[3]see e.g. 'good will' and 'care'

at social groups from whom they can recruit sufficient data at low cost, such as university students or elderly, and where a sociologically interesting theme can be further developed, e.g. race, age, gender, sexual preference groups. Self help books focus usually on a single theme that is presented as the single point solution to all the reader's worries about the subject. All these approaches are valid and serve a good purpose of knowledge generation and distribution, but fall short on building a general understanding of the topic of friendship.

I tried a different approach, which can loosely be described as lumping by theme. Any content qualifies as 'valuable' irrespective of its academically validated or on-the-spur creation (blog pieces on Medium or Youtube), with the connecting pieces being the themes addressed. Any descriptive material is considered. I end up with a framework or theory, but I view the merit of this text not in showing own exposition of what friendship is and provide a theory. The goal is to collect neutrally (at first) what others have written about it, contrasting views on issues or simply showing collective agreement on the important issues. A side aspect is a clarification of language and concepts, addressing Fischer, 1982 and Rath, 2006's concerns. In some texts the concepts are of course clear, however just like friendship or love, words like positivity, pleasure or companionship can mean different things in different contexts. By offering definitions I hope to support future clarity and the possibility of creation of conceptual mappings. Thus the concept of 'companionship' as employed by e.g. Rath encompasses a common experience, reliability and time spent in close proximity. A situationship as often heard in Expat circles is a friendship marked by a strong sense of respect for privacy and independence knowing that at some point in the future you will geographically part ways, but you appreciate and enjoy each others company for this moment, possibly even to pursue a joint hobby. Similarly, other subcultures have their own labels for types of friendships, and using the themes explored in the coming chapter it becomes easier to describe and categorize them.

People like to look at the big picture. It always sounds good. However, this is not what this book is attempting to do. If you think about all these books and texts about friendship above mentioned like beautiful wall tapestries, then what I suppose I do is turn them around, look at the (ugly) back, and simply look at the cloths and materials that were used to construct the grand stories and theories that concern friendship. And by categorising them and describing them, it might help other people to construct their story or theory. The parcellisation of snippets of course has its disadvantages, and there is something wonderful about well argued books with a Theseus like red fathom leading the reader through the Minoan labyrinth[4]. However, the big theme here is to show the commonalities between ancient and modern theory on specific issues. I want to show how some statements from Aristotle and Cicero line up rather well with modern sociological and psychological theory[5], and how on other themes the schools of thoughts are most strongly at odds with each other[6]. Having reviewed the different themes of all these books, I have concluded however that a single leading fathom to explain friendship is not possible. The phenomenon of friendship is more like a

[4]In particular Nehamas, 2016 is a brilliant book on this front. It has great depth, is very balanced and wonderful to read.

[5]e.g. those on the importance of goodwill and trust

[6]Privacy, the interpretation of loyalty commitment, the necessity of virtue

set of 50 different fathoms or materials, each of which is important on its own merit as a beautiful aspect, and only together do they provide a web of friendship like a Bayeux Tapestry. The four chapters on personality strengths, relationship attitudes, activities and resources, which represent the core of the book, will go through these. All books on friendship create a reasonably specific definition, but the used definition for this text is based on a selection of a limited set of conceptual building blocks. But their composition and emphasis diverges in different friendships and friendship theories, sometimes substantially so.

There is a second danger to this approach of synthesising themes based on excerpts, and that is citing out of context and either intentionally or unintentionally misconstruing arguments. The problem is particularly well known in the discipline of theology, where it is said that almost any opinion and its opposite can be argued based on a suitably chosen set of bible quotations. It is my hope that the weights of the frequency analysis (see F.1) prove to be relatively robust to this criticism, and that specialists reading the material might not identify too many such mishaps. But for this reason I included the respective verbatim quotes and precise locations to invite readers to challenge their understanding of themselves if an argument does not meet their pre-held intuition.

2.3 Introduction to the framework

Method of generation of themes

This coming three chapters 3, 4 and 5 are the core of this text. Rather than focussing on networks, functions, resources or process models, I focus on a single question: 'What do people say is good about a friendship'. What do they say they appreciate in their friends' personality, what do they appreciate in their attitudes and behaviour towards each other, what aspects do they find valuable or enjoyable. Sometimes when we look to find out what is relevant or special about human behaviour, we pose the hypothetical question how you would explain love/money/any other social construct to an alien visiting on earth. This usually results in a description of key attributes and observables rather than a deep philosophical theory. According to Rath, 2006, p.79 'only 30% of people find it easy to describe what each friends contributes to their life.' from which he deduces the need for a common language for description of friendship. This perceived inability or shortfall in people's capacity to describe friendship has been my guidance when looking through all the various texts on friendships. At first I was making a list of sentences and statements and after about 1000 such elements started a first attempt at grouping into keywords and overarching themes. The now achieved classification of recurring themes of friendships was a result of slow iteration and expansion. At around 2500 tags, most of the key themes were identified and their subthemes divided up. At this point the division into personality, relationship attitude, activity and resource started to emerge as a conceptual possibility. In the end I ended up with about 10000 tags of about 300 keywords to sentences in the literature. Loosely the friendship personality strengths are inspired by the VIA[7] Character Strengths of Seligman, 2004, the friendship attitudes by the general sociological literature (Hall, Adams, Blieszner, Degges-White, Matthews, Oswald

[7]'Values in Action Inventory' at https://www.viacharacter.org/about

and De Vries to name but a few) and the activities by the friendship books such as Shumway, Greif, Degges-White and Rath. Sociological research frequently (e.g. in Blieszner and Adams, 1992) wrote also about the exchange of resources, however frequently those resources were disguised personality traits (love, knowledge), and thus I designated genuine resources (money, health) that are [external to personality]. Finally Lewis, 1960 draws a clear distinction between gift love and need love. Following this logic there is the necessity of a typology of psychological needs for systematizing friendship. Contrary to the exploratory approach I took with the traits and attributes, using a preexisting typology accepted by psychology research would be best. I found a sufficiently suitable fit in the one provided by Max-Neef, Elizalde, and Hopenhayn, 1992, having experimentally mapped the keyword list into it. I should note that I only looked at the broad category of non-fiction. Doing analysis of themes in classical literature such as the Metamorphoses or Iliad, or more recently a variety of novels such as Huckleberry Finn, Chronicles of Narnia and Enid Blyton's five friends was out of my scope for now and given my decidedly non-literary background outside my competency profile.

Describing the properties and their emphasis in context

Thus the focus in the coming chapters is really getting the observables right, noting where sources define a particular attribute as defining/necessary property or more a descriptive but non-essential desirable. Each section is - as described in the introduction - split into into three subsections. A description of the attribute or theme with its defined subthemes is followed by an explanation of the nuances of the theme in literature on friendship. As mentioned, for the understanding section, I have focused on using prior material, bringing other people's contributions together rather than generating an additional dataset. I usually do not try to argue for a specific interpretation, but want to display the variety in statements leaving the reader to think about it and see what reasonates with them most. The final part is then the thought or improvement suggestion, with a small collection of thoughts or question to trigger reflection on how this theme impacts the readers friendships. There is also a reference to the appendix, where citations of **quantitative studies**, such as Hall, 2012b, Apostolou, Keramari, et al., 2020 or Roberts-Griffin, 2011a are collected. I partitioned the list of factors or variables into **six impact groups** from **(1) high impact**, significance or relevance to **(6) low impact**. Thus I intend to provide oversight of which of those factors have explicitly been studied and what resulting impacts were recorded. Also in the appendix is the result of the counting study (F.1) for this trait and proposed sentences for further querying. Please look into the appendix in section E for summaries of the sources, the logic for their choices and the groupings.

Defining friendship by its properties

Resulting from this set of personality traits, relationship attitudes and activities it is possible to take Aristotle's original goodwill and virtue based **definition of friendship** and generalise it.

Friendship is a free relationship of two or more people,

1. who bring into the friendship some personality strengths conducive to forming a relationship and attractive to the respective other,
2. who develop an attitude to, appreciation and understanding of each other through past interactions,
3. who repeatedly act out their friendship with and towards each other through a variety of activities.

The personality of the participants, their attitude towards each other and the joint activities come together and all end up satifying the so called friendship needs as defined by Max-Neef and elaborated upon in section 6.11. This meeting of needs is enhanced by the resources that are accessible to the two friendship participants. The schematic of this relationship is shown in figure 2.1, which provides a context for the elements of the chapters 3 to 6.1. The full picture will then be brought together in chapter 7 when the general process is mapped out.

The approach of defining friendship from its properties rather than presenting a all-encompassing general definition was championed by Claude Fischer. Concretely Fischer, 1982, p.289 makes the claim to report observations, i.e. correlations but no causalities[8] when it comes to friendship.

Fehr, 1996 describes friendship development processes at great length, though for the purpose of this definition it is a start to note that both 'Friendship by Spark' style or the 'Takes time to Grow' friendship are proposed as natural in literature. It is thus not easy to decide whether the existence of friendship determines the attitude and activities, or whether activities and a developing attitude builds and develops the friendship.

The process of finally deciding on the key themes within the personality-attitude-activity triad came after a review of the classification of keywords. The basis for making a group of keywords into a theme by itself also was not so much finding a well sounding label of something that should be important, such as 'positivity' or 'understanding'. It was more the realisation of having a collection of 3-5 typical descriptive keywords that collectively described an important aspect but varied in nuances[9]. Roughly at the point of fifty themes further merging would have created themes that encompassed potentially different[10] statements grouped, and thus I stopped. I will now go through the fifty core themes and explaining what they mean or how they could be defined. Additionally to describing their core sentiment I will exhibit their main supporting sources and the variability of emphasis and importance assigned to the respective trait within the friendship liter-

[8]'And no causal claims are made, only claims of correlation. The fact that associates with whom respondents discussed their hobbies were especially likely to be called friends could mean that discussing hobbies determines whether an associate will be called a friend, or it could mean that respondents were especially likely to turn to people they called friends when they wanted to discuss their hobbies. Either causal interpretation would be appropriate.'

[9]Thus the theme of 'honesty and integrity' would be composed of 'X is honest' (general trait), 'X is trustworthy', 'X is authentic or genuine', and 'X gives honest feedback', all sentences which are not identical in meaning, but could be plausibly grouped together. A theme 'humility' would bring items such as 'is interested in others', 'listens well', 'is proud in their friends', and themes of conflict resolution together.

[10]Potentially different in the sense that I felt like I can see a person doing A, but decidedly not B. Thus I can love to explore and discover with a person, but I would not think of that person as someone who teaches me or whom I teach.

ature. Thus I would point out how Aristotle sees virtue as key to understanding friendship, or C. S. Lewis sees mutual understanding through a shared object of interest as core friendship enabler. On the contrary it might be the case that e.g. modern sociological surveys on friendship completely might exclude virtue from considerations, and C.S. Lewis might exclude emotional understanding and affection. Indeed I think this observation of omissions of themes is really helpful for general understanding and overview. To provide context I will also provide the summary of how across the entire data set of key word tags the different themes occur in frequency in figure 2.2.

2.4 Instructions for casual reading

Before you set out reading the following sections, particular if you do not class yourself in the hard-core sociologist academic category, a little mental image or story might be helpful for context. Imagine yourself on your classical deskjob, with the usual 8.30-5.30 working routine day in day out. A good civic life, a rented apartment where you live together with your partner, work during the week, social life on weekends, the odd holiday - life is good. Tuesday evenings is pub night with your old university friend, lets call him Clive. Clive is different, he is a free spirit, a writer and bon-viveur, who never gave up on bohemian life. His Tuesday consists of getting up when you are already at your desk, and rocking up to the local cafe and pub around 9.30 for breakfast. He then starts his reading for the book he has been writing for a while and which he is in no rush to finish. At 11 he embraces the oldest of British traditions - the liquid lunch - also known as the 11a.m. pint[11]. The afternoon is his push of productivity and creativity, as he writes, inspired by conversations and snippets around him. In the evening after your days work is done, you join him for another pint. Most such nights your partner joins you too given the sheer positive cheer, entertaining stories and cringeworthily awful but glorious jokes that Clive embellishes the evenings conversation with.

One day he starts the conversation on a different note. 'You know, a most curious thing happened today. I was having my morning pint, when the door opened and three fellows from the local college entered. I am not sure whether they were well read high school teachers on an hour break or lecturers of the local undergraduate college, but it was an odd mix. One was a classicist or theologian, the other one a psychologist or sociologist, and the third more the self-help self-taught general social worker. They clearly had known each other since early student years. And they began talking about friendship, and how they had been hanging out for a long time, yaddiyaddiyah and how it was just so precious to them. In short, I rather enjoyed listening in on their conversation rather than just continuing with my reading that I actually came here to do.' As you questioningly look at him and ask what was so interesting about it, Clive continues: 'well, since you ask, today they were talking about honesty, and what role it has in their friendship'. Having always been blessed with an annoyingly good memory, he starts to lay out to you and your partner whatever he remembered from the morning

[11]On loan from Hodgkinson, 2005, p.52 'There is nothing so perfect as pinball and a pint at 11 a.m.'. In a similar fashion JRR Tolkien and CS Lewis were often known to go for a pint or two at 1130 at Keeper's close to the Magdalen grounds.

conversation. With his recalled summary complete you order another round of pints and off you go into an evening filling conversation.

Reading instructions for casual reading:

- Flick through the chapters 3-6 and just read whatever catches your eye. [a]
- The best way to read a full chapter is sitting in a cafe or bar being slightly early and waiting for a friend to join you.
- The book is not designed to be read cover to cover, it is designed to be read until you have a thought to ponder on or come across a new potential habit to experiment with.
- The two chapters that are specifically designed for the casual reader are chapter 8 - Maintenance and 11 - Recommendations for practices. Those should not be missed.

[a] The other excellent location beside the bedside table is of course the restroom to pick it up repeatedly over the course of a few months and flick through whenever a convenient moment arises. That way an inspiring practical takeaway or suggestion for thought can be directly implemented in the course of the remaining day.

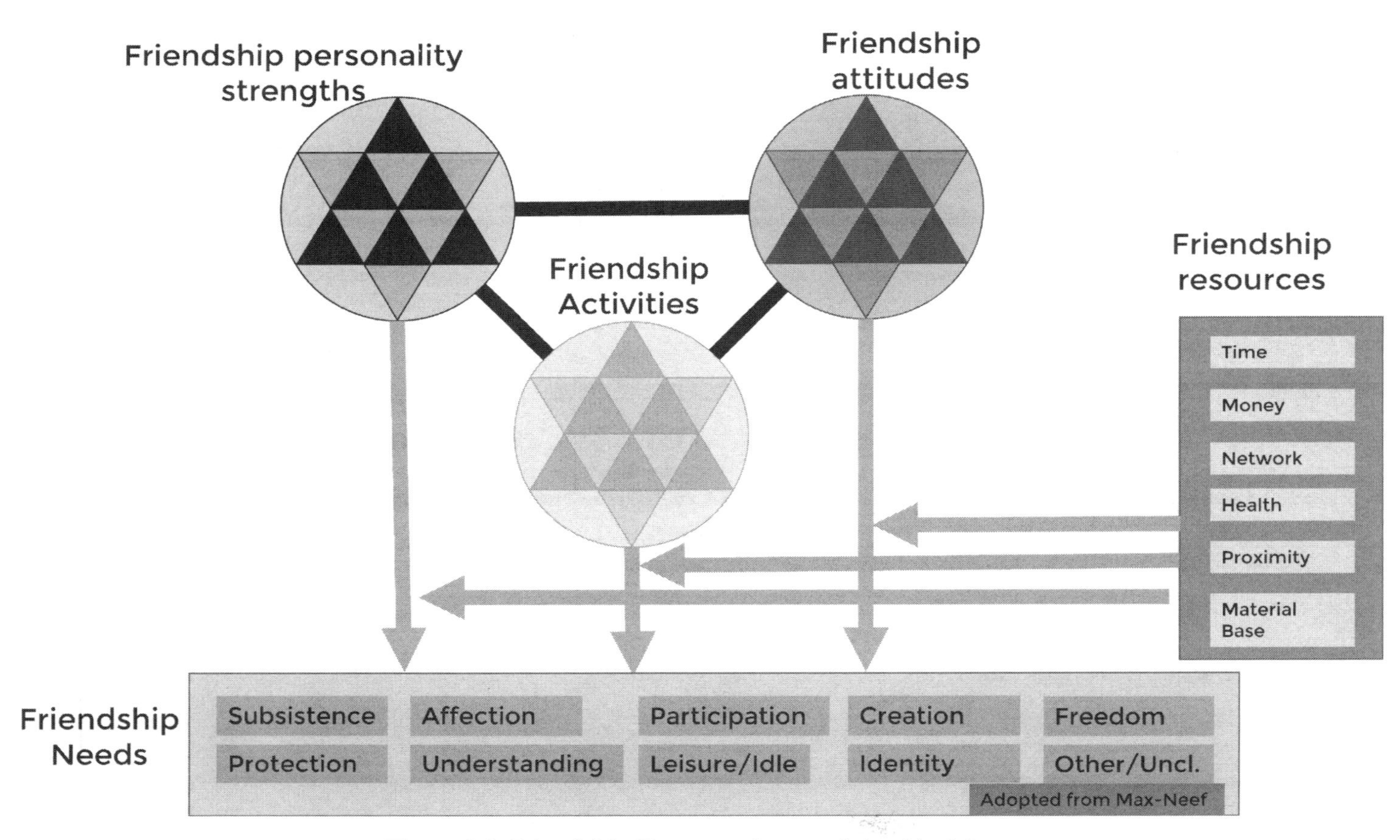

Figure 2.1: Friendship Framework as explained in 2.3

Personality %	22.9	Relationship %	48.1	Activities %	23.7	Resource %	5.2
Honesty	3.5	Shared History	4.5	Dirt Time	4.2	Proximity	1.3
Acceptance	2.2	Affection	2.8	Work Together	2.8	Content	0.9
Humility	2.1	FS Quality	3.7	Expression of Self	2.7	Health/Athl.	0.7
Reliability	2.0	Consideration	2.3	Being there	2.7	Network	0.7
Fun	2.0	FS Priority	3.6	Pract. Help	2.0	Time	0.4
Kindness	1.8	Loyalty	3.5	Circle	1.5	Material	0.4
Virtue	1.7	Independence	1.5	Encourage	1.4	Money	0.3
Intelligence	1.6	Enjoyment	3.4	Communion	1.2	NoMonPower	0.5
Positivity	1.4	Understanding	3.1	Effect Change	1.2	Attract.	0.1
Proactiveness	1.4	Reciprocity	3.0	Guidance	1.0		
Energy	1.2	Trust	3.0	Discovery	1.0		
Agreeableness	1.1	Openness	2.6	Teach & Learn	0.8		
Peace	1.0	Pride	2.4	Generosity	0.7		
		Benevolence	2.3	Vocal Support	0.6		
		Mut. Interest	2.2				
		Mutual Belief	2.0				
		DiffBG	0.2				
		Respect of Priv.	1.5				
		No Ind RespPriv	0.5				

Figure 2.2: Total Summary

Percentage figures from themes counting study F.1

Chapter 3

The personality traits

All sections are for casual reading

> Perfect friendship is the friendship of men who are good, and alike in virtue.
>
> Aristotle

Introduction

The personality traits, as written in the introduction, are strongly influenced in their composition by Peterson and Seligman, 2004. Their rationale comes from Aristotle and his insight that the goodness of the friends must be recognized and causal for the friendship to be good. Something is a personality trait, if the corresponding statement is 'I am friends with X because X is ... honest, kind, fun, intelligent.'. The personality traits or personality strengths loosely contribute 25% of the weight what people think is important in a friendship (the cluster centers are between 15% (old age) and 35% (young age)). This is a far cry from the all-importance of the virtuous character as postulated by the classical philosophers, but it does show remarkable significance.

Tot	OP	CP	TW	SH	CM	QS1	QS2	OA	YA	YS
23	24	20	25	25	24	20	24	15	34	NA
Weight share of personality traits										

The weights are from the frequency analysis explained in section F.1, the categories are OP: Old philosophers, CP contemporary philosophers, TW theological writers, SH self help, CM contemporary media, QS1 qualitative sociologist studies, QS2 quantitative sociologist studies, OA old age sociol. st., YA young age sociol. st., YS youth study.

3.1 Honesty, authenticity and integrity

We instinctively all know it when we see it in people. That **sincerity**, that 'this is genuinely me' aura honest and authentic people have about them. We

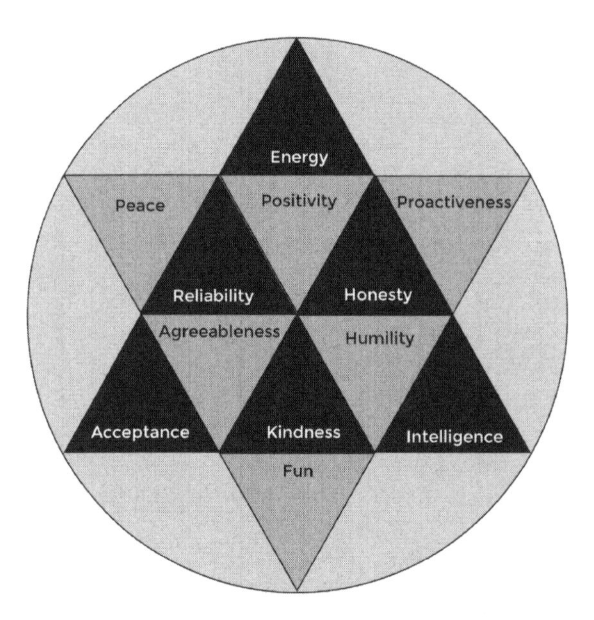

Figure 3.1: Personality Strengths

	Tot	OP	CP	TW	SH	CM	QS1	QS2	OA	YA	YS
Honesty	●	●	●	●	●	◒	●	●	◒	●	◒
Acceptance	◒	○	◒	◒	●	●	◒	◒	◒	●	◒
Humility	◒	◒	◒	●	●	●	◒	◒	◒	◒	◒
Reliability	◒	◒	◒	◒	◒	◒	◒	◒	◒	●	◒
Fun	◒	○	○	○	●	◒	◒	●	◒	●	◒
Kindness	◒	◒	◒	●	◒	◒	◒	◒	◒	◒	◒
Virtue	◒	●	●	◒	○	◒	◒	◒	◒	◒	◒
Intelligence	◒	○	◒	◒	◒	◒	◒	◒	◒	●	◒
Positivity	◒	◒	○	◒	◒	◒	◒	○	○	◒	◒
Proactiveness	◒	●	◒	◒	○	◒	○	◒	○	◒	◒
Energy	◒	○	○	○	◒	◒	○	◒	◒	●	◒
Social Ease	◒	○	○	○	○	◒	◒	○	◒	◒	◒
Peace	◒	○	○	◒	◒	○	○	○	○	◒	◒

Figure 3.2: Personality Strengths

trust our words to be safe with them. We feel that there is no 2nd person hiding in there behind a mask, but that word and thought are congruent, that they are straightforward and genuine.

At the foundation of building a relationship is our trust that what we experience with the friend is true, that the good will is sincere, and that we can trust our feelings and perceptions. This necessitates that the friend is honest with us. This need for **honesty** is almost self evident and assumed, but its importance comes in the breach. The feeling of betrayal or disbelief when you figure out that the friend is different to the one you thought you befriended, or the nature of your relationship is different to the one you thought you had (see 9.3). Now if you realise your view of the relationship was because of assumptions you made (erroneously), there is no issue: you adjust and move on. However, if a disappointment is because of dishonest statements of your friend regarding the relationship or facts about themselves, it becomes a substantial issue to the core of the relationship. Both Aristotle, 1925, 9.3[1] and Cicero, 1923, p.139[2] thus stress the necessity of truthful and honest interaction in friendship. The authors of psalm 28:3[3] condemn people who are not honest with their friends. Being honest and speaking truthful is also part and parcel of traditional virtue concepts, and thus also strongly related to virtue of the friend as per section 3.7.Alberoni, 2016, p.38[4] follows up on this, however more emphasising the issues of developing a friendship further limited by topics off-limits for self-disclosure. Note that this is consistent with his otherwise high regard for privacy and independence. The capability of easier lying and more difficult verification on social media based communication as Asatryan, 2016, p.24 elaborates, is one of the biggest obstacles to developing close relationships online.

The hallmark of an **authentic person** is that when they say something in general or to you, it reflects what they actually think[5]. There is an old school dictum 'to say what you mean and to mean what you say' that describes this well. A second level is the assurance that they do so, saying some behaviour is not OK (honest feedback), disputing nonsensical statements[6] or stating clearly when something substantially inconveniences us (c.f. Nelson, 2016, p.68[7]). Specifically, the explicit statement of inconveniences and impossibilities can be important in the long run, and can include things like expressing limits to resource availability (not having time, not having the funds to go to a fancy restaurant). As the alcohol in wine and beer has a tendency to make us speak more openly and truthfully, the function of eating and drinking together is also from this perspective a friendship enhancer ensuring the 'ground-truthing' of the friendship (see R. Dunbar, 2016 for a general discussion). More colloquially you may also think of the phrase 'in vino veritas' and the concept of 'nomunication' in Japan[8]. However, honesty is also

[1]'But one might complain of another if, when he loved us for our usefulness or pleasantness, he pretended to love us for our character. For, as we said at the outset, most differences arise between friends when they are not friends in the spirit in which they think they are.'

[2]'For while it is true that advantages are frequently obtained even from those who, under a pretence of friendship, are courted and honoured to suit the occasion; yet in friendship there is nothing false, nothing pretended; whatever there is is genuine and comes of its own accord.'

[3]'Those who communicate their good will to their friends, but evil in their hearts.', see also Olyan, 2017, p.43

[4]'The friend who has hidden his faults, but never asked the other to do anything evil, adheres to this rule. This type of friendship is a true friendship, even though it holds within it something fragile. One of the two has something to hide. He cannot be honest, cannot confide, cannot say anything important about his life. Friendship is a getting to know each other in ever greater depth. In this case there is an insuperable obstacle.'

[5]It is a different question if a person has to express it when they are of a different opinion or whether they can remain just silent and keep their air of honesty or authenticity. My hunch is that if a person is silent in a non-threatening environment (friends) when statements drastically opposed to their values are made, voicing of the disagreement is necessary.

[6]The colloquial expression here is 'calling out my bullshit'

[7]'One of my closest friends and I have a spoken agreement: We promise to ask for what we need, and we swear we will say 'no' if we can't.'

[8]'Nomunication'is the joining of 'nomu'- to drink - and communication and emphasises the role

something you bestow and gift to a friend. In our current society of woke culture and thin skins, being honest with a friend is a sign that you trust in their character to listen to you and take a potential comment with care and a degree of generosity for not always getting the wording right. Honesty expresses the trust that you listen to the sentiment and intention of what is being said and assume a spirit of good will, rather than strain the friendship or worse use what was spoken against the speaker by getting offended.

In section 4.13 on difference of background I describe how Nehamas, 2016, ch.0 conjectures a personality-per-friend thesis, and its evaluation in the context of authenticity might be controversial. I would take a definition of personality-authenticity to mean that a friend could be fully authentic in general settings, but that in the relaxed state of spending time with a close friend and when exposed to the wit, the intellect or the warmth of that friend, certain parts of our personality truly come to shine even further. The friendship rather than creating a different person enhances our base authenticity in the true sense of the phrase 'our friends bring out the best in us'[9].

We cannot put on an act with our friend. Alberoni, 2016, p.102 thus defines friendship to be free of and antithetical to the **theatrical roles**, which Erving Goffman claims underlie all human relationships[10]. In a similar style, people who put personal gain before authenticity and sincerity by feigning admiration - flatterers - are the personal bane of both Aristotle and Cicero, as well as hipocrites[11]. The need for authenticity in friendship is echoed at length in Wiest, 2020-04-30 arguing that true friendship must never become a performance. On the other hand, authenticity is also dependent on the listener. Asatryan, 2016, p.56[12] points out that in the presence of rose-tinted glasses it is likewise not possible to develop an authentic closeness in a relationship.

It is both a philosophical question as well as personal preference, whether and to which degree authenticity and integrity is universal in a person or has to be assessed specific to a relationship. But there are many examples in human interactions where people treat other people dishonestly or change their behaviour for advantages, yet act with perfect integrity towards their friends and families. Thus also in this case I split the theme into a personal trait, that is assumed to apply to anyone or most people the friend interacts with, and a relationship specific component that develops over time.

There is a level of trust in society that extends to people on an initial level, trust in reciprocity and in a range of other good characteristics and the name we apply

of alcoholic drinks in establishing honesty and trust in a developing relationship.

[9]Note that to bring out is the exact meaning of the word educere - education - the bringing out the personality from within- and thus an apt image for a different interpretation of authenticity in friendship.

[10]'Goffman analyses all interpersonal relationships like theatrical roles. Regarding each other men act as if each were his own public relations man.' using this analysis as describing the American society accurately and thus as sufficient argument to corroborate the claim that 'Of all contemporary societies America places the least importance on friendship and love.'

[11]Cicero, 1923, p.199 'Moreover, hypocrisy is not only wicked under all circumstances, because it pollutes truth and takes away the power to discern it, but it is also especially inimical to friendship, since it utterly destroys sincerity, without which the word friendship can have no meaning.'

[12]'In other words, if you reveal more about yourself over time yet find he doesn't believe you because these disclosures don't match his early idea of you, that's a problem. That's a red flag that he's falling for a fantasy of you.'

to the trait in which we place the trust is integrity[13]. Greif, 2009, ch2 states that 'Trust was a key component of friendship, and it does not always mean the same thing to everyone. Robert Putnam, in his book 'Bowling Alone', describes trust as the cornerstone of social connections. If you do something for me, you must trust that, at some point, I will do something for you. Without trust, friendships do not work.'. This is general trust, and ultimately it is based on the integrity of the other person. Putnam here references to reciprocity of benefaction, but the principle is more general than this. At the foundational level there is a belief whether any person is trustworthy that you have just met and who you have a first impression but no major first hand information about. This is generally uncontroversial, indeed believing someone saying the truth is the human default according to Levine, 2014. The second level of trust is then to apply it to a specific person on account of references of other friends and a gut feeling based on some level of interaction. Do you believe that they are an authentic person and act with integrity? That is personal trust. The third level of trust is the relational trust you develop within the interactions over the years, as a friendship develops. This is what I describe as trust and confidentiality in the Relationship Attitudes.

The conventional setting of confidentiality as the gold standard and the corresponding condemnation of gossiping however is controversial. Indeed R. Dunbar, 2004 points out its need in early evolution to identify free riders, and these mechanisms are still very active in a multitude of social contexts, last but not least the work place. McAndrew and Milenkovic, 2002 analyses uses of gossip today and finds that 'exploitable information in the form of damaging, negative news about non-allies and positive news about allies was especially prized and likely to be passed on.'. Thus integrity or avoidance of gossip is on two levels. One is the high integrity, and that is that no information is passed on. That is often the religious view. The second 'weak' form of integrity is that no damaging information about allies is passed on. A further dimension is general informational trustworthiness (general personal habit of non-gossiping) or person-matter-oriented trustworthiness (matters of confidentiality within the friendship). I will return to a liberal attitude towards gossip in section 6.3 on resource content.

Practical takeaway

As friendship is a relationship of person to person, it needs to be the real person who is participant in it. Even if you have a public persona in your professional life, you need to be your 'real you' with the friend. This friendship may take time to grow, and there might be caution at first, but once you are in 'steady state' you need to be honest and authentic with your friends and they with you.

Suggestions for thought

[13]Again, one could argue that this concept of integrity is indeed a weak form of virtue and thus argue for the combining of this section with that on virtue.

- To what degree are you willing to make a leap of faith and give someone the benefit of doubt of being trustworthy?
- Do you believe you can accurately gauge whether someone is being honest with you?
- How honest are you with your friends?
- If you observe a friend behaving differently with you than with others, is that an issue to you or not?

For statistics in sociological studies, question suggestions and weights in counting see H.

3.2 Acceptance, tolerance and flexibility

True friends don't judge each other, they judge other people together.

Emilie Saint-Genis

Acceptance is the capability to separate between action and person. It is the affirmation of the other as a person and being undogmatic about aspects of disagreement. **Acceptance** is the favourable reception of a person, whereas **tolerance** is the patient endurance of a persons traits or actions that resonate less well with you. The statement that 'a friend accepts you as a person, even when others don't' comes up often in characterisations. The opposite of it is judgement where you make explicit which traits or acts you disapprove of, often on moral grounds. Delaney and Madigan, 2017, Nehamas, 2016, Blieszner and Adams, 1992 and the MBTI characterisations emphasise this characteristic.

Despite the frequency of mentions of acceptance and tolerance in literature, this is not uncontested. Christian doctrines emphasize non-judgement and acceptance as character virtues. The philosophical tradition however in their focus on the virtuous character of friendship implies that friendship is established only after a mutual judgement or assessment has been made and the respective other has been judged worthy of friendship. Compare Alberoni, 2016, p.35 'I hold him responsible for what he has done. There is no passion 'above and beyond us.' I judge him on moral grounds. We are morally demanding of our friends, much more so than of other people.' These are no words of acceptance and tolerance. Even after the friendship is established no stopping is indicated. Cicero, 1923, p. 193 emphasises the initial testing but then explicitly requests a more accepting attitude as the friendship progresses: 'You should not appraise him after you have begun to love him'. Indeed, the free will involved in choosing to be friends with someone can be seen as an act of judgement, and thus the acceptance so valuable. Whereas family 'has to' accept us[14], the possibility of the friend to judge us and thus reject us confers value on us in the positive case.

[14]Cuddeback, 2010, p.52'It has a special quality of gratuity having been completely freely given, and a quality of objectivity that love from inside the family does not necessarily have.'

But whereas acceptance or tolerance of moral issues is contested, other aspects are consistently demanded to be subordinated to the friendship. It is also clear that the gold standard of friendship is acceptance. Tolerance can be a temporary state, but essentially endurance of traits we do not like should not be a constant theme in a well functioning friendship. For this context I view weak acceptance as accepting and loving your friend how they are for the moment and the immediate future, but hope for change and still think about how to effect it in the long run. Strong acceptance is accepting and loving your friend fully as he is including his less desirable traits now and also for the immediate and distant future.

I would put it that in the western world the contemporary general consensus is calling for strong acceptance on gender, age, difference of ethnicity, religion, wealth, education, profession and the likes, once friendship is established. Lewis, 1960, p.103 puts it like this: 'In a circle of true friends each man is simply what he is; stands for nothing but himself. No one cares twopence about any one else's family, profession, class, income, race, or previous history. Of course you will get to know about most of these in the end. But casually. ... This love (essentially) ignores not only our physical bodies but that whole embodiment which consists of our family, job, past and connections.' Note that here we are talking about Lewis, a traditional and deeply conservative man who still fought in the trenches of world war I, not a 21st century modern suffragette or woke social activist. Yet the stance is uncompromisingly clear. In the pursuit of friendship, none of the superficial background traits can or should matter. This of course is much at odds with actual experience, and a substantial portion of the effort of sociological studies looks at to what degree homophily impacts our friendship choices (see 4.13 on mutual background and the aspects of money, content, status in 6.1).

The distance and continually voluntary nature of the friendship as opposed to a romantic relationship can also allow for a significantly higher leeway on acceptance of lifestyle choices that would *never* be permissible in romantic relationships. A night life lover can happily befriend an early rising bird or an OCD level cleaning disciple of Marie Kondo[15] can befriend the worst comic hoarding messie. Likewise, a conservative priest can befriend a promiscuous poly-amorous philanderer (as long as no adultery is involved, upon which the matter becomes sensitively moral) or a freedom loving travelling weed smoking hippie can befriend a law abiding disciplined lawyer. I think the list of cliches has been extended enough, but the matter is clear. As long as there is a live and let live, and no judgement is passed on the other persons lifestyle choices, friendship is possible. However, breaches of this are possible. Whereas we can frank with bemusement observe differences and comment life style choices, there are limits to it. Here the respect for the other person and their autonomous choices needs to keep underlying the communication. This specifically concerns life style choices away from our own. If we are single it means accepting that a new mother has limited energy for going out drinking and partying. Or if we are still in a frugal mindset, we may regardless have to accept that a former travel buddy does now start enjoying wearing expensive suits or plush dinners, and not to nag them or try to keep them in a former version of themselves that suited us better.

[15]Marie Kondo is a japanese 'tidy-your-house' consultant with a modern interpretation of feng shui.

Proceeding there are three further contentious issues on acceptance: **acceptance of emotions**, **acceptance of morals** and beliefs, and long term **acceptance of personality** vs. challenge to change. Acceptance of emotions is a key aspect of emotional support, listening and understanding. Sometimes in life we may have strong feelings that can surprise us. We all at some time in the past may have been angry, because someone cheated us. We may have been sad because a partner broke up with us. We may have entertained a frivolous thought for a man or woman who is married. After a relative of ours died we may have been a mix of sad and angry at life - god - the universe. All of these are what in convention are normal or acceptable behaviours. However, it might also be the case that we felt emotions far beyond that. To the point that it is perfectly clear that these emotions are wrong, unhealthy and not at all like anything we would attribute to the general positive image of ourself. We may internally boil with rage for days or weeks over the minor insult a colleague levelled our way, imagining lending a hand in a reenactment of purgatory on earth. We may feel all sorts of rage and other emotions over the loss of a breakup - oscillating through several cycles of Kuebler-Ross's grieving cycle. Or we might feel nothing over it, emotionless passing over it. We may become completely infatuated in a really unhealthy way with a married colleague, actively planning out romantic conquests, or be in an abusive relationship and rationalise and suppress our emotions. The death of a dear relative may leave us completely distraught and depressed, or it may leave us completely cold without the blink of an eye and a second thought dedicated to the matter. Note that according to secular moral, as long as no harm to any third party is done because in line with classical Greek philosophy, the differentiating factor between human and animal is the capability to control action and restrain it according to personal and social norms. Regardless of the individual case, we may have strong emotions that we perceive as different to conventional moral norms, and to make sense of them would like to talk to someone. Of course there are shrinks, but for most of us this would be a matter for a highly trustworthy, empathic and accepting friend. The conversation would of course involve some observational judgement, like 'that is some crazy stuff', 'that is really not like you' or 'yep you are really screwed up, I always knew it', but beyond the comments there would be a person who would stand by us as we emote through our dilemma and not run for the hill to call 911.

Acceptance of morals is more difficult. As friends see each other as part of the themselves and themselves as part of each other, they consequently expect a high degree of morals (see 3.7 and 4.1). But it is possible that moral or social views can be different. Humans are unique, and no-one is flawless. Thus someone who we think of befriending, or may have been a friend for a long time, might disclose a moral perspective which we just find reprehensible; this is not the curiosity inciting mind expanding trait of appreciating different beliefs and backgrounds, this is a potentially sexist, or racist joke that wasn't even funny thirty years ago, this is the casual mention that they voted for Trump, Bolsonaro or Brexit. This could be the open proposal that refugees should be left to drown. Others say that women should stay at home and not have jobs. Yet others may imply that all men are clandestine rapists in waiting and white people on a wide scale collaborating to persist white supremacy. The list of statements reprehensible to the listening friend goes on... A moment of truth where you wonder what made you like the person in the first place. How on earth you got here through all these years? And we are not talking of a nasty rumour being spread which you can disavow as gossip. This is a moment of clarity, and the rest is up for you to choose. There is the virtue signalling self righteous but also morally consistent and upright immediate or gradual split. You decide that the character deficiency is unacceptable. You decide for correcting your cognitive dissonance (X is horrible, a friend must be of upright character, X cannot be a friend - see section 3.7) and part ways. Unfortunately, there are many examples of this in current literature, with friendships (and families) splitting over many controversial issues. Or - you swallow your need for consistency and accept. You choose, at least for the moment, to forego judgement, not sever the connection, with a view to effect change (see 5.9). The Christian view postulates this as the right path, and in friendship this may need to be echoed. 'Bear with each other ... whoever throws the first stone ... hate the sin, not the sinner'. There will be a time to discuss these matters. Acceptance for the moment means not to reduce the other person's validity to this one view or trait, as reprehensible as it is, but still keep the entire person in view, including remaining positive traits. This is a skill probably best coined (moral) flexibility, however it doesn't hold much currency these days. But the price is functioning discourse on a societal and civil level. Curiously, Nehamas, 2016, ch.1[16] is positive about people being able to split off such vices and maintain a positive view of friends.

The final version of acceptance is that of long term **acceptance of personality** vs. **challenge of changing**. Here I would say the consensus is that friendship does not do that, neither passively nor actively. Some friends feel they are unconditionally loved and accepted as friends no matter what. However, most friends would agree to the statement 'I love you the way you are, but I love you too much to let you stay that way'. We want our friends to grow. We may be humble enough to know our limits in being able to support them in that, let alone decide what is good for them. But seeing our friends and understanding them includes us seeing their weaknesses and faults, and for their wellbeing we should support them in becoming better versions of themselves.

Finally, acceptance and tolerance comes with an offsetting cost. If you accept anything and anyone, then the validation function of the friendship is offset. I do not encourage that you see yourself as morally superior to your friends, but having high standards and in part holding your friends to it does confer value and validation to them. How do you feel validated as a friend, if your friend has another friend, who is behaving like a total jerk. Now I do think that partial virtues exist, so someone might be an illoyal gossip or drug addict in 90 % of his life[17], yet the special bond to that friend might have grown over the years. But friendship, whilst freely given and accepting of the person, also needs to be earned and validated.

When acceptance of emotions, morals and personality come together, and are accompanied by a sense of trustworthiness, kindness and patience, (so we are not

[16]'Aristotle's scheme, in which friendship is limited to a rarefied few, turns out to be at odds with what we know through experience. We are all of us mixtures of virtues and vices, and all of us know that even our best friends have their shortcomings. True, it is unlikely that we can be friends with people we consider evil. But we often have no trouble excusing our friends' failings, both trivial and, often, serious.'

[17]'Things we lost in the fire', with David Duchovny, Halle Berry and Benicio del Toro

asking here for too much, really)[18] it sets the scene for **allowing expression of self**. Allowing expression of self is in a way one of the gold standards of friendship. It is the sentiment that you really feel yourself in the company of a friend, free to say whatever comes to your mind, emote, explore and figuring things out. The emphasis is on being able to voice opinions and thoughts, that you would be also deeply uncomfortable voicing to others. It is the state where mutual understanding is enabled, and deep listening takes place. There is the sentiment that we can come to our friend with whatever we have on our mind, fun, crazy, troubling, sad, and can tell them. This represents an optionality, and for us it is incredibly important[19]. Thinking there is no one we 'can' go to and share is one acute expression of loneliness.

Whereas acceptance and tolerance is about acceptance of difference, **forgiveness** takes it one step further. Forgiveness according to the Oxford English Dictionary is both the action of forgiving, e.g. the pardon of a fault or also the remission of a debt, and secondly the disposition or willingness to forgive in general. It is a key Christian virtue, and Lewis, 1952 dedicates an entire chapter to it. One sentence from a sermon stuck with me always 'Not forgiving is a poison with which you want to hurt someone but you drink it yourself.' N. Lee and S. Lee, 2009 cite Martin Luther as saying that 'forgiveness is not just an occasional act it is a permanent attitude'. And therefore it is part of the personality traits rather than the relationship specific aspects. We all screw up sometimes. This is not about Christian 'original sin', but it is just an observable statistic in our own lives. Without forgiveness we would over time be all drifting away from each other in alienation. Writing about the 50 themes in this book, each coming with their own do's and don'ts it also brought me back to many episodes in the various friendships I have and have had where I screwed up. My suspicion would be that this is probably no different for you, that you also can think of a few episodes where things went wrong in a friendship. Forgiveness is the mechanism, graciously wielded by the screw-up recipient or victim, to prevent this having lasting damage onto the friendship. Forgiveness is a response. It needs the apology to be effective. An effective apology needs the insight and understanding of the offence committed or inflicted. Millington, 2019, p. 94 makes this point: 'My rule is to give them one chance. Have a conversation about how one example of their behaviour made you feel and explore it with them. If that behaviour doesn't change, make a conscious decision not to spend time with them. People often aren't aware of how hurtful their actions and words can be when they are so caught up in their own pain, and sometimes pointing out that what they said was hurtful and rude can be enough of a wake-up call to stop the behaviour and get your friendship back on track.' The insight needs to be sufficient to allow for future change of behaviour.

Once the apology is expressed and forgiveness is granted, it is permanent and final (see Alberoni, 2016, p.32 'Usually friendship absolves, forgives. If there is forgiveness, forgiveness is definitive.'). Thus forgiveness purifies the relationship. For several situations it is also the only way to restore the relationship, as simply

[18]The nature of acceptance of self being such an interconnected theme also made it really difficult to allocate it to one of the key themes.

[19]People living in large cities often emphasise the fact that they can go to different restaurants, theatres or museums even though they hardly ever really go out. The car provides the option of mobility, our hundreds of books allow for wisdom to be gained. Even though we don't follow up, we value the optionality.

letting a matter rest and be forgotten is not an option. Forgiveness can be a powerful connector. If you screw up, and your friend has a moral right to feel and express anger at you, but chooses to forego this for the benefit of your mutual relationship, it is a sacrifice on his part.

Practical takeaway
At the core of friendship is the sense that your friend is OK. Your friend is appreciated for 'whatever' in his core, and certain peripheral quirks and quips can be (mostly) tolerated. If you have any red lines, then it is good for these to be known, at least in principle. Especially for friends - 'treat your friends as you wanted to be treated by them' holds true.

Suggestions for thought

- To what degree do you 'accept your friends'? Do you really think you are oblivious/indifferent of the social or cultural background of your friends?
- How accepting are you of their moral and political convictions?
- Have you ever felt judged by your friend? Was that justified? Do you think judgement or acceptance is more important?
- If you think about the times when you screwed up with a friend and they forgave you, how did the friendship develop after this?

For statistics in sociological studies, question suggestions and weights in counting see H.

3.3 Humility and interest in others

Humility means taking a genuine **interest in others** and in particular your friends first, or not being jealous but being **quietly happy at their good fortunes** and happiness.

Lewis, 1952, ch.8[20] elaborates on the effect of pride on friendships, effectively negating the feasibility of friendship among proud people. If you disagree with the Christian doctrine consider this description of a humble person: 'Probably all you will think about him is that he seemed a cheerful, intelligent chap who took a real interest in what you said to him. If you do dislike him it will be because you feel a little envious of anyone who seems to enjoy life so easily. He will not be thinking about humility: he will not be thinking about himself at all' (also ch.8). It is this sentiment of someone with ease being interested in you that just so many people long for in a friend, and one reason why humility merits a place of its own in the friendship virtues. One famous quote associated with friendship making

[20]'Other vices may sometimes bring people together: you may find good fellowship and jokes and friendliness among drunken people or unchaste people. But Pride always means enmity-it is enmity.'

is from Dale Carnegie: 'You make more friends in two months by becoming genuinely interested in other people than you can in two years by trying to get other people interested in you.' and it explains why humility might be the dark horse in friendship creation. As Sira M., 2020-06-14 observes: 'Let's be honest for a moment: when someone is curious about our job, passions, and goals — or whatever makes us tick — it makes them more likable to us. It usually makes us want to talk and spend more time with them.'. As such, humble is yet another one of those additional qualifiers that are used to elaborate why or in what way a specific person is a good friend to us.

Humility is of course a difficult trait to self-assess or even to solicit feedback on [21]. However when it comes to friendship there are a few good questions you can ask yourself. When you are sharing, is your mental focus of the story more on you or on the stories relevance to the conversation? Can you let a story that your friend shared stand and let him bask in the glory of a performed joke or an interesting anecdote, or do you feel compelled to 'one-up' and share an even 'better' story by yourself? How often do you think and express (spontaneously) 'wow that is so cool!' about your friends acts or stories. To what degree do you think success and attention are zero-sum games? When we make things about the other, the friend, we meet their needs for being listened to, to shine, to be appreciated. Thus humility is an enabler and enhancer for a number of the relationship traits.

The key mark of being interest in others is your capability of getting to **know personal facts** about your friends and retaining the knowledge. Keeping little anecdotes or preferences signals the value we place on them. Using such knowledge can make our gifts more meaningful or thoughtful. According to Shumway, 2018, p.53 'memory is perhaps the most underrated area of friendship fitness'. In the prep school days of my childhood we used to have friendship books for people in our class and social surroundings, where people pasted in a small photo and then wrote details such as birthdays, hobbies, favourite music or dishes, toys and dreams for later professions. In hindsight it was just such a phenomenal idea[22]. It is thus a good question to test yourself after you have known a friend for say 6 months or so, whether you could from your memory fill out a specimen sheet for your friend. In friendship literature there is a general consensus on women being better at this[23], though I would find an investigation interesting whether it applies in quantity or is just a difference in focus[24]. Thus regular catchups over a beer allow us to keep this knowledge about the other's state updated.

A second reason however makes humility even more important in friendship. During the course of almost any friendship, misunderstandings arise. The friend does not seem to be quite so attentive anymore, or worse seems to have betrayed

[21] Peterson and Seligman, 2004, ch.20 elaborate on this and refer to June Price Tangney, 2000 for an overview of themes and measuring difficulties

[22] It was a great idea if you had friends, and a painful realisation of exclusion, if the other kids did not want to write into your book or didn't ask you to write in theirs. Kids can be incredibly cruel, and though in some sense the disappearance of such conventions may be a blessing in disguise for some children.

[23] See Greif, 2009, ch.14 'she can tell me about what each of these women did' or Degges-White and Borzumato-Gainey, 2011, ch.1 'Girls enter this world better equipped to observe and remember emotional details.'

[24] As men might put focus e.g. on their interest rather than the person, it might be important to see that the friend retains good knowledge of matters of that interest, be it a proficiency in DIY skills or good rule knowledge of the strategic but complex board game.

your trust or committed another friendship offence. The key word here is 'seems'. It is however clear and real that your feeling is that of hurt. And the human instinct - fuelled by pride - is usually revenge. This word sounds ugly, but essentially it is simply a result of 'tit-for-tat' being an optimal strategy in game theory, a lesson we learned through thousands of years of evolution of our social system. The key however to successful conflict resolution is **holding our hurt ego back** until really all the facts are known.

Conflicts by themselves are nothing bad in friendship. Whereas the old philosophers[25] emphasised similarity of thought and consequentially absence of discord on account of the virtuous character, current thought is that it is perfectly OK for friends to fight - within bounds. As Olyan, 2017, p.92[26] notes that in the old testament with Ben Sira reconciliation becomes a topic, and reconciliation between friends becomes a feasibility. However, in all of those cases the link to humility is not drawn, it is more the later christian writers that make the link explicit.

The importance of humility reoccurs in the later part of the resolution phase. You have sat down with the friend giving them the benefit of doubt (loyalty), you have heard them out (listening, patience), you have given him your view of the matter (honest feedback), you have told them how it made you feel (openness/vulnerability), but now everything is in the clear. There are two options: your friend has actually committed a transgression and genuinely apologizes, or you realise (because you consider accepting your friend's viewpoint over your own ...) that there was actually no transgression, or the conflict was blown out of proportion. At that point, you need to make the choice to forego or let go of your right to be angry, to want to punish the slighting of your personality. Intellectually everything is clear, but emotionally you need to let go of your hurt pride. This situation will invariably arise in any friendship and at some point. And humility is then literally the make or break variable in the equation.

Practical takeaway

1. Few people are genuinely humble, and everyone loves when being listened to and less so listening to others. But we should monitor ourselves how much we monopolize a conversation or how well we are really listening to our friends stories and arguments.

2. Organizing such a child-like friend's book for a birthday present for someone during the pandemic or later might be a corny yet endearing gesture of community affection. With digital photobook printing services, it is also really easy to create !

---

[25]Cicero, 1923, p.187'For nothing is more discreditable than to be at war with one with whom you have lived on intimate terms ... no discord should arise between friends, but in case it does, then our care should be that the friendships appear to have burned out rather than to have been stamped out' - again for context remember Cicero's background being the Roman civil war.

[26]'According to 22:21-22, he who draws the sword or speaks against a friend (literally, 'opens the mouth') can still achieve reconciliation, but he who reveals a secret dooms a friendship.38 Ben Sira 27:21 is similar, stating that 'there is reconciliation for contention'—meaning that after a falling out there is the possibility of making up—as long as the split was not occasioned by the revelation of confidences.'

Suggestions for thought

- To what degree are you genuinely listening to what your friends are saying rather than just waiting for a moment to share your story?
- To what degree do you think your arguments, wits or stories are sounder or better than your friends?
- Have you ever experienced a full blowout with a friend? If you remember how the conflict came about and developed, to what degree might it have been your fault for not being able to back down?

For statistics in sociological studies, question suggestions and weights in counting see H.

3.4 Reliability, consistency and persistence

> It is not so much our friends' help that helps us, as the confidence of their help.
>
> Epicurus

While sometimes surprises are good, it is good to have a stable element in our life. **Reliable and consistent** friends are with us and don't just change their behaviour on a whim, but who will show up if they said they would. They also are sure not to drop off the radar but to maintain a stable affection for us and become one of those key elements in life to give us comfort and stability. People refer to their friends as 'reliable' or 'dependable', 'steadfast' or 'a rock', and the message is clear. If they behaved this way with me yesterday, it is likely that they will continue to do so today and tomorrow.

Aristotle, 1925, 8.8[27] recommends steadfastness as a key criterion according to which you should select your friends to make the friendship long-lasting and beneficial. Cicero, 1923, p.173[28] wholeheartedly agrees.

Dependability or reliability is also a key requirement in modern times. Alberoni, 2016, p.77[29] insists friendship should be predictable and boring. Greif, 2009, ch.2 seconds: 'A true best friend is someone you can count on in all circumstances, under all conditions'. Likewise for more female friendships, authors such as Nelson, 2016, p.39[30] emphasize the importance of consistency. However

[27]'for being steadfast in themselves they hold fast to each other, and neither ask nor give base services, but (one may say) even prevent them; for it is characteristic of good men neither to go wrong themselves nor to let their friends do so. But wicked men have no steadfastness (for they do not remain even like to themselves), but become friends for a short time because they delight in each other's wickedness.

[28]'We ought, therefore, to choose men who are firm, steadfast and constant, a class of which there is a great dearth; and at the same time it is very hard to come to a decision without a trial, while such trial can only be made in actual friendship'

[29]'We expect adult friendship to be staid, serious, predictable, boring exactly like the friendship between buddies or like those at the club, whether or not that is actually true.'

[30]'It's the repetition or regularity that develops patterns, rituals, and expectations in our relationship. It's from this consistent time that we come to predict consistent behaviors that leads to us feeling like we can rely on each other.'

in modern newspaper articles, e.g. Khan, 2019-11-15, a lack of reliability and predictability ('flaking') under the pressures of modern city life is lamented, making interactions such as meeting for coffee or dinner (i.e. spending time together 5.1) increasingly and unnecessarily rare. And when looking at reasons for the termination of relationships, being let down is one of the key accepted reasons for dissolving a friendship.

A controversial topic on reliability is whether it is permissible to test friends and in what way. The classical writers generally mandate it, though do not give specifications whether this automatically happens through the passing of time and in due course, or whether specific tests have to be done. It might however be pointed to the friendship virtue of honesty and integrity, with which the artificial creation of a friendship test might be inconsistent (you should not feign an emergency).

Practical takeaway
Life is busy and hectic, but don't flake. What kind of message do you send when you say your friends are really important to you, but just cancel by text message 30 min. before meeting up for a coffee. Being predictable and consistent as a friend is a base trait, and it is not exactly rocket science.

Suggestions for thought

- To what degree do you think can you rely on your friends and in which situations?
- Have you ever let down a friend and what was their reaction?
- Do you think all friends need to be reliable? Could there be an exception, someone you consider a close friend but who you know is just not reliable at all?
- How much time do you think you need to have known someone to be sure that they are reliable?

For statistics in sociological studies, question suggestions and weights in counting see H.

3.5 Fun and humour

> I can tell by your sarcastic undertones, rude comments, and sheer lack of common decency that we should be best friends.
>
> Unknown

Being able to make people laugh is a great trait. Laughter is good for us all, and bringing it out in people is a wonderful capability. There are four themes

- highly overlapping to this: (1) Having fun together through activities and in conversations, (2) appreciating the humour in the friend's personality, (3) being able to laugh a lot in the other's company, and (4) a healthy attitude towards joking and teasing of each other.

(1) **Fun** can be the differentiating element, why hanging out with friends is just 'better' than almost any other activity. For some it is to friendship what the spoonful of sugar is to Mary Poppins, an ingredient that makes the whole better. They turn mundane moments into fun experiences. To some, it is the key and single purpose to friendship. Fun can come from the activities or hobbies (see Greif, 2009, ch. 10, ch. 11, ch.12[31] or from harmless flirting and bantering, it can also arise from rituals reminding us of funny anecdotes. The experience of fun is a common theme when people talk about the experience of time with their friends. Indeed, for some time with the friends is where most if not all fun in their life stems from.

Some fun of friendship can come from some (moderated) leading astray. While Cicero and Aristotle look to friendship for virtue, every now and so often our friends challenge us to do something 'really stupid'! It is in those moments that bonding memories are made, that will last the rest of your lifetime (provided no one got hurt). Speaking autobiographical, the best experiences from University and bonding moments with friends included those where rational adults would have just rolled their eyes, and a phrase you hear sometimes decades later is 'I can't believe we did this ...'. When we are around friends, we can destress and let go of the usually rigid social norms. It is a sign of trust and safety, as making a joke involves getting it wrong sometimes and not being judged for it.

Fun is in the surprise, the difference. In our optimized and streamlined lives, the friend who is a little clumsy, different, can provide a great counterpoint to our daily routine, pointing out the absurd, and seeing the fun side of life can be a great source of joy. Some friends are imaginative, having ideas for new fun activities.

A downside issue however is entertainment management on our side. Few of our friends are fun all the time. Jokes can become repetitive, and sometimes our friends are not in a good mood. No one can compete with the constant 3 laughs a minute staccato of comedy sitcoms popularized by Friends and Seinfeld and successors (see Feigel, 2020-07-04[32]), and we should not see our friendships with the consumer attitude we have to so many other aspects of our lives.

(2) Some people have a knack for **making other people laugh**. Whether at work or in private life, we love hanging around them. They just make our day (e.g. Rath, 2006, p. 118[33]). A wealth of funny anecdotes, jokes and memories of movie scenes or standup lines can add great entertainment to our conversations (see resource content 6.3). Linguistically gifted people twist around sentences and point out ambiguities. Theatrically gifted people can act out jokes in a group .

[31]Ch. 10: 'It's play for me. Play music, play cards, play tennis or frisbee ... I guess it all comes across as play to me because if I'm with friends, I'm having fun.', ch. 11 'Friendships should be largely about fun, companionship, and a shared perspective on life.' and ch.12 'We single guys can go to dances and a lot of functions here where we can have a lot of fun.'

[32]`https://www.theguardian.com/books/2020/jul/04/love-beyond-sex-money-and-property-a-case-for-friendship`

[33]'There are days when I just want to tear my hair out. Whenever I am feeling this way, I stop by Josh's office, and he inevitably cheers me up with some funny story or imitation he likes to do. He cracks me up. I always feel better after having a laugh with Josh.'

Humour is also an expression of personality. Our jokes reveal our values, our attitudes, even our political convictions. It is because of that that humour becomes such a personality connector. If we share the same humour, we are of the same metal or make. Thus quite correctly, if we deeply care about say LGBTI matters or BLM[34], an insensitive joke will reveal a fundamental incompatibility in our mutual personalities. However self censoring humour might not be the answer. Essentially, we just mask a part of the personality from our surroundings and in particular the friendship. We need to rediscover affectionate humour, that - while it might make fun of a particular attribute or stereotype- regardless affirms again the right of the person to wellbeing and dignity. Thus, rather than questioning the defect of character that a certain joke is purported to reveal, it might be more helpful to accept temporarily the joke. You can use it then as a starting trigger later to have that conversation on values, respect for human rights and right to non-discrimination, without immediately calling the humour of the joke-teller and by extent their personality into question.

(3) A natural and free **laughter** (in most cases) is also a powerful relationship reinforcer. If I laugh about someone's joke, I affirm their humour and by extent I affirm their personality. I forget everything else, and in that moment the person does indeed have my full attention and appreciation. I am also relaxed, and if I am relaxed, then I signal that I feel safe with them, and vice versa they can feel safe with me, as I am not about to turn around and threaten them. Laughter is an indicator that our time with the friend is enjoyable. When looking at interview material, it is often unqualified, it just 'is there' or 'occurs' as a natural phenomenon and side-effect of a delightful conversation. It indeed occurs so often (e.g. in Dumagane, 2018-11-26, 82 % of adolescents name humour as one of three key values in friendship) as a comment that simply by observation it may be described as a necessary (but not sufficient) condition for friendship.

Laughter is also a human need, it is one quintessence that makes life worth living. It is good for our health (for details see e.g. R.A. Martin, 2002) both physical and mental, and whilst daily life provides material, often the prime source is friends. I often heard an adapted version of the 'An apple a day keeps the doctor away' to 'A laughter a day keeps the doctor away'. Thus if we establish, e.g. by robust psychometric research, that laughter really is a fundamental human need, by extension the need for friendship almost immediately follows.

(4) Inside an affectionate friendship, good friends get away with almost any **joke** at the expense of their friend. Good humour is then defined by the ability to 'take it'. A long good friend has an entire arsenal of anecdotes to hurl at you to get your eyes rolling, and the richness of this is a credible indicator on how much the friendship means to him. As friends improve in friendship, inside jokes taking aim at each other convey intimacy, history and connection strength. Being able to make a good joke about and to your face is advanced territory, but it (for some) can be the declaration that by being able to make this joke, I believe that our friendship is at such an advanced and close level. It thus becomes - more for non-expressive men than emotionally expressive women - an effective signalling or self-disclosure mechanism about the perceived quality of a friendship. I was also pointed out by one reader that the limit of pranks is given by the friend's personality to relax after it. Some people after a successful prank on your behalf

[34] Black lives matter

may never be able to relax in your presence again, always being on guard for the next trap, even if it is well intended. That is obviously not the result you want, so do be careful.

However, when that goodwill is being questioned, almost all jokes are evaluated against it. The jokes just feel a little too close to home, some almost like insults. They don't feel like jokes, but more like veiled criticism or disrespect disguised as jokes. We worry about further opening up to not give ammunition to further potentially hurtful jokes. The ultimate element of this is the best man's speech, and it is such a tightrope to walk, but usually mishaps on part of the groom told with great affection are expected, and the juicier the better (excluding former romances). Teasing without goodwill however is not friendship, but is merely bullying disguised in the package of a friendship. Cultural context matters here, too. In some context self deprecating humour allows and invites humour made by others from the same angle, in other cultures it is forbidden. When entering the territory of making jokes towards the friend, we need to pay close attention to his reaction, our motivation to tell the joke, and our surrounding.

Having fun is a key element of enjoying someone's company (4.5) and it is the key element of the reward function of the friendship process (7.3).

Practical takeaway
Seeing the fun in life with friends is so good and refreshing. Telling each other jokes, even and especially really stupid ones, can just make you giggle and see the day a little more positive. Send each other memes and jokes, links to Youtube standup comedy sketches and funny anecdotes to keep smiling. And throughout the year, have a list of little pranks you can do, or plan ahead for a good April fools joke.

Suggestions for thought

- To what degree is it your friends who make you laugh vs. any other social circle you are in?
- Do you have any key insider jokes or anecdotes with your close friends?
- How easily do you get offended when your closer friends make jokes about you / to your face? Or do you on the contrary appreciate it?
- Have you ever had a joke that crossed a border / line ? What did that result in? How did you resolve the issue?

For statistics in sociological studies, question suggestions and weights in counting see H.

3.6 Kindness, warmth and loving nature

This is love and affection shown both spontaneously and over longer times. It is the warm hug, the caring smile, the meal prepared for us, the card sent to wish us well or a speedy recovery. All these are signs that the person genuinely cares for us from the bottom of her/his heart. Particularly religious literature including Lewis, 1960 but also Blieszner and Adams, 1992 stress the importance of this trait.

While affection is primarily a directed emotion, it can be a general attitude. We sometimes set ourselves the challenge to do an act of kindness, but there are some people who just do it continuously without the reminder. A passionate argument for such an attitude is made in Shinyashiki, 1987 to have an affectionate general behaviour contributing to a loving environment all around. Fully affectionate people may seem anachronistic and tactless to us in western, distanced culture. But when we do meet them, there is something incredibly warming and positive about them. I was fortunate to spend some time in Brazil now more than a decade back, and there was reporting to a boss who literally came in and gave a full hug to her entire team when she was coming into the office. The first time I saw this I was stunned, and then over my time there grew to appreciate it as an actually really warm and caring gesture that only was a symptom of an all round affectionate and warm personality. And this wow factor is something that, when we encounter it, makes some of us then think - gee, I wish that person became my friend.

We instinctively value **kindness** as one of the highest qualities people can have. Cuddy, Kohut, and Neffinger, 2013 in Harvard business review[35] write that the key characteristic we evaluate when we meet someone is warmth, before competency and even in a professional context. Kindness likewise is a trait that is much appreciated by children, as they decide whether to engage with a non-kin adult, e.g. a friend of their parents dropping by for a coffee. Mentioned in the old testament[36] though not prominently, kindness (chraestotaeta as in Colossians 3:12), rose to be considered as a key Christian trait. The problem is that whilst people cite that kindness is a Christian virtue, the actual term denoted as the 6th Christian virtue by Gregory I in 590 AD is humanitas. This (different) term originates with the Roman philosophers importing 'Philanthropia' into Latin. After several centuries of incorporation of Greek and Roman philosophical concepts into Christian doctrine, it could cover many different connotations and meanings[37]. Kindness is even important in the 'male' classical friendships which use honest feedback and rebuke to develop virtues. Cicero repeatedly emphasised that criticism of character should not resort to harsh (aspere) language. Thus even if we broach a potentially difficult or painful subject, kindness as an underlying attitude enables the safety and sense of good will necessary to openly discuss a disagreement or criticism. I sometimes think as kindness as the salt in the soup of friendship, though arguably you can have a lot more kindness in a

[35] https://hbr.org/2013/07/connect-then-lead

[36] Job 6:14 'He who withholds kindness from a friend forsakes the fear of the Almighty.'

[37] See Brill New Pauly by Helmut Storch entry Humanitas: 'In humanitas as 'humanity' the following features emerge: 1. philanthropic respect, especially compassion (misericordia), 2. intelligent and tactful affability (urbanitas), 3. feeling for natural human solidarity (sensus humanitatis), 4. cultured humanity (eruditio, doctrina), 5. civilization (cultus). As early as Cicero's oration, Pro Sex. Roscio (84 BC) almost all shades of these can be found.'

friendship than you can have salt in a soup. But without salt, something just is missing. Kindness and warmth are mentioned or implied as attributes or qualifiers in a lot of statements on friendship: 'X has a kind personality', 'X warms my heart', 'X is thoughtful', 'X makes people welcome'. They are not so much mentioned as key character-defining trait. In the anecdotal evidence there seems no difference between genders on persons displaying it. There is a second kind of affection-attitude described by the word 'sweet' and it occurs often as a positive trait when people, especially young people talk about an impression. Someone is sweet means they are pleasant, kind and gentle towards other people (Collins Dictionary), and indeed this is a trait that is specifically in youth relating literature (see Delaney and Madigan, 2017).[38].

Practical takeaway
Hug (not in Covid times), but establish it as a rule to finish a meetup with a hug. It is warm, it is wonderful. For guys, maybe stop after 15 sec even if it feels wonderful.

Suggestions for thought

- Mentally going through your friends and acquaintances, who do you think are those that exemplify kindness? What effect does that have on you?
- Do you think you act in a kind manner, not just on occasions but in general? If not, why not?

For statistics in sociological studies, question suggestions and weights in counting see H.

3.7 Virtue and good character

> I don't like to commit myself about heaven and hell – you see, I have friends in both places.
>
> Mark Twain

For Aristotle, 1925 and Cicero, 1923 virtue is one of the key aspects of friendship, as virtue begets friendship and vice versa. For the contemporary philosophers Alberoni, 2016 and Nehamas, 2016 it is a more nuanced and compromising matter, but the general relevance is likewise discussed at length. The study of virtue is of course one of the key themes of philosophy, and the question of what virtue (arete or virtus) is can fill libraries. The concept of virtue and a virtuous character is not uniquely defined and has changed over the years. In particular,

[38]Linguistics like these need to be considered when designing future queries to estimate relative trait weight

its scope can be extremely wide. Nowadays a virtuous character would probably have a connotation of somewhere near integrity and a secular sainthood. In the old days virtus or arete were all-encompassing concepts[39], the width of which our current use of the word virtue doesn't do justice. The adoption of these terms into Christian thoughts by Augustine and Aquinus added to the width of the term, and when Christian writers in the 20th and 21st century now write about people having a virtuous character, this is an incomplete statement without a reference of which canon of virtue they actually mean. For modern science (psychology) the discussion reached an interesting summary with the publication of Peterson and Seligman, 2004 organizing their 26 character strengths into the key 6 virtues of wisdom and knowledge, courage, humanity, justice, temperance and transcendence. This however has only partially concluded the question for the domain of psychology. Within theology or philosophy, traditional and modern schools with substantially diverging concepts remain. Regardless of the concept, there is the claim that the virtuous nature of character of both friends is important if not conditional to a potential or existent friendship, most markedly made by Aristotle.

There are four subthemes to this explored in friendship literature: (1) Virtue is essential to friendship and only virtuous people (or people striving to be virtuous) can be genuine friends, (2) Friendship is necessary to develop virtue and the development of virtue is the justification for the institution of friendship, (3) it is through appreciation of the virtue of someone (or weaker - general positive attributes of their personality) that the desire to enter into friendship and maintain it is caused, (4) whilst full virtue is not required, a morally bad action is a sufficient justification to end a friendship. (1) - (3) is usually argued for together, though emphases vary. (4) is a view that can be commonly held even without accepting (1)-(3).

(1) The **exclusivity of true friendship to the perfectly virtuous** is a thought that was the essential conclusion of Aristotle's writings, and has persisted unaltered and unquestioned (for some) through the ages (see e.g. Cuddeback, 2010, p.3 or 33)[40]). A detailed discussion of the exact relationship of virtue and friendship in Aristotle's writings is provided in Pangle, 2008, but two key passages exemplify the close tie.

> 8.3 'Perfect friendship is the friendship of men who are good, and alike in virtue' and 8.4 'but good men will be friends for their own sake, i.e. in virtue of their goodness. These, then, are friends without qualification; the others are friends incidentally and through a resemblance to these.'

In this phrase for me the key takeaway is that only virtuous people can have their friends' interest at the core of the friendship, i.e. genuinely feel good will (4.11) and consideration at their own sacrifice (4.3). Cicero, 1923, p.127[41] agreeing that virtue is a prerequisite, expands its role to be causal in creation and maintenance:

[39]An illustrative exercise is opening an old Greek (Liddell and Scott) or Latin (Lewis and Short) and be amazed at the breadth of connotations and nuances these words have and cover.

[40]p.3 'Why do we not have true friendships? The answer is startlingly simple. We cannot have true friendships if we are not virtuous. The kind of life required for friendship is a virtuous life.' and p. 33 'one need not be perfectly virtuous in order to have a true friendship; yet at the same time, to the extent that one fails in virtue, one fails in the ability to have a full friendship.'

[41]This, however, I do feel first of all — that friendship cannot exist except among good men;

> p. 207 Virtue, I say, both creates the bond of friendship and preserves it.

The benefit of perfect characters however according to Cicero is the absence of such discord[42]. At the time of writing 'de Amicitia' the civil war was dividing the Roman society, and thus the theme of civil discord strongly influenced Ciceros thinking. My takeaway is that depending on the tolerance of the parties involved and how central this theme is to their friendship concept, a sufficient philosophical agreement or overlap of what the 'good enough' or virtuous character needs to be in place (e.g. no lying, no drugs, charity). Both people pass the moral test exacted by their individual philosophies in each other's eyes. Violations of this perceived code - that I believe is not universal but specific to the friendship - will put the friendship at immediate risk. It is thus good practice to be aware of the ethically acceptable boundaries of your friends, so that even if you yourself do not share them, you do not actively transgress them in their presence. [43]

(2) The potential to **develop character** is of course highly correlated with the friendship activities of guidance and effecting change. There are of course different ways how our friends help is grow the virtue, be it by inspiration and example, challenge, discussion, guidance or teaching (see 5.10, 5.9 and 5.12 or Pahl, 2000, p.85[44]). The key when helping people to grow in virtue is to accept that virtues and strengths are general, but they are differently relevant to different people. However the interaction with friends and the capability to speak things through and construct mental scenarios and hypothetical actions also allows us to decide which virtues are relevant in which scenarios, and which virtues we want to concentrate on in our development. Seneca, 1917, 9.9[45] develops this saying that whilst friendships are unnecessary (really like anything, as the stoic prioritizes self sufficiency over everything) they should be pursued as it is the natural context in which virtues can be exercised.

(3) Nehamas, 2016 whilst acknowledging the Aristotelian tradition, offers a more nuanced approach. Genuine friendship is possible among less than virtuous people, and often one element of our friendships are (minor) vices of theirs which we hold dear. Lewis, 1952, ch.8 goes even further 'Other vices may sometimes bring people together: you may find good fellowship and jokes and friendliness among drunken people or unchaste people'. The basis however holds, there must be something in the other personality which we like, find 'good', which we base our respect and trust on. The character traits in this chapter are all such examples which have been identified as relevant to a friendship. However, other positive characteristics can catch our attention and admiration. This can be attributes such

---

[42] p. 171 'When the characters of friends are blameless, then there should be between them complete harmony of opinions and inclinations in everything without any exception;'

[43] Note this is not a matter of hipocrisy, more of avoidance of offence. If I have a vegan or puritan friend, they may know and accept that I enjoy meat or am a little promiscuous, yet I don't need to chew on the bone of a rare porterhouse steak in their presence or start ostensibly and lasciviously flirting with a potential short term fling for later that day. Call it courtesy or respect rather than pretence.

[44] 'Part of the function of friendship is to provide the anvil on which we may individually beat out our own personal moralities. In this sense, friendship is a metaphor for morality. How to be a good and dutiful daughter, wife or mother is less likely to be discussed with a mother, husband or daughter than with a friend.'

[45] 'The wise man, I say, self-sufficient though he be, nevertheless desires friends if only for the purpose of practising friendship, in order that his noble qualities may not lie dormant.'

as empathy with elderly, courage in difficult situations or a strongly developed spirituality. These traits then cause us wanting to spend time with them, emulate them and develop our relationship with them. This is irrespective of whether we see the trait in us, or do not see it, but want to learn it from them.

(4) People may have different opinion whether a specific bad act that would qualify as a **breach of the moral contract** of a friendship needs to apply to them or can be a general act. Thus it could be asked whether A cheating on his wife with a general woman would be sufficient for B to break off the friendship, or whether A would need to sleep with B's wife for the termination of friendship by B to be justified. Lying, financial fraud, illoyalty, other immoral acts can also lead us to lose respect for our friends and may leave us not wanting to continue the friendship. We may say 'I would not accept my friend to commit act X towards me' or with wider scope 'I would not accept my friend commit act X towards anyone, irrespective of whether the victim is me or someone else.'. In some religious traditions accepted vices can represent such honor breaches, that they limit the possibility of further friendship (e.g. 1 Cor 5:11[46]). But rules of conduct can have many sources. As noted in section 4.13 when we make politics about character, we reinforce the 'us vs. them' sentiment. To the degree we identify ourselves with the friend, a bad action or expression also threatens our self identity, leading us to withdraw. People can be more or less compromising here (see e.g. Millington, 2019, p.10 talking about a simple revealing expression[47]). We might choose to still permit non-malicious jokes and humour, not wanting to relegate a history of comedy and humoristic culture to the dustbin and follow the line of need for free speech and a basic right to offend, but draw a non-compromising line on discriminating action. We might also make allowance for different cultural or generational backgrounds. But even if affection and the bond of the common memory remain, something will stay scarred from such a mishap. Once moral judgement is passed and fallen short of Alberoni, 2016, p.32[48] is even more pessimistic about the prospect of a friendship.

Among the secular self-help books, the centrality of virtue is more or less ignored, often after having paid lip service to Aristotle in the introduction. It is this divergence that is interesting to observe, whether our view of friendship has changed so much that thoughts on virtue are simply nowadays anachronistic, or whether sociologists have missed out on investigating the centrality of good character to a healthy friendship. My hunch, but I may be wrong, is that the phrasing of the question here might prove insightful.

[46]'Now, what I meant was that you should not associate with people who call themselves brothers or sisters in the Christian faith but live in sexual sin, are greedy, worship false gods, use abusive language, get drunk, or are dishonest. Don't eat with such people.'

[47]'A homophobic aside, a sweeping generalization about the LGBTQ community, language I would never use to describe people of colour - and all respect goes out the window.'

[48]p. 32 'Friendship has a moral substance. Once trust is lost, it is lost forever. A crisis in friendship is, therefore, a process. The past is invoked to be judged, the future evoked because it must be determined. And the decision can never be appealed.' and 36 'There is no passion "above and beyond us." I judge him on moral grounds. We are morally demanding of our friends, much more so than of other people. We say, "a friend should never make me do such things."'

Practical takeaway
Few people are saints, but if you have a friend who could qualify, let it rub off. Let yourself be inspired, join the charity run, pay attention when they challenge you to 'up your game'. And look how they relate to their friends including you, and imitate them in that.

Suggestions for thought

- Do you have a friend who you admire for his virtues? Do you think the feeling is mutual (even if not for the same virtues)?
- Are you aware of what virtues your friends prize? Do you think you meeting these requirements is a contributing factor to your friendship?
- Have you ever unfriended someone (not just on Facebook) for something they did or said that showed bad character?

For statistics in sociological studies, question suggestions and weights in counting see H.

3.8 Intelligence, knowledge and curiosity

Some friendships are defined around intellectual discussions driven by interesting topics, an innate curiosity and a mutual understanding of each other's thinking on the matter. **Intellectual stimulation** and reaching 'flow'[49] in the engagement are clear signs of the matter. What is of importance is that the respective other is intellectually sufficiently capable to understand the matter (intelligence), knows enough about the matters (knowledge) and is interested in expanding this knowledge even further (curiosity). Whilst intelligence and curiosity are personality traits, knowledge can be also partially seen as a component of the resource content and will be addressed as well under this aspect in section 6.3. In psychological literature, several characteristics can be identified in here. Referencing the character strengths framework of Peterson and Seligman, 2004 all of Ingenuity, Curiosity, Critical Thinking, Love of Learning and Wisdom - and thus almost all aspects of the 'Wisdom and Knowledge' cluster - resonate with this personality trait. St. Augustine highly valued the discussions exchanges and the book pleasures with his friend.

Whilst sport is the clear path to gaining positive reputation among adolescents, for some of them a combination of intellect and fun is quite appreciated too. 'Smartass' or smart is a positive trait in this group according to Delaney and Madigan, 2017. This is a factor strongly driving homophily and especially prevalent amongst academics (e.g. see Greif, 2009, ch.8[50]). Indeed some people see the

[49]See Nakamura and Csikszentmihalyi, 2014 for an explanation of 'flow' as a concept from positive psychology.
[50]'All of my friends are M.D.s or Ph.D.s, and I think these types have stereotypical behavior.'

key purpose of friendship in being an 'intellectual friend' (see Greif, 2009, ch.2, 11[51]).

For the philosophers intellectual capabilities are also essential, both per se (cf. Alberoni, 2016, p.37[52]) and to enable 'good conversation' forming intellectual virtue (cf. Cuddeback, 2010, p.66[53]). This trait is an enabler of good discussions that are stimulating. The variety of topics, interest and the quality of arguments are all driven by an acute and alive intellect. The love of learning and teaching enables great interactions that are by design memory building for friends too. Again being more a capability than a virtue, it is put forward by Rath, 2006 and the MBTI descriptors. Intellectual capabilities are however not just necessary for intellectual discussions, many of which revolve around mutual interests (4.12), they also support the giving of guidance, practical help in several situations, and the benefit gained from collaborating. Thus the trait of intelligence and curiosity correlates with the Rath roles of collaborator, navigator and mind opener[54].

A variant theme of this is also **wisdom** which whilst not being intelligence is closely related to it in the sense that unless discussing nuclear physics confers similar benefits on the friend. When good thinking capabilities coincides with virtue, the result is wisdom. We sometimes refer to both smart and empathic people as 'wise beyond their age' for their good insight and counsel (c.f. Cicero, 1923, p.115[55]). This also echoes with several other traits like prudence valued by Aristotle and the early church fathers.

Curiosity is also in the cluster. Curiosity in new topics and experiences leads to the acquisition of the resource content. It is underlying the key activity of discovery and exploration and thus is highly connecting. When you are curious, you are also willing to adapt and be changed by your experiences, and if you make those changing experiences together with a friend, it bonds. If you are curious about a range of new topics, then automatically you are interested in the people proficient or at least more experienced than you, allowing you to learn from them.

Defining the capability of the friend to engage in intellectual discussions or other intelligence- or knowledge-based activities however can become a burden on the friendship when one partner of the pair develops faster and the other partner stagnates. This already was noticed by Aristotle, 1925, 9.3[56]. It is in this context that the personality trait (in combination with the resource content) becomes a limiting factor and thus a resource. This effect can be observed in the experience

[51]'Rick was my 'intellectual friend'; he taught me about astronomy, chess, and word games.' or 'I have some friends who are just so smart. They remember everything they read.'

[52]p. 37 'With our friend we appreciate good intellectual qualities'

[53]'Good conversation is in fact crucial for the formation of both moral and intellectual virtue, but it has a more immediate relevance to intellectual virtue.'

[54]`https://theweek.com/articles/739502/8-kinds-friends-need-happy-life`

[55]'men are wont to call you wise in a somewhat different way, not only because of your mental endowments and natural character, but also because of your devotion to study and because of your culture'

[56]While Aristotle talks in the original text about virtue, the phrase 'remained a child in intellect' implies that the intellect component of virtue is emphasised here: 'But if one friend remained the same while the other became better and far outstripped him in virtue, should the latter treat the former as a friend? Surely he cannot. When the interval is great this becomes most plain, e.g. in the case of childish friendships; if one friend remained a child in intellect while the other became a fully developed man, how could they be friends when they neither approved of the same things nor delighted in and were pained by the same things? For not even with regard to each other will their tastes agree, and without this (as we saw) they cannot be friends; for they cannot live together.'

of school friends leaving for University and one of them developing into a more intellectual direction. It can come down to any kind of experience where intense or different directional development of intellectual capabilities occurs, such as periods of living in a different country. This is sometimes phrased as the Expat / McKinsey / Ivy League / Oxbridge curse. Having been exposed to an environment with a high percentage of driven and highly intelligent people, it becomes easy to forget that the general world is not like that and indeed values other traits to intellectual capacity equally if not higher. The result is a big reverse-culture shock, and people find that 'they have little to talk about with their former work colleagues, school peers, friends from home...'. It is in this context of disparity that the returning person feels or can feel somewhat arrogant and discriminating in reflection. In Christian circles the moral expectation is not to choose friends by their status, and thus self-reporting of a high significance of this trait may likely be self-censored.

Practical takeaway
I think curiosity is the key thing here. You should stay interested in the stuff your friends do, read or hear. It can be tempting to stay in a comfort zone of old topics and passions, and I am definitely not advocating a religious zest for truth on high philosophical standards, but an openness to new topics that your friends might bring to the fray. One aspect is being OK at explaining, that is breaking down what is currently in your mind, and on which you might be a super specialist, to a level where your friends can engage with you on it.

Suggestions for thought

- How important is intellectual capacity in your friends for your friendship? Is it more a capacity or an attitude issue?
- Do you have friends who differ significantly from you in terms of their intellectual capacity?
- What do you think would happen to the friendship of your key friends if it stopped being intellectually stimulating (e.g. because of an accident, impairment of brain function, dementia, etc.)?

For statistics in sociological studies, question suggestions and weights in counting see H.

3.9 Positivity, hope and seeing the good

Positivity is seeing the current good in people and situations now, and the potential better in the near or distant future, and making others around you see and feel it too. The result of this are positive emotions that people have in the positive person's company, but apart from positivity there are also different pathways to that. Thus positivity as defined here is substantially more narrow than the general concept of positivity as per Nelson, 2016[57] and Nelson, 2020, which is capturing in its loosest terms how a specific friendship enhances the lives of the two participants to it. Here we are concerned with the general personal trait a person exhibits in their daily life, to others but also towards the friend.

The first theme of positivity is generating **positive** energy or **emotions all around you**. N. Lee and S. Lee, 2009 put it like this: 'Having people around you who make you feel good is one of the first steps to human happiness.' It is a fact of human nature that smiling is infectious. Even the most miserable of people have difficulty resisting the smiles and giggles from a little baby trying to get their attention, and break into a smile themselves. Rath, 2006, p. 118 mentions the adult version in the case of a receptionist, whose smiles helped people start into the day on a positive note. When analysing the statements of the MBTI friendship characterisations[58], cheerfulness or good cheer were frequently mentioned items. People with a high positivity are characterised as 'able to make me feel good', 'never fail to make me smile' or 'create positive moments in your life'. In the qualitative material from discussions, words like joyful or joyous were mentioned for emphasis. Positivity helps in all situations - at work, at home, with other friends, with strangers. Gottman in his research on what makes marriages successful looks at whether couples succeed in making interactions or memories positive. Downey and Condron, 2004 uses the 'capacity to express feelings, ideas and opinions in a positive way' in explaining how suitable children are for friendship. Joyfulness also opens both us and other people up for connection, life is just easier, and we relate to each other on a positive note, and remember each other on a positive note when we see each other again. The trait is particularly valuable when positive people lift us up when we are down. They can take our mind of things, and **cheer us up**. Via affection[59], positive humour, quirkyness or even dark humour, they lift our spirits in difficult situations. It is important for us to realize that we have this need, and appreciate this function when we get cheered up. In the moment it usually comes as a surprise, almost serendipitously. It might be a completely inappropriate comment, yet we giggle or chuckle. It might be giving a perspective on things and a missing piece of information, that gives us hope again.

The converse is true too. Aristotle, 1925, 8.5 blames lacking positivity ('sour') for an incapability to make friends[60]. It is one of the self-fulfilling prophecies of depression that the negativity of the people makes all but their most steadfast friends turn away. Being a friend in such a situation requires patience with

[57]Nelson, 2016, p.36'So the foundation of our Frientimacy Triangle is built on positivity—it's how we'll decide whom to spend more time with, why it worth the effort, and how each relationship enhances our lives.' or on the converse Nelson, 2016, p.7 'We are lonely because those friends don't always leave us feeling better for having spent time with them.'

[58]MBTI is the Myers-Briggs Type Indicator, a psychological test resulting in a classification of 4 traits and thus in one of 16 personality types. A derivative of it is the 16 personalities classification. Based on those types, several authors made descriptions of what these types are as friends, which I summarized as a source.

[59]This is one of the reasons why animal therapy is often very effective at lifting people's overall spirits.

[60]'Neither old people nor sour people seem to make friends easily; for there is little that is pleasant in them, and no one can spend his days with one whose company is painful, or not pleasant, since nature seems above all to avoid the painful and to aim at the pleasant.', see also 8.6

the situation, but this often fuelled and aided by being made positive elsewhere. Other authors also warn of the dangers of negativity to maintaining friendship (cf. Shumway, 2018, p.40[61], Nelson, 2016, p.48[62], or see Anonymous, 2018-08-10 with a similar description of a dysfunctional friendship[63] or Degges-White and Borzumato-Gainey, 2011, ch. 3[64]. The most pointed summary came in Cormie, 2005: 'You will not succeed in building and maintaining close friendships if you are always sucking the life out of everyone.' The Aristotelian argument for a baseline of positivity is also consistent with general psychotherapeutic practices, which focus first on solving or addressing depressions before encouraging and supporting people to build relationships in general and friendships in particular[65].

The Christian term for positivity is **hope**, and it is a bit more far-reaching than classical positivity. Being hopeful[66] means believing that in the long run, things will be OK. For Christians, this comes from their faith[67]. However, it is a universally good trait. Indeed it is - bracketed with optimism - one key character strength chosen by Peterson and Seligman, 2004, who define it as 'positive expectations about matters that have a reasonable likelihood of coming to pass'. This can give us strength to persevere. The theme resonates incredibly strong in us and whether or not we like it, inherently we admire people with it. At its heart, the entire Star Wars Saga is a story of hope[68] and perseverance against the odds[69].

Seeing people's strength is a powerful connecting capability. A key moment in the TED talk Flowers, 2016 is the phrase 'When I could not believe in myself, she believed in me'. Chapman, 2009 states affirmation as one of his five love languages and affirming someone's strengths is the essence of it. And while sometimes in our weak moments we according to N. Lee and S. Lee, 2009 'have a tendency to put other people down to make ourselves look better', when we can overcome this and express our recognition and appreciation of peoples strength it can make a real difference to them. Seeing other people's strength is a positive habit different to flattery. Affirming someone's strength is about them, and the intention of their benefit and authenticity thereof is key in expressing this. The counterexample to seeing people's strength and affirmation is criticising people and friends in front of others, and this is a reliable way to put a friendship in peril. Critique is allowed

[61]'Although it can sometimes feel nice to vent and bellyache to other people, too much of that can deter even the most compassionate friends. People who are continually complaining about their stress and worry tend to come across as needy or difficult to manage.'

[62]'Healthy people aren't looking for needy whining, drama-filled, complaining, negative people with whom to spend time.'

[63]Conflict of wanting to help, but not wanting to be exposed to the negativity `https://www.theguardian.com/lifeandstyle/2018/aug/10/my-friend-is-single-and-lonely-but-demanding`

[64]'A regretted example of this was shared by a 62-year-old divorcee. After her divorce was finalized, she chose to socialize exclusively with other divorcees. Although this shared experience offered the women a unique sense of empathy for one another, our interviewee said that she eventually felt overwhelmed by her friends' negativity and entrenched unhappiness.'

[65]Discussion with Prof. Qualter 2021-5-19

[66]Literally 'being filled with hope'.

[67]see e.g. Lewis, 1960 'I must make it the main object of life to press on to that other country and to help others to do the same.'

[68]The 'first' Star Wars movie is called 'A New Hope'. This is acknowledged and emphasised in the last lines of Rogue One with Leia saying 'What is it they've sent us? Hope'

[69]It can be thought of the key connecting element of Leia and Han, with his key phrase being 'Never tell me the odds!'

up to a limit, but it needs to be against a backdrop of bottom line appreciation for people's positive traits in the friendship.

Practical takeaway
Ask yourself how you can make people feel good about themselves in your daily life. Believe in them, point out their strengths, say thank you. Sure, sometimes bad things happen, and we can curse and be a bit cynical. But overall life is good, and this is something we can try to radiate.

Suggestions for thought

- If there are positive people in your life, have you expressed your appreciation, gratitude and encouragement to them? Even though they may blush a little, it will go a long way in refilling the tank.
- Are you a positive person? Do people smile around you?
- Can you see the strengths in other people? Do you tell them what you think is great about them?
- If you have a friend who is down or in a difficult situation. Can you give them hope to persevere?

For statistics in sociological studies, question suggestions and weights in counting see H.

3.10 Proactiveness and consideration

Consideration is the regard for the circumstances, feelings, comfort, etc. of or thoughtfulness for another. This trait implies **perceiving** your friends or other people's **needs** and being willing to actively meet it, both at smaller and larger physical, emotional, financial or time cost to yourself. In the more pronounced level this is the spirit of altruism. It is the preparedness to sacrifice personally to benefit others. Degges-White and Borzumato-Gainey, 2011, ch. 1 argue this to be a more female than male trait : 'It makes sense that a girl would be willing to endure a level of personal sacrifice in order to access the neurochemical reward that arises from social success.' The attitude this extols can be argued to be at the core of the 'care ethics' so strongly featured in feminist social theory. Consideration is a powerful signal of character virtue, as it signals that you at least occasionally put other people first and not yourself. The Christian virtue **caritas** or charity is the theological term for this trait. Lewis, 1960 'The rule for all of us is perfectly simple. Do not waste time bothering whether you 'love' your neighbour; act as if you did. ... we do good to another self, just because it is a self, made (like us) by God, and desiring its own happiness as we desire ours'. Fromm, 2000 makes a powerful argument that selfishness is inherently an incapacity to love (in our context, to be a friend).[70] I would argue that Fromm's argument is uncompromising, and that indeed preferentialism is part and parcel of friendship. This preferentialism to the friend is one reason Kierkegaard partially rejects the notion of friendship as desirable from a Christian moral perspective. But love is antithetical to selfishness, and people monitor such behaviour[71]. Generally we expect selfishness is the default behaviour. The problem with selfishness and transactional attitude[72] is that should the benefits a friend has from our interactions ebb off temporarily, it might render the friendship obsolete in their eyes, which is undesirable. Even if we don't act entirely selfless, a certain preparedness to forego our interests is crucial[73]. N. Lee and S. Lee, 2009 include proactiveness in their guide to how to relate well as 'meeting other peoples needs' - doing what makes them happy or better. Cicero, 1923 repeatedly has Laelius extol the concern Scipio had for his friends and not just wishing them good, but actively doing whatever he could for them, as well as his family[74] and the general public. Why is this so important? The key here is that ultimately we have a non-utilitarian instinctive view of friendship. Of course, great psychological benefits accrue to us through it. But it is not a calculation like a transaction in a store. Statements such as 'X does not expect gains from the friendship', 'X is selfless in our friendship' repeatedly appear in interview material on friendship. Outright selfishness is considered a no go, and before becoming friends, we look out whether a person is selfish or transactional in his general dealings with others. When a person is behaving altruistically, i.e. acting to our benefit with no likely avenue of direct benefit accruing to them, especially if it is towards us, it is a powerful friendship initiator[75]. It is also good for the psyche[76]. I believe this positive trait is the reason volunteering both for a general community (selling cakes at the annual school event) and for vulnerable communities such as elderly or refugees can be such a powerful generator of new friendships[77]. People meeting in this context credibly signal that compassion and concern for others is a key and time-costly trait of theirs and thus find a strong mutual element of themselves in the other.

An ambivalent property for someone is **being of low need**, that can be met by other people. If you live a simple life, content in your situation, or are affluent

[70]'With regard to the problem under discussion this means: love of others and love of ourselves are not alternatives. On the contrary, an attitude of love toward themselves will be found in all those who are capable of loving others. Love, in principle, is indivisible as far as the connection between 'objects' and one's own self is concerned.'

[71]See also Grant, 2013

[72]A transactional attitude is the opposite of being person oriented. Thus you may just be interested that a barber is cutting your hair in a certain way (transactional), or you may have a conversation with him with genuine interest how they are doing and what their daily concerns are (person oriented).

[73]Alberoni, 2016, p.98 'We have seen that friendship is possible only when friends have the capacities to limit their desires, to reduce their needs, to do without.'

[74]Cicero explicitly mentions Scipio caring for his sisters. This would have been unusual at the time as they would not extend the family power quite as much as the males in Roman society. It was thus a beyond the norm signal of a general generous and caring attitude.

[75]Degges-White and Borzumato-Gainey, 2011, ch. 3 'As a corollary to our belief that friends provide support without expecting repayment, an unsolicited offer of support can lead to the development of friendship.'

[76]Sira M., 2020-06-14 'Helping others simply feels good. Try to do things for others without expecting nothing in return. Believe me, life becomes much easier.'

[77]Millington, 2019, p.24 'My advice: if you're looking to make new friends, start with volunteering for a local charity and you might just meet friends for life.'

and capable of meeting your own each and every material need, then people are unlikely to suspect you of a hidden agenda or transactional view seeking your own interest. Interest in the other person then is clearly interest in the other person for their sake. Cicero, 1923, p.143 makes this point thus: 'Now what need did Africanus have of me? By Hercules! none at all'. The conflict here is with reciprocity(4.7), equality(4.10) and possibly vulnerability(4.9). It is a great boon to be able to do a good or a favour to a friend, and by being of 'low need' you prevent them being proactive and considerate to you.

This does not mean that we are outright naive about selfless nature. Of course, most of our daily living is transactional. Nehamas, 2016, ch. 4 phrases it thus 'I know what I want from them and my interest in them is exhausted by the specific qualities that allow them to perform their particular function.' and in our initial transactions we spend time with a person because they might be entertaining, interesting, or profanely because we have a commercial or romantic interest. But the necessary condition in order to develop this relationship into a friendship and keep it thus that over time a genuine interest in the other and a consideration of their needs will become an overarching theme in the relationship.

Practical takeaway
When we say 'do an act of kindness a day' the key word is the 'do'. Friendship should not be transactional or utility-oriented, but if you see something that you can do to bring a little joy to your friend, just do it. Second, and even more important, asking for a favour from a friend is not being transactional. It is giving your friend an opportunity to show their concern for you and express their desire for your well being by doing something.

Suggestions for thought

- Do you have a transactional attitude to people? How much do you look out for yourself?
- How aware are you of other peoples needs? Do you even try?
- If you are Christian, to what degree do you practice loving your neighbour?
- If you are looking for friends, have you thought about volunteering at a local charity whose goals you share?

For statistics in sociological studies, question suggestions and weights in counting see H.

3.11 Energy, excitement and adventure

Having energy is a resource, applying it in the service and for the enjoyment of your friends is a trait. For most experiences that determine our good friendships someone took the initiative and made us do that hike, that trip, engage in that project or volunteer action, and inspired us or cajoled us into it with his sheer determination to do it and involve us too. This theme has the following subthemes:

- being positively healthy and being energetic,
- having an exciting personality,
- being adventurous,
- not being limited by one's health both in participation in sports as a young person and general social life as an elderly, which will be dealt with in the section on health as a resource (6.4).

(1) Being positive is part of (3.9), but there is a different kind of positive energy that people radiate and inspire their friends with, and that is a kind of freshness that is challenging to do things. Cicero, 1923, p.121[78]speaks here of 'viriditatem' - **freshness** in the sense of greenness or briskness. Thus people appreciate those who are full of energy or lively. High energy and agency levels are one of the most frequent positive characteristics in the MBTI friendship profiles. Doing things with friends creates good memories, and thus people who are full of agency and precisely encourage their peers to do things with them will thus enhance the friendship experience. For starters, they have the agency and energy to rise from the couch, switch off the TV and get out of the house to do *something* with a friend.

Rath, 2006, p.117[79] finds this aspect of energizing your friends also sufficiently important to create a role of the energizer, though basically it is a combination of positivity (3.9) and fun (3.5). My hunch is that Rath didn't go deep enough. It is not just fun and positivity, some people literally recharge your energy or batteries. I don't mean spiritually, or in a laying on hands. But there is effect that in the presence of a friend a mountain is not quite so steep (here I am not talking about support in grief). In the few unstructured interviews which I conducted in preparatory exploration for this book, one interviewee described friends pushing us along to go beyond our perceived capacity in the gym, or us studying longer in the library simply by their example. I mean, they literally give you the energy (maybe via peer pressure and that sickening good cheer and attitude) to not break off the hike but to persevere till the end. You tell them you hate them for it, but continue. And after you spend time with them, you feel energised or refreshed. It is worth here looking at the opposite: probably the most frequent word used with 'toxic friendships' is 'draining'. Now I really dislike the phrase 'toxic friendship'. It is illogical, an oxymoron. But in this context the phrase 'draining' is suggesting a correct intuition, as it contrasts the expectation we have from spending time with good friends, which is feeling energized.

This does not just refer to physical energy, but mental as well. Some people, though physically handicapped, can still develop a remarkable capability to focus and mental energy that is nothing short of inspiring to witness. It enables them to

[78]'...,tamen aufert eam viriditatem, in qua etiam nunc erat Scipio.' - 'yet it does take away that freshness which Scipio kept even to the end.'

[79]'Energizers are your 'fun friends'... `https://theweek.com/articles/739502/8-kinds-friends-need-happy-life`

still take part in life with friends. Sometimes energy and determination are taken equivalent to ambition and competitiveness. Here I would argue it is difficult to decide the balance. On the one hand, ambition is essentially an American virtue admired in others, and most friendship surveys are based on samples of American college students. On the other hand, ambition is antithetical to humility so emphasised in section (3.3). There is no fixed term for this in sociological research in the friendship context.

(2) Some people with their colourful, creative and **exciting personality** bring something different into our world. They are the natural partners to discover and expand the world with (see 5.8). With them in tow, the world just becomes a little less predictable. They are usually also rich in content (6.3) . When we grow up, so many people stop believing that the excitement of play, adventure and fantasy is still for us. We have friends who however don't follow that process. They can still see the world through the eyes of a child, the excitement of a good prank, the awe at nature and dragons, the joy of a really silly joke. When we interact with them, it is something of a world lost to us, and somehow at least some of us wonder what we lost.

It is those friends who have the potential to put us slightly off the path of true virtue. We may go on sailing trips, but we maybe even try weed or a bang cookie. Fun events that are slightly wrong but build glorious memories. The really stupid idea that was ... well stupid ... but that you will laugh about for decades to come is usually coming from them. When it applies to friends, 'crazy' and even 'reckless' is consistently a positive attribute.

(3) While the end of the New Testament probably didn't classify as **adventure** story, many of the miracles probably made the time the disciples spent with Jesus exciting: Driving out demons[80], raising the dead[81], sailing in storms[82], camping on mountain tops[83] - not a bad time for three years. The unconventionality of Don Quixote and its resulting appeal on Sancho to have adventures is singled out by Nehamas, 2016, ch. 3 and is made vividly graphic in the musical Man of La Mancha with Peter O Toole.

One of my favourite movie quotes (Rumour has it) is 'Life has to be a little nuts sometimes. Otherwise it's just a bunch of Thursdays strung together.', and this is what our Energizer friend can do for us. It is about taking calculated risks to enable an adventure. Alberoni, 2016, p.71[84] describes the friendship in particular in childhood and adolescence as perpetual adventure. Rath, 2006, p.123 tells the story of one interviewee being taken along to a volunteering trip in Kazakhstan. Some people need adventure like other people oxygen. They are not that frequent, but their surrounding profits from it. As they become experienced in adventuring,

[80]Luke 9:1 'When Jesus had called the Twelve together, he gave them power and authority to drive out all demons and to cure diseases'

[81]Luke 8:40-56, Matthew 9:18-19

[82]Matt 8:25 'The disciples went and woke him, saying, 'Lord, save us! We're going to drown!' He replied, 'You of little faith, why are you so afraid?' Then he got up and rebuked the winds and the waves, and it was completely calm.'

[83]Matt 17:4 Peter said to Jesus, 'Lord, it is good for us to be here. If you wish, I will put up three shelters-one for you, one for Moses and one for Elijah.'

[84]'Why are we never bored with our friends? Because true friendship is always an adventure, an exploration of the mysteries of life, a searching. This is how friendship grows in childhood and adolescence. Two children who become friends invent new games, liberate the imagination, go on to explore the big mysterious world surrounding them. '

they can make the adventure 'safe' for less adventurous friends, and take them along for the ride.

Practical takeaway
Next time your friend is wondering about a slightly crazy idea they always were wondering about, encourage them to do it and invite yourself along for the ride. Think Nike 'Just do it'.

Suggestions for thought

- To what degree do you value energy levels in a friend?
- Do you have an exciting friend? A friend who brings the unexpected and surprising life into your friendship?
- With which friends do you feel energized or more active after you have met them?
- What is the most exciting and adventurous thing a friend made you do?

For statistics in sociological studies, question suggestions and weights in counting see H.

3.12 Social ease, agreeableness and connectibility

Social Ease is 'being good with people', making them comfortable to relax, integrating them, being able to do the small talk and taking the initiative to it. Despite being the killer application among child oriented friendship literature, it actually is hardly mentioned by the philosophers and also only receives subpar results for adult friendship literature.

The theme has several subthemes: (1) general agreeableness and friendliness, (2) showing initiative and reaching out to others, (3) making new friends quickly and (4) managing a network of 'weak' friends well by interconnecting them.

(1) general **agreeableness** and **friendliness**: We are not friends with everyone, but we can be friendly with all people. We like our friends to be 'nice', 'easy to talk to', or plain old 'friendly'. This attitude in part is overlapping with general kindness (3.6), but it is more about creating ease in an initial interaction. Of course the other friendship personality traits like a peaceful disposition, positivity, humility, humour and acceptance likewise contribute to this effect. If I approach an agreeable or sympathetic person, my intuitive assessment of likelihood of rejection (which carries psychological pain to my ego) is reduced. This can describe individuals, but it can also describe communities and societies with words like 'welcoming', 'warm' and 'friendly'. As we evaluate people who we want to get to know and become friendly with ourselves, we often observe how people treat others and in particular how friendly they are to strangers, as a proxy for how

we are likely to be treated. Even Cicero, 1923, p.175[85] recommended us to pick friends who are 'sociable and sympathetic'. Romans 12:16[86] encourages to pursue this habit thus encouraging better interaction in the early church communities.

Whilst discussion of soft skills and the need for agreeableness is a lot featured in management talk, our general civil attitude towards unrelated others might be declining. According to Degges-White and Borzumato-Gainey, 2011, ch.2 this may even be brought about by the general public[87]. Affected is the way both how we interact with strangers and general acquaintances, as habits of casual mutual support slowly decline even in traditional rural areas. Interesting in this context is a story by Hunt, 2018-09-07 of a Tesco[88] becoming the social center of a community on account of the approachability of the staff[89]. The fact this example became such a newsworthy story shows how different to the actual norm such behaviour has become.

It is not just people that can signal agreeableness and friendliness, but places and communities too. I know of churches that have posts for 'welcoming team' - literally people waiting at the door to strike up a conversation to new faces entering to make them feel welcome and at home.[90] And even if they don't actively reach out, they signal a 'I don't bite, come talk to me if you have a question'.

(2) showing initiative and **reaching out to others** is one of the key characteristics of extraversion. It shows in sentences like 'X reaches out spontaneously', 'X will break the mould' or 'X initiates with people'. Alcock-Ferguson, 2018-05-16 shows the power this has on other people. Particularly the small gestures of acknowledgement and conversation can make a big difference to some people, and possibly be the only kind gesture they experience that day. Thus even if it is not your nature, picking up a habit of such micro-reaching outs is a great new year's resolution.

The difference between an introvert and an extrovert is the power to reach out to people in a kind way. While this is natural to some, behaving like an extrovert is a skill you can learn (see Baranski et al., 2020). Training extraversion only applies to behaviour, not retraining the personality, which is unlikely to succeed. I am thus not saying you need to become a completely trained extrovert, but literally practicing to initiate with people will bring you benefits, even if you fall on your nose a few times. Are there rejections, sure, but over time the benefits to your happiness by the connections you have built you would not have had without reaching out will tip the balance. It is really simple, in order for a connection to be created, someone has to make the start. It may be awkward, but it is a necessary condition. Section (1) is all about making it easier for others to approach you, but still the best practice for you to go to them. As the saying goes 'If the mountain will not come to Muhammad, then Muhammad must go to the mountain.' For some of us this is really hard to learn because of past painful experiences of rejections

[85]simplicem praeterea et communem et consentientem - frank, sociable, and sympathetic

[86]Traditionally 'live in harmony with each other' but is sometimes translated as 'be friendly with everyone'

[87]'Social scientists have found ...'

[88]British supermarket chain

[89]https://www.theguardian.com/voluntary-sector-network/2018/may/16/loneliness-charities-voluntary-organisations-communities

[90]That awkward moment when you extend your hand and they go for the hug. http://www.kappit.com/img/pics/74711790ichch_sm.jpg?

(see Atwood, 2005[91], but in order to enjoy friendship the faster and more effective we overcome this, the better. As you start this journey, you will also enjoy it more. As you see how interesting people (sometimes) are you become curious about meeting new ones and their stories. And yet it also makes you more appreciative of the friends you already have, as you see the stories of their lives, which they graced you with, from different angles.

For some people friendly and positive reaching out to others at every step in their life is part of the DNA (see e.g. Greif, 2009, ch.13[92]). I have been privileged to meet several such people over the course of my life, and it is always amazing just to see them getting acquainted most cordially to people on the spot. I have done it striking up conversations with sympathetic strangers in cafes, bookshops, trains, and other occasions. I love it and thrive of the positive energy such an encounter can generate. I know people who feel the same. I also know people who literally hate such a behaviour, and prize their noise cancelling headphones and broadsheet newspapers. On a trip I did with a friend which incorporated a longer train ride, I struck up a conversation with a stranger who had been reading a book I had read a prior month. Now I enjoyed myself and given how long the conversation and overall enthusiastic went, I assume the other person too. My friend was shocked in disbelief at my flagrant disregard for the strangers privacy and right to be left by himself. Today we laugh about it, but it reminded me to check for little cues such as eye rolls or heavy breathing at the start of a conversation with a stranger who is stuck in his seat in a train and cannot really run away - just in case.

The habit of reaching out to others is strongly dependent on our level of energy. This habit suffers when we are drained from work and commuting, but we also need to recognize that everyone else suffers from it too. We collectively need to counteract and initiate. And thus keeping a habit also to reaching out to old friends to organize that beer evening in the pub, or the next barbecue is key to keeping the gang together (5.6). And many people appreciate this (see Nelson, 2016, p.74[93]). On the other hand, there is the danger of overreaching. This can be particularly the case if there is a case of expectation and role mismatch (9.3). If you feel this is the case then a slightly nerdy recommendation might be of help: if you value the connection but do not want to become a nuisance then you might follow a geometric progression [94] of reaching out - this could be 1 day after meeting, 1 week, 1 month and then 3-6 month or annually. It of course depends of whether you get no response, an outright rejection, or a can't do - busy now but look forward to hearing from you later. The converse recommendation is that if you are the one to whom someone is reaching out, where you do not for whatever reason see a way forward, a courteous but clear rejection is probably the best way forward, rather than ghosting on repeated reach outs.

[91]'We've got to learn how to overcome the fear of rejection. And that's difficult for some of us because another big reason we're afraid to initiate is that we've experienced some very painful rejections in our lives.'

[92]'Women are better than men at making friendship ...', which is attributed to reaching out and cordial and rapid exchange of information.

[93]'It means so much to me that you invite me out so often....' one person expressing regret at not naturally reciprocating.

[94]https://en.wikipedia.org/wiki/Geometric_progression

The habit of reaching is automatic in friendly organizations. One frequent backdrop against which reaching out to friends and potential friends occurs is that of organization based social activities. You see your friends at an after service coffee at church; you see them as they bring their kids to the kindergarten. At that point, this trigger, you remember it has been a while since you last had dinner or coffee together and initiate. The converse effect is now seen in companies all across the industries in Covid times - the loss of the coffee corners increased the cost of reaching out in the office with a drastic impact on information exchange and relationship development.

The habit of reaching out can also define societies and cultures. In some pubs in the Rheinland, and particularly during Carnival, you can just enter and casually get acquainted with whoever stands next to you. In other regions in Germany or the world, striking up a casual conversation in a pub will be less in line with local customs. Some societies are remarkably hospitable, offering food and shelter to random travelers passing through their village, others are commercially minded and close their doors. It remains also to be seen, what the effect of locking down for a year will be for the world.

(3) Some people **make new friends** quickly. At the same time they maintain loose friendly relations without seeing the need to let go of people if they do not progress to true friendship. Friendly relations are not simply to be condemned as superficial. It is possible for acquaintances to be for years in the situationship category, only then to find the spark that they have a true passion in common. Nelson, 2016 speaks of common friends, people we are happy to meet at church or parents' evenings. Greif, 2009[95] calls these friends 'just friends', arguably a more complimentary title than the 'weak ties' of Granovetter, 1973.

There is a particular word of connecting people within this loose connection 'weak tie' circle, and it is the word '**schmoozing**'. According to the OED[96] it is 'To talk or behave in a charming, ingratiating, or insincere way, esp. as a means of gaining favour or an advantage. Also: to chat, gossip.' I find it sad that the dictionary implies insincerity. 'Working a room' at a party to enable guests feeling welcome and having a good time, both if you are the host and the guest, is one of the lubricants of society. Another great phrase - not to be confused with fun and humour as in the next section - is 'humouring people' or 'entertaining people'. Spencer and Pahl, 2006[97] also sees a vital role for schmoozers as social lubricant.

(4) managing a network of 'weak' friends well by **actively interconnecting** them. **Networking** and the phrase 'social network' has an ugly utilitarian instrumental sound to it in our time, it however needs not to be. Networking is about creating and maintaining connections. Consider the following advice of St. Paul: 'Greet all God's people in Christ Jesus. The brothers and sisters who are with me send greetings. All God's people here send you greetings, especially those who

[95]These friendships I call just friends because these people are, in fact, just friends. They are a little closer than acquaintances and are pleasant to be with, but we don't expect to socialize outside of our poker game. Just like guys who get together out of an interest in basketball, golf, or stamp collecting but gather only for sports- or hobby-related contact.

[96]Oxford English Dictionary

[97]'These have traditionally been seen as more virtuous than circles of friends gathered together for pleasure or mutual help. But here the authors rehabilitate the informal schmoozers, who may join nothing formal but who may play a critical role in holding friendship networks together and in holding communities together, below the radar of any official measures.'

belong to Caesar's household.' (Philippians 4:21-22). This is a textbook example of a skilled network manager strengthening the ties within the network. When you greet someone in someone else's name, you have something to talk about (that person). On that part, positive gossip is great[98]. If you exchange a positive but funny anecdote about this person (which the person would be happy for you to share), you immediately connect via your goodwill for this person with mirth. You connect over a person, also by expressing concern for her or his good will, or by bringing just general news. But it is about more than that.

Friendship networking or 'schmoozing' is both an attitude and art[99], and a resource and asset if done well (6.5). People recognise this with sentences like ' X seems to know everyone. ', Whenever I tell X of a problem, he usually has a suggestion of who might help me' or 'I have met several friends through X'. As a networker you know what your friends and friendly relations are passionate about, and thus you can spark people who are friendly relations on their mutual passions, travels, thus giving the opportunity of friendship. You enable by putting them in the spotlight in a way they would not feel good doing it themselves (X has a great taste in wines and makes a wonderful Sunday roast with his secret family bread crumb recipe, Y knows everything about early Roman history, Z has travelled extensively in Turkey and the Near east - aren't you travelling there, ...).[100] This is in particular a most helpful service you can render to your less extroverted and outreaching friends - see this testimony from Rath, 2006, p.111: 'My business partners mind is like a database of people. It's amazing because she knows so much about them too. She introduces people based on what they have in common. I think she wants to get to know people better — just so she can bring them into her network. This helps me meet new people every time I am at an event with her.' It is thus no surprise that Rath, 2006, p.111[101] creates a full 'vital friends' role called 'Connector' for this, however I would think that in most

[98] I define positive gossip as information about that person that is de-classified for sharing with someone who is also positively disposed towards this person. This information can include funny anecdotes, recovery from illness, success in life, a new girl or boyfriend, anything that allows you to express your genuine goodwill towards that person in the presence of a mutual friend.

[99] Disclosure - if you find my emphasis of the importance of the schmoozer too strong, then I would acknowledge that you may be right. I am a schmoozer by the book, privately as in my company life, and I acknowledge that there are differing opinions on the value of this function in organizations and society. I have over the course of the years met however several true masters of the trade: there was a priest at university who I recall to be extremely effective at matchmaking his flock. Not only did he sponsor romantic couples, but also introduced dozens of pairs for mutual interests and general friendship. He was literally all over the place, in and out of conversations, and always with a cheerful smile and social encouragement. There were several managers who simply knew everyone in the organisation informally and who were just highly regarded by everyone on account of their good cheer. Likewise, I encountered local butterflies who were the spiders in the web of the expat scenes of Sao Paulo, Tokyo and Hong Kong. I am in awe of these people and have always tried to learn. The world is just a better place because of people like that.

[100] I love introducing people who share mutual interests, went to similar schools, have similar work contents or anything you can have a hunch from that they just might fit well together for a good conversation. In fact the personal key motivation for undertaking the research of this book is to figure out what the characteristics are how people can be best matched platonically. how you best develop a hunch to bring people together, to play platonic cupid. Not for romance, not for networking benefits, not for business deals, but simply to have a pleasant and interesting conversation and leave the barbecue, dinner party or lunch with the thought 'that was time well spent for having met X, I really hope we manage to follow up for a coffee or beer in the future, that was fun.

[101] `https://theweek.com/articles/739502/8-kinds-friends-need-happy-life`: 'A Connector is a bridge builder ...'

cases the connector is not a core link but a weak link as you are an element in the network of his like many others (See 9).

In my view, the most effective habit of friendship networking is that of a circle bridge, where you are part of different circles and can introduce across boundaries. Thus you match people who have a high friendship compatibility, but would - mostly sticking to their own circles - otherwise not meet. A habit of hospitality (5.7) helps in bringing such people together in informal gatherings.

Practical takeaway
Gift one friend every year by facilitating a friendship. Continuously think about who of your friends might have a good chemistry and introduce them to each other when there is an opportunity.

Suggestions for thought

- How easily do you think you can be approached by a shy person who is interested in getting to know you? Do you reach out to other people at events?
- How good are you at spontaneously reaching out to others? To what degree do past experiences hold you back from doing so, even if a person seems sympathetic and interesting to get to know?
- How active are you in loosely maintaining your friendly relations? What do you do to ensure the contact doesn't die off?
- How good are you at introducing friends of yours to each other across circles, making use of what you know about them?

For statistics in sociological studies, question suggestions and weights in counting see H.

3.13 Patience, peace and calmness

People that radiate internal peace make it possible for other people to relax and calm in their presence. They can be the rock in emotional turmoil. In their talk on 'How to relate well', N. Lee and S. Lee, 2009 separate between peace and patience and name them both as key relationship enablers (along with positivity and proactiveness). **Patience** is described as absence of a quick temper resulting from internalised anger. Thus Colossians 3:12, on which N. Lee and S. Lee, 2009 is based, states 'Clothe yourself with ... patience. Bear with each other ...', and indeed arguably also in the four gospels patience is one of the virtue Jesus himself extols. Children of course notice it in adults and kids, and are usually turned off befriending kids who frequently throw tantrums. Even non-explosive passive anger can be a turnoff for friendships, e.g. see Ball, 2020-05-18 who labels passive-aggressive comments as toxic behaviour. Patience as a characteristic of friendship is echoed also in Alberoni, 2016, p.11, 24. Along this line, Asatryan,

2016, p.27 illustrates the cause of the lack of patience in our time and the potential obstacle it poses to relationships: 'As we integrate these products [smartphones etc.] technical deeper into our lives, the central principle they were built around ' efficiency' seeps deeper and deeper into our minds. The more we expect perfect efficiency from interactions with our phones, the less patience we have for interactions with people.'. When describing friends who have patience for 'repeatedly talking about the same problem' or 'our ranting about X, again' Nelson, 2016 shows how exercising patience can be an emotional gain. Shumway, 2018, p.2 emphasises the need for patience in the teaching and learning activity with a friend, which is central to his concept of friendship. Andrews, 2019-12-19 relates a story of a dear friend she has, who through tempers caused by an illness had lost friends, but who became a better friend again as her friends bore with her in patience. All in all, while patience is not the be all and is all of friendship, it is necessary for some roles that involve emotional understanding and support. Being patient is a great trait, and our friends will appreciate us showing it.

N. Lee and S. Lee, 2009 define **peace** as the result as the absence of stress. Likewise, the Bible stresses the importance on internalised peace on good relationships between the disciples. It is however not only that. Some people achieve a 'Zen' or 'Buddha' like attitude to life. These people are not saints but usually simply people who are at peace with who they are. But stress is usually the key reason for us not being at peace, and thus when our own life is in turmoil, be it because of a breakup or a redundancy, talking things over with that person helps. It is in such cases not even a talking things over, but more a 'venting' so that anger and turmoil at least temporarily evaporate. In romantic relationships the capacity of one partner to provide calm and perspective is often lauded, some people have it with their parents, and in friendships this is just the same. This is not the same as 'good empathic listening', though it may be part of it. Peace and Patience are not a must have, indeed, various roles such as Energizer or Clown need not have it. However, it is a trait we can value in friends specifically for situations of crisis and emotional turmoil.

Practical takeaway

Forgive. Keep forgiving. I mention within-friendship forgiveness elsewhere with acceptance, humility and loyalty for its immediate effect within the relationship. But even if the transgression towards you has been committed in a completely different context, you will only have peace in the other parts of your life if you manage to completely lay it at rest. It will also make the conversations with your friends much more enjoyable. Remember Aristotle - nobody likes sour people![a]

[a] I totally credit N. Lee and S. Lee, 2009 for that recommendation.

Suggestions for thought

- Even if patience isn't your virtue, do you check yourself what the causes of your impatience are?

- Are you at peace with yourself? Are thoughts storming through your head or are you basically fine? If you are a peaceful person, do you give enough time to your friends to benefit from this?
- On the contrary, have you had friendship breakups or crises because of your bad temper? What was the issue and was it connected with your friendship? Do you know what triggers your temper so that ideally you don't let it spill over into your friendships?

For statistics in sociological studies, question suggestions and weights in counting see H.

Chapter 4

The relationship attitudes

All sections are for casual reading

Introduction

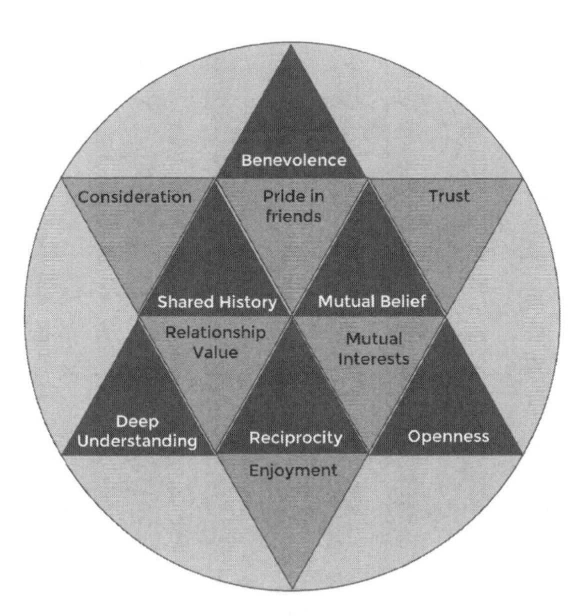

Figure 4.1: Friendship Attitudes

The relationship attitude carry about 49 % weight according to the frequency analysis (see F.1), with the cluster centers lying between 40 % and 54 %. This is where the weight lies, the meat of the friendship. These traits are generally also at the core of the psycho-sociological analyses and reasonably well researched. These generally are described by 'X behaves to me in a certain way...', 'my relationship with X is characterised by ...' or 'I am connected to X by ...'. It is thus an exclusive element. Whereas X might be intelligent at any point of time, or affectionate with many people, relationship traits are inherently bilateral. 'X pays attention to me, even though they behave completely narcissistically with everyone else' is a perfectly feasible statement about the quality (priority) of the bilateral relationship. In some such cases the bilateral attitude taken towards each other can differ dramatically from public general behaviour or the inherent personality of the friend without accusing the friend of acting hypocritical or inauthentic. It is also the part of the friendship that usually needs to be developed. Whereas the personality is (initially) outside the relationship, and starts it off, and the activities are just started based on initial platonic attraction, the relationship traits need to be discovered, developed and built over time.

Tot	OP	CP	TW	SH	CM	QS1	QS2	OA	YA	YS
49	54	54	49	49	45	49	49	48	40	NA
Weight share of friendship attitudes										

	Tot	OP	CP	TW	SH	CM	QS1	QS2	OA	YA	YS
Comm. Mem.	●	●	●	●	●	●	●	◒	●	◒	●
Affection	◕	◕	◒	●	◕	◕	◒	◒	◕	◔	◒
Love of friend	●	●	●	●	●	◕	●	◒	●	◕	●
Dir. Consid.	◒	●	◒	◕	◔	◔	◒	◔	◔	◔	◔
Priority	●	●	◕	◕	●	●	●	◒	●	◕	◕
Loyalty	●	◕	●	●	◒	◔	◕	●	◒	◕	◒
Independence	◔	○	●	◔	◔	◔	◔	○	◔	○	◔
Enjoyment	◕	●	◕	◒	◕	●	●	◕	◕	●	◕
Mut. Underst.	◕	◔	◕	◒	●	◕	●	◕	◕	◕	◒
Reciprocity	◕	●	◒	◒	◕	◒	●	●	◕	◔	◕
Trust	◕	◒	◒	◕	◕	◕	◕	●	◒	◕	◒
Open. Vuln.	◕	◔	◔	◒	●	◕	◕	●	◔	◔	◔
Resp. Appr	◒	◒	●	◔	◕	◒	◔	◕	◔	◔	◔
Equality	○	◔	◔	◔	○	◔	◔	◔	○	○	◔
Goodwill	◒	●	●	●	◔	◒	◔	◔	◔	◒	◒
Mut. Interest	◒	◔	◕	○	◔	◔	◕	◕	◕	◕	◒
Mut. Belief	◒	◕	◕	◔	◔	◔	◒	◕	●	◔	◕
Privacy	◔	○	◒	◔	◔	◒	◔	●	◔	◔	◒
No Privacy	◔	◔	◔	◔	○	◔	○	○	◒	○	◔

Figure 4.2: Friendship Relationship Traits

The weights are from the frequency analysis explained in section F.1, the categories are OP: Old philosophers, CP contemporary philosophers, TW theological writers, SH self help, CM contemporary media, QS1 qualitative sociologist studies, QS2 quantitative sociologist studies, OA old age sociol. st., YA young age sociol. st., YS youth study.

4.1 Common memory and history shared

This is the hoard of joined stories and experiences that both of you collect and value. The memory of our past interactions makes the relationship unique and irreplaceable, and no one can take it away from us. Nostalgia is a proven happiness drug in particular in old age, as already Cicero, 1923, p.125[1] noted.

Common memory is what we share directly, it is not the similar experiences as elaborated on in section 4.13. It is the actual memory, not the next best thing. It is the context of us understanding what shapes us and how it shaped us into who we are. We are not limited by our capacity to retell a story or their imagination of a situation, but we have the same firsthand experience of the situation. Some experiences are of the 'you had to be there' type. Indeed, we can rely on them to complement our incomplete recollection of an event with details that we forgot about.[2] In that through the memory of a friend we have a more detailed and potentially more objective view on the past we lived through together.

Common memory opens up optionality in conversations. It creates the opportunity to make 'insider' jokes referring to past anecdotes; it allows you to understand your friends' actions and emotions against a range of prior experiences of them, it creates a predictability as you have a track record of how they have behaved in the past towards you and others. Ultimately, your common memory is a bridge that links part of their person to yours in a unique bond. It should be noted that of course our actual memory is retaining 10 % of an event and filling in the gaps (see Gilbert, 2009). When we are with a friend, there is more retained between the two of us, and usually the filling in the gaps process happens complementary. This leads to a richer and more entertaining re-discovery, and of course this effect compounds in a circle of three or four friends. As our current mood and general attitude can influence our view or reprocessing of our memories, habits of positivity, affection or gratitude will further enhance the positive impact common memory has on our friendships and by extension our well-being, potentially creating a feedback loop.

As far as memories go, there seems to be a rough rule of 'the older the better'. As little as the experience might be relevant to later adult life, memories of kindergarten, primary or early secondary school have a certain innocence but also a 'when the world was still good and worry free'[3]

The **length of time** which you have known your friend has a direct impact on the quality of your relationship. There is a saying 'there is no such thing as new old friends'. As you know someone for a long time, you gain context. You can make comparisons of what they were like at different phases in their life. There is a difference of course between the statements 'we have known each other since X' and 'we have been friends for a long time', and in the later case this is a complete state-

[1] 'Still, such is my enjoyment in the recollection of our friendship that I feel as if my life has been happy because it was spent with Scipio.'

[2] Nehamas, 2016, ch. 3 'They told one another the stow at great length, each supplementing the other's recollections; and when they had finished: "That was the best time we ever had," said Frederick. "Yes, perhaps you are right. That was the best time we ever had," said Deslauriers.'

[3] Of course I am aware that the childhoods of many people are deeply trouble some, with bullying, financial worries and insecurities all around. However it is part of the human brain's capacity to over time rosetint most experiences and leave us with a positive image of our past, with which we then like to connect via nostalgia.

ment with a range of implications for the quality and type of friendship. Cicero, 1923, p. 179 'as in the case of wines that improve with age, the oldest friendships ought to be the most delightful'. Elsewhere Cicero, 1923, p.145[4] points to a weeding out process taking place as time passes. Contrary to Aristotle, 1925, 8.3[5], who also speaks of the dissolution of friendships of pleasure and utility, Cicero however in the light of the civil war acknowledges also other reasons for friendships to dissolve. As friends consistently spend time with us throughout the decades, they become like family to us, and even Alberoni, 2016, p.120[6], otherwise focused on friendships of mind, excellence and mutual recognition, speaks of friends 'of habit, who are a little like family'. As such, friends who have stuck around for such a long time are adequately compared in nature to actual kin (see Rath, 2006, p. 106[7]). It is this aspect via which a good romantic relationship also gains the nature of a close friendship over time, as the couple builds a positive common memory and narrative, and just becomes really acquainted with each other. The mechanism of simply letting time pass is effective for building intimacy in male friendships. Some men who have difficulty opening up, do so with time and discover step by step that a more personal relationship is possible (see Greif, 2009, p.62).

Greif, 2009, ch.1 coins the phrase 'rust friend' and his description is insightful, singling out the relationship and gained acquaintance, and this allows us to fall back into old patterns in which we can relax and be (former) selves[8]. This novel way of interacting is precisely what Nehamas, 2016, ch.0 records of his reunion: 'Every one of us, of course, has also undergone many changes, and at least some are to the good. Most important, we can appreciate what we once were and liked about each other without the insecurities, the resentments, and the competitiveness of adolescence: our interactions are now easier, milder, and more consistently affectionate, even if they are less dramatic or passionate than they were at the time.' I have first hand experienced this effect a few times, taking the opportunity of meeting up with old school or college acquaintances and can assert to this effect. Some of these meetings reveal clear out flat that there is no interpersonal chemistry lost, and it is a onetime catchup. But sometimes you meet with them on a hunch, and despite not bonding too much ten, twenty or thirty years ago, they have turned out in remarkably different ways to how you imagined, yet the sense of familiarity and fondness is simply there because of the long acquaintance. I would thus always recommend - given the opportunity - to go for a coffee with a long gone acquaintance from school or university days.

While I will come to the aspect of a friend's death later, when a friendship

---

[4]'Now he, indeed, used to say that nothing was harder than for a friendship to continue to the very end of life; for it often happened either that the friendship ceased to be mutually advantageous, or the parties to it did not entertain the same political views; and that frequently, too, the dispositions of men were changed, sometimes by adversity and sometimes by the increasing burdens of age.'

[5]'Such friendships, then, are easily dissolved, if the parties do not remain like themselves'

[6]'There are however, other friendships that last a lifetime that are not characterized by common creative activity and the intensity of encounters. There are those friends whom we rely on out of habit, who are a little like family; like when children call someone uncle or aunt, simply because they have begun to do so when they were little, and cannot explain the difference between an uncle and a friend.'

[7]'My friend Ben is someone I have known since second grade. He knows me better than anyone except my wife, and in some ways, he knows me better than my wife.'

[8]' When I see them, I may ...'

ends, the natural context of our memories dies. Whilst Cicero, 1923, p.211[9] says that through our memories our friends live on in us, the joyous nature of our joint exploits looses its luster. A joke based on a specific anecdote will never be quite understood the same way as telling it with a friend who was there (see Lewis on loss). If certain things in our life had a certain meaning, and the person dies, that meaning in part also dies. In the sense that at the end of a good friendship the risk of loss is also the greatest (see e.g. Matthews, 1983, p.146[10]).

Common memory has a key cross-fertilizing or enabling effect with fun and humour. The capability to make jokes, to see and show the funny side in things is a key desirable trait in a friend. However the good laughter is that on old anecdote. Some great conversations with close friends can comprise little else than a rinse-repeat of old humorous anecdotes, quotes, often not just about the two friends, but their friends in their wider circle. 'Do you remember when X did Y - oh my god, I still am laughing about it' is a frequent contribution to such a conversation. The amount and quality of such insider stories is a direct indicator of the mutual affection and quality of the friendship developed over the past.

Practical takeaway
There is no such thing as new old friends. Cherish your memories with your close friends. Delve into nostalgias unapologetically. And some anecdotes from childhood are there to be repeated every time at a friends reunion.

Suggestions for thought

- Do you give good long-lasting gifts to your friends? Do you keep the ones that you receive in a good prominent place to show you appreciate them?
- Do you have a habit of keeping good photos and even putting them up on a wall?
- When you engage in nostalgic anecdotes with your friends, do you incorporate the kids as well?
- If you are looking for new friends, try your old primary, secondary or college reunion. You might make new friends of old acquaintances.

For statistics in sociological studies, question suggestions and weights in counting see H.

[9] 'But those experiences with him are not dead; rather they are nourished and made more vivid by my reflection and memory;'

[10] 'The availability of a lifelong friend - a friend whose particular identity is important — is a precious asset, but also may make the old person vulnerable to a great sense of loss when the person dies.'

4.2 Love and affection

Whilst love and affection are usually mentioned in romantic love, expression of love and affection have been used in classical nonromantic friendships both between men and women throughout the ages. Recognising the pure love and affection a friend holds for you is greatly affirming and friendship enhancing. And thus sentences such as 'X really loves me' or 'I feel genuinely loved by X' speak of such deep love friends can feel for each other.

Friendship is a love, which the greek called 'philia', alongside 'storge', 'eros' and 'agape'. It is in this context that Lewis, 1960, p.87 includes friendship as a love: 'To the ancients, friendship seemed the happiest and most fully human of all loves; the crown of life and the school of virtue.' As such, this aspect of the tradition goes beyond Aristotle, and initial discussion of it among Greeks and extends to e.g. the Lysis of Plato. Aristotle, 1925, 8.8[11] puts philia-love as central to friendship. Cicero, 1923, p.163[12] sees it less as an activity, but more as an enabler. Whether the friendship of David and Jonathan was as initial and deep as claimed by a multitude of Christian sermons and commentaries or as formal as Olyan, 2017 analyses the actual Hebrew to be, I will not pass judgement on, but it developed into a full friendship over time. David's obituary of Jonathan thus states: 'Wonderful was thy love to me, passing the love of women.' However to qualify it is a difficult task. Perhaps the key distinction from the romantic love is simply that it is by convention non-erotic or non-sexual though this has not always held true both in antiquity as well as modernity. Contrary to the passions of antiquity, with Achilleus raging over Patroclus death, love within friendship in our time is expectedly quiet, though arguably most romantic relationship quieten down over time, too.

Many other relationship attitudes described above can be seen both causal for and resulting from or enabled by this love. Nehamas, 2016, ch. 4[13] argues that we fulfil this attribute if we move from appreciating aspects of our friend's features to loving the whole person.

Love for the friend expresses itself in affection. Showing affection - specifically among male same-sex friends - in the macho traditions is often frowned upon. This however is in contrast to historical behaviour[14], where showing explicit affection to a friend to express the love was common as Lewis, 1960, p. 93[15] points out citing examples from Roman legions and Hrothgar and Beowulf. In

[11]'Now since friendship depends more on loving, and it is those who love their friends that are praised, loving seems to be the characteristic virtue of friends, so that it is only those in whom this is found in due measure that are lasting friends, and only their friendship that endures.'

[12]'not so much the material gain procured through a friend, as it is his love, and his love alone, that gives us delight'

[13]'Perhaps the answer is that to love your friends is to be attracted not to one or more of their features but to every single one of them—to love them for everything they are. Yet. first, many of our friends' features are irrelevant to our relationship, and. second. I suspect that most of us have friends whom we love not because of. but despite, the defects they, like everyone else in the world, inevitably have.'

[14]It is interesting contrasting this to the attitude openness and vulnerability, hardly mentioned in antiquity, but very much en vogue now.

[15]'On a broad historical view it is, of course, not the demonstrative gestures of Friendship among our ancestors but the absence of such gestures in our own society that calls for some special explanation. We, not they, are out of step.'

this context I find the expression Lewis, 1960, p.105 uses to describe this sentiment very fitting: 'while at the same time an Affection mellowed by the years enfolds us.' The Latin word caritas, employed by Cicero, 1923, p. 131[16] to complement goodwill is in this context translated as affection, the word's meaning having only later been fully extended with the development of Christian theology and its assumption into the catalogue of Christian virtues. This affection also includes our friend's weaknesses, especially the idiosyncrasies and minor vices contrary to popular opinion. A beautiful scene for this is in the musical 'Man of la Mancha' when Sancho is asked, why he follows his master despite Don Quixote clearly being somewhat peculiar: 'I like him ...'[17]

Affection is also closely linked to generosity and caring. Specifically, small-scale but regular generosity is suitable to convey a general attitude of affection to your friend. Affection can show itself in simple and small acts such as sending a text before an important presentation. Finally affection is shown through physical touch, i.e. for friends mostly hugging. Affection can be expressed with a variety of methods. Also, when it comes to language, both spoken and written, affectionate is an adjective that qualifies it as loving. In particular, the letters of friends including male same-sex ones from in the middle ages right until the last century were full of words of affection.

Practical takeaway
This is one mostly for the guys, most women know this already. Friendship is a love, and as such needs to be expressed. This can be a hug, this can be through words, or other ways of expressing affection. We don't need to start kissing like Beowulf and wailing like Achilleus, but it is not unmanly to express one's friendship.

Suggestions for thought

- To what degree do you think friendship is a love or something entirely different? What would make it unique and separate to romantic or parental love?
- How appropriate or necessary is it to feel and show affection for and to your friends? Does this hold for all your friendships?
- How strict do you think is the boundary between friendship and romantic love?

For statistics in sociological studies, question suggestions and weights in counting see H.

[16]'benevolentia et caritate consensio': 'For friendship is nothing else than an accord in all things, human and divine, conjoined with mutual goodwill and affection, and I am inclined to think that, with the exception of wisdom, no better thing has been given to man by the immortal gods.'

[17]`https://youtu.be/G13jzheosNE?t=155`

Loving close and best friends

> Best friends are like teeth - when they are lost they cannot be replaced with an original.
>
> Unknown

A special aspect of seeing friendship as a love is the sentiment that someone is your best friend on the same level of significance in your life as a romantic spouse. It occurs where a friend grows beyond 'a good friend' to become a best friend, a true companion. Such friendships have been deep in Western Lore, and many dream of finding such a friend (or a few of them) as much as finding a spouse. In our time it is now expected that the two searches merged and we expect our spouse to be that person. Whilst the term 'friend' has lost a bit of its ring and luster no small part because of Facebook encouraging us to 'friend' or 'connect' with hundreds and in many cases thousands of people, the 'best friend', or 'soulmate' is still a well-defined concept without dilution.

The desirable property we are searching for is closeness, intimacy or connection strength. Loneliness is not so much the absence of many friends, but the absence of 'true'/close/'proper' friends. We speak of a bond between people, and indeed when we do, our understanding is a lot closer to the 'covenant' of the bible than the modern 'Facebook friend'. When such a friendship ends, we speak of a 'bond being broken'. Whereas differences in priority and closeness are acceptable for general friends (see 9.3), it is not acceptable to differ in priority and closeness for best or close friends. Reciprocal commitment is and must be unquestioned. Luckily we are better at defining and assessing reciprocity in close friendship than the boundary between friendship and acquaintance.

A **best friend** is a friend like no other. Whether it is David and Jonathan, or Scipio and Laelius the sentiment is clear: 'For I am indeed moved by the loss of a friend such, I believe, as I shall never have again, and — as I can assert on positive knowledge — a friend such as no other man ever was to me.'. Montaignes friendship to La Boetie was legendary, and also other friendships have been referred to in this context. As I will note elsewhere, it is an interesting question of what we should demand of a best friend until we knight her or him to that title. Is it a list of requirements (see Cerri, 2019[18] or Millington, 2019, p.7[19]), or is it just obvious once the state is there, a clarity you perceive once a certain amount of time has been spend or connection 'level' reached. Common is usually the passing of time allowing us to assess reliability and loyalty, which we may compromise about in other friends, but not in the best friend.

Whether it is a best friend or a very small number of best friends, this is a very exclusive attitude, and from Aristotle to Dunbar everybody points to the high cost of time and effort to naturally lead to the limitation of such a circle. Greif, 2009 is like me also a supporter of the small number version, defining the term 'must friend' to denote 'a best buddy, a member of the inner circle, the closest of relationships.' I for my part don't think the list of classical traits however are

[18] 'This type makes the best friend because they have all the traits you look for in a BFF: they're loyal, caring, trusting, and dedicated. ...'

[19] 'The ultimate best friend, her honesty, kindness, loyalty and empathy know no bounds and have set a very high bar for any female friends in my life.'

the key about it. Degges-White and Borzumato-Gainey, 2011, ch. 3[20] notes the durability of such friendships. In a similar fashion - whilst I have my doubt about the 'pickup' possibility (8.1), the property does seem to apply specifically to best friendships. Needless to say, true friendships are not unnecessarily put to the test either.

A special type of friendship is that of **companionship**. Whereas it is a pair, companionship often is marked by a potential difference in status, with a senior (king, warlord, main protagonist) and a companion (butler, shield-bearer, supporter) who however is a close friend, and completes the pair. Thus Frodo would not be complete without Sam, Asterix without Obelix, Wooster without Jeeves[21]. In antiquity and Arthurian legends the shield-bearer and squire would be a constant companion, and trusted friend. Alberoni, 2016, p.31 points to Virgil accompanying Dante down to hell. In all these images the themes of reliability, loyalty, trust and solidarity combine into one key theme of companionship, that Rath, 2006, p.105[22] invokes when defining his vital friends role 'companion'. Images such as sitting in front of a campfire or standing by each others side facing a foe easily spring to mind. Lewis, 1960, p.105[23] associates companionship more with the classical male [collaborator] model of friendship and thus diverts from the original term. For the context of defining a best friend or a close friend, the desirability and richness of association of imagery with the antiquated words companion and companionship is an interesting phenomenon in current times.

One very contentious issue for close or best friendships is the question whether you tell your friend how much this friendship means to you. Indeed, do you **talk about friendship** per se at all? Historically friendships were public. David and Jonathan made a covenant. Medieval monks explicitly let their affection and love for each other known (see Pahl, 2000, p.28). In Native American culture the ritual of becoming blood brothers[24] essentially affirms a close friendship, Kirk explicitly addresses his core crew as 'my friends'. Thus there are plenty of positive examples for naming a friendship a friendship. Aristotle's insistence on the declaration of goodwill towards the friend also implies an explicit affirmation of the friendship. Female friendship literature (e.g. Nelson, 2016, p.70 and Millington, 2019, p.44) emphatically endorses the explicit declaration of affection to friends.

This is in direct contrast to the male-philosophical understanding of friendship as exemplified by Lewis and Alberoni and acknowledged by Millington, when she writes about friendship as the 'unspoken promise'[25]. Lewis, 1960, p.91 flatly as-

---

[20] 'True best friendships are able to withstand significant challenges and poor behavior that would likely lead to the breakup of less close friendships.'

[21] Jeeves and Wooster is a book by P.G. Wodehouse, brilliantly enacted by Hugh Laurie and Stephen Fry, and a great example of such a companionship

[22] `https://theweek.com/articles/739502/8-kinds-friends-need-happy-life` 'A Companion is always there for you...'

[23] 'For they will seldom have had with each other the companionship in common activities which is the matrix of Friendship. Where men are educated and women not, where one sex works and the other is idle, or where they do totally different work, they will usually have nothing to be Friends about.'

[24] See `https://youtu.be/Gf02dZNcl6U` for that of Winnetou and Old Shatterhand in the America saga of Karl May

[25] Arguably this statement is in the context of describing male friendships ... p.151 'Men don't need to reinforce this with words or big gestures.'

serts that 'Friends hardly ever [speak] about their friendship', whereas Alberoni, 2016, p.8 even states that friends talking about the friendship 'not only threatens the bond, but likely augurs its end.' I will let this conflict stand here, my take is that friendship if invoked is likely under threat, but deep appreciation and genuine gratitude can and should (on occasions) be expressed. I also think it is helpful to voice and address potential misunderstandings.

As great as it is to have such an ideal of friendship to aspire to, it might not be a healthy attitude. If every friendship is benchmarked against such a lofty ideal, and found short, then this ideal might do more damage to actual friendship lived out than benefit. Specifically, being picky is singled out by Apostolou and Keramari, 2020 as a key obstacle to making new friends. Pahl, 2000, p.64[26] notes an analogous scepticism about attainability of true friendship. It is the key concern of this book to argue against this, that while it involves time and dedication, it is a wonderful and attainable goal to strive towards.

Practical takeaway
If you have a Sam or Obelix in your life, someone who never leaves your side, who is a true friend, make sure you appreciate them and do not take them for granted. They are one of the best gifts life has to offer.

Suggestions for thought

- Do you have 'a' best friend or more like a few really close friends where you cannot decide who is 'the best'?
- What makes your very close friends special? What traits are and have they in common?
- If you had to choose between never having met your best friend or your current partner what would come to your mind?

For statistics in sociological studies, question suggestions and weights in counting see H.

4.3 Consideration and prioritisation of friends needs

> Greater love has no one than this: to lay down one's life for one's friends.
>
> John 15:13

This is taking your friend's needs into account, potentially taking one for the team. It means you not chatting to that pretty girl or handsome boy because you

[26]'On balance, as the rest of the book will reveal, I lean towards Silver's view, although, following Rochefoucauld, I would feel that 'However rare true love may be, it is less so than true friendship."

know your friend has a crush on them or you recommending a friend for a job even though you might have liked it yourself. It can be going to the cinema even though you might have preferred the theatre, or actively coming to your friends help at financial, emotional or time cost or sacrifice to yourself. The overlap to the personality trait is clear, but there is a difference. As a relationship attitude, it is your willingness to sacrifice for your friend, but not necessarily anyone else.

1. It is the desire to do good for the friend (beneficence),
2. and really putting your friend first in his time of need, potentially at great sacrifice to you,
3. caring by meeting your friend's needs in practical concerns,
4. not being selfish,
5. duty and obligation.

(1) The desire to **do good** for your friend has a long tradition, even though utility is not at the heart of friendship. But if there is the possibility of doing something for your friend, conventionally, it would be seen as important to do it. This may be even coming at a minor sacrifice to us, and yet be deemed the path forward (see e.g. Shumway, 2018, p. 101[27]). Beneficence and minor sacrifice is also a great way to initiate a positive connection leading to friendship, which according to some is the purpose of Matt 5:40[28]. Contrary to major sacrifices, general beneficence should be issued without being asked among good friends (see e.g. Greif, 2009, ch. 14[29]).

Trust in reciprocity here is important, but this also includes an expectation of reasonableness. We expect the friend to come to our aid, but are expected not to impose such situations unnecessarily and unreasonably both in severity and frequency.Nelson, 2016, p.68[30] points out that we gain the possibility of not unwittingly taking advantage of our friend by the knowledge and assurance that they can and will say no, if fulfilling a wish of ours would put them at a major inconvenience.

(2) Making a major **sacrifice for a friend** is one of the oldest themes in friendship literature and mythology and in this context strongly connected to loyalty (4.4). Orestes and Pylades (see Aeschylus, 1926 or Phintias and Damon (see Diodorus,

[27]' ... we would rather use our free time to relax and use our money to buy things for ourselves, but friendship calls for some sacrifice'

[28]'40 And if someone wants to sue you and take your tunic, let him have your cloak as well. 41 If someone forces you to go one mile, go with him two miles.'

[29]'Most of them are not (must) friends—they will not do something for someone without being asked. Maybe women will do it—most men won't. Now, many, many men, if you ask them to do something for you will do it, but you have to ask them to do it. Men would not say 'I will do something for you" without being asked. There is one heck of a difference between the two. No one has ever done it for me—I don't resent it either.'

[30]'One of my closest friends and I have a spoken agreement: We promise to ask for what we need, and we swear we will say 'no' if we can't. In fact we joked that we both needed to say 'no' a few times just to prove that we could trust each other to do so. There is something so gratifying about knowing that, if either of us needs support, it's on its to ask for it — not on the other to guess it or psychically infer what we need! And we don't need to worry about imposing or intruding on our friend - it's their job to say 'no,' not our responsibility to preemptively decide for them.'

1933) are but a few examples of friends offering to die for the other. The Bible as in John 15:13 likewise in unambiguous in commending sacrifice for ones friends: 'Greater love has no one than this, that someone lay down his life for his friends.'. Nehamas, 2016, ch.1[31] writes of friends helping each other even at the expense of their own welfare, then later (Nehamas, 2016, ch.2) extending this with the phrase 'A friend helps you move house; a good friend helps you move a body.' According to Fischer, 1982, p.290 asking for a 'sizeable loan' is something that could be done within the friendship and be reasonably expected to be complied with (see also 6.8). Lewis, 1952 is most radical in stating that 'particular cases of distress among your own relatives, friends, neighbours and employees, which God, as it were, forces upon your notice, may demand much more: even to the crippling and endangering of your own position.'[32] Whilst our friends normally deeply appreciate a sacrifice to their benefit, it needs to be 'worth it'. I do not advocate making a drama out of it, and it should be clear that no moral debt is incurred, but when we do make a sacrifice, or feel like we are making one, the other side should know. It is pointless to make a substantial sacrifice only to bring a minor benefit to the other side, as lack of some appreciation will breed resentment.

One theme of sacrifice is the avoidance of conflicts in matters of love and romance. It is a clear rule of loyalty, the 'bro code'[33] and with similar arrangements amongst groups of female friends, not to compete for the declared love interest of a friend. And yes, if your interest is more 'short term' , then absolutely it is not worth it to get into a discussion with a friend. But if things are really serious, then it is a matter for a heart to heart chat. Maybe if your friend had known of your interest, they would have gladly encouraged it and taken a step back themselves. Don't sacrifice the potential love of your life for a friend to have an enjoyable but passing snog on the dance floor. In a similar matter don't help your friend to move his heavy furniture if you have a bad back and are at risk of permanently damaging it. At the same time there are moments when we have to drop everything and come to our friends rescue. This could be breaking a promise for a romantic holiday with our partner if your friend through a shock of life (breakup, redundancy, the usual...) suddenly finds themselves in a bad spot. The theme of sacrifice for one's close friends is gaining in part also a renaissance, as strong family ties are reducing. As people are getting older, more people living alone, and also due to different circumstances they live together with friends, who sacrifice substantially for the benefit of their friends (Vries, 2018).At the same time, our time shies away from these extreme views and obligations. In a consumerist mindset, sacrificing for your friends is not anymore the done thing. Even asking for help with moving is making us feel uncomfortable and Degges-White and Borzumato-Gainey, 2011 justifiedly ask how it has come this far.

(3) caring by meeting someone's needs in practical concerns is covered by (5.4) and (5.14). Aristotle, 1925, 8.14 acknowledges the convention that friends should meet their friends needs and look out for each other, in particular if there is an im-

[31]'And everyone is aware of its indirect benefits, especially the willingness of friends to help one another personally, professionally, and financially in their hour of need, often sacrificing their own welfare, sometimes even their own life, for their friends' sake.'

[32]This is not without its irony, as in other parts he does advocate more a privacy-independent style of friendship.

[33]The 'bro code' is a convention between male friends, c.f. `https://en.wikipedia.org/wiki/Bro_Code`

balance of affluence. Epicurus even more emphasises that supporting friends and meeting their needs is core to the goodness of friendship. In order to be able to do so, we need to listen closely to our friends complaints, as complaints essentially are voicings of unmet needs (see Asatryan, 2016, p.91).

(4) is simply about general consideration of the friends wishes, particularly when we are feeling down or having a bad day. Whilst we can indulge our misery a little, throw a little tantrum and playingly demand pity, ultimately we do not want to be self-obsessed or selfish, but to have a good time with our friend. Thus we may need to restrain some of our needs or whims. Thus we may want to look glorious in public, but if we can just put on a track bottom to jump out of the door to meet a friend for coffee, putting back our need might enable spontaneous and precious together time with our friend. We may love a perfect house and our friends having a great impression of us, but if we suppress this feeling and invite our friend over for a quick bite even though the living room is a big mess, we put back our 'need' for the benefit of our mutual joy of connecting. This is the key enabler of spontaneity (see 8.5 for an overview to what degree people manage to live this trait).

(5) One topic between loyalty and consideration is the theme of **duty and obligation**. According to this not only are you by yourself desiring to help or sacrifice for your friend, but once a friendship is established, convention demands that you feel a sense of duty towards your friend. This is at odds with independence and the voluntary nature, but has a strong biblical and classical context.

Practical takeaway
Sacrificing for a friend is a good thing, and in our selfish society taking one for the team is really commendable. But ultimately the greater the sacrifice the more important it is to do a quick check with our friend. Not to prepare fishing for eternal gratitude and appreciation, but basically don't do something silly.

Suggestions for thought

- To what degree do you value acts or benefits friends do or give you?
- How would you feel about asking your friend for a genuine sacrifice on their behalf? How would you feel if they rejected you, even with a good reason?
- Do you think pointing out the magnitude of a sacrifice is appropriate when or before doing it? If you sacrificed in your view a lot on a single measure or act, but it actually wasn't requested or required at the time, how would you feel when told about this?
- What do you think about people saying that sacrifices should not be a part of a friendship? Do you agree with this?

For statistics in sociological studies, question suggestions and weights in counting see H.

Making friendship a priority

Making your friendship a priority is a general life choice and attitude,

1. by giving your friend priority, time and space in your life when you are not around them,

2. by giving your full attention.

In the casual discussions supporting this book, two reasons emerged why you would go out on a limb for your friends. One reason was that the situation simply demanded it, but a second theme that separate to the person of the friend, some people treated the relationship as an object or habit to be upheld. Thus the second theme to prioritizing that such people saw cultivation of friendship as a defining characteristic of their personality. This is what I will discuss here. Friendship priority goes beyond loyalty or reliability, it confers upon the friend a sense of value, a signal that they matter. The clarity and its importance are exemplified in its opposite state. Saying to your friend that 'you are busy' is the exact opposite of this attitude, implying that just about any and every other activity is more important than making time for your friend,[34]. There is little that can kill a friendship so fast as a repeated application of the word 'busy' without a good excuse[35]. Shumway, 2018, p.95 agrees: 'They say that time is money, but what they mean is time is value we spend time on the things that matter to us. People who do not have time for relationships may not value them as much as other things.'. According to Greif, 2009, Ch.1[36] attitude can be learned in childhood. In our current time-scarce society, conferring value to our friends by giving them time or making time for them is the key expression of priority. The phrase 'carving out time' describes exactly that. However other resources may be equally costly and valued. If you choose to live close to friends, if you spend money to travel not just to attend your friends wedding, but maybe also do so to show up in a personal crisis or just as a surprise visitor to their 37th or 62nd birthday, you show them that the friendship is a priority for you.

Some people say that 'Most of us count our friends among our most precious treasures.' (see Degges-White and Borzumato-Gainey, 2011, Ch.0). Fromm, 2013b would be highly critical of the expression of 'having friends' with the connotation of 'owning them like objects' . But for some people maybe not owning them, yet knowing friends are around them is important to their state of life. If there is anything that this book argues for, it is that friends are good for you, and that you should dedicate time and resources to make sure you keep them. Self interest is a

[34]Compare: `https://www.psychologytoday.com/us/blog/the-art-closeness/201510/is-the-one-word-can-kill-friendship`

[35]In analogy of the 'F*** word' which is recommended to be not used in conversation, it could be argued to designate 'busy' as a b-word and likewise make a conscious effort to not use it. If there are genuine other issue, any friend will have sympathy. Just try not to use the plain unqualified 'Sorry, I am busy'.

[36]'Children get a sense of the value of friendships by hearing their parents discuss juggling time spent with friends versus time spent with family and at work.'

perfectly acceptable reason to invest time in friendship. If you agree with the tenet that it is friends through whom you acquire virtue, and acquiring virtue (or call it personal and character development with 21st century wording) being a life goal of yours, then making and maintaining friendships should be a key activity in your life. As Kim, 2018 argues, in this sense even though Aristotle postulates that people need to love friends for themselves, his concept of friendship is deeply egoistic and utilitarian, even though the secondary goal (virtue) is a good and indeed the supreme goal. But ultimately current convention is that friendship is not about its utility, but a good in itself, an institution that makes life just better. As in many cases, Lewis, 1960, p.103 says it best: 'Friendship is unnecessary, like philosophy, like art, [...] It has no survival value; rather it is one of those things which give value to survival.'

Both Aristotle, 1925, 8.1[37] and Cicero, 1923, p. 127[38] agree about this being a core belief in life. Even utilitarian Epicurus agrees on friendship being a good by itself according to Mitsis, 2014, p.99[39]. Note that treating Friendship as a public good - to be pursued not just because it is good for the individual but also the polis city state - is not a purely an Aristotelian argument. In times of fracturing families sociologists also nominate more and more friends to take over support and social functions (see section 5.14 or Pahl, 2000, p.1[40]).

The theme is relevant also for conflict resolution (8.10) and in that closely related to loyalty, as if you assign a high value to your friendships, you will not dump them on a whim. Valuing friends and friendships highly is also a signalling ex-ante when people decide on who to befriend. You ostensibly valuing friendships decreases the probability of their initial time investments in you being wiped out because of a potential capricious disinterest on your side.

The issue and problem with assigning a high value and priority to your friendships is that not everyone agrees, as some people genuinely have other priorities, such as work, family, personal training goals. Even those who agree may not do so in the way you want them, and they might have really close friendships they absolutely prioritise, but not prioritise the specific friendship with you (see 9.3). Thus such an attitude could be disappointed on occasions.

The second theme that is important, specifically in our smartphone infested world, is giving our friends our **attention** when we are with them, when we are listening to them or playing board games with them. We should do anything but signalling with body language that we are mentally in fact elsewhere. This is reflected in statements like 'X and I ensure we are attentive to each other and check in', 'X is engaged with me' and 'X pays attention to me when we talk'.

One of the key items in J. Gottman, 2001 is his characterisation of the interaction process in romantic couples as a continuous bidding process for the other partner's attention with the hope for a positive affirming result. It is like a contin-

[37]'For without friends no one would choose to live, though he had all other goods;'

[38]p. 127 'all that I can do is to urge you to put friendship before all things human; for nothing is so conformable to nature and nothing so adaptable to our fortunes whether they be favourable or adverse.' and 193 '... all believe that without friendship life is no life at all, or at least they so believe if they have any desire whatever to live the life of free men.'

[39]'At Gnomologium vaticanum 23, Epicurus says that all friendship is choiceworthy for itself apart from its instrumental benefits, 'pasa philia di' heauten hairete?"

[40]'Friendship may be seen as an increasingly important form of social glue in contemporary society.'

uous process of micro-transactions or more romantically signals of affection. As the process plays out over time it builds the relationship. I think part of the friendship process follows exactly the same pattern, though significantly more relaxed and more inclusive/ less jealous. There is a certain intensity, when you pay attention. In our time of smartphones and multitasking it is almost scary when people do give us full attention. On the other hand, when people consistently do not give us attention we notice and start questionning the quality of the friendship. This is not an instant but a process and we should be aware that life is messy. Sometimes our friends may have problems or other concerns in their life, and indeed us paying full attention we should notice this. But in normal circumstanes we should be assured of our friend's full attention.

It is worth it to ponder about the statement 'attention is money'. The concept of the attention economy for cyber space was formulated by Goldhaber, 1997 in his seminal article 'Attention Shoppers'. What is of relevance here is that we think about time budgets and allocation, and what we really could and should think about is our attention budget. Specifically we can think of which proportion of it we allocate to the TV, Smartphone or funny cat videos, and what proportion we dedicate to our friends? I think this concept is now intuitively understood by most people in modern society, even though they might viscerally dislike it. However, the proof is in the value we assign to our friends giving us undivided attention. We speak of the 'gift of attention' and it often is valued by us higher than financial or material gifts. Of course attention is now really expensive. Essentially the genius trick of Facebook (and the other apps, smartphones, ...) is that they made something so addictive that they got our attention, and sell that to the highest bidder (see Kwon et al., 2013, Archer, 2013, essentially in Facebook you are not the consumer or customer, but you are the product plied to easily be manipulated for purchasing decisions.). According to a study of D. Miller et al., 2021 the smartphone has literally become the place where we live.

The excellent book of Turkle, 2017 describes this situation and its side effects on our relationships in great detail. Two effects are particularly worth noting:

1.) Opportunity cost in case of full attention: Turkle cites an interviewee talking about the expectation of full attention on calls: 'They're disappointed if I'm like, not talking about being depressed, about contemplating a divorce, about being fired. ... You ask for private cell time, you better come up with the goods'. Essentially, it creates an ubiquitous fear-of-missing-out opportunity cost on simple plain-old time spent together (5.1). It thus lessening the enjoyment of this normal hanging out experience. 'We are more distracted in each other's company, and we know it. Recent surveys report that 89% of Americans say they interrupted their last social interaction to turn to their phones, and 82% say that the conversation suffered for it. ... Studies show that if two people are having lunch, a cell phone on the table steers the conversation to lighter subjects, and each party feels less invested in the other. It is not surprising. Each person in the conversation knows that with a phone on the landscape, you can be interrupted at any time.'. Various articles in popular media (e.g. Sira M., 2020-06-14) echo the frustration with this effect.

2.) Multitasking, inauthenticity and (dis-)interest in others: Turkle, 2017, p.293 describes youths having three Whatsapp conversations at the same time plus reading something on the internet or another one doing emails while skype-calling her grandmother. All the same they are content with only getting to know superficial and partial perspectives of their 'friends' online identities. Over several pages she concludes 'Young people don't seem to feel they need to deal with more [of the other person's actual off-line personality], and over time they lose the inclination [to get to know it]. One might say that absorbed in those they have 'friended', children lose interest in friendship.' Finally an effect is that this constant being switched on is taking a draining toll on our mind and mental capacity (energy), leaving us less energy to go out, meet friends and be attentive when we are with them. The opposite of attention is being ignored when you reach out. Being ignored not only signals rejection and breach of attention but also lack of respect and care. Not returning calls, text messages or Whatsapps over longer periods thus creates ruptures in the friendship. On the other hand, our increase in messaging inevitably also raises the cost of time in constantly returning messages. Balancing feeling completely unattended to and not making excessive demands on your friends is something to pay attention too.

Another negative aspect of prioritisation is the possibility of codependent relationships. These are relationships where the prioritisation results from a position of need or ulterior motives such as insecurity. Thus prioritisation of friends is a given, it is an unexpressed choice to meet their needs, to give them time in our life. I will get in the maintenance section to 'toxic friends', however on prioritisation I would say that general prioritisation (e.g. going to have a beer with your friend rather than going to some other social function) is always given, never demanded or required. But when given, it is appreciated.

Practical takeaway
Stop using the unqualified 'I am busy <insert shouldershrug>' , at least with your actual friends. If you really have something on, say it. They will understand. And then initiate to set up an alternative time. Not a 'we really should see each other more often' but a 'how about Wednesday next week or Friday the week after?'. Good friends who live reasonably close by should be able to set a committed date within a month even for busy schedules[a]. Compromise on location, and go for the opportunity when it arises, who knows when the next one arises.

[a]Good friends are always really understanding in actual emergencies

Suggestions for thought

- How central to your life are your friendships?
- How easily does the 'busy' word roll off your tongue? What do you think that says about your priorities?
- When you are with friends, do they have your undivided attention? How accepting are you of friends being glued on their phones or for some other reason not giving you their full attention?

- 'Make friendship a priority. Find the time to be with friends even if it means letting the lawn go unmowed or the dishes unwashed for a while.' (found in Meador, 2001-11-16)

For statistics in sociological studies, question suggestions and weights in counting see H.

4.4 Loyalty

> When you're in jail, a good friend will be trying to bail you out. A best friend will be in the cell next to you saying, Damn, that was fun.
>
> Groucho Marx

The Oxford Dictionary defines **loyalty** as faithful adherence to a promise or oath, government and by extension thus also to a person. This is about really appreciating the relationship that has built up, and not giving in if the going gets tough. It includes the commitment to engage in conflict resolution act of forgiveness in order to salvage the relationship in crisis. The general propensity to forgive is however more a character strength. Loyalty is at the core of friendship and sees the friendship as a value by itself. Olyan, 2017, p.16 in his characterisation of biblical friendships emphasises this important trait: 'Loyalty (hesed), like love, is also a term native to treaty discourse; in covenant contexts, it means conformity to treaty stipulations', and arguably for people using biblical stories to emphasise aspects of friendship, this is a sine qua non. It is also a consequence of old testament friendships being closer to vassalage contracts than modern day western friendships. The proverbs (17.17) emphasis loyalty as the hallmark of a friend, as does the book of Ruth (1:16 'Do not urge me to leave you or return from following you. For where you go I will go.'). Ancient literature additionally emphasises the loyalty of Damon and Pythias, who are willing to die for each other when plotting against Dionysius of Syracuse. Cicero, 1923 has Laelius emphasize the importance of 'fides'.[41]. The condition for the capacity of showing loyalty according to Cicero is a set character and personality. Even Epicurus - as Rist, 1980 notes, pursuing to avoid suffering in life, accepts that suffering for a friend in need is tolerable for the greater good of the friendship[42]. Loyalty being a built up friendship trait, it can be fast-tracked through intense joined experiences, such as living through war times or catastrophes (see e.g. Junger, 2016 on the narratives of the Croatian youths).

[41]Cicero, 1923, p.175 'Now the support and stay of that unswerving constancy, which we look for in friendship, is loyalty; for nothing is constant that is disloyal. Moreover, the right course is to choose for a friend one who is frank, sociable, and sympathetic — that is, one who is likely to be influenced by the same motives as yourself — since all these qualities conduce to loyalty; for it is impossible for a man to be loyal whose nature is full of twists and twinings; and, indeed, one who is untouched by the same influences as yourself and is naturally unsympathetic.'

[42]Rist, 1980, p.128 'Clearly loyalty to a friend—the price which has to be paid for confidence in that friend, and that which each man in turn expects of his friends—may entail personal suffering, not merely in the form of sadness if that friend is in trouble, but even, so Epicurus holds, to the extent that it is as painful to have one's friend tortured as to be tortured oneself. 62 'On a friend's behalf the wise man will endure very great pains,63 presumably in his own person; sometimes the wise man will give up his life for his friend."

The betrayal of a friendship is the violation of loyalty, and it is probably the supreme violation of friendship expectations. Alberoni, 2016, p.88 states that 'Friendship dies through trauma when it is betrayed'. In the New Testament, great emphasis is laid on Jesus' disappointment with both Judas betrayal and Peter's disavowal. Blieszner and Adams, 1998 estimate that about of the about 25% of friendship endings that were done intentionally, the usual cause was betrayal. The interesting aspect of betrayal of course is that what constitutes a betrayal is often very conditional on what concept of friendship predominates. Thus it can include everything from 'not standing up for me' (Vocal support), 'telling secrets' (trust and confidentiality) or 'not being there for me when I needed them' (General support and practical help).

A variant of loyalty is commitment. Typical statements here include 'X is committed / dedicated / devoted to me' or 'X honours commitments/follows through'. When this is phrased generally rather than person oriented, this becomes a statement about general reliability and consistency (i.e. 3.4). Commitment is a key time driven and proven relationship trait. It expresses that you are in for the long haul with that friend.

Commitment is also not uncontroversial, as commitment to a friend can mean helping them before other strangers (time preference) or doing things for them that you would not do for strangers at all (general preferentialism). Commitment can also be in competition to other relationships, such as a romantic relationship[43]. This is the natural state of friendship, as Nehamas, 2016, ch.2[44] notes. It is on the other hand this preferentialist side of love, that Kierkegaard[45] so disapproves of. It is tied in a second way to reliability, in the sense that commitment expresses itself by being true to promises, thus e.g. showing up both to a party and the moving of the house. As much as we love commitment, there is a sense of it being a bit of a lost art in some circles, as our continual inability to find appointments and time for each other show effective disregard for our friendships. As we outsource all kinds of services that theoretically could be done by friends, we likewise eliminate opportunities for commitment to be developed and shown, leaving our friendships the poorer.

A joined theme of loyalty, the duty to sacrifice (4.3(2)) and virtue in friendship is the question of whether there is an obligation to stand with a friend in case his actions or intentions are not virtuous. Cicero, 1923, p.147[46] asks whether it is right to support a friend against the state and concludes that loyalty and the duty to sacrifice covers even potentially illegal activities within limits[47]. Pylades helped

[43]Consider David Duchovny brushing off the request of his wife Halle Berry in 'Things we lost in the fire' to stay with her rather than driving away to meet his old school friend now drug addict Benicio del Torro for his birthday.

[44]'Friendship, however, is inconceivable without thinking that it is perfectly all right to treat some people differently from the way we treat everyone else, to give them preference and pride of place, simply because they are our friends.'

[45]According to Kierkegaard, giving our friend preferential treatment over a stranger is contrary to the Christian impartial love of the neighbour, and thus to be deplored.

[46]'Wherefore, let us first consider, if you please, how far love ought to go in friendship. Supposing Coriolanus to have had friends, were those friends in duty bound to bear arms with him against their country?'

[47]p. 171 'even if by some chance the wishes of a friend are not altogether honourable and require to be forwarded in matters which involve his life or reputation, we should turn aside from the straight path, provided, however, utter disgrace does not follow; for there are limits to the indulgence which

his friend Orestes kill his mother Clytamnestra. Generally, the consensus even among the virtuous-loving ancients is that within limits friends have to oblige to support. Only in extreme cases of [treachery] can they absolve themselves from their duty and say **no** to **illegal actions**. Current wisdom sometimes quotes E.M. Forster with his saying: 'If I had to choose between betraying my country and betraying my friend, I hope I should have the guts to betray my country.'

Loyalty contributes to conflict resolution, as essentially commitment to the friendship counterbalances potential grudges and differences. In fact, it is loyalty to the friend and the friendship that makes you continue to engage with the friend in a painful discussion despite already condemning evidence. The phrase 'they deserves a full hearing out' comes to mind, and the 'deserves' is precisely the result of loyalty of the potential victim. Loyalty is then about seeing the bigger picture of the overall friendship vs. focusing on the current transgression. Shumway, 2018, p.57 elaborates 'Everyone makes mistakes. We say things that inadvertently offend and cause hurt feelings. We overreact and retaliate with anger and sadness.' It is loyalty to this friendship, that reigns in this desire in us. Nelson, 2016, p.77 expands on this: 'There will always be tough conversations, hurtful words, neglect, and unmet needs in a relationship but none of those means we have to withdraw our goodness.'. Thus we should not only reign in our desire to retaliate but still act as a friend to the person despite our feeling of having been wronged. In modern research and literature, loyalty also comes out as a hallmark. Millington, 2019 refers to a study that 62% of survey participants would rather forego a promotion than a friendship. Greif, 2009 repeatedly picks up on loyalty as a key characteristic of friendship when analysing the friendships of his study participants in his testimony sections.

The loyalty and bond between friends creates an in-group effect that creates **separation** them **from** the **others**. Lewis, 1960 describes this at length - but the key phrase is 'To say "These are my friends" implies "Those are not."' Apart from a common cause, interest or belief system, this effect is also driven by a common memory. This is the most difficult to penetrate, as other people say may share the same dislike of a political group, but will not be able to acquire the same memories. The separation effect insulates our personality even in non-personal environments, such as the military or prisoner camps. Knowing that there is someone close to us who is our friend creates resilience and affirms us in our personality. Yet it is open, anyone who shares the core is welcome to join. The first two would be glad to find a third and building a group is a key friendship activity (see 5.6). Cuddeback, 2010, p.76 sees such groups not as separated from society as Lewis does, but as building blocks of communities: 'Friendships thus provide 'mini-communities' within the larger community; they are a basic unit, as it were, of striving for perfection. In this way the mini-community of friendship is very similar to the most basic, natural unit of society, the family.'. But in his analogy with the family likewise he acknowledges them as loyalty-bound groups inside but separate from the wider society. Some also emphasise that this separation extends to norms: whereas in wider society status, financial wellbeing, attractiveness or other characteristics matter, inside the friends group only the fact that the other is a friend matters. It thus inverts societies norms, and because of that separation from society enables us letting down our guard and relax in the company of

---

can be allowed to friendship.'

friends. But this separation can also become a negative effect, as Nehamas, 2016, ch.2 points out: 'they then turn into a clique and become oblivious to their own faults.', enabling vices and crime that the group of friends inflicts on the outer world.

Practical takeaway
Be clear about the level of commitment and loyalty that can be expected of you. Expectation management and moving slow is substantially better than leaving your friend in the lurch when they thought they could count on you.

Suggestions for thought

- A clear expectation of a good friend is to stay loyal in the relationship. What this concretely means will be specific to your friendship, but if in doubt whether to do something that is not completely illegal out of loyalty, you probably should. Do you agree?
- Loyalty is built up over time. Start small in the friendship and build from there. What does it take to prove loyalty to you?
- If you have a crisis or a falling out with a friend, remember to give your friend a fair hearing. Forgiveness is your choice, but some time and attention to hear the other side's case is a duty from loyalty. How much do you think loyalty compels you to hear a friend out?
- 'A friend helps you move house; a good friend helps you move a body.' - would you help a friend even if you thought the activity was immoral or potentially (marginally) illegal?

For statistics in sociological studies, question suggestions and weights in counting see H.

Independence

> If you love a friend, let them go. If they come back with coffee, it was meant to be.
>
> Unknown

The voluntary nature of friendship is one of its key defining features. Unlike family, friendship is a chosen relationship entered freely by both parties. Whilst friendship is freely given without obligation, more interesting is whether this attribute stays true throughout the friendship's course. The emphasis of general freedom of volition is in friendship literature termed by independence.

There are five subthemes to independence in friendship:

1. the freedom of choice in becoming friends (generally uncontested),

2. the independence of our lives while being friends,

3. the limitations to duties as a friend,

4. the freedom of choice of limiting a friendship in its scope,

5. ending a friendship.

(1) Beginning a friendship is an **free choice**, an active decision. This does not need to be all formalised, but it needs to be clear to both that this choice has been made.

The free volition of entering a friendship is (almost) universally accepted as a key feature of friendship. Lewis, 1960, p.103 writes: 'I have no duty to be anyone's friend and no man in the world has a duty to be mine.' Already Aristotle, 1925, 8.13[48] notes our free choice in who we associate and spend time with. Olyan, 2017, p.4[49] points to an implied voluntary nature in old testament Hebrew. In current sociology and psychology the phrase 'friends are the family we choose' defines the sentiment (see Degges-White and Borzumato-Gainey, 2011, ch.3 or Pahl, 2000, p.2). The active choice to become someone's friend confers meaning and value to a person as a positive judgement on his personality.

Whilst most people accept this tenet, an interesting question in this context however is that of friends of friends or peers in groups. To what degree are we expected just to be civil to people or actually befriend them is not always an easy question. The composition of play groups is a tension ridden question right from the get go in kindergarten. What happens if you have a friend A and they have a friend B, who you dislike? What happens if friend A has a friend B who you don't mind but your parents don't like B's parents? What happens if there is a kid in school your parents like but you (initially) do not? Later in life, at college, in sports groups, there will always be situations like that. One side effect of 'friend' being used so ubiquitously and having lost so much of its meaning, that we almost need to say 'real friend' to get to the original sentiment, is that 'acquaintance' explicitly implies distance and at least a temporary rejection of friendship. And if we give credence to Alberoni's argument that friendship is moral and judgement based, then the rejection of friendship is likewise a negative statement about the person's personality we choose not to associate with. Rejection stings. It is the possibility of rejection that on the one hand makes friendship so valuable that has led others to criticise it. This is at the core of Kierkegaards criticism of friendship (see e.g. Lippitt, 2007) as contradicting the demand for christian universal love to everyone.[50] Likewise Fromm, 2000 argues that an attitude of loving cannot be partial if it is to be authentic. I would classify these objections as more theoretic and utopian rather than recommendations for conventional human life, however the arguments from a general ethical view do at least question whether we may withhold our love and friendship from a person. Also regarding cultural conventions,

[48]'Nor do complaints arise much even in friendships of pleasure; for both get at the same time what they desire, if they enjoy spending their time together; and even a man who complained of another for not affording him pleasure would seem ridiculous, since it is in his power not to spend his days with him.'

[49]'...both meaning something like 'to associate with' or 'to affiliate with', suggesting a voluntary dimension to friendship.'

[50]It should be noted that Kierkegaard's criticism of friendship, and likewise that of Augustine and the early church fathers, is much more nuanced, and quite complex - for an overview see Lippitt, 2013.

it should be noted that for millennia Confucian tradition in China emphasised priority of the family over friendship, and friendship was subject to approval of the father or elder brother. To a lesser degree today, but plenty of examples exist of interethnic, intersocial[51] or interreligious friendship prohibitions implemented by societies, also limiting the freedom of choice in entering a friendship. Thus the full freedom of choice to enter a friendship is a sign of progress in our society.

(2) Another often mentioned differential to kinship, particularly marriage, is the relative independence of the lives of friends. The way they conduct their lives affects us little. Yes, there is plenty of evidence of inspiration and exhortation, but there is no expectation to give up our individuality. My friend is free to do whatever he wants without interference from me. The only exceptions might endanger their health or general wellbeing (which might conflict with my desire to care for them - see 4.11) or morally dubious activities which might provoke me to review the basis of our friendship. Unlike in a marriage, they can wear anything, work in any job, pursue hobbies I have zero interest in (except the fact that my friend draws enjoyment and satisfaction from it), can eat anything (assuming I am not the judgmental type on meat consumption) and live their life independent of mine. Independence here means that my life is not affected by their life choices. Friendship in this line of thought is thus a partial relationship, focusing only on the items that are of mutual benefit and enjoying these activities.

(3) The limitation of duties as a friend is one of the libertarian interpretations of friendship. Lewis, 1960, p.105 writes in the Four Loves 'and no one has any claim on or any responsibility for another'. This is of course in stark contrast to the 'endangering of your own position' he elsewhere demands in a friend's distress.[52]. This set aside, having **no obligation** represents the school of thought that friends have specifically no legal or social duties towards each other, but only do good to each other when they are disposed to. Phrased this way independence represents thus a refutation of loyalty as a friendship virtue. Whilst people agree that some level of duty exists to the friend, statements like 'don't mix friends and money' partially imply this, as by following this tenet you are essentially absolving yourself to support your friends financially in time of need.

(4) I will come to **matching expectations** in a separate chapter in (9.3), but here the theme is a nuance or corollary of the freedom of choosing to enter a friendship. In the same way as (1), we are also free (not) to 'upgrade' or 'downgrade' a friendship from friend to close friend to best friend and vice versa. This may happen explicitly or latently over time, as we choose to spend less time with a friend. Maybe we don't enjoy spending time with them so much, or because of beliefs, e.g. that a close friend should be also close in proximity to ease interaction and that after a move of either of us this no longer is warranted. This does not need to be a malicious or punishing move, e.g. after the choice of withdrawing because of a betrayal of trust, it can simply be a neutral observation. It is simply the fact that we need to accept it if someone does not want to develop the relationship beyond a certain level or indeed acts to cool it down (see also Millington, 2019,

[51] By intersocial I mean across class or social associations

[52] Lewis, 1952, Charity: 'Particular cases of distress among your own relatives, friends, neighbours or employees, which God, as it were, forces upon your notice, may demand much more: even to the crippling and endangering of your own position.'

p.29 and 83[53]). As a disclosure, I really find this very hard. There are a number of occasions where I had a great vibe about a person as we spent some time together, but as their lives developed, time constraints developed when the start of a family occurred, the friendship waned. More difficult still is when you realise that people made an active choice to limit the relationship and keep you at a distance, for whatever reason, when you think but obviously are wrong that given the fun you have with each other should warrant more potential.

(5) The last theme of freedom of choice is that both parties are free to step away from the friendship and stop it altogether. We are not here talking of stopping the friendship after a mortal sin, such as betrayal or sleeping with the friend's spouse. This **freedom** is the possibility of **ending a friendship** simply on the grounds of 'it having run its course'. In particular friendships can go stale because of boredom, which according to Alberoni, 2016, p.73 [54] is antithetical to friendship. When Lewis writes about 'no duty to be anyone's friend' it should be noted that he uses 'to be' and not 'to become', thus explicitly entertaining the possibility of freely stopping to be someone's friend. Pahl, 2000, p.62 concurs 'We create and keep our friendships by conscious acts of will.' implying the end of the friendship if the will dissipates. I would argue that the intentionality of this process does matter, i.e. whether I decide to let a friendship slip, or whether it slips simply because I 'forgot about it'. Self help author Millington, 2019 is most explicit in her treatment of the matter and advocating a conscious decision process, listing 'I know when it's time to let a friendship go' as one of her key learning of her thirties. She continues to elaborate how to do a 'Marie Kondo of friendship circles'[55] (coll. for cleanup). Other famous self-help authors also include the review of status of friendships in their end-of-year rites, including potentially a ritual 'cleansing cum grieving process' by dropping cards with 'scrapped' friends into the fire. Despite all sentimentality to the contrary, it is an observable fact that over our life course our friendships do change, and not all survive. How to steer this process to the degree this is possible will be discussed in section 11.1.

Whilst few people in principle dispute the basic freedom to end a friendship, the psychological cost incurred and damage caused however provide reason for concern. My hunch is that specifically Lewis' position is inconsistent with his other writings, given his great value of what is lost upon the death of a friend, and the dissolution of a friendship has a similar effect, as common memories and future options to enjoy times together are effectively invalidated. I am also uneasy how Alberoni, 2016 would condone the self-interested decision (avoidance of boredom) to stop being friends with someone to the lofty ideal having seen (and continuing to do so) the friend as an end in their self (rather than an instrument of pleasure of boredom avoidance). This is however a subject that could be easily debated at length outside the scope of this book. I am also not sure whether

[53]'Accept that some people see you as an acquaintance when you'd like to be a friend. Unrequited friendship is painful but it's not you, it's them.' and 'but respect the person's boundaries and enjoy any time you do spend with them.'

[54]'But when there is boredom, repetition and monotony there is no friendship. Friends, as we have seen, don't bore each other. If they do. it means they are not friends or that somebody else has intervened and has disturbed the encounter.'

[55]p. 43 'So when you're looking to 'Marie Kondo' your friendship circles - looking at those who bring you joy and you want to keep, while thanking those who served a purpose and letting them go - know you are doing it to improve your quality of life, health and happiness!'

the possibility to exit a friendship freely should be posited as the antithesis of loyalty. Essentially independence assigns a positive probability to the friend leaving the friendship without a causing breach. It also is antithetical to the being needed component of reciprocity. An independently lived friendship is still reciprocal, but it is (more) difficult for the friendship to gain deep meaning and value, as people hedge their bets and vulnerability to limit fallout from the ending happening with positive probability. Indeed, commitment and loyalty oriented people may choose not to enter friendships with independently minded people as they cannot agree on this fundamental attitude. This cost may be acceptable to bear for independently minded people, but it still needs to be noted as a cost!

Practical takeaway
Listen to your friends take on independence. Do they need a bit of distance and are you overwhelming them? Check yourself for feelings of jealousy - friendship must always be free.

Suggestions for thought

- Do you think it is important to give anyone a chance who is seeking friendship or is it sufficient to e.g. decline politely on a first hunch or for any other reason? Could there be a situation which would oblige you to offer friendship beyond mere acquaintance?
- Do you believe that as a friendship develops and becomes close, certain duties start applying? To what degree might this reduce the independence and voluntary nature of friendship?
- Do you believe people are justified to walk away from a friendship without major justification, on accounts that it does not feel right anymore, or that you simply feel it has run its way?

For statistics in sociological studies, question suggestions and weights in counting see H.

4.5 Enjoyment

Be it because of the fun and laughter, the positive energy, the interesting discussion or the warmth experience, a key theme is that friends again and again come together is because they experience thorough joy in their encounter, making them want to continue meeting. Whilst Aristotle, 1925 makes his preference for the virtuous friendship clear, he does however repeatedly come back to the point that many people maintain pleasurable relations which accrue great benefit to them. Thus he positions enjoyment or pleasure even to the virtuous friendship as a necessary though not sufficient condition. Both the sociological writers[56] as

[56] Adams, Blieszner, Greif, Degges-White

well as the self-help writers[57] likewise highly value enjoyment as a facilitator of friendship.

There are three key themes to this. The first is the enjoyment of being in the presence of the friend, the second the benefit of having good conversations and the third theme is our friends making us destress.

This can be the enjoyment of specific friends' company or the general enjoyment of socializing, being with friendly people, bantering, conversations. The two overlap and are only separable with additional information. Enjoyment in some form or another is a necessary in a friendship. If it is not met, people will not on their own account continue meeting up with the friend in spe. Agreement about this is almost uniform: Aristotle, 1925, 8.13[58], Alberoni, 2016, p.19[59] or Ball, 2020-05-18[60]. I would not be as harsh or uncompromising as Aristotle or Alberoni, but if you had a few encounters with a friend where in the post action review (i.e. mentally just going through how it was) you have the feeling that it wasn't all that enjoyable, this would lead you to question yourself of what changed. Nehamas, 2016, ch.3 puts it best: 'The truth is that in our habitual intercourse with others, we much oftener require to be amused than assisted.' and I whole heartedly agree. The enjoyment of the company is also a key element in building positive long-lasting memories (see 4.1). Depending of school of thought, mere enjoyment of each others company is not seen as sufficient for a good friendship. Cuddeback, 2010, p.28 cites 'two fraternity brothers who have a friendship primarily because they party together.' as a friendship not to be emulated. My hunch is that there is no harm in these situationships, and they are the basis from which proper friendships start. The joy of spending time with each other leads to step-by-step self-disclosure and other activities, and then either the friendship envelops other themes, or slowly die down as repetition stales the experience.

It is this theme of experiencing the joy of being together where scars from conflict come most heavily to light. No matter if an offence is forgiven, or a contentious topic (such as the election Trump Biden) is excluded from the friendship by mutual agreement, we sometimes find that in such a situation we still somehow cannot enjoy our friend's company just quite as we used to. Something just feels different and the polish is off. Whilst people often emphasise the need for openness in a friendship, including honest feedback and personal criticism, they intuitively understand this effect, and thus hesitate really to put the friendship to the test. Specifically raising the question whether both people mutually enjoy the friendship can tear away the veil of mutually agreed illusion.

Enjoyment of company is the key theme describing the Aristotelian pleasure friends and similar labels continue into present time. Note that the Aristotelian concept of 'hedone' from which we get our word hedonism however covers much more ground than our current day association of hedonistic pleasure. Of course pleasure primarily appeals to the senses, but can also include the pleasure of studying and learning and many other activities. Indeed the pursuit of virtue of-

[57] Rath, Nelson, Shumway, Millington

[58] '... even a man who complained of another for not affording him pleasure would seem ridiculous, since it is in his power not to spend his days with him.'

[59] 'Friends seek to have a good time with one another. If they fail to do so they tend to leave each other or to put some distance between them.'

[60] 'People will make an effort to spend time with you if they enjoy it. If they don't, they'll make an effort to be as far away from you as possible.'

ten creates true pleasure in the virtuous. For the Epicureans this general pleasure has an even higher purpose, it is the core meaning of life. And just like Aristotle states that friendship is necessary to develop virtue, Epicurus believes 'that friendships are necessary if pleasure is to be maximized.' according to Rist, 1980, p.122. Thus particularly from an Epicurean standpoint, asking yourself whether you feel good as in pleasurable about a friendship as a test of it makes perfect sense. In a similar way being concerned about your friends pleasure of your company should be a concern too. There are different ways and occasions how that pleasure materialises. You are delighted to see these friends in group meetings at organizations you are a part of, you like hanging out with them over a beer, but whatever you do, looking back after the event you find you had a good time. Their company makes a long commutes pleasant (cf. Rath, 2006, p.21), which otherwise would be a major drag on life happiness (cf. Stutzer and Frey, 2008). For those with friends (and not in the early 'honeymoon' phase of a romantic relationship) usually prefer conversations with friends to any other interaction, and our need for it is never exhausted or fully satisfied (see Nelson, 2016, p.8[61]). Good conversation connects to fun, intellectual stimulation, self disclosure and listening. Augustine states about his friend 'We could talk and laugh together' Lewis, 1960, p.105 repeatedly refers to the conversations with Inklings[62] and other friends as one of the great boons of life.

The joy of conversation is consistent through the ages, and having a good conversation is a great starter for an acquaintanceship. Hunt, 2018-09-03[63] writes about the joy of meeting strangers in Vienna over a conversation. Greif, 2009, ch.2[64] points to the growing appreciation for communication with friends. As you build acquaintance with a person, the depth for jokes, personal observations and discussion of mutual interests becomes greater. A good relaxed conversation usually is not just focused on a singular topic, but can range far and wide (e.g. Dooley, 2020-02-26[65]).

The quality or enjoyment of conversations is also a clear thermometer for our relationship with the person, the mutual understanding and the quality of conversations in our life a measure of our loneliness (c.f. Asatryan, 2016[66]). Whether it is the lifeblood of intellectuals such as C. S. Lewis or general socialites, or just an aspect that makes life just a bit nicer, good conversations are important to most of us as part of the good life. For the classical authors and their modern disciples

[61]'We simply have room for far more affirmation, laughter and honest conversation than we're actually getting'

[62]Group of Oxford literati including also JRR Tolkien, who regularly met on Tuesday mornings in a pub to write their books and discuss literature.

[63]`https://www.theguardian.com/cities/2018/sep/03/two-hours-stranger-questions-open-city-vienna`

[64]'Men increasingly recognize and want a friend as they age who they can communicate with and who is accepting.'

[65]'At our non-dinner, non-Scrabble party, we talk about college, empty nesting, aching limbs, aging bodies, husbands (or no husbands), and the possibility of legalized marijuana in New York state. I love talking about all of it, love that I don't have to perform for these women or compare myself to them. I am genuinely interested in their lives and they are genuinely interested in mine.'

[66]'This new type of loneliness is not like hunger, which is always satisfied by food. Even if the meal isn't delicious, it still sates you. A stale loaf of bread satisfies genuine hunger as well as a freshly baked one. Yet somehow a mediocre interaction with other people does not alleviate loneliness. It usually makes it worse.'

	F	M
Work	3.3	3.4
Love Life and Family	4.0	3.7
Personal Projects	3.6	3.6
Ideas	3.6	3.5
Feelings / emotional sharing	3.9	3.0
Other mutual friends	3.1	3.2
We don't talk, we 'do' (sports, crafts, ...)	2.3	2.2
Interests: Politics, Philosophy, Literature, News, ...	3.5	3.3
Other / None of the above really	1.9	2.1
What do you mostly talk about with your friends? Scale from 1 (hardly) to 5 (very often) Data from habits study F.3		

Table 4.1: Conversational topics

such as Cuddeback, 2010, p.69[67] good conversation is the pathway to character development and enjoyment.

Sociologists usually are also interested in gender differences playing out in society. Whereas the stereotype of women preferring to talk about emotions is confirmed in the habits dataset (see F.3), for almost all other categories differences are negligible.

Good conversations are enabled by suitable places that offer drink, food and good seating. Pubs and cafes are great for them - as is the private home. Conversely analysing what differentiates a great pub or cafe from an OK pub or cafe is the former giving rise to a community of regular customers getting to know each other and having good conversations (Hunt, 2018-09-07[68] anecdotally and as theme running through the entire book - Oldenburg, 1999).

One of the effects of being around our friends is that we automatically and instinctively relax and can let our guard down. They **make you relax and de-stress**. Phrases such as 'X makes you forget the stress in your life', 'X makes me slow down', 'With X I can just be myself', 'With X I don't have to worry about anything' or 'with X I can calm down' all exemplify this effect. Not for all but for many of us, stress is a general blight of our lives. Whereas being able to feel stress kept us from being eaten 10000 years ago, the higher cortisol levels are now affecting our immune system, and leave us susceptible to cold and flu and other ailments. There is no single way how our friends make us relax, some because of their calming personality, some by giving good advice showing us a way out of a difficult situation, some by making jokes leading us to forget about an issue. At

[67]'True friends want good conversations and will help one another and draw one another into good conversations. Friends will benefit from the insights of one another, as they constantly share the fruits of their personal meditation and contemplation. And in fact, some truths will be discovered in conversation, which each friend never would have discovered separately. There is something irreplaceable about two minds working together, in a context of mutual affection and trust, to uncover the deepest truths.'

[68]`https://www.theguardian.com/cities/2018/sep/07/on-the-bike-path-i-feel-a-connection-to-people-your-shared-spaces` describing how a local supermarket became the village meeting place.

least for the time we are with them life just seems a little easier and better, we stop worrying and we are relaxed.

But even outside the stresses of life, the relaxation enjoyed with friends is a good by itself. Not wanting to promote alcoholism or skiving, but there is nothing quite as deliciously relaxing as taking a day off (best on a Friday) with a friend with the sole purpose of meeting up in a pub to start the weekend early at 11am with a pint and a chat (see Hodgkinson, 2005). As Harald Juhnke, the legendary German entertainer frequently said[69], 'the joy of life can be found when you have no appointments and are slightly tipsy' when he was referring to the meetups of friends in his house when his calendar was empty. Lewis, 1960, p.105 likewise describes such a scene of relaxation: 'Those are the golden sessions; when four or five of us after a hard day's walking have come to our inn; when our slippers are on, our feet spread out towards the blaze and our drinks at our elbows'. For me it always was an item of wonder how fast sometimes this process works out. Of course, there have been moments when you have been under continuous stress for maybe even days or weeks[70], but then it is over, and you meet up with a few friends in a bar over a beer, and you literally feel stones drop off your shoulders. And yes, part of it is the fact that the audit is over, but the difference is that on your own the process of realising this period of stress is over might take a weekend, whereas I have experienced it run through in under an hour when hanging out with good friends. Try to remember the priceless moment where you realised you just had had an hour of joy and fun, and had not thought of [the audit / closing / report / presentation] at all. And this being able to let go and leaving it all behind you is something that friends are - along with children - uniquely positioned to do in your life.

The opposite of relaxation and de-stressing is 'drama', and this features mostly in the female friendship literature. Friendships of children are always filled with drama - both to the concerned parents' amusement and worry - and there is little to be done about it. The norm however is that this dissipates as the children grow up and enter adolescence and adulthood. Still, it apparently persists at least to some degree for women, but not so for men, at least not to the same level. Men - or so goes the stereotype - simply do not have patience for drama, and when it becomes too much of a problem, they just leave the friendship or put it on ice. That having been said, it genuinely seems to be less of a problem, a fact often observed by women with a tinge of jealousy (e.g. Millington, 2019, p. 151[71]. Despite their dislike of it, in several narratives women do put up for it for a surprisingly long time with few mitigation or self protection measures (e.g. Ball, 2020-05-23[72]). I tried with the might of Google to find a good definition of what 'drama' is, and yet, little of what I saw really convinced me comprehensively[73].

[69]'Keine Termine und leicht einen sitzen'

[70]For the accountants amongst you - think year end closing or the annual visit by corporate audit

[71]'My male friends seem to be more laid-back in their approach, more casual in locking in plans and chilled if you have to rearrange them. I know this isn't because they don't care, they just don't feel the need to overstate something;'

[72]'I can't stand drama, but it seemed like every time I picked up the phone to talk or text with Debbie, I was being drawn into some. I began to dread every time I picked up my phone and saw her name on the screen.'

[73]Tantrika, 2020-09-13 provided a definition by listing eight traits of a drama free girlfriend, other equate 'drama' to emotional toxicity.

A 'thorough search' of Quora[74] responses yielded the following items - usually in the context of why guy friends are less drama than lady friends: less competition, less upset after a potential badly phrased comment, less judging and less 'bitching'. Coincidentally and curiously so, the items 'less competition' and 'less judging' also held prominent positions the other way when men compared their female platonic friends to their male ones, without however specifically using the term 'drama'.

In summary, I don't just find enjoyment of company crucial; I think it might take a key role as the reward function in the friendship, incentivising to repeat the encounter. For this reason, I build the review element of the friendship process in section 7.3 around this.

Practical takeaway
Don't monitor or become obsessive about it, but ideally when hanging out with your friends everyone should really feel fully relaxed. Time should fly, outside worry forgotten, and the focus on the activity or conversation. It should just feel easy - and should do for everyone in the group. If it doesn't ask yourself why and what factors are leading to tension. But don't overthink.

Suggestions for thought

- What is it about being in the company of your friends you enjoy most?
- Is enjoyment of the time spent together actually your biggest motivator to continue a friendship, or are other factors more important?
- Do you know in what kind of situations you enjoy conversations?
- Have you found a local spot, your favourite cafe or pub that is particularly conducive to good conversations?
- To what degree do you relax with your friends or more on your own? If both, how are they different?
- Setting aside 'toxic friends' have you ever felt your friendships as sources of stress over a prolonged period? What did this do to the specific friendships?

For statistics in sociological studies, question suggestions and weights in counting see H.

4.6 Mutual understanding

Friendship is about finding people who are your kind of crazy.

[74]Quora.com is a website where users post questions and other users answer them.

Unknown

Mutual understanding is the capability of understanding the other and the feeling of being understood on a deep level. It enables the creation of quality time, that Chapman, 2009 writes about in his love languages. Note that this is not just emotional understanding, but also context or factual understanding, such as two professionals being able to talk shop and understanding what the other person is saying. It also includes the ability to be at ease to say what you want both emotional and factual, knowing that the other person will understand you. For the purpose of this book it might be difficult to parse the difference between the state and capability of understanding each other and the activity of listening and sharing that leads to it, and thus there will be a bit of overlap with that section.[75].

Thus there are three levels of mutual understanding. (1) First it is being able to rationally or intellectually understand what the friend is saying and is connected also to intellect. (2) It is also understanding the feelings that the friend is having even though we wouldn't share them - what I call weak empathy. Finally it means (3) being able and identify with the feelings that friends are having - strong empathy. All three items are then supportive of (4) gaining understanding of oneself through the interaction with our friends.

Any understanding we reach of the other comes from **sharing our stories and experiences**. For the more sensitive stuff we need openness, vulnerability, trust and a base level of confidentiality. However here I simply mean that we share *something*. We share general stories (information), humorous stories, general narratives. We share matters that concern us and that we have an interest in. We can also share experiences (personal information, captured in 5.3). We give the friend the opportunity to get to know us, to see whether they appreciate our traits such as our humour. We create familiarity, which in turn enables trust beyond the initial platonic attraction or gut feeling. The key skill here is good storytelling. This bonding over mutually interesting stories, that are relatable, leading to the seeing ourselves in the other person is particularly relevant in explaining why couch surfing worked so well (in the years that it worked well). It was a community of international travelling people, on a tight budget and with a joy of connecting over this kind of conversation. Hunt, 2018-09-03 also explores the Vienna coffee house conversation, where the stories and sharing builds up trust in just over two hours. The counterpart to listen well to other people's stories is at this point not empathy, we are initially not focussing on emotions, but imagination and relating from our experience. Can we see our acquaintance having fun in a going to a local carnival party in Brazil. Can we see the fascination with a certain sports and appreciate the pain in practicing hard for a year to excel at it. Can we relate to silly pranks we played in school or nights and days of D&D sessions[76]? Do we 'understand'? We share by having common experience with them, and bond through that, or through our relating to their experience.

Rational understanding or **non-feeling understanding** is 'being understood on an intellectual or professional level'. This is closely related to the activity of working together or pursuing interests together, but the activity here is not essential. It can also extend to humor or cultural understanding (which is close to

[75]Note that a significantly more extensive definition and discussion is in Coplan, 2011

[76]Pen and paper role playing game

mutual belief). The phrase 'X just gets what I am saying'. This can be another doctor understanding problems at work, people in a corporate career understanding why a boss demanding Y or departmental politics or alignment processes can be such a problem or nuisance. It is about being able to support in rational problem-solving processes, that you are capable of follow a person's thinking and the issues involved. It extends to travel experiences and captures a lot of the reverse culture shock [77], which is not just of an emotional nature. As you explain certain experiences such as cultural differences in work places or in food habits, and people including close friends and family look at you with a question mark in their eye because they just cannot relate or understand what on earth you are talking about and lack the imagination. It can be as mundane as trying to explain to someone why Star Wars is 'better' than Star Trek[78] or whether a certain speaker or sports equipment piece is better than another .If the other person retorts that they have neither seen Star Wars or Star Trek, do not listen to music nor have been out on a run since school finished, you may not even know where to start. They just would not understand and you might as well not even try. That is one instance when you can feel lonely. If men do not feel understood, at least in several cases this is what they mean.

The second item is **emotional understanding**. This is understanding that and why our friends might be angry, anxious or in love. This is the more common implied meaning of understanding. It is a contextual understanding, seeing what our friends are going through, what pressures they have. Sentences in this context include 'X has an uncanny ability to sense my true feeling', 'X deeply understands my feelings', 'X will understand what I mean even before I say it' or 'X understands me better than I do myself'. It does often not require active assistance in problem solving, which is probably one of the biggest misunderstandings between men and women both in romantic relationships[79] and friendships. It can be a step towards problem-solving as a friend might be better placed to provide critical review and help in interpretation of our feelings. To make this precise: A might be in a state of confusion. Something has happened and we are at a loss. When we are in a confused state about something, we can ask them 'I am not sure, does what I am saying make sense to you?' A friend unperturbed by the situation and ideally with a long history of familiarity with us is then ideal to untangle such a conundrum while at the same point validating their feelings. Indeed, whilst Vazire and Carlson, 2011 has made the argument from a psychological view, the phenomenon is age old.

It is a strong characteristic in friends according to Bennett, 2018[80]. And arguably, it is not just stereotype that females are better. Degges-White and Borzumato-Gainey, 2011, ch.1 explain the difference: 'Girls enter this world better equipped to observe and remember emotional details. They are also able to comprehend the nonverbal components of communication, including vocal tone, facial expres-

[77] Reverse culture shock is the emotional and psychological distress suffered by some people when they return home after several years overseas. This can cause unexpected difficulty in readjusting to the culture and values of the home country, now that the previously familiar has become unfamiliar.

[78] Classical semi-religious debate between science fiction fans

[79] S. Feldhahn and J. Feldhahn, 2008

[80] e.g. 'The INFP is your therapy friend, and this is because they're naturally gifted at reading and empathizing with their friends. Not keen on shallow friendships, the INFP friend is typically always down for deep talks and can help you clarify situations you just want to chat to your bestie about.'

sions, and body language, and to assess meaning more successfully than males.' The result of emphasis and importance of emotional empathy in female friendships highlights the need for female friendships outside the marriage, as men frequently fall short of expectations on this front, as Pahl, 2000, p.39[81] explains. A key question is whether certain cultural or religious backgrounds will inhibit this factor. I would argue that it can but doesn't have to. However, sometimes religious convictions can lead to emotional difficulties[82], and in such situations a friend of a different conviction needs the maturity to step beyond their own convictions and at least be prepared to see the situation from the friend's perspective. Thus whilst not going as far as Cuddeback, 2010, p.37 I acknowledge the potential for misunderstandings. Likewise, age, ethnicity and other background differences can lead to mostly an absence of experiences that might be necessary to empathise with emotions a friend feels in a specific situation. Misunderstanding situations hand can consequently also lead to disconnect. This is specifically reported for nagging behaviour after a change in situation, such as request for continued hanging out to friends who switched from being single to having young children or who worked long term hours and thus did not have time (see also Alberoni, 2016, p.24[83]).

The ultimate level is that of emotional identification, according to Asatryan, 2016, p.10[84] emotional 'worlds that are close enough to touch'. I would not go as far that it in its extreme is a complete merging of identities or thinking, a 'Pacific Rim' style drift without the technology of the Jaeger[85], but a deep mutual emotional intimacy certainly can be achieved on rare occasions in long and very close friendships.

The second large theme of understanding someone is **'knowing** the **person'**. When looking at the statements regarding knowing they usually are a bit different to understanding. 'X really knows me' can mean a multitude of things. But at the base level it is just a deep acquaintance. It is not a 'X does this because he thinks this will get him B' but a 'I just know X does this'. We are aware of the little

[81]'It is frequently asserted that there is 'gender asymmetry in emotional expression' - a theme explored in depth in a series of essays by Jean Duncombe and Dennis Marsden. Men are often unwilling or unable to respond to their partner's needs. As one of Harrison's respondents put it: Well, my friend Rose is very intuitive. I could be telling the exact same story to my husband and he just wouldn't get it, you know? I mean, he would completely miss the point! But Rose would understand - I'd get a much better response from her. She'd give me good, considered advice. And I know that she would be really listening to me, and not just pretending to be listening from behind a newspaper. Thus, for many middle-class women, while they may wish their partners to be their best friends, it is often their female friends who more closely meet their emotional needs. Karen Harrison suggests that, given the high incidence of divorce and single parenthood and some realistic pessimism about the longevity of marriage, it was a good, rational strategy for the women she investigated to develop close, personal relationships outside marriage."

[82]E.g. the age old question of whether and when pre-marital intercourse is permitted, advisable or to be delayed

[83]'But then it turns out he doesn't understand, has no interest in our problems. Now our disappointment is great and we feel alone.'

[84]'A person's inner world includes her thoughts, feelings, beliefs, preferences, rhythms, fantasies, narratives, and experiences. When two people are close, he knows her beliefs and can easily speak to them. She recognizes his rhythms and can easily move in time with him. He can feel her feelings. She knows what he's thinking. Your inner worlds are — metaphorically — close enough to touch.'

[85]Modern Science fiction, where two people merge their consciousness to jointly steer a giant robot (called a Jaeger) to battle oversized dinosaur-like monsters. See `https://youtu.be/2rGVxfP8n4U` for a description. If you know the movie, you may again reflect also on other symbolisms of the understanding, loyal hetairos played on in the film.

quirks, the traits. Some we appreciate, some we might not. Some may be morally or emotionally relevant, some not. But over time we have come to know them, and it is through this knowledge that we can interpret X's actions. It should be noted that this is not yet endorsing the mirror process view. Our friend knowing us deeply is not the same as me knowing myself or getting to know myself through my friend. I would also argue that words matter, and 'knowing a friend' is a theme profusely used. Olyan, 2017, p. 127 cites 'meyudda - one who is known to me', Lewis, 1960, p. 104: 'One knows nobody so well as one's fellow.', Flowers, 2016: 'One person who knows your true hearts desire', Matthews, 1983, p.148: 'Her lament about her current situation was not absence of associates but absence of ... *someone who knows about me*', Rath, 2006, p.106: 'My friend Ben is someone I have known since second grade. He knows me better than anyone except my wife, and in some ways, he knows me better than my wife.'. Nehamas, 2016, ch.4[86] quotes Thoreau to emphasise the nonverbal, intuitive acquaintance with a close friend. Being truly known by a friend is incredibly reassuring and confidence building.

It is in some sense the precondition for understanding, but also for respecting and appreciating one's friend (cf. 4.3). It provides meaning and validation. The better someone knows you, the more respect, appreciation and admiration (4.10) are meaningful. Someone knowing you deeply means they have undergone efforts to get to know you, have had a deep interest in you. As Asatryan, 2016, p.52 points out - 'love at first sight may be real, but 'knowing at first sight' is not.' - it is costly. It is the absence of this costly mattering to someone, that can make loneliness so acute and difficult to ignore in old age. Furthermore, if used in form of a mirror function, it can go to remarkable depth, even predicting our longevity accurately according to Jackson et al., 2015[87].

The three forms of our friends understanding us then can support us in learning to understand ourselves. The friends **help discover** the self. One of the interesting aspects of education is its literal meaning - educare means to lead or bring out of something that is already inside. We associate this usually with teachers and parents, but bringing out our personality to its full shine and potential is also a key function of good friends. Support in discovering one's identity is the key role of friends for children and adolescents. They discover themselves, and get support both from elderly who have a good view on them as well as from same age friends who are on the same path and situation as they are. With friends we can experiment, we can express our views, and get moral, intellectual, emotional feedback. Only a friend who knows us can respond meaningfully 'this is not like you at all, why would you say that or think that?'. Nehamas, 2016, ch.5[88] states that we are happy to admit that our close friends may know us better than we do. However at the same time the friend will not hold it against us permanently, but understand the hypothetical nature of a deliberation. We can thus try ourselves out. The stories we hear from our peers are also inexpensive thought experiments, and if we can visualise and relate to them we do not have to repeat mistakes ourselves. We can even discuss with friends how we ought to have handled in a

[86]'Thoreau said it best: 'You know about a person who deeply interests you more than you can be told. A look, a gesture, an act, which to everybody else is insignificant tells you more than words can."

[87]Their paper is aptly titled 'Your friends know how long you will live.'

[88]'When our friendship is strong, I am quite content with the idea that you may understand me better than I understand myself: we often depend on our friends to help us see things about ourselves that we can't recognize or admit on our own.'

situation, and potentially get feedback on how they think we would have acted. Whilst certainly our need to discover and shape ourselves decreases with age, and at some point our personality is reasonably set, it is estimated that we however change 10-20 % over every decade. Sometimes substantial changes, such as life events or illhealth leads us to or even forces us to substantially redefine ourselves. In that process of exploration, rediscovery and reshaping a good friend, in particular someone who has known us for a long time is invaluable. Alberoni, 2016, p.26 summarizes it as: 'To speak with a friend makes me realize who I really am; why I am really myself only in relation to what I think I can be.'. It is both the affirming but just assessment of the present as well as the future.

Practical takeaway
A deep understanding and knowing of your friend should be the goal of any friendship. Your friend will change, there will always be something new to discover. Some people share slower than others, but over time your friend should not remain a black box. This does not mean to categorize the friend, but to develop over time an understanding of their values, thought types, preferences and ways of argument. It also includes an idea of what they do not like, be it activities or values. Get to know your friend !

Suggestions for thought

- Do you feel understood by your friends? Is your definition of being understood more the intellectual or the emotional understanding?
- How well do you think your friends 'know' you?
- Do you think your friends understand you (partially) better than e.g. your family?
- To what degree do you think you learned to understand yourself through your friends.

For statistics in sociological studies, question suggestions and weights in counting see H.

4.7 Reciprocity and feeling needed

A friendship being one of equals is a recurring theme in literature, and this means that both friends are both giving and receiving, though there might be differences in timing and kind. But imbalanced relationships usually end up breeding resentment. It is important to note that not always the takers are the problem. Human nature has long inbred reciprocity according to Gouldner, 1960, and being in a relationship where effectively you cannot meaningfully contribute is deeply dissatisfactory. In such a scenario, the receiver and incapable giver will distance themselves to restore balance, unless a meaningful way is found how they can return favour and express their benevolence by active beneficence. This is a key factor particularly in old age, as elder people appreciate the care or favours bestowed upon them, but get frustrated as they feel incapable of doing anything that genuinely benefits younger friends and family.

In literature starting with Aristotle it is almost everywhere named, though not always emphasized as absolutely essential. Aristotle, 1925, 8.2 'goodwill when it is reciprocal being friendship.' or 'and in it each gets from each in all respects the same as, or something like what, he gives'. Cicero, 1923, p.137 'so that by the giving and receiving of favours one may get from another and in turn repay what he is unable to procure of himself.' These definitions are fairly general and essentially refer to magnitude in utility and affection. The golden rule of do as you are done by emphasises a general reciprocity. However, it is a minimum standard established also outside friendship. In Matthew 5:46 it is written 'If you love those who love you, what reward will you get? Are not even the tax collectors doing that?'. Christianity is of course preaching non-discrimination (see Kierkegaard), but I would deduce that within a Christian friendship significant diversions from reciprocity from the giving friend to the one in need (see consideration 4.3) can be tolerated, and thus placing a lower value on actual reciprocity. Indeed, I would argue that the reason reciprocity is at all on the radar of the Christian writers like Augustine and Aquinas is not because of a biblical background but because of the Greek and Roman influences.

Rath, 2006 emphasises the often different nature of roles friends have to each other, and thus we need to think about a general reciprocity rather than a reciprocity in kind. There is also the concept of reciprocity and diversions from it in time. Thus, reciprocity is achieved simply by having trust that the other person will rise to the challenge if and when the situation arises with complete disregard to actual reciprocity. This criterion is e.g. put forward by the motivational speaker Simon Sinek as his defining feature of friendship[89].

Likewise when Alberoni speaks about reciprocity, he emphasises the balance of power that a mismatch in reciprocity or utility brings. Thus a king might afford many benefits to his subject friend. Arguably the friendship of Laelius was also such a case, with his emphasising Scipios seniority in status and affluence. This would be a principle of proportion, which Aristotle, 1925, 8.14 and 9.1[90] acknowledges. According to Olyan, 2017, p.86[91] in biblical stories differences of wealth and status were common and the principle of proportionality applied. David receiving gifts from Jonathan was thus not an expression of utmost love, but a suitable consequence of the wealth difference in the just completed suzerainty covenant. Such an attitude can work or not work in our society depending on the character of the friends involved, whether generosity or the suspicion of being taken advantage of outweigh each other. Kale, 2020-02-11[92] tells the story of an

[89] What Friendship Really means: 'I could do a thousand things for someone and they do nothing for me, but I walk around with the absolute confidence that the one day that I need something I know without a shadow of doubt they'll be there.' https://www.youtube.com/watch?v=5UlP7g36ono

[90] 'In all friendships between dissimilars it is, as we have said, proportion that equalizes the parties and preserves the friendship'

[91] 'Thus, even a friendship between people who are not peers in every respect requires behavioral parity. Just as the suzerain of a suzerain-vassal treaty has obligations to the vassal, so a friend who has greater social status or wealth owes his friend loyalty and other goods of friendship.'

[92] https://www.theguardian.com/lifeandstyle/2020/feb/11/the-wealth-gap-how-changing-fortunes-tear-close-friends-apart

affluent person feeling uncomfortable with the thought of being expected to pay for group bills because of his exceeding wealth.

On the other end of the spectrum, a positive extension of proportionality is the attitude of paying it forward or a general trickle down. Thus it is expected to reciprocate to others according to one's means. This would allow me with no second thoughts enjoy the partially one-sided benefits of visiting a more affluent friend, possibly enjoying a good wine outside my classical price range, and on a different day taking out less affluent friends on a dinner in town with me paying the bill. As long as everyone is on the page with that, it works. Paying it forward as a principle is why communities like Couchsurfing worked for so long, in the sense that I host for free without feeling taken advantage of in the assumption that the people I host have hosted or at some point will host other members of the community[93].

Reciprocity in spirit is another theme that occurs in long-lasting friendships, especially during old age. This is essentially accepting imparity in the relationship based on the hypothetical mutuality. An example would be one friend taking care of another friend who in old age has become frail or even demented. The classical 'benefit' of the relationship is gone, as the intellectual capacity is impaired. Thus the classical friendship is over. Still, there are several anecdotes of such situations, with the only justification being that 'they would do the same for me if it was the other way round'. Here the imbalance is caused through no fault of the friend after a long period of actual reciprocity. Another theme of reciprocity is that of matching emotional disclosure and understanding, which Degges-White and Borzumato-Gainey, 2011, 3.29 and Nelson, 2016 mean when using the term reciprocity. This theme is included with openness and vulnerability.

A big theme of reciprocity is allowing love of the friend respecting the friend's desire to feel useful or needed. One party being a 'non-taker' can be an issue of equal importance to the imbalance of the one friend being a taker. This is a frequent theme in romantic relationships and marital counseling, but it also applies to friendships. The imbalance here is because of the choice in behaviour of one partner of the pair, of not accepting favours, gifts, or acts of service from the other one. This can be a dysfunctional consequence of virtue signalling. By not accepting any benefits, A trying to show to the other person that he is just in the friendship for spiritual wellbeing of B (and himself) and not any mundane worldly benefits he might receive from B. However this is bereaving your friend of opportunities to show devotion to you, and express his goodwill in ways which he can. The benefit of a gift or a service is not just in the receiving, but can also be in the giving. Thus the good is in 'permitting the act of giving'.This is even more relevant for people who have little opportunity to give elsewhere, e.g. on account of financial or health difficulties towards the end of their life. Meaning in life is a key human existential concern according to I. Yalom, 1980, and though usually meaning is sought elsewhere, mattering to people and continuing to being able to provide joy to friends is a contributing factor to happiness and meaning in life. Reciprocity means then acknowledging this need and allowing beneficence enacted by your friend. Even at the start of getting to know each other, think twice before rejecting an acquaintance reaching out with an act of service, gift or kind

[93]It is in the breakdown of the trust in this principle generally observed between 2016 and 2018 that the community started suffering.

deed to you. Even if you want to maintain independence and avoid 'reciprocity-debt', it remains a rejection and thus a stopping of friendship development in its tracks. One result of overemphasising independence is not accepting good services from a friend or potential friend. Thus by the mechanism of reciprocity of course you do not enter debt or dependency and ultimately avoid the associated vulnerability. Some people who value independence highly really avoid good deeds given to them like a vampire avoids sunlight. However, by doing so perhaps they are making the development of deep friendships much more difficult for themselves on account of such 'principles'. Indeed they may inadvertently signal a rejection of friendship, that might per se be actually welcome.

Ensuring reciprocity is difficult. Measuring benefit or utility is incredibly difficult, both on the positive and the negative according to Nelson, 2016, p.63[94]. If the relationship is going well, I do not want to think about it. If it is not going well, measurement is going to suffer from hindsight bias, where we allocate greater importance to our activities. My hunch is that exact reciprocity is difficult, but that it should be possible to reasonably steer a corridor, if that is the desire, monitoring extreme imbalances but choosing not to pay attention to details. Finally, I would mention the theme of the estimation or establishing of reciprocity in quality of friendship in light of Pentlands research (i.e. mutual levels of affect and relevance). This I will discuss in (9.3).

Practical takeaway

Don't be just a giver. Accept the good. Give, but also allow to be given. Allow yourself to need your friend. Ask your friend for favours and be willing to reciprocate. 'Trading favours' isn't a transactional attitude but one key mechanism of deepening a friendship.

Suggestions for thought

- What is your understanding of reciprocity in friendship? Do you believe reciprocity in kind or more overall reciprocity?
- At what point do you classify a friend as a 'taker' and take remedial action not to be taken advantage of? Over how long a time and under what conditions would 'taking' be tolerable?
- Do you allow yourself to depend on a friend, to be in a situation in which you need the friend? What does it take to get you to acknowl-

[94]'Scorekeeping is problematic. Do I get the credit for calling all the time, or does she get the credit for listening to me do most of the talking? Do I get points for always hosting girls' night, or does she get points for always driving the distance to reach me? Am I gifting her with an invitation to my special dinner party, or is she gifting me by paying for a night of babysitting in order to come? And talking about babysitting, if I watched her two hyperactive kids tear apart my house all afternoon, we even if she watches my three obedient angels the next day- or did give more? Was the generosity in asking my friend a lot of questions her life, or was the generosity in her being willing to share and reveal all those stories to me.'

edge or accept such a situation?

- How clear are you in your expectations in friendship? Are you consistent towards yourself?

For statistics in sociological studies, question suggestions and weights in counting see H.

4.8 Trust and confidentiality

We'll be best friends forever because you already know too much.

Unknown

Trust and confidentiality means keeping secret or confidential stories or items confidential. This is a virtue mostly valued among contemporary common friendships, much studied and evidenced by the sociologists. There is not a lot of variations in the statements, but it has its context: 'I can trust X to keep what I tell him confidential'. 'X is worthy of my trust'. Trust is based on tested integrity over the course of the friendship. Honesty, integrity and consistency are traits of the person, which are general and which a person acts with towards anyone. Trust is personal. I can trust X to act in a trustworthy way regarding the interactions with me. Rath, 2006, p.105 cites an interviewee: 'It is very hard to win my trust. I expect a lot from myself and those around me. When I find someone I can trust, I know they will be a lifelong friend.'. This is a definition of person-specific relational trust. Aristotle, 1925, 8.3 confirms that trust is a necessary condition in friendship: 'nor can they admit each other to friendship or be friends till each has been found lovable and been trusted by each.'. In the same sense, Alberoni, 2016, e.g. p.11 defines trust as one of the basis elements of friendship.

Trusting is part of the disclosure journey, and we need to do it, albeit slowly, in order to deepen the friendship. You need to trust to have your trust validated over time, which is necessary to trust more. Trust is earned through acts proving trustworthiness. Given its naturally slow build up over time, trust is thus inherently linked to relationship length. Trust can also be selective. There may be at the start aspects with which you can trust the other person, and stories, emotions or other items on which you don't wish to give your trust quite yet. Given that it is selective, it is perfectly normal to only have a few people in an inner circle whom we trust completely. Trust is one of the key issues in questioning the validity of online friendships. I will get to an overall discussion later, but as Asatryan, 2016, p.24 points out that on the internet, specifically on dating profiles, everyone lies a bit. Some more, some less, but the principle is clear. While people can lie in person too, the internet with its anonymity and the reduced interaction information makes flexibility on truth a lot easier.

Confidentiality also means that the information is tied to a context within the friendship, you give information about yourself to a friend in a certain role, e.g. as a confidante or to work through things. However, it is possible that the role changes - thus a friend suddenly might become your boss at work, or one of you develops romantic feelings for the other. Though either situation may not be helped, this creates an instantaneous trust issue. At the time of information provision there was an unspoken agreement that the information was given to deepen the friendship, and no personal gain may be extracted from it. This agreement may be difficult to uphold, if the friend has information about some professional weakness of yours. Similarly, it might seem unfair that the friend may reject your approaches based e.g. on your past behaviour with a different ex-partner[95]. In both cases however even the consideration that past information could be used may imply a breach of trust and confidentiality, that will place a strain on the friendship.

Reflecting on this matter where I found confidentiality most important was on hypothetical discussions. We have a politically charged environment, with a global standard of political conventions. Now the goal of course is noble, of better acceptance of parts of the population that are discriminated against. However at the same time words like 'woke' or 'cancel culture' have made it a risk to even discuss controversial items, leading to echo chambers. In Germany there were discussions whether the AfD made racism OK for public debate, or whether Leave.EU made xenophobia acceptable to the british public. I will not wade into this debate here, but what I maintain is that it must be possible within a friendship to discuss openly items that are contrary to public convention. If I have read an article - say with a rather horrible conspiracy theory - but which I find plausible, i.e. attach a positive probability of truth to it - it should always be preferable, even from a societal perspective - that I take the discussion to a friend whose critical mind I appreciate. This friend may fast debunk it - rather than me 'doing internet research' and by virtue of Googles algorithm end up gobbling more junk[96]. And I must be sure that me entertaining certain thoughts must be confidential whilst they are still forming. That having been said, if they subsequently sign the AfD membership form, that publicly confirms the conclusion of the thinking process and adoption of a set of morals that I may then disagree with.

On the other hand, some people cannot be trusted with sensitive information. Maybe they are gossips, maybe they get drunk. Breaches in confidentiality in part can be avoided as a problem if people communicate this openly. Some people cannot lie, act or pretend that they do not have a certain information, making it easy for an adversary to obtain it. Some of you may remember series 5 of Friends where Chandler and Monica get together, and then when Joey finds out, make him promise not to tell. The rest of series 5 he spends in agony trying not to give it away[97]. There are some people like that, and there is no blaming him. This situation can be made more complicated if say it is information about an action of your friend you or they themselves morally disagree with, which can range from taking or having taken drugs to cheating on a friend. I am not talking

[95]There is no shortage of mental scenarios here, nor of movies or stories of friend turning romantic interestee

[96]My unsubstantiated impression is that Google in 2010 was a genuine help for information search, in the way Google Scholar still is. But the general Google engine combined with widely deployed SEO strategies is now just a consumption and advertising pushing channel. An illustration: Google has a calculator in it. I wanted to check the calculation $30/e \approx 11$ and indeed it came out with 11.036. However the next 3 items were adverts for lingerie and bras, followed by vape juice and an electronic designer yacht.

[97](1) https://youtu.be/XZVHmRvfDHM (2) https://youtu.be/KyJJ6vi26uA?t=142 Though the scene with him subsequently blackmailing Chandler and Monica is hilarious - (3) https://youtu.be/FNgAlglarPg

here about a mortal sin that causes you or them to question the basis of your entire relationship. But it may be impossible for them to keep a straight face or continue to feel comfortable when the topic is broached in company. Different value systems, that may not matter in other parts of the friendship, may come full out into the open. It also may conflict with other items, such as putting your friend in a good like ('X is not like that, you guys don't know it, but he actually did Y to help Z'). SIRC, 2006 discusses the issue of confidentiality and reveals that 'Over a third also believe that 'There are different types of secret. Some I would pass on, some I would not'.'. I am not making a defence of breaking someone's trust, however want to make it clear that the theme is not completely uncontested.

The issue is, as a popular meme goes : 'It takes years to build up trust, and it takes suspicion, not proof to destroy it'. If you know yourself to be a of not the highest confidentiality standards person, it is in my view then OK to come to terms with one's own imperfection, and to decline to be privy to certain particular information. That does not have to completely [preclude] the friendship. I do not need to trust a clown and energizer to enlighten me when I am down. A mind opener does not need to trusted with the most intimate personal details to enter with them on deep discussions on politics, AI and other topics. I can trust a companion to be there to help me in really important practical matters, without entrusting them with the information that it was me who played a certain prank on a teacher. But I need the mentor or my emotional support and confidant to be absolutely trustworthy in order to open up to them to such a degree that they can console my sorrows and advise me on my life's decision. There is no gender divide: While women engage more in sharing activity, men, when they do share, expect the volunteered stories or experience to underlie confidentiality all the same. I have touched on the issue of gossip including positive gossip elsewhere, but negative or even malicious gossip on a friend that draws on confidentially given information is a direct breach both on benevolence as well as trust. This basic truthism is also recognized from ancient times, as Proverbs 11:13 and 16.28[98] set a clear standard.

Beyond the trust of confidentiality being kept, there is a second type of trust in the ultimate benevolence and loyalty of the friend. Indeed, it is difficult sometimes to parse the difference between trust and loyal in statements on friendship, as the implied statement really often is 'I trust my friend to act loyally.' Once trust is destroyed, destruction is difficult to repair and almost permanent. It also leaves scars beyond the concrete friendship, as the betrayed person will in future not be just on guard in this relationship, but in most others too. Thus the once scarred person will be inhibited in their potential for opening up that is necessary to develop deeper friendships.

[98] "No one who gossips can be trusted with a secret, but you can put confidence in someone who is trustworthy." Pr. 11:13 "A troublemaker plants seeds of strife; gossip separates the best of friends." Pr 16:28

Practical takeaway
Either be trustworthy and keep things confidential, or be open that you find it difficult to conceal private information. Whilst being trustworthy is of course preferable, both are better than being untrustworthy yet enjoying the thrill of getting inside information.

Suggestions for thought

- Is there anything that prevents you from trusting your friends? If so, is it something holding you back in general, or is it something about a specific person and relationship?
- There is no need to rush, moving slow but consistently is perfectly OK. Are you aware of your speed in getting to trust people?
- Have you ever broken confidentiality and trust? How did that affect the friendship?
- How do you rate your own trustworthiness at the moment?
- What do you think about a person you would in all other counts consider a friend, but who cannot be trusted with very sensitive information and freely acknowledges it?

For statistics in sociological studies, question suggestions and weights in counting see H.

4.9 Openness and vulnerability

The tandem of openness and vulnerability is the key element of the disclosure process in emotion based friendships. In our time, the two major proponents of the benefits and value of vulnerability are Brown and LMSW, 2012 and Nelson, 2016. So what are the two terms about? **Openness** is about disclosure of information about yourself of increasing depth. It is the opposite of emotional privacy. You can see it as the read access right to your heart and mind. **Weak vulnerability** is a read access[99] to significant weaknesses and elements of shame. **Strong vulnerability** is about being open to be touched and changed. It is about being open to the painful possibility that we may have to change our mind and heart. It is the write-access right to your heart and mind. Scary stuff! And yes, you want to restrict that in part, just not to everyone. Whilst openness is acknowledged as a necessary condition in friendship ('With X I am a completely open book, X is very open with me, I talk to X about my intimate personal problems...') people viscerally shy away from vulnerability. It hits just really close to the mark.

That openness and disclosure is important if not fundamental to friendship is uncontroversial. One of the two widely accepted theories of friendship develop-

[99]I find the image of read or read/write access from computers really precise as an image to describe this aspect.

ment - the social penetration theory by Altman and Taylor, 1973 - is more or less based on this process. Interestingly, neither Aristotle, nor Cicero, nor the old testament either by direct quotation nor in its interpretation by Olyan had anything that I could construe as openness or vulnerability. Of course I am happy to be proven wrong, but for now I do find it a remarkable observation in the sense that it represents a genuine shift in nature of a relationship. This sentiment changes in the New Testament. Contrast this with Matthew 26:37-38 'He took Peter and the two sons of Zebedee along with him, and he began to be sorrowful and troubled. Then he said to them, 'My soul is overwhelmed with sorrow to the point of death. Stay here and keep watch with me.' '. For someone who is the son of god and a master rabbi, this is about as open about your raw feeling as you can get, in the sense of weak vulnerability. I would argue that weak vulnerability is also included in James 5:16 'Therefore, confess your sins to one another and pray for one another, that you may be healed.' As anyone knows who went to own up and apologize for a major screw up to a friend, actual confessions[100] are difficult and situations of genuine vulnerability.

Moving forward, I will now summarize how far the different authors go in supporting openness, weak vulnerability and strong vulnerability. Openness is the most common denominator. Besides the short definition given above, I also think Asatryan, 2016, p.54 provides an illustrative definition: 'The ability to self-disclose essentially means being willing to reveal parts of one's inner world to someone else. It wouldn't be an exaggeration to say that this is the fundamental ability required in creating closeness. At its core, self-disclosing means openness and honesty, as well as a desire to share a range of information about oneself—both factual and subjective.' In order to follow through in this process, I essentially need to have trust in the other persons goodwill connecting the three concepts. Alberoni, 2016[101] discusses the limited openness a friend engaged in criminal activity can exhibit, and how in extension it limits the friendship. Given the wording, I would argue that Lewis, 1960, p.103[102] argues for openness and weak vulnerability. Nehamas, 2016, ch.1 acknowledges openness and weak vulnerability[103]. Shumway, 2018, p. 39 and 114[104] acknowledges difficulties and effects of openness and vulnerability.

It should be noted that tact and appropriate speed are important considerations in disclosure. Degges-White and Borzumato-Gainey, 2011, ch.3 note that

[100] I.e. not the catholic one in the confessional in the side alley of a church with a priest you see, but where you go to the dad to tell him you scratched or crashed his car Ferris Bueller style. (`https://youtu.be/bqjK6jjt6gk?t=145`) In defence of catholic confessions it has to be said, that the conversation with the priest included not only the absolution, but usually also an explicit request to right the wrong or at least own up to it when your pocket money was not enough to purchase a new set of mums favourite plates you had dropped and blamed on the family dog.

[101] 'One of the two has something to hide. He cannot be honest, cannot confide, cannot say anything important about his life. Friendship is a getting to know each other in ever greater depth. In this case there is an insuperable obstacle.'

[102] 'It is an affair of disentangled, or stripped, minds. Eros will have naked bodies; Friendship naked personalities.'

[103] 'Others believe that the essence of friendship lies in the ability of friends to be completely open with one another and share their most intimate secrets.'

[104] p. 39 'Vulnerability can be one of the most challenging friendship skills. This is particularly true for people who were raised in homes that discouraged emotional expression and open sharing.' p. 114 'When we are open with our friends, we invite them to understand our inner selves. We also tend to feel more drawn to the people that open up with us.'

'TMI, or "too much information," revealed too soon in an acquaintanceship can halt a potential friendship in its tracks'. Thus openness needs to be dosed. When we are starved of friendship, and suddenly find a kind and friendly person to listen to us, giving the full emotional download can feel so good ... to you. The strongest arguments against openness come in the interviews are recorded in Greif, 2009. Not that the author argues against it, much on the contrary, but his in-depth interviews resulting characterisations of friendship philosophies record aversions to emotional openness among males of various ages[105]. Matthews, 1986, p.35[106] gives an example that such attitudes are not only male.

Weak vulnerability preconditions acceptance as we emote on more sensitive topics, and is not uncontroversial. Whilst the psychological and self-help tradition argues for weak vulnerability with close friends, it also has its opponents. Citing Kant, Nehamas, 2016, ch.4[107] strongly argues that section of our personality are off-limits to our friends. Pahl, 2000, p.36[108] citing Simmel also acknowledges the argument.

Strong vulnerability with its preparedness to let the friend actively touch me and change me besides trust in goodwill requires also confidence in my friend's intellectual and moral capability to do so, as well a deep understanding. Given the delicate nature of such a situation, kindness and warmth are also a strongly supporting personal traits. Without a question, this is a strong hurdle to jump over. For this reason reaching this state in any friendship is rare, but when it is reached, it is precious. One supreme example might be Abraham Lincoln being persuaded by his best friend not to dissolve his engagement with his betrothed, but to proceed to marry her (as told in Strozier, 2016).

---

[105] See e.g. Greif, 2009, ch.11 'Showing vulnerability is not something that could be afforded during the year's of Michael's youth—a guy can give help, but he cannot ask for it. Friends have to anticipate it—that is how he is taken care of. For men in their 60s, vulnerabilities are creeping in to their everyday thoughts. Understanding that feelings of vulnerability are normal at this age can help men to relate to each other. Definitions of friendship may have to change so that men can ask for help, although not all men will want to talk about frailties or self-doubt. Friendships should be largely about fun, companionship, and a shared perspective on life. But they can be deeper and more satisfying when all topics can be discussed.' or Greif, 2009, ch.12 'In some of his answers, he reveals an independent side of himself that borders on the emotionally inaccessible. ... Anything about feelings? I asked. "No—men will shy away from that. We won't get into that."'

[106] 'No, I am a very private person. I always lived by the rule "no explain, no complain." When you say too much you are revealing too much about yourself. You should retain a little bit of your privacy and thereby you get pride and you get self-discipline. The very private things you keep to yourself.'

[107] 'Some subjects, though, may remain beyond the reach of even our most intimate friends. Kant was not being completely unreasonable when, in one of the dark moods of his late years, he warned that there is always a need for reserve,not so much for one's own sake, as for that of the other: for everyone has his weaknesses, and these must be kept hidden even from our friends ... so that humanity should not be offended thereby. Even to our best friend, we must not discover ourselves as we naturally are and know ourselves to be: that would be a nasty business. There are many things I might disclose to a physician, a psychiatrist, or if I were religious, to a priest or minister that I would keep from my friends. Such precautions aside, however, there are almost no limits to the aspects of ourselves that enter our friendships. Our instrumental relationships are clearly circumscribed: our interest in each is focused on satisfying some explicit need or desire. But our interest in our friends goes well beyond whatever specific expectations we may have for our relationship.

[108] 'Indeed, the century began with the powerful assertion by the German sociologist Georg Simmel that modernity is inevitably destructive of friendship - in the sense used in classical debates.' and 'Such friends would not be expected or try to probe into the depths of a person's soul. For Simmel, the modem style of friendship would be based on reserve and discretion. Modern people have too much to hide.'

Practical takeaway
Sharing with openness is a necessary activity for your friend getting to know you. You can take your time, you can experiment, you can test your friend's capability to react adequately to emotional information, but bit by bit you need to learn that vulnerability is the price you pay for being deeply known by your friend, and it is worth it.

Suggestions for thought

- Are you comfortable opening up with personal information to your friends? If not, why? Specifically is it a general attitude of yours (e.g. such information only belongs with the family) or is it about your current friends and acquaintances, that it doesn't feel quite right yet?
- If you think of what defines your personality, to what degree do you think you have told your close friends how that came about? And how much of your current emotional thinking do you share with your friends?
- Have you ever admitted to a friend an activity that was really wrong and discussed it?
- To what degree are you willing to have your friends discuss and make recommendations on personal decisions?

For statistics in sociological studies, question suggestions and weights in counting see H.

4.10 Respect, appreciation and pride

> Anybody can sympathize with the sufferings of a friend, but it requires a very fine nature to sympathize with a friend's success.
>
> Oscar Wilde

There are three levels to the esteem you have your friends in: It starts with **respect**, which is a kind of basis of friendship. Respect according to the dictionary is the feeling that something is right and you should not attempt to change it. You cannot be friends with someone whom you don't respect. The second item is that there needs to be something you appreciate in your friend, a positive trait, a habit (see also 3.7 (3)[109]). The third level is showing pride in your friends, which gives them confidence. It is affirming them, openly stating towards them that you approve of their character and are proud to be their friend.

[109] 3.7 is about the friend *being* a good person, this section is about you recognising and appreciating this

The key personality trait to show respect to other people is humility (3.3). It is in this sense that Shumway, 2018, p.141[110]defines the litmus test of respect whether we see our views as superior. You need to entertain the possibility that the other person's opinion is valid, and at least as likely to be valid as your own. Thus respect is also vital to the functionality of giving feedback and advice (5.10) as you do not get offended or sulk if your friend listens to it and gives it due consideration, but decides to reject it. Respect for his free will and person means we accept this without detriment to the friendship. Finally, respect necessitates the absence of moral deal breakers (i.e. vices that are core to your own moral code, see 3.7 (4)). Respect is thus also tied to a value judgement, the fact that we have evaluated the character of the other person and by enlarge, approved it as suitable company. Friends have respect for each other if they have 'equal power and dignity in each other's eyes.' (Alberoni, 2016, p.10). Whilst this assumption should not be again and again revisited, there are moments of shock that can eliminate respect and, as a consequence, the friendship.

A number of activities can betray the attitude of respect: Slander is one thing, which is displaying to others that you do not have respect for a person because of potentially false facts (see Alberoni, 2016, p. 99[111]). The most direct way to break a friendship is to show contempt (see J. Gottman and Silver, 2015[112]) , and is probably even worse for friendships than romantic relationships in the absence of physical attraction. The act of 'ghosting' I will discuss elsewhere (4.14) but its painful sting is also related to the absence of respect for the other person's need for closure in a relationship, regardless of what is the issue. It can even be referred to as an active attempt to harm the self-respect of the ghosted person. The last act to betray respect to be mentioned is the act of belittling or 'gaslighting'- be it in front of others or even just in a private conversation (e.g. Millington, 2019, p.99[113] for an example and appropriate response).

Whilst Aristotle and Cicero hardly mention respect, it is clear that it is expected in their societal context. However it is expected not just between friends, but essentially between normal citizen participating in public life too. Likewise, when the old testament talks about friendships, and specifically more the covenant - suzerainty formalised ones (Olyan, 2017), showing honour and respect was part and parcel.

The second level is **appreciation**, and this is the key thing. Appreciation can be experienced and expressed for two 'objects' - the person/friend and the friendship. Appreciating the role a friendship (see Greif, 2009, ch10[114]) has in your life is part of showing gratitude (4.2) and also as a result assigning it a value in life with a corresponding priority (4.3). I will focus here on appreciation of the person and

[110]'However, many of us are guilty of seeing our own views as being better or superior. When we assume our perspective is the right one, we communicate disrespect for anything different.'

[111]'Friendship is esteem, respect. One way to hurt it is to put it in doubt through slander.'

[112]Alternatively see `https://www.gottman.com/blog/the-four-horsemen-contempt/`

[113]'If they laugh off the comment or dismiss your attempt to open a conversation about it, repeat what you said: 'But I was hurt by what you said/did.' No one should dismiss your feelings, and this should be a strong boundary set so the behaviour isn't repeated in the future. If they still don't take what you're saying seriously or suggest the hurt is due to your sensitivity instead of their actions, try: 'I understand it might not have been your intention to offend me, but your words/actions did."

[114]'And he has turned friendships into a life preserver, a guard against loneliness. He appreciates them now more than before. He hints at the understanding that life is not going to go on forever and that he better appreciate the good things he has.'

her/his traits. Appreciating the friend is noting the uniqueness and value of the person, both generally and specifically to you. Appreciation for your friend generates the feeling of appreciated by you in her or him, and this is acknowledged in interview statements such as 'X thinks my ideas are important and worthwhile', 'X appreciates a skill or character trait of mine' or 'I feel appreciated and/or cherished by X'. It is a matter of philosophy and linguistics of whether appreciation of traits and 'of the person as a whole' is necessary and where the difference lies, but I shall treat it for now as one and the same. Likewise, I will treat esteem or high esteem for a friend as a synonym for appreciation based on context, rather than the more basic respect. . Whereas Aristotle, 1925, 8.3[115] sees appreciation as necessary for the friendship, Cicero, 1923, p. 133[116] phrases it more as an aspect of friendship with consequences[117].

There is no rhyme or reason of what people find worthy of appreciation. Of course classical virtuous traits are common, but minor details feature nonetheless (see e.g. Adams, Blieszner, and Vries, 2000[118]). Whereas larger services or sacrifice trigger our gratitude, little tokens of affection build up our appreciation. This could be a postcard, a drink, a joke shared with us just at the right time when we needed it. It could be a quirky habit, the way she/he makes jokes - be it dry, crazy or just plain old silly, rolls her/his eyes or a dish that only she/he can make just that way[119], or the warm bear hug a person gives to you. Nehamas, 2016, ch.1[120] on this issue substantially diverges from Aristotle's 'only virtue is lovable' dogma.

N. Lee and S. Lee, 2009 note the self-reinforcing of appreciation: 'the more we express appreciation to each other, the more appreciative we become of each other'. It is thus no wonder how Nelson, 2020, p.68 includes it among her sustainable positivity builders. Chapman, 2009 includes 'words of affirmation' as one of his love languages for couples, and there is every reason to believe that this holds for friendships too. In the same sense Lewis, 1960, p.104[121] places appreciation as qualifying element of friendship as a love. Of course the way and frequency with which appreciation is expressed, will undoubtedly differ relative to the romantic relationship, but it surely cannot hurt to make it a point to on occasions tell your friends when an action or trait triggers the sentiment in you.

The meaning of what appreciation is also becomes clear in its opposite when you are put down by a friend. A friend knows us, and whilst that knowledge can ground us if necessary, it should be taken with caution and goodwill. Also, being taken for granted over the long run is also not ideal, but not every good deed

[115]' ... nor can they admit each other to friendship or be friends till each has been found lovable (worthy of love) and been trusted by each.'

[116]'...so great is the esteem on the part of their friends, the tender recollection and the deep longing that still attends them.'

[117]p.133 'Wherefore friends, though absent, are at hand; though in need, yet abound; though weak, are strong; and — harder saying still — though dead, are yet alive;'

[118]'It may be features like about the individual, their sense of humor, an admiration that I have aside from that in the way they stand up to the problems that I've known them to experience.'

[119]This is no joke, I had people say about me that the best thing about becoming friends with me is the foamy hot chocolate I make.

[120]'Aristotle is absolutely correct: we can't be friends of people in whom we find nothing to appreciate. He also believes, though, that only a few features—the virtues—can be truly admired. ... I think he is wrong, but reversing his view in some respects can point us in the right direction.'

[121]'Hence, as he rings true time after time, our reliance, our respect and our admiration blossom into an Appreciative love of a singularly robust and well-informed kind.'

we bestow on a friend demands its immediate acknowledgement and appreciation. Some people are better at expressing appreciation than others and do it more regularly. Discovering a structural lack of appreciation in the friendship however can be quite problematic, as it signals often that a friendship that might have been considered being close, might have been a lot more superficial or instrumental (see Cuddeback, 2010, p.31 as well as section 9.3).

The significance of respect and appreciation emerges in the receiving. One key function or addressed need of friendship particularly in adolescence is identity building, and that happens through validation and ego reinforcement. Kids often say that our parents are supposed to love us and think we are great, and thus it 'isn't worth anything'.[122] Respect and admiration from friends however needs to be earned. Later in life we may know the shallowness of some people liking us for our status, good looks, network or other support capabilities, when all we want is being appreciated for who we are. Friends provide this independent affirmation and validation for our personality and identity. They may not do that all the time, indeed if we do something morally bad they will probably call us out. And some of them will not miss an opportunity to play an embarrassing prank on us. However, overall we should leave encounters with our friends feeling better about ourselves and our personality than when we went into the meetup. It should be a matter of 'my friends like and appreciate me, so I can't be that bad after all'. In that sense the positive affirmation received from friends insulates us from social adversity from all other walks of life. Paine, 1969, p.507 puts it like this: 'the affective meaning and value of friendship is the sense of worth [...] it imparts to the person enjoying it.'

Practical takeaway
For each of your good friends, ask yourself what you appreciate and possibly admire in their personality. You do not need to tell them or discuss it with them. You also will not reduce their entire personality to those two or three key features. But having two or three positive traits in your mind that you associate with your friends will enhance your predisposition towards them.

Suggestions for thought

- How often do you catch yourself arguing with friends and thinking in the back of your head 'why doesn't she/he get it'? Where you think your opinion or information is just slightly better or superior?
- Have you ever thought about what exactly you appreciate in your friends?
- How do you feel about expressing your appreciation to your friends? Are you sure they know you appreciate them?

[122] Of course it is important, but a 14-18 year old may not think so for a while.

- If a friend expresses her/his appreciation of a trait or activity to you, how do you feel? How do you decide which appreciation is sincere and where does it for you become flattery?

For statistics in sociological studies, question suggestions and weights in counting see H.

Equality

Equality in rank and financial resources initially was a subcategory of reciprocity, however on second reading of in particular the philosophers it became clear that at its core is a different issue. Nonetheless, on several occasions equality and reciprocity are used as substitutes[123]. The theme of equality is that friendship is only possible between people of equal social status, because only thus can one not gain socially from the other by the friendship, but is in it only for its sentimental value[124]. Thus equality really means that both do not depend on each other for any commercial or other utilitarian benefit, potentially giving one person power over the other of which Alberoni, 2016 warns. It is an equality in the eye of the beholder, thus even a vast difference in wealth or societal status can be casually ignored if the two friends define that the core of their friendship is their intellectual capacities, love for poetry or athletic prowess. This argument is made forcefully amongst others by Lewis, 1960, p.103[125] and Alberoni, 2016, p.10 and 48[126]. Aristotle, 1925, 8.5[127] in his definition treads much closer to reciprocity, considering the benefit that accrues to each party as crucial measure of equality. According to Rist, 1980, p.125[128] the Epicurean philosophy however was a highly equalizing one, only caring for attitude and character ('right thinking') and effectively disregarding background by accepting women and slaves even when this was highly untypical of the surrounding society[129]. It should be noted that this first of all did

[123]E.g. Millington, 2019, p.10 'There has to be equality in a friendship - equal amounts of time sharing your good news and bad- Naturally, the need to be there for each other will ebb and flow, and life can throw a spanner (or a whole toolbox) in the works every now and again, but conversational hijackers must not be tolerated.'

[124]e.g. Kale, 2020-02-11

[125]'No one cares twopence about any one else's family, profession, class, income, race, or previous history. Of course you will get to know about most of these in the end. But casually.'

[126]p.10 'To be equals does not presuppose that friends inhabit the same social position. They are equals because they encounter each other as sovereign individuals who do not question each other's social standing, but who have equal power and dignity in each other's eyes.' and p.48 'And so friendship is perhaps often avoided antagonism. Thus, friendship is the encounter of two people that decide to put themselves on the same level and who identify as sovereign individuals with little questioning as to who is superior or inferior. It is an activity of equalization.'

[127]'Each, then, both loves what is good for himself, and makes an equal return in goodwill and in pleasantness; for friendship is said to be equality, and both of these are found most in the friendship of the good.'

[128]'Epicurean from how wide a circle of humanity can one's friends be drawn. The answer seems to be "Any right thinking person, man, woman, free, slave, is acceptable." If that seems striking in an ancient city, we should recall that Epicurean society is overtly nonpolitical, that is, indifferent to the polis; hence, women, and slaves are not barred. They can be treated as of equal merit if they live in the right spirit.'

[129]The story of Epicureanism is particularly interesting, as it essentially refutes the novelty of Christianity's equality teachings in the Graeco-Roman world. The concept of equal rights communities

not hold for the friendships of antiquity. Achilleus and Patroclus, Gilgamesh and Enkidu, David and Jonathan[130] had a clearly defined senior. While the philosophers more emphasize the capability of the mind to abstract from matters such as wealth, others are more insistent on actual equality, e.g. Shumway, 2018, p.152 'Ideally, all friend relationships would be equal in power and respect.' or Pahl, 2000, p.20 'Equality of status is a necessary condition for a reciprocal friendship.' . I deal with money in the section on resources, but 'class' is an important factor still in a range of societies. But even power and status is contentious, and two cases stick out - that of boss and employee or team member, and that of teacher and student. In both cases there is a significant power difference, which according to the above argument renders friendship impossible. It is one observation that formally the friendship is conceived in many cases only when the power difference is eliminated, that is when the student stops being a direct student of the teacher or the employee stops being a direct report. There are however different cases, and it is unclear whether in this case 'the exception proves the rule' or indeed not so. Greif, 2009 notes on this matter that Mitch Album and Morrie return to their preassigned roles despite spending so much time in intimate conversation. In a similar fashion one might wonder whether Sean (Robin Williams) would befriend Will (Matt Damon) after the movie's storyline conclusion in Good Will Hunting[131]. What is true I think is that the circumstances never leave the relationship, the teacher or boss will always continue to be to some degree the 'senior'. Even if overall the relationship moves beyond this, stories foundational and constituting to the common memory of the relationship will keep referring back to the initial stages of acquaintance.

For me the question is to what degree admiration and deep appreciation are consistent with equality. This may happen with musicians, artists and poets expressing deep admiration for each other's feats and outputs. However this mutuality may be breached, say my friend is a great musician, and I am only a mediocre orchestra participant, and passion for music is actually at the core of our friendship, I or they may not feel equal in skill. On the other hand, we may feel equal in passion, just with different innate capabilities. Equality also works the other way, and one particularly annoying thing is 'false humility', where we appreciate a trait or skill in a friend, and they denigrate themselves with statements 'oh, it is nothing'. It is something for the pure reason, that I may want to kill to have this skill myself, be it a grasp of mathematics, how to chat to a romantic interest in a bar or the capability to run or row really fast. It is for this reason that I cluster equality as a side theme to appreciation and admiration, as accepting appreciation and admiration on both sides is key to upholding equality.

Note that equality and reciprocity, whilst resonating with our egalitarian instincts, are not unquestioningly a norm without alternative. **Proportionality** where each has to contribute according to their capacities can also be an accepted and agreed upon measure (see e.g. Alberoni, 2016, p.46[132]).

---

including women had already been established three centuries before Paul went on his missions.

[130] David and Jonathan is an interesting case, because while in the later part of the relationship, Jonathan becomes the junior, he starts off as the senior in the dyad bestowing David with presents as is customary for the suzerainty overlord, see Olyan, 2017

[131] `https://www.imdb.com/title/tt0119217/` see also `https://youtu.be/rzUkLB9vJnU?t=180`

[132] 'Concretely speaking, this means that he who possesses superiority and power must put every-

Suggestions for thought

- To what degree are you aware of the general societal status of your friends? Do you have good friends who from a societal perspective would be substantially beneath or above you? How do you feel about that?
- Do you believe it is possible to ignore a difference in status?
- In your society, which elements of status (class, power, ethnicity, looks) do you think are still most predominant, at least subconsciously, when people consider friendship potential?

For statistics in sociological studies, question suggestions and weights in counting see H.

4.11 Benevolence and care

> If it's very painful for you to criticize your friends — you're safe in doing it. But if you take the slightest pleasure in it, that's the time to hold your tongue.
>
> Alice Duer Miller

Wishing your friend well and being interested in their wellbeing is the defining element of friendship. This is the classical precondition of friendship. 'Eunoia' (well mindedness) is the term Aristotle, 1925 uses repeatedly for goodwill, which gets transformed by Cicero, 1923 into 'benevolentia', as which it survived as the term benevolence into current day English. This term still might seem old-fashioned, but it is highly relevant. When you feel goodwill, you care about someone and you are rooting for him[133]. You want to see them happy and successful and generally well.

There are four themes to this:

1. the classical goodwill of Aristotle and Cicero and non-instrumentality of friendship,
2. the modern care and caring,
3. the need to express it and,
4. the theological virtue of compassion.

---

thing into the friendship. The other, however, must not use that power, must learn not to feel the need to. Then the friendship can exist because it is not based on inequality and need, but on what particular value each friend for himself brings to the making of the other's personality.'

[133] A great illustration of this is the ending of George Bush Senior's letter to Bill Clinton on Jan 20,1993: 'You will be our President when you read this note. I wish you well. I wish your family well. Your success now is our country's success. I am rooting hard for you. Good luck, George'

(1) According to Aristotle, 1925, 9.5, 'Goodwill seems, then, to be a beginning of friendship, as the pleasure of the eye is the beginning of love.'. And once it is perceived to be mutual, friendship starts: '**goodwill** when it is reciprocal being friendship.'. It cannot be understated how important goodwill is to a friendship. Cicero, 1923, p.129 rightly says 'if you remove goodwill from friendship the very name of friendship is gone', and Alberoni, 2016, p.129[134] agrees in equally strong terms. It is the attitude with which we approach our friendships, and motivation is everything (see Nehamas, 2016, ch.3[135]. As such, most of us may know several stories, where a friend screws up practically[136], but you just roll your eyes because you know they have your interest and well meaning at their heart. Even criticism that may be painful needs to be listened to if given with our interest at heart (see Cicero, 1923, p.197[137]. Trying to find a functioning definition of goodwill was a little harder than I expected, with literature interpreting Aristotle often giving preference to abstract definition. The most workable one I found in Nehamas, 2016, ch.4 - the 'desire to see good things happen to one's friend independently of one's own welfare'. 'Independently of one's own welfare' here is the important thought, as a phrase humorously coined by Gore Vidal displays: 'whenever a friend succeeds, a little something in me dies.'

(2) The modern word goodwill is 'to **care**' and it has had quite a renaissance in recent years. There is now a full school of thought called 'care' ethics since the seminal works of Gilligan, 1982, focusing on emphasising emotions and care over the theme of justice emphasised in the Platonic and Aristotelian tradition. The theory has been extended into friendship by Friedman, 1993 The word care has two prime uses - one is to care for someone and to take care of someone, the latter is the subject of (4.3). This word is repeatedly mentioned in words qualifying friends: 'X cares for me', 'X expresses concern for me', 'I feel cared for by X'. You want to see that your friend is alright and worried when they are not.Alberoni, 2016, p.11[138] includes it as a key characteristic of friendship. Caring prompts us to help the friend when we can. When we ask a friend for a favour, we do so on the assumption that it will be granted out of goodwill and concern.

Goodwill and caring are enablers in friendship. They are necessary and the other person needs to be convinced of your goodwill. There is a word of wisdom attributed to Teddy Roosevelt[139] that says 'Nobody cares how much you know until they know how much you care.' Caring for your friend confers meaning to you. Rath, 2006, p.8[140] shows how destructive it is for someone to feel that nobody cares about them anymore. When you listen to people's stories about their life (cf. 5.3) it shows you care about them and what moves them. That 'just knowing there is someone who cares about us can be a strong emotional uplift' is

[134]'In friendship there can be no deception, no ill will. Never. Not even once.'

[135]'Like courage, it can be manifested in all sorts of different, even conflicting, ways of behaving. Whether a particular way of acting is an indication of friendship or not depends on the motives with which one behaves as one does.'

[136]e.g. when introducing you in a most cringeworthy way to a potential love interest, teasing you but end up insulting you, ...

[137]'both advice and rebuke should be kindly received when given in a spirit of goodwill'

[138]'Mutual trust, care, affection and respect as key indicators'

[139]The source is disputed, with alternative sources John Maxwell and others.

[140]'But I had one last question: 'Who expects you to be somebody?' Roger paused for a moment, took a deep breath, and said, 'I don't think anyone does anymore."

according to Degges-White and Borzumato-Gainey, 2011, p.128 well supported by research. An interesting question in this context raised by Nehamas, 2016, ch.1[141] is whether we do or ought to continue to care for one's friends once the basis for the friendship disappears, which he advocates. However, the norm in practice an 'out of sight, out of mind' attitude holds true at least for some. The opposite of care is the stopping to care or abandonment of the friend. The transition from feeling cared for to realising one is on one's own, abandoned to the wider world, can be deeply painful. Olyan, 2017, p.40 cites various passages in the old testament where friends or family have abandoned the speaker (e.g. Job 19:13). However, most figuratively for the pain of abandonment is the image of Jesus' final outcry 'Why have you forsaken me'.[142] Here the friend's role is to ensure that this sentiment doesn't set in, and to reassure of his care.

One issue and problem with 'care' is that it has been now saddled with so many meanings. Adams, Blieszner, and Vries, 2000 include the Affective Process 'Care' in their analysis, however the description[143] is rather vague and relates more to affection and friendship quality (4.2). Finding appropriate survey questions will be key in looking into this trait in the future.

(3) Expressing friendship or talking about a friendship is a no go for many men. But as Aristotle, 1925, 8.2[144] says, goodwill needs to be expressed. Indeed one hypothesis in this context I would like to pose is that importance of and goodwill for friends is equal for both men and women, but that women surpass men by far in frequently expressing affection, care and appreciation. And this does make a difference. Indeed, this old wisdom has been rediscovered of lately and after decades of guys fearing the expression of love in a platonic relationship, this is now starting to become more popular. Even in the seventies and eighties, there would have been good role models though, in that Captain Kirk and Spock frequently express their affection within their friendship.

You can also express your care in nonverbal ways, and that is by signalling that your friends are on your mind. In part it is making your friends a priority (see 4.3), but also by keeping up the communication when you are off site, by from time to time checking in, asking how they are doing and seeing what is going on. The act of 'staying in touch' is essentially maintaining a low but consistent level of communication over prolonged periods of time. A particularly affectionate way is doing so by letters(see 5.13).

(4) Compassion is a mix between goodwill and empathy. According to the OED compassion is 'the feeling or emotion, when a person is moved by the suffering or distress of another, and by the desire to relieve it; pity that inclines one to spare or to succour.' It is thus a more powerful version of goodwill and directed towards a suffering person. In a way it is the emotional impulse that triggers

[141]'... one should still care for one's friends even if they have undergone serious changes—provided, though, that they have not become "incurably" vicious.'

[142]I am not sure whether this moment qualifies as a question mark to the 'knock and you shall receive' expression of goodwill of God towards humankind.

[143]'Care was described as a criterion of friendship for one middle-old woman in Vancouver: Just the way they come across to me as a friend, which an acquaintance doesn't. You feel close. You get close to them, whereas an acquaintance, they are distant, you can't get close to them, they are just an acquaintance and they stay that way. A young-old man from the same sample incorporated care as follows: Someone who likes you as much as you like him or her.'

[144]'To be friends, then, the must be mutually recognized as bearing goodwill and wishing well to each other'

then thoughts of how such suffering can be relieved (4.3) and the action of going about it (e.g. 5.9). Given that in compassion much focus is placed on the suffering persons needs, it is difficult to divide it between goodwill and consideration. The uncompromising nature of compassion is also noted by Alberoni, 2016, p.127[145] and exemplified in our days by Mother Teresa (c.f. N. Lee and S. Lee, 2009 'Mother Teresa treated thousands of Lepers and Got Alongside'). While friends rarely want pity[146], when serious sickness hits, compassion is required of the friend. It is in these situations that one's worth in the friends' eye becomes brightly clear, as they join the family in attending to us. It is the affirmation of all that was good in the friendship.

Practical takeaway
Express your joy in your friends successes. 'I am really happy that X worked out for you'. When they have an exam, send them a text. Make it clear that you wish them well and care for their happiness.

Suggestions for thought

- Asking yourself honestly: to what degree do you feel the sentiment of 'whenever a friend succeeds, a little something in me dies'?
- How do you feel about expressing your goodwill or care for your friend? Are you comfortable to do so or does it feel strange? Why? How do or would you feel if a friend says she/he really cares for you?
- Have you ever been in the situation where you stopped caring for a (former) friend, just literally stopped? Or have you ever been in a situation when you realised a friend had stopped caring for you? How did either make you feel?

For statistics in sociological studies, question suggestions and weights in counting see H.

4.12 Mutual interest

> The royal road to a man's heart is to talk to him about the things he treasures most.
>
> Dale Carnegie

[145] 'The true friend, however, must conduct himself as if he were a brother, a father, a mother, a lover. He loves, loves, loves and asks for nothing, it is this love that has inspired Christianity. Christian caritas is a total, heroic love that turns to the leper and kisses his wounds. The imperative of caritas universalizes parents and brothers love.'

[146] Short of a little sympathy in case of a manflu, pain from being sore after exercise and other minor ailments

Mutual interest binding friends together is a predominant theme albeit mostly modern one. Interests and life goals, fascination for sports, political or social causes (with the actual intent to do something about it), all lead to a range of joined activities. Statements towards this include 'we have a mutual understanding of passion', 'X and I talk about shows we have seen or things we have read', 'we share a passion for sports, hobbies, religion, work, politics, food, music, movies or books' and 'we can discuss ...'. Mutual interests or passions for the arts are not a key friendship criterion in antiquity, biblical or early christian texts. The theme starts occurring in the literature of friendship in the middle ages, where monks bond over mutual passions for poetry, nature or music, and collaborate in activities pursuing those interests. As the renaissance takes off, groups of artists, poets or scientists convene at king's courts and early universities to discuss matters of interests. In this context Alberoni, 2016, p.16 names Dante, Cavalcanti and Gianni, or Montaigne and la Boetie. In the 19th and 20th century, collaborations between writers such as Marx and Engels and similarly the Oxford Inklings (CS Lewis and JRR Tolkien and others) enhanced creative output and provided the backdrop for deep friendships. It is thus no surprise that Lewis, 1960[147] emphasises mutual interest enjoyed in a circle (see 5.6) as the key theme of friendship.

Mutual interests are a powerful connector when starting a friendship as Millington, 2019, p.9[148]notes. This holds in particular also for children (c.f. Werner and Parmelee, 1979). Greif, 2009 in his narratives picks up consistently of similar interests being both an initiation connecting element and the key element of a stable friendship of men to convene to pursue such an interest.

There are different themes to why mutual interests apply to friendship. In the initiation phase it provides content for a conversation, it provides an incentive to come together and thus maintain the friendship. It provides understanding that family and other social circles maybe don't provide (e.g. if your hobby is uncommon) and can generate appreciation for the other.

The desire and real potential of people to connect over mutual interests gave rise to a startup meetup.com, which, having launched in 2002, has gained 44 million members on the platform and 330000 meetup groups by 2020, which generate about 84000 meetup events per week. Passions for specific interests have spawned platforms by themselves. Expat platforms such as 'A Small World' and 'Internations' are successful because of the possibility to create interest based groups. One key feature of Facebook gaining in importance is the provision of groups where people can connect regionally, often over hobbies and interests. Pursuing mutual interests beyond conversations often leads to collaboration - often within enabling institutions (5.2) or in small groups (5.6).

The more intense level of mutual interest is the **common cause** or common passion. Stamp collection, tennis, reading philosophy or a shared religion is for

[147] p.91 'Lovers are normally face to face, absorbed in each other; Friends, side by side, absorbed in some common Interest.' p. 95 'This pleasure in co-operation, in talking shop, in the mutual respect and understanding of men who daily see one another tested, is biologically valuable.' p. 97 'All who share it will be our companions; but one or two or three who share something more will be our Friends.'

[148] 'If you're going to spend time with someone, it's clearly important that you like doing some of the same things - and a shared passion is always a good way to kick-start a friendship. Whether it is sport, films, politics, music or books, having pastime you're both passionate about means you'll never run out of things to discuss.'

many people a connecting element that adds a bit of colour to the friendship and provides a starting point. Yet for others such an interest takes on much more intensity and constitutes a life's purpose. This could be the artist devoted to create art pieces of a certain beauty, Wilberforce desiring to abolish slavery or disciples of a certain religion being interested in spreading the good news. As the interest becomes a cause in their life, the connecting power of this cause also increases. As they find their causes are the same, they can decide to join forces and fight the good fight together. Jesus in his commission (Mark 6:7) sending the disciples out in pairs of two to drive out demons is exactly an image of this, joining pairs over an emotionally charged good cause. Anecdotal evidence from Mormon's prosyletizing[149] corroborates the intensity of the experience and suitability to form bonds. Beauty, art, music, poverty, science, all such themes can evoke great passions.

Practical takeaway
If you have friends from childhood or adolescence, try out your old childhood hobby. If it was Lego, and you have both kids, join in with them one afternoon. If you played AD&D or DSA[a], meet up for one weekend and play again. If you liked riding horses or playing hockey, but haven't done it in decades, do that. Embrace that you were once your happiest doing that activity and just relish in the freedom and nostalgy.

[a]Old school pen and paper role playing game

Suggestions for thought

- If you are interested in making new friends, have you checked out meetup.com, Internations or couchsurfing hosts in your region?
- Do you know your work colleagues or general acquaintances interests to connect over? If you do and you figured out you have something in common, have you initiated to pursue it together on occasions?
- If you think of your close friends, do you more bond with them due to their character, wit or general personality or more because of mutual interests, hobbies or activities?

For statistics in sociological studies, question suggestions and weights in counting see H.

[149]The Church of the Latter Day Saints - or Mormons - send out their youth in pairs to tell others about their faith.

4.13 Mutual belief and cultural background

> Agreement in likes and dislikes - this, and this only, is what constitutes true friendship.[150]
>
> Sallust

Having the same beliefs or cultural background offers a common ground from which to build trust and closeness. It is so much a part of classical theory, that a specific term homophily was coined to describe the phenomenon (see e.g. McPherson, Smith-Lovin, and J.M. Cook, 2001). In sociology, this usually extends to similarity between gender, age, race ethnicity or class, but can include other sociological classifiers too.

This theme can be divided up into four different aspects: (1) a similar value system (religion, ideology and politics), (2) a similar cultural background and (3) a similar life situation or (4) a general shared belief or truth on a particular topic (such as 'Marmite[151] is delicious'). Sharing any of the four enables mutual understanding (4.6) even without great empathic capability. It makes identification with the other person easier, as there are genuine views that are part of ourselves in the other person too. Degges-White and Borzumato-Gainey, 2011, ch.3 point out that thus validation is increased as our new or old acquaintance will automatically agree with our statements rather than put them into question.

Homophily, or the preference for similarity in character and belief system, and dislike for strong opposing political views was already picked up by Cicero. It is the background against which Cicero wrote 'de amicitia' (about friendship), as the Roman republic was tearing itself apart with the three factions of Caesar, Pompey and the republican loyalists. In the process, many Romans who hitherto had been friends and family found themselves on opposite sides. Aristotle, 1925, 9.6[152] was mostly concerned with harmony and good civil interaction in the city state and whilst acknowledging similarity did not include it at the heart of his exploration, Cicero, 1923, p.125 and p.171[153] much more so.

This can be exploited while looking for friends, as joining organisations that represent our core belief, there is anyway a natural pull towards this. There is thus a high likelihood that other people in such an organization share these beliefs. Alberoni, 2016, p.66[154] singles out Catholics or Communists for such behaviour and the increased trust we exhibit towards the in-group members. This in-group

[150]Idem velle atque idem nolle, ea demum firma amicitia est.

[151]A very polarizing British salty yeast extract used e.g. on bread. Some people think it is the best thing since sliced bread, others find it abhorrent and disgusting, with few in between.

[152]'Unanimity also seems to be a friendly relation. ... but we do say that a city is unanimous when men have the same opinion about what is to their interest, and choose the same actions, and do what they have resolved in common.'

[153]p.125 '... enjoyed that wherein lies the whole essence of friendship — the most complete agreement in policy, in pursuits, and in opinions.' and p.171 'when the characters of friends are blameless, then there should be between them complete harmony of opinions and inclinations in everything without any exception;'

[154]'Such solidarity also characterizes members of political or ethnic groups with a strong organizational structure. Italian Catholics or Communists have between them a bond of sensibility, of reciprocal trust, that leads them instinctively to prefer someone who is from their own world to someone who isn't.'

feeling - sometimes referred to as Asabiyya - is however common for many religious and political organisations, and often entire belief systems are tailored to reinforce this attitude amongst its members (c.f. van Schaik and Michel, 2016). Indeed, Christian books on friendship usually recommend ensuring friends are of the same faith, quoting Corinthians 15:33[155] or Proverbs 13.20[156] because our friends usually influence us over time for better or worse (5.9) and disregarding that genuine friendship (and hospitality) is the best context to convince our friends of the worthiness of our cause.

As beliefs change, so do our capacities to connect and find common ground across the fault lines. In most cases, differences of conviction and belief are viewed as negative impact for friendship, as it introduces friction (the contrary case will be discussed in the next section). I have in the past decade observed or heard of splits because of US Politics (see e.g. Eldredge, 2020-11-10), Hong Kong's evaluation of independence and police violence[157], Brexit (see Leaver, 2019-01-24), Corona safety measure adherence and refugee politics in Europe. Mahdawi, 2020-07-01 gives a Corona example on the need to distance from a friend who does not comply with distancing conventions. The theoretical groundwork of it is provided in Baldassarri and Bearman, 2007, and Lauka, McCoy, and Firat, 2018. I think the key here is that politics morphed from being an opinion issue (which could be respected) to a moral issue (which essentially provokes moral judgement). If this tenet is accepted, then political or religious conviction becomes a matter of character (3.7) and only allows a yes or no answer to people for whom character is a friend (de-)selection criterion.

(2) **Cultural background**: Junger, 2016 describes the positive feeling people develop when they are in a home group, a tribe. Without being able to point to extensive research, I think the identification of 'one's tribe' is one of the most important steps in life. The community in which you feel comfortable and where you feel at home can be the make or break whether you go through life enjoying it or feeling alone. Mentally cycling through my friends of acquaintances a statement of 'I feel I have arrived here' where the 'here' not only includes the family, job or house but also the surrounding area and the people living in it is one of the key drivers of happiness in life. There are several elements to it, but probably one of the biggest is the ability of being able to enjoy the same things and rituals. This can be enjoying the Carnival in the Rheinland and everything that comes with it. Or it can be long nights in Italian Osterias discussing and chatting with the neighbours, the pub atmosphere of local establishments in England or a warm and welcoming church community. You look around and feel - this is home, and this is my tribe. When people say that 'friends are your chosen family', in the context of the tribe this sentence becomes 'this chosen family - tribe - are also my friends'.

Cultural background however also extends to the negative cultural experiences. Poverty or difficulties in the job market especially experienced in ethnic groups lead to further discriminations in general social life. Black people in the US still today feel the aftereffects of slavery and Jim Crow laws and an ongoing litany of further measures implemented to stifle their participation in public life. Rawl-

[155]'Do not be deceived: Evil company corrupts good habits.'

[156]'He that walketh with wise men shall be wise: but a companion of fools shall be destroyed.'

[157]Anecdotal evidence points to a clean split of pro-establishment and anti-establishment - see Lo, 2019-06-08

ins, 2008 explains how certain experiences can only be really understood in-group, thus the humiliation of repeated racial profiling will be difficult to be empathised with by a white middle-class male. Also on positive experiences, it may be difficult for a friend to empathise with your expansive travel experiences or working in different cultures, if they have never left the local area. A similar cultural background creates an illusion of a common memory or experience (4.1). This effect is strongly observable in Alumni organizations, where people across generations can bond over having had the same experience such as rowing in Oxford or having attended a boarding school. And as much as elitism based on such rituals is to be deplored, it provides a mechanism of creating an intergenerational in-group where people connect based on common experiences essentially as equals. This effect is something that other institutions would do well to emulate. Indeed, one of the most iconic movies of German cinema, the 'Feuerzangenbowle'[158] revolves about a group of old friends reminiscing about their school days. Upon discovery that one of the group did not attend school and thus did not share this experience, they recommend him to catch up to fully relate to their experience.

(3) Similar **life situation**: The third common element can be a common problem to overcome in life, such as school, pregnancy, old age or the likes. Whilst because of the dearth of time most people usually reduce their circle of friends in the child rearing decades, outgoing parents often make friends via their children. This can be via the parent teacher association, organising play dates, shuttling services to sports and cultural events of the schools and then hanging out there waiting for the kids to finish[159]. This effect of course works in the reverse, as fractures are created among friendships of people in different stages of life. As Degges-White and Borzumato-Gainey, 2011, p.128 note, in old age (2) and (3) particularly become interlinked, as friends of same age 'are often more likely to share the same perspective on the world and the same morals that were prevalent during the years in which [they] were coming of age.'

(4) **Shared truth**: People can bond over almost anything, but one really effective item for people to come together over is that of a mutual enemy or a strong preference for something really peculiar, such as Marmite or fish with ketchup and chocolate. A wonderful example - if a little ethically questionable - is given in the movie 'About Time', where our time travelling hero having been given the insight of his love interests true passion[160] uses it to sweep her off her feet completely. Discovering you sharing the same favourite composer, movie director, book author, culinary dish, travel experience can all create this commonality effect. For this reason again friendships are sometimes easier to establish intra-generationally.

My hunch on general similarity and homophily is that it is vastly overrated as a variable in friendship. It is of course easy to access in terms of getting data from a sociological standpoint, but I would say that other relationship variables merit far higher attention. I would certainly not agree with Degges-White and Borzumato-Gainey, 2011, ch.3 that the 'level of similarity between two potential friends is directly proportional to the chance that a friendship will be launched'.[161]. Thus

[158] On IMDB at https://www.imdb.com/title/tt0036818/

[159] The life situation here leads also to a strong propinquity effect - see section 6.2

[160] 'Do you agree that the magic of her lies in her history? ...' `https://youtu.be/ww7Vfr3ErxQ?t=48`

[161] Indeed I disagree that Rodin, 1978 is a sufficient evidence for making such a sweeping assertion.

even elevating this trait to a rule or recommendation, as done in Millington, 2019, p.20[162] is definitely too constraining. However, I would say that the shared truth aspect of triggering a 'spark' is definitely underrated. Serendipitous moments can create a powerful illusion of acquaintance, accelerating trust and subsequent sharing and time investment. The unfortunate correlate is that similarity and proximity can become powerful reinforcers as societal stratification and gentrification occur.

On a final note, I would also acknowledge that much of this comes down to the scope of definition of homophily. As an example, R.I. Dunbar, 2021[163]speaks of the seven pillars of friendship: (1) having the same language, (2) growing up in the same location, (3) same educational and career experiences, (4) same hobbies and interests, (5) same world view (moral, religious, political), (6) humour and (7) music. That captures a lot under one roof, and of course defining it this way, homophily is overarching. However in the approach chosen in this book language is assumed, growing up in same location can overlap with common memory and mutual understanding, hobbies and interests is a separate category, world view is partly in this category, but also overlaps with virtue[164]. Humour likewise I would not count as a homophily category but as a personality trait, and finally music splits into preference and activity[165]. Thus I advocate more for a narrow but operational definition of homophily.

Suggestions for thought

- If you reflect through your circle of close friends, to what degree are they similar to you in gender, age, education, political or religious conviction?
- To what degree did that matter at the start of the friendship?
- Have you had a falling out or slow distancing / cooling with a friend over political or religious differences?
- If you meet old friends who are at different life stages or did not share substantial experiential elements of your life (university, time abroad, periods of unemployment), do you feel a disconnect or is the core of your friendship unaffected?
- If you know your friend holds a distinct political opinion than you, at some point it might be necessary to either agree to disagree, but essentially converge on a mode of dealing with your difference.

---

[162] 'First rule: be the person you'd like to be friends with! You'll attract the people who share the traits you find the most appealing.'

[163] See also Launay and Im Dunbar, 2015

[164] We generally have a world view that gives us an opportunity to shine in some respect, and thus appreciate traits which we are 'good in'. But generally Aristotle would maintain that we appreciate other friends for their good character, which only secondary or accidentally is then similar to us.

[165] There is a common bond when people find out the other person also plays a musical instrument - triggering common memories of practicing, toiling, band camps and orchestras.

For statistics in sociological studies, question suggestions and weights in counting see H.

Difference in background and belief

When joined and mutually agreeable activities are seen as the key of friendship, often people make recommendations on looking for similarity in background when trying to make friends. There are however opinions that recommend the opposite, as only different friends can suitably act as mirrors to oneself for self-discovery and the challenging of one's own thinking. There are two lines of thought, one is that difference in background should not matter (which essentially is another way of phrasing equality (4.10)) and one that a difference in background and worldview is good for the friendship to be enriching and character developing. This line of thought has a long tradition - going back to Aristotle, 1925, 8.1[166] who points further to Heraclitus. Augustine agrees - 'If we sometimes disagreed, it was without spite, as a man might differ with himself, and the rare occasions of dispute were the very spice to season our usual accord.'. Alberoni, 2016, p.23[167] even constitutes a need for difference for a good friendship. When our friends have a different experience in life because they essentially have lived different lives, by the powers of imagination and simulation we can put ourselves in their shoes, and learn from their experience. In this context an observation or even a conjecture of Nehamas, 2016, ch.0[168] is really relevant - do we not just behave but think differently in the company of specific friends. There is the statement of 'with my friends I can be just myself' usually stated in context of the trait of acceptance (3.2), hinting at an authentic inner personality that gets distorted in public life, e.g. in the job. But here the conjecture is that we literally have a (slightly) different personality tailored towards the specific good friend. Little, 2000, p.41 agrees 'Different friends bring out different aspects of us.'. Whilst I am per gut feeling sceptical about this, on second thought there is a lot that can be said for the plausibility or validity of this. I think there is a lot to be said for the personality per language / culture theory. This states that bilingual or trilingual people behave according to a trained innate personality dependent on the language they are operating in. Grosjean, 1982 describes this phenomenon at length. It is thus analogously possible, that spending time with a friend over time, we establish our own unique culture, and by extension, shape a subset of our personality as belonging to that friend, that comes out to full bloom when we are in this friends

[166]'Heraclitus that 'it is what opposes that helps' and 'from different tones comes the fairest tune' and 'all things are produced through strife"

[167]'in fact, the other needs to be a little different. That difference is precious precisely because it provides us with a new perspective in whose direction we would otherwise not have looked. That new perspective can also constitute a confirmation that what we are thinking is correct. '

[168]' Another was driven home to me by my reunions with my school friends. My meetings with them occur within a context significantly different from the context of many of my other relationships, and I found myself behaving and thinking differently in the company of these friends than I do in the company of others. ' and 'We adjust to our different relationships, and what some particular friends see of us is very different from what is evident to some others: We have as many sides to our character as we have friends to show them to. Quite unconsciously I found myself witty with one friend, large and magnanimous with another, petulant and stingy with another, wise and grave with another, and utterly frivolous with another. I watch with surprise the sudden and startling changes in myself as I pass from the influence of one friend to the influence of another.'

company. I do think that certain aspects of our personality do particularly resonate with certain friends. Candidates here are with friends that have something strong in common, thus I will fully experience my passion for Greek and Roman history with a friend who also shares this. But similarly, friends who are substantially different to us will then enable us to diversify our personality with traits, insights or habits, we would have otherwise not developed. It is possible that by virtue of being different, some friends cannot relate to part of my personality and daily life, and this can be a most refreshing experience. For example if you are in the corporate world, a banker, or a lawyer, and you identify as this in your daily life, but you have a close friend who say became a free-spirited artist to complete the cliche. Then, because of this friend having no emotional connection to your working life, you can reconnect with the artistic side of yours, which you may have suppressed in the course of your studies and working life.

What I find an interesting question to consider is 'when people say they have friends who are different to them, then just how and in what way they actually are different?'. Is it a matter of politics, race, religion or educational level? Based on my limited anecdotal experience, I observed that only in a few cases people are genuinely different: commonalities that might not be so apparent, far outweigh differences that might be currently en vogue and in public focus. As written in the introduction, whilst cultural differences may remain, I don't think anyone would blink an eye over cross-ethnic friendships or friendships with gay people, that would have been viewed critically years back. However, when people say they have diverse friendships, the currently relevant question would be how many genuinely poor or uneducated people are in the fold (see e.g. Atwood, 2005[169]). If you are an agnostic essentially indifferent to religion, it can be easy to befriend both Buddhists and Christians superficially, but if you are a 'true believer' about something, only then can you challenge yourself to befriend someone of diametrally opposed views. Or what about someone holding an opinion that is really contrary to 'acceptable' public opinion such as militant anti-abortionism, denial of climate change, the necessity for refugee pushback or other topics where most people might be aghast. This is not to condone any of those views, but to provide a litmus test of how truly you cultivate a 'diverse' friendship circle, or whether it is morally or politically homogeneous and just diverse e.g. in geographic origin (see e.g. Millington, 2019, p.90 vs. 10[170]). Indeed it might be a moral challenge in our time to maintain friendship bonds across such boundaries, though people disagree.

Tomlin, 2010 specifically demonstrates that 'the rich' Christians need to befriend the poor not to have an object for the commanded act of charity, but need to befriend them in order to learn from them about key features of Christianity. In similar fashion when volunteers go out to volunteer in situations marked by

---

[169]'Befriend the people who really need a friend. Don't worry about becoming the friend of the rich and famous – concern yourself with becoming the friend of the poor and destitute, the sad and lonely, the homeless and the hurting, the man or woman or child with AIDS, the persecuted believers around the world.'

[170]p.90 'Many of my friends have different views to me on politics and religion - two topics that are notoriously controversial - but we can still enjoy discussing them because we respect each other.' vs. p. 10 'A homophobic aside, a sweeping generalization about the LGBTQ community, language I would never use to describe people of colour - and all respect goes out the window. Shared values and a moral code are the pillars of any friendship.'

poverty (c.f. Deen, 2017-06-22), they gain themselves as persons from befriending their 'clients' for their own personality, views and habits. It is this image that probably best describes the benefit that a truly different friend can bring to us in. If the biblical recommendation of going the extra mile is interpreted in the context of friendship[171], then it would be about initiating friendship across societal boundaries.

Suggestions for thought

- How homogeneous is your list of core friends? I don't mean your 500 to 2000 accumulated Facebook friends, but the core group of 5 to 10?
- To what degree have you got one or two friends who genuinely have a different life philosophy where either of you really would not want to live the way the other one does? How about political or religious views?
- Do you have a friend with whom you genuinely behave and think differently than with other people? Why do you think this is?

For statistics in sociological studies, question suggestions and weights in counting see H.

4.14 Respect of privacy

The respect of privacy is a controversial item. Alberoni most of all, but also Lewis, 1960, Millington, 2019 and Degges-White and Borzumato-Gainey, 2011 stress its importance, whereas Aristotle, Cicero and others stress the importance of joined living.[172]

Respect for privacy and needing time alone is important for introverted people, who value their alone time as really important. However, even extraverted people who are completely in the limelight might wish to cordon off aspects of their life, even from their friends. There are different kinds of sentiments that convey this, such as 'X understands that I sometimes need a break without contact', 'X knows that I sometimes disappear for a few weeks to chase other dreams', 'X respects my privacy' or 'X respects that I do not wish to share about certain aspects of my life yet or never'.

Respect for somebody's privacy is closely linked to independence, but it is not quite the same. There is (1) informational privacy, this is maintaining a life that is partially hidden or kept separate from friends. And the other theme (2) is maintaining a life that is separate from those of friends, in essence compartmentalising

[171]Under Roman occupation law, a legionary carrying a backpack of 20-30kg could requisition a peasant or general civilian and make him carry the pack for a mile. The request of going the extra mile thus implied spending unnecessarily time and effort with essentially an oppressor, with the possibility of initiating a friendly conversation on the basis of this voluntary act of service.

[172]As a disclaimer, my personal bets are firmly on living together. I have no sense nor need for privacy, but hope the following passage presents the case for respect of privacy as strongly as the substantial argumentative and statistical evidence merits.

one's life. Thus you may tell them about it, but keep e.g. business and friendship or family and friendship rigidly separate. Respect of privacy is thus about the way how to conduct friendship (but not questioning it) in a mutually agreed upon or accepted form, whereas independence of friendship includes the possibility of one party unilaterally downsizing or walking away from the friendship.

(1) Privacy of information is not letting everything on, keeping some information about my person, habits, preferences to myself. It is thus a selected opting out of openness on information. Pahl, 2000, p.36 points to Simmel explaining the boundaries of such information. [173]. Nehamas, 2016, ch. 4 agrees with the need for informational limits[174]. When we choose to withhold information from a friend and it is clear that it is due to choice, the friend needs to respect this desire for privacy. The friend needs also to respect choices that result on account of things at the basis of this. In this sense nagging is both lack of respect of privacy as well as lack of respect. Essentially, privacy assumes that there is some information that B might have to explain their actions that A is not privy too. For example, B might not exercise because of a disease she has however not told A about. Nagging about exercise and not realising it is about something else will turn into a sore point. This is equal both for women and men (see e.g. Greif, 2009, ch.12[175]). In our times, this sense of and perceived need for privacy is a key seller for internet relationships. If it is important, privacy is perfectly ensured, as you can effortlessly keep the other person at bay, and indeed the informal code of conduct of online friendships seems to be sensitive of personal boundaries in a way physical space friendships usually do conform.

(2) The habit of compartmentalizing one's life's activities is particularly culturally driven. It is no accident that it was also Simmel making observations about this trend in the starting twentieth century, as described by Pahl, 2000, p.36[176]. This can be that we need time where we are alone, or we might pursue activities that we simply do not wish to share with friends. In Germany, most people explicitly do not wish to mix friendship and work. Rath, 2006 reports similar attitudes in American corporations, though partially on the way out. For hundreds of years homosexual relations were frowned upon or simply illegal in both western and eastern societies, leading to millions sequestering their love life from their public daily life. Finally, there might be the very profane situation that I might be friends with two people who simply cannot stand each other, or who become intolerable when they are together. Here I will ensure to keep my friendships with them separate, and they will have to respect me for staying friends with the other person and respect my privacy for not involving them in it. But even without a reason,

[173]'Such friends would not be expected or try to probe into the depths of a person's soul. For Simmel, the modem style of friendship would be based on reserve and discretion. Modern people have too much to hide. ... The assumption is that friends would respect the boundaries of these differentiated relationships: if they had common interests in travel and holidays, for example, they would not expect also to share their deepest thoughts about religion or their sexual proclivities.

[174]'Even to our best friend, we must not discover ourselves as we naturally are and know ourselves to be: that would be a nasty business. There are many things I might disclose to a physician, a psychiatrist, or. if I were religious, to a priest or minister that I would keep from my friends.'

[175]'Don't push the other guy too much. If they are not feeling well, if they are quiet, then I try and recognize that they would rather be left alone.'

[176]'The modem way of feeling, he suggested, produces differentiated friendships, implying that we would have separate friends for particular interests and activities. We would lunch with one, play sport with another and complain about our partners to another.'

but maybe driven through our introverted personality, we may wish to limit the time spent with friends or a certain group of friends. Pahl, 2000, p.87 points to people who say 'God protect me from my friends. I need space and a bit of peace for myself.' but uses this expression as a sign that 'some people cannot be good friends.'

For Alberoni, 2016, p.8[177] privacy goes beyond this and strongly overlaps with the need for independence. Encounters are within intervals which the friends spend separately. Additionally, friends according to Alberoni should have little interest in what they get up to separately from each other. Little, 2000, p.52[178] likewise seconds the view of Alberoni on having liberty between encounters, and likens this relationship to that of children. However, this freedom, which is also seconded by Lewis, is precisely questioned and criticised by Nehamas, 2016, likewise specifically pointing to the friendships of children[179].

Whilst some case can be made against this item on general grounds (see next section) and from openness and loyalty, it is a necessary attitude in the starting phase of a relationship. Shumway, 2018, p.104[180] writes about 'friendship obsession' as an effect of 'rehydration following dehydration'. As a result, if you observe yourself suffering from this, pace yourself and your demands on information and time spent with the new friend. This way you will not overwhelm them and push them away or love-suffocate them. However, such self-reinforcing situations can also occur later in friendship. At its basis is the thought: just because seemingly your friend has nothing to do, she/he should want to spend this time with you, and reacting inquisitively or questioning if that doesn't happen. As the person at the other end notices this, they are incentivised to let on even less when they have nothing on for fear of immediately being called upon. This turns the thought of friendship into a burden and shows by itself that the friendship is severely fractured.

A second habit that has become prevalent in recent years and is difficult to categorise exactly is 'ghosting'. It is the complete cutting out of a friend of all parts of life, ending the friendship by simply disappearing and cutting contact. At its extreme end it is malicious, leaving the friend to second guess causes, blaming her or himself, and makes a direct attack on the friend's personal value. At that, it forbids itself as ethical action in anything resembling a friendship. However, normal people do not resort to such drastic measures, but exiting an increasingly one-sided relationship can eventually become the only viable strategy. This often depends on the level of miscommunication in the deteriorating relationship, as not all 'warning' communication issued may be noticed by the pursuing party.

[177]'When we talk about the future, it is not about a common future, but about two separate futures. Encounters live side by side. Intervals are insignificant. Time is insignificant; as soon as it takes on meaning—usually in times of relationship crisis—the friendship dissolves.'

[178]'Free to come (and warmly welcome in that) and free to go, much like the prodigal son the crucial finding is that the child develops a self not from being held tight and filled up with love, nor from being sent away or thrown in at the deep end, but from being free to come and go, free to leave yet warmly welcomed on its return.'

[179]'C. S. Lewis described friendship as a relationship that is 'almost wholly free from jealousy.' Surprisingly since he wrote so well for children—he seems not to have kept in mind how desperately hurt children and adolescents can be when they are abandoned by their friends.'

[180]'The trick to rehydration after dehydration also works with relational obsession. You feel starved of the thing you need, and the temptation is to take in as much as you can while it lasts. Instead - take small sips, send fewer texts, and ease into the relationship slowly.'

As conflict resolution is an emotional costly exercise, the pursued party may just want out when their emotional budget is exhausted. They may then not enter a discussion where they suspect the other party will not accept feedback, try to argue any point and not accept the proposal to 'put the relationship on ice for a while'. Thus the pursued party may choose the easier road of just exiting the relationship without further ado and last comments.

Suggestions for thought

- How do you feel about rejection and being left out of your friend's life? Do you accept it or let it leave you disappointed or even angry?
- To what degree are you aware of the privacy needs of your close friends? Do you have a friendship where your friendship feels conditional on you respecting their need for privacy (and independence)?
- How do you have parts of your life that you do not wish your friends to know about? Why? Do you fear the vulnerability? Do you fear the judgement? Do you just want to keep it separate?
- To what degree do you compartmentalize your life? How would you feel if maybe some of your friends know your boss or colleagues?
- To what degree do you just need some part of your life, not for secrecy or keeping friends away from your professional life and vice versa, but really time and space for yourself. Why?

For statistics in sociological studies, question suggestions and weights in counting see H.

Living together and waiving privacy

> If you can survive 11 days in cramped quarters with a friend and come out laughing, your friendship is the real deal.
>
> Oprah Winfrey

Whilst privacy is important to some people for good reason, both a strong fundamental case and a more pointed nuanced case focusing on contemporary culture can be made against it. It should be noted that the following arguments only concerns personal privacy towards our close friends, not the wider public, big data or the state institutions.

The strong case is made by classical sources of friendship advice. Aristotle, 1925, 8.5 asserts: 'Those, however, who approve of each other, but do not live together seem to be well-disposed rather than actual friends.'[181]. On this he includes also the 'friendships of pleasure' of the young in Aristotle, 1925, 8.3 'But

[181] Rackham translates this as 'Nothing is more characteristic of friends than that they seek each other's society' - the word used is 'suzaen' which is unambiguously living together, indeed the word is composed of 'together' and 'to live'.

these people do wish to spend their days and lives together; for it is thus that they attain the purpose of their friendship.'. Liu, 2010 issues a deep analysis of its context, which as with all assertions of Aristotle draws in a multiple of complex philosophical concepts. But nowhere does Aristotle insinuate that living together only means every second Friday of the month! Aristotle much more would probably applaud the highly intrusive habit of Paul Erdos, one of the most eminent mathematician of the 20th century. Paul Erdos literally showed up at other mathematicians doorstep with no prior warning, invited himself in and stayed with them for weeks to 'do maths' and befriend the person in the process. Thus if people insist that friendship needs to respect your privacy and you can or want to share only a part of your life with your friends, at least according to Aristotle that would be make-belief, but not friendship, at least not any friendship worth its title. Aristotle is not alone in his assessment. Jonathan and David - a much analysed and cited Bible bromance - not only had 'knit souls together', but actually lived together - 'from that day Saul kept David with him and did not let him return to his father's house.'. I would argue that the continuous interaction resulting from living under one roof was just as vital for the development of their friendship as the initial spark. If you follow the argument made in the introduction, that Jesus and his disciples can be seen as a group of friends, then it likewise can be observed that this resulted from of a three year intense bonding process, of travelling, eating, sleeping together on the road. Privacy - most likely none. Cicero has Laelius attribute his friendship to Scipio amongst others to 'living under the same roof at home' (p.125) and 'together not only in our military campaigns, but also in our foreign tours and on our vacations in the country.'(p. 211). Again, even roman officer tents afforded little private space below legate or tribune rank. I thus have some limited issues with sociologists and psychologists for citing Aristotles triad of utility, pleasure and virtuous friendship but ignoring this aspect of living together. It strikes me however as most surprising that the contrast of these arguments to Alberoni, 2016 and Lewis, 1960 insistence on independence and privacy were not at least addressed in their writings. This insight did not stop with antiquity. Strozier, 2016 tells the story of the friendship of Abraham Lincoln and Joshua Speed, who lived together for several years and build a most close and affectionate friendship, allowing Speed to intervene at a crucial time in Lincoln's life to save his marriage. Other close friendships are also known to have developed from such intimate settings, voluntary or forced.

Children likewise understand this, preferring sleepovers for the intense bonding experience to just play afternoons. Interestingly, Alberoni, 2016, p.69[182] picks up on the habit of spending excessive time with each other for children. In due course however he only comments about the aspect of the pair separating from the wider group but drops the habit of continual presence of child friends as a potential natural state for friendship to be likewise aspired to, contrary to his insistence on independence and privacy. Speaking autobiographically, specifically in 5th to 8th grade, sleepovers with a group of friends was the norm rather than the exception. Not only did our parents enjoy the quietness (essentially two of

[182]'The passage from individual friendship to electing an individual group is, especially in childhood and adolescence, often imperceptible. The transition is exemplified by two 'inseparable' friends—friends that are always together, that confide everything to one another, that cannot stay apart for even a few minutes. In such cases, parents may jest where the boy has left his 'fiancé'.'

three families got rid of one of their kids for 48 hours and only one family had to ensure that we had some food and did actually switch the lights off at some point), for us it was an uninterrupted time of fantasy, dwarves, elves and demons, which was a highlight which we could enjoy every fortnight.

Where friends start living together (and don't fall out over dishwashing duties) they can bond for life. A personal anecdote is that of my grandfather who went to Aachen to study engineering, and as the family jokes could have shared a single bed and desk with his close friend as they had mutually exclusive day schedules for sleeping and studying. This effect of course ties in closely with proximity (see 6.2) as it simply maximises also time spent together (5.1), and if one person is hosting the other, then living together becomes a prolonged case of hospitality (5.7). But these components or aspects do not by themselves explain the full extent of the effect of living together in the development of a friendship. Even if not living under one roof, in rural neighbourhoods or with good neighbours in cities, open-door policies signal the waiving of privacy. Compare the following definition of 'solidarity' by an interviewee of Adams, Blieszner, and Vries, 2000, p.127: 'They'd come in the house and out of the house almost at will, the same way we did.' and in their study this aspect scores high with 29 % and thus is allocated in group (2). At least some people in the elder generation who live on their own having moved from a rural setting into a city do acknowledge missing this sort of sentiment of living together. I would not use the word solidarity for this concept, but turning back to Latin would find the word conviviality ideal and fit, unfortunately it has already got a different meaning (Cambridge Dictionary the quality of being friendly and making people feel happy and welcome). Cohabitation is also a great term, again it has these days the additional connotation of romantic entanglement.

Living together is sharing the maximum of our lives together. There is no presenting the best of us, our friends see all of us. Thus in a way judgement and acceptance are absolute and including contentious issues such as dishwashing, apartment hygiene and bedtime rules. Whilst Couchsurfing is arguably not quite living together because of the short time of stays, there have been several occasions where I invited couch surfers to prolong their stay, as we got on well. These added few days significantly increased the likelihood of still being in good contact years later. A few times in my life I also was fortunate to have friends come and live with me for about a month or two. These were intense times of getting to know each other, and our friendship was always for the better, significantly so. In one case this was not just a dear friend, but the entire family of four, leading to a wonderful experience as you also see the children grow up. Even if privacy is important to you, having a friend in need over - for a prolonged time at a sacrifice of privacy and living convenience - is a statement of how much the friendship means to you.

I would thus argue that if it were not for a marriage to get in the way, living together is a natural state of good friendship. This is echoed by the experiences or desires of people to move in with friends if their spouses die (c.f. Degges-White and Borzumato-Gainey, 2011, p. 131[183]).

[183]'One woman said she was only half-joking when she shared that she and her best friend have decided that because they would most likely outlive their husbands, they were already planning to take up housekeeping together some year in the future when they found themselves both widowed.'

The right to privacy has one further countering concern. In a friendship, one sometimes needs to balance it with a legitimate expression of concern for or by a friend. Is it my friends' freedom to live an unhealthy life - be it drugs, lack of exercise, smoking, or any other of the myriad of unhealthy habits we can adopt. If my friend spends a lot of time alone, she/he may be genuinely happy to do so, but she/he may also be lonely but just too reluctant/proud to admit it and reaching out by her/himself. At what point does my genuine concern for his wellbeing expressed in exhortations (e.g. to eat more vegetables, exercise a bit more or go to the doctor, or simply join a few friends of mine for a beer on a Friday) stop being legitimate and turn into the nuisance of nagging described in the prior section. On the other hand, is my not addressing my concern out of respect for his privacy just a cheap excuse to avoid a confrontation? Is the friendship so weak that I don't feel justified to express my worries about my friend's health or social habits? I find this choice difficult, and practically have always erred on the side of concern rather than backing off, but know this has not always been welcome and come at a cost.

A further charge against privacy in friendships or social relationships is led by the research of Cacioppo and Hawkley[184]. According to this our desire for privacy is a self protection mechanism to prior negative social experiences. However as with all such mechanisms, the cure can become worse than the sickness, and thus insistence on privacy is one of the steps that drives our isolation rather than supports our capability to build relationships. Thus our need of privacy can be interpreted as a symptom of the psychological disorder of loneliness already having gotten hold of us (see Layden, J.T. Cacioppo, and S. Cacioppo, 2018), as privacy essentially suppresses our clan-like social co-living shaped by the millennia.[185] I will elaborate on this in section 7.5.

[184]See e.g J.T. Cacioppo and Hawkley, 2009 or J.T. Cacioppo and Patrick, 2008

[185]I am aware that many readers will protest heavily at this suggestion of connecting desire of privacy and their beginning social dysfunctionality, but it is simply good evidence based psychological research catching up with Aristotle's theoretic observations and conjectures on human nature. I would not be surprised if post-pandemic further robust evidence here will built up rapidly. Indeed a certain parallel to the Freudian theory of suppression of animal instincts by modern societal conventions almost naturally jumps to mind.

Suggestions for thought

- How do you feel about Aristoteles' assertion that true friendship is not possible without letting go of privacy?
- How do you feel about the interpretation of need for privacy as a coping mechanism with loneliness?
- Have you ever lived with a friend under one roof? Was it your home or a shared home (i.e. equal rights to the place)? If not, why not with actually anyone of your friends?
- Have you got friends you could never imagine spending continuous time with, continuous for minimum a week or maybe a month? Why? What would be mostly an issue of concern?
- Have you ever 'invaded' an area of privacy out of concern? Possibly even insistently? How did your friend react to that? What about the other way round?

For statistics in sociological studies, question suggestions and weights in counting see H.

Chapter 5

The activity habits

All sections also for casual reading

Introduction

The activities describe what friends do together. This is how the friendship expresses itself and materialises in each others lives. 'X and me do ... together' or 'X often does ... for/with me.' are typologies for this trait. The activity habits likewise carry about 24 % of weight just as personality. Contrary to the stereotype that men's friendships are all about doing and women's friendships are all about listening and feeling, the actual activities are secondary to the fact that they are happening and what comes out of it. The activities result in the deepening of the relationship over time by building memories and setting the background against which assessments of loyalty, enjoyment or goodwill are being made.

Tot	OP	CP	TW	SH	CM	QS1	QS2	OA	YA	YS
24	20	24	24	23	26	26	22	27	23	NA
Weight share of friendship activities										

The weights are from the frequency analysis explained in section F.1, the categories are OP: Old philosophers, CP contemporary philosophers, TW theological writers, SH self help, CM contemporary media, QS1 qualitative sociologist studies, QS2 quantitative sociologist studies, OA old age sociol. st., YA young age sociol. st., YS youth study.

5.1 Dirt time and hanging out

This is the pure spending time in each other's company. It doesn't so much matter what you do, or how you do it, but that you **spend the time together** and thus build up a greater familiarity. Playing cards, taking walks, anything really as long as you are together with your friend. Nehamas, 2016, ch.6 emphasises that the casual regular interactions are much more the backbone of friendship than the grand moments[1]. The difference between spending time together doing something (5.1) and working together (5.2) is the purpose, the former being focused

[1] 'We spend considerably less time offering our life in exchange for theirs, sacrificing our happiness so that they can live with the love of their life, or generously helping them out of bankruptcy than we

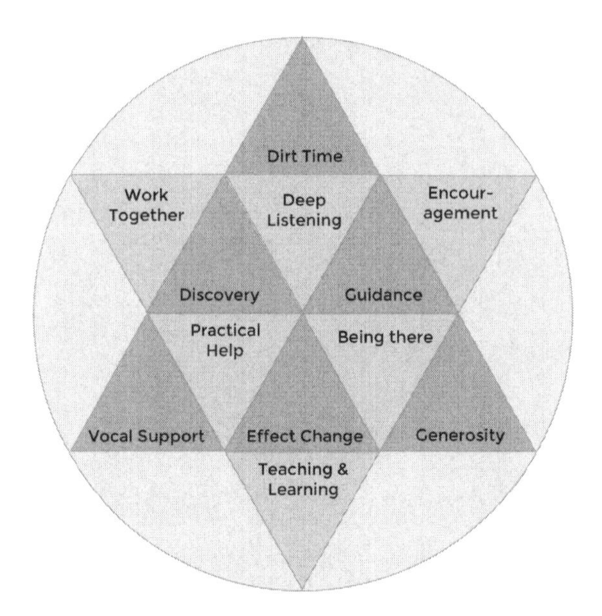

Figure 5.1: Activity Habits

	Tot	OP	CP	TW	SH	CM	QS1	QS2	OA	YA	YS
Dirt time	●	●	●	◒	●	●	●	●	●	●	●
Work tog.	●	◒	●	◒	◒	◒	●	◒	●	◒	●
Listening	●	◒	◒	●	●	●	●	●	●	●	●
Being there	●	●	◒	●	◒	◒	●	●	◒	●	◒
Pract. Help	◒	●	◒	●	◒	◒	◒	●	◒	◒	◒
Circle Bond	◒	○	●	◒	◒	◒	◒	○	◒	◒	◒
Hospitality	◒	○	◒	●	◒	●	◒	○	◒	◒	◒
Enc. Chall	◒	◒	◒	◒	◒	◒	◒	○	◒	●	◒
Eff. Change	◒	◒	●	◒	○	◒	◒	○	◒	○	◒
Guidance	◒	◒	◒	◒	◒	◒	◒	◒	◒	◒	◒
Expl. Disc	◒	○	◒	◒	◒	◒	◒	○	◒	◒	◒
Teach Learn	◒	○	○	◒	◒	◒	◒	○	○	◒	◒
Generosity	◒	◒	◒	◒	○	◒	◒	○	○	◒	◒
Vocal Sup.	◒	○	○	◒	◒	○	◒	◒	○	○	◒

Figure 5.2: Activity Habits

on the activity itself and its enjoyment, the latter focused on striving towards a goal outside the friendship. Greif, 2009 uses the example of a biweekly card gaming session to show how friendship develops as a side product of the activ-

do exchanging news and gossip; discussing books, movies, and love affairs; going places; or just being together—conversation and everyday activity, mostly casual, are what friendship lives on.'

ity. Degges-White and Borzumato-Gainey, 2011, ch.3[2] also illustrates this process of friendship developing as an accompaniment to shared activities. Lewis, 1960, p.111 puts it bluntly: 'Where the sexes, having no real shared activities, can meet only in Affection and Eros, cannot be Friends.'. Other issues can arise too, such as when the chosen shared activities are time or financially expensive, either excluding former members of a group or putting them under unreasonable pressure to keep up and make sacrifices elsewhere (c.f. Kale, 2020-02-11). Shared activities can be casual, such as card gaming or hanging out, emotional (see 5.3) or intellectual (5.11), still any such activity is likely to lead to deep enjoyment and 'Flow'[3]. Alberoni, 2016, p.106 captures this beautifully: 'Friendship flourishes beautifully where activity is at its most intense, where relations between people multiply, when we are full of fervour, where we most active, when we are seeking others with whom we can travel the road together'.

Whilst the specific activities subsumed in 'dirt time' might differ across gender and age, the theme is consistent across. Time is precious, more precious of course in the thirties and forties, but our society has successfully implanted the concept of opportunity costs in all of us. Instinctively we all are aware of fear of missing out, measuring the joy or benefit of what are we doing now against a host of other imaginary potential activities which we also could be doing. Spending time with friends thus is a choice and alone for that matters enormously. When we look back on our life, we look back also on the time we spent with friends, and usually these are fond memories. When reading the likes of Kübler-Ross, 2011 and Ware, 2012 a key theme is the regret at not having spent as much time with friends as we could have done. On the contrary, where people developed deep friendships and held them closely until the end of life, it provided sources of great joy. See Cicero, 1923, p.125: 'Still, such is my enjoyment in the recollection of our friendship that I feel as if my life has been happy because it was spent with Scipio, with whom I shared my public and private cares; lived under the same roof at home; served in the same campaigns abroad, and enjoyed that wherein lies the whole essence of friendship — the most complete agreement in policy, in pursuits, and in opinions.' While the 'pickup' theory is widely acknowledged[4], the counterpoint that spending time together is a clear indicator of the quality and state of the friendship, and picking it up should be more the exception driven by life's circumstances than the rule. Lewis, 1960, p.116 puts it quite blunt: 'People who bore one another should meet seldom; people who interest one another, often.' Prolonged times (i.e. days) spent in each other's company are one of the best ways to bond closely. Roosevelt and Churchill spend days together during WW2 and forged a most affectionate and close friendship. Children understand that sleepovers are much better experiences than just play afternoons.

The time we spend together is driven by the **frequency of our contacts** and the **duration** of the encounters. I would say that occasional prolonged full encounters really keep the friendship going, but would not discount the familiarity bred by a multitude of micro-meetings, such as when neighbours interact with each other in

[2]'Next, as our friendship commitment grows and we begin to enjoy shared activities, we learn even more about each other through mutual interactions; this self-disclosure helps the relationship transform from acquaintanceship to friendship.'

[3]Nakamura and Csikszentmihalyi, 2014

[4]See 8.1 for discussion

a cordial and consistently friendly way. Time can be spent one-on-one, in a small group of three to five (see 5.6), or in general company, and all of those have its purpose or function. While time spent one on one is obviously the gold standard friendship, I would disagree with Alberoni, 2016, p.73 that activities such as parties are not conducive to friendship[5]. Whilst arguably they do not support deep bonding, they create common memories, new content for conversations and the possibility to meet new people brings with itself the opportunity to adopt new people into a circle of friends.

The key activity for children to pursue with their friends is to **play**. It is an activity of exploration, of practicing certain social behaviours, exercising restraint and consideration. Alberoni, 2016, p.71 writes of the 'vital, creative and adventurous aspect of friendship' for child's play. Kernan, 2020-07-12 describes play as 'the great unifier. If you could play, you were in.' and I totally think it is correct. Unfortunately, only few adults keep this passion. When they do, it allows to establish habits such as game afternoons or weekends. It also provides a natural background to integrate visiting friends with spending time with the family and everyone having fun. Enjoying play and finding people to play with is also a good item in older age. Several positive experiments were made getting elderly people also into video gaming[6], and the results are positive, both socially (see Theng, Chua, and Pham, 2012), for physical health (see Brox et al., 2011) and for cognitive health according (see Kuehn et al., 2014). Playing games where pursued is almost a stereotype activity to be done with friends, as you have fun and relax doing so.

There are also substantial benefits of **organizational belonging** for increasing likelihoods of re-encounters. The [benefits] for friendship development are only fully reaped with active engagement in organizations, and I will come to that in the next section. Yet the amount of time we dedicate to activities with friends is also determined by how convenient this is both geographically and practically. Being part of organizations such as a tennis club, a local community center, or an alumni association which we attend frequently increases the probability that I will run into people again, increasing interaction. Of course, there is also the aspect of similarity in interest and background. If we come to such places with sufficient time, such as going to a cafe with a book, it can be a welcome surprise to see a friend and thus have a tea with her. At an alumni reunion it is pleasant to make new acquaintances and bond over experiences shared (see e.g. Greif, 2009, ch.11[7]). It is even better if you see an actual friend coming there by chance, to withdraw to the sidelines for a while and spend some minutes in bilateral conversation before rejoining the general fray. Furthermore, there always is the option to seclude themselves after the event and appreciate the fact that without the lucky occasion the opportunity for this encounter might never have realised in the first place.

[5]'Its [the party] purposes are multifarious: to pass the time, to get to know new people, to do business, to put oneself in the limelight, to seek an erotic adventure and a thousand other things. Friends at such gatherings have little to say to each other because they are separated from one another and because they must conform to social rituals. They tend to spontaneously seclude themselves in order to chat.'

[6]Yes, the much deplored violent ego shooter team tournaments turned out to provide competition and fun, as teams of four elderlies started taking on 15 year olds - see e.g. `https://www.swp.de/digitales/wenn-senioren-zocken_-der-aufstieg-der-_silver-gamer_-24129596.html`

[7]'I will go back to the Academy for some reunion and meet people who were in school with me who I never really knew, and I come to talk with them and they are fantastic people, and I say to myself, 'I wish I had known them when we were in school together because they are such great people."

The effect of good social organizations supporting the creation and maintenance of friendship works in reverse, too. We like showing up at events of organizations where we may run into our friends. We come to specific church services in the course of the Sunday because those are the ones our friends attend; we go to specific networking events at Internations, Couchsurfing or Meetup because we know our friends are there. A benefit of the Facebook 'service' or functionality is Facebook Local, where you can see which events your friends are going to, so that you might not just enjoy the event, but effortlessly coordinate with friends to attend jointly.

One way to spend time together is to **travel together**. With my closest friends, I have had holidays together, and the joined experiences made for long memories. The extreme case of spending a lot of time together is living together, and this is what Aristotle advocates for the best of friends. The time you need to spend together to form and maintain a really close friendship is often quoted as the limiting factor for the number of close friendships. The quoted number here is no more than five close friendships. In part I agree, though I would say that the core intensity is in the buildup, once the base is built, usually close friendships can reach a slightly less intense steady state of maintenance. My caveat with this argument more is that it almost treats the rest of our busy lives as given. If people say I don't have time for more than say three close friends, you could interpret that as an alternative statement: 'There are a hundred other activities I choose to pursue. And after deducting TV watching and Facebook/Instagram scrolling from that I have indeed no further time to spend with friends'. On the other hand, while lamentable, of course this time scarcity is part of today's reality. How large is the time availability effect? Rath, 2006, p.22 estimates that the third of our time we spend with friends in adolescence drops to 10 % or less in adulthood. If you put this next to the famous U-bend curve of Happiness of Stone et al., 2010 then at least a correlative association becomes clear[8]. And this is why the allocated time budget to hang out with friends matters so immensely.[9]

Practical takeaway
The spending of our time with our friends is the base of our friendship. How, where, when, is all secondary to that we spend time with them. Be grateful for all the time with your friends, and take every opportunity to make time for them.

Suggestions for thought

- How much time do you spend with your friends during the week

[8]A mere overlap of plausible curves is of course only limited evidence, but co-correlates such as control over time use, and thus ability to also choose to spend it with friends is a plausible connector. See also the discussion on proximity and time resources.

[9]The difference between the theme of spending time together, and the resource of time, is that of action and choice vs. availability and possibility. Person A might have little time and choose to spend every bit of it with their friends, whereas B might have lots of time, but just not bother to spend it with friends.

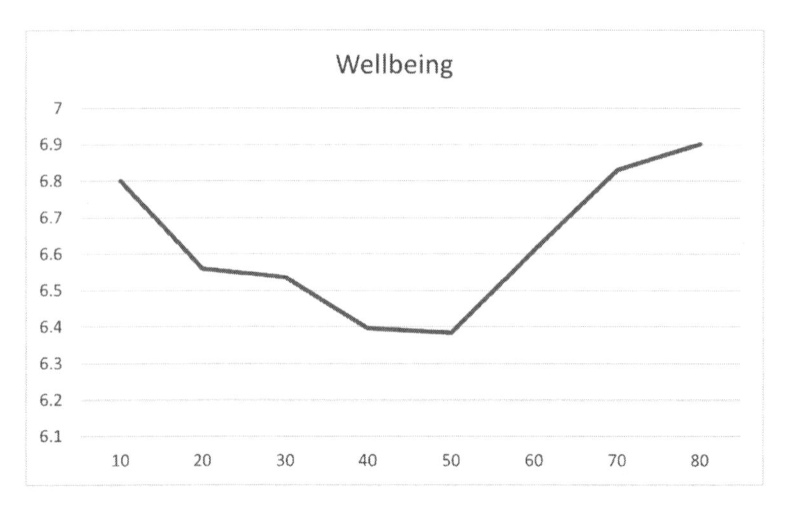

Figure 5.3: Stone 2010 U-Bend curve

and on the weekend?

- How do you spend it, and how has it shifted? Are there things you used to do which you stopped doing because of lack of time?
- Is for you more the frequency of spending time together or more the duration of time when you are together important to the development of the friendship?
- When you meet friends, do you more hang out and chat or is it usually centered on a pastime such as a sport or board game?

For statistics in sociological studies, question suggestions and weights in counting see H.

5.2 Work together or pursue common goals and interests

Here the unifying element is the common goal or task. This is about doing something together, not just as a pastime, but with a specified goal. This can be brought about by being together in a company working on a project, or in an association and serving on a board, or being inventors and collaborating. Working together builds acquaintance as you learn to appreciate the other's approaches, energy and thinking. There is also a companionship element and bonding, as you work towards the goal. Some writers on friendship define collaboration as the core element of 'male friendship'.

This theme splits up into

1. having a unifying task which you pursue,
2. intentionally being part of an organization that pursues your goal (you are there primarily for purposes other than a salary - intentional participation),

3. being part of an organisation that provides a social setting (you are there for the salary and/or the social environment - situational participation. Arguably this in nature is more like unproductive 'dirt time', but in common understanding it is still covered by 'working together'.).

In all cases, the result is that you spend a lot of time together, and most of it intentionally. In the work context you get to observe each other in day-to-day life, you see the other person taking decisions, get to know their thinking and other character and personality traits.

(1) The creative process of **working together** towards a goal is also connected to exploration and discovery as well as mutual challenge but at its heart is not just the enjoyment but the passion for the goal. And in the pursuit of this goal you engage with the person. Lewis, 1960, p.104 emphasises the need for the common activity as the bonding element: 'You will not find the warrior, the poet, the philosopher or the Christian by staring in his eyes as if he were your mistress: better fight beside him, read with him, argue with him, pray with him.'. Indeed, this was the basis of the Inklings fellowship[10]. It is this artistic connection that also features heavily in the friendships of Chinese friendship lore (see e.g. the friendship of Du Fu and Li Bai described in Christensen, 2011) that are not of the 'master-loyal-follower' type. The friendship thus has its core in the activity's intensity according to Alberoni, 2016, p.106[11]. In its highest form it is experiencing 'flow' together (see Nakamura and Csikszentmihalyi, 2014), and bonding over the experience. This can then be the 'shared truth' basis of a friendship and also be a sufficient condition to feel fully understood by the friend (4.6).

(2) **Voluntary or intentional organizational belonging**: Whilst artists can band together in small groups, most larger causes both commercial and non-profit demand larger teams coming together to pursue this. Where people join this organisation intentionally and for the purpose of making an impact through this organisation, this can be a powerful bonding experience. Thus researchers even from different topics meet at university and bond over their passion for research. People join the military, especially when it is voluntary or for the same (non-forced) reasons also can bond as they spend considerable time together under stress. Cicero, 1923, pp.125, 151 has Laelius recount the joint military campaigns and joint consulship as times of bonding.

The sense that it is beneficial for a friendship to develop and be maintained if one works together in an organisation is strong. Putnam argues that the social networks provided by PTAs, bowling clubs, alumni networks, church communities and the likes are the matrix and breeding ground for our friendships, and I fully agree. The theme of participating in something common or being part of a joint association is according to the Oxford english dictionary fittingly captured in the term 'communion'.[12] One might now say that in a lot of these associations we mostly take part passively as consumers, and maybe just attend reunions, church services. If we participate actively by serving some of our time to further the

[10]The Oxford Inklings were an informal literary discussion group, also including JRR Tolkien, known for regularly meeting in the Oxford pub institution's back room Eagle and Child on Tuesday mornings.

[11]'Friendship flourishes beautifully ...'

[12]Whilst in sociological literature communion has been used for openness e.g. Zarbatany, Conley, and Pepper, 2004

goals of the organization, our experience is more intensive and the bonding with other active members more effective rather than passive showing up and just consuming. You become a contributing member of the chosen tribe. Both Putnam and Degges-White and Borzumato-Gainey, 2011, ch.2 note that 'Women also provide much of a community's unpaid work and social collateral, such as church committee service; nonprofit, volunteer work; school-based organizational leadership (e.g., PTA committees); and neighborhood organizational tasks'.[13]. When you actively - e.g. by serving on a committee or handing out cakes and coffee - participate in a social organization, you interact with more people on a more frequent basis. As you spend more time at and in the organization's service, people perceive you more positively, as you are making their experience better (assuming a minimum amount of competence). Service-oriented organizations both secular (Lions, Rotary, ...), Churches and social action (refugees, poor, homeless) are particularly effective as they unite their members with a purpose and automatically get them to serve together. It is overall not surprising that volunteering can be considered as a best practice for making friends (see e.g. Millington, 2019, p.24[14] or Alcock-Ferguson, 2018-05-16). Being part of an organization increases proximity (lowers effort cost of meeting friends) as you automatically run into positively disposed people and friends, creates a common memory of anecdotes and context with the people around you also serving the organization, provides also opportunities for other activities (parties and hospitality).

(3) **Situational and economically motivated organizational belonging**: Even for those who are at work not for the whole-hearted passion for the organizations goals, it still needs to be recognised that we spend a good 40 hours per week at the workplace. In times of COVID many of us started working from home and thus we may be out of each others presence and sight, but in normal times this is substantial time spent in each other's presence. By presence I mean physical presence, with the immediate option to retire into a coffee corner or meeting room to discuss something, ask how the respective other is. Online our name might show up as a participant in a teams room, but it just is not the same. Given the general statistics on productivity and engagement increase if people have good friends at work (Rath, 2006, p.53) it seems also a good policy to support this from management. As Rath, 2006, p.66[15] shows, this support from management is highly effective. Setting aside the benefits on productivity and engagement, general happiness in life increases if we spend more time in the company of friends, including at work (see e.g. Cohen, 1992). For enabling this, nothing is quite as effective as the British Friday 5pm pint custom as a way to end the working week on a positive, relaxed and cheerful note, as groups from work head down to the pub. At my own employer, BASF, the monthly wine tasting organised by the company's wine cellar likewise offered a similar informal opportunity for new entries to connect with their new colleagues or old colleagues to integrate their new team members. It became a welcome and joyous fixture in the social calendar. Presumably there is

[13]For Putnam this holds mostly in the past, i.e. the sixties, seventies and eighties, and the decrease in community activity is because of a higher participation of women in the workforce and men not compensating sufficiently. For Degges-White it is mostly about the still existing current day imbalance.

[14]' My advice: if you're looking to make new friends, start with volunteering for a local charity and you might just meet friends for life.'

[15]'When managers discuss friendships with employees on a regular basis, it nearly triples the chances of employees having a "best friend at work."'

also a difference in impact for introverts and extroverts, or other elements of the personality (independence in work vs. team orientation and integration).

There is also a school of thought according to which people want to separate their professional and private lives, sometimes rigorously. Misunderstandings and rejections can occur when sympathy and good collaboration are mistaken for an initiation of post work friendship. It is then important to simply just respect that. It might also be healthy depending how many other interests you share, or whether work is your prime connector. In the latter case, the temptation is there to bring work problems also into the private life and end up discussing company strategy or department politics when other friends are there.

Another issue with having friends at work is the transfer of status once you leave the organisation, be it because of a job change or retirement. Once you are out of the environment, you can be less interesting as a source of company gossip, and it might be difficult for you to take part in company happy hours. Note that here exceptions are however quite possible, in some organizations with a good company culture it is common for ex-colleagues to still join the social gatherings. Also, during my secondments I experienced that people talk to their colleagues, who are out of the local physical loop, more easily about the items slightly too sensitive for the coffee machine chat. Some ex-colleagues of mine were still very socially up-to-date on departmental gossip years after they left. However, in particular at retirement the effect is hard, especially for those who in part defined their status and self worth through validation at work and the respect and integration with the colleagues.

Practical takeaway
One of the most intense bonding you can do is pursuing an intense project or task with a friend. This can be the collaboration on a book, or the long term serving in an organization. With one of your friends, find a common purpose and pursue it to the joy of both your hearts.

Suggestions for thought

- Are there people at work with whom you could imagine striking up a friendship?
- Are some of your friendship centered on a productive purpose, such as collaborating to create art, a book or volunteering?
- Do you meet your friends directly or do you maintain your friendships within organisational membership, such as a sports club or a church?
- When you are a member in an organization, do you at least for some time get actively involved in a serving role? Put differently, do you currently actively serve in one voluntary or social organization?

For statistics in sociological studies, question suggestions and weights in counting see H.

5.3 Deep listening and expression of self

This section describes the activity of one side opening up and the other one being deeply attentive in order to enable it. Depending on the needs of the situation, this can be one-sided (in a crisis) or interactive (general sharing encounter), and over time builds a deep understanding towards each other. Some writers on friendship define this as the core element of 'female friendship'. The theme is literally ubiquitous in writings on female friendship. There are different ways of listening and different ways of sharing, and I will go through them one by one.

In order to enable sharing, you need to listen, and this requires focus on the other. In order to focus on the other properly, you need humility - the capability to put yourself second and the other first. Listening shows you care. It is a key skill people look for in potential friends throughout the ages (see e.g. Degges-White and Borzumato-Gainey, 2011, p.134[16]. And people appreciate their friends for it :'X will quietly sit with you', 'X will listen without making any judgement', 'X always listens when you need an ear' or 'X really listens what you have to say'. Biblically one might remember likewise the recommendation of James 1:19 'Everyone should be quick to listen, slow to speak and slow to become angry'.

I am unsure when you listen to someone's experience, how much parallel processing is allowed or natural or cannot be prevented. People take up information and can process in different ways, such as by imagining the experience themselves. It is a classical trope of male-female mismatch in communication that men listen too little and directly want to fix an identified problem. Of course, often this is true, but at least sometimes this is down to a lack of technique (not understanding what slow listening is all about) vs. a lack of care (trying to make the problem go away as fast as possible). I think that one-upping is at least sometimes more a case of poor technique to be unlearned rather than bad style. Sometimes it is wrong, but on other occasions it is genuine processing, and trying to understand and validate by sharing a story of your own that is close to the other's; Not to interrupt, but to use an example so you can relate to that what you have good emotional access to. You want to see whether you correctly captured the emotion the speaker was communicating to you. Of course, there are better ways of validating and processing. What I want to highlight is that if you are the sharer you might support the sharing process by paying some attention to how your listener is processing what you are sharing and accommodating this.

There are different listening styles too. The website marketing91.com lists 18 styles of listening, many of them typologies of bad listeners (unactive, one-upper, distracted, ...), or types of recipients of Powerpoint presentations, which I will not go into here. From what I read across the rest, I consider the following a reasonable summary of the styles that our friends might employ:

1. Sympathetic and supporting listening - This mix between empathic and active listening is not aiming for full connection between the sharer and

[16]'a lady in the mid sixties talking about the friendship with her daughters: ' I find that now with them in their forties my role as protector is lessened, but the role of listener never ceases."

listener, but just to make the other person feel better. It can be required when your friend underwent a self-inflicted train wreck, such as complaining about hangover pain after a heavy night of drinking. It can in lighter cases even involve (limited) jokes at their expense, as long as the goal is building them up - it is there to support the sharing process.

2. Therapeutic listening - Empathic is really understanding the friend's point of view and in the process helping them reflect it.

3. Critical listening - sparring and giving feedback, calling you out, it is partially judgmental (see 5.10).

4. Active listening - This is listening in an active conversation, asking questions, encouraging to share more on a topic, good for explorative discussions.

5. Deep or reflective listening - Whilst listening or in breaks you process the thoughts and ideas given to you, read between the lines, understand context, ... the kind of catch all. I only know very few people who I would assign the genuine capacity to do this.

At the extreme interpretation, listening well is an art according to Fromm, 2013a. An interesting image is to think about listening as a muscle, which you need to exercise in life. The metaphor works very accurately, as the muscle can be tired out (e.g. from zoom calls, long discussions), and it takes practice. Essentially, psychotherapists are in this view professional sports people. Fromm, 2013a[17] sets out requirements to achieve the state to bring this art to fruition.

The theme of sharing has a range of subthemes, but they all require listening skill and attitude:

1. Sharing for emoting and processing what currently concerns us,

2. Sharing emotions for therapeutic listening,

3. Sharing for enjoyment and disclosure (i.e. for helping the other getting to know you),

4. Sharing for creating and affirming emotional closeness.

(1) 'I just can't believe what just happened to me'. If we are in a situation of shock, grief or trouble, we need the presence of someone listening. This is very close to the general support of (5.4). Joyous occasions can require the same. A

[17]'1 The basic rule for practicing this art is the complete concentration of the listener.
2 Nothing of importance must be on his mind, he must be optimally free from anxiety and from greed.
3 He must possess a freely-working imagination which is sufficiently concrete to be expressed in words.
4 He must be endowed with a capacity for empathy with another person and strong enough to feel the experience of the other as if it were his own.
5 The condition for such empathy is a crucial facet of the capacity for love. To understand another means to love him — not in the erotic sense but in the sense of reaching out to him and of overcoming the fear of losing oneself.
6 Understanding and loving are inseparable. If they are separate, it is a cerebral process and the door to essential understanding remains closed.'

typical misunderstanding is when a guy is in hospital witnessing the birth of his baby and is overfilled with joy, yet an hour later he runs off to tell his soccer friends about it, leaving the mum in the hospital. Asked later why he did it, there is little he can say apart from 'I just had to tell them'. We process our emotions by expressing them to others. This is listening without at all incorporating your 'listening skills'. You acknowledge your friend's emotion and share their grief or joy. You let them be just what they are in this moment. Listening is also a key activity helping a friend overcome grief. It is both simple and difficult. Simple because there is no real wrong as long as your friend knows you care. Difficult because you need to believe that yourself. Stepping up is the decisive part.

(2) Therapeutic listening is very close to (1) allowing someone just to say what comes to the head, and it is the key theme of this topic. It is an interaction, as you ask questions trying to help your friend process and clarify their head. You do not want to change them, or make them change their mind, but you facilitate and interact with their thought process through clarifying questions. Tact and respect permitting, you try to build your friend up very slowly after a breakup. You really try to understand what their key concern is. And you really want to just help your friend in the situation. And the best thing you can do is to listen patiently and with empathy.

The norm is of course that this activity comes as trust has been built and the friendship is close. But there are moments when there is a need, and someone unexpected steps forward. It is not a matter of TMITE[18] - but compassion in that concrete situation. It is these moments of compassion and deep connection, that then jump start a deep friendship. Whilst with serious problems such as drugs or depression of course psychotherapist professional help needs to be sought, for most emotional problems a good friend is the first port of call. Specifically, when thinking about marital or other family problems, a well meaning long friend, who knows the history and nuances, is invaluable as a listener and sparrings partner. If this friend knows not just us, but also has a longtime acquaintance with the other people in the drama of our mind, they can give objective advice.

Arguably as the interaction increases we enter sparring which is covered in guidance (5.10), but between therapeutic listening and sparring/guidance there is an activity that Paine, 1969, p.507 calls 'explaining one to oneself', which I think is a very precise description of full understanding intimacy. As our friend is from our joint history acquainted with our background yet in emotional situations a bit detached himself, they can offer objectivity. They can make conjectures on our motives or hypothetical actions, support in simulation, sound things out, potentially point us to past fallacies and self-cheating, all the while providing affection and a safe environment.

(3) The theme of sharing to get to factually and emotionally know the other person features in male friendships, however, it is usually a side process rather than intentional. Sharing anecdotes and in that context describing occurring emotions is the most effective way of sharing emotions in male friendships. Information is kept and the anecdote including the shared emotions passes into common memory (see 4.1), allowing at a later stage the friend to make clarifying comparisons such as 'So is this a bit like when you did when X happened'. But this ac-

[18]Too much information too early

tivity has limits, as Matthews, 1983, p.146[19] points out, in the friend's capacity to relate to it in his own personality and experiences. The sharing of stories and emotions also has a signalling effect, as by sharing more sensitive stories and emotions we make a statement how far we think the relationship has progressed in terms of trust and prepare for larger and more sensitive material (see Shumway, 2018, p.115[20]).

Apart from focused discussions on AI or other topics of direct interest to us, the sharing of stories entertaining and revealing is one of the prime joys in conversation - at least for some of us. It is just nice to be listened to or vividly to experience an anecdote or a humoristic moment of our friend. We expand our mind in much the same way as we read a book, only with the difference that we can ask the book and see the principal actors emotions. It is an interactive process of exploration of our friend's life, formation and experiences. Sometimes with this sharing, there is no further point to it than literally just sharing it. The experience and emotion needs to get out in a most positive way. A splendid example is that of responding to kids passions, when they discover something new, like Lego not only having knights and castles but also space ships, or when they learn something new in school, and really allowing them to express their passion for it. This children like passion usually wanes with adulthood, but a few people maintain, protect and cherish their capability to be genuinely excited for little things. In these cases you may not share the passion, certainly not with the intensity of your friend, but friend has something to tell, and it needs 'out' and they have chosen you as the love object they needs to tell it to.

(4) Emotional sharing is the intentional sharing of emotion to build closeness with the other person. This is probably the stereotype weak point of male friendship. A sentence I heard repeated verbatim again and again from female friends is 'I have never understood male friendship, the lack of sharing would just not work for me'. As with all stereotypes, there are exceptions, but it is true enough to warrant detailed analysis on both causes and possible interventions. The book Garfield, 2016 describes one such consistent and sustained effort. Greif, 2009 likewise points to a deep unease at intentional emotional sharing. On this matter Nelson, 2016 is clear that building the connection with your friend is a purpose of the act of sharing, and women find it deeply satisfying and enjoyable. The process of sharing and exploring each other's perspectives has even been incorporated into the philosophical schools by Friedman, 1993. I am not aware whether there is conclusive evidence of whether men who do not share do so because they do not want to, do not need to or are not able to. I think it is a case-by-case situation, and probably a bit of all three. Additionally to the 'not want-not need-not able' the speed and focus of disclosure may be different, thus making a direct comparison between male and female sharing inappropriate. There is a possibility that

[19] 'If you have the idea of a friendship as one in which you can share things more or less completely, how are you going to re-create whole sections of your own past for the purpose of an individual you have come to like very much, but who really has only known you since you were 50 years old?.. .You can say, 'Well, yes, when I was in Brazil', or 'When I drove a cab in New York City', and then you watch someone's eyes widen... You can't tell them. You can only skip over the high points.'

[20] 'Your friends may be trying to open up to you in small ways all the time. Even small self-disclosures like their favorite foods or their feelings about a television show are ways your friend is trying to be open with you. Do not take small sharing for granted- Your friends want you to know them better just as much as you want them to know you.'

the fascination with one's car, Lego collection or computer games genuinely is foremost on a man's mind, and if they talk intensely about it, then everything of relevance has been shared[21]. It might be even said that in this respect men stay much more emotionally like children in their object orientation and fascination. If you or your friend is at odds with aspects of their current situation or identity, friendship offers the opportunity to leave this behind and escape with a friend to a space where only the interest such as poetry, sport or good discussions are in focus and everything else does not matter. The absence of emotional sharing then is a bonus and not a detriment of the friendship.

On a positive note, although the process of emotional sharing can distress men, the result of sharing is being understood (4.6). This result is equally and highly desired by both men and women (see Greif, 2009, ch.2[22]), and thus finding a personally acceptable way of emotional sharing is more a matter of technique and getting used to it.

Being fully connected and fully attentive is important at all levels of this activity. This means to actively listen, you need to be able to see the sharer, you need to see their entire body making gestures and not just a section on it on a 5 inch phone screen. You need to hear the nuances of the voice and not just the transmission of words through a phone. This is described in the 'layer theory' of Asatryan, 2016 (see 11.1) and is particularly relevant here. As people age and lose their health, the capacity to hear well and thus to participate in sharing and listening is one of the most painful losses according to Degges-White and Borzumato-Gainey, 2011[23].

Practical takeaway
Good listening is a muscle, which you practice best with your friends. It is an art and skill employed to the best benefit of your friends. The SHUSH[a] framework of the Samaritans is also really helpful for thinking about this.

[a] Show you care - have patience - use open questions - say it back - have courage `https://www.samaritans.org/how-we-can-help/if-youre-worried-about-someone-else/how-support-someone-youre-worried-about/what-do-if-you-think-someone-struggling/`

Suggestions for thought

[21] Note how Lewis, 1960, p.103 casually dismisses e.g. family, profession and previous history as non-topics in a friendship, arguably the background from which a good number of anecdotes and stories might be shared from. 'In a circle of true Friends each man is simply what he is; stands for nothing but himself. No one cares twopence about any one else's family, profession, class, income, race, or previous history. Of course you will get to know about most of these in the end. But casually.'. The 'casually' corroborates the non-intentional sharing as part of a side activity and not as a goal by itself.

[22] 'Everybody wants to be understood and accepted by others. This is the cornerstone for men. Whether the men interviewed talked about this issue in terms of communication, giving feedback to someone, or having a friend to share with, being understood was essential for the majority of men.'

[23] 'Mary shared that the loss of her hearing was the hardest part of aging for her and research shows that age-related hearing impairment is a much greater blow to women than to men.'

- How good do you think you are at listening? Which listening styles fit your personality best?
- Do you have a friend who listens really well? What is it about their style that makes it resonate or feel good with you?
- Is your sharing style more intentional or more byproduct of hanging out?
- How good are you at retaining information or stories shared with you?

For statistics in sociological studies, question suggestions and weights in counting see H.

5.4 Being there & Crisis Support

It comes in different themes:

1. being there (physical presence)
2. unspecified emotional support
3. unspecified general support

(1) This activity is being there when your friend needs you, be it at a funeral, after a romantic breakup or a visit in the hospital. No advice, no practical help, no deep listening, which are usually explicitly mentioned in interviews. Sometimes you just need to be there. This activity is likewise uncontroversially endorsed by all, though the quiet being there also resonates more with men than the more listening and sharing approach of women.

One of the best examples of this I actually find in the bible in Job 2:11-13, where the three friends come and visit him[24]. In the biblical tradition they are generally criticised for their actions and words[25]. Not all what they say in the passage would be considered what we now call helpful or emotionally sensitive or smart. In the very text, both Job and God end up annoyed with them. Contrary to mainstream convention, I would argue that at least in their initial reaction their behaviour is spot on as could be expected. They hear about the misfortune that Job is in, and they show up, and they sit with him in his suffering. And in times of grief or emotional anguish, that counts. You show up, and you don't bugger off when you get bored. They sat with him for a full week, showing their support and commitment.

[24]'When Job's three friends heard of all this evil that had come upon him, they came each from his own place, Eliphaz the Temanite, Bildad the Shuhite, and Zophar the Naamathite. They made an appointment together to come to show him sympathy and comfort him. And when they saw him from a distance, they did not recognize him. And they raised their voices and wept, and they tore their robes and sprinkled dust on their heads toward heaven. And they sat with him on the ground seven days and seven nights, and no one spoke a word to him, for they saw that his suffering was very great.'

[25]e.g. `https://www.theologyofwork.org/old-testament/job/jobs-friends-blame-job-for-the-calamity-job-4-23`, I do look for a better discussion on this.

'My friend was **there for me** when I needed them' is with 'my friend has my back' one of the strongest general phrases to express a good friendship. The difference is that whereas 'having someone's back' involved personal risk to life or reputation, 'being there for me' usually just involved time. The expectation here is that the friend will put almost anything to the side to come to your support (see also consideration in 4.3). It can be a support in really difficult times, or just momentary attention, such as responding to text messages that have minor questions. It can mean for example accompanying your friend to the doctor or dentist. The theme is the prioritisation of your friends need for your presence over your own preferences e.g. to go to the cinema or whatever else you actually would have wanted to do in that moment.

(2) Mostly among women, friendship there is a specific category of **emotional support**. Again this highly overlaps with other themes, but the emphasis here is on the emotional benefit of the friends' help. Stereotyping here with significant caveats applied, men care about the result of the help (car is fixed, work problem discussed and solved, feeling understood by friends) and appreciate the effort involved. Women care about the process and how the support of their friends makes them feel supported (emotionally) and appreciate the result of the help (see also S. Feldhahn and J. Feldhahn, 2008. This is emotional support in the wider sense. Emotional support in the narrow sense is essentially producing the result that I feel I am not alone in my emotions, that there is someone supporting me in whatever I am grappling with in my head. How this assistance comes, is secondary. It does not need to be guidance how to solve it, or sparring[26], but can involve it. As such, emotional support in the narrow sense is most likely covered by deep sharing and listening (5.3).

In sociological literature the term emotional support seems to be used without wider differentiation, and interpreting results thus implies significant value judgements of what activities actually lie in the scope of 'emotional support' (e.g. Blieszner and Ogletree, 2017[27]).

Disregarding the issues of lack of exact definition, emotional support is a key desirable in friendships at work and at home (see e.g. Nelson, 2016, p.2[28], Greif, 2009[29]). Lacking sufficient emotional support from their husband in the form they need it, women in third part of life turn to develop friendships to make up for the shortfall.

(3) Sometimes being there is not enough, your friend really also needs your help apart from presence. So you need to show you have your friends' back. You help and it doesn't matter how you do it or what you do. You know you are **there for your friend** and their wellbeing, you do whatever it takes, without emphasis on the actual activity. Your friend feels 'that' you support him without going

[26]Sparring is a method of critical or constructive discussion, see (5.10)

[27]'Both unmarried men and unmarried women, whether never married or previously married, were more likely to be high exchangers of instrumental and emotional support with friends than were their married counterparts.' and 'Encouraging friends to engage in meaningful activities together, visit back and forth, and telephone or send caring messages can also be foundational to emotional exchanges. Even friends living at a distance can offer emotional support if in-person interaction is infrequent or impossible.'

[28]'Emotional Support is the key item they want from the group.'

[29]'Aykroyd felt as if he had lost a brother. Gone was the business partnership, and the strong friendship, which had provided for both men an emotional support system'

into details. See Cicero, 1923, p.195 'Thus nature, loving nothing solitary, always strives for some sort of support, and man's best support is a very dear friend.' This 'do-what-you-must' attitude resonates in Lewis, 1960, p.101[30], though he considers it only peripheral to the nature of friendship. The effect of a friend of standing by to support us can help us in various ways. It is both physically and mentally good for us, as can make pain more tolerable, hills or mountains less steep, and reduce stress. Whether intuitively or explicitly people are aware of that, they express gratitude for friends standing by them in difficult situations.

The stereotypical example of helping in difficult times is **support in grieving** processes. When a loved one dies, be it parents, spouse or worst - one's children - our worlds get fractured. Friends coming to our side and support us in our agony. From personal experience I can say, this is both easy and difficult. Easy because as a friend you don't actually have to do much. You just have to be there, listen, and not be selfish. However, most people realise that it is not an emotionally easy situation, because in it we all are confronted with our own mortality. Thus what is required is that we bear this tension. Thus our personal availability is the first step (cf. Shumway, 2018, p.152). The message is 'you are important to me, so here I am'. Showing up to a funeral, taking the friend out to dinner, allowing him to switch off. Depending how large the family is, and what skill sets are there, practical help can be invaluable. In our smaller families with increased longevity, people don't die as often as they used to 100 years ago, and hence dealing also with administrative processes etc. is difficult for everyone. If you have practical skills such as a knowledge of legal issues, tax, or two right hands and lend one of those for clearing up a space, that is really valuable help, especially if your friend is overwhelmed. Whilst humor is not always appropriate, and some tact needs to be shown, following the death of a parent, spouse or close friend, people don't want to be miserable the whole time. Even if you classify yourself more the clown than the deep listening therapist friend, your role might be valuable in allowing your friend to have a night out with laughter and thinking neither about grief nor the grind of the administrative process. Our realisation of mortality is also a moment of full honesty and with it vulnerability. Emotions are bare, and this is a moment of responsibility, but also a moment where the friendship can rise to the challenge. The emotional bonding during such a process resonates for a long time. It is quite common when mentally flicking through the different events in a friendship, that 'she was there for me when X died'. Events other than death can also induce grieving processes. These are moments of loss, such as of a job and the meaning of it (status, meaning in life, value, self esteem) or a romantic relationship. The loss of health, particular in old age, when you realise you stop being able to do certain sports or other activity dear to you, will cause grief (cf. Matthews, 1983, p.147 on the loss of mobility[31]).

[30] 'A Friend will, to be sure, prove himself to be also an ally when alliance becomes necessary; will lend or give when we are in need, nurse us in sickness, stand up for us among our enemies, do what he can for our widows and orphans. But such good offices are not the stuff of Friendship.'

[31] 'Informants who were still able physically and financially to visit out-of-town friends made a point of doing so on a regular basis. Those who no longer were able, experienced a loss tantamount in many cases to the death of the friend.'

Practical takeaway
Sometimes all that you need to do is drop everything and come to the side of your friend to be there. You will know when such a time comes.

If a friend tries to help you appreciate the effort and the intention. Our friends are not trained psychotherapists, they may feel deeply uncomfortable in their element. You don't need to take everything in, and you can point out to them when something is unhelpful or hurtful, but appreciate the showing up and commitment more than a temporary stupid or ill-advised comment.

Suggestions for thought

- Have you had a situation of intense difficulty where a friend stood by you? How did that make you feel?
- What does emotional support mean to you?
- Have you ever been in a situation where you needed to be the pillar of support to a friend? What demands did that make on your time and emotions?

Suggestions on supporting and being supported in grief as a friend

- When including a friend in your grieving process, trust your gut feeling. If you want to be alone, that is OK too. Everyone is different.
- When a friend is undergoing a grieving process, offer, but don't be offended if your offer is rejected. Everyone grieves differently, some people need people by their side, some don't.
- Strong grieving processes bring chaotic emotions. Cut your grieving friend some slack if they go off radar for a while, but keep up the invitations.
- If a friend of yours is undergoing grief, and you think it is on you to step up but feel uncomfortable, there are great resources on the web. Of course you will never be a trained professional, but all that is necessary at first is to give you some context what benefit you can do.

For statistics in sociological studies, question suggestions and weights in counting see H.

5.5 Practical help

Practical help refers to the meeting our friends practical need by our investment of time and effort to their benefit. It means knowing you repeatedly are there to support and get your hands dirty is a powerful display of valuation and appreciation. Chapman, 2009 puts Acts of Service as one of his key love languages. In a household context, i.e. the married or cohabiting couple, it revolves around household chores such as vacuuming, doing the dishes or general cleaning, cooking, taking care of the kids at certain parts of the day, making sure the car is always filled with petrol, taking care of taxes, the list goes on. These are the little things that often go unnoticed or undervalued. Whilst less regular in friendship, it is present, and it is plausible to assume that people whose romantic love language is acts of service, will just as much react by feeling loved if a friend helps them in their daily life.

In the social-economic sphere, services include help at finding a job, such as doing mock interviews, looking around for suitable positions, reviewing a CV, proof reading applications or helping with elements of studying. Aside from network services (see 5.14 and 6.5), practical support can be helpful from the wider communities.

The history of friends helping on practical matters is likewise long documented. Aristotle, 1925, 8.1[32] thinks of older people and their support. A very pragmatic example is given by John 13:5-6[33], and the theological explanation usually revolves on humbling oneself. There is however a very profane non-theological explanation: roads in ancient times were really dirty and dusty, and most people would wear open sandals, meaning that at the end of a day of walking your feet would be literally covered in a crust of dust and sweat. Jesus' act of washing the feet was thus not just theologically significant, but an extremely pragmatic act of service to his exhausted friends.

The activity of service increases in significance as financial assets of a person decrease. It is now our current social consensus that if you have money to outsource a service, you should not refer to friends to do this. This of course results in the increase in service industries from home work support, nannies, shopping delivery services and care homes. For poorer communities this is no option, and thus specifically in families that came from poor backgrounds to higher middle class, still narratives of the strong social connections in the past remain (see Degges-White and Borzumato-Gainey, 2011, Ch.2 'My grandmother tells ...'). Other items would be substantial support, such as giving a loan or lending expensive equipment (cf. Fischer, 1982). Whereas sometimes crisis assistance is emotional consolation, or support by presence (both dealt with in previous sections), often the need is of a practical nature. The crisis is a crisis, as a friend cannot solve a given situation by themselves. The biblical covenant-friendship, as Olyan, 2017 describes it, is essentially a mutual insurance policy for such crises. Even in a friendship, support in a crisis is not unconditional. A key question was whether it is avoidable, and the inconvenience to the friend could have been mitigated. Some people are

[32]'it aids older people by ministering to their needs and supplementing the activities that are failing from weakness.'

[33]'After that, he poured water into a basin and began to wash his disciples' feet, drying them with the towel that was wrapped around him. 6 He came to Simon Peter, who said to him, 'Lord, are you going to wash my feet?"

disorganised, yet so endearing. We expect them to get into multiple minor crises simply on account of their incapability to get things done and we forgive them, albeit with a bit of eye rolling. However some crises can be predicted, and then calling up a friend on the last minute in crisis mode, whereas a week's warning to prepare could have been easily given, is a breach of consideration and respect. By involving the friend earlier, the crisis could also have been avoided. A crisis does however not have to be a onetime moment, but can also have continuing circumstances. Thus a divorce or a sudden death of a loved one can trigger a general or emotional crisis lasting months. It is an interesting question whether support in a crisis can be predicted or should be prepared. This is not a manipulative exercise, but more a thought exercise in human psychology. Can we credibly assure our friend that we will support them (and being supported by them) in a crisis, if we have cut out or sourced out most minor favours to third party services? Thus we routinely hire a babysitter instead of neighbour, we call a taxi rather than plan for a round-robin drive home after a night of drinking, and we buy a ready made meal from the super market rather than share food with a neighbour. All of this is super convenient, but it cuts out the transmission of showing our friend we care for them.

Even in modern times, adolescents are grateful for friends supporting them. The internet influencer Akana, 2018 commends her friends for baking muffins or helping with a towed car. Shumway, 2018, p.23[34] lists fairly profane services friends do for each other, which regardless are meaningful to the recipient. Millington, 2019, p.55 cites a famous actress on friends helping her to start the day by getting her dressed and out of the door. Anecdotal evidence amongst youngsters points to roles such as substitute girlfriends and boyfriends helping single friends with chores that would be normally expected from a partner, such as helping to pick clothes, technical tasks such as fixing a computer/mobile or wake-up phonecalls before interviews. Practical help is the general function of how neighbours get to know and appreciate each other. Over time, it builds a track record of reliability (see 3.4) and consideration (see 4.3). As certain needs are predictable, it is also easy to reach out and do things on a hunch for a friend. The theme of older people requiring assistance from friends mentioned by Aristotle is getting increased attention by sociologists in recent years (see e.g. Vries, 2018 or Blieszner and Ogletree, 2017). With declining physical and health capabilities, services such as giving a lift to the community center, doctor or church service, helping with fixing things around the house or coping with modern technology become increasingly valuable to the elderly as family ties are fraying.

[34]Sometimes, we just need a ride to the airport. Friends can also meet some of our practical needs, take notes for you while you are out or watch your cat while you travel; they can bring you Taco Bell when you forgot your lunch at home or give you an extra call when they suspect you might have hit the snooze button on your alarm one time too many.

Practical takeaway
Do not think of practical help as outsourcing, but free. Think of it as an opportunity, how you can express your benevolence and devotion to your friends and they to you. It is the key avenue in how the meaning of relationships is demonstrated. If you don't believe it, talk to your grandparents.

Suggestions for thought

- To what degree are you aware of what your friends need on a practical level?
- How do you feel about helping a friend on a matter which they could alternatively outsource, e.g. moving house or babysitting? How would you feel about a friend offering or even insisting to help you on a matter which you would otherwise outsource?
- Where does a favour end and a genuine sacrifice start? What is the most important dimension of it (time, finance, pain or effort)?
- Do you know your key strengths, skills or assets are how you could help friends?

For statistics in sociological studies, question suggestions and weights in counting see H.

5.6 Embedding and circle bonding

This is about embedding the pair-wise friendship in a group of three, four or five people, each of whom complementing each other, enhancing each other's jokes, insights, listening and understanding capabilities and advice giving.

'But two, far from being the necessary number for Friendship, is not even the best' is how Lewis, 1960, p.91 starts his argument for multilateral friendship. He goes on to explain how two would 'delight to be joined by a third and fourth'.[35] Groups of four or five friends over a long time seem to have significant advantages over just disconnected bilateral friendships. I am not arguing that bilateral friendships are bad, but that bilateral friendships are best if they are embedded in a group of four. The theme of group friendship is for me the key takeaway of Lewis, 1960 'Four Loves' chapter on friendship. The key effect is 'Especially when the whole group is together, each bringing out all that is best, wisest, or funniest in all the others'. An economist or sociologist would rephrase this as 'the total is greater than the sum of its parts', and it is this effect that I find missing in

[35]'Hence true Friendship is the least jealous of loves. Two friends delight to be joined by a third, and three by a fourth, if only the newcomer is qualified to become a real friend.'

the classical sociological and psychological research on friendship[36]. Admittedly, the data requirements to quantify any effects of this type would be specific and enormous, and I will address the issue in the section 9.13 on smart bubbling.

As deep as our understanding and appreciation of our friend might be, there will still be aspects for the discovery that only other friends with their personality and humour will bring out. Lewis, 1960, p.92 makes this point about the death of a friend: 'Now that Charles is dead, I shall never again see Ronald's reaction to a specifically Caroline joke. Far from having more of Ronald, having him "to myself" now that Charles is away, I have less of Ronald.' Groups of friends thus exhibit humour and a quality and vivacity of discussion, that individual pairs in most cases will struggle to maintain. Whilst it is a matter of major cultural contention and discussion, I partially for this reason always preferred the game of Doppelkopf[37] over the game of Skat[38] as the accompanying side conversation just is a bit more diverse. Whilst not specifically referring to friendship circles, Rath, 2006 recommends us not to be just content with having one close friend at work, but according to research from Gallup significant additional benefits accrue with up to three close friends. While this is not guaranteed, often these won't be disjoined pairs, but the natural state at work is small circles who can go to lunch together. Anecdotally while many people do the network lunches bilaterally, the more social and relaxed lunches which come closest to the friendship style, are often groups of three or four, even though they are difficult to organise in times of busy outlook schedules.

Addressing the role of friend's circles in organisations and causes is a chicken and hen discussion. Lewis puts the friendship group at the founding of the social movement. He is criticised for this explicitly by Alberoni, 2016, p.62[39]. I would say that both paths are possible. A unifying cause is a platform on whose back friendships can be made well (see (5.2)). But Lewis' converse argument still holds. There are many examples, last but not least, of friends founding companies, where the friendship of the group underpins the entire exercise. Thus the movement or cause brought them together and exposed them to each other, but the friendship becomes deeper in the process than the movement would have warranted. The friendship is also the reason the collaboration works in the way it does and succeeds. Churchill and Roosevelt were united by the war against Hitler, but their key biographers write with detail on the deep friendship they developed and maintained throughout the years 1939-1945 and how it shaped their collaboration and trust at a foundational level going far beyond the day-to-day needs of effective coordination. This hints at the friendship being the dominant

[36]As a qualifier - sociological research is very aware of these mini-networks and circles, and societal properties such as homophily regarding gender, race, age etc., and studied to a great extent their role in society in providing support or giving advice. The criticism is more on the failure to addressing the mechanics in it, which factors give rise to their longevity and quality, whether it is humor and enjoyment, or simply acquaintance and knowledge of the other person etc.

[37]Doppelkopf is played with four people with 2 teams of 2. As partners change and with the possibility of one person dropping out, the game can perfectly accomodate even five people in an evening, allowing always one person to drop out to get beers, go to the restroom or answer a text.

[38]which is played as three - with one battling it out against the other two

[39]'Lewis errs because in reality the friendship group does not pre-exist the movement. There weren't twelve apostles and Jesus that at one point decided to create a movement. ... Of course, we make friends in movements. But it isn't the group of friends that makes the movement, it is in the movement that friends are made.'

theme on a personal level, even in the presence of a major common cause.

The building of small communities is a core theme in the early Christian church. Jesus himself either directly convenes his disciples[40] or strengthens the intra-group bonds in his group of friends[41]. Jesus doesn't ask his best friend to come to Gethsemane, but three closest friends (coincidentally the same number of friends that join Job in his trials). In fact, when you read both the gospels and the acts from the perspective of friendship, I find it quite remarkable how almost strategic both Jesus and Paul go about in fostering friendship in the early church community. In the movie 'Passion'[42] from Mel Gibson, this sentiment doesn't quite come through. The recent and in many regards rather unremarkable movie 'Risen'[43] however places a great emphasis of the apostles with Jesus in the middle as primarily a group of friends, who are then sent out on the mission. It is the warmth of the group that ultimately also envelops the Tribune Clavius played by Joseph Fiennes. As noted in Cuddeback, 2010, p.x[44] the formation of close friendship groups continues within the Christian tradition.

On a practical note specifically in looser social ventures (i.e. not corporations or movements for world peace) such as meetup.com groups, Internations regionals or expat oriented get-togethers, a small group of friends is the best way to run a social organisation or venture. Well-run Meetup or Internations groups almost always revolve around a small circle of friends, who pull in other friends to build a base critical mass. The base group comes and uses the occasion to set up a regular habit of coming together, whereas newcomers profit from the warm atmosphere and vibe established already. School or University reunions likewise are best organised and functional, if there is a core group of people who have maintained the friendship over the decades and provide a base for the others to latch onto.

Whereas Nehamas, 2016 example of a (rather dysfunctional) friendship triad ultimately breaks apart, I would argue that groups of three or four are also highly conducive to conflict resolution. There might be misunderstandings and fallout between two friends, but the opportunity to talk it through with a 'neutral', objective and moderating party allows for an effective discussion of the issue without loss of face. You may consider Matthew 18:16: 'But if they will not listen, take one or two others along, so that every matter may be established by the testimony of two or three witnesses.'. It is easy to notice that the existence of a mutual friend will usually be a sufficient pressure at least ensure an attempt of reconciliation. There is also a significant cost of failure to resolve. Whilst our pride and anger at one friend may be larger than our will to compromise for the sake of the friendship, the commendation of our other friends to 'just get over it' imposes the danger not only of loosing one but two or three friends if I continue to grandstand.

[40]Matt 17.1 'After six days Jesus took with him Peter, James and John the brother of James, and led them up a high mountain by themselves.' John 6.3 'Then Jesus went up on a mountainside and sat down with his disciples.'

[41]Mark 6:7 'Calling the Twelve to him, he began to send them out two by two and gave them authority over impure spirits.'

[42]https://www.imdb.com/title/tt0335345/

[43]https://www.imdb.com/title/tt3231054/

[44]'If we peel back our sometimes overly pious perceptions of the saints we will see something amazing - they almost always come in clusters. It is not by accident that when we think of St. Augustine, we think of Monica and Ambrose, when we think of St. Francis we think of Clare and Bonaventure, when we think of St. Ignatius of Loyola we think of Francis Xavier.'

Rather than the full blowout of the friendship as depicted by Nehamas, the test of friendship is usually the asynchronous development of different life circumstances. Some friends may be still single, others in a committed relationship, and yet others may be fully enveloped in family duties of work and children. It is then often down to the effort of a schmoozer to keep the team together (see Pahl, 2000, p.x[45]).

If friends are the family we choose, then circle building and fostering of mutual friendships is a key activity of managing this. And introducing new links in the network strengthens the whole. It is in this context that Paul in Romans 16 offers an absolute master class. He mentions no less than 26 friends of his to be greeted, including personal details on how he is connected to them. By putting their names into a document, it allows for anyone with access to this document to follow up on it and get to know them. He specifically commends Phoebe to be included in his friends' community. The practice of such recommendation letters for befriending has also a long tradition between monasteries in the middle ages, and in Mediterranean societies (e.g. see the role of the Ferman in Karl May's writing, or the role of introduction letters in medieval Jewish trading networks). The practice continues in our time in expat circles. When relocating from one expat community of an international metropolis to another, often the last months are filled with current friends recommending people to search out in the new location, who might share an interest or compatible personalities.

For me personally, creating such links is one of the most fulfilling activities imaginable and boons of a good network. Whilst some thought must be given, finding common ground between two people, such as a compatible humour or a personal mutual interest, are often sufficient grounds to make a first introduction, and much less contentious than playing cupid. In this sense bringing friends together over a party, barbecue or a dinner and just seeing links develop is also simply enjoyable, as in their interaction you find out new aspects of your friends you yourself would never have suspected. A mutual friend is probably the most powerful friendship totem to gift to another friend.

Practical takeaway

This is - with hospitality - my personal 'most important' activity. Friendship is most beautifully experienced in a group of four. If you had a group of friends in school or university, consider yourself 'on a mission from god - you got to get the band back together.'[a]

[a] Blues Brothers - `https://youtu.be/Q3ypX22-SYY?t=236`

Suggestions for thought

- If you compare your friendship groups of three, four or five friends with the bilateral friendships, how do they differ?

[45] 'But here the authors rehabilitate the informal schmoozers, who may not join anything formal but who nevertheless may play a critical role in holding friendship networks together and, indeed, in holding communities together, below the radar of any official measures.'

- Have you got a friends group that stayed together for a long time? If you had, but it disintegrated, what is to stop you from 'getting the band back together?'
- How good are you at introducing friends to each other or 'gifting a friend'?

For statistics in sociological studies, question suggestions and weights in counting see H.

5.7 Communion and hospitality

Best friends don't care if your house is clean. They care if you have wine.

Unknown

In German there is the saying 'love goes through the stomach', and Aristotle, 1925, 8.3[46] likewise says that strangers need to eat salt together before they can become friends. Eating together, and in one's home is a strong bond.

The theme of communion, commensality and hospitality can be split up into four themes:

1. sharing food to facilitate conversation,
2. inviting someone over for self-prepared food,
3. the bond of classical hospitality in ancient literature and traditional societies (which I will start with for chronological reasons I start with),
4. full hosting (stay-over).

Hosting someone (Xenia) is the oldest form of friendship-like bonding extended, and people even remembered it for years. One very early example is the anecdote of Diomedes and Glaucon in the Iliad 6[47], who are about to do battle, when they discover their grandparents ate together, and decide that their bond (friendship) extends to them also and that they should not fight. As the gods travel often disguised to test mortals (also see the stories of the angels in Genesis 1819 and Hebrews 13.2[48]), the practice of showing hospitality to strangers was justified by self-interest in order not to offend gods. The socially beneficial role in creating bonds is recognized all around. Olyan, 2017, p.5[49] likewise mentions sharing food as a characteristic of friendship in the Hebrew bible. The intensity of

[46]'as the proverb says, men cannot know each other till they have 'eaten salt together'; nor can they admit each other to friendship or be friends till each has been found lovable and been trusted by each.'

[47]Perseus link `http://data.perseus.org/citations/urn:cts:greekLit:tlg0012.tlg001.perseus-eng1:6.191-6.231`

[48]'Do not neglect to show hospitality to strangers, for by so doing some people have entertained angels without knowing it.'

[49]'In addition, the friend is described in Ps 41:10 as 'okellahmi, "one who eats my food," suggesting a role for hospitality, including commensality, as a component of friendship.'

the bond that hospitality is supposed to create is illustrated also in the universal condemnation when it is broken[50].

Indeed, it is a hallmark of Jesus and the disciples, as they recognise him through the breaking of bread, a theme followed up by Christian books and sermons such as N. Lee, 2015-07-01. In this context there is also the significance in the initiation, as Jesus frequently invites himself[51] to someone's house to initiate the friendship (a thought that would of course abhor freedom and independence advocates such as Alberoni). To add insult to injury, not only would he invite himself, but subsequently on occasion suggest to his hosts that they should also invite all the poor people out from the street until the house is full. There is an urban legend[52] about Henry Nouwen often quoted on this matter in sermons:

> Henri Nouwen, the great spiritual writer, was going to a monastery for a retreat. The monks observed vows of silence, and the retreat was to be meditative and prayerful. Nouwen was delayed and was late getting to the monastery on that miserable, rainy night. He rang the bell, well after bedtime, and was met at the door by one of the brothers. The brother warmly greeted him, took his wet coat, brought him to the kitchen and made him a cup of tea. They chatted in the late night hours and Nouwen began to relax and feel ready for the retreat. But he knew this monk was supposed to observe silence, so he finally asked him, "Why are you willing to sit and talk with me?" The monk replied: "Of all the duties of the Christian faith and the rules of my order, none is higher than hospitality."

If Christianity is all about connecting with people, then hospitality is an if not the golden road to it (see Willis and Clements, 2017)[53]. The Church of England's Alpha course likewise brings people together to bond over food, with the church hosting for the meal. Anecdotal evidence here is that many a friendship was created in this context. Secular supper clubs apply the same principle to bring people together and bond them over time. And it is not just dinner or a simple meal - Jesus loved parties (see wedding and turning water into wine), indeed the parable of the lost silver piece is sometimes translated as the woman throwing a party for her friends and neighbours[54] as the right line of action. Sharing a meal is simply connecting. It is in my view no coincidence, that two of the key scenes in the New Testament of Jesus reconnecting with his disciples and friends are over shared food (Emmaus breaking the bread, eating Peter's broiled fish at the lakeside). Providing food (and drink) is sustaining, it is meeting your friends' need on a most basic level.

---

[50]See also Matt 26:23 'The one who has dipped his hand into the bowl with me will betray me.'

[51]Luke 19.5: 'When Jesus reached the spot, he looked up and said to him, 'Zacchaeus, come down immediately. I must stay at your house today.'

[52]Following up this lead with the Nouwen foundation - thanks to chief archivist Gabrielle Earnshaw for following up on this - it was classified as unverifiable, the original quote seemingly coming from Rev. J. Burton Williams, 'The reward of a disciple'

[53]'Since people will sooner enter a living room than a church, hospitality is a natural and effective way to build relationships for Christ'

[54]Luke 15:8-9 'Or suppose a woman has ten silver coins[a] and loses one. Doesn't she light a lamp, sweep the house and search carefully until she finds it? And when she finds it, she calls her friends and neighbors together and says, 'Rejoice with me; I have found my lost coin."

But also in contemporary times, Nelson, 2016 and Shumway, 2018 emphasise eating and drinking together for friendship bonding. R. Dunbar, 2016 devotes an entire report to the importance of people sharing a drink for social connections. The easiest way to get together in western culture is indeed over a drink. This can be a pint in the pub or a few cans shared when sitting out on a park bench or somebody's back garden or living room. Whilst alcoholism and substance abuse are social ills of grand significance, alcohol by itself in limited quantities has pro-social effects, and has supported western society for millennia. Hockings and R. Dunbar, 2019 explore the phenomenon of alcohol in the formation of social ties at length in an edited volume.

The modern youth phenomenon of Couchsurfing, where people open their homes to travelling strangers in a bid for good conversation, companionship and in no few cases ultimately friendship is a further indicator that eating and drinking together is incredibly helpful in the establishment of relationships. Being a good cook - as evidenced by profile reviews - is a good selling proposition on a profile. The push from distanced coexistence with neighbours to initiation of friendship development can also most effectively be done over food. Degges-White and Borzumato-Gainey, 2011 point to sharing food on the porch of the house. This imagery beautifully features in the film 'Gran Torino', where Clint Eastwood's grumpiness and disregard for his neighbours is broken down, essentially inundating him with food[55].

Habits are best build around food. When talking to people about best practices to maintain friendship, repeatedly food was involved. Extending invitations there is the closed and open form: extending an invitation to a selected closed group extends value to the invited. You are spending time and effort specifically for their benefit. You potentially tailor drink and food composition to their needs. On the other hand there is the issue of exclusion. Inviting four colleagues[56] out of ten leaves the other six out. Inviting 20 people to a wedding leaves 40 out not invited. Yet it is still better to invite people over than not to do it at all, and specifically in dense cities the limitations of space are a clearly acceptable excuse.

On the other hand there are open invitations. One habit I thought particularly suitable for copying was to hold a regular open house. A family of four designated a fixed weekday of the month as the friends' dinner evening, cooked a simple but ample meal like a spaghetti bolognese or a stew, and any friend of the family could swing by[57]. It was a fixture in the diary of many of their friends, and people tried to make it. When I was living in Tokyo, with friends we started a monthly food and movie night, and it was also one of those regular fixtures for us. Such an activity is also really effective to build and maintain a circle of friends (5.6), be it one for board games, philosophical discussions or just hanging out, a few bottles of wine and a pot of food is all such an evening needs. And if your cooking skills are bordering on the likelihood of inflicting physical harm, you can always just provide your space and kitchen and get a more talented friend to volunteer their skills. Finally treating friends for dinner at your home is more time costly, but financially substantially more efficient (provided you have the space), and thus

[55]'No more, please... is this that chicken dumpling' `https://youtu.be/s4MLZ4WsXc4`

[56]The number choice of course depends highly on the facilities, but generally the three couples - six people seemed to be the optimal mix of liveliness and ease of preparation.

[57]Thanks to the freezer it is possible to aim for a bit more and let nothing go to waste.

can be more inclusive if you have differences in affluence in your friends' circle.

Where because of space or other circumstances having people over for a meal is difficult, the availability of third places is important. Oldenburg, 1999 emphasises how various social strata and groups bonded at these great good places over eating together. Conversely, well designed social places with affordable food often have communities developing around them. The canteen of a workplace is a designated social space, and can facilitate people at work get to know each other and bond as they keep having lunch together.

The more intense form of hospitality is hosting, where the guest gets to stay a night or several. The activity of hosting is substantially shorter than the activity of living together as explored in 4.14. The principle is however the same. Having someone stay with you for a few days opens up your home differently than if you have them over for dinner. It allows them to be part of your life, to see you in real life. For the friendship it doesn't matter whether it is at the beginning of a friendship, like on hospitality exchange sites, or later, when friends not only come to visit you in your city, but lodge on your couch for a few days. It is just great for bonding. Making it a priority to have a guest room or a convertible couch is also a costly but incredibly effective commitment to maintaining friendships. And once you have the capacity to host, you will find yourself wanting to see it being used.

Practical takeaway
If your apartment or house allows it *somehow* consider an open door pot luck once a month. Pick a fixed date within the month, and let your friends know they are welcome to barge in. They can let you know a day before or just swing by, and it might be just four of you or ten. You can make it a movie night, game night, chat night, philosophy night. But food on the table, some drinks and good conversation is all that is required for a great evening.

Suggestions for thought

- How did you feel last time you were invited to a friend's house for lunch or dinner?
- How suitable is your apartment for having friends over for lunch or dinner? Have you got a spontaneous cooking plan for such opportunities? If not, have you ever thought about doing a pot-luck lunch[a]?
- Can you have friends staying at your place for a few days? Have you ever tried?
- Do you think you could adopt a hospitable attitude in general?

[a] A pot-luck lunch is where you provide a place and some drinks, and each of the attendees brings a dish. This way your time-effort to organize it is substantially reduced. Great for people without cooking skills, but a good place.

For statistics in sociological studies, question suggestions and weights in counting see H.

5.8 Encouragement and challenge

> I don't need a friend who changes when I change and who nods when I nod; my shadow does that much better.
>
> Plutarch

> Good friends don't let you do stupid things...alone.
>
> Unknown

This is about our friends seeing the best in us but holding us accountable to achieve it. This is both stick and carrot, cajoling our friends to push towards their goals, and challenge them whether they are doing enough, and helping them to keep up the spirit in difficult situations.

Human condition is (often) riddled with insecurity. We dream, but we are unsure of whether we can attain it, and even when we set out in pursuit of a goal we tire out and lose sight and hope. In these moments a friend can come alongside us, and encourage us to go for it in the first place, or pick us up and put us on the path again. Encouragement is about telling your friends that you believe in them achieving a certain goal of theirs and that their life will be better if they gave it a shot. Words of affirmation is one of the key love languages, and it is not just about appreciation, but a lot of it is encouragement like 'I believe you can do that'. Stories of this theme usually include the job change that a work friend might be planning. It might be risky, but if it is good for him you grieve a little for yourself and the decreased time for interaction you will have with your friend, but you encourage to pursue the new opportunity. Even if you don't believe the goal, friends can be encouraged to go for it as you accept it is really in their desire and they need to have a stab at it before being able to let go (if pursuing it will not have major financial or health risks).

If your friend has already set out on the path, encouragement means fuelling the hope in the friend that she/he is going to persevere. It means maintaining the positivity level as they are grinding through tedious and mundane activity, it can be accompanying them on a jog and pushing them along. In the extreme case, it can mean Sam picking up Frodo and carrying him towards the cave entry of Mount Doom[58]. Examples here include friends pushing you to stay in school or college and not drop out. Encouragement can also include casual reminders of not so active but recommendable goals, such as to take care of ourselves. In particular, in our busy lives, with work, children, and all the obligations, we often just prod along. We know that we should give ourselves some rest and recover but often just do not. It is our friends who can see this development more clearly, and can and often do encourage us to take a step back, ensure we recharge our batteries.

[58]Movie Lord of the Rings - Return of the King `https://youtu.be/BKIgv8AhffA`

Encouragement is a deeply Christian activity and mentioned several times particular in Paul's Epistles (1 Thess 5:11[59], Hebrews 10:24[60] and Ephesians 4:29[61]). Building up the people around you is a typical activity of a positive and humble mindset. Rath, 2006, p.87[62] identified this important function and built a whole role from it in 'Vital friends'.

As with all aspects of friendship having an influence on us, the limits of what is appropriate can differ from person to person's comfort level and the quality of the relationship. One key item is choice of place, and this primarily means not in front of others (Millington, 2019, p.11[63]). The other is having an agreement to challenge or criticize your friend. There is the phrase of accountability buddy, who is a friend specifically given both permission and duty to hold you accountable against agreed goals, even though this might not be welcome to hear at a future time (Wiest, 2020-04-30[64]). The pattern is particularly frequently applied with painful or frustrating themes such as finishing a dissertation, sports goals and weight loss. Despite the agreement to follow through and be held accountable, this does not always end well as Degges-White and Borzumato-Gainey, 2011, ch.3[65] gives an example of.

It is also not always the right thing. Sometimes critical feedback is required more than encouragement. Sometimes we need that friend to tell us 'I see you are really excited or have made your decision, but that is a really stupid idea'. This is if your friend is e.g. about to sink all his assets into a business idea that you think is really not going to work. Your duty of caring then involves at least voicing your concern, rather than 'loyal' encouragement. Sometimes we have been in a difficult situation and now see a way out. This may include a difficult relationship or a really hard job. Then sometimes encouragement means the friend telling 'I think you are right, cut your losses and run, it will work out' and sometimes it is 'leaving your partner would be really [stupid, bad,...], hang in there it is going to get better'.

Taken to the next level, encouragement becomes the 'pushing out of the comfort zone'. Whereas encouragement respects boundaries of privacy and comfort, pushing out of comfort zone is defined by breaking through these. The 'kick in the rear' is an appropriate image showing this caring but determinate transgres-

[59]'Therefore encourage one another and build one another up, just as you are doing.'

[60]'And let us consider how to stir up one another to love and good works, not neglecting to meet together, as is the habit of some, but encouraging one another, and all the more as you see the Day drawing near. '

[61]'Let no corrupting talk come out of your mouths, but only such as is good for building up, as fits the occasion, that it may give grace to those who hear.'

[62]`https://theweek.com/articles/739502/8-kinds-friends-need-happy-life` 'Builders are great motivators ...'

[63]'They motivate you and bring out the best in you. Good friends challenge you to take risks and encourage you to fulfil your potential. They don't egg you on, don't mock you or belittle you in front of others.'

[64]'The friend who holds you accountable is the one who privately, and gracefully, points out your patterns, tells you that you deserve better, who reminds you of commitments you didn't follow through with.'

[65]'Don't nag your friends and do try to make them feel good. A friend and I decided to join a weight-loss club together last spring. I needed to lose a lot more weight than she did, but she was 'über eager' for us to help each other stay motivated. This worked fine until I got sidelined by some personal struggles, and rather than being empathic and accepting, my friend started nagging me about going to the meetings, exercising more, everything. Support I wanted, guilt-tripping I didn't need!'

sion. The necessary condition is having faith that your friend can do something that will be highly beneficial to the person, even though they lack this faith themselves. A statement about friends to this end is that 'they will do everything in their power to push you forward and fulfil your dreams'. Accepting such a statement pre-absolves your friends from several potentially intrusive acts[66].

I have to admit I am a big fan of this habit. Autobiographically speaking, I would not do any sport if it were not for the persistent coaxing of my friends. I intellectually understand that some exercise is necessary to maintain the body functional, but when it comes to going on that jog, I have had zero desire and energy. And it was only a combination of persistent reminders of some friends to start back up and then keep at it that has in the past decade prevented me from substantial weight gain and further loss of fitness. It is necessary to point out that with such activities one reminder or one person - even if it is the best friend - is usually not enough. With doctoral theses and similar projects, it is common that towards the end you just don't want to deal with it anymore. However, all your friends asking you 'So how is the dissertation going?' is really annoying, but the irritation does (usually) translate into energy to get the darn thing done. Similarly, knowing that your friends will ask you about your latest jog or last gym session might prompt you to ensure that the last such activity was not a month ago. Examples I have heard are ringing friends out of bed in the morning to go jogging, under protests and 'I hate you for doing this' comments, but general appreciation for the effort and concern. On this I have been both at the dealing and receiving end. The attitude with which such activity is usually licensed is 'I know you hate me for making you do this, but I will be there with you, investing my time and undergoing pain myself'. Rath, 2006, p.124 provides also an example[67] of a woman giving in to her friend Kathy to join her doing sports to sort out a painful back. It can be also really helpful to very introverted people, such as playfully threatening to end the friendship if the shy friend doesn't accompany you to that terrifying social event (e.g. dancing classes in high school). All of course - and this is the important bit - needs to be motivated by their benefit: the experience needs to expand their mind or confidence - you need to be confident that they will be better after experience. I am a big fan of this aspect within some limits: some agency and free choice still needs to be ultimately remain with the friend. It would be too far to burn a 'bridge of no return' (though you may pretend that you did). There are two parts to it - one side is that given how close the friendship is, your friend owes something to you, and the other side is acceding to it and saying, yes, I will probably hate it, but because it is you, well, looks like you are serious and hence I will have to indulge you. And it is a quid pro quo, if you make your friend do that 5km run they really don't want to do, there is no way you can chicken out of attending their improv-comedy event with audience participation for good measure.

Apart from sport, degrees and work at crucial life events or situations, this activity is important to get us up on our feet. While friends usually are not equipped to deal single-handedly with a major depression, they are uniquely positioned to cheer us up and push us to move forward. When loosing a partner in a painful

[66] E.g. ringing your doorbell at 6 a.m. for a joint jog or temporarily emptying your stashes of chocolate and ice cream while you are away.

[67] 'My good friend Kathy ...'

process, i.e. death or an acrimonious separation, it is often friends who push us to go back 'out there'. We might feel not ready, and be totally sure that we really do not want to date, but allow ourselves to be strong armed into going for that date. It is trusting in the capability of our friend to assess our state better than us.

Practical takeaway
The first step in encouragement is knowing what to encourage and challenge your friend about. What is their dream that they want to achieve? It allows you to from time to time enquire whether they still have their eyes on the goal.
You can also ask a really old friend for an activity that they would want you to try. Up the ante by committing to do it before hearing the answer. They may come up with your childhood aspiration you long forgot about.

Suggestions for thought

- Would your friends see you as a source of encouragement in their life? What items do you mostly encourage to pursue?
- How happy are you to receive encouragement? Have there been key encouragements in your life that came from friends?
- How happy are you for a friend to push you or to hold you accountable to your goals? How far are they allowed to go with it?
- Have you ever really hard-pushed a friend for the last stretch because them reaching this goal was important to them, even though it became temporarily strenuous for the relationship?

For statistics in sociological studies, question suggestions and weights in counting see H.

5.9 Effect change

> We've been friends for so long I can't remember which one of us is the bad influence.
>
> Unknown

Our friends influence us, while we spend time with them, but often long beyond that, potentially even after their death. The habits, jokes and life improvements stay with us for a long time. Friends influence us in a variety of ways:

1. First there is an automatic **imitation** of habit. There needs to be nothing specific about it, we just do it, because we see it done or because we just do it as well without thinking about it. An example is young children learning words from their friend. They hear a joke or a word, and then continue to use it themselves.

2. A second path is **direct inspiration**. People see friends study hard or excel in sports or push through a stringent diet or do non-alcoholic lent, and they take the inspiration to copy them. Indeed, as they see themselves in their friends, they can infer from them the capability that they can complete the program themselves too.

3. The third path is **direct encouragement** of friends. If they are concerned with us say eating unhealthily or not taking care of us, they can say that they have noticed something and that they would recommend or ask us to at least think about doing something about it. This can be even anticipated encouragement. We see what our friends like and we form ourselves in order to conform. Peer pressure, even if just implicit, is a powerful force: all but the most independently minded of people essentially want to be part of the tribe they are in and be respected by it. This aspect is dealt with in 4.10.

4. The fourth and most extreme path is that our friends use the friendship as a **leverage** to get us to do something . This can be negative, such as criminal behaviour, or positive for us. Whilst friendship is a loving relationship, it is usually not an unconditional and unlimitedly accepting friendship, but also a just and partly judgmental friendship. Examples here could be friends threatening to withdraw from a friendship if certain destructive behaviour is not stopped.

Aside from our parents or spouse, our friends know us best, and hence they are also the most effective in getting us to change, whether by active suggestion or passive example. But change of personality is not just a matter of good and evil, or virtue, but also of personal nuances such as humour, interests, preferences and eating habits. All those items however could be covered between encouragement, challenge and guidance. The separation of effect and change from these comes from the theme's fundamental nature. Thus the question arises whether it is a necessary item of friendship that we change through it tangibly and beyond how e.g. a mere acquaintance or coworker would change us? In being prepared for the friend through our interaction in the relationship to change us, whether actively or passively, but definitely in substantial ways, we show trust, validation and choice.

Apart from the direct impact vectors given from (1) to (4) there is also a fifth theme to be considered - observed by Nehamas, 2016, ch.6: it might not be our friends directly who change us, but we change and develop ourselves in the safe space they provide us with to explore ourself and our ideas. Our friend also has impact on us through the interaction, by exposing us to other ideas, people, mentioning jobs, themes. We might meet other friends through them and maybe also our future or current spouse. All of this results in us growing in the context, not melding or growing towards each other, but definitely incorporating parts of the other person in our own personality. And as a result, when we look back on a friendship, maybe after many years, we don't just remember the fun we had, but we are aware of the impact they had on our lives, and in most cases are grateful for it.

In the ultimate consequence, part of us becomes **part of our friends** and vice versa ('Part of my personality is defined by X and the experience with them'). We hear a joke from a friend and completely internalise it. We copy a way of sniggering, a peculiar phrase or a certain way of arguing for something. The legacy of certain defining moments stays with us forever. Knowing our friend changed (ideally for the better) because of us will stay with us. I am not an immortality fanatic; I think many of us dramatically overstate the significance of what we do and the need to leave a legacy. However, the parallels of the effect we have on people and Harry Potter's horcruxes[68] can be interesting to think about. We do not of course need to split our souls in an excruciating ritual, but our time spent with our friend over the years compounds to a significant part of our life. And when the friend dies, and all those memories and changes die with them, the parallel to Voldemort's agony with Harry Potter picking off the horcruxes one by one may be very similar to the experience of an elderly, who is the last of a close circle of friends who all die before them (cf. Nehamas, 2016, ch. 6[69]). The **see part of oneself in the friend** theme thus has two parts, the simple 'similarity of thinking, background and values', and the substantially more precious of similarity of little traits mutually acquired through years of friendship.

For the ancient philosophers, the key and purpose of influence was the development of virtue. They were however acutely aware of influence working both toward virtue and vices, and thus used the argument of social influence to recommend a thorough vetting of potential friends before exposing ourselves to this influence. This concern of choosing friends of good character echoes in modernity (see J.R. Miller, 1897, ch.5[70] or Cuddeback, 2010, p.63[71]). The agony of parents of 'choosing' the right kindergarten or school for their children to a large degree comes down to perceptions of the social (and hence moral) quality of the peers at the institution, from which their offspring is likely to choose her/his friends and thus become influenced by. For adults, many people quote a saying attributed to John Rohn: 'You are the average of the five people you spend the most time with'. The extent of the 'are' is however doubtful, indeed it is limited by research of the school of positive psychology, which points to about 50 % of our personality being fixed by genetics, another 30 % by nurture and only 20 % varying over the decades (see e.g. Seligman, 2004). However already our parents and some work colleagues shape us a bit, thus what our friends can influence is most likely within the 5-10 % range (ignoring the worst-case scenario of our friend getting us into deep crime or drugs). Still, within the possible variability, arguably our friends can substantially contribute to our personality and thus happiness, and detract from it both by absence and being 'bad friends'. They can also influence anything from our habits to our diets (see Fletcher, Bonell, and Sorhaindo, 2011).

---

[68]An object into which a dark wizard puts part of his soul and thus themselves in order to make themselves immortal - see `https://harrypotter.fandom.com/wiki/Horcrux?jwsource=em` and `https://www.youtube.com/watch?v=OGtMGiqJRYw`

[69]'Friendship provides many such benefits and their loss can be painful, but mourning the end of a friendship is not mourning the loss of its benefits. It is mourning the loss of oneself.' Nehamas explains how we mourn for ourselves for the options of activities we lost, but also the part of ourself we had in the friend and now lost.

[70]'Nothing in life is more important than the choosing of friends. Many young people wreck all by wrong choices, taking into their life those who by their influence drag them down. Many a man's moral failure dates from the day he chose a wrong friend.'

[71]'Thus, it is of particular importance that the young have friends of good moral character.'

Practical takeaway
Allow yourself to be changed. Take your time, ponder over advice given, wait for a second opinion, but eventually know that your friends have your best interest at heart.

Suggestions for thought

- To what degree are you aware of changes in your life, where your friends had a substantial impact just by being there with the right comment at the right time?
- Did you ever experience a change in yourself more because of the consistent effort of a key friend?
- Do you have a friend who credits you with a major shift or change in his life? How does that make you feel?

For statistics in sociological studies, question suggestions and weights in counting see H.

5.10 Guidance and giving direction

Helping a friend make sense of a situation, talking through the pros and cons, asking questions that helps him/her structure and get perspective and using our own experience and insight to support the decision process is helpful and meaningful for our friends wellbeing.

The process of character development with friends has four levels:

1. allowing the friend to emote and think through by himself. Guidance or interaction is minimal, the key is the expression of thought (This element is covered in 5.3),
2. providing observational and honest feedback, which can include normative specific elements ('You were a jerk, stop it'). This is what the emphasis is on here,
3. the friend acting as a sparrings partner or a collaborator on equal footing,
4. the friend acts as coach or mentor (i.e. senior to me).

The key function of giving honest feedback has several elements. For the friend to give appropriate and effective honest feedback, several requirements need to be in place. We must be convinced of the authenticity and honesty of our friend[72], we must have trust in him, and we must be convinced of his goodwill and respect. Finally, honest feedback needs to be delivered with a minimum

[72]It was difficult to decide whether honest feedback was more in a bracket with the feedback part of guidance or the honesty part. The general sentiment seems to be that that both relevance and actual proof of honesty are providing honest feedback.

of kindness. The function of the friend to give honest feedback is the key benefit to friendship according to Cicero, 1923, p.197 and p.199[73]:

> As, therefore, it is characteristic of true friendship both to give and to receive advice and, on the one hand, to give it with all freedom of speech, but without harshness, and on the other hand, to receive it patiently, but without resentment, so nothing is to be considered a greater bane of friendship than fawning[74], cajolery[75], or flattery.

The Bible[76] likewise recommends the use of honest feedback as a conflict resolution tool on several occasions (see 3.3). Honest feedback I think is this way the key to understand the mirror function of friendship (7.1), where 'each can be said to provide a mirror in which the other may see himself' Pahl, 2000, p.22. This mirror can range to the most mundane trivia to sensitive aspects of the friendship (see Millington, 2019, p.11[77]). This mirror function however only works, if the other party is willing to accept the feedback without kicking up a fuss (see Greif, 2009, ch.9[78] or Nelson, 2016, p.32[79]). Feedback is important, particularly for young people, and not just the guidance from elderly, but the on-the-spot feedback from people who understand their situation. Feedback in this sense is often not highlighting a completely blind area, but emphasising criticism of something that is usually known. It is however the friends' comment that gives it value. As Cocking and Kennett, 1998 puts it: 'The evaluative creative content in the interpretations offered by my friend makes them dynamic; they will often change the way I view myself and how some character trait of mine is realized, even when the trait in question is already well known to me.'

With all the eulogy on honesty and feedback, there is also timing to be considered. More in the romantic self-help literature, one key issue over and over emphasised is that patience, empathy and understanding must come (chronologically) first before feedback induces a potential problem-solving part of the conversation, and friendship is little different (see also Greif, 2009, ch.2[80]. There are situations, in particular, when you are still in public, when loyalty in form of vocal support is preferred from the friend before privately being told how and where you might be wrong.

---

[73]See also p.197: 'for friends frequently must be not only advised but also rebuked, and both advice and rebuke should be kindly received when given in a spirit of goodwill. ... but much more troublesome is complaisance, which, by showing indulgence to the sins of a friend, allows him to be carried headlong away.' and p.199 'Now we must despair of the safety of the man whose ears are so closed to truth that he cannot hear what is true from a friend.'

[74]displaying exaggerated flattery or affection

[75]Coaxing or flattery intended to persuade someone to do something.

[76]Matthew 18:15 'if your brother or sister sins against you go and show them their fault just between the two of you if they listen to you you have won them over.' and Proverbs 27:05-06 'An open rebuke is better than hidden love! Wounds from a sincere friend are better than many kisses from an enemy'.

[77]'Don't have a fringe cut, they just don't suit you.' 'He seems a great guy but since you've been with him you always talk about the issues you're having rather than the joy-' 'I love going out with you but you are a messy drunk at the end of the night and it spoils my fun.'

[78]'For instance, if someone does something I think is wrong, I can just tell them about it without us getting all worked up about it. That is part of what a friend can do.'

[79]'knowing you can trust each other for an honest reply without it reflecting on the relationship'

[80]'... people who can be there for you at the same time they can give you both kinds of feedback—they can give you the positive, and they can tell you when you are ridiculous.'

On a more general level, the trust that my friend provides honest feedback enables a range of processes. Feedback is one of the key function of (3) collaborating with a friend (see Alberoni, 2016, p.117[81]), e.g. by having them proof read a book, discuss projects at work, improve presentations and the like. And of course it also is a sine qua non for any (4) coaching and mentoring.

(3) The next level of guidance is **sparring** with your friend. You don't give direct guidance, but ask questions and discuss. This covers statements such as 'When I have an important decision to make, X talks me through pro's and cons', 'X helps me figure out how to get what I want'. You let your friend to do the work themselves, but ensure that if they take the decision, they have thought through all eventualities. You are the sounding board. Methods here can be adversarial sparring, playing devil's advocate, or creative sparring with pointing out opportunities and other alternative options. You skirmish, you dispute, you raise objections, all to improve the decision-making capability of your friend. Potentially you also actively help to break the decision down. This process partially overlaps with encouraging and challenging. You help to think things through and visualise scenarios. Proverbs 27:17 says about this - As iron sharpens iron, so a friend sharpens a friend. Apart from general exploration, contribution of interesting topics and narratives, sparring is a key function of the 'mind opener' role of Rath, 2006. Sparring requires several traits, apart from honesty and integrity it requires also critical thinking (3.8) and a good understanding of your friend and his potential weaknesses (4.6). Sparring and discussion also takes patience, as you do not seek to just solve the problem, but just enhance the process of problem discovery and solution your friend is on. I find yet another great image of this in the walk to Emmaus, where Jesus rather than blurting out the solution spends the entire time walking with his disciples and discussing the issues, and only at the very end of the day provides the 'give-away-clue'(Luke 24:13-35). Rather than pushing a decision, it is a very effective after-action review and of great meaning to them developing an understanding for the prior events. As you try to overcome your own subjectivity and bias of a situation you struggle to understand, you can discuss it with a sparring friend.

(4) **Giving advice** both asked for and unasked for is deciding to have a direct influence on your friend. These are statements like 'X points me in the right direction', 'X give you advice', 'X always knows what is best for you, but you don't always listen'. Aristotle, 1925, 8.1 says that advice given by the friend 'helps the young, too, to keep from error'. Cicero, 1923, p.157 and p.199[82] emphasises giving and receiving of advice as a key function of friendship. The Bible likewise advocates the giving of advice to friends (e.g. Proverbs 27:09[83] or Colossians 3:16[84]). YouTube talks (TED and others) on the roles of your important friends always

[81]'All we want from our friend is an honest, impartial assessment. This is precisely what Gerber says when he writes to Jhering that the latter's problem is a consequence of his being an inventor. He gives his friend the recognition he deserves but that others can never give him.' The capability to give feedback is a qualifying criterion for the friendship of the two lawyers.

[82]p.157 'in friendship let the influence of friends who are wise counsellors be paramount, and let that influence be employed in advising, not only with frankness, but, if the occasion demands, even with sternness, and let the advice be followed when given.' and p.199 'As, therefore, it is characteristic of true friendship both to give and to receive advice and, on the one hand, to give it with all freedom of speech, but without harshness, and on the other hand, to receive it patiently, but without resentment'

[83]'The heartfelt counsel of a friend is as sweet as perfume and incense.'

[84]'Let the message of Christ dwell among you richly as you teach and admonish one another'

mention one friend to give you advice in key situations. The MBTI friendship classifications[85] emphasize the different types of guidance and advice given by various types of friends. Rath, 2006, p.129 designs a full role around the concept called the Navigator[86]. Guidance can also be provided by giving good books as gifts or forwarding good articles to your friends (c.f. Hunt, 2019-12-13). I have always appreciated people giving me books, and there are a couple of books I keep giving out to as a top 5 on general life advice.

The function of guidance is interesting for friendship because it so clearly elaborates an aspect of reciprocity, and that is at least for guidance reciprocity is not 'in kind' (see Rath, 2006, p.78). Giving guidance inherently means that one person is the 'higher', the 'wiser', the 'more clever', at least in this moment. In return the advice giving person is receiving the appreciation of his competence and the trust in his character, which might be equally affirming, enjoyable and meaningful. Possibly such an element of disparity is structural in the relationship, giving credence to a role model of the friendship process rather than insisting on the Aristotelian symmetry of character and status (see 9.3).

One item of sensitivity is the giving of unsolicited advice. For some people giving unsolicited advice signals disrespect and a putting yourself above the other. This action thus violates the tenet of equality. On advice and guidance, I have erred on the side of too much rather than too little. My opinion is that showing options to choose from expands the picture and is in almost all situations positive, unless fast decision making is necessary. Maybe one might not put it as guidance, but phrase it as 'here is a thought you could consider too'. The justification is that I have benefited tremendously through the advice from friends. Virtually every time, as even the process of thinking about such proposals and conjectures made by a friend is beneficial to the eventual decision. I have benefitted specifically several times where people overstepped their boundaries of propriety on advice giving. I think the key of giving advice is not being tactful about it, on that side honesty and frankness dominate (see Cicero). But more important is not sulking or feeling rejected by the advice receiver if they think the advice doesn't resonate with them, maybe at that point in time or maybe never. There have been several recommendations made to me that needed to sink in or needed to be reinforced by others over time. It is unrealistic to expect your friend to change his life just because you recommend a change of behaviour. But you expressing precisely one aspect of criticism or suggestion (you should exercise more, you are a bit of a blabbermouth), it opens the opportunity for me to remember it three months or three years later. And when somebody else repeats the suggestion or criticism, I can observe 'funny you should say that, A and B have said exactly the same some time ago' . I can then adopt the feedback at the third time or fourth time it is made. When we get into situations where we do not accept someones advice, only to do so some time later on someone else's suggestion, we should give credit to the first contributor[87].

---

[85]See E.2

[86]`https://theweek.com/articles/739502/8-kinds-friends-need-happy-life` 'Navigators are the friends who give you advice and keep you headed in the right direction...'

[87]The classical stereotype is of course that parents or best friends can suggest us for years to quit smoking, start dieting or go exercising, yet at the first hint of a suggestion from a potential love interest we stand ready and throw the cigarettes away. Sometimes life is just unfair and discriminating, even to friends and family.

Regardless of whether it happens via just listening, sparring or direct guidance, the role of friends is crucial to us not just in adolescence, when we shape our identity. It is our friends who we turn to most when we notice that we need to review our identity and make adjustments in order to master the years still ahead of us. And as - according to Seligman, 2004 - we change approximately 10-20 % every decade, this process of change never stops, and neither does the need for our friends to support us in it.

Practical takeaway
Change is two-fold: I think if you think your friend can improve their life in some way it is more important they know this than to adhere to respect of not giving unsolicited advice. As a friend with good will it is your job to think how your friends can become 'better', whatever that means. Say what you think openly but with tact and only once. And then you need to forget about giving this recommendation. Change will come when they hear the suggestion the third or fourth time from a different person. You did your part. The rest is theirs.

Suggestions for thought

- How good are you at receiving and accepting negative feedback from friends? How comfortable are you in telling a friend off when they show inappropriate behaviour to you or others?
- How much guidance do you receive from your friends vs. your other circles (work, family, ...)? In what way does the advice differ?
- To what degree does the process of reaching a potential insight matter to you? Do you prefer more the discursive Socratic way of discussion or the flat advice given straight?
- How do you feel about unsolicited (but well meaning) advice? Is it a show of concern or slightly disrespectful?

For statistics in sociological studies, question suggestions and weights in counting see H.

5.11 Exploration and discovery

Exploration and discovery is the joined activity of exploring - both physically out into the world, museums and new places, as well as mentally to new topics, theories and experiences, satisfying our mutual curiosity.

There are two themes to this:
(1) discovery through a person where the friend with all his experiences is the gateway and facilitator to new insights, or
(2) where we explore together by bouncing ideas and thoughts off each other.

(1) Through our friend's experience we are exposed to new topics and interests. We **discover** new ideas and theories. This is often unpredictable as we get to know them better as the friendship develops, but even after decades of friendship we may be surprised that a friend has picked up a completely different hobby or interest that we just did not have on the radar at all. Through our friends our mind gets opened (see Rath, 2006, p.123[88]). In our current time information is ubiquitous, and we can get documentaries on National Geographic, and anyway, there is an information overload. But just decades ago really intently listening to travel stories of friends or doing evenings of slide show documentaries was a great pastime, as we imagined how they visited those places. Pahl, 2000, p.80[89] likewise supports this view, as does Alberoni, 2016, p.10[90].

(2) In childhood a significant function of play is the discovery of the world around us, together with a friend. We are equals, entering fantasy worlds of Tolkien and George Lucas' making, **explore** the wild west and outer space. To our friends at the age of 10 it is not silly to combine different worlds, and hypothesize whether Gandalf had access to the force, or what the missing horcruxes were (before JK Rowling published book 7 of the Harry Potter series). We can let our minds roam, each of us contributing from the power of their imagination and reinforcing the mutual other. Note how C. S. Lewis writes: 'the whole world ... opens itself to our minds as we talk.' as the epitome of conversation with friends. The safety and acceptance if not coupled with challenge and critical thinking and the separation from main society can render groups of friends as ideal sources, however not just of grand theories, but also of self spiralling conspiracy theories. Whilst most people grow up and get completely mired in daily life, a lucky few keep this fascination for discovery and child like awe for the world around us. Some keep at least enough of a memory that can be triggered in the company of a similarly minded friend. Of course the topics change, but the joy stays the same. Curiosity is key character strengths according to Peterson and Seligman, 2004 and the process of exploration a key activity resulting from it.

Discovering a new topic or area is best done with a creative and curious friend, as you can bounce thoughts off each other, and see where the discussion carries you. There is an element of creative chaos in such a discussion, as you are bringing different insights and bases of knowledge to the discussion. In either case, whether it is through or with a friend, the discovery of new activities is highly effective at creating positive memories, as our brain is wired to save 'firsts' accurately and for a long time (see Wiking, 2019). If we have a high enjoyment at these moments as well, this activity, whilst not for everyone, will create effective and long-lasting bonds between us and the friend. The activity of discovery doesn't just restrict to discussions, or discovery of new activities, as one of the common activities bonding with a friend is going on a trip, small scale to a museum or city nearby, or longer travelling for months. Whereas part of the effect is surely the

[88] `https://theweek.com/articles/739502/8-kinds-friends-need-happy-life` 'Mind Openers are the friends who expand your horizons and encourage you to embrace new ideas, opportunities, cultures, and people...'

[89] 'Close friends can open up new areas of interest, activity or intellectual concern. We may respond to our friend by exploring some new area with him; we take up an interest in orchids or contemporary poetry because that is the passion of our friend.

[90] 'More than simply mirroring each other, friends are open to being lead by the other into new terrains of activity and new ways of looking at the world.'

close spending of time together (time spent, waiving privacy), the overarching theme here is the joint exploration. You make jointly new experiences together with the friend, see places, and are enriched for being able to discuss it there and then with the friend. The excitement and intensity of experiences will create a common memory with the friend that will sustain the connection for a long time.

I

Practical takeaway

- On Wikipedia[a] there is a list of different hobbies, about 200. Read through them carefully and then pick one of them to try out with a friend or two. Better still, pick one every year.
- Spend time with kids and see how their minds work when exploring. Be in awe how cool the world is!

[a] https://en.wikipedia.org/wiki/List_of_hobbies

Suggestions for thought

- Who among your friends is most likely to give you new ideas?
- Have you ever invited a few friends around to a 'show some photos from your favourite travel tour'?
- Do you have a friend with whom you can let your mind wander? Who is the same kind of crazy as you are? With whom you can reawaken that child inside of you?
- Have you ever been on a trip with a friend (not to a hotel resort)? How was that? How did the memories you made differ from other trips?

For statistics in sociological studies, question suggestions and weights in counting see H.

5.12 Teaching and learning

Both teaching and learning from each other is a deeply memory building experience as you invest in each other's growth. It often occurs in tandem in working on a joined goal or passion, but also conveys caring.

As the end goal of friendship in antiquity was the virtuous life, friendship was the vehicle to get us there according to Aristotle. Whilst support in seeking virtue was mostly seen as guidance and advice, no doubt teaching about the core disciplines such as philosophy or rhetoric viewed necessary to attain it was part of such a virtue seeking relationship. Such discourse was not just seen as useful, but older men according to Cicero, 1923, p.209 'find delight also in social intercourse with still younger men'. In antiquity the friendship model alternate to the battlefield companion was that of the teacher having a younger disciple to pass on the wisdom (see also 5.10). However, Aristotle does not follow our classical view of classroom teaching or knowledge transfer, but more proposes the awakening of the spirit for the people then to discover and develop virtue and knowledge themselves[91]. Arguably Jesus teaching the disciples in the New Testament should not be read too much into as a best practice among friends, as that was more the actual rabbi role than friends learning from each other. Augustine expresses this theme more explicitly: 'Each of us had something to learn from the others and something to teach in return.'

Love of Learning is key character strengths according to Peterson and Seligman, 2004 and thus learning a key activity resulting from it. While studying on one's own is often more effective, the real learning is done best in discussion with other people, and outside university friendship is a most suitable forum. And the best way of actually learning the finer touches of a subject and ensuring full understanding is to teach it to someone else, and who could be better suited than willing and interested friend. On the other hand, teaching can be a deeply rewarding experience. If our friend really makes progress, we feel we are contributing to his life. And it can be so much fun. Finally, as we teach, in the discussion we often increase our depth of the subject, as new connections become apparent, often through the question our friend asks.

When we pick up a new interest from a friend and get them to teach us the ropes, it reinforces our friendship in a range of ways - we spend more time with them, we validate their capability and thus personality and we validate the quality of their choices. If we teach the friend, we invest time and effort, and validate her/him as someone worth teaching. For this reason Shumway, 2018, p.115 includes both learning and teaching separately as friendship fortifiers citing his own experience with his best friend Dan[92]. Rath, 2006 has the key roles 'builder', 'champion' and 'mind opener' all teaching their friends in some capacity or another. Thus he puts substantial emphasis on the theme of teaching to and learning from friends.

While it is true that learning is not so essential anymore in the old age, this doesn't hold for all people. For some elderly learning remains a key theme in their life, and they really appreciate in particular younger friends from whom to learn about technology and the modern world. While perhaps the association of learning with the young is ageism, I find it is quite the reverse, with elderly who are engaged in learning processes feeling young and mentally staying younger. In German this phenomenon in its converse is described by the proverb 'who rests, rusts'[93].

In modern terms, the goal of a virtue seeking friendship would be 'mutual growth' and it is conceivable to see teaching and learning in a bracket with exploration and discovery resulting in a joined and larger theme of growth. As a general observation - this activity is only partially emphasised: a defining and elemental theme for some friendships, but completely omitted in other books and

---

[91]Discussion with Prof. Karen Nielsen

[92]'Although Dan learned some valuable lessons about strength training and made incredible physical gains, the time and focus of teaching to lift provided us with a chance to become much closer as friends.'

[93]'Wer rastet, der rostet'

descriptions.

Practical takeaway
Explore what your friends can teach you about. You discover your friend's passions, you gain new appreciation for them and you discover topics and thoughts outside your traditional field.

Suggestions for thought

- Is learning a key activity of yours or are there other activities which you enjoy more. If the latter no worry ...
- Did you ever go through the experience of either teaching or learning from a good friend? How long was the total time spent together?

For statistics in sociological studies, question suggestions and weights in counting see H.

5.13 Generosity and making gifts

> There is nothing better than a friend, unless it is a friend with chocolate.
>
> Linda Grayson

Whilst in our affluent society gifts are a little out of fashion, well placed and thoughtful gifts have historically been a key ritual and habit for people to build connection. Not by accident is this one of Chapman's key love languages and arguably a bit of a lost art. The book by Grant, 2013 describes the general attitude of generosity and its appreciation by society. While Grant estimates that only a small percentage of all people are actually givers, it is the matchers[94] who protect them from being taken advantage of by appreciating their societal contribution. Giving gifts is a specific application of this general attitude.

Aristotle, 1925, 8.6[95] identifies generosity as one of the sign of pleasure friendship being better in quality to utility friendship. Cicero, 1923 noting Scipio's generosity as a positive trait[96] however is focused of the antonym of generosity - greed- and its impact on friendship: 'the greatest bane of friendship is the lust for money' (p.147). Showing thus generosity with gifts is thus a (though surely not the only way) to signal friendship. Olyan, 2017, p.92 points out that in Ben Sira

[94] TED talk summary at `https://youtu.be/YyXRYgjQXXO`

[95] 'Of these two kinds that which is for the sake of pleasure is the more like friendship, when both parties get the same things from each other and delight in each other or in the things, as in the friendships of the young; for generosity is more found in such friendships.'

[96] 'Why need I speak of his most affable manners, of his devotion to his mother, of his generosity to his sisters, of his kindness to his relatives,'

people are expected to be generous, both materially (particular to poor friends) non-materially.

The cultural significance and context are nowhere so explicitly emphasised as in Marcel Mauss, 1925 treatise on the importance of gifts when humans establish relationships. He exhibits many motivations are possible for gift giving, such as manipulation for reciprocity or indebting. In friendship however, it should always be motivated from love and used to express affection or esteem.

Chapman, 2009 identified gifts as one of his five love languages, noting its role in the exchange of rings in weddings[97]. He describes the significance thus: 'A gift is something you can hold in your hand and say, "Look, he was thinking of me," or "She remembered me." You must be thinking of someone to give him a gift. The gift itself is a symbol of that thought.'.

As time has become the scarce commodity in our current era, Chapman, 2009, p.81 also links being there for somebody to gift giving[98]. And indeed 'X is generous with their time' not only emphasises the value of time but also how it expresses the attitude of their generosity. Hospitality expresses generosity similarly. Whilst generosity should not be taken for granted or exploited, there is a wonderful sentiment to just accept generosity and not feel obliged to reciprocate immediately. I find it indeed really pleasant to decouple invitations of friends and bringing something to it. So rather than comply with a convention of bringing a not so well thought out gift on time, I find it much more effective in conveying appreciation to keep a lookout for small but really fitting presents for close friends, and then bringing it along when the opportunity arises. Gift giving is enhanced by an element of randomness, of free gratuity, of the surprise in the moment.

Gift giving is an aspect where thoughts of proportionality (see 6.8) are significant. Whilst most people agree that the financial value of a gift is of secondary nature, it is often at least partially valued against the affluence of the giver. But general thoughtfulness and effort dominate financial value in the consensus that a 'thoughtful' present is better than a 'lavish' one. Given our heightened need for appreciation and affirmation of individuality, gifts are a way to convey our knowledge and understanding of as well as affection for our friend by finding a gift that uniquely fits his personality.

Whilst ulterior motives are usually not intended in gift giving, perhaps what is actually frowned upon, are hidden ulterior motives. When we know our friends well and their affection and love for us is beyond reproach, gifts can contain an element of teasing and even self interest. It is possible to show up to a friend for dinner with a delicious bottle of wine and the hint that this would fit really well with the dinner made. Making a photo album of the joined trip together is one example of what Shumway, 2018, p.111 calls the friendship totem, a gift that ensures occasional reminding, other potential examples include a DIY tool that would be used regularly, a painting for the wall, or a plain bottle of wine to be drunk at a different future occasion. There is a whole art to the habit of book gifting as Hunt, 2019-12-13 explains. Gift giving expresses the attitude of generosity, which

[97] p.77 'Gifts are visual symbols of love. Most wedding ceremonies include the giving and receiving of rings. The person performing the ceremony says, "these rings are outward and visible signs of an inward and spiritual bond that unites your two hearts in love that has no end."'

[98] 'There is an intangible gift that sometimes speaks more loudly than a gift that can be held in one's hand. I call it the gift of self or the gift of presence. Being there when your spouse needs you speaks loudly to the one whose primary love language is receiving gifts.

expresses general consideration and special consideration towards friends.

Practical takeaway
Use gifts to surprise. Rather than doing an obligatory gift that time of year when the birthday party comes around, off-season small thoughtful gifts that come as a surprise, e.g. when you casually meet up for coffee or a beer. Gifts are not designed to display magnitude of generosity, but thoughtfulness and affection.

Suggestions for thought

- Do you have a little notebook for remembering good ideas for present for your friends?
- What gifts do you think are best to give among friends?
- Never reply to receiving a present 'That would not have been necessary!'. Your friend wanted to give you a present and it thus was necessary for them! Say 'Thank you, I really appreciate it.' and that is all that is required.

For statistics in sociological studies, question suggestions and weights in counting see H.

5.14 Vocal or visible support

Vocal support means having your friends back vocally - even when they are being criticised by others. It also includes introducing them to other people in your network and commenting positively in their presence and absence. Thus the topic splits up into

1. the standing by them in moments of danger,
2. supporting them vocally in presence or absence though without major cost

There is a story frequently mentioned in sermons that exhibits the first trait beautifully: 'Jackie Robinson was the first Black American to play baseball in the major leagues. Breaking baseball's color barrier, he faced hostile crowds in every stadium. While playing one day in his home stadium of Ebbets Field in Brooklyn, he committed an error. The fans began to jeer him. He stood at second base, humiliated, while the crowd booed and got right nasty. Then, without saying a word, shortstop Pee Wee Reese went over and stood next to Jackie. He put his arm around him and faced the crowd. Suddenly the fans grew quiet. Robinson later said that that arm around his shoulder saved his career.' (taken from Coltrain, 2004).

The simple phrase 'the friend **has my back**' evokes potent images of steadfast friendship. The expression carries so much connotation, reliability, consistency, loyalty, companionship, the image of warriors standing shoulder to shoulder in a battle (apart from the gory entertainment I believe the image of the large shields covering also companions of men standing side by side was one of the biggest emotional appeals of the movie 300[99]). The image of the 'hetairos', the man-at-arms companion standing at one's side would continue for millennia to come.

The theme occurs in movies over and over again and evokes powerful emotions in all of us. The key person stands alone in the middle, but then is joined from left and right by friends who 'have his back'. Guardians of the Galaxy, Avengers, Justice League, it triggers thoughts of loyalty and the image of age old battlefield tested companionship. Olyan, 2017, p.39 emphasises the words of 'clings closer than a brother' vs. 'stand at a distance' as a feature of friendship in the Old Testament. The bad friend fails to come to the aid of the friend in need, he fails to show up and stand by his side. Alberoni, 2016, p.124[100] speaks of the friend coming alongside us. Showing our visible support and endangering our position is the ultimate test of loyalty, it is the activity resulting from the relationship attitude of loyalty. The danger need not be physical danger faced in battle, but can be likewise moments of potential embarrassment, such as a prom ball or movie concert[101].

The trait's disappointment is absolute, if the friend refuses to show up or stand up for us and stand with us, and we know it when we have failed the test (see Peter at Jesus' trial[102]. Jesus did not expect or want his disciples to fight for him physically, but he was disappointed with their absence at his side, first falling asleep and then dispersing). This behaviour however do not just happen in grand anecdotes or movies, it also occurs in daily life and are just as meaningful there. Rath, 2006, p.11 relays such a story where the memory of being publicly affirmed as a friend is 'seared into Maggie's memory for good'. In his view, the Champion is the one to embody this virtue ('Champions stand up for you and what you believe in. They are the friends who sing your praises.').

The second theme is supporting your friends by positive affirmation to others in their presence. This is not the life saving support, but more the positive networking and promoting. If your friend has a business - you can mention this to other friends. You can sing your single (and looking) friend's praises to suitable other bachelors and bachelorettes. If your friend is looking for a job, it is asking other friends for recommendations and leads as well as encouraging them to link your friend up to suitable opportunities. You are your friend's advocate. And I know this is a contentious issue, and people may disagree, but I believe all this comes together in a concept I denote as 'positive gossip'. Positive gossip is marked by affection towards the friend. When I am having a coffee with friend B, we also update each other on what is going on in the lives of mutual friends C and D. We want to know they are well. And if they are not well, we want to find

[99] https://youtu.be/2ba2ZinGL14?t=97

[100] 'The true friend comes alongside us when all others disappear. A true friend stands the test of the struggle because the struggle implies choosing. He chooses you in place of another.'

[101] A beautiful scene for this is when Hugh Grant supports his younger sidekick at the embarrassing school concert - aptly titled 'killing me softly'. That is 'having someone's back'.

[102] Matt 26:74-75 'Then he began to call down curses on himself and he swore to them, 'I don't know the man!' Immediately a rooster crowed. Then Peter remembered the word Jesus had spoken: "Before the rooster crows, you will disown me three times." And he went outside and wept bitterly.' - see also https://youtu.be/5mZZhVtECD4?t=126

out if there are ways how to help them.

Our capability to stand up for our friends stems from our knowledge of the person. In particular, it is not just blind loyalty, but it results from us having judged the friend and found worthy of friendship. On this basis, we can give our perspective on our friend when they are being criticised. As Little, 2000, p.12[103] writes 'they explain us to other people who only saw our failures and limits'.

The opposite of this trait is slander, and it is unacceptable in friendship. Alberoni, 2016, p.93[104]. It is this trait also in a way that emphasises privacy when criticising, as even well meant and justified criticism, if it occurs in front of others, does not lift us up or improve our standing in the eyes of the third party bystanders (see Greif, 2009, ch.12[105]).

Suggestions for thought

- To what degree is standing up for you and your beliefs important for you as an expected behaviour of your friends?
- How good are you at pitching your friends within your network, be it for business opportunities, romance or jobs?
- Did you ever have to take a stand for a friend? How did you feel?

For statistics in sociological studies, question suggestions and weights in counting see H.

[103]'Friends take the trouble to think us out, as it were, and, where appropriate, they explain us to other people who only saw our failures and limits. A friend sees our ideals where others only see us.'

[104]'A friend does not spread rumours about us. If others gather to badmouth us, he will either defend us or leave immediately. He will not even stop to listen in order to let us know.'

[105]Donald was hurt by a friend and deeply resented his lack of support. "Funny you should ask that—something happened with me recently, with my tennis playing buddy, where I felt he didn't back me up. Essentially, I felt he rejected me. (This is the first hint of vulnerability he has expressed since he said he has no close friends, although in this case he faults his friend and not himself.) I don't want honest feedback from a friend. I want him to back me up. I didn't think he backed me up in this one situation.'

Chapter 6

Resources, needs and summary

All sections until 6.9 are for casual reading

6.1 The friendship resources

Figure 6.1: Friendship Resources

As noted, resources - once given at a basic level - are peripheral to the functioning of friendships, mostly in total only meriting 2-10% of emphasis. The priorities are for young adolescents valuing athletic capability and physical attractiveness, the middle-aged valuing spare time, and the elderly valuing mobility, financial security and proximity. Other than proximity, no individual resource consistently has a score of higher than 1%. But essentially, resources are only significant as they enable people to participate, be it in school or clubs via physical prowess and fitness, or be it in civic life of town clubs, church and neighbours by still being mobile and reasonably healthy.

Tot	OP	CP	TW	SH	CM	QS1	QS2	OA	YA	YS
5	3	2	2	4	5	6	5	10	4	NA
Weight share of friendship resources										

Why do I classify them as resources and use the strict sense of this word? It is because these characteristics can be limiting factors, they can be scarce resources, becoming either an impediment and enhancer. If we have little time, we will not be able to spend it with our friends. If we do not have any financial resources, we may find it extremely difficult to participate meaningfully in society. If we are obese, we may experience discrimination, as people may ignore you[1], if you have

[1] Obesity discrimination is mostly studied in three contexts: workplace discrimination, schools and health discrimination. In a youth context, Schaefer and Simpkins, 2014 document a 30% preference for

nothing to say people might be interested in, it will be difficult to get a meaningful exchange. Should you be unable to get out of the house for health reasons or live far from your friends, interactions may be limited. On the other hand, resources are characterised by clearly diminishing returns. Thus they are not so much enablers in abundance, but more just limiting factor in absence. Particularly in old age there can come the truly tragic moment where two long friends might still be alive but unable to live out their friendship of decades. This can happen because they are in care homes at a distance from each other and cannot visit each other because of that and ill health without substantial assistance, which they may not be able to afford [2]. The alleviation of these situations could be one of the greatest human benefits of self-driving automobiles bringing down transport cost.

	Tot	OP	CP	TW	SH	CM	QS1	QS2	OA	YA	YS
Proximity	◒	◒	◒	◒	◒	◒	◒	○	●	○	◒
Content	◒	○	◒	○	◒	◒	◒	◒	◒	◒	◒
Health	◒	○	○	○	○	◒	◒	◒	◒	◒	◒
Network	◒	○	○	○	○	◒	◒	○	◒	◒	◒
Time	○	○	○	○	◒	◒	○	○	◒	○	◒
Well off	○	○	○	○	○	○	◒	◒	◒	○	◒
Wealth	○	○	○	○	○	○	○	◒	◒	○	◒
Attract.	○	○	○	○	○	○	○	◒	○	○	○

Figure 6.2: Friendship Resources

6.2 Proximity

Even in the digital age, proximity is a key driver of the possibility for a friendship to develop. It simply determines which time or financial costs are associated with seeing each other. The difference between this definition and geographic proximity as the bird flies is crucial. In large cities people can be only 3 km apart, yet completely inhabit different worlds. Examples in my own life included Hong Kong and Tokyo, where despite living in the same city travel distances could be up to an hour. Contrasting that in rural Germany or America, it is not uncommon to just drive 20km down the street. Putnam, 2000 singles out urban sprawl and associated commuting habits as culprits for our deterioration in social interactions. Degges-White and Borzumato-Gainey, 2011, ch2 seconds this, pointing to 'an average commute of 100 minutes a day ... [which] creates a chasm between our work life and home life. We may seldom socialize with our work colleagues.'.

Proximity is the prime enabler of almost all friendship activities. As Pahl, 2000, p.8 says: 'Caring for a sick child who has to be collected from school in an emergency almost certainly requires the help of a local friend.' In the developmental

non-overweight friends over overweight friends amongst adolescents. Like all such studies, effects might decrease for later ages, but unlikely ever disappear.

[2] See e.g. Matthews, 1983

phase it is necessary for access to a person (cf. Greif, 2009, ch. 1). Thus kids are playing with neighbour kids, school children befriend those they are seated next to, college room mates become friends, soldiers befriend those in the same platoon or whom their bed is placed next to, old people in care homes befriend their neighbours. In research, this has been described as the mere exposure effect. Thus simply the gross amount of time we are seeing someone will affect our liking of that person and being physically close to them increases this. Asatryan, 2016 labels this as 'situational proximity'.

I am not sure whether this factor is more important along gender lines. Already Aristotle, 1925, 8.5 cites a saying usually associated with male friendships: 'But if the absence is lasting, it seems actually to make men forget their friendship; hence the saying 'out of sight, out of mind." However, a temporary absence is usually less impactful on men friendships, who are much more happy than women to pickup a friendship after some time lapse. In old age, as Matthews, 1983, p.147 points out, it becomes a key determining factor of feasibility of friendship: 'Both decreased physical health and lack of monetary resources meant that the friends might never again be in each other's physical presence.'. This of course also inhibits the possibility to make new friends by simply reducing our daily interactions with new people.

If you want to improve your friendships, then one advice based on this is to improve the proximity to your friends, i.e. cut down the transport distance. Lewis and Hooper, 1979 writes 'If I had to give a piece of advice to a young man about a place to live, I think I should say, 'sacrifice almost everything to live where you can be near your friends."[3]. Aristotle, 1925 goes the one step further to recommend living together with friends, and Cicero, 1923 agrees by having Laelius emphasize the time he spent with Scipio in close proximity on the military campaigns. Millington, 2019, p.76 describes when the converse happens: 'Other mates might move to another town - or even country - and while you stay in touch on social media, visiting them is just not a priority and the friendship slowly fizzles down to Christmas cards.'

Proximity by itself is not sufficient. Proximity lowers the cost of meeting friends, indeed if you are living door-to-door costs are at a minimum, but still you have the cost of initiation. In particular in large cities, sure, sometimes our friends live really far, but even if they don't and it could be just so easy to meet up, people do not rise from the couch after they return home from work. A frequent conversation on alumni reunions is the mutual apology for not having actually met up in a long time, despite living geographically close. But it is a good start and makes the keeping of new year's resolution to spend time with friends much easier.

[3]As a disclaimer - this was part of the plan of moving to Oxford for the sabbatical. Whilst the productivity part worked, and I managed to write this book, the social plan of hanging out with all my friends failed of course miserably. Yet I would do it again, and I fully echo this sentiment.

Suggestions for thought - local

- If setting out in a new city, do you analyse the location to move in also for proximity to social infrastructure?
- Have you talked about optimizing routes in your city with your friends to see whether there are times in the week where you are physically close and thus could easily squeeze in a coffee or pint?
- To what degree do you use opportunities when you are close to friends elsewhere, e.g. because of a business trip, to make sure you see them?

Suggestions for thought - general

- How does geographic distance affect your friendships? Do you stay well in touch over a longer distance?
- What do you think about C. S. Lewis advice to move where a cluster of your friends is living?

For statistics in sociological studies, question suggestions and weights in counting see H.

6.3 Content

Having things to say and thus being interesting is a core feature of friendship. Content is the stimulant of conversations, the general chat, the intellectual conversation, having tea with someone. Originally I was going to bracket this theme simply with intellect and curiosity, but two examples convinced me of the contrary and treat it as a resource, and that is the effect its absence has on conversations and how it comes about.

Content is generated in and through our lives. We live and by living create stories and narratives. This creates gossip. Whilst malicious gossip is of course undesirable with plenty of bible quotes and managerial guidance books to prove it, as a fact most of us do it, according to some statistics up to 50 minutes a day (Robbins and Karan, 2020).We share the stories with our friends and discuss them, laugh about them, learn about them. It is part of the social process. We notice the world around us. We read, we watch TV, we study, we visit places, we make experiences. All this creates content that can be shared with people. In this sense it is highly linked to the factor of intellect and curiosity, which determines our content acquisition propensity, but also linked to themes like mutual interests, working together and discovery and exploration.

On the other hand, content also has a half-life and an applicability. They say that nothing is so old as the news of yesterday. Content receives its value in the interest of the other person. If I know everything about good bars in Hong Kong, but the other person neither has been there, never will be there nor is interested in anything that goes on outside the county borders, then this content is irrelevant. For content to be a resource, there must be a match of existence and interest. Economists would talk about the marketability of the resource content. Sometimes we are simply in the wrong place, where we have content, that other people would be interested in, but we are not in their proximity. This happens when we change locations, companies, interests. What we used to know and be able to summon to contribute to a conversation lost its relevance. It can even happen with friends, as they or we change. There is a terribly awkward moment when two former friends who however haven't met for a while meet again, only to find that they have nothing to say to each other. They might still have memories and affection for each other, but essentially the content of their life is mutually disjoined, rendering any path forward back to reestablishing the friendship difficult.

The problem however arises when we stop gaining content that friends are interested in. There are two examples to this. One currently plays out in the Covid pandemic. Whilst early in March and April Zoom calls with friends were frequent, interesting and fun, and everyone got used to the medium, people still had content from the prior 6 months. People had broken up, gotten together, gotten new jobs, and we had all missed it for our 2nd and 3rd tier of friends and acquaintances, respectively. However as lockdown continued, and people just were passing their time working a bit and then with lots of time on Netflix, active content that could be shared got less and less, and by this, also the zoom calls became less and less stimulating. In a similar fashion as people retire, they also lose access to the gossip networks in the company [4], and thus, while being interested to hear what is still going on in the old place, they have nothing to contribute anymore. This effect leads them to feeling less valued and superfluous after retirement, and can be a second painful process after the act of retirement. In particular, as people retire to care homes and are pressed into a culture of sedation and compliance with a daily nonstimulant routine, it is tragic to see how fast intellectually capable and alive elderly people comply and enter mental hibernation essentially giving up on content acquisition.

In the more abstract qualitative sociological studies on friendship, resource exchange includes the resource information, but it is on a lower relevance.

Suggestions for thought

- Have you ever had the experience of sitting together with a former good friend and found you had nothing left to talk about? Did you think about how that came about?
- What is your attitude to gossip and stories of your mutual circle of friends and acquaintances? Have you heard of the THINK[a] rule?
- Are you aware of what sort of topics you mostly spend your time finding out stuff about?
- What do you do to stay interesting?

[4] There are exceptions, some former colleagues were simply in the know on *everything* that happened in the company, as people thought it would be 'safe' to share it with them, rather than people in the office.

[a] True, helpful, inspiring, necessary, kind c.f. K. Miller, 2020

For statistics in sociological studies, question suggestions and weights in counting see H.

6.4 Health and fitness

> We will always be friends until we're old and senile. Then we will be new friends.
>
> Unknown

Health and fitness is important both at the adolescent age, enabling participation in sporting activities and thus conferring status (Hall, 2012b) as well as in older age conferring general mobility and thus participation in community events outside one's household (Matthews, 1983).

One should note that Hall's group is mostly 18-22, and sporting prowess or at its other end, obesity can be a severely enabling or limiting factor in social participation in young ages. Essentially, there is little more that awards social status amongst children as athletic capability. This book here is mostly only addressing adult life, but it is relevant as being discriminated or completely excluded as a child for obesity, as can happen, may cause perturbed socialisation, fear of rejection and lack of trust for some people for the rest of their lives. In adult life whilst some rise above it because of good cheer and laughter and an affective nature, obesity is on the whole still a factor that can impede our capability to have a full social life.

The capability of participating in sports is for many people an opportunity not just to live healthy life styles, abstracting for the moment from the various sports injuries every half serious sportsman seems to be plagued by at regular intervals, but to camaraderie in teams. In schools, university, rural areas and other such communities, a remarkable share of social life revolves around sports activities. Where good athletic capabilities of course confer social status, my concern here is simply the capability to participate. The competitive nature however gives meaning and a unifying purpose to groups to form teams. It is a major loss of a social resource if frailty prevents us from meaningfully participate in team sports. The emphasis on such an activity to bond is particular important for male friendships, and thus in turn the loss of participating in it is equally damaging to the continual development of them.

As ill health bears on us, it also severely affects our mood and can lead to depression (absence of positivity). There are broadly five impact vectors how ill health can affect us, in later life and for some people even before:

(1) **Energy** and capability to take part in social life: One item appearing in seeing time as a resource is the energy or residual will to go out, e.g. after a long day of work. If we don't maintain a minimum energy level, but are constantly fatigued from our daily life, then meeting up with friends can become a chore, something we should do because we know in a way is good for us (like dieting or

exercising), but not something we do for the sheer joy of it. The limitation of this can occur through work and burden of children, but also energy draining illnesses such as chronic fatigue or long Covid can bring this about. I do not elaborate on the social effects of depression, as this is clearly outside my area of competence, but it is obvious that a depression will likewise affect energy levels for socialising.

(2) Getting out / **physical mobility**: Another limiting capability and thus resource is the capability to go out of the house. Unless our friends can and do come to us, we need to go to a bar, sports club, their home or anywhere to meet them. Often we don't meet our friends directly, but for some social occasion like a concert or at or after work. But our mobility may be impaired because we temporarily break a leg or the frailty of our muscles, joints or bones makes going out difficult even with a wheeled walking frame. We may get an illness that gives us a higher danger if we get sick and hence need to isolate at home, or indeed a global pandemic forces us all into our homes with an occasional trip to the supermarket or pharmacy by concern for ourselves or on account of government regulation. This puts us at a severe obstacle to meet our friends and adds to loneliness.

(3) Capability of **seeing and hearing** (see e.g. Degges-White and Borzumato-Gainey, 2011, p.134[5]). In the section on good communication later, I will elaborate how much nonverbal and emotional information is flowing in conversations that goes beyond the exact words. Now blind or deaf people usually compensate, developing their skills in the capabilities that they still have, e.g. listening extremely well to nuances and tones, or being attentive to details in face expression. But something gets lost in the capability to connect, and the impact on being able to maintain friendships is felt. Perhaps a lesson to be taken away is to make the most of it while we still have full command of our senses and enjoy the wonderful conversations to be had with friends.

(4) **Dementia** meaning reduction of memory capacity and social interaction is a real problem, however milder forms of dementia can make friendship even more precious. Dementia in earlier or middle stages is selective and often allows for the keeping of long-term memories. Thus an old lady might not remember what she had for lunch, but still with major clarity tell you the seating order in her school class in 3rd grade. Thus dementia makes the development of new friendships difficult, but on the contrary might be a really key motivator to maintain at least your key old friendships.[6]

(5) **Mental difficulty** of dealing with ill-health on our side or our friends' side: As I. Yalom, 1980 elaborately argues, many people have a visceral unresolved attitude to mortality and death. As we get sick, potentially with cancer or other terminal diseases, this leaves us with a lot on our plate. Our friends being close to

[5]'The value of easy communication could not be understated by Mary, who acknowledged that she had become increasingly hard-of-hearing as she approached her seventy-eighth birthday. Mary shared that the loss of her hearing was the hardest part of aging for her and research shows that age-related hearing impairment is a much greater blow to women than to men.'

[6]If you think this argument is selfish or calculatory, you may think that in a friendship you maintain at 40 you don't know who is going to get Dementia. It might be you being the friend with access to your dementia-suffering friend's world and helping them relate to it.

us then face a variety of dilemmas how to deal with this issue within our friendship, all with the potential to both deepen and disrupt the friendship. We can choose to emphasise the levity and joy of the friendship, to continue to have fun and declare friendship a sickness free zone. We can count on the emotional and practical support of our friends for those difficult times. And we may need to respect the fact that some friends will withdraw because of an incapability to deal with the situation. This may be a painful experience, but even if we come to grips with our drastically decreased life expectation, we may not expect the add-on effect. Us dying will be really difficult for some friends, too, and even though they might be physically perfectly healthy, the confrontation with mortality that our situation imposes on them may need to play out in a different speed. Also in this sense the fact that two friends are perfectly healthy and can live their friendship worry free, is a resource and fortunate situation that may change. So make the most of the time of health while you can!

It should be noted that good friendships create via this factor a positive feedback loop, as there is ample evidence that good friendships are actually also good for our physical and mental health. We have lower stress and cortisol levels, and ideally positive influence from friends to e.g. eat better and exercise more. As Degges-White and Borzumato-Gainey, 2011, p.129 points out, while men (if married) get their social support and health benefits from their wives, their wives get it from children and friends. They postulate this feedback loop particularly for older women [7].

Suggestions for thought

- Have you ever been in the situation where your ability to interact with your friends was limited through a health issue? How did that make you feel?
- If this situation lasted for a longer period, did you feel there came a point where interest waned and friends started dropping off?
- Have you had a friend who was in such a situation? How did you adapt to it? How long did you adapt to it?
- Are you still participating in a team sport? Have you thought of taking a team sport up again?

For statistics in sociological studies, question suggestions and weights in counting see H.

6.5 Network

As part of the personality traits, I already included the trait of social ease, which is about the person. However, because of this personality trait, but also

[7] p.137 'There is a positive relationship between friendship interactions and health—the healthier older women are, the greater their involvement with friends. Having friends seems to provide some sort of immunity factor that promotes good health.'

because of job or family connections, involvement in organizations or general social life, people can gain networks. The activity of utilizing your network for your friends is also covered in the activity of vocal support, where you stake your reputation or interests in with those of your friends, ideally thus motivating others to help them. A wide network however is simply a description of the resource that enables this state. Whilst some networks have strong links, networks are the famous 'weak links' of Granovetter, 1973 that are effective in letting us find information from out of our circle, and I will discuss this in section 9.9. But it is not just useful information on jobs or business connection, the best benefit of friends with a wide network are that they can create links for friendship, thus helping their introverted friends.

A good network of friends is an enabler on a lot of other levels, too. It can support the organisation of events and socials, it can mean that whenever you decide to host a dinner, there are people to provide the critical mass on the one hand[8]. At the same time a constant new acquaintance with new people allows to diversify attendance and thus maintain a variety of conversation themes within a social group. In particular in expat lives, where a change in city often occurs every 3-5 years, building an international network is essential to landing on your feet well in a new city, ideally with a few references from friends from past locations for people to have a beer with. Even romantically it can pay off for you and your friends, as the pool from which and in which you can make suggestions grows.

Whilst I would put 'having a friends network' more down to agreeableness, it is nevertheless a resource in some senses as well. As people perceive you as having good friends, not necessarily many, but the capability of maintaining good friendships, they likewise want to be a friend of yours. Furthermore, other good friends of yours introduce you to their friends. Whilst transitivity is not a given (see 9.10), a recommendation and endorsement will usually help to make new bonds.

Suggestions for thought

- To what degree do you intersect your network with your friends' circles?
- Do you have a friend who maintains an extensive network? How does this play out in your friendship with them?

For statistics in sociological studies, question suggestions and weights in counting see H.

6.6 Time

Time is the scarce currency and **resource** for adults in their prime years. Alcock-Ferguson, 2018-05-16 cite a statistic that almost half of the UK adults say their busy

[8]This ensures viability of planning events. It simply makes a huge difference if you get together e.g. in a social club planning a bar night to know that between the two or three organizers' friends circle, ten or fifteen people will simply show up for the company, or whether there is a significant probability of literally no-one showing up.

lives stop them from connecting with others.

However, actual time scarcity in our society has ambivalent evidence. Putnam points to the liberation of time for adults through the automation of domestic chores, and both Degges-White [9] and Putnam point to the sizeable share of time that TV takes up in our life. Official figures from Netflix estimate that every user spends on average 2 hours a day on the platform. As Netflix currently only captures 10-12% of all video content time in the US, it is plausible to assume that for non-Netflix subscribers TV or cable times are approximately of similar height. If we chose to make it a new year' s resolution consciously to spend more time with friends, this is where we could effortlessly wring a few hours of time from to head down to the pub, bar or cafe to meet a chum.

Childcare of course is a significant factor for time shortage, according to Dotti Sani and Treas, 2016 mothers spend nearly 100 minutes (fathers only 50) on childcare on each day, with substantial variation in different cultures, levels of affluence, education and number of children. This, of course, is just a number and does not yet reflect the emotional fatigue potentially coming from dealing with the daily tasks from nappies to reviewing homework and consoling on the emotions of fights with 'best friends'. There is no getting around, optimising or streamlining these chores. When people have kids and take their development seriously, it is a black hole for disposable time. Whilst I treat time and energy (health) as separate resources, this example shows the two concepts are closely related. The amount of blocked time increases further when other household chores are counted in, where equal disparity continues to exist between men and women. In traditional rural neighbourly communities, some of this time would be spent in the company of neighbours as families were essentially in and out of each other's houses. In modern city based living or the likewise more privacy oriented suburbia, this pool of time is blocked for combining with friendship oriented activities. Child care thus represents a direct opportunity cost on our time availability.

Several studies have been conducted on the commuting times in both Europe and the US (and no doubt about other parts of the world too), and analysing the impact on 'social capital' - see e.g. Besser, Marcus, and Frumkin, 2008. According to Statista average commuting times in the EU range between 43 min (women, UK, children $\leq$ 6y) and 70 min (men, also UK, children $\geq$ 7y).[10] Similar statistics show sizeable percentages of the population having commutes of more than 90 min per day. For most people, having such a commute is not a choice but a necessity to maintain their income. Most people I know are perfectly aware of the detrimental effect their commute overall has on them. However, there are ways to improve the situation, and that is to try to combine the commute to coincide with a friend's schedule, or even an acquaintance who can become a friend over time. In my personal experience, the morning tram from Mannheim to the main BASF site of Ludwigshafen was such an opportunity. Also outside my own, I know of a few friendships that were formed by showing a mutually friendly face on the tram and having a pleasant chat rather than just staring outside or dozing.

[9]'Today, according to the American Time Use Study (ATUS), we spend more than 50 percent of our discretionary time in the company of the cast and characters of our favorite television programs and only about 13 percent in the company of our friends and neighbors.'

[10]Interestingly, there seems to be a robust gap of about 15 min between men and women, thus partially offsetting the longer time women spend with household chores.

From a sustainability and avoidance of traffic perspective several large corporates in Germany have started app-supported commute-sharing initiatives, and again anecdotal evidence here shows that this is likewise supportive of friendships developing, as people use otherwise 'dead' time for relationship building. Another example was the TubeChat Campaign launched on the London Underground in 2016, that allowed people to put up a pin on their collar to signal being happy to be talked to.

Time availability then improves once people come closer to retirement as they often reduce their working hours already in the late fifties. Parallel to this as children become independent and leave the household further spare time becomes available, which can be converted into friendship fostering activities. From the middle of their sixties, time often is not anymore a constrained variable or resource and can be used for enabling friendships.

One hypothesis about the resource time in friendship is that in adulthood people with similar time constraints seek each other out, as otherwise imbalances place a strain on the friendship (e.g. Pahl, 2000, p.86 [11]). On the contrary, people with substantial time constraints might be grateful for their friends with more flexible and free schedules. Their friends' availability increases the chances of the few prized hours that can be wrung from a life of work and family come to fruition in a few joyful hours having a spontaneous drink with a friend. My hunch is that if people are genuinely short of time and energy, being additionally picky with friends who do have time and show flexibility is a luxury that should be prized and appreciated, not criticised.

Asatryan, 2016 [12] highlights seeing time as a resource or currency, with our drive to live our life efficiently. Some things however require patience and time, and a breakup consolation cannot just be adequately addressed and completed within an allocated time budget of 90 minutes. Thinking about time as a resource to be managed - specifically as friends are concerned - is one step to developing a transactional view of people and friends that has been criticised in prior chapters. And yet, expressedly **giving or making time** is an active choice that recognizes opportunity costs but thus directly confers value on the friend and costly and credibly signalling how they are important to us (see friendship as priority).

Suggestions for thought

- Are you aware of how much of your time you spend with your friends? Does this allocation reflect your values?
- Are there any holes in your daily calendar that could be spent with friends? Are there any other activities that could be moved to make time blocks available?

[11]'Those with unequal time burdens are unlikely to form close friendships: the one with the greater time will be perceived by the other as too demanding. If one is already suffering from emotional overload, a call late at night from a friend with relationship problems may be the last straw. Some people cannot be good friends. 'God protect me from my friends', they complain. 'I need space and a bit of peace for myself."

[12]The underlying discussion appears over and over again, even in Steven Covey's Habits of highly effective people.

- Do you mostly develop your friendships with people of similar time budgets? Alternatively do you use imparities of time budgets with one of you making allowances for the other? [Rephrase]
- Have you thought of combining your commute to spend with friends if possible?

For statistics in sociological studies, question suggestions and weights in counting see H.

6.7 Material

There are several studies that show that perceived life quality improves until a certain level of income, e.g. Kahneman and Deaton, 2010 reports such a boundary to be at 75k USD p.a. using 450k responses from the Gallup-Healthways Well-Being Index. A certain amount of property and income enables certain friendship activities. This can be a guest room that enables people to stay over, a living room that enables hosting for dinners, and a certain financial independence allows for participating on a night out, even if they go a little over budget.

However, in times of increasing youth unemployment but also inadequate pensions for a wide number of elderly, sufficient disposable income to take part in social activities is not available to many and directly inhibits their friendships and friendship opportunities. In the current climate, one of the impact of many people in their 20ies continuing to live in their rooms with their parents for financial reasons, they are likewise restricted in social functions such as hosting and going out[13]. Degges-White and Borzumato-Gainey, 2011, p.128 points to direct choices in the construction of personal social networks, as women in poorer circumstances favour developing family relations over those with friends because of the increased permissibility to ask them for practical help.

On the contrary, people with a stable income may live on their own, in socially more desirable neighbourhoods and have more time for socialising, as they can externalise household chores. Often the availability of institutional support networks depends on the local affluence, with richer councils being able to offer more services of benefit to those hitting a temporary rough patch. Variance in disposable incomes may also break up a group of friends, as people with better resources go out of state or abroad to university and financially more restricted students stay local or do apprenticeships (see Greif, 2009, ch1), or elderly move out of established neighbourhoods to better care homes leaving less affluent neighbours behind. Even if this occurs, the availability of disposable income for travelling allows the occasional visit, be it for an afternoon or a long weekend.

Inequality is presumably an inevitable characteristic of our current socio-economic system, and the roots and overall impacts are completely out of the scope of this book. However, if we have a reasonable material base, then we can count our blessings and use it also in the benefit of our friends, whilst maintaining their dignity and not putting pressure on them to keep up. This is in particular of

[13] For a limited few the reverse may partially hold, as saving money this way whilst holding down a full-time job may likewise liberate funds for going out.

significance for the dreaded 'wedding season', as people are no doubt happy for their friends getting married, but dread the implied cost of a wedding invitation, as that can rack up to 500 EUR or more for a multi-day wedding with need for a dress, transport and hotel. But even without this, finding good habits to maintain friendships across difference of affluence might be a good habit to pickup over the coming years, and practices such as pot luck meetups might be something.

Suggestions for thought

- Have you ever hit a financially rough patch where you were inhibited from socialising ? What happened with your friendships?
- If you have reached a certain level of income, does your hospitality and generosity match this?
- Are you in your group of friends aware of who is genuinely capable of affording the general group's lifestyle? How do you ensure that you are not excluding someone on financial terms?

For statistics in sociological studies, question suggestions and weights in counting see H.

6.8 Money and status

Once basic viability is established, the benefits of beginning affluence allow to invite friends for meals effortlessly, stay overs and travel for friendship maintenance. Beyond this Alberoni, 2016, and other philosophers, point that larger imbalances in financial status will introduce inequality to a friendship, rendering it a liability and strain on it. Wealth and status have been included in several studies, with wealth related indicators tested in Hall, 2012b, mostly among children and adolescents. It was uniformly shown to have with low impact on friendship, and definitely subordinated to personality, attitude or activity traits. What however has not been included in the design of the surveys or question is the option to give a negative response which the philosophers would assert.

A substantial disparity in assets or status causes two strains on the friendship. One strain consists in the suspicion of seeing the friend in terms of benefits they can bestow on account of the assets rather than as an end in themselves. The other is the suspicion of greed or stinginess of the friend if they are too withholding. 'Having is a result of keeping' - 'Haben kommt von Halten' is an old german proverb. With people who have money there is the usual prejudice of 'being good with money' also coming with stinginess. If a friend thus is substantially rich, but makes it a virtue to be frugal - to live the simple life and make his friends take part in this, questions can be quickly asked. This compounds in a much worse fashion, if your friends find out that you live lavishly in say your family life, but keep your friends on the short. Such behaviour conflicts with the tenets of affection, consideration, goodwill and generosity.

However from childhood on, most of us have stories where we have feigned affection or friendship for benefits. This could be that the 'friend' had a Playstation or a Computer when we didn't, they had the big barbie selection, maybe the friend had an elder sibling who could take us to a party where there was alcohol, had a car, better connections, the better wine collection or the fancier apartment to have a party at. This leaves our more well-endowed friend wondering about the motives of our affection to them.

Essentially, with this line of argument you enter an adversarial situation: by one side testing the hypothesis, the hypothesis of the other side gets confirmed, and vice versa. Both cases lead to no mutually satisfactory outcome. The theoretic possibility is proposed by Alberoni, 2016, p.45 - it is the solution through 'behaviour opposite the instincts'. [14]. Alternatively there is also the possibility of stratification, i.e. of choosing and aligning your friends to be equal to you in wealth (looks, intellect, ...). The result of status-homophily is widely investigated and supported by strong evidence.

I would posit there is a third way out, and that is observing general behaviour and deducing generosity, selflessness and renouncement of instrumentalisation (i.e. a non-transactional attitude) from that. It is not foolproof, but essentially you will eventually weed out the transactionally oriented people by having an attitude of being forthcoming to people who are visibly forthcoming to others. For a functional friendship, it is more important that the disparity is not felt by either side. The moment that a genuine measurement of financial equivalence or proportionality is effected, the resulting suspicion has the potential to implode any friendship, especially developing ones.

In my personal attitude I for some time kept a mental target budget of a standard social interaction of say approximately 20-30 Euro for an evening including drinks. Some adjustments would be appropriate given the occasion: an Oxford ball or a formal dinner would of course be higher, whereas a dinner at a local restaurant while backpacking in India would not allow for the expenditure of that entire sum even among a group of four. If a substantially more affluent friend took me out to a really fancy restaurant, I would speculate on being invited myself. On the contrary- if it was me determining the location in the knowledge that it is outside the budget for my company, likewise I would budget to pick up the total bill.[15] Different practices of course abound, and everyone's preferences towards finance are different, but I would say that if the friendship is valued, then effort must be undertaken for the suspicion of greed or stinginess not to enter the friendship. It is just not worth it.

I have introduced the principle of proportionality and paying it forward already when dealing with reciprocity. For the attitude of paying it forward to work, however, an external fortune view is probably the most helpful, not too dissimilar to how the Romans and early Christians saw affluence. Affluence was an external gift bestowed by the goddess of fortune or a situation or challenge given by the

[14]'Concretely speaking, this means that he who possesses superiority and power must put everything into the friendship. The other, however, must not use that power, must learn not to feel the need to. Then the friendship can exist because it is not based on inequality and need, but on what particular value each friend for himself brings to the making of the other's personality.'

[15]Before you accuse me of arrogant behaviour, this may not just be preferences of the palate, but also preferences of food hygiene when travelling in remote areas. Some people have a proverbial horse's stomach and can eat the often ridiculously cheap food from the street stands, others need to watch certain standards, and pricing often signals a certain reliability. And I would much prefer pay two dinners than spend three days suffering from another instance of Montezuma's revenge.

Christian god. In the former case, wealth was nothing inherent to character to be proud of, and thus of little value to be withheld. In the Christian case, it came with the explicit requirement to be used and shared [16]. If wealth is a gift of fortune, it is mostly independent of the person and their 'value', totally contrary to our contemporary attitude of equating power to consume with the value of the person. A Roman could casually and without the blink of an eye accept an invitation that was extended on grounds of differential affluence. The modern American or European would be stung and feel slighted by the veiled devaluation.

Substantial difference in resources might also result in different perspectives on matters, even when resources cannot be shared. The more affluent side A may need to exercise tact because other friends might still have real-world problems. As an example - if A complains about renters in one of their six apartments not paying on time, and their friend B is wondering how to make rent payments themselves to the landlord. Additionally, B's landlord may be still four months behind in fixing the heating and ignoring complaints about that, and suddenly A and B find themselves in a serious disagreement on values. Analogous scenarios can be constructed for a range of other attributes, such as attractiveness, intellect, even metabolism. There are few things more odious to listen to than someone complaining that they cannot do anything to gain weight when at the back of your mind you are painfully aware that a single Magnum ice cream will demolish your weight maintenance target for the week.

On the positive note, if a friend is affluent, has status or other attributes, and finds a good modus operandi with her or his friends, it can be a great boon. It allows for the entire group to make better experiences as they share in his pleasures. Such a friend has the power to help his friend in need, to support them in crucial moments of their lives, and the only necessary and sufficient response of the friend is gratitude.[17]

Suggestions for thought

- Have you got friends who in terms of financial assets, looks or social status are substantially below or above you? Does it sometimes matter or are you keeping it separate from the friendship?
- Have you ever gone separate paths with a friend because of such issues?
- Do you think having money is good for the friendship because of increased activity options or bad because of the above mentioned issues?

[16] The comment of moths eating up treasures apply to 'unused treasures', and condemns the owner of wealth that is just being stored rather than being put to good use towards fellow citizen and the poor according to Graham Tomlin, 'Wealth and Poverty', HTB Focus 2010, sermon now publicly unavailable (I have an MP3 copy).

[17] With all the differences and fights within the movie Spiderman 2002, the friendship of Peter Parker and Harry Osborne shows how across such social differences a benevolent and true friendship can be built.

For statistics in sociological studies, question suggestions and weights in counting see H.

6.9 Attractiveness

Attractiveness is a fairly minor resource on the grand scale, however like financial assets it is an interesting case as it can set up substantial differences in social status and motivation. Being rated attractive has substantial benefits in life. Simply by being attracted to someone we have a higher disposition to them, which makes befriending at first easier. This is not just a matter for romantic mating. Often attractiveness-homophily can be observed in same-sex friendships, as it is a trait where people seek friends of similar levels to themselves (see Cash and Derlega, 1978). There is the ubiquity of advertisement usually transported on the back of bodies and faces, all stating the same message: that good looks are universally good and socially desirable. It is no surprise that across all commercialised societies effects of tangible benefits and positive disposition are observable. Having a high attraction increases contact frequency across the spectrum. However, even more so than with financial assets it leaves the recipient of such attention open to the question of how altruistic and platonic the attention genuinely is. The alternative hypothesis is how much forthcoming attention is motivated by currying favour to improve the likelihood of later romantic involvement of whatever longevity[18]. The probability of the alternative hypothesis varies with relationship status, gender, general availability and other variables, but ultimately its existence can spoil the development of an authentic platonic relationship. This uncertainty of even the option of romantic interest is the major reason for difficulty of cross-sex friendships, and a high attractiveness increases the difficulty gauging of authenticity of friendship interest substantially. Additional effects include the potential triggering of insecurity and competition in same-sex friendship, such as when on social outings romantic potentials mostly converge on the more attractive one leaving their friends on the side. It can also be felt when partners of current same-sex friends implicitly - even if unconsciously - signal interest.

Suggestions for thought

- Do you have a platonic cross-sex friend who is substantially more attractive than you? How did you resolve the potential uncertainty?
- Do you have a same-sex friend who is substantially more or less attractive than you? Has this ever been an issue between you two? How did you resolve this?

For statistics in sociological studies, question suggestions and weights in counting see H.

[18]S. Feldhahn and J. Feldhahn, 2008 on survey on response to attractive female conference speaker. It is unfortunately both a cliche and yet a relatively robustly evidenced issue that men react far stronger in attention and behavioural change to an attractive female than the other way round.

6.10 Discussion of resources

The themes of resources are heavily codependent, and it is not always easy to separate them. Most of the resources, except for Time and Content, are essentially about one factor: 'Resource availability enabling participation'. Resources are essentially insignificant for the establishment of friendship, as long as a minimum amount is met. However, once this threshold is not met, they become prohibitive. Couples with small kids or investment bankers or consultants becoming so time scarce that there is simply no way to get out of the house to meet friends. People who lose their incomes and simply cannot go out with their friends to restaurants anymore, or live in really tight accommodation that they cannot host people coming for dinner. Shy people coming to new places, and in the absence of 'any' network, do not feel comfortable to join social events. Teenagers not conforming to physical norms (attractiveness, fitness = suitability for sports) ostracised in school or adolescence. Elderly people or long time unemployed or recently divorced who believe (often through no fault of anybody else) that they have nothing to say that anybody might be interested in and withdraw from society. Elderly who are vulnerable (specifically in current times of COVID-19) can be rendered stationary by disease or other health conditions. And finally there are people whose friends move away, or through a move inside a city or cuts in public transport suddenly find themselves transport-topologically further away from their friends. Transport can be expensive both in time and money and thus adversely affect activities of friendship maintenance. A particular example is the metropolis phenomenon[19], where people who self-profess to be friends, but living in different suburbs go through months without seeing each other despite a maximum distance of 5 miles as the bird flies.

Other candidates for resources: Separate to time another candidate for a resource was the capacity to pay attention, to listen and to be emotionally available. This seemed more natural as an activity and a trait, but arguments can be made for its nature as a resource. Whenever we linguistically correct apply the word 'my X is exhausted', it points to a resource mentality. Thus we speak of emotional capacity, with some people listening for hours when we need to emote and offload, and some people not having patience longer than 10 minutes. Attention and focus is another general resource increasingly in short supply (c.f. Turkle, 2017), though arguably this is a subset of resource time or energy.

6.11 The friendship needs

> Unlike sexual desire, friendship can neither be satisfied nor self-satisfied.
>
> Alberoni

Categorising needs as mentioned above, I did not want to generate this exploratively from the key word frequency analysis (see F.1), but utilize a pre-existent studied and reviewed framework. On the back of the excellent summary of human development scales in Alkire, 2002 and her given criteria on how to evaluate

[19] A metropolis is a city of more than 5 or 10 million people, such as London, Tokyo, New York or Sao Paulo

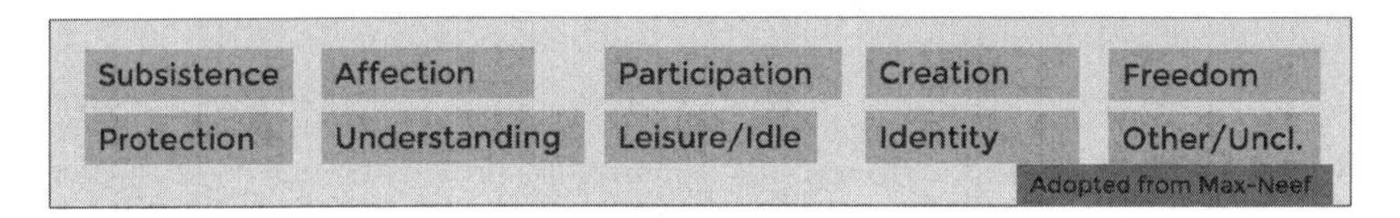

Figure 6.3: Needs

them, I tried out a few of them that were focused on psychological needs rather than the general measures of poverty and human development. The framework of Max-Neef, Elizalde, and Hopenhayn, 1992 provided the best fit to friendship and social connectedness. Natural here I mean the degree to which common sense and intuition provided a natural fit when trying to map the correspondence of friendship keywords to the need categories. Intuitively I found the categorization almost like a perfect description of 'love languages for friendship' (in exactly the same sense that Chapman, 2009 writes about love languages for romantic couples - the frequencies on which signals of love are both sent and received, if the partner is open for reception, see section 7.2).

Subsistence: Apart from physical health, this includes mental health, humour and sustainable living. It is the stereotype strict 'Need-love' as defined by Lewis, 1960.

Protection: This encompasses caring for other people, helping and protecting them. This in a way is a strict 'Gift-love', and thus naturally paired with Subsistence.

Affection: Affection includes emotional caring for other people, sharing and listening to emotions and thoughts, building relationships etc. Like all the other needs this is both a gift and need love. This need is mostly emphasised within the sociological group.

Understanding: This is the brain oriented expansion need, thinking, investigating, exploring and analysing. This is probably not a universal need, but much emphasised among the philosopher group.

Participation: This is our need of connection to the wider community and society. It is driven by the herd instinct, the need to belong, and to cooperate with other people.

Leisure: This is the need to destress, to relax in each other's company, to play, fantasize, laugh and indulge in nostalgia.

Creation: The need of creation, to leave a legacy, to work together. Doing is in a way at the heart of 'male' friendship, and characterising many great friendships such as Marx and Engels, Cicero and Atticus, Chinese artists and western musicians collaborating to create works of literature, art or music.

Identity: Building a positive story about oneself, a sense of identity and self worth is a key human need. Friends are core in this discovery process and can support this need probably better than family or wider society on the back of the trust and mutual understanding slowly built within the relationship.

Freedom: The sense of liberty, independence, openmindedness and separation from others is innate in many of us, though probably the most fraught with cultural differences from all the other needs above.

Using these categories and an approximate transformation matrix, I could then also transform the keyword weights of the literary texts into weight vectors of needs. The exercise proved its utility in demonstrating how different the various authors imagine which needs are being met by friendship. It should be noticed of course that this concept of 'friendship satisfying a need' or 'friendship being a need to be satisfied' is strongly argued against in Alberoni, 2016. Evidence for the possibility of satisfying this need is provided by evolutionary biology and general psychological research, and its tradition ranges to Aristotle (Humans are social animals) and arguably the earliest part of the Bible (it is not good for man to be alone ...). I would argue that it is a bit of both. Individual 'low-level' needs can be satisfied, in the sense that some people can be made to feel good (and some absolutely fantastic) simply by spending some time with their friends over a hike. For other aspects, in particular questions of meaning or identity, the long-term effect is important. A further tangent is the fundamental nature of these needs. I. Yalom, 1980 in his reference work describes four ultimate concerns as fundamental psychological questions that every person needs to answer for her or himself: Death, Isolation, Freedom and Meaninglessness. In a way you can partition the above terminology into short-term affective (Subsistence, Protection, Affection, Leisure), transcendent (Creation, Identity, Freedom) and in-between (Understanding, Participation). Thus you can see that the transcendent and in-between friendship needs directly cater to the needs of isolation-connectedness (participation, understanding), freedom-responsibility (freedom), and meaning (identity, creation). But being specific here will help in identifying what need or love gaps people have when they complain about being lonely. This holds true for all ages, but specifically is necessary when trying to devise intervention programmes or policy for the elderly.

Loneliness and Needs

The general tool of choice for loneliness measurement is the Gierveld scale defined by Gierveld and van Tilburg, 2006. It comprised 11 items that were shortened via confirmatory factor analysis to a 6 item loneliness scale or a 3 item emotional scale and a 3 item social loneliness scale. To be clear, the value of the instrument cannot be overstated for the overall measurement of loneliness. However, it is less suited to give us information on the underlying causes of loneliness (see table 6.11). Participation (having people around, best friend, circle of friends) is covered adequately. Leisure is likewise somewhat covered by the pleasure of company, but not in different types of enjoying leisure. Trust and 'feel close to' seem overlapping. Not covered explicitly are understanding (I miss someone who really understands me, close friend can do that, but can also qualify via loyalty and trust) and creation (I miss someone with whom I can do / create something together). Whilst subsistence is covered, protection and active affection are also missed out - lonely people might be lonely because they feel useless as they cannot provide or care for someone else.

The other scale for loneliness measurement is the UCLA scale (see D. Russell, Peplau, and Ferguson, 1978, D. Russell, Peplau, and Cutrona, 1980 and D.W. Russell, 1996 for the various versions). This one does have a few questions that are tailored to finding out things about the existence of quality friendships, however from a full response to the 20 items scale a mapping to the Max-Neef Needs is somewhat difficult (see table 6.11).

It needs to be said that these may not all be equally relevant to all people. It is likely that the needs diverge, so the result of a Max-Neef type Loneliness scale would not measure overall loneliness like Gierveld, but would focus of pain felt from loneliness in different social needs categories.

Why is this 'gift-need love' dimensionality important? For an illustrative example, I will turn to the popular test for loneliness developed by Hawthorne, 2006 Friendship Scale with six items:

1. It has been easy to relate to others.
2. I felt isolated from other people.
3. I had someone to share my feelings with.
4. I found it easy to get in touch with others when I needed to and others felt they had to help me.
5. When with other people I felt separate from them.
6. I felt alone and friendless.

It is an excellent scale however it mostly serves the purpose of answering 'is a person X lonely' or 'how lonely does a person X feel'. It does not answer the question 'why or in what way does a person feel lonely'.
One thus might devise a different loneliness scale dependent on whether the individual friendship or connection needs are being met. The following could be an example, however, only there for illustration.

1. There is 'someone' who supports me in my day-to-day life.
2. There is 'someone' I can take care of and support.
3. There is 'someone' with whom I exchange regular signs of affection.
4. There is 'someone' who understands my thoughts and with whom I can discuss politics, daily news or other interests.
5. There is 'someone' with whom I can together participate in civic life, be it church, association, local events.
6. There is 'someone' with whom I can relax, play games, laugh and indulge in nostalgia.
7. There is 'someone' with whom I can engage creatively, write, paint, make music and make stuff.
8. There is 'someone' who helps me discover myself, with whom I can discuss personal issues and my personal growth.
9. (difficult) There is someone who does (1)-(8), but respects my privacy and independence, with whom I do not have to conform to societal norms.

It is a hypothesis that behind all the items (1)-(6) of the Hawthorne scale or similar scales hide one or more items from the friendship needs group. These trigger the perceived lack in connection relative to a state of satisfied friendship needs. By identifying the strengths of needs for groups of population (e.g. academic widowed women in care homes who might have a need for intellectual stimulation or men in early retirement who just want a friendly fellow to head to the pub with and engage in work nostalgia) and how they contribute to feelings of loneliness we can develop targeted policy to mitigate this felt lack in connection. I will return to this point in the research outlook 9.11 once I have introduced roles.

As a final comment - using the Max-Neef needs as loneliness categories, one can also look at the loneliness definitions of other authors writing about loneliness. The chosen words in their definition of loneliness will often reveal which friendship need they mostly emphasise. Thus when e.g. Hertz, 2020 speaks of loneliness as 'not mattering' or 'not being seen', this can be easily classified as protection (mattering - providing use to someone) and participation. As noted above, most of the sociologically influenced literature has a subsistence (support) and affection/understanding (discuss problems) perspective. Social organisations offering befriending often have more holistic views, emphasising affection, leisure and participation. At this point I would argue that it probably is indeed helpful to have a focused view of loneliness for evaluating certain social problems and interventions, but from a generalist analytical perspective, overall figures (which needs are met to what degree in which parts of the population) should be desirable.

6.12 Conclusion of framework

This concludes the chapter of all the important traits and other characteristics. Now whilst the categorization can be disputed, and indeed at the time of writing I expect that substantial discussions will still be necessary to hone the allocations of positive traits, I wish to reiterate the claim of exhaustiveness. The claim is that all sentences of the type: 'my friend is X, feels or treats me a certain way Y, or does Z, ... which is important to our friendship' should be somehow covered. It is not a short or parsimonious list, but contains about 50 traits, attitudes, activities and resources. But it is reasonably exhaustive, in the same sense that other lists such as the character strengths in Peterson and Seligman, 2004 are reasonably exhaustive. Future discussions will show to what degree and how this list will still have to be amended.

The merit in this compilation on themes is in being able now to think structurally on the differences in attitudes and philosophies. First we can think about ourselves, our friendships. What can we now say about them? Can we appreciate something more that we didn't before? Are there habits which we want to improve or change? How do we interpret differences in opinion between the philosophers of old and modern self help or psychology? Maybe Aristotle and Cicero were onto something that is important? Maybe the study of their texts shows us aspects that have gone out of focus for us, and our friendships are poorer for it. Maybe authenticity and honesty are substantially more important than even the current modern psychometric evaluations see it? Or maybe their rigid virtue oriented approach did not age well [20]. Maybe by focusing on emotional availability, listening and appreciation of individuality our friendships are all richer for it, far beyond what Aristotle or Cicero could have experienced. If we are Christian[21], how do we live our friendships? Do we subscribe to a biblical 'hangout, eat and bond' philosophy that marked Jesus and the disciples? Or do we subscribe to the neo-aristotelian virtue view that developed in the middle ages and is currently advocated by Cuddeback, 2010, but has suprisingly little in terms of biblical foundation? There is no right or wrong here, but I hope that in reading the richness of options has become clear.

When people hear that I study friendships and friendship maintenance, immediately the next question is 'What is most important?'.This can relate to traits, aspect or activities, but it can also relate to maintenance strategies. Is there maybe not a single trait but a cluster of traits or activities that is the most important. I don't think this is possible to be answered conclusively. I will come to the analysis of clusters both in the appendix as well as in a separate quantitative paper. Indications are possible, but overall the answer remains 'It depends'. My current sentiment is that there are a few items that are universally important (loosely I would put into the category good will, consideration, loyalty, honesty, reliability, enjoyment of company and spending time together), but only make up for maybe 40 % of the picture of an individual friendship. Explicitly I would exclude homophily [22] from this list. That begs the question how to deal with the 60 % that changes between different close friendships. The answer will come in the roles section. Before I get there, I will however try to give a picture on how the collection of themes could give an illustrative picture of what happens inside a friendship, so to speak the 'mechanics' of it. That is the theme of the next chapter.

[20] Aristotles statements about women and slave-ownership likewise have not aged well and are now generally frowned upon.

[21] I apologize in advance for having covered little of Confucian, Islamic or Buddhist thought, despite reading material, I did not have the feeling of being able to appreciate the material sufficiently to include it.

[22] If you dispute this, ask yourself whether you would say 'I am really blessed that all my friends are so much like me' in the same sense as you might say 'I am really blessed that all my friends are so funny, loyal or enjoyable'

Gierveld and Max-Neef					
	Max-Neef	OES	OSS	SES	SSS
1. There is always someone I can talk to about my day-to-day problems.	Under. & Ident (?)		X		
2. I miss having a really close friend.	Part., Under., Ident (?)	X			
3. I experience a general sense of emptiness.	Unrel.	X		X	
4. There are plenty of people I can rely on when I have problems.	Subs.		X		X
5. I miss the pleasure of the company of others.	Part&Leis	X			
6. I find my circle of friends and acquaintances too limited.	Part	X			
7. There are many people I can trust completely.	Gen.		X		X
8. There are enough people I feel close to.	Aff.		X		X
9. I miss having people around.	Part.	X		X	
10. I often feel rejected.	Unrel.	X		X	
11. I can call on my friends whenever I need them.	Subs.		X		

Gierveld and van Tilburg, 2006 subdivides the 11 questions in 4 different scales: Original Emotional Subscale (OES-6), Original Social Subscale (OSS-6), Short Emotional Subscale (SES-3) and Short Social Subscale (SSS-3), which are mapped out by the X's.

UCLA and Max-Neef			
1.	I feel in tune with the people around me.	Understanding	General
2.	I lack companionship.	General	Friends
3.	There is no one I can turn to.	Subsistence	General
4.	I do not feel alone.	General	General
5.	I feel part of a group of friends.	Part + Und + Id	Friends
6.	I have a lot in common with the people around me.	Ident + Und.	General
7.	I am no longer close to anyone.	Aff	Friends
8.	My interests and ideas are not shared by those around me.	Creat + Leis	Friends + Gen
9.	I am an outgoing person.	General	General
10.	There arc people I feel close to.	Aff.	Friends + Gen
11.	I feel left out.	Part.	General
12.	My social relationships arc superficial.	Und. + Ident	General
13.	No one really knows me well.	Underst.	Friends
14.	I feel isolated from others.	Part.	General
15.	I can find companionship when I want it.	General	Friends
16.	There are people who really understand me.	Und. + Ident	Friends
17.	I am unhappy being so withdrawn.	Part.	General
18.	People are around me but not with me.	Affection	General
19.	There are people I can talk to.	Leis. (?)	General
20.	There are people I can turn to.	Subs.	General

The last column distinguishes whether this statement relates to the general social environment or just friends.

Chapter 7

Process of Friendships

For casual reading, please just look at 7.6 and 7.7

> Laelius on the friendship with Scipio: 'there was one home for us both; we had the same fare and shared it in common, and we were together not only in our military campaigns, but also in our foreign tours and on our vacations in the country.'

Cicero

> Friendship arises out of mere Companionship when two or more of the companions discover that they have in common some insight or interest or even taste which the others do not share and which, till that moment, each believed to be his own unique treasure (or burden).

C. S. Lewis, 1960

> To become good/best friends 200 hours intentionally spent together are likely needed over 6 weeks.

Hall, 2018

7.1 Review of theories

This chapter develops a conjectural description, how friendship 'works'. I want to describe it as I would describe how a machine works[1] or a complex dynamic system. It is the attempt at synthesis, bringing the themes together to see whether the whole construct makes sense. It is also a model, in the sense that in the end the description is a simplification for explainability. If your interest is non-academic, this chapter can be skipped, though it might be helpful to spend a few minutes on the description of the conjectured process in section 7.3 or with the graph 7.1, as I will refer to it in the subsequent chapters.

[1] See `https://youtu.be/HkB4c0nv3qk` for a good style of description of such systems (DE - die Dampfmaschine).

Over time, various theories on friendship processes have been proposed and tested, though with varying levels of rigour and suitability. Hammering out the friendship processes was in focus in the seventies and eighties culminating in the volume of Fehr, 1996, which collected and summarized the state of research of that period. Fehr distinguishes in the work five types of friendship models - reinforcement (1), interdependence (2), equity (3), cognitive (4) and developmental (5) model/theory.

1. **Reinforcement** theory states that 'we are attracted to people who provide us with rewards' (p.22). Fehr rephrases this as 'If another person happens to be present when something good happens to us, we are likely to be attracted to him or her' (p.22). Note however that the first represents a causal explanation vs. the second providing a coincidental explanation. In this context, Clore and Byrne, 1974 posit that our attraction can be represented as the weighted 'sum' of positive reinforcements and implies a causal relationship. B. Lott and A. Lott, 1960 investigate the coincidental explanation labelled the classical conditioning approach. Social exchange theories try to move beyond attraction and explain the mechanics of continuous relationships.

2. Kelley and Thibaut, 1978 **interdependence** theory applied to friendships according to Fehr means 'we develop a standard, the comparison level, for what we feel we deserve in a friendship. The theory would predict that we feel satisfied with friendships that exceed this standard, and dissatisfied with friendships that fail to meet it.' The level of the standard we compare it to is generally dependent on the number and quality of alternatives. Rusbult, 1980 proposes an **investment** model that considers level of rewards, cost incurred, availability of alternative friendships and investment in the friendship and predicts us to remain in a particular relationship if the benefits outweigh the costs and opportunity costs. Argyle and Henderson, 1984 expand on the reward theory by defining a set of key rules both to be kept and actions to be avoided. However, the rules they are considering are not so much costs but in a way penalties on perceived transgressions.

3. The **equity** theory of Hatfield and Traupmann, 1981 'predicts that we will be satisfied with a relationship only if we perceive that our outcomes are comparable to those of our partner.' To be clear, we are dissatisfied in both cases of our benefits being higher OR lower than that of the partner. In both cases we will try to reestablish reciprocity, which can happen by changing our efforts (up/down), reject or encourage efforts of the partner or change our perception or interpretation of the benefits.

4. For cognitive belief theories, Fehr singles out Newcomb, 1961 **balance** theory, which states that the beliefs of two friends also need to be balanced towards other objects, i.e. the environment. The model is a theory built around the theme of mutual belief and worldview, postulating a strain in the relationship if our friends hold different attitudes towards other people or objects (politics, values, interests) that are significant to them.

5. In the **developmental** theory (e) there is foremost the social penetration theory by Altman and Taylor, 1973, who posit that 'relationship development is characterised by an increase in both depth and breadth of intimate self-disclosure' with the four phases: 'orientation, exploratory affective exchange, affective exchange and stable exchange'. The result of this process is full disclosure and mutual awareness.

Related to the developmental model we also have the **mirror** theory. The mirror view originates with classical philosophers and is formalized by Cocking and Kennett, 1998, p.513[2] in the philosophical school of thought. The phrase 'We become closer friends the more we see of ourselves in the friend who takes the shape of a mirror' (see e.g. Cicero, 1923, p.133[3]) however shows that mirror doesn't quite capture it either. In the same essay, they also discuss the 'secrets view' which is the philosophical label for the social penetration theory. As Pahl, 2000, p.80 notes: 'Neither the mirror nor the secrets view is able to capture with complete success the essential features of the close or companionate style of friendship.' Cocking and Kennett, 1998 conclude with proposing a '**direction and interpretation**' account of friendship, which loosely captures understanding, guidance, effect change and common memory. Their description of examples is close to the mark of essence of close friendship, but again its specificity leaves out affection, creation and simple enjoyment. Concluding I would say that the economic (reward, cost, equity) or single feature (balance, reinforcement) theories all substantially fall short of the mark. This becomes specifically clear when taking note of the richness of features friendships can be shown to exhibit in the previous chapters on personality, relationship and activities.

7.2 Requirements for an explanatory friendship process

I believe that a model for a process needs to feel right - it needs to reflect intuitive thinking. Friendship is not calculatory or keeping count of benefits given to each other, even though reciprocity is important. It is not just positive reinforcement (Enjoyment of company, Fun, most activities), though positive emotions are a substantial element of it. Friendship has long-term investment features, specifically as common memory builds up and trust, loyalty and awareness of mutual affection and goodwill. Whilst the sociological and psychological literature has been excellent at identifying effects and measuring them, philosophy and the 'self-help' literature has been substantially better at identifying suitable images for explaining the friendship process on an intuitive level. I will explore four of them.

Alberoni's encounter

One key idea in Alberoni, 2016 is that friendship is lived discontinuously. Not lived together, but lived as a sequence of meetings or conventions in the literal sense[4], which he calls encounters. Friendship manifests itself in these encounters

[2] 'A friend therefore is like an ideal mirror. Now it occurs to us, that as an ideal mirror, a friend might provide more than just an image of what we should be.'

[3] 'Again, he who looks upon a true friend, looks, as it were, upon a sort of image of himself.'

[4] convenire - to come together, gather

and by doing so comes into existence. Alberoni specifically positions the nature of the encounter as the antithesis to the market or exchange model of the likes of Adam Smith (which the sociologists then adopted in later course). It is much more about the experience of friendship and the friend in the moment, as you explore topics and the friend's personality, discuss theories, smile and laugh. In its highest form, it feels like a miracle. Alberoni is not alone in his assessment. Lewis, 1960, p.47[5] also singles out the momentary experience as the pinnacle of friendship, the moment where everything comes together and you are fully immersed in the conversation with your friends. Little, 2000[6], labelling his preferred or pure friendship the communicating friendship, also emphasises the vitality of these conversations and places them at the core of the friendship purpose. In particular, he notes that in the coming together and leaving again friendship much more than any other relationship reflects the natural state of interaction of children with each other. Children come together to play and then head out again, or come to mother or father, interact, and then head off again. Whilst all three writers emphasise the conversation based moment, it needs to be said that there are moments other than intellectual conversation, where likewise friendship manifests itself meaningfully. These can be moments of grief, where the friend stands by your side and comforts you - an experience marked by long silences. It can be mundane catchups over a beer or a coffee, or meeting at the football pitch where the kids practice. But the memory creating unit so to speak is the moment, hour or day spent together.

Gottman's positive bid

To categorise Gottman's positive bid theory as self help is deeply unfair, as it is built upon a thirty year rigorous research program identifying predictors of marriage success using his observation lab and coding interactions of couples who are or are about to get married. On a micro-process level, it is probably the most extensive dataset out of all the relationship-process theories described in this section, and capturing not only self-reporting data but also medical indicators enriches the dataset enormously.[7] The key to understanding his theory are the cumulative responses to positivity and bids for connection. J.M. Gottman, 2002, p.308, Experiment 7 observed that couples constantly bid for each other's attention and reaction, and the reaction of the partner can be described as turning towards or turning away. If the turning towards occurs, e.g. by voicing interest, concern, joy, or affirmation, the 'signalling handshake' is concluded positively. If it is ignored or

[5]'Especially when the whole group is together, each bringing out all that is best, wisest, or funniest in all the others. Those are the golden sessions; when four or five of us after a hard day's walking have come to our inn; when our slippers are on, our feet spread out towards the blaze and our drinks at our elbows; when the whole world, and something beyond the world, opens itself to our minds as we talk; and no one has any claim on or any responsibility for another, but all are freemen and equals as if we had first met an hour ago, while at the same time an Affection mellowed by the years enfolds us. Life - natural life- has no better gift to give. Who could have deserved it.'

[6]'They seem to dwell in conversation, always looking for talk, investing time and energy in it, enjoying it as an end in itself, treating it as both work and play. Witty or earnest, disjointed or smooth, angry, troubling or pleasing, a patchwork of light and dark of strong feelings and cool, sharp ideas, a conversation is life in a microcosm.'

[7]Heyman and Slep, 2001 however maintains that further independent validation on larger and more diverse samples is required, and the high prediction rates are most likely a result of in-sample over-fitting.

rejected, disconnection is signalled and loneliness is created in the partner. Whilst Gottman applies this to romantic couples, it is easy to see this process is also taking place at the very core of the friendship development. We signal interest in our friend's concerns, we engage with the friend on our interest or hobby of choice, we value the friend's opinion, we laugh about the friend's joke. Alberoni's encounter as described in the previous section can thus be dissected into hundreds of mini-handshakes with positive outcome, and all of them involve a trigger from one or several items of the personality, relationship attitude and activity sets. Conversely, I believe that this is a two-way street, and the transmission mechanism, via which all (sic!) the aforementioned elements transfer into our perception of friendship quality, consists of such mini-handshakes or positive interactions.

Nelson's triangle

The key concept of Nelson, 2016 and Nelson, 2020 is a triangle of so to speak the three dimensions of friendship which she labels Positivity, Consistency and Vulnerability. In order to develop a friendship fully, Nelson claims all three must be increased bit by bit and roughly in sync of each other. As noted in the sections before, the terms cover significantly more components than the same labels in the friendship framework explored here, and yet I think they are still not quite spot on. They are no doubt important, but I would not be surprised if slightly different focus arises in the future once more studies like Hall, 2012b generate datasets of friendship preferences and employ factor analysis techniques. The key take-away for me is the idea of describing the state of a friendship as a triangle of three different descriptors or indicators which need to be developed and worked at simultaneously and over time. Thus a single factor such as vulnerability, degree of self disclosure or positivity (aka reward) will never satisfactorily 'explain' friendship and the potential imbalances in it. The codependency and slow growth of the descriptors is key to what I call the '**takes-time-to-grow**' hypothesis, meaning that friendship needs to be developed, and is thus antithetical to the '**spark**' hypothesis.

Chapman's love language and tank

Chapman, 2009 is another classic in the marriage self-help and advisory genre. There are two key concepts (images) in his book. The first concept is that of a love language, a way how to express love to a person and how that person can perceive that love is being expressed by a specific action. The claim is that out of the five options Chapman offers - words of affirmation, quality time, receiving gifts, acts of service and physical touch - we usually only speak one language natively, i.e. express our love by it and perceive love expressed to us. As a corollary he posits that most marriage issues are because of mismatches in love language spoken by partner A and expected by partner B. Egbert and D. Polk, 2006 and D.M. Polk and Egbert, 2013 subject the concept to some validity tests, as do M. Cook et al., 2013 and Surijah and Kirana, 2020. But beyond the validity testing, the concept of love languages is cited in over 500 academic publications[8], and thus by sheer impact can be considered as accepted or at least as not outright refuted. Interpreting

[8]Google Scholar citation index

love languages as transmission vectors, Chapman then expands this theory by postulating a virtual 'love tank' inside each of us. This love tank gets filled as love is expressed to us. But - and here comes the crux - the love tank has only one of the five openings fully open and all other openings half or completely shut. Thus even as love is expressed abundantly by people around us, if it is not on our wavelength we do not register it. As a result, we may be left with an empty love tank and feeling lonely. The consequence is that while making demands is frowned upon both in romantic love and in friendship, making sure that we are aware of our needs and ensuring that our family and friends can know what is effective at making us happy by good communication is a healthy habit.

7.3 Conjecture of Process

With these images or concepts exhibited, it is possible to expand the identified elements of the friendship framework of chapter 2.3 into a process model. To be clear, this model at the stage of writing is a conjecture or hypothesis, not a validated concept. What it is however trying to do is to bring the elements together to an intuitive view of how friendship 'works'. When explained to a lay person the description should elicit the response 'yep, that sounds about right'. It should resonate with the layperson's experience of his friendship in the way the above mentioned concepts do.

I sketch out in figure 7.1 how I piece all these elements together. The core element is that of the encounter or coming together, much in the fashion Alberoni describes but extended also to the non-conversational other meetings. I think indeed every encounter with friends is singular. It happens within a context, but it is the unit. It is where our personalities and our relationship history and status come together and play out in activity. As this happens a myriad of micro interactions create positive feelings, as we smile, laugh, joke, discuss, play games, give counsel, listen to our friend's worries or support our friend in day-to-day matters. In the friend's presence we are reminded of their personality, all their positive traits, the humour, their character, their kindness and the energy they radiate. And in it our relationship is affirmed, as we remember old stories, we feel the loyalty and devotion to us. We know we are important to the friend as they pay close attention to what we say and recognize how we have over time gained a deep knowledge of each other through sharing stories and thoughts. We see all that is common such as our interests and yet again also discover novel aspects in the personality of our friend. We meet eye to eye one person to another.

When the encounter is over, we part ways, and on the way home, or that night before going to sleep, or on the way to work, we think about it again. At that moment we recall what happened. With this act we commit the result to memory, the key scenes, jokes, moments of affection. We incrementally adjust our relationship attitudes, our assessment of our friend's loyalty, how much fun we have in their company. This is not an exercise in going through a mental spreadsheet, ticking elements off or giving grades. It is like a fast forward of the evening, only a minute or two, a flick through images in our mind and associated emotions. We gauge to what degree our friendship needs were met on this evening, whatever they were in our particular case and situation. We look at both of our needs observing reciprocity, we ponder whether our friend had as much fun, enjoyment or increase in life quality from meeting us as we did. Gauge here means just that - in a very rough way: the fundamental question is 'did it feel right or good' without looking into details. We also however reflect on what might have been substantial transgressions. These in most cases will be nonexistent or immaterial, but our friend may have said something offensive, or something inconsistent with the image we have of them, or may have acted in a way we would not expect them to (in a way that it questions our friendship). This then is the moment where we reflect on it and try to understand what might be the issue (see Argyle and Henderson rule breaches). We reflect on what might have changed, and how we might deal with it, and how much of an issue it is. Thus we either initiate the conflict resolution or reconciliation process or in the most severe case accept the need to disconnect.

But in most cases the outcome of the assessment will be positive, and because of the reflection, we not only adjust our relationship attitudes by a little but also two concepts that I would see as the short-term and the long-term memory of friendship. The short-term memory could be labeled 'positivity' and essentially represents a superficial short-term assessment of the friendship. It is a measure of how fun or enjoyable our recent interactions were, how good they made us feel, and thus how much we anticipate of meeting up again. This comes first to mind, when we think of the friend again, specifically when we are thinking of whether it is time to meet up again.

The second item is the long-term common memory, and this is the built up awareness of the value of the relationship. It is the full treasure of shared anecdotes and stories, our awareness of mutual knowledge and affection. I think this is the equivalent of the Chapman love tank within that relationship. The cumulation of all that was good, how our friend aided or changed us in crucial moments, the good times we had, the meaning this friendship has assumed in our lives. The love tank so to speak is the collective memory of what is all good about the friendship and makes me want to pursue it and invest in it in the long-term. It also captures the gratitude and privilege that we feel in response to the friendship's history. Most of the activities given in section 5 are not chosen as key activities because they give short-term enjoyment or positivity, but because they create long-term memories that are key to sustaining the friendship.

This is the state we are in when we consider re-initiating the next encounter. We think of the fun we had at the last meetings and look forward to the new experience. Sometimes however the last meeting was really far back, as we lost contact, e.g. during times abroad, child caring or intense work periods. Here, our desire to re-initiate an encounter is also driven by considerations of the overall relationship and a general affection from the past years. We may also feel guilt for having let the contact slip. At this moment we also consider the resources (as explained in section 6.1) that we need to muster - whether our busy life allows for a suitable time slot, or whether our financial situation allows the expenditure of transport and expected cost of drinking and eating. Finally, and specifically in age, there is the question whether my health condition predictably and comfortably allows me to go out of the house and venture to meet the friend. Whilst we can thus speak of 'cost of the meeting' it should finally be considered whether the initiation is a full decision to be made, or whether there is a habit or rule that substantially reduces the cost of the decision. A monthly game night with friends needs no further coordination - it is simply there in the diary. Hosting a grand party or visiting a friend on the other side of the planet however requires a greater decision over costs in terms of time, effort and financial ones. Finally there is the mental cost of overcoming fear of rejection. If we initiate, we expect our friend to respond positively. If our friend rejects the initiation, depending on our personality and security, we can shrug it off as a side effect of busy life and other circumstances, or take it personally and thus put our friendship potentially at risk of fracture, however minor. Whilst for some people this is no issue, this rejection risk can be an obstacle to reaching out and initiating an encounter.

In an ideal case this process repeats itself in a virtuous cycle (positive feedback loop), building the relationship in the process and reinforcing itself, as the encounters get richer and more rewarding as intimacy is being built with the accompaniments of mutual understanding, affection, common memory and appreciation for each others humour.

7.4 Assumptions and implications of the model

Placing the encounter or meeting in the middle of the friendship development and maintenance process is a significant statement. Friendship is thus a highly interactive and direct relationship. Conversely, it asserts that without encounter there is no friendship. Not that friendships cannot last a long time even in the absence of a friend, e.g. because of prolonged residence in a different country. But it assumes that the desire to see the friend again is always there to a substantial degree. It is assumed that we will initiate, and make some effort to get together if there is an opportunity for just such an encounter, e.g. by being in town or finding out we have some spare time on our hand when we know our friend is most likely to have time as well. The moment the anticipation for the encounter dies and the efforts to arrange it with it, the friendship is dead, as Alberoni, 2016 argues and is echoed in the relationship attitude 'making friendship a priority'.

Hall, 2018 using 500 participants from the Amazon Mechanical Turk service deduced that it takes about 50 hours to consider someone a friend and 200 hours to consider someone a close friend, something I call the 'Takes-time-to-grow' friendship concept. This insight is built into this model, as repeated encounters slowly build the relationship attitudes that make up the core element of the friendship's nature.

7.5 Improving friendship within the process

This process model is at this point only a conjecture, and will need to be validated and tested, both empirically but also simply by scholarly discussion but also in conversation with lay people, whether it resonates with them and reflects their intuitive understanding.

If the model however is validated, it provides the benefits of offering precise levers or instructions on how to develop and maintain a friendship. It is clear at what points we can change our behaviour and improve our friendships, provided the other party is willing to walk on the path with us. We can bit by bit initiate to raise the temperature of the relationship, but it takes two to tango.

We can reduce the costs of initiation by clear communication and signalling. Being spontaneous, fast and uncomplicated in responding to bids of initiating an encounter lowers the cost for a friend taking the initiative with us in organising a get together. Being overall respectful of privacy lowers the impact of rejection of a date suggestion if it has to occur because of other circumstances. If we have to reject we can also ensure that we emphasise the situational aspect by encouraging a future initiation ('I cannot make it on Thursday, but I hope we still manage to catch up in the next two weeks, how about next week Wednesday after work'.). Again the best way to reduce the cost of initiating is the establishment of a habit like a girls' night, boys' night, open door dinner or board game evening.

We can try to improve our encounters. This of course is easier said than done. It comes down to whether we continue to meet each other's friendship needs, whether intuitively or explicitly. This sounds very market economy exchange of services like, but it is not. It is striving to make our friend leaving from the encounter a little better and happier. Variation might help, such as going to different restaurants or cafes, trying different activities or naturally changing and stimulating activities (such as having an opera or theatre subscription). But essentially the logic of the love languages applies here, with certain activities more resonating with our friend's needs more than others. Thus, whilst not being strategically manipulative, we just are attentive to not just what makes us happy, but how our friend is doing, what mood they are in and how we can set activity and setting to ensure they have a genuinely good time.

Using the post action review in the right way, we can make memories more lasting, creating gratitude and love for each other. Habits here can be gratitude diaries, taking photos, making sure we remember details. We can also review our expectations and at certain times cut our friends some slack. A friendship is not immediately in danger if a few encounters are less than spectacular. Sometimes friends have other worries, leaving them unable to savour the joy of the meeting. Sometimes we may even fight and need to swallow our pride to realise that actually we were wrong, and it is up to us to apologise.

These are examples, and I will elaborate more in the coming sections. But this concludes the formulation and construction of the friendship framework and friendship process. For the remainder of the book I will assume that the framework and process are reasonably robust, acknowledging that validation work remains to be done in the future. Based on this assumption I will show how the elements of the framework can be then used like a lense to look at Friendship Maintenance, Roles of Friendship and how to improve our own approach to friendship and that within organizations and civil society.

7.6 Formation and platonic attraction

Whilst I maintain in this book that romantic relationships and friendships are different in nature, there are some parallels that are closer than one might think. One such item is the role of attraction. Whereas in romantic relationships this more often than not boils down to physical attraction, I found the forming of friendship also much more understandable by conjecturing a concept of 'platonic attraction'. The concept is not new; it is also widely employed in LGBTQ literature. Again Asatryan, 2016, p.49 provides a great definition: 'But attraction simply means the experience of feeling drawn to someone - feeling interested in getting to know him or her better.' - and further on - 'It was the smallest, simplest moment of meeting someone and thinking, "I like you!"'. This attraction can have a host of different reasons and may be as difficult to explain or rationalise as romantic attraction (this is more difficult, as the obvious biological motivations for reproduction are non-relevant by prior definition). Part of the intended research for this book was to figure out the key elements of this process, but at this point I am not sure how the key candidates could be captured to measure impact or validate the concept.

My hunch is that it boils down to rapid imagination. When we talk to the person or maybe just observe, our mind makes a blitz on us, imagining us having a good time over a beer, sharing our favourite activity or sport, or feeling really understood in a good conversation. This imagination is fuelled by nothing but a first gut feeling or impression.

The **'spark'** hypothesis of friendship formation then says that if two people simultaneously discover a mutual strong platonic attraction, the friendship starts on a spark, and strongly takes a leap of faith right into the middle of a friendship. By bonding over a key theme, the two participants jump past the first 20-30 hours of acquaintance and find themselves speaking to each other as if they had known the other one for a long time already. It is not like a complete friendship by lightning, but it creates a strong initial illusion that makes us act as if we had a full strong friendship. Thus the foundation of the actual friendship catches up fast, friendship formation is much faster than on traditional terms. This friendship by lightning is most strongly proposed by Lewis, 1960[9]. The spark hypothesis is the platonic analogue of 'love-at-first-sight'.

This book is not at its core about friendship formation, but one aspect of this platonic attraction is of key interest to me, and that is its predictability. I 'know' that it is predictable to some degree, because there are people who can predict or guess chemistry between people with a remarkable accuracy[10]. Sometimes in good close communities you have the proverbial spiders-in-the-web. They seem elusive and have only superficial acquaintance with most members of the community, but are blessed with an incredible instinct on which people they need to introduce to each other for friendship making. Whilst operating on little more than hunches, as their actual knowledge and acquaintance with the 500 or 1000 people in their community or congregation is by virtue of the sheer number very limited, nevertheless they operate almost with a 'Facebook'-like mind. They work their magic to ingest newcomers to the community and integrate them with like-minded and welcoming veterans and connection groups. Of course a lot of this is experience, but if insight into friendship formation by formal research could capture some of this magic and 'teach the trick' to others, this would be a great boon in the fight against loneliness.

The antithesis to the spark theory is the **'takes-time-to-grow'** hypothesis, essentially states that whilst platonic attraction is also necessary to take the first step, its role is substantially smaller. Consistency in spending time together, a slow

[9]'The typical expression of opening Friendship would be something like, 'What? You too? I thought I was the only one.' We can imagine that among those early hunters and warriors single individuals—one in a century? one in a thousand years?—saw what others did not; saw that the deer was beautiful as well as edible, that hunting was fun as well as necessary, dreamed that his gods might be not only powerful but holy.'

[10]And no, this is not just remembering hobbies or attachment to a particular political party, but almost more like alchemy and instinct.

gradual mutual discovery[11] and self disclosure build trust and affection over time (c.f. Alberoni, 2016, p.64[12]). As with most general observations on the nature of friendship, Aristotle, 1925, 8.3, 8.6[13] noticed this pattern in friendship formation. This hypothesis is related to the disclosure and investment process models and its key evidence of the need to invest time was tested in Hall, 2018. I think the key of this hypothesis is not only that friendship building takes time, but people might be on different mental speeds. Some may be prepared to call someone a friend after a few months of hanging out and having fun, whereas others only take the plunge after years. Whereas friendship necessitates reciprocity, these different speeds may strain this requirement. Shumway, 2018, p.114 agrees on the importance of expectation management on development speed, and that at the start of a friendship, respect for privacy and independence must be observed.

7.7 The perfect end state - the circle in movies

This section uses a lot of film and gaming references for examples

As a corollary I would follow that the natural perfect 'end state' of this process is not the dyad, but a circle of three or four friends[14]. The encounters get richer, there are more personality facets shining brighter. What I would just like to point out though is that courtesy of the entertainment industry we have the examples right in front of our eyes, the examples of stable rich friendship circles we feel drawn towards. I apologize now to people who dislike Star Wars, Star Trek, Bollywood movies and computer games or discount it as admissible material in a semi-scholarly text: the imagery was simply too powerful to ignore and leave out.

A good circle is marked by three elements in no set order: an all-encompassing **affection and warmth** for and towards each other, an element of mutual **humour** and **laughter**, and a **deep bond**. The difference of having a group of friends with a good chemistry at the heart is an if not the key ingredient to make a good movie a great one. The team of Han, Leia, Chewie and Luke in Star Wars IV-VI[15] possess this key ingredient, always coming through for each other. They are mocking each other in moments but fond, affectionate and deeply committed. This group effect is simply not developed to the same level in both the series I-III[16] and VII-IX[17]. Indeed, and I hope I am not being unfair, I think the reason VII-IX is still better than I-III is that the last trilogy profits to no end of the warmth triggered by the reunions from IV-VI[18].

---

[11] Lewis, 1960, p.104: 'Every step of the common journey tests his metal.'

[12] 'To know the true personality of another, time and evidence are required.'

[13] 8.3 'for a wish for friendship may arise quickly, but friendship does not.'
8.6 'One must, too, acquire some experience of the other person and become familiar with him, and that is very hard.'

[14] I cannot scientifically back this up why personally I think four is better. An equally good argument can be made for three. However, I would think that five, while equally arbitrary is too much. And I am not sure how to test this, though the Gottman method of inviting best friends groups to an observation room and coding their interactions might do the trick.

[15] A New Hope, The Empire strikes back, Return of the Jedi

[16] Phantom Menace, Attack of the Clones, Revenge of the Sith

[17] Force Awakens, Last of the Jedi, The Rise of Skywalker

[18] 'Chewie we're home' `https://youtu.be/bdrErkGQPB0?t=14`, or the scene were Luke joins Leia in the old rebel base before busting them out. 'I know what you are going to say - I changed my hair'

The friendship theme as foundation is strongest in Star Trek (for a full analysis, see Selley, 1986). It is explicitly expressed at key stages in the series. 'I have been, and ever shall be, your friend' makes it absolutely clear, and 'I could not deprive you of a revelation of all you could accomplish together, of a friendship that would define you both in ways you cannot yet realise.' picks it up and puts it also into the core of the series[19]. But whilst the dyad is at the core, there is Bones and in the new series also Uhura in the inner circle (e.g. going after Khan, being the leader of the captured enterprise crew in Star Trek Beyond.). The scenes where Kirk refers to his inner crew as friends[20] are likewise hallmarks for the bond and affection in the team. If you reflect on it - affection, humour, deep bond - is exactly the recipe to describe that band. And the reason that the reboot of Star Trek worked so well, is that the new series replicated this chemistry.

The Fellowship of the Ring, so strongly hailed and convened at the start of the Lord of the Rings, breaks up, but it breaks up into teams. Sam and Frodo set out to Mordor, Aragorn, Legolas and Gimli set out to rescue their friends, the other two hobbits, who end up then joining up with Gandalf after the defeat of Saruman. The end scene chosen in the film is not the Frodo-in-bed scene where everyone comes in to say hi, but the four hobbits sitting in a pub drinking [21], where finally Sam picks up the courage to chat to the girl, and where it is now clear that they are back.

Other more humorous movies likewise clearly carry the message, that two is not enough. In 'Blues Brothers', Jake and Ellwood try to figure out how to save their old orphanage. The revelation from 'God' - when Jake 'sees the light' is to get the band back together. And one by one, they all come together. Also in non-Hollywood folklore the 'circle of friendship' recipe, if done right, is something that speaks to the hearts. One of my favourite Bollywood movies, 'Dil Chahta Hai', is likewise about three close friends, who go through life, fall out with each other, but in time of need come back together again and discover what a bond they have in each other.

The recipe also extends to a different private entertainment genre, the computer game. Again, the last two decades got us lots of shooters, 4X, and other games. However, there were three story lines I would like to single out that never quite got paralleled. Mass Effect[22] and Dragon Age[23] not only had a quest to defeat the evil, be it the 'Reapers' or the 'Arch demon', and not only do you build a base, but much more you build a team that ultimately all become friends. The games include literally days of voiced original and funny dialogues, and you have side missions where you help your teammates out to build up the bond with and get to know them. The depth of this underlying side story developing this fellowship again is a less recognized but strong differentiating factor on the appeal of the

https://youtu.be/BZWeriwu8yI

[19]A humorous analysis shows how the bromance with Kirk takes precedence over the actual romance with Uhura throughout the entire new Star Trek Into Darkness https://youtu.be/P1qjUN9ZLQg

[20]E.g. when stealing the Enterprise to rescue Spock https://youtu.be/c-8WOuTV19M?t=246. The explicit addressing and naming of friends as such can represent a male role model on screen expressing strong friends-emotion even as early as the 70ies and 80ies.

[21]https://youtu.be/J3oXr7XVuhc?t=62

[22]https://www.ea.com/games/mass-effect/mass-effect-legendary-edition

[23]https://www.ea.com/en-gb/games/dragon-age/dragon-age-origins

games in those two storylines, much more than the potential romance to pick[24]. And the quality of the humour of the dialogue and depth of character is directly correlated with the game's reception by the fans. The Witcher, before the current movie a successful game trilogy, essentially is also not just the story of the main character Geralt and about his bonds with the companions Yennefer and Triss, but also Roche, Zoltan and Dandelion and in III, Ciri. My taste in movies or computer games is personal and of course absolutely can be disagreed with. But I wanted to use the popularity of both the movies and the games to point out the attraction of the picture of a group of close friends. In particular, if marked by the triad of affection - humour - bond - this image is a truly powerful and appealing one.

The circle seen in the light of the process has a few reinforcing mechanisms. Rather than one out of two reaching out or initiating, it just needs to be one in four to initiate and the other three to follow peer pressure not to cancel. The conversations can be both richer and lighter. Problem solving becomes more productive, as three friends complement their understanding and insight with that of the friend. The jokes, rather than bouncing like a tennis game, circle around the room like a frisbee. I thus completely agree with C. S. Lewis placing the experience of friendship in such a group as the highest of human experiences.

[24]See e.g. https://www.usgamer.net/articles/mass-effect-2s-final-mission-was-the-apex-of-the-series

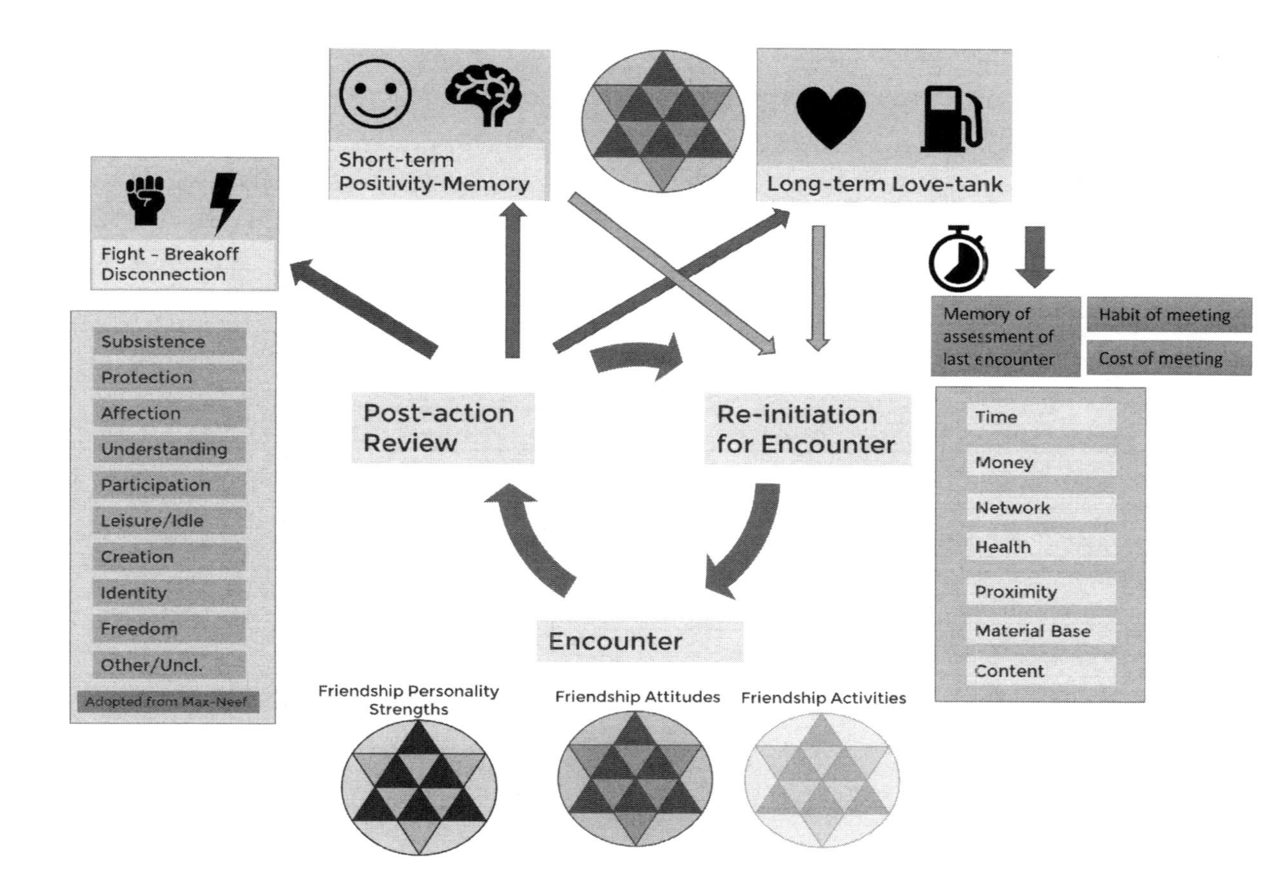

Figure 7.1: Process Conjecture

This figure is explained in section 7.3

Chapter 8

Friendship maintenance

For casual reading, all sections are relevant.
Jump to those where headers are of interest

A man, Sir, should keep his friendships in constant repair.

Samuel Johnson

In this chapter I will first go more through the positive and descriptive habits of maintenance, whilst in the second part commenting on aspects that can derail a friendship and looking at the process of how it happens.

8.1 Ease of 'pickup' and reverse culture shock

One hallmark mentioned for good friends is the ability to **pick up** the friendship as if not much time had passed in between. Seamlessly, we resume the conversation as if we had just met the prior day. It is mostly reported in male friendships and used as a quality indicator for the friendship. Proponents of this property can emphasise the difficulties of modern life, in particular as far as finding suitable time slots is concerned. In the discussions I had it was also largely mentioned by expats living in Hong Kong or Tokyo, who had been away from home for a while and found it assuring to still find this level of connection when they were visiting their parents once or twice a year and then catch up with a few old friends.

Within the Friendship Process model, the pickup property implies a powerful role of the long-term memory and a low decay rate for relationship attitudes such as trust, loyalty and enjoyment of company. It also signals a high independence and respect for the need for the friend to live their life. Friendships for which this holds can be described as low in affection, not per se, but without the need for a continual display of affection. Thus the dropping out of sight like a submarine submerging is not taken as a personal rejection but simply accepted as part of the nature of the friendship.

Others doubted the prevalence of it, quoting the reverse culture shock. This meant that as people went home after a long time of absence, or reconnected with old friends, they found them to have changed. Topics that several years ago would have excited both of them and given material for long discussions had lost their lustre and appeal as one of them had changed. Especially if the friendship had been a side-by-side friendship with an interest at its core, this could then form a constitutive disconnect in the friendship. This shock however is not just reserved for expats and globetrotters. Changes in life circumstances can likewise imply personality, interest and priority changes with similar effects.

There is a second subtheme to the pickup property, and that is making a new friend from a former 'just friend' or even peripheral acquaintance. This is a pretty interesting experience to describe. The classical scenario is having spent substantial time in mutual social periphery (e.g. a school, university, sports club or work environment) however only marginal interaction took place directly. Partially this is because of an intuition that e.g. interests are now different, and the wavelength just is not the same anymore. Maybe you had 'enough' other friends or for whatever reason it just didn't click. Years later you meet each other and chatting a little you completely hit it off again. The traits that were back then an obstacle are gone, and you instantly connect over potential gossip on updating each other on the mutual social circle of old (A married, B even has kids, C went off to country Y, D started a band, ...), you rekindle the old anecdotes that were common lore, and via indulging in nostalgia about the old times you connect in a way that you could not do with a new acquaintance. I observed this effect several times during my time in Sao Paulo, Tokyo and Hong Kong, where I met up with old school acquaintances also in the location and was genuinely positively surprised by the pleasance of the conversations. Thus the fact that we associate the pickup property with good friendship, can also be used in reverse to fast track development of friendships when coming to a new place or life situation.

Suggestions for thought

- Have you experienced this feeling of a 'pickup' with a friend where you met after a long time and it was just like it was yesterday?
- Have you likewise experienced the feeling of really looking forward to meeting up with an old friend after a long time, only to find that both of you are sitting there trying to find common ground with a mutual awareness that the lustre is simply gone and both of you have changed out of each other's orbits, at least for the moment and immediate future?
- Have you made the experience of catching up on the opportunity with an old acquaintance who also is in your geographic proximity? How was the gut feeling and how did the conversation go?
- Do you have a friend with whom you think you have this 'pickup' status, but who you haven't seen in a long time? What is preventing you picking up the phone and setting up the next coffee/beer/dinner?

8.2 Consistency by continuity

The opposite of allowing for friendship to be just picked up again is the theme of maintaining consistency. This is ensuring in a disciplined manner that not too much time passes between contacts. These contacts do not have to be long evenings spent together, but ensuring that we are on each other's radar, and aware of each other's issues.

When people say that women are 'better at friendship' then this is one aspect they mean. Speedier responses to communication, keeping birthdays or other dates in mind, **checking in** from time to time as the stereotype goes, are associated with female behaviour of showing continuous affection. Whilst this raises the overall level of required effort within the friendship, it does however keep the short-term positivity alive. In a reasonably continuous stream of communication, it increases also the number of potential triggers to initiate a meeting.

I think checking in from time to time and keeping a steady interest in meeting up is a very good habit to have about friendships. Of course with limited time, we might not manage every week, fortnight or even month. But the value of a short catchup to see how the other is doing and whether to our knowledge of our friend we need to add novel details is significant. The quick check-in for the opportunity for a proper beer or activity in the coming weeks or month can be managed and signals a certain consistency to our friend. This should not become an obligation from either side, but a call up also with the diary open and two or three suggestions of dates when a proper meetup would be possible is a great idea. Indeed, I think it is often men who are better at keeping their friendships with low maintenance, and thus a reaching out is an act of genuine volition and anticipation. I know sometimes it is difficult to find a mutual acceptable time over a long period. But, unless something is wrong in the underlying friendship, you should keep trying. Analogous to Peter asking Jesus how often he should forgive, I would recommend not just to reach out for a beer seven times, but seventy-seven times.[1]

Some authors (Alberoni, Shumway) argue that a friendship should not become stale, should not become repetitive. Friendship must change continuously, it must continuously provide stimulation. I would argue that this may hold for some friendship roles, in particular the collaborative or identity development ones. However, some friendships may be just good because they don't change. Even if the jokes are 'the same', somehow they don't stop being funny[2]. The familiarity with the affectionate smile, the signature dish at the annual dinner invite, the attempt to still play our favourite sport together even as our bodies age and we clearly are past it, some things are good simply because they provide stability and consistency in our lives that are changing anyway continuously outside this little oasis of peace. Friendship provides the space where we can relax and be maybe for a moment a past 'better' version of ourselves. It also depends on people's natures. An analogy to think about might be that some people never want to watch a movie twice. Other people however have favourite movies or sitcom se-

[1] Matthew 18:21-22 'Then Peter came up and said to him, 'Lord, how often shall my brother sin against me, and I forgive him? As many as seven times?' Jesus said to him, 'I do not say to you seven times, but seventy times seven."

[2] Just like movies like the Exorcist `https://youtu.be/N8x8xqZzD8w`

ries, the key scenes of which they can go back to over and over again experiencing no sense of staleness.

One example showing the important of consistency and continuity is its absence in changing circumstances. Especially when people retire, and people whom they considered reasonably good friends at work do not make an effort to stay in touch, this can lead to questions to what degree the friendship experienced, potentially over years of work, was genuinely felt or just situational. Thus regularity of contact does not necessarily imply consistency, but when people take it for it and find out the contrary, the pain of disappointment is clearly felt.

Suggestions for thought

- Do you have friends with whom you are in reasonably frequent contact, and not just social media, but at least quarterly meetup or monthly phone or video call? What is different to those without this?
- Do you find the establishment of a regularity habit helpful or constraining?

8.3 'Minimum maintenance'

One core question of this book is if there is such a thing as minimum maintenance for a good friendship? The pickup property says it doesn't exist: if you are good friends with someone, you can literally put the friendship on ice if you are genuinely busy or far away. The consistency property says the reverse, that you need a somewhat material interaction with a friend to keep even the pretense of friendship alive.

The point of minimum maintenance rather than complete freezing of the friendship is to keep the threshold of re-initiating contact as low as possible (to put it into the fridge so to speak). If you have not seen or heard from someone in years, then suddenly appearing out of the blue might just feel weird to some. It also increases the risk of rejection to the person reaching out. Thus a habit of 'minimum maintenance' is respecting of the circumstances that one party to the friendship might have an interest in keeping it going, however simply really little time, and for the foreseeable future (think single mothers or fathers). The point of the exercise is ensuring that the door is kept open. I mean this literally kept open with a standing open invitation to come and visit whenever a suitable time slot eventually appears. The credibility of this approach hangs on the actual obstacles (time scarcity, proximity) to meeting up. Laziness or 'cannot-be-bothered'-ness is not among those. But in order for reaching out a minimum amount of information is necessary: area of the country or city currently lived in, likely working hours or occupied hours, loosely what even might be good times to drop by.

Whilst the concept might seem manipulative or insincere to some[3], I am interested in its benefits for one key reason, and that is that it might hold the key to combating loneliness in age. I will come to the importance, nature and good

[3]Some private discussions I had show that some people would consider such a strategy indeed manipulative or insincere, and indeed there are some egoistic traits to it.

practices of friendship in age in chapter 10, however it is an observation stressed already in the introduction that loneliness is particularly painful in later life. A habit of maintaining a social network of 'minimum maintenance' friends, with the view of reviving it when collectively everyone emerges from parenting and working life with substantially more time might be a winning strategy to address this.

Suggestions for thought

- Do you have friends with whom you have such a minimum maintenance strategy, such as an annual or semiannual regular phone call
- Would you spontaneously call up such a friend for a coffee or beer if a spontaneous opportunity arose
- How relaxed would you be about the possibility of rejection. On the contrary, if such a friend reached out to you out of the blue on a whim to see whether you have time for a coffee, how would you feel?

8.4 A version of regret avoidance

One important argument in advocating consistency over letting friendships hibernate and picking up at a later point is a variant of regret avoidance. I think questions like 'what would you do if you found out you would die tomorrow, or at the end of this year?' are unreal and hypothetical. As such, they hardly ever spur us into action. If we are of good health currently, even if we get diagnosed with cancer or similar, most such diseases are these days treatable. Five years however is a time span where substantial uncertainty still applies, and can apply also to your friend. Thus 'if I knew that a specific friend was going to die on a five-year span, then what activities would I want to have done or experienced' is a very good question to reflect on. It is a time span long enough not to change calculus too much, but it is a time span to provide some sense of urgency not to push out things for too long either. A possible answer of course could be that the 'friend' and I are actually not close enough or affectionate enough that in such a scenario we would want to spend whatever time is left together. Then that is also helpful to realise. But for sufficiently close friends I would have a (limited) bucket list to follow up on, which might include a weekend away, or to go back to our post school pub once more for a pint. It might be indulging us in one more round of Warhammer gaming, a spa or wellness day, or whatever really made you feel good. And what then might be an idea is to share the key item with the friend and set it as a target say for the coming two years to deepen the friendship (maybe without the semi morbid justification of 'I was thinking what I would have liked to have done with you in case you died in a few years from a car crash - don't say that!').

For your top five or top ten friends write up a bucket list with one item per friend to be completed in the next two or three years.

8.5 General Habits

I come now to the part of what people do together. Whilst the response of 150 people (plus 30 partial answers) was good to get a general overview of habits, the number was not large enough to get statistically robust impressions of e.g. gender, age, marital status or regional divides. Substantial differences emerged, from which I mostly would deduce that it really depends on one's individual situation, what is appropriate or welcome. However, it gives a suitable backdrop against which you can reflect your own interaction habits. Two elements were queried - the annual frequency of the activity and the happiness of the response it triggered. As a minor comment, I find the term social media rather badly defined. I for my own language use distinguish between in-time communication (telephone, facetime, skype call), near-time asynchronous communication (whatsapp, ICQ, other messengers, short voice message) and off-time asynchronous communication (email, letter, long voice message). This subdivision is not canon, but I just found it helpful in discussions on effectiveness of friendship based communication[4].

Some observations that I took from it:

- About a third of people does not participate in 'meme/joke' communication[5] and does not like it.

- About a third of people does not participate in voice message communication and does not like it. This is interesting as according to the layer theory, voice messaging is more personal and memory building.

- Postcards and letter writing is almost extinct, however people do still value it. Letter writing polarizes even stronger, presumably because people feel obligated to respond and may not want to. This is however offset by an equal number of people who are ecstatic about receiving postcards and letters.

- About a quarter of people do not use the phone for voice communication between friends and a sixth actively dislike phone conversations.

- Short meetups during the day and dinners have equal value, however dinners are preferred for convenience of organization.

- Prolonged time spent together involves more visiting a friend rather than taking time off and going together to a 3rd destination.

[4]If some communications scientist can recommend me a better suited taxonomy, I would be grateful.

[5]This is the continuous receiving and forwarding of funny jokes, memes or anecdotes via near-time asynchronous media.

Communication habits					
	Not 1/y	1/y	m/3m	w/2w	1d/3d
(1) Short message	9	8	31	49	85
(2) Send funny meme	48	10	47	39	38
(3) voice message	71	16	55	28	12
(4) postcard	105	47	27	3	0
(5) letter	160	16	5	1	0
(6) check in call	20	11	91	51	9
(7) long call	33	14	96	35	4
(8) activity	22	16	77	53	14
(9) meetup	3	5	72	87	15
(10) dinner	5	4	114	57	2
(11) 3 day visit	58	81	41	1	1
(12) 3+day trip	70	91	19	1	1
* = or less often, but more than next category Data from Habits survey F.3					

Happiness on response					
	Average	1-3	4-6	7-8	9-10
(1) Short message	5.1	29	135	15	3
(2) Send funny meme	4.2	68	102	11	1
(3) voice message	4.2	66	104	11	1
(4) postcard	6.4	18	90	51	23
(5) letter	6.4	35	57	54	36
(6) check in call	6.0	23	87	61	11
(7) long call	5.8	34	69	72	7
(9) meetup	7.4	4	58	79	41
(10) dinner	7.4	10	48	76	48
(11) 3 day visit	6.3	29	69	47	37
* = or less often, but more than next category Data from Habits survey F.3					

Survey items in full length

(1) Send Facebook/ Whatsapp/Wechat/Line message of 5 lines, (2) Send funny meme or photo via Facebook/Whatsapp/Wechat/ ..., (3) Send a voice message / leave a message on an answering machine, (4) Send a handwritten postcard, (5) Send a handwritten letter of 2 pages or more, (6) Call a friend for 10 minutes to check in, (7) Call a friend for 30-60 min for a full phone conversation, (8) Do an activity with a friend for 1-3h (sports, board gaming, card playing), (9) Come out to meet a friend for a 1-2h coffee, lunch, beer, chat, (10) Have dinner with a friend for 3+h , (11) Visit a friend for 3 days, (12) Do a trip or a joint activity with a friend for 3 days or more.

For the happiness of response (8) and (12) were omitted for a reason I no longer remember.

The other key aspects of determining our ability to hang out with our friends are availability (i.e. proximity and resource time) and priority in our calendars. This combines to spontaneity. As expected, a clear divide between singles and married with kids was visible in the data. Also, a quick drop in at home was easier realised than having a coffee or beer in town. Weekends were planned out and required planning or were reserved for the family.

Spontaneity					
	0	1h	1d	1w	1m
(1)Coffee / Beer in town	30	37	70	41	4
(2) Lunch or dinner in a restaurant	11	21	69	66	15
(3) Coffee / Drop-in at home	55	41	55	25	6
(4) Lunch / Dinner at home	13	19	52	76	22
(5) Activity on the weekend	4	7	55	79	37
Data from Habits survey F.3					

Survey items in full length

Answer options were: 0 None - ready straight away, 1 One hour before, 2 One day before, 3 One week before, 4 One month before

Writing Letters and maintaining address books

My friends are like my pen collection, I have 30 but only one writes.

Unknown

Writing physical letters and postcards has been mentioned already as a key friendship maintenance strategy. In fact, writing postcards for me has always been the silver bullet. The key of letters and postcards is the element of surprise, therefore it is also counterproductive to ask people for their address before or when you send the letter. However, as it has become so rare that people actually write postcards or letters, it is inherently difficult to find out the actual address. I actually have numbers on this, as in order to recruit participants for the general friendship practices survey I wrote about 200 postcards from Hong Kong and Japan to friends or acquaintances with whom I shared some fond memory. From actual friends to people who I had hosted on Couchsurfing, to former work colleagues to people I had shared a few beers with when travelling in South America, Europe or Asia in Youth Hostels and with whom I would love to re-initiate contact for the opportunity for a beer in the future. It was an exercise that taught me much on the availability of public data and the absence thereof. Whereas between Facebook, Linkedin and the national telephone book you can usually find out the job location/employer, the last holiday destination, current relationship status or similar, less than 20 % actually had maintained an easily retrievable physical address. Comparing current residence location (Facebook) or job location (Linkedin), I would say 80 % of addresses in my address book were provenly out of date[6]. Thus I have the habit of recommending everyone to cultivate a base address, an address where you can be reached even if your current living parameters change.

A letter of course is the gold standard (see e.g. Turkle, 2017 in her conversations with youths). If time and dedicated attention are considered resource and currency, then a full-blown letter is the equivalent of a Rolex watch for Christmas. The writing of a proper letter of say 3-4 pages takes about an hour. Whilst Mark Twain is reported to have said 'I didn't have time to write a short letter, so I wrote a long one instead', letters can be assumed to take time roughly proportional to

[6]I assumed a maximum 30km commute

length and thoughtfulness of writing. In current times, this is compounded by our sheer ineptitude and custom to do so. Most of us have not written a text longer than a page with a fountain pen for a long time. Some of us may not even own a fountain pen anymore (I do strongly recommend writing with a fountain pen if after reading this you consider now embarking on a trial, it makes the ductus or writing style better almost by itself).

Of course a letter with a delivery time of a week or more is the ultimate asynchronous social medium, with a certain unpredictability when it will arrive and when - if ever - it will be answered. But this timelessness is also what makes the receiving of an unexpected letter so joyous.

In the discussion with a friend[7] I was told that she had switched from letters to sending longer recorded video or voice messages to her friends. I think this is also an excellent idea to try out. It might seem weird at first, but like a letter you can theoretically save it in your Dropbox and somewhat safely retain it. It also marks a significant time investment, and exchanges the personality of the handwriting (which for some people might seem undesirable) with the personality of voice and face. So a great tip!

Suggestions for thought

- If you think of your close friends and the circle of semi-close friends, say the top 15-25 friends, how many of those would you be able to still reach by snail mail, i.e. because you have their address or parents' address[a]?
- How many postcards or even letters did you receive and send respectively in the past year?
- How high is here your tolerance for reciprocity? Do you insist on approximate balance, or a factor relationship (e.g. three postcards from you for one in return) or do you just write postcards to your friends regardless of whether they write postcards to you in return?

[a]Some of us think of the house of mum and dad not just as a bank or hotel, but also of a permanent post office - in German 'Postamt Mama'

Near-time asynchronous social media

The impact of social media on our friendships are amply debated in various publications such as Delaney and Madigan, 2017 and Jeske, 2019 on a general level and in publications like Erin M. Bryant and Jennifer Marmo, 2012 in journals. Overall, the evidence seems to be ambivalent. It doesn't help that from research data generation to full publication there is a gap of at least a year, often two, at which point usually standard practices have started to become prevalent. Whilst frequent use in particular of scrolling social media (Facebook, Instagram) is asso-

[7]Rachel Roberts in Japan

ciated with depression and isolation (see Blease, 2015), some benefits however can be identified.

First of all, it is now nigh impossible to literally completely lose contact. With the use of the networks LinkedIn, Facebook (including Whatsapp and Instagram) and the classical messaging platforms (Wechat, Line, Viper, Threema, and the various others) we usually stay 'connected' or 'in contact' to almost anyone we meet. This circle of general contacts extends far beyond our actual friends. Secondly, with a limited use of social media it is possible to keep up a regular though superficial loose contact with limited time effort, in particular of dead time slots. It can be a lifeline of contact in particular to people with erratic schedules and thus difficulties to properly meet their friends physically.

What is however key to the use of social media is to keep in mind to use them to facilitate actual encounters, not replace them. As Asatryan, 2016 argues and as I will elaborate on in section 11.1 the obstacles to meaningful interaction on social media are remarkably high, and I would thus doubt that proper friendships can develop and thrive online. On the contrary, I would posit that online behaviour has to be consistent with offline behaviour. A person who likes everything we say on Facebook or LinkedIn, but leaves our initiations for a meetup unanswered is not a friend, but just a reciprocity-utilizing flatterer (aka friend of conditional mutual utility) aiming to increase her or his circle of 'influence'.

The reason I am critical of social media is that they are inherently not good at memory creating. If you want to do a quick test, ask yourself how many of your friends posts even from last week you are actually remember. My hunch is that you probably don't remember that gorgeous looking blueberry pancake your friend posted a photo of on Instagram, even if it had been the most delicious blueberry pancake ever created and you even applied a 'like' or a 'wow that looks delicious' - comment to the post. Let us suppose you however had met your friend that evening after his eye-opening breakfast, and your friend had still been raving on the sheer delight of those squishy hot and sweet blueberry pancakes. I dare you being able to tease him about his guilty pleasure a year on. Now if Facebook and Instagram somehow introduce features that improve long-term memory retainment of the key items (and they are trying to get to reposts of key photos from x years back), that might change the game.

Practical takeaway
If you live sufficiently close to someone that a physical meeting is possible, try to meet that person, and save up news and snippets for these meetings. Don't let the feeling that you roughly know what is going on in their life through social media keep you from having a beer together.

Suggestions for thought

- How much time do you spend on social media, and how is it distributed between consumer and interacting social media?
- Do you spend substantial time on interacting with people with whom you actually could physically meet up?
- Have you ever taken a social media addiction test?

Phone - in-time synchronous social media

When the telephone was introduced into society in the late 19th century, it became quickly the social medium of choice. Copper wires went everywhere, and were soon supported by connecting stations. With a few changes in operation model, technologies and reach we are now at a stage that we can call anyone anywhere anytime (if we have their details), not just via the telephone but also via the voice functionality of Whatsapp, Facebook messenger and Skype.

The problem with the voice-only aspect is multi-tasking. On text-based social media we all acquired the habit of multitasking and peripheral attention, and this does not work so well for phonecalls, especially if a competing task is attention intensive, like reading or playing computer games. Turkle, 2017 dedicates an entire chapter with the telling title 'no need to call' with the disenchantment of the current young generation and the telephone, and describes how the difficulty of multitasking while phoning is key for understanding this.

On the other hand, calling is incredibly easy, and really suitable for dead time slots. This can be waiting for the bus, or - if you don't have an overly loud voice - something to do on your daily commute. Thinking a little further afield from friends, making it a habit to call your grandparents every two days for 10-15 min during the commute is a great one to pick up. For them it doesn't matter that you fill dead time with it, it matters to them **that you call - regularly**. Once you have this habit, it will spill over to other relationships. It is in connection with this 'dead slots' calling that I would find an automatic time slot matching app really useful, where somehow the app would discover dead time of mine or I could switch a certain time slot as available and likewise check spontaneously, who of my social circle friends might also be available for a short casual chat. The key here would be to minimise searching cost. Ideally, you would know whether your call is convenient for your friend before you place it.

Of course, as seen above on the habits survey, not all people like phone calling. If you are not a caller, or have a friend who calls but you don't enjoy it, ask yourself why you don't like it. If you appreciate the friendship, but just dislike calling, let them know that explicitly. Otherwise continuous calling and not getting appreciated for the effort will feel one sided and lead to a strain.

Phone calling can be casual and deep, it could be a quick check in or a deep call where you need to console someone over a breakup. I think the capability of being able to call our friends when we need them is incredible, but maybe they do have time for a 10 min chat, but not for a 60 min consolation discussion. Openness here is key. You want to tell your friend that you value them, and want to give them the time, but that you are constrained because of a meeting or a deadline. I think in most cases your friend would prefer to delay the conversation to a point when your mind is genuinely free and at rest, and can focus fully on the call and interaction.

I think one can make a culture of good phone calls, or indeed video calls. Having a comfortable chair with a side table to put down a beer and video and proper sound function gets reasonably close to simulating a pub situation. I think there is a substantial difference in holding up a 6 inch iPhone display, or having your friends face on a 42" screen, sitting relaxed and arms free and also talking free without the little headset dongles, but with either proper loud speakers or HIFI headphones. Continuous eye contact also assures us of the full attention that might be doubtful in telephone calls.

Whilst according to Asatryan's layer theory the phone or video calling would be less preferable and intense to meeting up, it would be an interesting analysis to compare peoples' depth and length of conversations during social distancing in the pandemic, whether a change in topic, self disclosure and emotional intensity occurred over time. Once the medium is put back on the map as suitable for exchanging emotions, it might have quite a renaissance.

Suggestions for thought

- Are you a caller or do you more dislike it?
- When did you last time have a long phonecall and enjoyed it? With whom? What made it 'good'?
- Have you ever tried having a digital coffee or beer with a friend? What worked, what felt weird?
- Do you pay full attention when phoning or do you multitask? How do you feel when others multitask?

Reciprocity expectations

The key to good casual communication is the management of reciprocity expectation. If a friend writes me a long letter, are they disappointed if I don't write one back. Same goes for postcards. How soon should a phonecall be reciprocated? How about a message? Whatsapp and iMessage have 'read receipts'. We all can all overanalyse the status of our friendship and the meaning of rejections of calls, yet being ruthlessly cold-hearted and agreeing simple and effective protocols might point a way forward. This could include:

- If I am busy I will just push you away or better - pick up, say that I am busy, that I will call you back within 24 hours and then hang up. I call it the 30 sec protocol, that allows for checking whether the person on the other side has had a complete breakdown and is in overriding need of urgent attention, or whether it can wait an hour, or until the end of day.

- If I am busy I will just push you away, but please send me a message if it is super-urgent[8], and I will look back 5 min later at the phone. On the contrary, if someone pushes me away, I usually send a message even if it was nothing of importance. Letting them know I just wanted to chat takes me off their mind, and allows them fully to get back into the conversation without worrying or wondering.

- I hate WhatsApp and the Facebook, I like to take things slow and not be under constant bombardment. I only check it once a week.

Whatever you go for, and even if it feels cold-hearted, the key is here making your reaction or behaviour predictable, and excluding the possibility that your friend feels rejected when there is actually any of the hundred other reasons that their message goes unseen. The key to making pushing away permissible is the reliability by which you call back within a reasonable amount of time.

Some people also feel burdened by thoughts on reciprocity and fear of rejection in the context of the protocol of ending a phonecall. Some people avoid phonecalls because they don't like the ending it, e.g. when it gets boring or when they have to go to the next appointment. Some people are brutal and just cut a conversation short by stating a simple 'Sorry, but I have to go now, talk soon, bye'. Others - especially if they feel lonely - can happily talk on for hours, completely oblivious of the fact that their friend has been trying to get off the line for the better part of half an hour. I think cutting off a call in a direct and clear manner is much to be favoured over indulging in the moment but in the future having to think about the likely length of such a call. Talking on the phone to a friend should be a joy (unless you have to do it out of friendship duty as you have to console them over a breakup or coach them towards an interview they are panicking about) rather than a chore. You need to maintain the voluntary and anticipatory nature of the call at all costs. Cutting off the call when you really need to go should be respected. Some people try to mitigate time loss and then start multitasking by reading email rather than telling their friend that they need to go or get back to work. I think being honest here is probably the better path.

Suggestions for thought

- How good or comfortable are you at ending a phonecall? Do you sometimes 'over-talk' or more 'cut short'?

- Do you have a rough policy on calling back your friends? Do they know it?

Research:

There is plenty of research in communication studies on the use of social media and transformation of the use of the phone, however I have not yet found a conclusive large scale study on the matter focusing on the use of media among close friends and effects on closeness maintenance. I would suspect though that despite some google scholar searching, it does exist waiting to be found.

[8]My car broke down in Transylvania and it is getting dark, my water broke, my husband is AWOL and no taxi is coming, ...

8.6 Money, Loans and Business

> The holy passion of friendship is so sweet and steady and loyal and enduring a nature that it will last through a whole lifetime, if not asked to lend money.
>
> Mark Twain

While I write about money as a resource in the section on resources, in discussions on the nature of friendship the possibility of mixing money and friendship is often raised. There are three themes in which this can occur - running a business with a friend, transacting in business with a friend and giving a friend a loan. All three have both good examples to follow as well as bad examples.

The first of running a business with a friend is the closest such binding. Effectively the friendship is burdened with the responsibility of maintaining a successful business. There is no shortage of potential conflicts and causes of strains on the relationship. Yet friendship is by some exactly the attitude sought for by potential investors. When (some) venture capitalists evaluate companies to invest in, they primarily vet the team. And whilst business acumen, brilliance or other individual traits are of course at the center of the analysis, so is the capability of the team to 'work as a team'. The parallels to friendship are unmistakably there when looking at the traits sought for such as good communication, care for each other, good complementing of skills or a unifying passion for a specific cause. Thus a strong argument can be made that friendship is indeed a high desirable for running a business together rather than a reason to avoid going into a business. On the other hand, given the daily strains equally a lot of stories exist of friendships broke down in the running of a business (some acrimoniously).

Transacting on a business level is another item. In current society it is usually frowned upon with 'chumocracy' or 'nepotism' claims easy at hand. Given the ample supply of scandals of lacking scrutiny, this overall seems justified. I would say that the dividing line is whether in the transaction you are using your own money or someone else's. Giving preference to a friend with someone else's money, potentially with the owner of that money ending up with a worse service because of your choice, is plainly unethical. Hiring a friend over someone with better qualification in a firm owned by anyone but yourself is not right.[9]

However the duty to support a friend which comes part of the package of friendship, allows and indeed mandates several activities. If you know of a job that your friend who is looking for a job could fulfil suitably, you can give him information about the job and its contents. You can even prep him for a potential interview. If you are however the hiring manager, it is in such a case necessary to make your link to the friend known to colleagues and recuse yourself from the process. If your friend has a business and you know of the need for his product or service in the company you work for, you can make the connection and support your friend in tailoring his offer (with not confidential information, that does not put your employer at a disadvantage - 'you can demand any price, they really

[9] I would however acknowledge that trust is partially a qualification. If you know a friend can do a task X and compare them to someone who claims to be able to do something, but is not convincing, this can influence your decision. It still might be better to include other members in your unit to weigh in on the matter.

need it' is an unethical no go), as your friend submitting a tender increases the options your employer has, and a well-tailored submission reduces information costs.

If your friend has a business, such as a cafe or a restaurant, support mandates you to go there. Now if the coffee or food is shoddy, it comes with honesty to tell your friend just that. One must be supportive, affectionate and encouraging, but honesty comes with it. Now it might be also the situation that you are picky, and your friend's food is good, but really different to your palate preferences. Then you still have the option of taking another friend there who will like the food and appreciate your friend's restaurant, whilst you stick to garlic bread, the soup of the day and a glass of wine. On the product or service providing side, you need to be sure that your product or service is good, not just about adequate for the purpose. If you have a computer or second hand car shop and you sell your friend a computer or car, you essentially collateralize the warranty with your friendship. If the computer or car breaks down after a year or two, your friendship demands you to repair it, even if the warranty has expired. In purely economic terms, you may thus mentally price in the expected extended warranty in the deal and if that turns the transaction profit negative,[10] then it is indeed better to refrain from the transaction.

Giving loans within friendships works along similar lines. Whilst plenty of people also argue against it, giving a loan to a friend in need is defined as a quality mark in friendship. It is one of the key variables of the analysis of Fischer, 1982 in defining what friendship means. The issue comes two-fold. First when you give a loan to a friend, you essentially both collateralize the loan with your friendship. By implication, if the loan defaults for any but a most severe reason, the friendship is dead. Whilst your friend is still affected by the difficulties that got him to need the loan in the first place, there is no question of repayment. However as the loan remains outstanding over time, the question arises if your friend is doing the right actions to get himself out of the predicament. Whilst no financial bonds exist, it is purely his own responsibility to get himself out of the puddle. A freelancer on a rough stretch yet not feeling entirely miserable in this situation remains in their permissible range of life decisions to stay in the status quo. The loan may however remain extant indefinitely because your friend - as much as you appreciate him - is actually a miserable artist, cafe owner or accountant. Sticking to his life choice and potentially ignoring other more profitable activities and occupations, they remain incapable of generating the funds necessary to repay you in their current line of work. Their liberty to make their own life choices then conflicts with the moral duty of making efforts to repay you. On the other hand, your own consideration to their well being becomes also fused with your selfish interest to have the loan repaid. Thus it becomes for your friend difficult to gauge whether the advice to change line of work[11] is motivated by genuine concern for her or him or rather a less than subtle effort to recoup your loan in disregard for the implications of your friends mental wellbeing. Such evaluation of motivation and second guessing is poisonous for a friendship.

A loan contract among friends should thus include a wellbeing clause at which

[10]Think of low margin desktop computers or 2nd hand cars

[11]Maybe because you genuinely think your friend would be better off for herself as an accountant with a hobby of teaching yoga or art history rather than a full time yoga teacher or art historian.

point it is reasonable for the money to be expected back. This needs to be generously phrased so that by repaying the loan the friend is not pushed back into a situation of need. There is no harm in making it extremely explicit such as 'I will start paying back the loan when I make a minimum of 2000 EUR on a net basis', quite similar to student loans of the UK government. And until this condition is met, the loan becomes a grant, a financial support with no further strings attached. Needless to say, both partners will be relieved when it is being repaid. But in this scenario the repayment of the loan coincides with the friend generally being back on their feet financially. The joy over this relief then will overshadow the unpleasantness of repayment.

Investing in a friends business should also only come in the form of accepted high-risk equity capital. Depending on which statistic you read, between 90 % and 98% of all new businesses fail. An investment must reflect that, and the business failing, possibly because of stupid decisions on part of your friend ignoring your well-meant business advice, must not be reframed as a moral failing on part of your friend. The best way to think about such an investment, if conservation of the friendship is a goal, is of a generous gift to your friend and statement of trust and esteem in his business acumen with an attached lottery ticket 5 years down the line.

There is actually a powerful argument that can be made for giving loans within a friendship to the friend in need. I have throughout the elaborations of the friendship framework supported the tenet, that the biblical tenets or commandments on social life specifically given in the New Testament are a remarkably well-defined set of instructions for good friendship. One such passage is Luke 3:11 'Anyone who has two shirts should share with the one who has none, and anyone who has food should do the same.' The relationship trait 'consideration of friends' demands even major sacrifices for friends in need, and a limited financial loan is a substantially smaller sacrifice than a life or kidney. If privacy is important to you, giving a loan to pay for a friend's rent deposit and a few months of rent might be a smaller sacrifice than putting the friend up in your garage or living room. If you have the money 'spare' and your close friend needs it, I am afraid - unless you have an extreme definition of an arm's-length friendship - then help is demanded. By giving money outright however you put the extreme disparity in your friendship on display. Formulating the grant as a loan allows your friend to maintain their dignity by having the upheld option of repaying it at a later point. Given the emotional costs and strains, giving a loan within a friendship should only thus be a rare exception to usual practice. If you feel you should prioritise your potential psychological discomfort or the fragility of the friendship, that you want to keep the friendship 'safe' from a potential strain rather than addressing the actual need of your friend and the potentially substantial improvement to his wellbeing, you should potentially reflect on the value and quality of that friendship in the first place.

Suggestions for thought

- Have you ever given a loan to a friend? Or have you ever received a loan from a friend?
- After reading this section, how do you feel about doing so?

8.7 'Toxic Friends'

A lot of literature in the friendship self-help section is dedicated to the concept of 'toxic friends' and how to deal with them. If you type 'toxic friend' into Medium[12], you get your pick of thirty plus advice columns on how to deal with them. Barash, 2009, Degges-White and van Tieghem, 2015 or Zahiduzzaman, 2015 offer various views on strategies dealing with toxic friends. Probably the most helpful one [13] is written by Ball, 2020-05-18 with the focus on helping you discover whether you might qualify as a 'toxic friend' rather than deciding which ones among your 'friends' are 'toxic' and this should be cut. Tara Ball cites avoidance (Enjoyment), being judgemental (acceptance), controlling (respect of privacy), unapologetic (affection, humility, vulnerability), not taking responsibility (general personality), being a taker (consideration), taking things personally (humility, respect), not celebrating success of others (benevolence, pride), not keeping secrets (confidentiality) and passive-aggressive commenting (peace, positivity, affection) as the ten signs of a toxic person, and as I showed in the brackets, most of these represent shortcomings in one or two of the friendship dimensions mentioned in the prior chapter.

As a basic assertion, I would state 'toxic friends' simply don't exist. A 'toxic friend' is an oxymoron, a contradiction in itself, somebody is toxic for you or a friend, but not both concurrently without extremely stretching definitions of either toxic or friendship. I also highly doubt that a person per se by their very nature can be toxic, and certainly doubt that so many people are toxic that we need to make such a problem out of it. What I would say is twofold, and it boils down to the old Christian saying of 'love the sinner, hate the sin' - separating of person and action. A friend comes inseparable with respect, affection and appreciation. We are friend to someone if we see in her or his personality traits we think are commendable, admirable, 'good' in the most basic meaning of the word. If there are vices, then they are tolerable to some degree. A friend may be always late, disorganized, messy, might even have hygiene patterns that we might not want to emulate or endorse, but essentially the good outweighs the bad, and does so by a substantial margin. If I label someone's personality as toxic (and to do that in any justified manner) there needs to be a LOT that is wrong with that person. Of the top of my head I cannot think of a single person I met in the past ten years I would attach this label to, and I certainly do not have any 'toxic friend'.[14]

[12]Medium.com is a website collecting opinion pieces from thinkers and self-help writers all over the world.

[13]`https://goodmenproject.com/sex-relationships/are-you-toxic-10-ways-to-tell-and-how-to-stop/`

[14]Funnily enough I cannot even recall a conversation, where somebody referred to someone else as

What is possible is that we have acquaintances whom we consider as friends yet who display continuous behaviour that is inconsistent with good friendship. Some of these actions will cause a blowup and trigger an argument or fight. The subsequent conflict resolution leads either to the improvement of behaviour or dissolution of friendship. It is possible that some people who we consider friends display patterns of behaviour in aspects of the relationship, that breach the expectations of good friendship. Moreover, it does so continuously but to such a degree that the single action saps our energy, makes us unhappy in the moment, but not sufficiently to trigger a robust response including an honest and frank conflict resolution. Logically the damaging nature of the action must be unknown to the perpetrator, as knowingly doing an action that harms your friend in a malevolent way is an immediate and unrevocable signal that there is no friendship in the first place[15]. I will address stupidity in the next section.

Thus what remains of the concept of 'toxic friends' is the subgroup of people who in principle we would label as friends, but who may have one or two severely annoying, disrespectful or damaging habits that for a time have had the effect of you not enjoying the friendship quite so much. It probably can be likened a bit to a 'death by a thousand cuts'. Whilst victim blaming is usually not helpful, but in most such dysfunctional relations two people are equally involved, and it is an interesting question to ask why people don't take measures in a relationship they identify as dysfunctional. That however is an area which is inherently specialist and the domain of properly trained people. But on a more positive note, I would still posit that most people do not actively want to harm, damage or cause stress to people, least of all friends. Thus my take is that once a dysfunctional habit is identified, the first step is bit by bit bring it to the other person's attention and speak about it. It is at this point perfectly permissible to use expletives in the sense: 'You normally are a nice person, but when you do this, you behave like a real [insert favourite label]. This is so not like you!'. This eliminates the possibility of your friend not being aware of the negative effect. It also allows to clarify the misunderstanding and different interpretations. Maybe the negative habit is a protective reaction to a dysfunctional habit of yours (see ghosting as a reaction to obsession).

Even if the habit is identified, discussed and seen as valid, it might not disappear immediately. You may be lucky, and sheer awareness is sufficient for your friend to stop being late, making certain jokes at your expense, or whatever the cause of action is. But most likely it will not be done immediately. And that is where consistency, patience and persistence will be needed: patience to wait for the change to occur, but consistency and persistence in clearly continuing to point out your displeasure at whatever you perceive as the dysfunctional behaviour. This can be done even slightly escalating if the behaviour is really annoying you or detrimental to your wellbeing. But coming back to the list of qualifiers for 'being a toxic person' I would say that in that list there is nothing so severe that it cannot be ignored for a while whilst applying some mitigation measures to the

toxic, so I am genuinely puzzled with whom this concept resonates so much.

[15]I would exempt a spur-of-the-moment retaliation going bad from this, e.g. slashing your friends car tyres in a drunken stupor after (wrongly) believing he kissed your girlfriend is malevolent, but more an in-the-moment action, and one from which in a proper friendship there will be a path back. It will be a few severely awkward discussions, and even more so awkward discussions if he did indeed kiss your girlfriend, but essentially the action did not stem from a sustained dislike.

problem. In short, whilst there is no shortage of bad and destructive behaviour amongst people available, the hurdle to label someone a 'toxic person' should be far higher than it is done so in current self-help literature.

A final, even weaker labelling of 'toxic' is applying it to 'draining or tiring friends'. Indeed, it is normal that we should feel energized after we have met with our friends. They should leave us relaxed, we should enjoy our time together, laugh, and experience all or many of the benefits described in the framework. However it is possible, that our friends for a prolonged period are not in a good place, and rather than energizing us, need our support. That is however not being 'toxic', just being needy, whether justified or not. Sometimes the word was just used for imbalanced friendships, where one person clearly had a higher level of friendship in her mind than the other, and the request for more time was described as annoying or negative by the reluctant other party. Again, in all these cases, words like imbalanced or unmatched are far more appropriate and accurate than the sweeping and damning 'toxic' (I will get to an analysis of reciprocity, matching and roles in the next chapter).

To be clear, I am all for reciprocity, and one does need to loosely be aware whether a friendship is loosely balanced. But by telling people to monitor their friendship groups for potential toxic friends introduces a mindset of constant measurement of 'whether I am getting enough out of the relationship'. This encourages people to become transactional, inhibits them in forming genuine and trusting relationships, and thus by extended definition makes them become 'toxic' themselves. You can think about the old revealing psychic test that usually people are what they suspect of others (liars think most other people are liars, tax evaders think most other people are tax evaders too). Thus my hunch is that people who worry about toxic friends are usually not the proverbial lambs who need to be taught to be wary of the wolves and blood suckers out there trying to take advantage. They are likely much more like Adam Grant's takers complaining that others are not just showering with graces as they surely must be deserving of it rather than the genuinely unselfish givers who regularly tear out a limb for undeserving friends.

Suggestions for thought

- Has the above argument convinced you to strike the word 'toxic friend' from your active dictionary?
- If you have experienced toxic behaviour from a friend, what has stopped you from addressing it with that person?
- Has anybody of your close friends called out such behaviour in you? How did you react? How many 'strikes' were you given?

8.8 Stupidity and making up

> It is one of the blessings of old friends that you can afford to be stupid with them.

Ralph Waldo Emerson

I think a key aspect of good friendship is the awareness that everyone is imperfect, and the potential for people to make mistakes is endless. Einstein said to have said: "Two things are infinite: the universe and human stupidity; and I'm not sure about the universe."[16], and this just applies to our friends too - and sometimes especially our close friends. Stupidity (and this is not just intellectual incapability, emotional or common sense failures can be just as bad too) is annoying and sometimes extremely destructive, but I would argue that the resulting fallout is mostly avoidable.

A lot of well meant, but badly thought through and really badly executed actions fall under this category. The amount of times I heard 'well it seemed like a really good idea at the time' when someone told me of a reason she or he fell out with an actually reasonably good friend at the time was substantial. On the other hand, matters of these kinds often make up the stories that are also told in good friendships years after it, and can mark a turning point for the better in a friendship. You need to consider intent and plausibility of the negative result from the perpetrator's perspective. With a number of 'stupid mistakes', there often preexists a history of minor items. Jokes, pranks or similar situations, that already were not quite so funny to the receiver or subject of the joke, however were indulged or tolerated. We don't want to be the spoilsport. If you address a minor transgression, it is easy to be looking petty. There is of course also a suitable occasion for everything, and if you confront your friend in front of everyone else about a joke they made, which you found less than funny, it immediately triggers a range of defensiveness mechanisms. However, a pointed bilateral comment on the lines of 'That joke of yours an hour ago, it hit a little close to target. Did you really mean it like that?' will not only clarify the situation, but more importantly prevent further unintended resentment. Mutual Understanding, emotional insight and knowing our friends are part and parcel of friendship, however, we are not perfect. Humankind has not yet been equipped to mind-read. It is always possible that a friend, who understands us on almost anything else, does not know or see that a specific comment or action did hurt us. We owe it to them to point it out, if it feels hurtful.

A clear sign of stupidity being in place is the genuine remorse once the full extent of the transgression becomes clear. Statements like 'I am so sorry, I had no idea it had such an impact on you.' will come spontaneously and unequivocally, once the penny drops. If repentance is genuine, the case can be closed fast.

8.9 The friendship sins

Friendships 'sins' are essentially actions that go diametrally opposite key friendship attitudes, specifically the 'more important ones'. They are Betrayal (Loyalty), Boredom (Enjoyment), Contempt (Pride and Admiration), Exploitation (Reciprocity), Malice (Benevolence) and Disregard (Consideration and Priority), Jealousy and Obsession (Respect of privacy). The offence lies in the diametral attitude or observation to the within friendship reasonable expected actions. Note that I am not

[16] `https://quoteinvestigator.com/2010/05/04/universe-einstein/` traces this claim inconclusively, and also links the statement to Alexandre Dumas

advocating here a perfect friendship of the saints, where all the friendship virtues are fully exercised all the times. Mishaps, mistakes and misunderstandings are common in friendship, and require conflict resolution skills. Nobody understands our weaknesses better than our friend (maybe except the parents) and makes allowances for them.

Friendship sins				
	Average	1-5	6-8	9-10
Dishonesty / Lying	8.5	8	65	88
Untrustworthiness	8.3	9	68	84
Unreliability (not being there when needed)	6.7	37	101	23
Chronic impunctuality	4.2	119	40	2
Disloyalty (e.g. sleeping with your ex, ...)	7.0	42	77	42
Negativity / Constant criticism of you	7.1	36	85	40
Becoming boring	4.9	97	55	9
Absentmindedness	5.3	95	55	11
1 = 'Not at all' , 10 = 'Reason to end a friendship' Data from Habits survey F.3				

However, an intentionally or carelessly caused but fundamentally hostile action is one that can instantly shatter even the best friendship. As Alberoni, 2016, p.20[17] suggests a single hateful action, once its negative nature is established, has the potential to end the friendship. Crucial here is the intent, with very high hurdles on assessing gross neglect.The table below compiles a rough overview of how strongly people feel about the individual friendship 'sins'. My take on it is that looking for implicit intentionality of harm, this seems indeed to be an explanatory variable to the responses.

Suggestions for thought

- Did you ever experience a capital friendship 'sin'? Was it intentional or grossly negligent?
- Did you ever perpetrate such a transgression yourself? What were you thinking in that moment? What were your motives? Did you experience regret afterwards?

8.10 Conflict Resolution

Samuel Johnson[18] is quoted with 'A man, Sir, should keep his friendships in constant repair.' The question is, what precisely does this recommendation mean. I think the key item is a good decision process of which issues are minor (i.e. annoying or irritating at the time but can be ignored or accepted) and which issues might become substantial problems over the long-term and thus need to be resolved. Thus for some chronic unpunctuality may be acceptable, whereas with others frustration will build up eventually leading to resentment.

[17]'In friendship, on the other hand, there is no room for hate. If I hate my friend there is no more friendship, it is finished.' in combination with 'friendship in crisis ...'

[18]Via Pahl, 2000, p.62

Seeing friendship as a covenant can be a stabilizing influence. The idea of a covenant is that you do not withhold your end of the agreement, even if the other party seems to breach it. This is important in the phase of the suspicion. There might be an issue, you heard a rumour, or you don't understand quite how something was meant. In this limbo, while you are still deciding on whether something is an issue or a non-issue, a covenant attitude can help not to set the friendship on a downward spiral. I have discussed the need for acceptance that can cover all sorts of traits. Our friend is not our romantic partner, and thus different standards apply. As at least to some part friendship is a less intensive relationship than a romantic one, it is often unnecessary to resolve a conflict.

The key difference between conflict resolution among strangers or business partners should be the predominant interest in the conflict resolution to save the relationship rather than to win the issue. Now I would say people are aware of this and thus restrain themselves. And a genuine flareup is I think a highly unlikely scenario. It does not matter if you win, but it matters that you understand the why. The friend does not want to judge, but he needs to understand. Getting the impression that your friend does not understand you is potentially also more threatening to the friendship than the original issue.

Even in good friendships, a different process is I think much more insidious, if a conflict is not resolved. Once a problem occurs, not only do we hold back our anger, but we hold back completely. We shy away from the confrontation. However, when we suppress the confrontation, but continue to hold the grudge, it has consequences in the relationship elsewhere. We suddenly monitor reciprocity, whether we are adequately compensated for our ignoring the issue that still matters to us. And in this case, you really kill a friendship by taking its temperature.

Being close friends also implies that it is necessary to raise an issue when it becomes important. If you believe that the resulting strain from a frank or stern feedback suffices to derail the friendship, then there are more foundational reasons and may not be worth maintaining. But if an important issue arises, you must confront the friend with the problem at hand. You want to understand and you want to resolve, not ignore or suppress. The capability to resolve conflicts between themselves is one key criterion of a good friendship, as Aristotle, 1925, 8.1[19] explains. There is no need of a 3rd party judge. The New Testament (Matthew 18:15)[20] agrees that first a potential conflict should be resolved bilaterally. For faithful adherents of the Christian faith, a conflict must be resolved. Either bilaterally, or the matter or sin is laid with God. The key message here is that once a matter is placed with 'the God', it is no longer with us, we are not to hold a grudge. This is the key message, that if a matter is identified as important in a friendship, it must be resolved and must not be allowed to linger permanently. Forgiveness either must be seen to be unnecessary in the first place, or it must be complete for the friendship to be restored. Degges-White and Borzumato-Gainey, 2011, ch.3 state that 'True best friendships are able to withstand significant challenges and poor behavior that would likely lead to the breakup of less close friend-

[19]'When men are friends they have no need of justice, while when they are just they need friendship as well.'

[20]15'If your brother sins against you, go and show him his fault, just between the two of you. If he listens to you, you have won your brother over' again on the assumption that adelphos (brother) can be seen also as instructions to friends

ships.'. True friends raise conflicts when they need to be raised, work harder at resolving them, and then bring them to resolution than weak friendships. (also see Abell, 2009, ch.12 for further excellent comments on how to handle conflicts among friends[21]).

Again, also in conflict resolution, circles are stronger. A third friend, unless the transgression is clear and unequivocal, will refuse to take sides between two friends of his, but insist on resolution. The friendship of the third friend however may be invoked to establish objectivity: if a fight started in their presence, they may interrupt adversarial arguing and provide with their neutral view point a common factual basis[22].

Thus even if there may be anger and no desire to reconcile between A and B, both being friends with C will force both to limit their wrath towards each other, and thus avoid unnecessary escalation and uncivil behaviour. A burning of bridges with B would be an almost malicious action towards C, thus the result of a falling out often is just a kind of armistice. Furthermore, the third circle member will always be a bridge, enabling reconciliation without loss of face. This theme is beautifully explored in the movie 'Dil Chahta Hai', where after a major falling out, in the end it is the friendship to Sameer that enables the reconciliation of Sid and Akash. The third friend will not be the judge, but may (and most likely will) be a mediator and reconciler. However it is important to note that only hostile activity is prohibited. The mutual and amicable agreement of A and B to henceforth limit contact and go separate ways needs to be respected by C.

Suggestions for thought

- What is your conflict style in friendship? Do you openly address items or cover them up/ignore them?
- How good are you at seeing your friends' point of view in such a conflict? How much can you control yourself to find a resolution rather than getting 'vindication'?
- How good are you at apologizing sincerely? Do you maybe even sometimes concede or apologize before actually having understood the issue?

8.11 Friendship discontinuation

There is the general phenomenon of friendship churn, but the focus in this book is on magnitude of the effects and roles in friendship. In the next chapter I will look at the circle theory (inner circle, social circle, acquaintance circle) and different roles of friendship (best buddy, clown, mentor, collaboration partner).

[21] The best thought is about the John Ortberg 10 % rule – 'Often after going through all the hard work of setting up a difficult conversation, we shrink back from saying the hardest but most important truth. We fail to say the last 10 %. We get vague and fuzzy precisely when clarity is most needed by the other person.'

[22] See also Matthew 18:16 'But if he will not listen, take one or two others along, so that every matter may be established by the testimony of two or three witnesses.'

But just as there is positive development and deepening of friendship, there is thus a dissolution and discontinuation process.

Cicero, 1923, p.145[23] already observes the phenomenon, stating that 'nothing was harder than for a friendship to continue to the very end of life'. Kuegler, 2020-01-13[24] claims that 'The Death Of Friendship Is More Of A Rule, Not The Exception' and broadly this is correct.

Whilst I find it rude in romantic relationships to break them off without a proper conversation, friendship allows for a lot more opaqueness. Not everything needs to be said, especially when reasons might be temporary. Sometimes value differences where we think 'how could he think/say this' do not lead to a conflict, but in its aftermath we simply lose the interest to interact. Something in the picture changed, and if we are honest to ourselves, that as much as we were looking forward to meeting that person a month ago, now, we just don't anymore. At least we do not anymore at this point. Sometimes this insight is clear, but sometimes it is not, and we just have a feeling that something is 'off'. I have always found this stage difficult, and discussing it is probably unhelpful. Once a friendship is questioned, it is thus ruptured. It is here in this situation that I found also friendship circles most helpful to figure out and move through such a period. Whilst the positivity in a specific relationship might have gone down, our jokes have become stale, or our interests diverged, our focus in life gotten to different areas, in the circle however there is still enough content to make it fun and interesting. A few years later there is the possibility still of convergence.

The depth of the friendship also has a great impact on the impact of the loss. Someone from the general support group (i.e. Dunbar numbers 6-20) would be an annoying loss, sad, however ultimately acceptable. Some friendship churn indeed is expectable. However, losses in the inner circle of close friendships are of a different metal. Long years of built-up mutual understanding and common memory are at risk of being invalidated. In the section on 'effecting change' (see 5.9) I compared a best friend to a horcrux, which we have tied part of our soul and identity to. The dissolution of such a friendship will kill that horcrux, and thus strong emotional reactions are expectable. Indeed, it is likely to trigger a full 'Kuebler-Ross' grieving process to get through it. Depending on the causes of the friendship dissolution, self doubt may creep in, as we doubt whether the friendship had been well-chosen and genuine all along[25]. Thus for a general friendship a temporary silent withdrawal might be acceptable. For a close friend address the problem and talk it out with a genuine attempt at reconciliation and resolution is a moral must that is demanded by the year-long loyalty, history, and benevolence to the well-being of the friend. This may be painful but is owed to the situation.

In Christian circles there is the parable of the judge and the criminal, generally used in sermons to explain the roles of God the Father and Jesus in how Christian salvation works with God judging human sin and Jesus' sacrifice paying the debt. Two children in school became close friends and were inseparable in their

[23]'Now he, indeed, used to say that nothing was harder than for a friendship to continue to the very end of life; for it often happened either that the friendship ceased to be mutually advantageous, or the parties to it did not entertain the same political views; and that frequently, too, the dispositions of men were changed, sometimes by adversity and sometimes by the increasing burdens of age.'

[24]I used to think that friendships weren't supposed to die. My father told me the other night that in all his years he believes that fizzling friendships are actually more of the rule, not the exception.

[25]The analogon here would be doubting the judgement which object to tie the horcrux to.

adolescence. However after school their ways parted, they moved to other cities and lost contact. Upon leaving school one went on to do a law degree, qualify as a barrister and eventually in his fifties became a judge. The other one also went to university, but because of financial difficulties eventually dropped out. Finding it difficult to find his role in society with a few mishaps and unlucky turns, he eventually became homeless and turning to petty theft. As the gods of fortune would have it, the judge was moved to a different court and ended up in his home town. Soon after he was sitting on yet another car theft case, when he recognised his old school friend as the homeless and pitiful delinquent accused. The case of the prosecution was clear, as he had been caught in the act, and being a just and diligent judge, he convicted his old friend, who had not recognised him yet to a fine of 10000 Euros for damaging the car, however avoided a prison sentence as no harm other than property damage had been done to anyone. Once the verdict had been read out, he put down his robe, stepped down from the pulpit and approached the surprised court clerk and paid the fine and other prior court debt of his friend with a signed cheque. He then revealed his true self to his surprised old friend, took him in and helped him over the following weeks to get back on his feet. I think this story is not only relevant on a theological level, but also a practical guidance for close friends who lose sight and contact. If you are genuinely close with someone, it is good to hang on to the affection and benevolence towards the former friend even as the friendship has passed.

8.12 Turning friendship into romance - a friendship sin?

Harry in the movie 'When Harry met Sally' famously claims[26] that 'men and women can't be friends because the sex part always gets in the way.' I disagree with the sweeping statement, but would acknowledge that it can put a strain on a friendship.

At the point when one party[27] to the friendship realises they have a romantic interest, things change. Essentially a switch is flipped, and several 'friendship sins' are automatically committed, even with no malevolent intentions.

Not seeking the friendship for personal gain is breached, as the fulfilment of romantic interest is at least to some part selfish[28]. Trust is breached as the friend might be privy to information that the other friend would never have given to a friend. Reciprocity, equality and 'balance-of-power' are strained, as the friend's attention and affection is now exceedingly more valuable and sought after. Jealousy - totally alien to friendship - may enter the fray. I am happy to share all my friends with other friends, and I am happy indeed if one of my friends said that they met up even without me with another mutual friend and they had a great time. Exchange friend for girlfriend in this sentence, and the sentiment invariably even if partially and in the greatest of trusting relationships may become more a 'errm, thats great'.

[26] `https://youtu.be/i8kpYm-6nuE` or lookup Hum Tum for the bollywood version and equal arguments exchanged during the movie, but with more singing

[27] For clarity, if A becomes infatuated with or attracted to B, I will call A the 'interested' and B the 'interestee', thus A is the 'subject' of the 'loving/infatuation' action and B the 'object'.

[28] Of course, many romantic stories are about sacrifice, love spurning us to great deeds to ensure our quarry's happiness, but at its core romantic interest is a non-altruistic biological drive and instinct.

Now as the interested has done all this, and thus partially fractured the friendship from his side, the second act of the drama commences once the interestee becomes aware of the conundrum. This can happen by explicit confession or confrontation, or the impossibility to ignore the starry-eyed vision, significantly heightened levels of requests for attention or provided tokens of affection ((See Crystal Duck `https://youtu.be/Yfi4sr_vlZA`). Romantic interest essentially (setting aside friends with benefits scenarios) demands a binary answer, at least in the medium term. Whilst friendship allows for degrees of friendship, such as best friend, close friend or just friend, serious romantic interest does not allow for a 'just a little bit boy-/girlfriend'.

This sets up a tribunal on the interested's person, with a verdict issued by the interestee. Given the substantial overlap of criteria for friendship and romantic interest, a rejection will in all but the best scenarios put the friendship in question. In the lucky case there are obvious (to both!) accepted obstacles, that are inherent to the two persons, and cannot be credibly changed by willpower. Items like religious convictions, maintained hygiene levels at both ends of the spectrum, clearly expressed preferences for physical features (e.g. body height, a compatible level of fitness and affinity to sport) or cultural traits (extreme but unshared passions for art, music) and conflicting views on family model including the number of desired children - all these characteristics can represent uncontroversial get out clauses. Personality based rejections will sting, as any such rejection has a likely interpretation (which may not at all be justified) of 'Well, it sounds like I am good enough as a friend, but not good enough as a romantic partner.'

Thus my hunch is that genuine friendship is possible for men and women once the possibility of developing a romantic relationship is credibly eliminated. It is best, if this proceeds without a direct rejection, but more implicitly by external circumstances (such as happily dating someone else). Now I do not want to disparage romance springing from a pre-established friendship. Friends becoming romantic partners is the best that can happen, if it works out well. The pre-established trust makes opening up and disclosure much easier. There is no question about the feasibility of establishing a friendship, because it has already been established. It really is the best of both worlds, having your cake and eating it.

The topic has been of substantial interest in friendship research, e.g. O'Meara, 1989. It certainly is not restricted to any age group, as elderly women report to refrain from pursuing cross-sex friendships precisely quoting the ambiguity of motivation on the men's side.

8.13 Sickness and death of a friend

When a friendship ends because of a fight, or fades out because of geographic relocation, there always remains the possibility and hope of reconciliation or other change of circumstances. However, since the days of Lazarus, resurrections have been in short supply.

Showing powerful emotions for grief of the death of a friend has been a consistent theme in antiquity. Achilleus lament[29] over Patroclus death in book 18 of

[29]'So spake he, and a black cloud of grief enwrapped Achilles, and with both his hands he took the

the Iliad is one of the dominant themes of the book. The grief over the death of the dear friend is the one emotion to overcome his legendary wrath. David also laments Jonathan after his death, ripping his clothes in expression of the agony. Roland avenges Olivier's death and subsequently dies himself. Of course quieter reactions are possible, yet even Laelius in his old age has his younger relatives concerned for his wellbeing after the death of Scipio Africanus. Their checkup visit on their grieving uncle and patron is the background of the 'de amicitia' dialogue of Cicero, 1923.

When we grieve for a friend, we grieve for ourselves. We lose possibilities of future jokes and stories, and we lose part of the context in which our own past has meaning. Indeed - if reciprocity was lived well within the friendship - we lose one avenue of meaning of our lives to others. We also are confronted with our own mortality, which can trigger all sorts of additional emotions in us (c.f. I. Yalom, 1980). Yet death is part of human nature and dealing with it is inevitable, the question is how best to do it.

I have above written about regret avoidance as a maintenance strategy and motivator, and I think that the mortality is one of the best warnings to make us think about what we value in life and what gives us the highest pleasure and satisfaction. Ware, 2012 writes that key regret no. 4 is 'I wish I had stayed in touch with my friends'. Thus the best way to avoid it is to cherish the friendship as you go along. Reasonably regular (and this can be annual) meetups or video calls are the best way to ensure that there is no 'I wish I had ...' wake-up call in the extreme case of that car accident or cancer with late stage diagnosis. Making sure you allocate reasonable time for a friend, such as visiting in hospital, is much better to show appreciation for the friendship than showing up at the funeral.

The Romans organized feasts to commemorate their ancestors, and I think that is one of the best legacy to leave. Especially as a circle of friends may lose one of its members, it can take the birthday as an opportunity to come together, drink and commemorate their fallen friend. Personally speaking, if I die and my friends come together for drinks year on year for drinks on my account, I would be thrilled. Integrating the widowed spouse into such a circle or helping them out in the years following the funeral can be also a last meaningful display of affection for the deceased[30]. Yet in some cases also long-term couple friendships may die, as encountering the friend may trigger painful memories for the widowed spouse.

dark dust and strewed it over his head and defiled his fair face, and on his fragrant tunic the black ashes fell. And himself in the dust lay outstretched, mighty in his mightiness, and with his own hands he tore and marred his hair. ... Then terribly did Achilles groan aloud, and his queenly mother heard '

[30]On that ground I find 'Things we lost in the fire' such a well-written and acted movie, where the widow takes it upon herself to help her husbands oldest friend out of his drug addiction.

Suggestions for thought

- If you hear of a close friend getting sick, make time to check in regularly. See it not only as a payback to them or a duty but also as part of the process of yourself getting closure. It can be the difference between a bad conscience, or - as horrible as it sounds - laughing on the funeral because you remember a silly anecdote.

- If you get terminally sick, unless there is a personal reason to do so, don't hide it from your friends. You are not a burden to them, but give them the opportunity to still really have a good time with you.

Chapter 9

Roles, circles and social networks

For casual reading, most sections are relevant.
9.3 academic except takeaway , 9.4, 9.9 - 9.12 academic

The personality traits, relationship attitudes and activities are defining aspects of friends and friendships, however per se a single such trait does not 'define' the friend. It is often the case that there might be five or even ten such themes that make a specific friendship as great as it is. And while we might have preferences or even 'minimum conditions' of what we expect in a friend, these may and will vary from friend to friend. What can however be useful to think about is how themes combine to roles and how they might be defined.

Even though I use the term 'role' or 'type', which in sociological terms is generally associated with Goffman, 1978 and Merton, 1968, their definition does not correspond to the concept of role used here. A role here is not a theatre act that you put on, a societal convention or function, that you perform or conform to[1]. It is - in its ideal - something that comes out from you deeply and naturally. It is the authentic you, and you are fully at ease. It is what Lewis means when he says 'each bringing out all that is best, wisest, or funniest in all the others'. The core role is a continuation of Chapman's love languages, just in a platonic sense and slightly more elaborated. The more peripheral social roles are closer to Goffman's concept, but that reflects simply the insight that the relationship has not yet reached its full potential, intimacy and understanding. I would not want to call them deficient, as I do appreciate the considerable social contribution also our general friends and good acquaintances make to our benefit, but they do not measure up to the full 'true' close friendship which must be authentic.

The first professional typology, and to date far the best out there, is that of Rath, 2006[2], which also is coincidentally a splendid book to read. Rath does however focus very much on the key functions, which he calls 'vital' friends, giving not enough credit to the wider circle. I will come to the discussion of circles after the definition of the roles, but theories of friends' circles often divide into an inner and an outer circle with a variety of different labels created throughout literature. In scientific literature, the most common concept is the Dunbar numbers. Sutcliffe, Binder, and Arrow, 2012 refer to this as the 'support clique' of 4-5 persons and the

[1] See key trait 'honesty and authenticity'

[2] `https://theweek.com/articles/739502/8-kinds-friends-need-happy-life`

sympathy group of '12-15'. It is estimated that we approximately spent 40% of our time with the support clique and another 20% with the sympathy group.[3]. Thus, I kept to this clustering and used it to distinguish between the close friends of the key support group or core group (the 'company of heroes') and general friends in the wider social circle.

9.1 The friendship types

For the following section please note that this typology resulted from an iterative process between reviewing at the literature (books, internet, ...) and finding additional aspects and nuances represented by a variety of statements about (good, best, close) friends. As a result of this process the categories of personality traits, relationship attitudes and activities were refined, and the developing list of types was remapped onto the parallel developing trait list. The list of types is non-scientific as it is not the result of a rigorous process that used machine learning on a large data set of structured descriptions of friendship traits appreciated in close friends. Such a data set that would need to be substantial in size in order to confirm role style groupings with factor or cluster analysis. It is however structured in the sense that for each role three to five key traits were identified and assigned, and the coverage of the trait spectrum from the framework was analysed for gaps.

The core group

These are the best and very close friends who we do (or should) spend a lot of time with. If you are lucky within your core group of friends, at least one exhibits this type in order to make your life just great overall. These roles correspond to the 'Vital Friends' of Rath or the 'support clique' of Dunbar. As much of my thinking is also influenced by the old school pen and paper role playing games, this would be analogue to the company of heroes ganging up to solve the problem (free the princess, slay the dragon, find the treasure).

Best friend: The friend from old times, who understands your history, and has been through the thick with you, loyal to the end. Supportive when you are in a pickle, and the one to stay with you when the others don't. [Common history, mutual understanding, loyalty, dirt time, trust, ...]

Coach: This is the one who pushes you forward. They know your goals, and know when you need a reminder not to lose focus. And when the going gets tough, they will be there by the sidelines cheering you on or pushing from behind. [Guidance, encourage and challenge, pride]

Partner in crime: This is the soulmate, the one with the passionate same goal. This is the Ive to Jobs[4], the two great minds coming together to solve the mysteries of mathematics or physics, the inklings composing their books together and reviewing them. In a way this one comes closest to the friendship of old, where a joined passion for a common goal and the power of appreciation for it creates the friendship almost by itself. [working together, mutual interests, intelligence, discover/explore]

[3]Until Facebook came along and made us spend all our time online with the 150 or 500 and much less with the key 5...

[4]Jony Ive was for decades the chief designer of Apple, working closely together with Steve Jobs

Clown: This is the fun one. Always producing a light giggle or roaring laughter in his company, the clown brings joy all around. We all need a Mrs. Doubtfire[5] in our life, our own personal Robin Williams. This is the one who teaches our kids to play pranks on us on April 1st, who sends us stupid memes on a dreary day, and now and then tests our capacity to forgive if a joke overstepped the mark a little. [fun and humour, enjoy company, dirt time]

Mind opener: This is the one who you get on well enough to enjoy the conversation with, but is different enough to add that random element to your life. This could be the hippie leftie who eats vegan but still talks to the carnivore in you, or the artist or musician who is free of constraints of a daily life defined by the struggles of family or regular work spending his time with the creation of inventive works of art. [discover and explore, guidance(sparring), energy / excitement]

Mentor: This is the friend who provides perspective and wise council before big decisions and along the way. They know you well, have empathy and life experience. [understanding, listening, guidance]

Mom: The mom radiates warmth, love, and affection. It is the safe house where you rock up, to find a full fridge, open arms and a warm hug, sweets and cake, and a patient ear to listen to your heart's sorrows. [patience, warmth, affection, love, support general]

Dad: This is the second version of the homecoming. They are quiet and caring, no big words, maybe just a 'good to have you back' nod when you visit. This function can be the one into which the actual dad or uncle morph into, as a person grows up, moves out and becomes independent.[patience, warmth, practical help, reliability/consistency]

The social circle

This is the sympathy group. Some of them may be deep connections too, but essentially not every friendship needs to be of the 'put down your life for each other' - type. In life it is the good friends, close but not super-close, that help us out in key moments and with whom we can just have a good time. Note that the cheerleader (champion), connector and daredevil(energizer) were in part included in the 'vital friends' core roles of Rath, however characterisations hinted at less close and committed base cases[6].

Cheerleader: This is the one to show up at our sports events, concerts, speeches or other events, whilst also behind our back be singing our praises and holding down the fort for us. [Pride, support vocal]

Rust friend: This is the old friend from school or general earlier days. You are acquainted, trust each other, and enjoy each other's company, but for now there is no pressure or desire to increase the frequency of encounters significantly. [common history, enjoy company]

Connector: The connector just knows everyone. They effortlessly connect to people around him, remembering the stories and introducing people. They know

[5]Comedy about a middle aged man dressing as female nanny `https://www.imdb.com/title/tt0107614/`

[6]In those cases where they denoted a best or close friend, this friend often had an additional role or key trait that was mentioned in the essential role circle.

people's needs and capabilities, and match them as they can. [agreeable, network, support vocal]

Daredevil: This is the power type[7], hiking, going on adventurous holidays, and prompting us try the things we always dreamed of, but never thought we would do. They bring us to go-carting, make us do Cross-Fit, laugh away our protests and complaints. When the deed is done, they bask in our expression of joy and fun, as we in the evening sit with them over a pint confessing that it was a great day out with them. [excitement, independence, encourage/challenge]

Neighbour: The neighbour is a classic, once domestic life settles in. This is the mutual support group for little favours, such as checking in on the house when you are on holiday. Coming over for a bottle of wine, a few beers or a dinner is enjoyable, and you encounter each other at various local social occasions. A very frequent variant is someone to meet in parents' evenings, where the kids go to play, and who is likewise living close enough to support with day-to-day items (especially those of the kids) if life overwhelms you. [Practical help, proximity, dirt time]

Younger sister/brother: This does not refer to kinship, but to the phenomenon that sometimes friendships can be struck across generations. An older guy/lady befriends a younger person who profits from their experience in life and in return draws them back into 'active life'. [teach/learn, affection]

Saint and idol: This is the one we wish we would be like (at least a little more). Whatever you admire in live, they embody it. Truthful, authentic, despite rough adversity still smiling and positive. Compassionate and putting other people first when we ourselves would have withdrawn or minded our business, the saint reminds us to appeal to our better senses and keep pushing forward with hope, love and integrity. [virtue, consideration, honesty]

Work pal: This is the one to make you want to go to work. They may provide you with a little funny gossip, or help you out with a task. They may just make some funny jokes here and there and brighten up your day. In meetings they have your back, and show appreciation of the work you do. After hours on a Friday a pint in the pub might let off some steam. Before important decisions or presentations they have an open ear to give you some perspective on the matters at hand, using their knowledge of the workplace to point out issues you have missed. [work together, enjoy company]

Discussant: The discussion partner is someone with similar interests, who appreciates the finer details of issues you are also interested in, be it poetry, politics, philosophy, art, music or contemporary events. It is fun to engage with the person and delve deeper, knowing that your passion is understood and mirrored. [mutual interest, mutual background]

Best Friends Partner: As the friendship grows, they also become a friend in their own right and adopt one of the pure roles. Often in career oriented couples, even with the best intentions one partner becomes a little amnesic of the old friends and the need for friendship, and the social partner picks up the slack, prompting to re-initiate contact, reminding of birthdays and other social occasions. The partner is aware of the deep importance of the friendships and out of

[7]With people like these, I always had the association of people with 4 Duracells up their bottom that keep them going and going and going and going. `https://youtu.be/zsKvomCiFRY?t=240`

love for the other partner ensures [that] they don't wither. [consideration, common memory]

Single Friend: This is the one who never settled, challenging us to go out and relive our glory days. The one who allows us to experience the troubles of single life by telling us all the stories of why it didn't work out this time. They give us perspective on also the benefits of our current life. [fun, excitement]

Running Mate: The relationship is not deep, but you are there for each other - reliably so, ensuring that the other's training schedule does not slack. Whether it is 6am in the parks for a jog, after work in the gym or on the weekend of the golf course, you keep to your schedule together. [health/fitness, challenge, reliability]

As one of the tools I will get to in the appendix, I structured a questionnaire of about 60 questions by which you can measure which role is strongest for a key friend of yours. It is my opinion that when people think of a specific close friend, they usually can accurately point the main role this friend fulfils. However, the feedback from the questionnaire and reading the results was that friends usually have one major role that is clear to the respondant and up to two minor roles that become clear only in hindsight. Finding out these roles as a response to the survey increases the appreciation we have for the meaning of this friendship in our life. This is precisely the purpose for which the friendship role tool was designed.

On the whole, I find qualitative type measures much more important in friendship research than quantitive attachment measures. It is more interesting to find out whether somebody has say a need for collaboration or having fun, and has developed a friendship with someone to pursue activities rather than whether somebody has a general nondescript friend to whom they 'feel close'. I also find it incredibly difficult to order my friends, indeed there are moments when the clown is really the most important person in my life, and there are other times when the collaborator or mentor is more important for our wellbeing. Likewise, there are moments when the connector in us is required, and in other situations we are just the best buddy hanging out over a beer. Roles add colour to a black-grey-white scale or social network description. They also give a substantial and important spin on the definition of matching and reciprocity, which I will turn to below.

Suggestions for thought

- If you mentally cycle through your close friends, would you assign them a key role or would you on the whole rather assign two or three roles to them to capture the essence of their contribution in your life?
- Do you have for every role of the 'vital friends' or 'support circle' a friend who fulfils this role for you?
- Are you aware of the key roles you fulfil for your close friends?

9.2 Instrumentality and Appreciation

One key issue in friendship and mapping roles onto such a friendship inventory is instrumentality. From Aristotle via Marx to Alberoni, philosophers have maintained that friends should be an end in themselves. The fundamental idea of this is that friendships should not be pursued for an ulterior motive. On the other hand, I postulate a specification of needs, that friendship satisfies needs and has tangible benefits to our life. In assigning roles to friends, in the extreme case I could be accused of reducing friendship to a team staffing exercise, strategic and utilitarian. I would acknowledge that a rigorous rational approach to friendship and its role in life would end up in such a scenario. The way out of this may be in defining the purpose of friendship about benefitting the other.

I also think it is not helpful to stop yourself thinking about concrete benefits from the friendship for fear of catching yourself to think instrumentally. I think seeing the undeserved privilege of friendship, and then passing the sentiment on like a gift or the christian love is one way to ensure you do not approach friendship in an instrumental attitude. In the movie 'Things we lost in the fire' the key message is to 'accept the good' - it is the quote and key thought underlying the film. I think it is probably my take on friendship, if I was to summarize a good attitude towards friendship, would be to echo this and rephrase it as a give and take, do good and accept the good. 'do et das' rather than the instrumental 'do ut des'[8].If you now take a portfolio approach, and the friendship inventory is precisely the formalisation of that, it could be seen as a narcissistic view of what you are getting out of your friendships. However, it could all the same be seen as a snapshot overview version of a friendship gratitude journal, showing you just how fortunate and privileged you are that these friends are in your life. Likewise, it would show you how you currently are also meaningful to your friends and can and most likely do support them. Using then such a tool is a way for you to remind yourself to live up to expectations of yourself to yourself, how to turn the love you feel for your friends into actions that benefit them.

A not transactional but functional or capability driven view of friends acknowledges that not every friend is good at everything and absolves them from being so. It thus relaxes the conditions of friendship and enables different forms of friendship. I grappled for a long time with the output of the dataset of Hall, 2012b, Study 1, that essentially postulated one major co-correlated factor of almost everything that is nice in a friendship (see for a detailed analysis in the appendix in F.4). It is however true that unrestrained by reality, we would like our friends to be loyal, funny, smart, kind, affectionate and a little admiring of us. We would like them to be some kind of mix between Robin Williams and Jesus, Wonderwoman[9] and Mary Poppins. Who would say no? That is however not what is on offer with normal people. Instead, we keep finding imperfect people still being wonderful friends, but maybe not in every respect. A person specific role approach, cultivating maybe two specific roles towards each other, and still filling for others in whenever we are needed and no one better is nearby, might just be the best that a real world might have on offer. It might also be the best we can ask of ourselves to be the best loving friend to others.

[8]'I give and you give' instead of 'I give so that you may give'

[9]Female hero in the DC Universe, https://www.imdb.com/title/tt0451279/

9.3 Matching expectations and reciprocity

One statistic discussed in recent times is the significant mismatch of reciprocity in friendships and our inadequate perception at realising that a friendship is reciprocal. The key study here is Almaatouq et al., 2016, and within that the reciprocity study. The authors got 84 members of an undergraduate course to ' score every other participant on a 0–5 scale, where 0 means "I do not know this person", 3 means "Friend" and 5 means "One of my best friends." In addition, participants were also asked to 'predict' how other participants would score them.'[10]. The often quoted result is that only half (53 %) of the edges are reciprocal, with authors like Millington, 2019, p.35[11] following up on it. As the following table shows, the numbers are actually substantially more positive than that.

	5	4	3	2	1	0
5	75					
4	61	54				
3	22	104	151			
2	8	27	295	686		
1	5	6	64	674	636	
0	0	3	11	150	285	169
Tot	171	194	521	1510	921	169

For the best friend category 5, 35 (so about 20%) are 2 or more categories distant, for the close friend and friend the 2+ category namings are 36 (so about 19%) and 75 (so about 14%). Thus whilst only 43%, 28% and 29% are exactly reciprocal, 'only' one-in-five friendship pairs is substantially mismatched. If two members from the 84 as outliers are excluded[12], the proportion of unreciprocated friendships with two differences category reduces to 9%, 11% and 12% respectively. Thus while minor differences in perception occur, as one close friend may consider the other one a best friend or 'just friend', substantial differences actually only occur as one-in-ten. Minor differences can occur because of differences in definition of close and best friendship, as well as comparison circles. The dataset of 84 management students is closed, but some may have only found their first true friends in the circle, whereas others might be benchmarking their new friends against the long friends of old from school or college. The argument here is that when I looked at reciprocity in section 4.7, the main issue of concern is substantial imbalance. Whilst it is a nuisance if my 'new' best friend has an old best friend from school or kindergarten, it is however no big drama. Friendship is free from jealousy and respecting. Some people are more affectionate than others, feeling or

[10]' Participants in the experiment were early career (age 23– 38) adults taking a university course in applied management. Gender balance was 40% male and 60% female.' This is significant as it implies that it is in terms of maturity and gender balance more representative of a general public than the 80 % female 18-20 year old first year psychology undergraduates who usually supply sample populations.

[11]'A 2016 study found that only half of perceived friendships are actually mutual! I hate to be the one to break it to you, but many of the people you consider friends only think of you as an acquaintance, and there are probably many people you have happily popped into your outer circle of friends who think of you as one of their closest! That's right, up to half of our friendships are actually unreciprocated!'

[12]An adjustment the authors make themselves for reaching the 775 edges mentioned, as the two members report substantial numbers of reciprocated best friends.

expressing feelings more, some are faster, so some imbalance is to be expected in a survey like that, with only the one-in-ten substantial difference being a genuine matter of concern.

Whilst I have a great fondness for the general social circle, the notion of trust, loyalty and reliability in close friendships is crucial, and with that comes that our notion to perceive it accurately. Fortunately, when restricting the analysis to categories 5 and 4 (one of the best friends and close friends) in the dataset of Almaatouq et al., 2016, 75% of us get between 60 and 100% of our best and close friends correctly categorised. This represents a remarkably encouraging result given the data, certainly substantially more encouraging than the statement that roughly 50% of our friendships are not reciprocated. However, in the converse, some people are actually quite bad at recognising who their friends are. As the 20+ category shows, the Aristotle inspired statement[13] 'A friend to all is a friend to none' explains uncertainty of actual reciprocal friendships. Additionally, there are about 20 % of people who are quite bad at correctly identifying their actual friends, and for those I would think it is both a problem, and without additional knowledge it is difficult to speculate on the actual reason. Here further research (probably then detailed qualitative interview work) is really necessary to identify the issues and start thinking of remedies.

	10%	30 %	50 %	70 %	90%	100%	Total
0			4				4
1-2	1		2			8	11
3-5	1		1	7	2	12	23
6-9		1	3	8	11	9	32
10-14			3	2	2	1	8
15-19			3	1			4
20+	1	1					2
Total	3	2	16	18	15	30	84

Practical takeaway
Most people are actually reasonably capable of judging whether a good friend of theirs considers them a good friend in reverse. Those who are 'friends to all' however struggle a bit to accurately identify their actually good friends.

Suggestions for thought

- How good do you think you are at guessing the reciprocity or matching between you and your friends?
- Do you have a friend where there is a substantial imbalance? Are you the more important friend or the less important friend?

[13] 'Those who have many friends and mix intimately with them all are thought to be no one's friend, except in the way proper to fellow-citizens, and such people are also called obsequious.'

9.4 Circle theory review and scoring friendship

With Dunbar being the most prominent one, several authors promote the idea of friendship circles[14]. The definition of those are essentially hierarchies of friends, with a core set of friends being very close (the best friends or 'must' friends), and a general social group still with regular contact complementing it. Whilst most people speak of best friends and close friends and differentiate them from 'just friends', I am hesitant whether I want to make the argument for the existence or possibility of an ordinal scale for friends. The validity of such a hierarchy is closely tied to the quality of the reciprocity-matching and perception as described in the prior section. Though overall the existence of such a hierarchy might be robust for most of us, how we mentally allocate our friends to circle one, two or three or in between might vary from person to person. Thus two people A and B might see each other in exactly the same way, loyal, trustworthy, been around for a while, and yet A might consider B a very close or best friend and yet B may consider A a close friend for the only reason that the circle boundaries are defined differently.

R. Dunbar, 2012 bases the structure of the networks on the 'social brain' hypothesis, that postulates humans being incapable of maintaining more than 150 relationship at any one time. There is evidence that we maintain hierarchies of concentric groups with each group increasing by a factor three in size from the other. Thus Sutcliffe, Binder, and Arrow, 2012 labels these the support clique of 4-5 and a sympathy group of 12-15, surrounded by an affinity group of around 50 ('band') and an active network ('clan') of about 150. The main investigated variable usually is time spent together, with group structure or functionality taking a second place.

Spencer and Pahl, 2006, p.215 construct maps of 'personal communities'. Whilst likewise these are built of concentric circles, the number of participants in each circle was not prescribed, nor was the number of used circles prescribed. Spencer and Pahl mostly focused on the closer community of say up to 20 people total, and how they related to the ego, regardless of whether it was kin or friendship as the bond. What is key to their material is that they include the functional dimension to label the relationship to the ego[15].Degges-White and Borzumato-Gainey, 2011, p.169 dedicates an entire chapter to guiding the reader through constructing a 'friendscape' ('landscape map of your relationship'). The 'friendscape' is likewise egocentric and looks at the support friends and family provide, and how they contribute to happiness and satisfaction in the life. A second circle is reserved for those whose company is enjoyed and limited self disclosure occurs. The image transforms into a garden, where friends can be repositioned, replanted, transplanted, weeded or pruned, a garden that may have open spaces or overcrowding, and encourages the perspective of having a goal, a normative state which you would like your 'friendscape' to be in. Subsequent questions focus on the cat-

[14]Note that this 'circles' is substantially different to the circle of friends' definition in circle building, which is about actively fostering specific groups of friends bonding together, and says nothing about hierarchy or quality.

[15]Spencer and Pahl, 2006, p.155 ASS: Associate/ single activity friend, FFD: Fun / sociable friend, FFM: fun family, FVR: favour/neighbourly friend, HLP: helpmate or helpful family (practical help), SUP: supportive friend or family (emotional support), CNF: confidant or intimate, SLM: Soulmate, AMB: ambivalent or 'heart-sink' relationship with friend or family, DTY: relationship based mainly on normative expectations, sense of duty

egories of instrumental support and emotional support. The chapter closes with several valuable recommendations on how to develop this, focusing on the emotional support landscape[16].

Greif, 2009 defines four circles of 'must', 'trust', 'rust' and 'just' friends: a must friend is loosely equivalent to the 'best friend' and a trust friend a confidante with less regular contact. A rust friend is a 'fossil friend' where the long acquaintance (e.g. since school or college) results in familiarity and easy reconnection/reactivation. Finally the just friend is a slightly more cordial and close version of an acquaintance, a version of the single context/activity friendship. Internet personal advice columnist Manson, 2018 likewise proposes a five-level system for the friends from best friend, close friend, mutual interest friend, polite acquaintance, bare acquaintance.[17]. He also makes a couple of assertions that I do think are really worth considering, namely that some people only have low-level friendships but no high-level friendships and some people are the exact opposite, and gives the recommendation that a balanced mix is probably the best course of action. Furthermore, he asserts that reciprocity of category implies an upper bound, i.e. the level the friendship operates on is the minimum of both parties' estimates in mid term[18]. Other 'classes of friends' I have come across include the label of 'situationship', which often describes the bonding of expats, hanging out and enjoying each other's company, but in a clear expectation that the friendship will end once one of the two moves on geographically.

Another way of thinking about friends categories is in terms of 'badges' or 'levels'. This is related to the concept of Guttman scales [19]. But this would be a cascade of ordered statements such as 'we occasionally have a beer together' or 'we help each other out', and the more statements higher up the merit order are answered positively, by conclusion the 'better' a friend is deemed to be.

I think more than thinking about ordering friends by quality, I would encourage the appreciation of different natures and roles. Thus specifically I would not want to decide (and don't think it is healthy to) whether the clown friend or the mentor friend is a better or more important friend. I would even partially cast into doubt the sole focus on time spent / attention that underlies e.g. Dunbar's studies to use 'number of contact initiations in a given month' as an indicator variable for closeness. As previously identified, time spent together of course is majorly significant, however even regular but rare encounters can work as well or even better as the foundation of a great friendship, if the time is well spent, thoroughly enjoyed and gives rise to long-lasting memories.

---

[16]It might be noted again for context that the book is written for women to improve friendship in a self help style, but thoroughly footnoted and based on sociological research.

[17](5) 'We're practically family' - the best friends that are to last the lifetime, (4) 'We are the same, you and I' with shared life experiences and humour, with mutual understanding and acceptance, (3) 'Remember that thing we both like? Me too!' - friendship of utility and pleasure with focus on a common activity, (2) 'Let's smile and make noises of general approval toward one another', (1) 'Hey, it's that guy'

[18]'Friendships naturally fall to the lowest level. So if we're friends, and you see me as a Level 4, and I see you as a Level 3, we will never pass Level 3. That's for the simple fact that I won't engage you on a Level 4.'

[19]The paper by Friedkin, 1990 unfortunately falls short in elaborating on this.

9.5 Designing a friendship inventory or map

Bringing the two concepts together - the friendship roles and the idea of concentric circles of friends - in order to design a helpful way of thinking about ones 'friendscape', one issue however is missing. One of the key issues I have with the landscape tools or maps mentioned above is the ego-centricity. The sole focus is on the benefit to your happiness and wellbeing, how your needs are being met. Friendship however is a bilateral path, and at least as much focus should be on the joy and 'benefit' that you bring to the equation. Thus a tool or friendship landscape should prompt you on how you can be a great or best friend and in what ways you can be there for your friends. What friendship needs are not just the ones that you need to have satisfied, but which friendship needs are you naturally good at satisfying.

If we think about friendship on an ordinal scale, I would strictly separate it from acquaintance. Thus on most of the above scales I would only consider the core two categories as actual friendships, and thus would propose three actual friendship categories:

1. the **very close / best friends**: this is the inner circle of 2-5 people, where you would be severely distraught if one of them were to die.

2. the **close / good friends**: this is a group of say 5-15 people with whom you enjoy activities, meet up intentionally, maintain close contact e.g. by writing postcards.

3. the **potentially close friends**: this is a group maybe also of 5-15 people, the potentials but not there yet. You have a great vibe, and have a hunch that you could become good friends, but the levels of trust and reliability are not established yet. [20].

Rather than considering them as delimited classes, I would more see them as fluid groups, with a bit of a grey zone between them. As noted above, friends move between categories not necessarily in sync, and it is plausible and indeed likely that minor mismatches occur and persist for a while. And rather than 'rating or scoring' them, I think it is much more helpful to focus on their role. Having a list or an overview that you look at occasionally however has one major benefit, and that is that it drives appreciation and gratitude. Indeed - in line with the common memory, appreciation and gratitude themes, I would recommend that once the 'list' is made, to get photos of each of them and find a place on your wall and put them all up there. Then on regular intervals you will get reminded of all of their existence, no matter how busy and chaotic your life becomes. If a full free wall is not available, one of those digital photo frames with changing photos can likewise do the job[21].

[20] Note that this is different to the people who are 'just friends' but where you think it will stay this way. It is perfectly fine to cultivate situationships, who are enjoyable but will never rise beyond this. This category may be called the 'not yet great friends' with the emphasis on the 'not yet'.

[21] Preparing this of course is also a must exercise in onsetting dementia.

Suggestions for thought:
Have a look around your room and apartment and look whether you have some space for putting some representation of your core friends up.

Don't rate your friends by numbers with statements like X is a better friend than Y. But do be clear to yourself who is in your core inner circle. It doesn't matter whether you draw it at 2, 5, 10 or even 15, but you should be clear who is in it, and prioritise them at least to some degree over all the other acquaintances and Facebook friends.

9.6 Choice and pronouncing the friendship

One difference in habits of friendship formation is the degree of formalization and **active choice**, with a slow and unacknowledged process as the alternative. In antiquity, a careful, explicit choosing and - upon making the choice - formal confirmation seems to have been the norm. This goes without saying for the covenants of the bible, but also it is implied in the 'goodwill expressed towards each other' of Aristotle's definition of friendship. Cicero, 1923, p.173 explicitly mentions to 'put the dispositions of friends to a preliminary test', presumably the results of which will be then acknowledged. Jesus appointed his apostles by declaration. The theme is that **friendship needs to be meaningfully expressed** to become effective[22], and cannot be assumed.

The proponents of independence - Lewis[23], Alberoni[24] and Millington[25] - take the counterpoint to Aristotle, Jesus (and Captain Kirk). Expressing friendship or **explicitly affirming** that the choice of **friendship** has been made **is a no-go**.

Whereas openness for friendship of course has implications on how many 'candidates' are identified, setting criteria and being careful with friends has implication on circle composition. Whilst they may be disappointed if they have not reached a certain level of friendship with someone, people respect being a little slower with bestowing approval, as it shows that the friendship will be properly valued as they would hope it to be, once it is achieved. Openness or caution for friendship is acquired and refined in adolescence, as people make experiences in school and see what kind of friends their parents developed a friendship with. There is also different attitudes, usually differing whether emphasis is more placed on personality traits (whether the potential friend qualifies because of certain traits such as virtue, fun or intelligence, loosely consistent with the 'spark' creation) or relationship traits (which need to be established over time, thus loosely consistent with the 'takes-time-to-grow' creation).

[22]Facebook friendship doesn't quite cut it as a public declaration of friendship.

[23]Lewis, 1960, p.91 'Lovers are always talking to one another about their love; Friends hardly ever about their Friendship.'

[24]'But for friendship to do justice to those who embody it, it must remain silent about itself. It is a virtue; and virtues do not speak of themselves, or rather do so only to exchange dignity for hubris.' and 'Unlike romantic love and erotic passion, and like all the virtues, it does not declare itself.'

[25]Millington, 2019, p.74 'Unlike marriage - we never exchange vows with our best friend. It's an unspoken promise to be in each other's lives'

Caution and showing care in selecting friends and the active element of such a choice is emphasised by several authors, and interestingly is a unifying element between both the friendship 'declarers' and the undeclared[26]. Thus J.R. Miller, 1897 points out that according to Luke 6:12, Jesus spends a full night praying, before choosing and appointing the disciples, despite having hung out with them on the road already for an entire year. It should also be repeated that an emphasis on caution and care is antithetical to the theme of acceptance. Being cautious and independent involves an element of judgement in the choice. This ensures good friends assuming there are plenty of people to choose from. Sometimes, e.g. in a small village community or church, the set from which we pick from is limited. In particular, in older age as people move to new areas, a retirement village or get more restrained in their mobility, being too picky becomes self-defeating in looking for connection. Yet for people with high friendship standards, compromising and spending time with people who actually do not understand you can create intense feelings of loneliness too.

Striking the balance between being too picky or judgemental and too accepting and setting oneself up for potential disappointment is difficult. It will depend on one's own personality, preferences, needs and the current life situation. It might be good to reflect on patterns, being aware of what traits are particularly appealing to oneself. Likewise, it is good to think about cases where giving someone a second chance after a bad first impression, or giving someone a bit more time to test their metal paid off.

Suggestions for thought:
Are you more a friendship declarer or a non-declarer? Either way, why?

9.7 The spouse as the best friend

> It is not a lack of love, but a lack of friendship that makes unhappy marriages.
>
> Friedrich Nietzsche

Much has been written about friendship in marriage and that marriage, or partnership, needs to include friendship. J. Gottman and Silver, 2015 most prominently states that the quality of a marriage depends on the quality of the friendship embedded inside. Having been single most of my life, I am in no position to offer any personal insight into the truth of this. I write these lines in a similar situation as C.S. Lewis wrote about friendship in the four loves, aware that he did substantially alter his views as he experienced married life later on. The phrase of the 'blind talking about colour' might be apt. In this book, I only address the friendship component of a relationship. Thus if physical attraction enters the fray, anything related to it becomes part of the romantic element and is considered out of scope for this book.

[26] those who insist that goodwill and friendship must be declared and affirmed - Aristotle - and those who insist that the friendship is not spoken about and not verbally affirmed - Lewis, Alberoni

What does it mean for a romantic couple to develop a close friendship? What realistic expectations can be held for on the strength and nature of such a friendship? I conjectured earlier on that a friend usually only fulfils two to three key roles well, and can substitute in temporarily for the others, but most likely not as in natural strength. I am not talking about the acquaintances here, but even the best of friends. What does hold for expectation management for even the best friend however must surely also hold for the spouse or partner! It is deeply unhealthy to expect a spouse to fill the shoes not just of two but of up to eight key friendship roles or functions. However, one consequence of our retreat into the privacy of our homes and detaching from friendships is - assuming we still have our natural social needs - precisely that we now expect our spouse to take up the slack. Given the exposition above, there should be no surprise that this is destined for disappointment and disaster. It might be much healthier to identify which three roles or call them strengths your partner has, but apart from that to see them as a 'primus inter pares'[27] with friendship needs. Then you look that other friends are covering for other roles. Indeed, one corollary of gender oriented friendship research is that it is healthy - if the stereotypes are to be believed - for married couples to have other friends to talk shop with and cater to needs of emotional understanding and listening. This does not diminish the spouse's role, indeed it allows specifically for cherishing and being grateful for what they do well and not burden them with the rest. Alternatively you might be in a situation that you are still single and have set your mind upon finding a spouse that has this friendship potential. It then might be good to know both what the key friendship needs and corresponding roles are in your life, and what roles you best fulfil, thus seeing for whom you can be the best friend they could look for in a spouse[28]. Again, this is a rationalisation of an inherently emotional and intuitive process or situation. I acknowledge you may not only disagree and object, but that I may change my opinion on this in the future too if further data on this is raised within future research.

The spouse also has most times an additional function, and that is likely the reminder and supporter. In our busy lives it can happen often that we lose sight of our friends, and sometimes it is the spouse who reminds us not to neglect them. In less fortunate circumstances, a spouse jealous of our attention or time may also become the biggest obstacle to maintaining friendships. Lewis, 1960, p.49[29] paints two pictures of wives, one (the 'sensible women') who encourages her husbands friendships and those who are interested in isolating their husbands. In my experience, even if the friendship precedes their romantic partnership with their spouse, also befriending the spouse is extremely enriching. Befriending the spouse convinces them of your general affection and benevolence, and is probably also a precondition of being permitted off-time in good spirit.

[27]Latin: first among equals

[28]As hinted upon elsewhere, this attitude has in practice worked not quite yet for me, so treat it just as a thought, not a sure-proof recipe.

[29]'But the conscious war against Friendship may be fought on a deeper level. There are women who regard it with hatred, envy and fear as the enemy of Eros and, perhaps even more, of Affection. A woman of that sort has a hundred arts to break up her husband's Friendships. She will quarrel with his Friends herself or, better still, with their wives. She will sneer, obstruct and lie. She does not realise that the husband whom she succeeds in isolating from his own kind will not be very well worth having; she has emasculated him.'

Suggestions for thought - ignore if currently single

- In what ways are you friends with your partner/spouse?
- Hands on heart - does the above description of expecting all friendship needs to be fulfilled by your partner fit to you and your partner/spouse?
- To what degree are you both accepting and non-jealous of friends who might be better at something than you are?
- Do you encourage each other to pursue and invest in high-quality friendships?

9.8 Friends at work

Another contentious issue is the feasibility, and the advisability of having friends at work. According to Rath, 2006 there are clear benefits, and his recommendation is to not only have one but ideally three close friends at work for full benefits. In favour of having friends at work is the fact that we spend 40 or more hours a week in the office and thus in the company of potential friends. Having friends around basically makes us more relaxed and enjoy our time at work more.

Yet it is also important to acknowledge potential issues: first at work we compete for attention, promotions, success. Of course ideally there is a sense of cooperation, of comaraderie, of working for a common purpose. But most companies are organized as hierarchies, and there is competition on the way up. Not everyone can go to the top, and as a friend may succeed whilst we don't, envy can set in. I have already written about trust and interest conflicts in such situations, though maybe not initially as you form a friendship with a direct colleague. But if, say ten years down the line, your colleague friend becomes your direct manager or even higher level senior manager, how does the relationship change? Your friend may know details about your capabilities or even work ethic that might be disadvantageous to you. There might be also the appearance of preferentialism, as people might be envious of the direct access you have to the senior manager, that they themselves lack. In the extreme case conflicts of interest can occur, as a senior manager is mandated to close a department and make the employees redundant, among which they might have a or several close friends. Alberoni, 2016 is sceptical that friendships can survive substantial power balances and conflicts of interest. If a genuine friendship was established way back, trust, affection and benevolence can be tested and affirmed. In a trusting environment established by a prior friendship, critical feedback can be given much more freely and without the context of second guessing personal interests.

Like in cross-sex friendships, instrumentality must be credibly excluded. The friendship with your coworker or manager must be clear to be formed on the basis of their personal qualities, wit, interesting comments and really anything other than being a means to an end to your career. That does not mean you cannot show appreciation for their contribution to your work, support when drafting a memo or presentation, advice on career choices, and compassion when you have a terrible day at work is part and parcel of friendship. But it must be clear that the friendship is one of genuine personal interest in the other and not their function/ jobtitle / organizational power or generally put - utility.

Also people like to separate their friends and their private life, often for a good reason. If most of your social circle is from work, and you meet with friends at a party where 50 % of people are from your same company, topics from work will automatically surface. Now this is not a bad thing per se, in particular where people are intrinsically passionate about their work, such as academia or social work. But it poses problems both for those who do not want to continue talking about work topics in their private space, as well as for 'outsiders' who are not familiar with the background.

Criteria for befriending work colleagues

	Average	1	2	3	4	5
Mutual Interest	3.6	8	11	41	52	33
Hobby	2.7	29	35	48	25	10
Political view	2.4	47	34	35	25	7
Humour	4.0	2	16	22	52	55
Good Teamwork / Collaboration	3.8	5	12	31	65	34
Loyalty	4.2	3	7	24	42	71
Discretion	3.9	6	9	35	40	58

1 ='not important', 5 = 'very important'
Data from Habits survey F.3

Suggestions for thought

- Do you think friendship on the job is a good idea? If not, why not?
- How is friendship at work different to an exclusively private setting?
- To what degree do your priorities or criteria for work friendship compare to the above survey averages?
- If you meet friends from work, to what degree do you still talk about work?

9.9 Strong and weak ties

Granovetter 'strength of interpersonal tie'

Ever since Granovetter, 1973 the social network world has been partitioning social ego-centric networks into weak and strong ties. In the original paper, the concepts of weak and strong ties were implied to correspond to acquaintances (weak) and kin & close friends (strong ties). This was confirmed in Granovetter, 1983[30]. Krackhardt, 1992 formalized a strong tie definition. The original paper

[30] 'The argument asserts that our acquaintances (weak ties) are less likely to be socially involved with one another than are our close friends (strong ties)'.

now has approximately 60000 citations under its belt, and thus while falling a little short of Einstein's Elektrodynamik or Lowry's Protein measurement, can be counted as one of the most influential economics paper of all times.[31]. The definition of tie strength as given in the original paper was phrased thus:

'Most intuitive notions of the "strength" of an interpersonal tie should be satisfied by the following definition: the strength of a tie is a (probably linear) combination of the amount of time, the emotional intensity, the intimacy (mutual confiding), and the reciprocal services which characterize the tie. Each of these is somewhat independent of the other, though the set is obviously highly intercorrelated. Discussion of operational measures of and weights attaching to each of the four elements is postponed to future empirical studies. It is sufficient for the present purpose if most of us can agree, on a rough intuitive basis, whether a given tie is strong, weak, or absent.' (Granovetter, 1973, p. 1361)

As a first comment this definition captures, allowing for a level of abstraction, pretty well a sizeable part of the relationship attitudes, and with reciprocal services arguably the activities in the framework. At this point the big observation is that the personality of the two participants as a feature of tie strength is omitted. 'Reciprocal services' is a classical sociological term (albeit an unfortunate one for friendship), and at this point I would assume that classical beneficence and mutual activities are subsumed here. Indeed, I would argue that Aristotle's 'does what is good for the sake of his friend' (NE 9.4) is much closer to the modern day services term than might be admitted by modern virtue-philosophers. By emphasising additionally emotional intensity and intimacy, the utility of the tie for information transmission is actually not part of the definition. As such, Casagrande and Castañeda, 2020's criticism of weak ties as 'fickle companies based on shared interests' and thus the opposite of 'true friendship (as in philia)' is actually not justified at this point.[32] It is a relationship and activity emphasising perfectly functional definition of friendship.[33]. Friendship or tie strength thus was in the original focus of the author's definition. Job search and information transmission represented merely an interesting traceable use case to test the conjectured theory of tie functionality in network[34]. It is a major missed opportunity that subsequent research focused only on the latter whilst at best paying lip service to the original 'rich' tie definition and the range of possibilities it allowed.

Krackhardt's definition of 'philos'

When close friendship is mentioned in modern management and organization studies, the definition provided by Krackhardt, 1992[35] is often referred to. The

[31] It beats Modigliani Miller by a factor of 2, or Hayek's knowledge in society by a factor of 3. In sociology it passes the 'Iron cage revisited' and leaves almost everything in the dust after that.

[32] In trying to find philosophical/psychological discussion of the weak ties I searched within the citations of Granovetter and Krackhardt for 'Aristotle', 'friendship', 'ethics' (for Nicomachean Ethics) and 'philia', but an actual direct comparison I did not find. I am still suspecting an oversight on my part and would be grateful to a pointer or reference.

[33] It would be a highly interesting exercise to expand the study of tie strength with character variables, but that for later.

[34] By traceable I mean it was feasible to generate good data and work evidence based, rather than on an abstract level with philosophical qualitative arguments

[35] 3245 references on Google scholar

'strong tie' or 'philos' definition[36] was coined as a response to the 'weak ties' of Granovetter, 1973. Krackhardt, 1992, p.219 defines three necessary and sufficient conditions for the 'philos' relationship. I also quote from the subsequent passage of the paper.

- 'Interaction: For A and B to be philos, A and B must interact with each other.
- Affection: For A to be philos of B, A must like B, A must feel affection for B. ... one may assume that in most cases such relationships are symmetrical. However one can imagine occasions when affection is not reciprocated, resulting in an asymmetric relationship.
- Time: A and B, to be philos, must have a history of interactions that have lasted over an extended period of time. That is, there is no such thing as instant philos.'

'But they also actively combine to make [...] trust. Interaction creates opportunity for the exchange of information, some of which may be confidential. Affection creates motivation to treat the other in positive ways [...] and time creates the experience necessary to allow each person to predict how the other will use any shared information.' Subsequently Krackhardt echoes the Fischer 1982 critique of inadequate preciseness of definition of the word 'friend'. He summarizes with 'But the face validity of the idea that friends are people who like each other, have known each other for a reasonable time, and frequently interact with each other is at least minimally defensible.'

In the analysis of this it is both interesting to see the terms included as well as the conditions relaxed or even omitted relative both to the classical or Aristotelian definition of 'philia'[37] that the choice of the word 'philos' doubtlessly invokes the question whether this corresponds to prior elaborations on the reality of practiced friendship in the workplace[38].

Interaction corresponds to themes of 'dirt time' (5.1) and a common workplace, thus both intentional and situational organizational belonging (5.2). Affection in this context is probably more a professional and general goodwill or care in the Aristotelian sense rather than the emotional affection or love for the friend.[39] Significant is then the relaxation of necessity for reciprocity[40], at which point Krackhardts concept of 'philos' departs irreconcilably from Aristotles 'philia'[41], which insists on mutual declaration and recognition of goodwill as a necessary condition. It should be repeated that in Granovetter's definition, services are also assumed to be reciprocal.

---

[36]The choice of the word is a curious bow to the classical tradition, unfortunately not followed by a literary reference just whose concept of 'philos' is actually meant.

[37]It might be mildly amusing to recall the quote of Whitehead 'The safest general characterization of the European philosophical tradition is that it consists of a series of footnotes to Plato.' (Alfred North Whitehead, Process and Reality, p. 39 [Free Press, 1979]) extended by the information snippet that Aristotle was Plato's most prolific student. Thus from a perspective of us living 2000 years later the duo can be arguably combined to a single school of thought.

[38]A re-edit might also adjust the wording to the classicist friendly 'A and B are philoi'

[39]This however is an interpretation based on what follows, per se the term is spot on and might include the esteem for the other person.

[40]This is specifically intended, see Carley and Krackhardt, 1996 for elaboration

[41]And thus by extension, also how contemporaries such as Nehamas, 2016 would define a philos too...

Finally Krackhardt subscribes to the 'takes-time-to-grow' school of thought, which is general social convention. Specifically, the assertion of the impossibility of 'instant philos' is however contrary to the observation that the 'spark' close friendships of the collaborative style particularly often arise in a professional environment with a high level of specialisation, such as between scientists, engineers, entrepreneurs, poets, artists or musicians. Implied in affection may be themes of respect and appreciation of the other person and the necessity of the pursuing the friendship or close tie for the purpose of the friendship and the other person as an end, not a utilitarian calculation. As Krackhardt mentions trust and confidentiality, loyalty and discretion can be assumed to be implied. Predictability is alluded to and may extend to the concept of reliability and consistency.

Essentially omitted are the themes of humour and good collaboration and teamwork. The theme of advice, guidance and sparring, often mentioned in qualitative studies of work friends, is likewise not included in the definition and subsequent characterisation. It is however often focused on in studies drawing on Krackhardt's base construct. The simple theme of bottom line 'enjoyment of company' however is missing. This I think is a critical omission for characterising work friendships, with all benefits such as information exchange, power coordination and mutual support, work collaboration and advice being secondary to that in importance. It not sufficiently covered by affection. On the positive side, it should be repeated that affection interpreted in a narrow sense is inherently person (and thus personality) oriented. This definition thus implicitly forebodes the inclusion of the relevance of person as posited in Kilduff and Krackhardt, 2008, p.10.

Friendship in SNA

Krackhardt and Kilduff, 1999 state 'The role of friend is well understood in society, as indicated by the high level of agreement within societies concerning how friends should act in relation to each other' citing Argyle, Henderson, and Furnham, 1985, p.92. This assumption is in stark contrast to the previously often cited Fischer 1982 or Rath Gallup survey on only 30 % of people expressing friendships accurately (see section 2), and the oversimplification through the assumption of binary yes-no nature of friendship could already be questioned at the time of their writing on the basis of the circle theory of Dunbar and others (see section 9.4). Indeed one might argue that the role of friend is intuitively well understood in society, yet still question whether it coincides with the sociological theoretical construct of it. Resulting from the lack of reflection on the meaning of the term 'friend' and 'friendship' in the literature on social network analysis a few problems persist, that from a friendship theory perspective can be resolved in a straightforward manner.

Tasselli, Kilduff, and Menges, 2015 thus pose the question: 'We examine three distinct positions, asking whether the people, considered as individuals with characteristic traits and cognitions, make the network; whether the network, through structural patterning, makes the people; or whether people, in their idiosyncrasies, and networks, in their differentiated structures, coevolve.' For 'philia' friendship there is a clear answer - **people** and their personalities **make the network**. The personality of the people is the starting trigger point of platonic affection and is the constitutive causal element of the good friendship. The network and environment may be supportive[42], but is peripheral (unlike e.g. power-ties or advice networks in corporations). Conversely, social network analysis that ignores personality may understand professional organizations such as companies and accurately predict behaviour and patterns in such utilitarian environments, but will categorically fail at understanding friendship circles such as the Inklings. Previously cited research from positive psychology[43] on how much of our personality and preferences is actually due to genetics and nurture, and if we further deduct for impacts of kin and non-work friends, it is clear that people predominantly make their social network and not the other way round.

The big drawback of these studies is that they sample work friendships or student friendships because this is where they are able to generate edge-level data. However good friendship usually needs both an informal as well as long-term environment, and both of these fall short on this front. Brokerage between Friendship cliques and exploiting structural holes is an issue in instrumental friendly-professional relationships in work contexts, but seems an artificially constructed non-problem in actual casual friendship networks. I will happily be convinced otherwise as data on church communities, care homes, sports centers, (science or humanities) undergraduate colleges or rural villages is generated and analysed. However I insist there are limits to which you can generalise from 'friendship networks' in employee groups in corporations and MBA classes onto general humankind, especially given the more utilitarian transactional ethos predominant among such groups which is by itself antithetical to good friendship[44]. Indeed a Rath/Hall style friendship role evaluation is likely to yield substantial differences in expectations between a set of work friends and a set of friends from school, football club or church.

Much of social network analysis' data is generated in corporations. However people act different in professional environments (work) than in informal environment (friendships, university). As an example take 'Thus, individuals in organizations perceive their friendship ties with others as more reciprocated than they actually are' Kilduff and J.W. Lee, 2020, p.162[45]. The cohort study of Almaatouq et al., 2016 shows that to the contrary even in an MBA class, nine of ten ties are actually not materially unreciprocated, but additional datasets and using continuous scales might yield better insights.

A further much investigated trait shows the alienation of such corporation and

[42]The environment may be conducive for A and B spending more time than usual getting to know each others personalities to decide on whether to form a friendship

[43]E.g. Seligman, 2009 on us changing our personality only up to 20% in our lifetime post-childhood

[44]An environment of competition, ambition and task over people orientation incentivises for lower levels of altruism, generosity, consideration, humility, time availability for managers, kindness and patience, all of which ceteris paribus would imply lower friendship quality, though exceptions are plenty.

[45]Compare this with the earlier practice of completing unreciprocated friendship ties - e.g. in Mehra, Kilduff, and Brass, 1998, p.444: 'Because the eigenvector analysis program handled only symmetric data, for this analysis we symmetrized the friendship matrix, using the rule that if either member of a pair nominated the other pair, then the pair was a friendship pair.' Almaatouq et al., 2016 demonstrated the danger of this approach, as usually there are two or three people who think of themselves as friends with everyone, but aren't. Indiscrimnate pair closing would however place them as central connecting points within such a social network, an error that Almaatouq et al., 2016 specifically correct for.

organization theory motivated perspectives on friendship - the high-low self monitors: 'Those high in self-monitoring resemble successful actors in their ability to play different roles for different audiences' Snyder, 1987. This is of course a trait that would leave Cicero, Fromm and Alberoni aghast to be used in a sentence (or paper) about friendship. You can read also descriptions of self-monitoring as 'active construction of public selves to achieve social ends' by S.W. Gangestad and Snyder, 2000, p.546 or how Snyder, 1987, p.42 describes that the lubricating techniques employed by high self-monitors 'would have warmed the heart of Dale Carnegie'. More interesting is the observation of Snyder, S. Gangestad, and Simpson, 1983 that low self monitors tend to be with the same friends across all activity domains [46] and high self monitors like the challenge and select on skill[47]. Some high self monitors may indeed do that. However it is also possible that other correlated traits (a fascination for a single mutual subject - need for understanding and creation) dominate their personality. Rather than using thus such a simplified scale for SNA, the path to raising a richer dataset on people's personality might just reveal a much more intuitive approach. Thus collaborative friendship style does (usually) require 'skill', but not because of needing a challenge but because it is a logical consequence that skill is built when pursuing a subject. In my anecdotal experience it was not only the high self monitors that were the go-betweens between disconnected others. It was precisely the opposite, warm connecting people but deeply authentic. Reasonably well-liked by most people, possibly for the wit or other positive traits, they make everyone at ease, however from a deeply founded personality. Grant's theory of givers, matchers and takers (see Grant, 2013) provides the appropriate intuition here, because supportive low self monitors are helpful to everyone, some end up on top by helping everyone and getting their own stuff done, and some end up on the bottom, as they help everyone but then don't manage to do their own work. Still organizations profit from having some of them.

The unreflected use of such terms does not stop with friendship. Homophily is similarly often very vaguely defined, and statements about its effects repeated without attention whether homophily of beliefs, character, gender, interests or simply shared dislike of marmite or raw tomatoes is leading to the effect conjectured. It needs to be recalled that most sociological definitions of homophily would be dismissed as irrelevant by writers such as C.S. Lewis[48] for 'philia' friendship. Now I would like to reiterate that I do not in general question the results and validity of SNA for work relations and organizations, it is a phenomenal field of research with great insight. I just posit that due to a semantic difference in 'friendly work relationship' of SNA and the 'good friendship' as defined by philosophy and psychology, substantial differences can arise that need to be considered when generalising results from friendly professional work networks to private and informal friendship networks. Just because Aristotle, Cicero and C.S. Lewis are 'pre-data' does not make their insights and assertions irrelevant to the modern sociologist.

[46] You may read: Select friends based on personality, virtue friendships

[47] You may read: Select friends based on utility, though skill 'can' also be capability of

[48] 'No one cares twopence about any one else's family, profession, class, income, race, or previous history'

Measuring tie strength

Given the fast recognition of the value of the insight of Granovetter, 1973 it was surprising that it took more than a decade to follow up on the operationalisation of measuring tie strength. Marsden and Campbell, 1984 was the first to take up the topic, using two constrained and one larger dataset. The latter used the variables closeness (acquaintance, good friend, very close friend), duration, frequency, confiding and topics (family, friends, politics, local events, work* and leisure*, of which work and leisure were most prominent). Now time spent together (frequency and duration) in a way is a catch-all variable, but inside the two additional factors might be hidden. Thus frequency can be influenced by proximity, convenience of arranging a meetup, utility or enjoyment, and time availability. Duration is likewise influenced by time availability and enjoyment or utility of the encounter. As such, variables suitable to gauge affection, creation, identity support and participation are not contained. Mathews et al., 1998 follow up a decade later and look at closeness (acquaintance (1) - friend (5)), frequency, duration, giving or receiving of advice (advice), discuss personal problems of A or B (confiding), hours per contact in network, proximity, class shared, same organization and relationship length. Their richer setup allows for a closer analysis of the underlying relationship variables. Thus they proxy for homophily (class shared age or topic focus, organization interests, relationship length trust and common memory). Advice and confiding serve as proxies for intimacy and understanding. Like Marsden they do not query for any personality variables nor the fun-leisure-creation complex.

Huszti, Dávid, and Vajda, 2013 use contact diary information with a more casual focus. Two population samples provided data, and the four variables raised were enjoyment ('In general how do you feel being with this person?' - dislike very much - like very much), frequency ('frequency of talking' less than monthly - every day), frequency of meeting (No of meetings during week), intimacy of encounter ('intimate contact' - not at all - very much), which was a combination of three binary variables of familiarity ('ego has been to alter's house'), meaningful sharing ('ego talked with alter about private issues') and presence ('ego spoke to alter face-to-face')). Key progress relative to earlier papers is the focus on enjoyment and intimacy (not just private issues but also way of interaction). Unfortunately, the method is difficult to replicate given its high cost of generating such data.

The most extensive survey, however gain more utility-social-support focused than quality-of-relationship is Wellman and Wortley, 1990[49] who look at 6 factors, of which emotional aid and companionship come closest to classical non-material friendship, with the other 4 factors addressing social support, but not friendship.

The weakness of all these tie strength survey designs is the base assumption that tie strength has a utilitarian purpose. The purpose of the Granovetterian or

[49]The following percentages are the reported frequencies of mention in their study: emotional aid 62% (minor emotional aid 47 %, advice about family problems 39 %, major emotional aid 33 %), small services 61% (lending and giving household items 38 %, minor household services 35 %, aid in dealing with organizations 10 %), large services 16 % (major household services 16 %, major services 7 %), financial aid 16 % (small loans and gifts 13 %, large loans and gifts 4 %, large loans and gifts especially for housing 4%), companionship 59% (discussing ideas 47 %, doing things together 39 %, participating together in an organization 19%)

sociological tie is support. This can be social support (advice), emotional support, practical help. It is ultimately egocentric or altruistic. But it is not in its nature person centered. It does not account that the tie is strong, because I like the person (Huszti does acknowledge it). It does not account for me seeking the encounter because I admire the intellect, because I enjoy the company. Think back to C.S. Lewis' view- 'friendship has no survival value - ... [it] gives value to survival'. What boxes on a tie strength survey would Montaigne tick saying with 'because I am I, because he is he'. When Wellman and Wortley observe that 'strong ties are also more likely to provide companionship', I would suspect that most people on their interview list would almost react in disbelief if they actually got asked 'on a scale of 1-5, how much does your friend provide you companionship'? I certainly don't think that Sam would consider himself as 'providing companionship' to Frodo on their venture into Mordor. What is wrong with 'being a friend'? All I think is that human relationships and their functions are of deep interest to non-sociologist lay person, and abstinence from jargon and returning to meaningful language could provide benefits in making this phenomenally interesting subject more accessible to the public.

A good step forward to use explicitly friendship oriented measures was done by Binder, Roberts, and Sutcliffe, 2012 using the four factors identified by Oswald, Clark, and Kelly, 2004[50]. In the next section, I will explore how this can even be improved upon.

A role based tie strength

I accept the argument that when generating data on tie strength, fifty questions querying all the different personality traits, relationship attitudes and activity habits is too long a list. However everything I have elaborated upon in the book so far evidences that the attempt to condense such a complex topic as tie strength into a 3 question combination of 'is a friend' - 'does favours' - 'can discuss problems' is fundamentally inadequate.

The compromise midpoint could be in condensing the above roles into five typical inner circle and five typical social circle roles. To build ego centric networks in a fast and efficient way these could then be rated with points, where the inner circle roles could be rated with 0, 1 or 2 points and the outer circle roles would be rated simply as a 0 or 1. After an initial calibration exercise cutoff points could e.g. be Weak tie 2 or 3, in-between 4-5, and close friend 6+. Rather than using factor analysis and a large dataset a good brainstorming, discussion and subsequent voting organised as a group session or a guided workshop in an international relationship conference such as the IARR could be a good process to reach such a role taxonomy.

[50]I explore the issues of interpretation of these factors in the statistics part in the appendix, but they are a good start.

Example social network of X Role focus											
Name	Tot	BuCo	Cl	MO	PiC	BF	Con	Work	Sing	Nei	CL
Spouse	7	0	2	1	0	2	1	0	0	0	1
Phil	5	2	1	0	0	0	1	1	0	0	0
Erica	2	0	0	0	0	0	0	1	0	1	0

Roles: total, strong roles: builder / coach, clown, mind opener, partner in crime, best friend, social roles: connector, work pal, single, neighbour, cheerleader

An alternative to measuring tie strength could be in measuring the contributions in Max-Neef needs (see 6.11) that a tie makes, again giving a scale of 0-2 as options.

Example social network of X Max Neef focus										
Name	Tot	Sub	Prot	Aff	Und	Part	LI	Cre	Id	Fr
Spouse	8	1	1	2	0	1	1	0	2	0
Phil	8	0	0	1	2	1	1	2	1	0
Erica	2	0	0	0	0	0	1	1	0	0

Needs: total, subsistence, protection, affection, understanding, participation, leisure & idleness, creation, identity, freedom

Both approaches may be theoretically desirable, yet I make no claims to feasibility of generating this data by any other method than self revelation by survey or interview. In particular, I find it highly unlikely that suitable data will ever be generated from social media such as Twitter, Facebook or Instagram. A full NLP[51] supported text and data mining of large WhatsApp exchanges could do the trick, but such a study will probably never be approved both from an ethical and data protection standpoint[52]. As thus such data generation approaches are expensive, it will remain to be seen when suitable data has been generated to subject past research assertions to replication tests with tie strength generated by above methodology. Before this is however included to measure tie strength, the validity and intuitiveness of the roles themselves and the design of the friendship needs survey must be properly reviewed and tested (see subsequent sections). Replicating and adapting the Rath-Gallup study on a suitably large data set should achieve this.

9.10 Transitivity in triad

In the sections on networks we wrote of the power of some people of being the spider in the web and introducing people. I will also come to this point in the section on how to create friendship-friendly organizations. Academics sometimes discuss the question of 'transitivity of friendship', and usually deny it. If A is a friend of B and if B is a friend of C, then certainly A is not by default a friend

[51] natural language processing

[52] However - quoting the german saying 'Ein Schelm wer dabei Boeses denkt.' - loosely put 'I would however not be surprised if ...': I suspect Facebook has internally in their social sciences research team done already precisely this and is preparing to use tie type of friends to support viral marketing targeting.

of C. Indeed 'broken triangles' are not uncommon, where A & B and B & C are friends, but A &C cannot stand each other. However, B as the middle person is uniquely positioned to give A & C a substantial push on their journey together should B wish it. B knows intimate details and thus can identify common interests, passions, world values, humour potential and many other traits that A & C might look for in each other, but would take maybe several meetings of mutual encounters to disclose to each other slowly. B can thus 'ignite' the friendship with a major 'spark', whereas between them it would 'take-time-to-grow'. B can ignite the friendship even past initial resistance and antipathy, encouraging both aspirants to give the respective other a second look or chance, as they might not have considered all the information or gotten off on a wrong foot. B can influence the first encounters to include activities and themes that are likely to generate positive feelings in both of A & C, thus kicking off a virtuous cycle (positive feedback loop). If A and C now become friends, B is said to have closed the triad. In my personal experience the 'Facebook' cue was the best introduction to set two people on a positive path together ('A also knows D as they went to school together. And C was the one who went with D on that long China trip he told us about back in the pub some years ago'), inviting both A and C to share positive gossip about a mutual friend D of theirs.

I was pointed out in a discussion with Bernie Hogan, the 'jargon words' for what I called transitivity that had eluded me in my review of sociological literature are Simmelian and Heiderian Triads. Simmelian triads are groups of friends that are created or stable because of a similar context, e.g. participation of an organisation or mutual interest. These themes are covered in 4.13, 4.12 and 5.2. The triad as a group is stable, as long as the enveloping organization or background is stable. This is essentially the same thought as Lewis' friendship, that is conditional on a common focus or object, and in a way traces back to Aristotle, if pursuing virtue is taken to be the 'good common background and interest'. Good men find to each other and stay friends as long as they are in pursuit of virtue and eudaimonia. St. Paul in his letters essentially keeps pointing out potential connections and suggestions for friendship - in sociological terms he actively promotes the closing of his Simmelian triads in the early church[53].

Heiderian triads are substantially more interesting, both in their positive and negative sense. Broadly Heider's balance theory maintains that triads that are imbalanced are not stable over the long run. Thus if A likes B and B likes C, but A dislikes C, this triad will not be balanced and face disintegration stresses. As I have argued above, the positive example holds, and B's friendship for C will exert positive pressure on A to extend friendship to C. But even if that does not occur, B's friendship to C will put a lower bound on A's treatment of C, and be it just out of respect for B.

Of the top of my head I know numerous examples where unbalanced triads can exist over many years, with active and explicit dislikes. However friendship is multidimensional in interests and focus. The friendship traits of loyalty, acceptance (+respect) and respect of privacy as a trinity effectively block negative spillover effects on 'good' dyadic friendships. Staying with the example of A ♡ B

[53]It would be an interesting thought to propose for future literature relabelling Simmelian triads into Pauline triads, given that St. Paul's recommendations and observations predated Simmel by a good 1850 years.

and B ♡ C, but A † C. Even if A and B's friendship churns in the end, this can be for dozens of reasons and none of which may involve A's dislike for C. A knows that as B is a good friend, B out of loyalty will not drop C. Out of respect for B's personality and capability of choice A will accept respect B being friends with C. As A and B generally do not spend every moment of their lives together, A being a good friend will not be jealous of the friendship for C, and just be happy for B getting pleasure also out of his friendship with C, even though the exactly how that works might escape him. This is however extremely simple to imagine. A might love B's appreciation for poetry and fine wit. However, B might also be an active football supporter of a local football team, who sometimes gets silly drunk with C, his friend from school days, who A may consider is a chauvinistic simpleton. Indeed, C may be the last person in whose company A would ever want to find themselves in. But knowing that B for some odd reason enjoy's C's company is sufficient reason for A to respect it, and A's good will towards B sufficient reason not to spoil this pleasure by unhelpful uncalled-for comments. The antipathy in this case may be perfectly mutual, for C to think A to be a self-righteous, arrogant intellectual prig, yet likewise will respect B's commitment to A, especially as C has no desire to substitute for B's interest in discussing 19th century poetry. Active confrontation is not permitted. If C waits after school for A and beats him up, B does have a moral decision problem. C inflicting this moral problem on B is committing an act of malevolence towards B breaching goodwill (see friendship sins). C thus reveals himself not to be a good friend, and hence pushes B to end the friendship with C rather than A. If A in a public discussion, e.g. at B's birthday party, intellectually humiliates and insults C, this would also be a non-physical but equally aggressive and offensive act. By thus expressing malevolence also towards B as C's friend, it likewise put the friendship with B at risk of immediate termination. Thus, by the dyadic nature of good friendship, I would argue that negative edges in a triad would effectively be neutralized by good friendships on the other edges. Furthermore, in several cases sudden emotional events may in an instant supersede any longlived antipathy. B's sudden passing or hospitalisation because of cancer or other terminal illness will have goodwill for B turn A and C into instant allies with a cause, historic antipathy there or not. Even if B's wife and I disapproved of each other strongly, if B asks me to help her or if he passes away, I will only in the gravest of circumstances not feel obliged to support her in her grief if I so can and she desires[54].

The weakening or even dissolution of an edge within a hitherto closed triad can however occur in a civilised manner. If I am friends with B and C, however B and C find over time that their interests have moved on and they just find nothing interesting in the other person's life anymore, then that is unfortunate and sad, however respect for their person and our friendship mandates me to accept it. I can occasionally try to bring people together, indeed it is likely that B and C will exchange anecdotes and good wishes if they reunite on account of their friendships with me at my birthday party, but their decision on maintaining the friendship is ultimately independent of their bilateral friendships with me. Kilduff and J.W. Lee, 2020 are thus erroneous in stating that 'Each member of the dyad is constrained in their abilities to sever relations because severance would

[54]The previously cited movie 'Things we lost in the fire' provides an analogous story.

affect the relationship with the third person.'. Severance is freely possible and to be respected as friendship is a voluntary and free association, only the manner of the severance must be conducted respectfully, kindly and benevolently.

Suggestions for thought

- Do you think not befriending the close friend of a close friend is an option long term? Does it come at a cost to either friendship?
- How would you classify the not-befriended close friend of a close friend?
- What would be permissible criteria for this situation?

The strong bridge conundrum

A key assertion of Granovetter's theory is the assumption that unclosed strong triads will close and thus not remain bridges: 'Thus, if strong ties connect A to B and A to C, both C and B, being similar to A, are probably similar to one another, increasing the likelihood of a friendship once they have met. Applied in reverse, these two factors-time and similarity-indicate why weaker A-B and A-C ties make a C-B tie less likely than strong ones: C and B are less likely to interact and less likely to be compatible if they do.' ... 'If strong ties A-B and A-C exist, and if B and C are aware of one another, anything short of a positive tie would introduce a "psychological strain" into the situation since C will want his own feelings to be congruent with those of his good friend, A, and similarly, for B and his friend, A.' ... 'Now, if the stipulated triad is absent, it follows that, except under unlikely conditions, no strong tie is a bridge'.

I would say that a role-view on friendship and the insight that close friendships are often contained in circles of three or four, the longevity of strong bridges is not an 'unlikely condition'. Intuitively speaking, and based on nothing but my own anecdotal evidence, I would even postulate it is the norm rather than the exception when it comes to 'true friendship' or philia, which as noted above, may diverge from the sociological tie strength definition. You may recall that I emphasised the omission of personality from Granovetter's tie strength definition, and I think it is crucial to the understanding of strong bridges. Friendships evolve over the life course and in different settings. The acquisitive friendship style usually retains one or two close friends from a typical life episode. Thus you may retain two close friends from high school, three close friends from university, one close friend from your first years at work and maybe one friend you inherited from your spouse. This will hold for each of your close friends.

If you reflect on the inner egocentric circles of your close friends, my assumption would be that you know them.[55] For each of your close friends' close friends, you may know rough demographics and a few anecdotes, both meaningful and/or humorous. What you should and probably do know however is the nature of your friend B's affection for his close friend C. By knowing your friend, you may know

[55]I am at this point heavily projecting from my personal experience and that of a few friends, with whom I talked about this.

how the third friend contributed to your close friend's wellbeing over the time. Maybe they helped move the apartment when you didn't have time. Maybe your friend met his partner through them. Essentially, you have an affection for them through gratitude for the wellbeing of your friend. The same goes - with the usual exceptions - for trust and appreciation. You personally have no prior experience or capability of judgement of C's character, trustworthiness or integrity. But you have (normally) every trust in the world in your friend B's capability of choosing a good friend. Thus if your friend B vouches for C, what matters is not the weak or absent link to C, but the combination of two strong bridges. It is at this point however not a matter of tie strength - i.e. relationship and interaction, but of character and personality.[56].

Even if you are in the same city or suburb, you still may have zero interest in hanging out with the third person C. When asked for tie strength for some of them, I would opt for absent rather than weak. We are aware of each other in our friends orbit, yet there may be zero direct interaction. This is consistent with a role view of friendship. It is consistent with the theme for respect for privacy for and independence of our close friend's life, which is also featuring in Simmel's theory and strongly advocated by Alberoni and Lewis. This strong bridge is a strong bridge without any tendency to close the triad or fragility to disintegrate. And if asked directly any of the parties A, B or C would sustainably reject the notion that the tie A-B or B-C is anything but very strong! If you remember the person-personality theory from 4.13 that states that with different friends I can let a different part of my personality come fully to fruition, then it would be logically optimal for me to actively prevent strong triads from closing, but appreciate the joy that with one friend I can fully discuss poetry whilst continuing with my other friends to play football and have a good night out drinking. This perspective is conceptually related to the vision of Feld, 1981 for a society divided into stable focus groups/circles with bridging elements connecting the different circles.

I would like to explore the theme of strong bridge ties further when it comes to utility, e.g. job search or 'mating support'[57]. Now general job adverts or general acquaintance making is obviously available through the weak links network. But the good stuff, the job you know that will be created in a few months in a neighbouring department but for which the ad is not yet out, the great and yet affordable apartment in central Oxford, Heidelberg or Boston, or the not-yet-public insight that your very attractive and nice friend X just dumped their partner - all these are not designated for your weak links. It is thus hardly surprising that Gee et al., 2017 in their comparative study of weak links across 55 countries conclude that the individual strong link is far more valuable than the weak link. After all, your own reputation is on the line too if you recommend a lazy acquaintance for a job, or if you put an equally attractive but morally questionable character on

[56]This does not preclude the possibility of you through your interaction, and yes, let's call it gossip, with B being aware of some of C's vices. Thus you may know that C likes a drink too many, may play pranks on his friends or be a source of rather inappropriate jokes, may tend to wander off and leave you in the lurch the moment they set their eyes on an attractive new bar-entry, or all sort of other semi-undesirable characteristics.

[57]Some young readers might find this hard to imagine or stomach, but in the pre-Tinder age the extended networks of friends was the prime recruiting ground for potential romantic partners. This theme is still featured in Apostolou, Keramari, et al., 2020 identifying a factor of mating support as a motivation to make friends

the courtship path with your friend. What I am arguing is that you are making a moral judgment, whether the beneficiary is worthy of the valuable private information. And this worth is transitive across strong bridges and does not travel via weak links. Weak links however make excellent partners for snippets of general information, from which we can get a feeling how our company is doing, whether housing prices in our area are appreciating or going down, which areas of the job market might be promising for us, and which companies might be good applying to.

Suggestions for thought:

- Do you know the genuine close friends of your genuine close friends? Which of these would you classify as close friends of yours, weak ties (benevolent acquaintances) or absent ties?

Observations:

- It should be noted that whereas initially it was a global assertion, this statement of instability of strong bridges was later specified to apply only to local strong bridges.

9.11 Research outlook on linking roles and needs

Structural mismatch

If a role / type theory of friendship would be validated as accurate description of how people live friendship, then this has also substantial importance on how we deal with friendship from what might be called macro-policy level in loneliness intervention. As you may have gathered by now, I am highly doubtful that economic or sociological exchange models provide a good way to think about friendship. Another economic concept - that of structural unemployment or mismatch however can provide a useful hypothesis to be evaluated for loneliness research. This is described at length in Cappelli, 2012 - the idea is that there are plenty of good and smart people willing to work, and likewise plenty of good paying job opportunities around. Yet because of a structural mismatch such as technological progress or other external influences the peoples's skills are unsuitable for the jobs offered. Thus there might be a number of engineers with skills long honed for the optimisation of combustion based car engines, however the electrical revolution essentially devaluates those skills and retraining for electronic engine or wind turbine design might take time. Furthermore pride or misplaced hope might delay such an adaptation process. Other explaining variables of structural unemployment are lacking mobility (the jobs being in a different part of the country), or institutional unavailability (where ability to exercise the job is regulated).

If friendship is considered a kind of virtual circular labour market, with participants being both employee and employer, then just like in such a job market there would be different kinds of jobs requiring different skill sets. Such a view would of course then come substantially closer to the resource exchange theory by E.B. Foa and U.G. Foa, 1980 and applied to friendship by Roberto and Kimboko, 1989. Such an analogy could go quite far: Many people like to be listened to but don't listen quite so well themselves, men crave for more emotional intimacy but do not have the skill set to share and listen caringly. In a similar fashion people in care homes might want self-improvement or youth like silly laughter, but only are offered board games and general social participation as this is what top down is expected to be desired. Note that these are only conjectures, but a validation could go a long way in analysing causes for loneliness in age. Geographical structural mismatch would be analogous to arguments of proximity where the people who could fulfil the need of the friendship live in a distance, financial worries would be analogous to a debt trap issue inhibiting skill development. A desire to enact public policy on loneliness could essentially experiment with an adapted handbook of unemployment policies designed to address structural unemployment. In the Appendix I attach a draft of such a role-oriented loneliness questionnaire the data from which could facilitate the validation this theory.

	Total	OP	CP	TW	SH	CM	QS1	QS2	OA	YA
Subs + Prot	16	28	11	27	12	11	14	24	15	15
Affection	18	11	14	22	26	19	15	18	14	16
Underst.	7	4	10	6	7	6	8	3	5	8
Partic.	17	14	14	13	17	19	18	13	28	10
Leis./Idlen.	11	8	7	5	11	17	12	12	12	19
Creation	4	2	5	2	4	3	4	6	3	7
Identity	21	24	26	21	21	20	21	23	16	20
Freedom	7	10	14	4	3	6	7	0	7	4

Allocation of weights per need in percent per literary category

The weights are from the frequency analysis explained in section F.1, the categories are OP: Old philosophers, CP contemporary philosophers, TW theological writers, SH self help, CM contemporary media, QS1 qualitative sociologist studies, QS2 quantitative sociologist studies, OA old age sociol. st., YA young age sociol. st., YS youth study.

Measuring Needs

It is one of the more daring conjectures of this book that the factors identified in research such as Hall, Apostolou, Oswald and others should not be identified as maintenance strategies or functions, but as a collection of needs and/or roles addressing those needs. Thus as people are asked what they value or require from a friend, it is their perspective that counts, and they answer what traits, relationship attitudes or activities they require in order to satisfy their needs.

Indeed, I see the needs from Max Neef described in section 6.11 as macro-roles or love languages, to be fulfilled / satisfied by the above mentioned example roles, many more can be found in conventional literature such as Millington, 2019. To recapitulate, the Max-Neef needs were subsistence, protection, affection, understanding, participation, leisure, creation, identity and freedom. Using the data from the keyword frequency analysis, we can get again rough indications[58] as to where the focus lies.

[58] I would like to emphasise that these are indeed just indications. Whereas I was reasonably confident for the objectivity of allocating my keywords to the traits etc., the allocation to these needs was a lot more vague and could be a subject of discussion. I still do think the proportions as in the table over-

A few high-level observations follow: The old philosophers and theological writers emphasise practical mutual support and loyalty. The mirror theory as proposed by Cocking and Kennett, 1998, Alberoni, 2016, Blatterer, 2015 and of developing identity is important and contained in 'Identity', but that also has elements of affirmation and self valuation in it. Self-help hardly surprisingly emphasises affection. The 'Lewis-style' co-creation is rather limited in focus, if classical unproductive shared activities are classed with leisure/idleness and intellectual discussion with factual understanding. Elderly people vastly emphasise participation over all other items. And the young, contrary to the expectations of the philosophers and sociologists, value a good share of having fun and affection and are not only concerned with developing themselves into matured adults. By allocating now the roles to the needs, one can see which types of friends people need according to which school of thought and stage of life.

	Role 1	Role 2	Role 3
Subs + Prot	Mom	Dad	Companion
Affection	Best friend	Cheerleader	
Understanding	Mind opener	Rust friend	Discussant
Participation	Neighbour	Connector	Work pal
Leisure/Idleness	Best friend	Single	Clown
Creation	Partner in Crime	Work Pal	
Identity	Mentor	Coach	Best friend
Freedom	Unclear		

Roles allocation

These are all indications and currently missing are good scales for these needs. I have included potential survey questions with all the traits, attitudes and activities, and essentially it will be necessary to select 3-4 representative questions for each of those needs categories. This should not be done ad hoc, but ideally take the form of an international workshop or collaboration, to define a standardized scale that can be then used in several different settings and easily aggregated to a meta study. This meta study could then compare life settings, cultural or geographic differences, and in particular look at the changes of needs throughout the life course.

This scale could be used both academically to gauge the prevalence of potential needs in society or in parts of it, e.g. the newly retired, general senior elderly, but also socially disadvantaged adolescents. On a practical level the scale applied to a single friend could identify the key benefits and roles that friend has, and thus be a building block to a scientifically validated friendship inventory tool. You can find a draft of such a friendship inventory in the Appendix, and future editions will be posted on the companion website to this book.

9.12 Roles in social networks analysis

At this point, the centrality of roles to the friendship relationship is a conjecture. I would argue that it is intuitive, relatable, and does have substantial evidence in its favour, but it is not tested. Furthermore really testing it was beyond

all are reasonable, but could perceivably change if the mapping data is recoded by a second person or discussed in a workshop.

the scope of the research project collating the material for this book. Once further evidence gathered that such a theory of roles is an accurate description of how people think about their friends, really interesting research designs on friends social networks become possible.

First the roles need to be verified, with the traditional methods of cluster and factor analysis employed in past research, analogous to Hall, 2012b and Oswald, Clark, and Kelly, 2004, just with an expanded dataset on characteristics and presumably a significantly more sizeable dataset[59]. This validated set of roles needs to be taken and complemented with a functional and concise questionnaire to efficiently not only query for connection strength between two people, but also unambiguously and relatably identify roles that shape this relationship. Figuratively speaking, this would not just get connection strength between two variables, but also determine the colours of the edges in a directed network[60]. This would then go substantially beyond the classical multiplexity of 'talk about important things / share personal problems / ask for help', as employed e.g. in Albert et al., 2020.

To illustrate this, consider two studies Kadushin, 1995[61] and McKay, Grygiel, and Karwowski, 2017[62]. Kadushin's analysis has as key observable (i.e. the edge criterion) a self reported 'Influences me' (plus a whole common background variables, such as school attended etc.) which corresponds to the 'navigator/mentor' role or the activities 'guidance' and 'effect change'. McKay uses creativity which in the study's context invokes themes like 'intellectual stimulation', 'collaboration', 'exploration and discovery'. Now the question they ask is exactly the right one, looking at how certain functions play out in networks and how it influences our friendships and our society. They take a multicolour network with maybe ten or twenty different roles, take a projection onto a single colour, and then try to deduce consequences from just looking at the structure of this one colour. A simple counterexample might be that maybe all friendships are such that you have a wise but boring person bestowing advice and practical help to the other friend, who is a creative clown who bestows fun and good ideas to the other one. Taking such an approach at looking at just one colour would result in an only unreciprocal 'friendships' network. Changing the colour by focusing on another role would result in the same network, just opposite direction. Of course reality is much more complex. The perfect study would be a repetition of Almaatouq et al., 2016 but including roles. These roles probably need to be vetted and standardized within a workshop or other format of discussion. Using a closed society (such as an MBA class, a cohort of an Oxford college or a retirement community, or ideally all three for comparison) all potential links within will have data applied, and a substantial percentage of total key friends of members of this group could be covered. I will include in the appendix a draft questionnaire, however at the time of writing I consider the set of roles listed above not suitably condensed or standardized yet to allow for this study to be conducted.

[59]Both in numbers and covering different strata of society, age, education

[60]For colouring the network, see e.g. Rainie and Wellman, 2012 and Deri et al., 2018

[61]I am unsure whether the title 'Friendship Among the French Financial Elite' is rightly applied, there is nothing in the paper that gives me the indication that the relationships would qualify as friendships under any objective criterion set out in this book, but apart from that the method is well explained and could be adopted

[62]An excellent paper that really uses standardised friendship attachment criteria.

Once these roles are standardized, and thus what Wellmann would call the 'colours of relationships' defined, the impressive toolset of SNA assembled over the years can be brought to bear on the new data[63]. At this point genuine insight can be expected, and the goal formulated in Kilduff and Krackhardt, 2008, p.10 achieved for non-corporate friendship settings: 'Our aim in this book is to bring the individual back into the picture - to account for the cognitions and personalities of individuals in connection with the structural patterns that constrain and enable.' Such insight would be most promising and valuable to employ in the fight against loneliness.

9.13 Smart bubbling

For me the holy grail of friendship research in the coming two years, and the faster the better, is getting insight into smart bubbling. I come to the benefits in the section on 'good practices' how societies susceptible to pandemics need to learn how to construct small social groups, that can isolate together. This is not the 'creating Mission-to-Mars teams' research of NASA, but simply how to take 50 people in a care home, in a residential community, in a block of houses in a city, and subdivide them into groups of six or eight so that they can continue enjoy social and friendly interaction with each other while social isolation or distancing rules are in practice in general society. Now my hunch is that the potential of this is going to be limited at the start, because the data is not there yet. But if we managed to get groups of elderly or groups of singles who are friends with each other to query what aspects make the group special, in the same way I collected data on just dyads, it could point the way to create functional support bubbles, e.g. via a non-profit app or a meet-your-neighbour website.

What data would sufficiently describe such a bubble? In figure 9.2, I posited one example. A core group of five people have been living in the same neighbourhood for a while: Steve, Peter, Kate, Ciri and Phil. Essentially, they spend most of their free time together. Once a fortnight they all come together for a drinks night in Ciris house. Steve and Peter play sometimes Tennis together. Kate is the clown of the group and makes everyone laugh except for Phil, who just eye rolls her jokes, but appreciates her for the laughter she brings to the others. Ciri recently befriended Tara on their mutual kids playground, and brought her along to the joint painting sessions she usually pursues with Phil. Peter, Phil, and Kate sometimes meet up for a book club. Steve, Peter, Kate and Ciri sometimes do a bridge afternoon, a game they enjoy but do not share with Phil or Tara. All in all, a loosely closed group that suffices for itself, but is welcoming newcomers should a mutual interest or affection provide an opportunity to come together. Such groups provide the back bone to what I would call 'social joy capital', that captures not social support or utility, but simply the creation of fun in our lives.

Having identified such bubbles as the key to our social leisure functionality, the question is how do they arise:

1. To what degree do these bubbles grow organically or can be created? How do group dynamics evolve? Do they arise from dyadic friendship by inte-

[63] See e.g. Hogan, Carrasco, and Wellman, 2007 for optimized querying methods for personal networks or the digital version 'Network Canvas' developed by Hogan.

grating others, or do they arise from larger communities (e.g. church congregations) and split off? What societal or community grounds are most suitable for their creation?

2. What are characteristics of good bubbles? What differentiates great bubbles from good ones? Are they the same characteristics of dyadic friendships (e.g. common memory and history, mutual affection, humour) or is there a different level of chemistry in place? Which friendship needs are catered for within-bubble (participation, leisure) and which are most likely catered for from outside (advice, identity support)?

3. From a societal perspective the most interesting one: how do we get socially disadvantaged, poor people or elderly into such groups? How do we establish such groups within elderly communities? Does bubble creation or bubble inclusion[64] potentially represent a more sustainable intervention than befriending services?

4. Are there patterns for roles? Does all such groups have a connector who brought them together and keeps them together? Are there needs that are equally provided by all, e.g. affection or collaboration? Is there a clown who provides fun to the others, a comedy duo, or are other aspects more important?

Answering these will require suitably generated data, and it will be interesting how such a data strategy can be executed.

[64]Pulling a socially disadvantaged person into an existing bubble

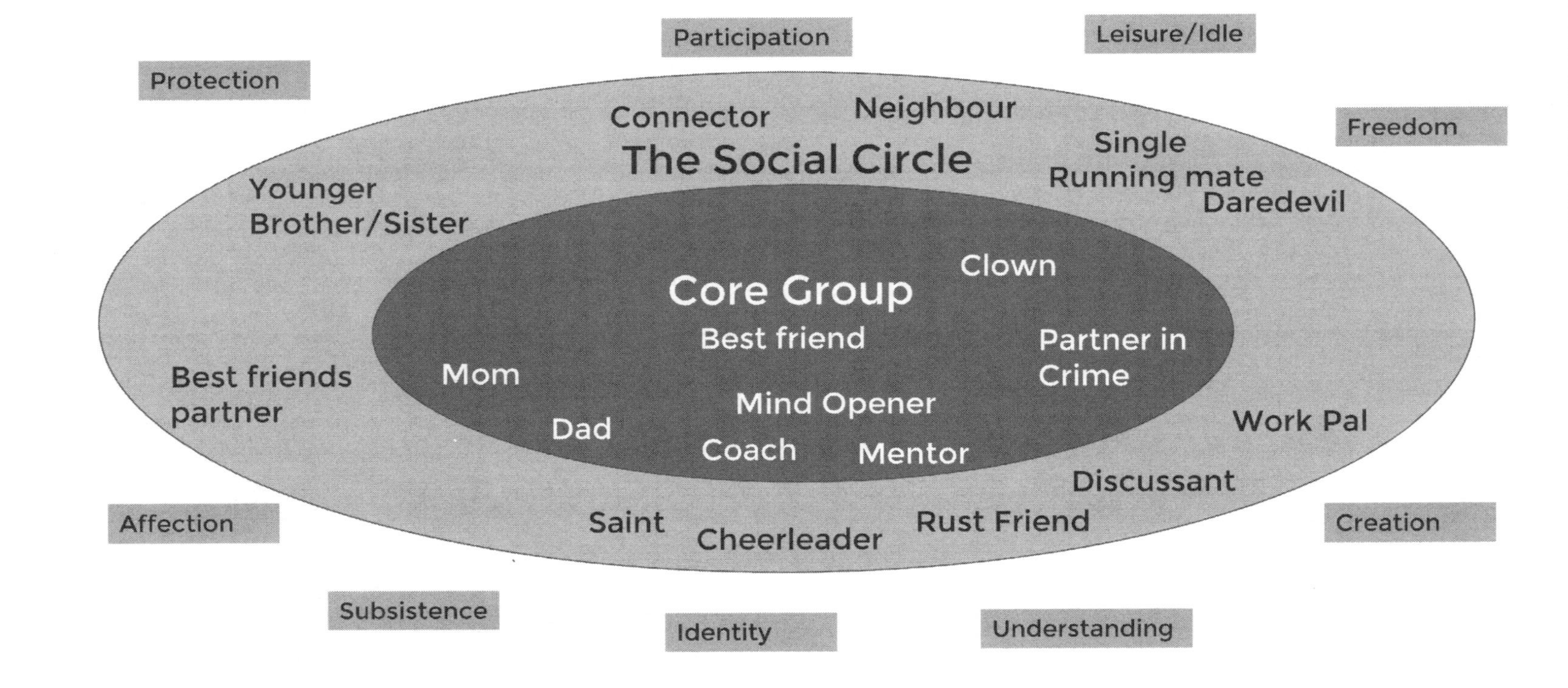

Figure 9.1: Core Group and Social Circle ordered by Max-Neef Needs

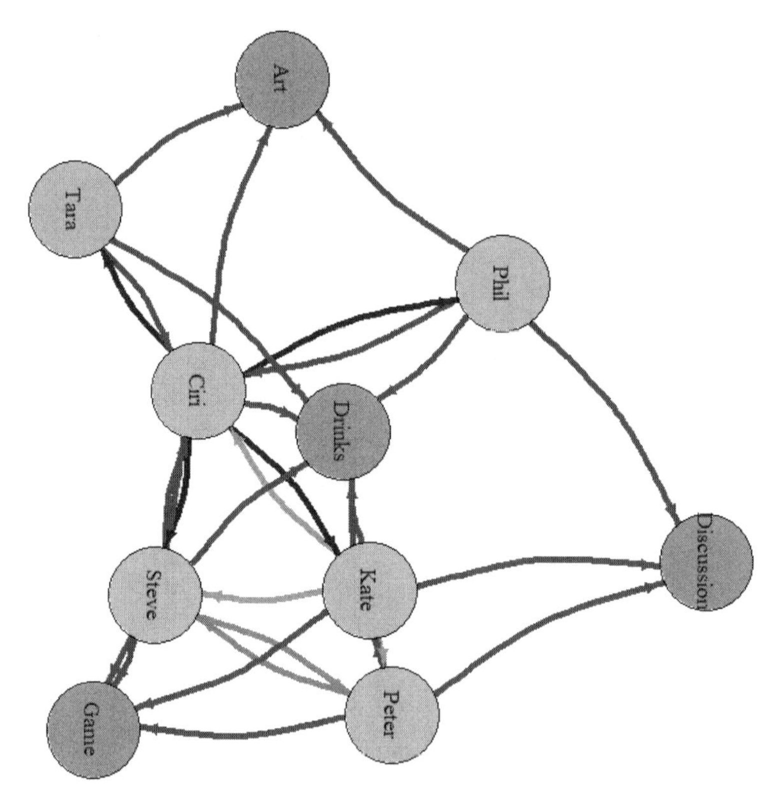

Figure 9.2: Smart Bubble

Chapter 10

Friendship in Old Age

For casual reading, most sections are relevant.
academic sections: 10.2, 10.8 and 10.9

10.1 Loneliness in age

In the introduction I have written that this book is to a great deal motivated by reducing loneliness among the elderly. Whereas a lot of initiatives currently focus on managing the crisis that the western societies have with a large number of elderly without a 'support network', I think just as much it is up to all of us to prevent the current generation of 30-60 year olds being the future lonely 65-90 year olds. In a connected way, I would also encourage the current generation of 20-50 year olds to think about their parents social life, and potentially trigger such thoughts while their parents are in the bracket of 45-65 (i.e. post child-rearing pre-retirement). I think with limited time investments in relationships in the period 30-60 we can do a great deal to prevent or at least mitigate potential loneliness in old age.

I would like to emphasise that I consider loneliness in age as different and entirely preventable or mitigate-able by limited long term structural measures for most people whom we currently classify as lonely. I do not want to oversimplify the issues of poverty, social exclusion, xeno- or other types of phobias, which I refer to in the appendix D. They all aggravate life experiences for millions of people. However, it should be possible to bypass these to reach out across society, to make communities welcoming and ensure that most of us find communities where they feel at home and where they develop a few close friendships as they spend time in such communities. Individual responsibility is there too, and whilst we should not allocate blame, we need to get the message across to people to keep trying even if it feels difficult:

- to keep trying to make some time for friends in busy schedules
- to keep trying to overcome fear of rejection
- to keep trying to pull away the eyes from Netflix
- to keep reaching out to old friends and keeping an open door

- ...

This may sound condescending, or oversimplifying an indeed multidimensional and multifaceted problem, but I passionately believe that if we collectively work on the bad habit of giving in to our convenience or staying in comfort zone at home, we can drastically mitigate the problem. Likewise, the rest of us actively need to encourage the 'at risk' candidates we know around us, to come out for a cuppa tea, coffee, beer, dinner, hike or weekend activity, no matter how tired we or they feel after the work week is done.

The payoff may come only thirty years down the line, but when I enter an English pub, a French bistro or a German-Austrian Konditorei (bakery with coffee) and see four elderly people having an intimate and joyous time laughing, teasing and talking together, I know that the effort to encourage people to keep their core friendships in good repair is worth it.

10.2 Needs in Age

Needs have been studied at length, and specifically Bruggencate, Luijkx, and Sturm, 2018 performed an extensive meta-study. However, most included studies were only partial, less focused on 'social needs' and more on the 'support needs'. If these presumed trends about needs are corroborated, whether overall or as statements about population clusters, differences between needs and existing social networks to satisfy these needs can be identified. Subsequently, and only then, will we be able to identify suitable interventions tailored to prevent felt social loneliness in age. Steverink and Lindenberg, 2006 evaluate the continuation of social needs in age listing 'the three human social needs' of affection, behavioural confirmation and status. They conclude that their importance doesn't wane in age even though their satisfaction may become more difficult with increasing frailty. The definition of those three needs is actually fairly encompassing, it covers a broad range of aspects, likewise the general scale framework provided by Nieboer et al., 2005 is robust. However, it suffers from the general defect of sociological studies that the questions are selected for capability of providing scales suited for high-level statistical analysis rather than data for root-cause analysis (see F.8 for an itemized discussion). Sources like this paper can, however, be included in producing estimates how needs develop with increasing age.

As age increases, so do physical needs and thus subsistence (uncontroversial). As frailty increases, it also negatively affects the capacity to take care of others (protection). However, the desire may still be there, and further dedicated data may corroborate this. I think the need for affection is unchanged by age, but determined essentially by preset personality, likewise understanding. With increasing age, fewer people may be capable to meet stable demand, leading to a relative shortage. All research is clear that participation is a clear priority in old age (see e.g. Bruggencate, Luijkx, and Sturm, 2018). As people are in the bracket 55-65 they may also enjoy their leisure time more as the kids move out of the house, opening up opportunities for new hobbies. Creation is a difficult to predict, first with little data, and with skewed priorities[1]. The hunch here is that for those personalities

[1] Creation or productivity is central to the personality of some people, and continuation of this capability, ideally in a community, central to the wellbeing and meaning.

with high creation self-expectations, continuing this will be important throughout old age as long as possible. Identity is very unclear, as the maturing of the personality relative to young people of course requires for much less shaping. They have lived their lives and do not need so much to refine their character and identity. On the other hand, existential questions on interpreting one's life meaning may increase demand for identity support from friends (see e.g. I. Yalom, 1980 and Carstensen, Fung, and Charles, 2003). Similarly need for independence is likewise stable, however decreasing financial and health resources and resulting dependence on other people may conflict with desires for independence. We can deduce that resources (in the classical sense) become much more important in old age than during earlier years. Financial constraints determine the capacity to take part in cultural activities, as does health. This all correlates with mobility (being able to go about to see people) and proximity (how far I need to go to see friends). If a single goal of friendship in age is necessary to be specified, it would be to spend a good and enjoyable time with each other, in a circle of agreeable people who can appreciate their history, ideally old friends with whom they can indulge in nostalgia, and with whom they have a shared value system.

	Likely Movement			
Name	Overall	55-65	65-80	80+
Subs	↑	→	↑	↑
Prot	↑	↑	→	↓
Affection	→	→	→	→
Understanding	→	→	→	→
Participation	↑	↑	↑	↑
Leisure/Idleness	→	↑	→	→
Creation	→	→	↓	↓
Identity	→	?	?	?
Freedom	→	?	?	?
Resource	↑	→	↑	↑

At this point this is little more than a plausible conjecture in need of further backup. As noted, not only general trends matter but also intensity clusters. Some people may not need understanding at all, as they get it from their spouses. Other people may not need leisure activity at all as they are permanent on-call babysitters with lots of laughter and exciting activities from grandchildren and great-grandchildren, and others gain identity support from them by passing on family legacy (see e.g. Schuler and Brito Dias, 2021). Only by a sizeable and representative study will we be able to identify what friendship needs dominate in which clusters of the elderly population. Using the datasets provided by the coding of Degges-White and Borzumato-Gainey, 2011, Ch10, Greif, 2009, Ch11-14, Matthews, 1983 and Adams and Blieszner, 1989 there is a combined dataset of 925 tags of friendship in old age. Thus in figure 10.1 the relative mentioning of themes gives a reasonably robust impression of potential subdivisions.

My hunch is that the needs can be grouped into two clusters of ease of satisfaction. Basic participation and leisure usually do not require very close friends. Most people can enjoy board games or other light social activities with relative strangers, who are reasonably agreeable and fun. Satisfying this need is literally down to opportunity (availability of a welcoming community) and willingness

	OA	Total		OA	Total		OA	Total		OA	Total
Personality %	15.2	22.9	Relationship %	47.7	48.1	Activities %	26.9	23.7	Resource %	10.1	5.2
Honesty	1.5	3.5	Shared History	6.8	4.5	Dirt Time	7.6	4.2	Proximity	3.2	1.3
Acceptance	1.5	2.2	Affection	3.2	2.8	Work Together	4.5	2.8	Content	1.0	0.9
Humility	1.1	2.1	FS Quality	3.7	3.7	Expression of S	2.9	2.7	Health/Athl.	1.7	0.7
Reliability	1.2	2.0	Consideration	1.0	2.3	Being there	2.3	2.7	Network	0.6	0.7
Fun	1.1	2.0	FS Priority	4.1	3.6	Pract. Help	2.3	2.0	Time	0.5	0.4
Kindness	1.4	1.8	Loyalty	2.2	3.5	Circle	1.9	1.5	Material	2.0	0.4
Virtue	1.1	1.7	Independence	1.6	1.5	Encourage	0.7	1.4	Money	0.7	0.3
Intelligence	1.4	1.6	Enjoyment	3.2	3.4	Communion	1.2	1.2	NoMonPower	0.3	0.5
Positivity	0.8	1.4	Understanding	2.6	3.1	Effect Change	0.6	1.2	Attract.	0.1	0.1
Proactiveness	0.6	1.4	Reciprocity	2.9	3.0	Guidance	0.9	1.0			
Energy	1.3	1.2	Trust	2.2	3.0	Discovery	0.8	1.0			
Agreeableness	1.8	1.1	Openness	1.4	2.6	Teach & Learn	0.4	0.8			
Peace	0.5	1.0	Pride	1.4	2.4	Generosity	0.5	0.7			
			Benevolence	1.7	2.3	Vocal Support	0.2	0.6			
			Mut. Interest	2.7	2.2						
			Mutual Belief	3.9	2.0						
			DiffBG	0.3	0.2						
			Respect of Priv.	1.6	1.5						
			No Ind RespPriv	1.2	0.5						

Figure 10.1: Friendship in Old Age

Percentage figures provided by theme counting study F.1. OA stands for Old age, Tot for the overall total summary to meet the offer and mingle. Understanding, Creation and Identity usually requires a much closer friendship that needs development over the years. If an old friend moves away or dies, the loss for not being able to fulfil these needs can be substantial.

Chopik, 2017 shows in a robust analysis how participants in his study who place a high importance on friendship consistently report better subjective health, happiness and subjective well-being.[2] This then provides a tangible benefit to be pursued beyond the idealistic perspective of treatings friendship as a good in itself.

Suggestions for thought:
Do you know your social needs for the time when you hit old age? Have you thought about them? Have you thought, how you will satisfy them?

10.3 Improving knowing and sharing

In age, the elderly have achieved their identity and are thus in a way set in their ways. That is not to mean that they cannot change, they do, even though they may insist on doing it at their pace. But on mundane habits of life, the discussions are well and truly dusted. You may have tea with or without milk, with or without sugar, but you have made your decision how you like it best some time in your fifties. There is no need for too much well-meant advice on potential self improvement in old age, and this is a key element of 'respect of privacy'. However, if this privacy is respected, then there is a genuine desire for connection. Elderly people (maybe not all) want to come out, open their houses, eat together and live closer to each other. Finally, there is a desire to enjoy mutual interests and hobbies together and be thus somewhat productive (i.e. work together).

The key is that as the personality has developed, it has also simply become 'larger'. In the work context of CV writing, a friend of mine phrased this insight succinctly by saying; 'Until being thirty you simply haven't done enough stuff to justify writing a CV longer than a page'. At twenty if I know what sports or hobbies you had during school time, whether you had a temporary romantic partner, and whether you had then proceeded to university or other paths, maybe taken a gap year, plus a few trivia such as favourite music or film, I know already a substantial part of your life's story. This is of course grossly exaggerating and simplifying, but you get the point. Conversely, by the time you are sixty or seventy, you have had a life full of experiences. You have been working in several jobs and careers, you may have been in different cities around the country or the globe, you had one long partnership or several shorter but still substantial, you may have kids and seen them grow up into adults, and indeed you may have experienced a fair share of psychological and physical suffering. In short, your life is book length. And for a new friend to know you adequately, they need to know much more of you. The hurdle is simply a lot higher until you would say 'they really get me'. Appreciation, respect and trust depend on knowing the other person and thus are also significantly more difficult to attain.

[2]Curiously the question in the survey is pointing to the valuation of friendship, not a self-reported rating of the social network.

In some sense, it is encouraging and helpful that usually elderly people are more pragmatic. Acutely aware of limited life span availability even in the face of a very successful pharmaceutical industry prolonging our longevity with every year of research passing, usually the goal is to make the most of what is left and not waste it. However, with friendship there is a key insight, and that is that it cannot be rushed. The key to facilitating friendship in age is thus enabling the elderly intent on developing friendship to open up in meaningful ways. By this they reach the state where they feel their counterparts 'know them'.

A practical activity is provided by good board games designed to get people to open up. One such board game is 'Therapy' [3] by Milton Bradley Game company. Other options are 'Better me' [4], 'Ungame' [5] or 'Vote-the game'. Finally, there are also story-telling oriented card and board games with however some adult content, which may not be to everyone's liking. Therapy is thus from a fun and story potential an ideal board game to be employed at facilitating relationship building among the elderly. As the focus is on competition and knowledge with the same game play mechanics as 'trivial pursuit'[6], it does not have the feel of artificiality to get to know people. As an additional bonus playing it to interact with younger people can be varied by using editions from different decades, with the first English edition dating from 1986 and representing psychological insight and values from the seventies, with the latest edition being from 2013 with updated knowledge questions.

A more formal possibility (which however will be potentially resisted as people feel uncomfortable with its formal and artificial nature) to get people to share are sharing clubs. These are informal copies of group therapy, only designed to get people to get to know each other in a structured way. This is in particular helpful to people who are not used to sharing and hesitant about opening up (see also Garfield, 2016 for descriptions of the 'friendship lab'). However, any kind of activity that facilitates being accompanied by conversation is suited for the job, and thus pursuing hobbies together like crafting, playing cards [7] or hiking groups will eventually see people opening up to each other, and via the sharing of stories and experience get better and better acquainted with each other. To be explicit, the yardstick is not the quality of the activity, but the quality of the accompanying conversation and its suitability to share stories.

The shortcut is to rediscover acquaintances who shared key periods in the life and thus can appreciate stories more than people who were not there. Suppose I shared a particular anecdote dear to me with a friend B in college. Suppose somebody C with whom I may not have had much to do at the time was also in the same college at the same time. This C will be uniquely positioned to understand

[3] `https://www.therapythegame.com`

[4] Targeted at improvement, however its obvious nature makes it feel a little artificial.

[5] Apparently more suited to adolescent therapy, and a little out of date these days, but apparently with good questions

[6] Popular board game distributed by Hasbro `https://en.wikipedia.org/wiki/Trivial_Pursuit`

[7] I always found the best setting for casual conversation to be provided by the German card game Doppelkopf (see `https://en.wikipedia.org/wiki/Doppelkopf`), which coincidentally I learned from my grandfather and grandmother. It brings together four people who play each other in changing teams of 2. Whilst strategic and requiring paying some attention; it is fluid and low intensity and rarely interrupts much the flow of the accompanying conversation, unlike Poker or Bridge, which require significantly more game related communication and concentration.

the context of this anecdote over any new acquaintance. C would know the character and habitus of B and could imagine how the anecdote came about or how a particular joke would have sounded given B's way of telling it. They would appreciate how a particular mishap might have embarrassed B to the bone or set everyone in the group laughing. Websites such as Stayfriends or other Alumni Network services of course can go a long way, but have not yet gone the consequential step of actually bringing people together. Whilst boarding schools and colleges are designed for young students, it might be a highly interesting concept to collect 'the leftovers' at the other side of life. Organising admission or allocation policies to retirement villages or care homes by school, university or work-based acquaintance would create such pairings. Similarly, commercial care home associations could cooperate with alumni organisations to analyse data from their cohorts, houses, sports teams and data mine old photos to identify recently bereaved people suitable to be contacted. These would then have the prospect of setting out with a group of old friends anew to form a shared apartment or shared house, sacrificing some privacy for the benefit of reliving their youth.

For socially isolated elderly, simply identifying former acquaintances might not be enough. Here dedicated coaching seminars on how to approach former old friends with confidence might be needed and very effective. This is partly what the friendship teaching programs of Stevens and Bouwman have done. Stevens, 2001 and Martina and Stevens, 2006 describe the initial offline version. Most importantly, they first measure the efficacy of the program to build relationships, and only then measure the impact on life satisfaction, positive and negative affect and loneliness. They also note that the engagement with friendship is not without its risks: heightened expectations on friendship may lead to realizations of deficiencies in current relationships and thus to an increased sense of loneliness. Bouwman et al., 2017 describes the expansion to an online program[8], and reports efficacy for it. Thus, while we can discuss how to improve on such programs, and also improve on their evaluation (see coming sections), as baseline method such programs seem robust and focusing on training initiation a likely promising first step. Thus the elderly could be made to initiate themselves, or a sponsoring organisation would invite suitable matches to an event. Depending on lack of social skills, such processes could additionally be supported both by volunteers and professional supporting staff. Thus rather than befriending a volunteer, the direct focus could be on help to help themselves establish friendships. Evaluating a program that combines seminars with subsequent matched re-initiation of contacts from school or early life could be a fascinating research project developing an alternative to classical befriending.

10.4 Support activities

Beyond this it is a key question how to further enable story sharing and recall, and specifically for lonely people who have no more acquaintances from the time, and furthermore for people with dementia. Whilst it requires time, surrounding them in their living room or bedroom with photos from their life can enable them

[8]The lesson blocks are 'Making new contacts', 'Maintaining relationships', 'Spending time alone', 'Becoming a better friend'

with memory triggers to stories they experienced. If being visited from family or other people, it enables those to ask questions. The photos can be printed and stuck on the wall, or kept as digital photographs and be displayed in a changing photo frame. In this context, I would also like to mention the most powerful case for postcards I have experienced to date. In my extended family, we had one case of in the end severe dementia. As our family had been quite good with sending postcards still in the 2000s, that elderly lady had a collection of about thirty postcards she had received over the years, and the live-in helper would lay a few of them out every morning or lunchtime, saying they had arrived. This gave the elderly lady immense joy as it showed to her she still mattered to people outside. I know this will not sit easy with everyone, but on the ethics of this I still remember acutely a panel on treating dementia patients I attended in the summer of 2010. A practitioner doctor dealing with dementia patients successfully debated a theologian and a philosopher that for dementia patients, the outcome of improving the life of the patient is the key benchmark. Thus anything that causes joy rather than suffering is preferred rather than pondering on considerations on truthfulness and respect that only at this point matter to the interacting person. The benefit of those postcards and letters in this case multiplied in the context of dementia, and I can thus simply encourage to pick up the practice of writing postcards, at least to your elderly friends and relatives. An ethically much more troublesome question will come in the coming years with the potential of deep fake technology, where with existing pieces of handwriting or voice samples we could literally generate postcards, voice messages or even telephone conversations from friends who have passed away. This would occur in much the same way as reviving Carrie Fisher as Leia in Star Wars[9] and have great potential in alleviating the suffering of lives of dementia patients, albeit in a deeply inauthentic way. Until then, generation, collection and preservation of suitable material is a good practice, and one that can be encouraged even from children of parents becoming elderly.

If people directly known from the past are unavailable, still groups in care homes or communities can be created based on matching of life experiences. Thus similar jobs, life experiences (military service, boarding school, universities, areas of growing up) can all improve relatability of life experience and thus a richer appreciation of aspects of each other's lives. Not that diversity is not important, but understandability and relatability are primary considerations at this level.

The final key concern from a policy perspective is what society and institutions can do to mitigate the restraints that dwindling health, mobility and financial resources mean. Whilst in most western countries a subset of pensioners have high pensions often backed up by private property and rents, financial limitations do severely limit parts of the elderly population . High care home and health costs often eat up all or most disposable income otherwise available for socialising. Currently, social institutions like churches or social initiatives feel the funding squeeze, especially as demand on basic needs support from them like food banks diverts budget allocations. Thought can still be given how to bring elderly people together for connection and friendship. The german 'Kaffee und Kuchen' is a splendid example here, and English afternoon tea likewise a wonderful tradition. However, the southerners given their pleasant weather might have the

[9] https://www.esquire.com/entertainment/movies/a30429072/was-carrie-fisher-cgi-in-star-wars-the-rise-of-skywalker/

upper hand here, simply wheeling or getting their elderly out to the park bench and bringing them together there for afternoons of chess, newspaper reading, local gossip and heated discussions, as I have frequently experienced when a tourist in Italy and Spain (see also 11.4).

10.5 A fitness program for friendships in aging

This section is a collection of practical ideas or themes that I think is good to keep in sight as you prepare to age or if you are concerned about an aging person whom you want to support.

Suggestions for the elderly person

- Update and maintain the address book, use your time to send cards, letters, call and visit as much as you can.
- Prepare a time capsule of photos, stories, happy memories you want to be reminded of in case you get dementia[a].
- Learn to videocall.
- If it is difficult for you, slowly learn to open up.
- 'Find a tribe' that ideally will stay accessible to you as your mobility reduces.

[a]See `https://www.liverpoolmuseums.org.uk/house-of-memories` for further information.

Suggestions for a younger relative of an elderly person

- Help organise the family photos and contact details and learn the names of your elder relative friends.
- Teach technology, in particular that of video calling.
- Play board games and cards.
- Help find out about transport facilities, local social organisations and their events.
- Learn about dementia, there are fantastic training courses.

Suggestions for a younger relative of a not yet elderly person

- Encourage your elderly relative to reach out to friends.
- Help them organise school reunions or round birthday parties.
- Ask them about the communities they frequent.
- Ask them about their favourite hobbies when they were young. Encourage them to find their passions.

10.6 Evaluating general interventions for elderly

As loneliness has been identified a major trend in society by psychological research, so has the research into potential intervention blossomed. Reviews of such interventions now routinely evaluate 70-100 publications of varying merit to condense it to common themes and evaluate overall efficacy. Masi et al., 2011 identifies four **intervention strategies**: (1) improve social skills (2) enhancing social support (3) increasing opportunities for social contact and (4) addressing maladaptive social cognition. Placing a slightly different focus, Bouwman, 2020[10]identifies four **subgoals of interventions**: 1) improve social network, 2) increase the sense of belonging, 3) increase intimacy 4) sense of meaningfulness, and identifies seven active elements of how most of these are achieved: 1) activities, 2) meetup, 3) practical support, 4) meaningful contact, 5) social skill, 6) realistic expectation, 7) meaningful role.

With so much effort having gone into it, it is surprising to hear that the overall quantitative evidence for efficacy of general interventions on reducing loneliness is less than encouraging. Gardiner, Geldenhuys, and Gott, 2018 report that 'quality of evidence base' on reducing social isolation and loneliness 'is weak'. As an aside I found the descriptions and designs of such programs substantially better documented for the studies conducted in the 90ies [11]vs. those in the period 2000-2020, which in some cases provided ample evaluation of test statistics but left the reader to guess what was actually done never mind the rationale behind it. Another frequently made criticism is made of methodology, i.e. lacking control groups or not implementing random trials. Now if several reasonably different but plausibly equally effective treatments or interventions are available, such methodology may be suitable and indeed advisable to further tweak insight. But I fully agree with Stevens, 2001, p.197: 'However, a procedure in which participants have no say in their own assignment to an intervention or control condition cannot be used in good conscience when the intervention is based on the principles of empowerment.' and thus randomized control trials is an element we will have to do without, especially when our basic data availability is still so scarce and weak in the first place.

Also in other ways the statements on weak evidence need to be qualified to some degree. A number of interventions such as humor therapy, bibliotherapy[12],

[10]https://research.vu.nl/en/publications/4c127925-a36d-47c5-8df6-62b97d6e38d6

[11]Stevens, 2001, Caserta, Lund, and Rice, 1999

[12]The targeted use of books as therapy in the treatment of mental or psychological disorders. Thus

robot or animal therapy are aimed at the general feeling and experience of loneliness. Other interventions that may not even be covered by this, may be family therapy to reconcile families and intensify the family bonds, possibly with cousins or within family like communities. Among all the intervention studies and reviews and reviews of reviews only a subsection is relevant to measures to foster companionship and friendship. I do not want to disparage these other studies and methods, they are however outside the scope of this text. In this book the question is to what degree which interventions can trigger meaningful friendships. Given the theme of the layer theory, I am not surprised that most online or tech-based solutions report lower than desirable efficacy.

It is superfluous to hypothesise on the outcome of those studies reviewed by Masi et al., 2011,Gardiner, Geldenhuys, and Gott, 2018 or Poscia et al., 2018 if other questions had been included in the evaluation. However coming back to the numbers of Hall, 2018 according to whom you need to invest 50 hours for a 'normal' friendship, and assuming a higher 'miss ratio' initially for people with low social skills, it would be curious to speculate on the outcome statistic to a question like: 'Did the intervention lead you to get to know a person with whom you subsequently spent a minimum of 50 hours?'. If the answer is no, then we should not be surprised that loneliness measures hardly budged for the participants[13]. Bouwman, 2020, p.95 picks up on this conundrum: participants do not get to the hours necessary to build connection, have cynical attitudes, experience more anxiety and perceive social situations as negative. Interestingly Stevens, 2001 include and comment on the explicit statistics of newly formed friendships by the participants of the program. If the observation is right that the obstacle consists in participants putting in the hours, then resulting we need to ask what intervention could push them to get there[14]. Furthermore, if receiving several rejections has given them a trauma, we need to learn how to make scarred people initiate and open up again. It is correct that an evaluation needs to get data on basic initial trust in people and past social scars. Such a program might work for non-scarred people and not work or need substantial modification for scarred people. At the time of writing I however did not find conclusive evidence of an intervention explicitly controlling for it. Including a grit measure as defined by Duckworth et al., 2007 may also yield good controlling data. Finally, the timing is important. Maybe some interventions need months or even a year to fully come to fruition.

The key performance indicator for such a social intervention should simply be how much relationship potential was created and how much was followed up upon by the participant. I am not so good in designing parsimonious questionnaires, and I am sceptical whether factor analysis is the best way to identify good questions. My hunch for evaluating the effectiveness of such social interventions is using a Hall, 2018 style terminology, and ask for the number of acquaintances

potentially for some people the reading of this book could be interpreted to be an anti-loneliness therapeutic intervention.

[13]Of course a pleasant acquaintanceship can help, and the inclusion in a nice church community is lovely, and having a dog really can improve our daily mood, but none of these are a substitute for friendship.

[14]By my wording you may guess that I am a fan of gentle 'forcing'. As we say in Germany, some people have to be 'carried to the hunt'. If an intervention can be shown to work robustly with a high probability of success and a robust outcome, then some initial discomfort and eye rolling is a worthy price to pay for it.

with whom 5h, 20h, 50h or 200h were spent with over a course of a year past the study. This is still imperfect, but people will make time for people who they feel close to and whose company they enjoy. Unreciprocated relationships are also unlikely to make the 50h or 200h mark. The development of proper friendship roles most likely also only happens robustly post the 50h mark. Note that I don't think the 50h is fixed, for some people and friendships it may take 30, for some it may take 70h. There is substantial variability and there is always churn. But an initial goal post of 50h is a very concrete and objective criterion that some level of chemistry and rapport was established. Including this criterion in future evaluations of social interventions may provide additional insight into the effectiveness and sustainability of the intervention.

Working on this assumption a friendship fostering program would be to maximize opportunity at the start, and then provide a setting to make it easy for people to push past the 20h, 50h and 200h goal posts[15]. Secondary to that continual mixing should also allow to review first impression and slowly extend the circle further. Given how important the setting is, such a program is best offered in connection with an established social organisation, such as a church community or community center with a regular and alive social program. Taking inspiration from John Wesley's proselytizing, the local village pub might likewise perfectly do the trick both to host the program and provide participants with potential test subjects for newly acquired conversation skills.

I will come to an actual course program in the next section, but if I were to sketch out a target map for socialisation, if asked how the whole 'making friends thing works' in a coffee corner, I would probably come up with the following road map:

The key principles would be first experimenting, second quantity, and third a slow build of quality. The most important realisation at every step might be 'this is not that hard'. And the contribution of the environment needs to make it not that hard. A socialisation step program might look like this:

Key steps for socialisation:

1. Level 1: **Meeting people**
   Get to know five people with conversations of roughly 30 min, follow up with two of them for a meetup and follow up a second time with one of them. If it doesn't work with five people, expand to ten
   Learning: It is OK if people say no to you. It is also OK for you to say no to people if it doesn't feel right. Just chatting or doing something with someone new is fun.

2. Level 2: **Expand**
   Get to five meetups with one person and try to find one more person with whom you would like to meet occasionally. Get to know another five people. Maybe join a community like a connect group at church or an interest group.
   Learning: Secretary or 'optimal stopping' problem[16] - knowing when to stop searching and start relationship building.

---

[15] See 11.3 for a description how Oxford and Cambridge have perfected this system to build welcoming environments for their undergraduates.

[16] `https://en.wikipedia.org/wiki/Secretary_problem`

3. Level 3: **Build**
   Experience the dynamics as you continually build time up to 20h with your two acquaintances from Level 1 and 2. Get to know another five people, but focus on your key two acquaintances. Maybe you have a common sport, interest or hobby to pursue. Don't pester or stalk them though, respect each others independence no matter how much you yearn for connection.
   Learning: Experiencing the gradual build up. Getting the feeling for gradual disclosure. Also learn to manage disappointment and accept it if one of your good acquaintances declines to take things further. But if you get to a loose 20h and feel the chemistry, enjoy the fact that you have found two potential friends.

4. Level 4: **Consolidate**
   Take your time to continue meeting with your two friendship potentials. Get to know the social network in the community you joined. What hobbies and interests do people have? What life concerns? Who is friends with whom? What connects them? Maybe you want to start helping out by preparing coffee or cakes at the coffee corner. Maybe you have other skills to be put to good use in another issue the community has. Try to help and see how it feels to contribute.
   Learning: You have spent 50h with two people and ideally each of you looks forward to continue meeting each other in the future. There are two people who value your personality, and there is a community that values you for your person and the support you provide. This is the platform you build on from now.

Key principles:

- **Be patient with yourself**: Some people will race through the above program in a month, some may take a year. Different levels may be of different difficulty to each of the participants.

- **Take your time** and allow others to take theirs, Rome wasn't built in one day. Relationships are always determined by the slowest one in the relationship, otherwise they break.

- **Fun first, then depth**: as a consequence of taking time the focus should be to ensure that people have fun first and enjoy themselves, this should include first easy successes in being social.

- **Statistics matter**: Some people get lucky, some don't. You can however influence your luck - by stepping out of the door, joining groups of people and paying attention to them and feeling for the chemistry.

- **Churn is expected**. The goal is to find people with whom you want to spend 200h! If say after ten hours your acquaintance partner decides that they don't want to embark on this journey with you, that is OK.

- **Not everyone can be a friend**, it is perfectly nice to know a number of well-wishing acquaintances in an organization without the immediate prospect of a deep friendship.

- The goal is **not** to become an extrovert or **change your personality**. The method is taking behavioural elements of socially adept people and imitate and experiment with them to see what fits you.

Note that this program would be designed for people without major preconditions. It would for me be an interesting question if such a program (with modifications as local requirements or experiences show necessary) can be shown to work for as normal conditions as possible. This could be 30 year old single professionals who realise that all of their friends are getting married and babied up, and they need to diversify. This could be 45 year old parents who moved recently and now need to build up some new relationships despite still having to take care of kids. It could be 60 year olds just entering retirement. I do not want to disparage the work done for special needs groups (blind/deaf, mentally disadvantaged, prisons, physical disabilities). Yet the key takeaway of the various reviews of loneliness interventions is the absolute scarcity of evaluation of interventions for the 'easy cases'. Once such programs have robustly been shown to work, possibly also across cultures, ages and genders, modifications can be designed to account for added difficulty levels (i.e. levels of decreased mental or physical health).

If particpants could be made to volunteer for research interviews, really valuable data on what people struggle with could in depth be gathered. As you might have gathered, I am a big fan of replication studies that work on a common basis. Having four or five such initiatives on different continents and gathering data on people's struggles with friendship initiations would be invaluable. The beauty of qualitative interviews of course is the flexibility of the interviewer to delve into depth on their instinct, searching for good insights particular to the interviewee. But a central methodology sponsoring university could prescribe five key questions to be asked in the course of the interview, one of which would be 'which part of the various levels did you struggle most with?'.

Suggestions for thought

- When is the last time you actively engaged in a conversation with the full intent to get to know the other person that lasted 30 minutes or longer? How long does it take you to establish a good rapport or chemistry with someone?
- When is the last time you actively engaged in developing a vague acquaintanceship into a friendship potential? How many hours did that take (10-40)?
- When is the last time you really made a friend? How much time had you spent with the person?
- How do you feel about rejection?

10.7 Course for connection

Dufton, 1986 proposes group therapy to address loneliness. Garfield, 2016 proposes it in particular for men's loneliness therapy. In the evaluations of studies I was surprised not to find substantially more group therapy interventions targeting loneliness, as the anecdotal evidence seems highly convincing. I would particularly see its role for people who struggle to achieve levels 1 and 2 of the preceding program. The guidance of a professional psychotherapist is the only thing that can really tease out underlying mental issues inhibiting social initiation and initial conservations. It is cost effective in the capability of dealing with five people at the same time, and could also be organized around other organizations publicly funded, e.g. within church or community center contexts. Hopefully, with increases in social prescribing in the NHS, this instrument will also be included in the evaluation on an extended basis. The caveat with group therapy is that people are generally explicitly discouraged from getting to know each other or meeting outside the therapy group. All interaction within the group is designed to be in the sight of everyone, including the therapist. It is thus good to repair basic social deficits, such as an incapacity to listen, a bad temper or other traits that if left uncheck essentially torpedo any attempt of building a sustainable social relationship. The slightly less formal version of these are so called T-Groups (trainer groups) or encounter groups, usually used to support psychology students and becoming psychotherapists in their path to self discovery. In the 1970ies a lively debate ensued[17] as to the suitability and effectiveness of the method with two camps effectively agreeing to disagree by the start of the 1980s (see I. Yalom, 1975, ch.16). I would however posit that development of future psychotherapists is a different goal to initial intervention on establishing habits useful in avoiding loneliness, and thus would leave it to the academic psychotherapy community to fully evaluate whether such encounter groups with full supervision of trained psychotherapists are useful for social skills training and loneliness prevention.

Following on from the theme, full group therapy or even guided encounter groups might not be required for most people. Indeed, most people who count themselves as reasonably functioning, would resent going to therapy. The solution might be to find a format where people can experiment with relationship building in a safe and mildly guided format. It could be marketed as social training or fun socializing for people who are just a little out of practice. The Alpha course of the Anglican Church offers a perfect design to be adapted[18]. The original alpha course invites 50-100 people to a parish center, where they go once a week over a course of 8 weeks. They are split up into tables of usually 7 participants and one designated table leader or table supporter. Looking at alpha groups and connect groups from churches cues can be taken on how you would train a loneliness connect group organizer to be a welcoming host. Where in alpha courses 'table leaders' were chosen or schooled to provide a reasonable competence in Christian orthodoxy (but not a priest), an 'alpha loneliness course' would most likely not require a full psychotherapist training with a specialisation in group therapy. However, designing a reasonably robust 'introduction to leading groups' course by psychology or psychotherapy specialists could go a long way. This could include basic group psychodynamics and an awareness of what mental issues require a specialist. Such a connection course would then be hosted by an

[17]Lieberman, I.D. Yalom, and Miles, 1972 and Kaplan, Obert, and van Buskirk, 1980

[18]Indeed to test the hypothesis, it might be ideal to approach the Anglican or Catholic Church to accompany a regional alpha course offering with a thorough intervention analysis for befriending group effects.

organisation or a community center, and involve inviting people who self-report to be at risk from loneliness to an 8-week course on building connections. These would be grouped into groups of 6 plus a trained table leader or group supporter. The mixing of groups could happen according to varying criteria. Whilst diversity is great, it might be advisable at first to match tables based on similar backgrounds and tempers via a questionnaire for vulnerable people to feel safe in comparable peer groups. Indeed I think a psychologist or trained social or community worker assigning groups intentionally might be a much preferred practice to let people assign themselves at random. A more diverse mixup can then be effected later on in the course. A platonic large data matchmaking[19] could help to lower initial threshold further, in return increasing external supportive pressure to bear with each other a little longer. This should be optional, as people don't want their agency taken away. However, some people might appreciate the ' computer support' if they have low trust in their own social skills for selection.

A hypothetical schedule can be as follows:

1. Introduction of table participants
2. Play board game 'therapy' - practicing disclosure and social humour
3. 36 questions for friendship - practicing deeper disclosure and Zeldin, 2000 styled conversations
4. Discussion Friendship virtues
   Homework 1-1 meetup in pairs from table
5. If possible feedback round [20]
   Homework Feedback exercise
6. Tryout Hobby - Hobby Bazaar - get people to present a hobby of theirs in a bazaar, or pair people to mutually try out their hobbies
7. Mixup tables - Introduction on new tables: practicing get to know with slightly more diverse people
8. Mixup tables - Play therapy with new table - practicing disclosure
9. Weekend away - like youth trip including finisher party.
   Hike, 36 questions for friendship round 2, game afternoon, ...
10. Feedback and new resolutions

A couple of observations: some of these activities may need to be switched around, for some groups more light social activities could be included, financial constraints or socio-economic inequalities need to be paid attention to not to exclude anyone. I think it would be best if - as in the Alpha courses - a light meal

[19] I programmed a prototype at www.lunchroulette.co.uk but it still needs further testing and optimisation.

[20] This of course depends on vulnerability of participants and the table leaders judgement on feedback being helpful. Potentially under psychologist supervision

was offered before every group session. Eating together is great for ice-breaking, and knowing that some food will be there allows people to come directly after work without the need for separate arrangements. Depending on vulnerability of the target group, the presence of a social worker or trained psychologist might also be helpful if not mandatory. Emphasis on strictly platonic intention should be made, if necessary tables should be sex separated, at least for the first few weeks. Of course people have romantic needs, but strictly constraining it first of all within a platonic context might be helpful for basic social skill building and feeling safe. Depending on the organisations resources and timelines, additional conversational elements and a different pace can be applied. If the connection course is for people who have been very solitary, then exploring the various options for public places and getting accustomed to them may be something also on the activity plan.

Depending on the profile of the participants, people may be coached a bit more actively for a **path in the middle**. Specifically very lonely people may feel like completely opening their heart - almost like flood gates - the moment some kind soul takes some time to listen to them. That can completely overwhelm the other person, especially if that person is also not used to general social contact. Observing if something like this occurs and calming people down can be a major support of a somewhat psychologically trained table leader in such courses. On the other hand people might be overly shy and not stepping forward at all. Gentle coaching and reminders that the goal is to also give an opportunity for people to get to know you may then slowly push people out of their comfort zone and into interacting with new people. Having two or three really kind and friendly people[21] available in the room might then offer this both safe space and social challenge to do just that.

Toepoel, 2013 points to 'active' activities being more helpful than 'passive' ones. I agree, however given people's diverse interests the more specific and engaging activities become, the more it also applies only to a smaller subset of the population leaving others disengaged. Statistics on the proliferation of hobbies and interests may be of help to find likely candidates for hobby-based engaging activities that include sizeable parts of the participant crowd of such a workshop series. Depending on composition of participant group other possible activities might offer themselves and can be probed for within the pre-course participant survey.

The **weekend away** can be a great opportunity for bonding. Many will have memories of school trips, some of which may not be positive. In anticipation, group leaders will need to figure out anxieties. Another possibility is to separate groups into those who want to go on such a trip and those who do not. But as an opportunity for connection it should definitely be considered being part of the spectrum. I. Yalom, 1980 reports on the power of a weekend away. A multitude of friendship virtues are also being triggered on such a weekend, such as building memories, spending time together, fun, collaborative activities, circle building and

[21]Think about it, you probably know one or two people who even the grumpiest and reserved person cannot say no to. The people who no matter what will have gotten you to tell your entire life's story in 15 minutes just by being attentive, positive, cheerful and warm. These people can 'be used' to break the ice with the more difficult cases, showing them that making a nice conversation that includes sharing is not that hard and actually quite pleasant.

communion.

The goal of this course would be for everyone to go through the mechanics of making a 20h acquaintance. For expectation management, it might be claimed and then calibrated over time that this will statistically only happen for say 60 % of all attendees. Some people have bad luck, however once they know the drill there could be shortened followup or -leftover courses. That sounds horrible, but might be necessary. Not walking away with a new friend from such a course may be bad, however it might be a perfectly workable message to say that x % just don't develop the right chemistry in the first round but manage in round two or three. This may also take the pressure off for some and relax.

One key element of the alpha course is its convention around a joined and emotionally charged topic - the discussion of the truth or validity of the Christian faith. Despite people stating that religion is divisive, in this context it acts as a positive and unifying trigger for intense discussions including personal self disclosures in the group. It is possible that copying the concept for loneliness reduction would likewise need a unifying theme other than finding friends and loneliness. The statement that 'making friends happens while you are busy doing other things'[22] may very much hold and need to be considered. However topics that are suitable to bring 50-100 interested people together in a room repeatedly are in short supply - suggestions welcome.

Such a program would also provide an opportunity of testing Apostolou and Keramari, 2020 in a practical setting. Whereas Apostolou surveyed a number of people adhoc, it might be interesting to survey people on what is keeping them back right after they have actually done it in an active and reflecting process. Maybe after a period of three months practicing they figure out that reaching out to new people becomes easy, but managing availability of time or transport might be more difficult than anticipated.

This program would be in particular effective for elderly people, as it would directly tailor towards their needs of participation in society. They would have a friendly conversation within the week, some activities and the opportunity to meet new people. If such a program is done at a community center, it provides a casual non-formal opportunity for their social worker also to see them in such a relaxed environment rather than in their home. Also on a general level such a program would be a boon, as spillover effects into other parts of their lives can be expected at least for some (see Stevens, 2001[23]).

[22]Adapted from the statement about becoming happy.

[23]p.199 'It is important to note that a small group of women did spontaneously report improvements in other relationships, with children and partners, following the friendship programme. Apparently what women learn in the friendship programme can be applied to other relationships besides friendship.'

Suggestions for thought

- What would it take you to go on such a course?
- If you think of friends or acquaintances of yours who might feel lonely - would you suggest to them to take such a course? Would you go as their wing(wo)man if they didn't want to go alone?
- Have you ever played the game 'Therapy'?
- When is the last time you went on a weekend away with people outside your family?

Comment I: If you have further suggestions of activities or items on such a course, I would love to hear from you!
Comment II: If you try out such a format in a lay organisation such as a church or a community center, and are likely to recruit a good group of people to it, please reach out to a local psychologist, the local psychology department of the university (they might have a very grateful master student looking for a topic) and use the opportunity to subject the participants to some questionnaires and surveys. There really is a dire need of further data on effectiveness of interventions. Even if your organisation does not have the competency to analyse the data, or by itself may not generate sufficiently large datasets for statistically robust statements, if you can contribute 30 or more cases of questionnaires filled out before the course and after the course, this may immensely contribute to a joined dataset. See section 12.3 for data strategy in research.

This concludes the practical part of friendship in ageing. There are two research related topics where academic investigation could generate additional insight to lead to measures to improve friendship in ageing, which I will now explore given the general discussion in prior chapters. If the roles hypothesis is verified, the aspect of attachment measurement will need to be revisited. Closeness may not be reducible to a single scale, but may require a multidimensional treatment (and by that I don't mean two or three dimensions but possibly six to eight). It will also make various evaluation research questions at first more complex, as we look at potential policy to reduce loneliness by fostering friendship and 'friendship-like' relationships. One of such policies is befriending.

10.8 Evaluating Interventions

Evaluating 'Befriending'

Befriending is a social service intended to reduce loneliness. Volunteers throughout the ages commit to regularly (usually weekly) call or (pre-/post-pandemic) engage in person with a lonely person. It is common to be applied to lonely elderly living by themselves, which is why I include it here in this section. Similar volunteer services for children, prison inmates or other people usually have a larger proportion of practical support (homework, mentoring) and concrete advice (re-socializing), whereas for elderly the social interaction element is the key priority.

The key question for evaluating befriending services in terms of loneliness reduction is whether the volunteer and the elderly did, after all, develop a friend relationship? Not whether the elderly feels supported, has a better wellbeing, or goes less to the doctor. These are all good goals, but they are secondary. The question, blunt and simple, is whether the elderly feels less lonely, and in what way? The definition or concept of loneliness and its opposite - connection will drive everything else in the evaluation. A role-based concept for friendship and a need-based concept for connection would change such a narrative substantially. We could structurally map out the relationship path and see where the obstacles were. We could look at whether a spark came about and in what context it came: was it a group activity, was it a 1-1 chat? Was it within the course of the planned activity program or did it come about serendipitously? How much trust was established at what point?

It could be very true that certain needs can be effectively met within the context of befriending and volunteering (e.g. participation or affection) whereas others don't work (e.g. identity development and collaboration). Using the items of the friendship framework also could provide the background of a rigorous evaluation why certain setups for befriending services do not work as intended. Maybe the volunteer is suspected to act out of do-good instrumentalism ('The elderly as a vehicle or object to good to, not a person to be friends with.' - the friend should be an end in themselves). Maybe reciprocity is breached (the elderly doesn't feel being needed, it is a one way street). Maybe - connected - it is the power disparity (the elderly are at the mercy of the volunteer who can - and in many cases does - break it off once priorities change). Maybe because of a difference in generation and experience the sense of humour is incompatible. Maybe no mutual object of interest for discussion or collaboration is found. There are a lot of maybe's here, and I will make no assertion or guess which one is the major one. What I will assert is that I looked into literature evaluating befriending (Balaam, 2015[24] for a general overview but also e.g. MacIntyre et al., 1999). If you contrast this with the narrative of Maggie and Jessica in Rath, 2006[25], the key of the entire exercise was not that Jessica would be relentless in her support, but that a publicly affirmed friendship had been unequivocally formed. The basis of this friendship, not friendship-like relationship, is what Maggie and by extension Rath attributes the following success of the case study, as Maggie transformed into a grown woman with a job, husband, family and thriving network of friends. Nothing less than that should be the goal. This may be difficult to achieve in some societal contexts, but given the substantial value of friendship quality, connectedness, mutual understanding, affection and authenticity in characterizing friendship, I struggle to see how befriending services could sustainably substitute for actual friendship.[26]

[24]'Both studies focus less on the nature of the one-to-one relationship and more on the way befriending can act to relocate the individual in a social setting, which then in turn brings about positive outcomes.' when writing about Gillett and Dixon, 2009 and Cattan, Kime, and Bagnall, 2011

[25]'Recounting their first outing together, Maggie became emotional as she described what happened when they bumped into one of Jessica's classmates at a department store. After exchanging the usual pleasantries, Jessica said, "This is my friend Maggie." Not only had these words been seared into Maggie's memory for good, but I could tell they had given her even more motivation.'

[26]As a disclaimer - I am only criticising the organizational setup and the artificiality of it, ensuring

Genuine friendships need the spark, if external circumstances are not bringing people together (like kids are brought together by spending time in school or adults are brought together by being in the same sports club or work department). It needs the casualness of the situation for generating the insight of friendship potential. Thus - not suitable for covid - the likely success case is probably spending time together in a group for a prolonged time before splitting of friendship pairs. Friendship is a mutual voluntary relationship, implying full and free choice on both sides. Being matched via an agency is totally contrary to this. A priest matchmaking platonically by sticking you two on the cake and coffee counter after the service might be hideously obvious and unsubtle, but yet again provides a totally casual environment for a potential befriending volunteer to meet someone who could use a friend. Even if such environments are created, it needs to be understood better what aspects lead to follow up and the initiation of a sustainable friendship development process (Positive experiences from hanging out trigger a vicious cycle of self-motivated re-initiations for meetups). What social infrastructure is best suited - cafes, public parks, maker-spaces, internet cafes for gaming, public libraries for studying together? As a hunch, anything that helps to forget the 'befriending' setting will most likely be beneficial. Lester et al., 2011[27] describe one exemplary case: 'I enjoy his company and he enjoys mine, I think ... I feel as though he is a friend rather than a voluntary worker.' But key for me is the evaluation what roles develop inside the friendship. Is it the fun, is it the intellectual stimulation, is it the affection, or is it the general reliability-consistency companionship that matters, and to which elderly personality type does it matter to. One befriending service that it might be interesting to do an evaluation of is ShareAmi[28], and it could pave the way for similar models, where elderly lonely people in English-speaking countries could work as freelance English language tutors online for a reciprocal befriending. Introducing or emphasising the role of mutual utility at the start of such a relationship will ensure reciprocity, allowing the rest of the relationship to develop from that.

To conclude evaluating befriending, I also think that other aspects will need to be evaluated in such a context, such as the impact of phone-only vs. alternating physical face-to-face meetings, the preference for activities, setting/location, age difference or others. Given recent discussions in fora such as the Campaign to End Loneliness discussion groups, I have little doubt however that comprehensive studies addressing this will be forthcoming in 2021.

Evaluating Social Prescribing

In the UK over the course of 2010-2020 the practice of social prescribing has become widespread in the NHS. Polley, 2017 provide an introduction: 'The terms 'social prescribing', 'community referral' and 'nontraditional providers' have all been used to describe a way of expanding the range of nonmedical options that could be available to healthcare professionals when a person has needs that are

that lonely elderly are connected to people in society is a central aim of this book.

[27]The collection of qualitative quotes from interview partners in this paper similar to Matthews, 1986 makes this an excellent paper to read not only to gain a theoretic overview of the matter but also an instinctive feeling awareness.

[28]`https://www.oldyssey.org/shareami` at `https://www.theguardian.com/world/2021/mar/07/french-senior-citizens-link-up-with-language-students-in-lockdown`

related to socioeconomic and psychosocial issues.' Such issues are described by the following: 'Factors contributing to health inequalities can include financial, educational, poor housing, low self-esteem, isolation, relationship difficulties, and physical and mental health problems. There are also more people who are living longer and struggling to cope and adapt to living with Long Term Conditions which can't be addressed by a clinical consultation.'

As can be seen, social isolation is one of the issues addressed, but generally the focus is on the general package of non-medical triggers to seek medical advice. Given the substantial spread of relative poverty in the UK[29], a statistically (and thus fiscally) significant number of people are seeking support from the health system, that really should be granted from elsewhere. Social prescribing is intended to address these issues, assigning social link worker to help with ensuring the person knows how to register for entitled practical social support, but also to link them up to social activities such as lunch clubs or walking groups to address isolation.

The holistic approach of course is exactly what is required to help these people, and on a macro-fiscal level these interventions seem effective in reducing strain on the health system and helping the many individuals manage with their issues. For the purposes of this research here it will be interesting to see to what degree the various interventions can be disentangled and the effectiveness proven in different areas of concern, specifically social isolation and connectedness. It is the hypothesis of this book that practical support (shopping, finding support within health system, effective financial advice, ...) and social joy (participation, connectedness, fun) are two different areas and need to be dedicatedly and separately surveyed. Note that I do not question the overall effectiveness of social prescribing in the slightest. What is of question is whether the social prescribing interventions in their current form sufficiently and effectively address social isolation and manage to create connectedness (participating in a community, making friends) or to what degree other organizations and people are better suited for this and need to rise to the task. Indeed Polley and Whiteside, 2020, p.20 cites a link worker stating 'what I find really frustrating is that the social prescribing service is only as good as the voluntary sector and community around it' which substantiates the hypothesis that social isolation (and the other issues) are mostly addressed in the interventions recommended through the initial social prescribing.

Thus the general hunch is here that in order to assess effectiveness on social isolation, it would be great to piggy-back onto a general wide evaluation and introduce friendship-tailored questions for the social factors in Polley and Whiteside, 2020, p.58[30].

[29] By that I mean poverty marked by indebtedness, squalid living conditions such as mould, disadvantaged position in the education system, etc., not the abject poverty that a billion people in the third world are suffering from.

[30] 'Reduced loneliness, reduced social isolation, increased independence, increased social identity, builds self-worth, feeling supported and listened to, increased self-awareness, builds knowledge, friendship, connectedness'

10.9 Weak ties and bridging in old age

My key concern in this book is how to improve friendship ties and reduce loneliness, predominantly in midlife with the focus on friendship maintenance, and then for the elderly with a focus on loneliness reduction. Reviewing the literature on ageing that also draws on Granovetter, their key focus is access to social support and health services. The information on available jobs is thus replaced by information on hospitals, doctors, care homes and community services. What I did not find[31] is how the strong tie - weak tie plays out for elderly with regard to human connection. Huszti, Dávid, and Vajda, 2013, Fig 3 report a relative lowering of contact to close friends for the elderly. Following up on this Albert et al., 2020 generate a new contact diary dataset focusing on only on elderly and considering Verbrugge's multiplexity of relationships[32], again in the usual utilitarian sociological fashion. It is really unfortunate that Albert and co. skip the enjoyment criterion employed by co-author Huszti in her previous study from 2013[33]. Huxhold et al., 2020 explicitly investigate the impact of good weaker ties in the elderly's network, but do not move beyond establishing an abstract impact on well-being. Thus they are able to establish a robust impact on lower depressed affect and higher positive affect, but are in no position to make substantiated statements on the transmission vector (social support, practical help, enjoyment, affection, participation).

Reflecting on the role of bridges in social networks of elderly might be valuable for an additional reason. As I have shown in 10.2, the key friendship need for elderly is 'participation'. In sociological speak - it means staying a connected node in the wider network of society. The elderly play the 'social connection game' with an added difficulty level. It is like a constant game of musical chairs, where nodes might be added through their reaching out or other actions, but valuable invested nodes removed at a higher rate as their old friends and peers in their cohort die. As health deteriorates, the capability of maintaining the emotional intensity in geographically distant edges also deteriorates. Thus the key question for analysing networks of the elderly is not whether the Heiderian-Granovetterian strong bridges close over time, but whether they get knocked out, for what reasons, and at what speed.

The function of the bridge also changes, with provision of information or advice potentially taking a back seat to real-life integration. The information travelling on edges might not be job or hospital information but good old gossip and interesting stories - whatever is interesting for older people and stimulates them[34]. This is enhanced when the strong or weak bridge provides a link to actual life communities in a real sense, e.g. by giving a lift on a Sunday to get to church and the post church coffee corner, or by bringing people together for a Wednes-

---

[31] But there is always the possibility that I missed the right or used the wrong keywords for the search.

[32] (1) How typical is it that you and the given person talk about important things? (2) How typical is it that you share your personal problems with the given person? (3) How typical is it that you ask for help/favor/money from the given person?

[33] The lacking scope in questions of course limits the power of their test of the functional selectivity theory (Hypothesis 3), and my hunch would be that including questions for the themes enjoyment - creation - leisure could indeed produce positive results.

[34] See the section on resource content in the friendship framework.

day afternoon bridge session. The currency is not job information but actually friendly faces. Access to new friendly faces means automatically new content and connection to the outside world. As an illustrative example think of the movie Gran Torino[35] where the old and grumpy Walt Kowalsky starts befriending his neighbours Thao and Sue.[36]. The young neighbours build Walt a bridge into their world (and access to a substantially different and tasty cuisine to a daily diet of beef jerky and beer). Note how in this example the bridge closes very fast as predicted by Granovetter. One can only assume that after Kowalsky's funeral at the end of the movie the Lor community and the 'local-white-elderly' community complete their social integration out of affection for Walt.

Thus moving even further from the theme of bridging information transmission in society and the whole practical support debate, I would like to point to another key purpose of weak ties. A good number of non-bridging weak ties in a community increase your familiarity and welcome. Aristotle would call this the integration into society. Junger would call this the factor of the tribe. These weak ties are highly significant to our wellbeing. They can be factors of whether we are homesick or not. Whereas introverts can have most social needs fulfilled with a few close friends, for extraverts a reasonably sized network of weak ties can be the difference of happiness and loneliness. This is the key benefit of voluntary associations, churches, and other types of communities. Bridges are then the welcoming connectors, who draw the single lone nodes in and 'build them a bridge' into such warm and social communities. It might thus be an interesting research question of what traits or situations are most conducive for people to build such contracting bridges that pull people from outer orbit into such a social center.

As a final comment on SNA analysis involving the elderly - much has been written about the need to integrate elderly, helping them continue to matter etc., but proper network data that elaborates on the roles of elderly in organizations and networks is scarce. Anecdotally in church organizations, in community associations some elderly have prominent roles e.g. as the treasurer or social secretary, but much more interesting is how many elderly embrace the role of 'social glue' - schmoozing without a title, helping out here and there with little explicit recognition in terms of titles. How about the veterans in football or rowing clubs, local archaeology associations, who support the younger members with advice, go to the club's home pub, cheer at competitions and talk about past glory days. It would be hugely interesting to get quantitative data on such associations, categorising how elderly assume roles in such environments at social benefit to themselves and others.

[35] https://www.imdb.com/title/tt1205489/

[36] https://www.youtube.com/watch?v=so3WZKpx7Uc

Chapter 11

Rules and Practices

All sections relevant for casual reading

I tried to deal as objective as possible with such a highly subjective topic in the introduction, the chapters on the framework, the process and the roles. The focus was on synthesising themes and content from other authors, only complementing from my life experience and personal assessment where I felt it necessary. The parts on practical takeaways or suggestions for thought were clearly labelled and separated from the neutral analysis. This is not the case in this chapter. The assertion in the following pages is that friendship is a universal good in itself, and should be sought. Thus this chapter concludes this book by bringing together proposals on how to improve the practice of friendship in your life, in organisations and in public society. As such, it also depends to a significantly larger degree on my anecdotal evidence and own experiences of what has worked for those whom I interviewed and myself. This on the contrary also includes the clear expectation that some of those practices or recommendations may and indeed will be unsuitable for some situations and readers. In this case I am looking forward to hearing back from you what you consider is a best practice or a rule to follow for inclusion in a future edition.

11.1 Individual Good practices

Expectations and selfishness

Expectations on others:
I think the most important thing on an individual level is clarifying one's own expectations towards friendship, irrespective of whether the current circle of friends lives up to these expectations or not. You may not have met the right people, you may have not invested sufficient time in them, you may have concentrated on other aspects of your life - there can be many reasons why the current state of your circle of friends is not quite how you want it. But the key question is what is important to you, and what activities you most would like to do with friends? If you look back at the section on needs, you can contemplate what kind of needs are strongest for you and which ones of those likely will best be met within the social

area of friendship. Some needs may be better met by the family, within church, at work or other social circles.

Meeting needs, calculus and selfishness:
Now in prior sections I have repeatedly emphasised that friendship is about the other, about seeing the friend as a good in itself. And yet it should be acknowledged that friendship answers to our deep need of connection and subsidiary needs within that. Staying with the image of the love tank of Chapman it is perfectly legitimate to look at how your friendship love tank is being filled, what key needs you have that are being met through your interactions with your friends. Friendship should not be about all sacrificing your own happiness to satisfy your friends, it should (mostly) be a joyous free spirited relationship that leaves you energized and loved. Being clear about what you need (without making demands) makes it possible and easier for your friends to tailor their expression of good will to you. Having your friendship needs met drives your positivity, energy and inner love, and on that front I really believe what goes around comes around. If you feel loved by your friends, then you will be capable of being a much better friend yourself. Thus rather than mentally accusing yourself of selfishness if you look out for yourself, think about keeping yourself in shape mentally, physically and emotionally, partially also to enable yourself to be a good friend to your friends.

Expectations on yourself:
The second question is what and how do you think you are as a friend? One frequent advice is 'be the (best) friend you want to have'. As I explained in the previous section, that is neither necessary nor desirable. We are all different, and that is fantastic. There are really different ways how we as friends can make the lives of our friends better, leaving them more cheerful, more thoughtful, more adventurous and colourful, warmer and loved. It is completely unrealistic to try to slot your feet into all these shoes at the same time. However, it is good to know and get a bit of feedback on what you are appreciated for, so that you can be sensitive and generous with your time when this is opportune. Thus being a great friend for a few people is I think the 'friendship goal' to aim for.

Tolerance and moral expectations:
As our society is getting more and more fragmented and some of us develop faster than others, or adopt certain conventions faster than others, one question might be how fast I expect my friends to 'catch up'. Indeed, is it necessary and essential to our friendship that they must sign on to changing social conventions as fast as I do for harmony's sake? Or is it more valuable to ignore the resulting conflict temporarily, but keep myself in orbit and available so that they may ask sensitive questions to topics that they are grappling with and where we may support with. We all have read plenty of argument, why it is not the duty of gay people to explain to the homophobic part of the population, why they are wrong. It is neither the obligation of people of colour to educate their white friends, for whom white privilege might actually have 'delivered' in the past decades. But the question is, if you unfriend your friend, because they voted Trump or Tory, how are they ever going to listen your argument that will change their mind? Isn't a period of grappling necessary before any meaningful change of heart, an investigation period, where you want to explore another position, maybe just hypothetically and from an intellectually safe distance, before you adopt it?[1] Thus I would say cultivating

[1]For myself I would say that there were a few cases where intellectually I understood the position

a virtue of acceptance and tolerance over finite time horizons may just improve societal understanding. And in the meantime, good and old friends are hard to find and close friendships take a long time to develop. You should think long and hard before dropping one over such a sensitive measure, even if this close to your heart. Finally, who is to throw the first stone? Maybe your carnivorous nature and frequent flyer status are just as offensive to their pro-climate thinking as their religiously conservative views are to you?

Resource availability and budgeting

If you decide friends are important to you and you wish them to have a substantial role in your life, make time for them. Think about which times in the week or on the weekend do not conflict with your primary duties of work and the family and then try to get into a habit of keeping some slots in the month free for socials with friends. You can even check whether other occupied slots - such as commute or exercise - can be combined with friends joining you on it. When you plan trips, do you emphasise the beauty of the place going to a hotel resort in some remote location, or do you plan the route taken with the help of your address book, trying to pick off a few friends on the way.

Also in terms of the other 'resources', how much do your friends figure in your decision making. In designing the layout and use of your apartment or house - do you consider the aesthetics of a couch as the key criterion for buying it for the living room or the sleep comfort it provides as a pullout bed when you have guests. Do you have a comfortable sitting corner, where you can have two or three or five friends sitting down for a bottle of wine or a meal? When choosing a location to live in, do you, as C. S. Lewis recommends, factor in where your friends are based, at least loosely, to facilitate increased social interaction?

Maintaining old friendships

As I have elaborated, it is much easier to maintain good old friendships than making new ones. The depth of understanding, the loyalty established over time, the affection known and the common memories have created a bond, that any spontaneous hunch or sympathy can hardly compensate. This even holds for friends of old whom you haven't been in touch for a while. I would say that one of the best practices to maintain old friends is lived spontaneity if possible, a continual trying to initiate or make possible spontaneous meetups, when an opportunity arises. This can be complemented by an annual date based habit, such as meeting a group of friends for dinner the day before Christmas.

The power of habit is indeed powerful, and my hunch is that establishing a genuine habit is far preferable over relying on the optionality of the pickup property, that you can simply temporarily discard but then pickup a friendship when you have time again. Combining such habits with hospitality, e.g. in the form

---

of a friend and accepted it as potentially correct. Yet it took me upwards of a year to change my emotional response to the issue fully and thus adopt the other position as my own. Some people may be able to change their opinion the moment they perceive new good data. Anecdotally I would suspect for most that they need to hear a good argument contrary to their position three or more times until they accept it.

of having a monthly Spagbol[2] open door are wonderful practices and easy to arrange. A quarter-annually pot luck lunch in the neighbourhood or church community is an extension of making a low-effort but regular joyous occasion.(see 5.7)

One issue these days is that of focus and priority. We end up scrolling hours on Facebook and Instagram with imaginary friends and long gone acquaintances and yet do not spend time with our close friends. Especially as we are skimped for time and energy, another solution can be thought of, the rule of six (non-Covid) of 'Jon and Zara' in Abell, 2009, ch.6[3]. Applying the rule of six you (and your partner) choose six close friends in your geographic proximity, and for a year prioritize them over all others, and you let them know that (and ideally they are fine with it). This will feel a little awkward and potentially brutal to all people who do not make the cut. But when asking people what they think of it, it does make sense to a lot of people, and you can always also tell people that maybe they will be next in the following year.

Suggestions for thought: Make it a goal to maintain your inner friendship - prioritizing them before all others. There is still a possibility that one or two drop off, but e.g. pick your six most important friends, and then behave in a way to ensure from your side that they are six close friends still five years down the line.

Skipping perfection for opportunity

Casual Visit:

The key to good habits of friendship maintenance is driving down the mental cost of a meeting as much as possible. An expectation of perfection is the enemy of the good. The best habit is creating opportunities with little or no additional effort for friends to get together with you, making allowances for the party that is more stressed with work or childcare. In Germany, having a good 'Abendbrot'[4] is a perfectly decent occasion to set a casually visiting friend in front of to join in. What is important is the time you spend with the friend, the conversation you have, the experiencing of each others life (which Aristotle would probably label the 'living together' and highly applaud), rather than the absolute intimacy and flow of the moment. What does not matter is the state of the apartment and the gourmet quality of the meal[5]. It is not optional to have a minimum amount of

[2]Spaghetti Bolognese is a classical scalable dish, where the meat sauce is freezer compatible in case you overestimate attendees, and on the other hand can be adjusted in ratio of meat sauce to pasta (which only has 10 min preparation time) in case a few more neighbours and friends show up.

[3]'We had an amazing group of friends - but we hardly saw anyone regularly. It felt like we didn't have any real community or any sort of deep, true, significant friendships with anyone. So we wrote a list of about 6 people and agreed that they would be the people whom we would really like to spend time with. We kind of sheepishly let them know what we were thinking (as it's an unusual thing to do) and asked if they'd like to get together more frequently etc. They were all really touched and there was a resounding yes'! Friendships take time (which is really tricky in the big city) but we now see them more often and have great friendships which flow two ways in both the good and bad times.'

[4]Traditional family get together over bread and cold cuts

[5]Unless a mutual passion for cleaning or gourmet food is the connecting passion of your friendship and understanding

attention for good conversation though, which however in a most transactional way can be traded for by making the friend lend a hand. If your friend drops by for an early afternoon or an evening, there is absolutely no harm in your friend playing with the kid for some time[6] to allow you to quickly also to get something else done. That in turn may allow you to have uninterrupted 1-1 time later in the evening. Finally it is important that no resentment develops, if the friend overstays his welcome. We all have our schedules, need to get up early, got things to do. If you are on a restricted schedule, it is good to announce that at the start of the hangout in order to set expectations, and then be rigorous in turfing your friend out when it is time to get the kids into bed. Of course by law of nature the time comes often when the conversation is at its best, but all this should be subordinated to not have regret impair the next decision to repeat the occasion.
Meeting up:
Of course we want to give our friends long hours of attention for long conversations, but if this is not available, sometimes a quick hour in between may also do just fine. What I have not yet come across is an automatic private coffee opportunity alert service that notifies you if you get within a kilometer or two of a friend where a meetup is due again. It could alert you, when you have idle time such as a long car drive, and the central server knows that another friend also has idle time, that it would be an opportunity to catch up by phone. Short coffee meetups do not compensate for long evenings over dinner or joint hikes, but they do keep our presence literally in each other's orbits much more than texting can. Again, the key here is spontaneity, with both sides being prepared to jump at the opportunity when it arises.

Integrating families

Joint families:
For the good friends you may think like treating them as extended family, quite literally. While the key god parents most likely will be recruited from family, there is always space for a 'funcle' or 'faunt' (fun uncle or fun aunt) to drop in and be out and about. There is no harm in having a spare baby sitter on hand, and they might enjoy having the kids for an evening. Even if they have kids themselves, it is perfectly workable to have an extra two or three for an evening to allow the other kids' parents to have a date night. Perfectly workable maybe not in our today's custom, but go back to the generation born in the 50ies and 60ies and ask them about parenting habits, and sure trading around kids for an evening was a thing rather than paying babysitters. Neighbours in rural areas would be in and out of each other's houses, often with doors staying unlocked[7].

Whatever role you assign to a friend in relation to your kid, my hunch is that some degree of 'formalization' is helpful, and I will get to the concept of 'secondary [godparentage]' below. If it is a mere joke or spur of the moment, then it

[6] Your friend however is not going to complain if you manage to place a pint of ale or a glass of wine within reach of his arm and yet somewhat protected from attack charges of the valiant Lego knights of your kid about to rescue the princess.

[7] I am aware that this assertion only applies to some countries and cultures. This is not the place to enter an extensive discussion on trust indices, however even in some low trust environments the 'gate' would be placed at the front of the community, and behind it doors could be left open for the in-group.

will wear off over the years. But a friend uncle or aunt may take the role a bit more seriously, and then really ensure a visit once or multiple times a year to catch up with you and the kid. It is also a credible sign that you both take the friendship seriously and believe it to last: if a friend has vested over a decade time and efforts in you and this relationship, then neither party would just drop out, e.g. because your interests or social circles change.

Time away and time together with friends:
One powerful way to maintain your key friendships can be that of dedicated time together. Now with family and our other obligations this is a difficult one, and I acknowledge nigh on impossible in countries where only e.g. 14 days of holidays are given in any year. But if in a close friendship between couples a ritual weekend away in the year is institutionalised, come what may, this may really be something. In marriage the weekend away is - if feasible and grandparents are on hand to take over the kids - one of the highly prized rituals (apparently). Yet its function to reconnect with the deeper parts in the personality, that is swamped in the nitty gritty of daily life, may be enhanced by having old friends around. It may be a friend from the era of the first years of the couple that brings out the childish humour, the adventurous nature or other traits, that stood at the start of the romance and attraction. At the same time when families also are compatible by having children of a similar age who also get along, joint family holidays might be a great way to connect. This could be by institutionalizing to come together in the same location, e.g. beach resort, camping site, hiking or skiing location every year.

Using technology to maintain and develop friendships

Whilst the book Asatryan, 2016 has been mentioned before as a good read for making friends, one aspect of her writing deserves special attention, and that is her **layer theory**. Whilst this is hidden away in 'A note on technology and questions' the following sentence was for me the main takeaway of the book: 'The best mode for investigating our inner world is the one that includes the most layers of communication.'(p.109). Asatryan goes on to elaborate what information is all lost when you don't see or hear the person, specifically singling out the possibility to interpret and value silences. Whilst not ditching the convenience of a quick phonecall or catchup WhatsApp message, I have because of the experience of one year of social distancing and lots of Skype calls tried to test this theory for myself. I found that indeed screen size, video quality, volume and sound quality do matter. For myself I have thus gravitated towards using a full screen computer monitor, a proper PC HD camera with onboard mic and a high-quality headphone for what I would call the 'focused conversations'. I reflected a lot on whether I was prepared to take on board the full implication of her claims, but at the time of finalising the draft now I would say it extends to refuting the possibility of genuine online friendships. We may after all be biologically wired to build relationships person-to-person. We not just need to see the face, but we need to feel a person. This feeling might be quite literal, as we part ways with friends on the convention of a hug. Until two people have met in person, I would thus - foregoing extreme exceptions - highly doubt it if people were to tell me they formed a friendship online. Now the get-out clause I would accept is that people developed a friendship with someone online, whose authenticity they had established before. Thus you may have developed a friendship over Zoom and Teams with a work colleague who you had met priorly only two or three times casually in the company coffee corner. But the possibility of establishing trust and emotional intimacy with someone whose core person you have not grasped with all your senses is in my opinion complete 'make-belief' - wishful thinking.

Photo sharing could also be a key item to be supported on a technological level. Facebook and Apple (and presumably Google inside the Android system too) incorporated functions for flashback photos, highlighting photos you look often to. But I do think there is potential for a great friendship - 'create-a-habit' - reminder app. One app I used over the years was CJournal (for contact journal) keeping track of postcards I had sent and long phonecalls. This served two purposes, first to make sure that there weren't close friends who didn't get any postcards, and secondly to keep the door open for rust friends[8] who I maintained an affection for, but for whom because of life circumstances on their side I had dropped off the priority list.

Another opportunity could be provided by fast scheduling apps to enable people to utilize 'dead time' to check in. Skype, Teams, WhatsApp all have enabled a status function that says whether you are online or 'busy', but what is still missing is an auto-scheduling app. The ideal case to enable contact maintenance among busy people would be to have an app with telephone and video functionality, where you could mark your key friends and probably divide them into the three layers of friends described in section (9.5). Then you could set your status to be free for a certain time in the week, and potentially also couple it with a location / area for possibility of a physical meetup. This could then within the system send alerts to your friends who perhaps might also be free at the time for a call, or who might be in the area and have time for a beer or coffee. Now of course, this takes the romance of reaching out etc. completely away. It is mechanic and unaffectionate. But such a system would be brutally effective, if time scarcity and energy is the bottleneck. If you think back on the friendship process in section (7.3), the bottleneck for really busy people is the time and energy to reach out and get that time slot where an encounter is possible. So any technology that reduces the cost of reaching out and setting a time and place for the encounter will help. What is important is to make use of 'dead time': when travelling in a car or commuting on a train, waiting for a doctors appointment or any other dead time, this is really key to maintain a base level of contact with the social circle. And if you are the busy bottleneck on a tight schedule, such a solution could enable your more flexible and free spirited friends to come out spontaneously and make use of available time slots, if they get the notification.

The app 'addappt' seems to be suited for solving the 'updating of contact details' dilemma. It is a no-other-purpose app, thus you are not sharing your address with Facebook or Linkedin if you don't want to. Of course the app also suffers the network effect, in the sense it is only made effective by the number of people in your network who go onto it. Convincing your wider network of casual friends to go onto it might be more of a hassle than enquiring annually with five to thirty people whether their address details have changed. Other apps like Covve that claim to solve the problem with AI at current levels of public databases introduce

[8]See Greif, 2009 and 9.4

more 'false friends' (pun intended) than actually improve data quality in your address book. Of course, making addresses public is a concern specifically for women, in times of stalking and other dangerous habits. Postboxes are also cumbersome to use, especially as physical mail has become so rare. Yet it would be really great to have physical DOIs, anonymized addresses that nevertheless allow for actual delivery of snail mail. This could take the form of a unique identifier for every person, that could be placed on a physical letter or postcard, and then within the postal system is mapped to a region, e.g. a county within a country. Once the post reaches the head office of that county, it is relabelled to be forwarded to the actual address there. I also really miss the app Plaxo, and hope it will at some point resurface.

One of the things that I loved about the various messenger apps is the possibility of sending silly jokes to friends and getting new ones back. Now I know not everyone loves that, but for a few friends of mine and me it is a real connecting element. It is one habit that I unapologetically will continue.[9] I genuinely think that the capability to send a good joke, meme, fun thought to a friend is indeed priceless. We can share a happy thought, a laughter, a giggle, instantly with any friend of ours wherever they are on the globe. Getting sent stupid jokes from friends whilst being in lockdown - as silly and awful as some of them were [10] - was one of the key contributors to keeping me sane. I can only encourage you to not underestimate the power of a little happy thought, conveying the message 'I am thinking of you and want you to giggle a little'. On the building memory front, I for one find that I do remember the good memes and jokes, as well as roughly when I was sent them and by whom. That may hold for few people admittedly in this strength, but for those it is a great way of keeping the sparkle of the friendship truly alive even over distance. If you want to start up this habit, a good point is subscribing to a few of the classic feeds on Facebook and Instagram[11]. What I would like to emphasise again however is that the sending of jokes and memes should not substitute or replace the actual meetings. The 'thinking of you' should always be complemented with an occasional and consistent 'It has been a while, how are you and when and how can we meet up again?'.

[9] There is a great short sketch on Youtube where Jimmy Kimmel explains to time travelling Marty McFly and Doc Brown Video Kimmel Back to the future -from Back to the Future (https://www.imdb.com/title/tt0088763/) how the key purpose of our super-computer smartphone is to send smilies to other people (https://youtu.be/QOVGR1EJewA):
After a bit of chatter Jimmy Kimmel takes out a smartphone and takes a selfie with Marty McFly and Doc Brown, and they discuss the concept of a smart phone (scene starts at 4:27: Doc Brown: 'Great Scott, it is a tiny supercomputer. This must allow astrophysicists to triangulate complex equations in real time' to which Jimmy responds 'yeah really well I guess it probably could do that but mainly we use it to send little smiley faces to each other, pictures of eggplants, that sort of thing ...')

[10] Here a selection: 'Why can't you see elephants hiding in trees? Because they're really good at it.' Or 'I thought I had caught Corona because I hardly could breathe, but then I loosened the belt one notch and everything was OK again' or simply cues/prompts to remember funny movie scenes, such as Spock's tracing necklace in Beyond, the Guardians of the Galaxy escape from prison conversation. *Anything* that will distract your friend for a second or two, and return him to the world with an eye roll, chuckle and smile really.

[11] Unvirtuous Abbey, Ruthe, Lynn Miclea, Chris Tilling, Tot aber Lustig, Postillon, Punhub to credit a few.

Suggestions for thought:

- If you live far from your friends have you thought about investing in a proper 'connection kit' (Large screen HD TV, High-Def Camera,...)?
- Have you experimented on a process to find good time slots with your other busy friend?
- Do you have a way of keeping your addresses and contact details updated with your friends?

Circle fine-tuning

A friendship circle is not something that you manage like a portfolio of shares and bonds. It is also not managed like a team at work or a professional network. However, a certain structured approach may help in avoiding pitfalls. In section 6.11 I described the needs that friendship addresses, and in section 9.5 I sketched out a tool to look at one's personal community or friendship circles. I will now come to the normative section, the recommendations on how I think it is helpful to approach friendship structurally. This is an opinion, not based on exact science, and may feel a little too cold or utilitarian for some. The principle I would propose is to not put too many eggs into one basket, or too many burdens on one shoulder. If you are aware what key needs are addressed or you need to be addressed by friendship, then the second step is to look who in your circle of friends does so. Essentially, this is filling out the friendship inventory in the appendix, but can also just be done on the back-of-an-envelope or just mentally running through it in your head.

The key theme to look out for then are the single points of failure per category. The key needs where only one friend knows how to press your buttons. For minor elements or key insights of course no friend is replaceable, indeed every friend is unique and cannot be replaced per se. But what is to be avoided is dependence. If your friend is the only one who understands you, or who can help you with key discussion issues understanding your spouse, or if you can only really laugh about the jokes your friend does and nobody else's, then a temporary withdrawal of your friend, becomes an existential threat to your wellbeing. You might think me to [overdramatize or overstress] this item, but please bear with me. I have elsewhere exhibited the opinion that I substantially prefer closeness and commitment over freedom and respect for privacy in friendship. I think that our emphasis on personal freedom, constant self-optimisation and non-committing is the great inhibitor to developing high-quality friendships in our time. However, it is a matter of fact that circumstances of life take their tolls, and it is perfectly reasonable for a person to not be emotionally available for a prolonged period, be it because of the birth of a child, new job or whatever reason. Such a temporary absence of mind must be accepted in friendship, even if the occasional hint that the door is open whenever time becomes available, I would classify as affection rather than nagging. If you have a friend who fulfils three or four core roles for you, then I would recommend immense gratitude for being so lucky to have found such a great friend. At the same time efforts of diversification to reduce dependence might really however be a healthy step forward. If seen from the other side, would you want your friend to say 'I don't really have an option to cancel on my friend, I am the only real friend they have got left'.

It is from this perspective that I find it so problematic that specifically married people retreat into their own homes. Now of course it is wonderful if a couple finds true love and develops a great friendship within this, and if the spouse can indeed fulfil several core friendship roles to meet friendship needs.

But the question is however whether it is healthy to set up the spouse as a multiple single point of failure in the network and burdening the spouse with the knowledge of that. Instead, by maintaining a circle of close friends we liberate the spouse to bestow goodness onto us when and where they choose. We stop making a moral unspoken demand upon it. Rath, 2006, p.33 with the story of Judy and Tim provides one such example: the wife's decides to turn to her best friend for encouragement and challenge, which she needs, but her husband Tim cannot provide the way she needs it. This frees up the marriage of the stress of trying to get it all within. It also allows her to appreciate her husband much more for all the humour, love and emotional understanding he provides with her. Indeed, it frequently (e.g. Degges-White and Borzumato-Gainey, 2011) is cited and stereotyped to a degree, that women diversify the marriage with a close friendship with a female friend. That way they receive the emotional understanding and affection that the husband is perhaps falling short in provision. Likewise, men diversify the marriage with close friendship to 'talk shop and sport'.

What I advocate thus in this section is just taking it one step further and think in a general circle and fostering and growing that rather than in single relationships. It also has consequences, as you perceive you are the single point of failure for a friend in a specific respect, to encourage that friend to go out and make new friends, so that if you become unavailable, their quality of life does not substantially deteriorate. This is also part of the watching out for a friend.

Memory building investments

Research exists that shows we experience events differently and memorize it differently when we take photos. Even this act leads to different experiences depending on the purpose - making a quick shot with the iPhone for later posting on Facebook is a far cry from the meditative experience of a photo-hobbyist trying to capture the essence of a specific landscape, venturing out in the darkness to get that perfect sunrise shot. Just like that I found that if you are at a party with friends, spending some time withdrawn on the edge with a good portrait distance lense [12] you can get some fantastic shots of your friends talking. Having good photos of key encounters really makes wonderful memories, and thus investment in a decent camera [13] and a pair of lenses that are both fast with one suitable to capture both candids and one wider designed to capture conversation moments is really that, an investment in memory building. Shumway, 2018, p.111 recommends a more physical and direct approach, giving a friend a gift that is going to keep you in his mind. As the phrase goes for some friendships 'out of sight, out of mind' such a gift, e.g. a photo-frame, a cool object brought back

[12] My manual Nikon 135 f2 was the toy of choice

[13] I mean a proper DSLR of the Nikon-Canon-Sony type in full format or APS-C.

from a journey (kitchen magnet, wooden statue of an Asian luck demon), printed and framed silly meme or stupid joke appreciated by both of you, anything that expresses really a key memory in your friendship will do.

Wiking, 2019, the director of the Happiness Research Institute, shows how the close link of how our effectiveness of making 'good' memories directly affects our happiness. Encounters with friends, especially if they add in elements of excitement, special affection or discovery and exploration can provide such memories. The good and potentially life-changing advice of a friend will stay with you forever. And by extension, so will the memory of that friend. What I found really effective in hindsight are the times where I spend full days rather than just 2h coffees with a friend. This could be visiting them and staying on their couch, or travelling with them for a city trip. In my three years respectively in Japan and Hong Kong, a few times friends came to stay, always resulting in special bonding and prized memories. As a curiosity, specifically cooking with friends is additionally memorable, and Wiking provides the explanation, as we additionally thus link the memory of that act to the smell and taste of the dish. Thus if a friend teaches us a recipe, or we both try out a recipe to see what it is like or whether we get it right, we may and probably will remember this act also the next times when we recook the dish.

Of course, if you have a bucket list of crazy things you want to do still, there is nothing better than to get a friend to join in on the fun. Historical reenactment donning old armours, flying a balloon or chopper, going paint balling or blowing glass - there are many activities which we don't make into hobbies, but want to try out once (or twice or...) in a lifetime. Even if it completely tanks, the fun of the memory will stay with you. In Tokyo a few friends and I had started a monthly movie night, cooking at 7pm and movie start at 8pm. On one evening, by request of one member, we picked Bill and Ted's excellent adventure, a movie with a respectable IMDB rating of 7.0 and which we had all heard of as being a bit of a classic. For him, it was 'the' movie he had wanted to see for a long time. So we kicked off and I think the movie per se was quite enjoyable. Our friend however was in agony over the perceived stupidity of the jokes, his assessment on the acting employed and the general awfulness in the movie. The last 30 minutes for us involved less actually paying attention to the movie and more teasing our friend on his excellent taste in movies and enjoying him squirm over our comments on the 'ingenuity' of the wit displayed. This anecdote seems meaningless, insignificant and unrelatable to anyone who wasn't there, yet it is a perfect example of the positive endearing memories of which friendship is built up. Embracing such 'funny failures' is also a key recipe for memory building employed by Wiking as such stories contribute to a common narrative of the friendship. Whatever those stories and experiences are, we can keep thinking about them and be grateful for them.

Suggestions for thought:
What do you do to build and keep your precious memories with your friends?

11.2 Starting out

Making new friends

The standard advice of making friends 'fast' of course holds, such as looking to people also pursuing your standard interests and acquaintances within existing social circles. This way you maximize compatibility and enjoyment, specifically in the initial 20 hours where no mutual bond or personal knowledge has been established yet. You can listen to your gut feeling or instinct how you click with people - usually a good indicator to go by. Essentially the book Asatryan, 2016 with the appropriate title 'Stop Being Lonely' is an excellent guide for this situation, if you judge your 'social skills / perception' to be 'in need of improvement'. Beyond that there are a few thoughts I would like to share which you can think about. Daring to make the leap of faith and giving somebody the benefit of doubt to be a kind and friendly person opens you up for new opportunities and is a necessary cost. Note that Apostolou and Keramari, 2020 identifies 'low trust' as one of the key obstacles to making new friends.[14]

First - and this may come across as calculating, cold or superficial - friendship is a **numbers game**. There is a difference of meeting a hundred people or just ten. Developing friendships is neither 'finding friends' nor 'making them', but somewhere in the middle. You find people with whom you click and then make them into friends by hanging out with them and getting to know them better. Depending on what makes you click, that click or spark may happen on sight or within the first ten minutes, or it may only occur after several hours of conversation. Now whilst this is not a perfect validation, within the Youth preference study F.2 there were two subset of questions, one on self assessment, and the second on preferences, in order to analyse matching qualities. A key takeaway of the dataset was that the scores of potential matches generated improved significantly once twenty people were on board. My hunch is that even if you are 'in the right room' you want to get to know about thirty or forty people until you start making choices on your end who to spend more time with to develop friendship.[15]

Second - let the power of organizations work for you. I write below about what organizations can do to become friendship fostering, but some do it automatically. You are welcomed and feel at home when you step into the door. Those are great places to make friends, as you regularly interact with the same people and get to know them casually. If you regularly attend a church, or if you are a regular in a certain Meetup group[16] or expat group like Internations[17], it takes away the pressure of needing to make good first impressions. You find yourself again and again in conversation circles with the same people, and you can make up your mind slowly, and so can they about you. If you are unsure of whether such an informal group is right for you or is likely to last, then try to identify whether

[14]Summarized in the appendix, Apostolou, Keramari, et al., 2020 and Apostolou and Keramari, 2020 are great evaluations of the motivators and obstacles to making new friends.

[15]The right room is really important. If you are in a room of 30 or 50 people and you have a 2% probability to click with someone, you still have a probability of about 55 % or 36 % not to click with anyone. If you raise this number to 3 % these change to 40% and 21%, for 5% they change to 21% and 8%. So it is really important to pick the right room / or to use an alternative phrase - to find the right tribe.

[16]www.meetup.com

[17]www.internations.org

at the core of it is a pre-established group of four or more friends that drive its energy and warmth and welcoming nature. If it does have such a core group and you like them and can see yourself interacting with them, then that is something to go for.

Third - and this may again be cold - consider the 'optimal stopping problem'[18]. The secretary problem is that of an administrator who wants to hire the best secretary out of a given number of (e.g. 30) available applicants. The optimal solution is for the administrator to interview roughly a third (to be exact n/e, roughly 11 of the 30) applicants, reject them all but takes down their scores, and then hires the first applicant (e.g. number 14) that is better than all of the first n/e applicants. Comparison with original problem delivers the following insights: you are not limited to one person, but you should not settle for the first one to come along. However at some point you need to stop searching. Friendship is only 25 % of the person of the other, and even that you don't appreciate fully at the start, the rest is developed over time and within activities.

Overview of friendship potentials:
However you might not be lonely per se, and thus not 'need' further friends. Instead, you may be motivated from the curiosity to meet new people, and meeting people different to you might prove very enriching. The right attitude is to pay attention to people who come to you in your daily life, almost like letting your karma attract people. Of course we are all poor at predicting the future. Specifically, we are poor at what we are like in, say, ten years' time (see Gilbert, 2009). Depending on lifestyle and life choices, it may be unclear in which country or city we will be living. You can consider spending thus some time in the year keeping a bit in touch with people where you had a particularly good vibe, even though geographic considerations didn't allow for a deepening of the friendship. But the idea would be to keep the beacon slightly higher than the general Facebook/LinkedIn social radar so that we would notice when a change in geography permitted spending more time together.

Also remember that it is both patience and a numbers game. As far as numbers are concerned, everyone is free to befriend people and cannot be forced. Whilst we might feel like we clicked with someone, this does not need to be mutual. Given that we might end up spending a substantial amount of our disposable time with this person, it is good to listen in on that click or connection. As noted before, Hall, 2018 shows it takes about 50 hours of time spent together until some sense of friendship is established. That is quite some time to waste if the desire for friendship is unreciprocated.

The art of the initial conversation

One aspect I was unsure about whether the art of the conversation needs to be taught. The argument against it is that conducting a conversation according to perceived rules may take the bliss out of it and make it feel stiff and artificial. However general anecdotal evidence seems to point that our conversations over the past decades have become shorter, more superficial and more distracted. The absolute expert on good conversation is Zeldin, 2000 and he points out that in

[18]Colloquially called the secretary or marriage problem - see `https://en.wikipedia.org/wiki/Secretary_problem` for details and explanation

Victorian times conversation was actually taught. After reading his book I am actually convinced that such a conversation training might be helpful to a lot of people and for broadening connection. A short well-designed course (e.g. 4 sessions of 15 minutes each) on how to improve casual conversations could be a great boon and confidence builder for those who are a little out of practice. His book is highly erudite and a wonderful pleasure to read, and a grand eulogy on the good conversation. It is however mostly preaching to the converted, i.e. those that already have a deep appreciation for the joys of conversation[19]. For a session in a loneliness intervention program some of it might need to be toned down and edited for practical takeaways. The last pages of the book are dedicated to 36 conversation starters for meaningful conversation.[20] For me the key takeaway (and there are many others) is the genuine desire to explore the other's thinking, to step out of our own world and into the others. This quest Zeldin sees beyond the conversation, he advocates people to step into the world of engineers, doctors and architects, to genuinely explore their worlds and way of thinking. His claims of teaching someone to learn to understand the thinking of a doctor, engineer or architect over the course of a few months is radical, and yes it might very much be true. Whilst the technical knowledge of course takes years to accumulate, something he doesn't dispute, he is interested in us exploring the mindsets and trains of thoughts.

I also see the key of conversations as an art to elicit the inert passions of people. This can be cooking or tasting food, travelling, raising children and observing their growth, the beauty of the world, plants or a great many things. For me there are three kinds of passion themes - the passions that I have, the passions that I don't share but can understand and sympathise with, and then passions that I have no connection to. I just don't get them. I understand that people are passionate about these things, and I can respect that, but it is just not up my alley. In order to connect, you need to be interested, and fully invested in the topic. If you are not paying attention over longer periods, switch the topic. If you are feigning interest, you are not polite, you are wasting both your as well as your conversation partners time. I don't mind so much get rudely interrupted in my story telling by someone who really wants to tell their own similar and related story, whose story connects to some element in the bit that I have told already. I do mind to tell my story into the dazed eyes of someone who cannot relate to it and just indulges me but essentially has switched off mentally and just keeps their eyes open for pretence. You don't have to be connected and friends with everyone. That having been said, if there are only two topics you are interested in, and everything else bores you, you are likewise making life difficult for yourself.

---

[19]During a longer conversation with Prof. Zeldin, who kindly provided me feedback on a number of items, it became clear that the goal of the conversation in his intent is a different one to the one I depict here. For Prof. Zeldin the conversation is an entry to someone's world and viewpoint. The goal is so to speak expansion of knowledge and an appreciation for the uniqueness and identity of the other person. If I understand the viewpoint of the other person, in the extreme I never have to talk to them again, but both of us are richer for this insight. In the context I refer to it I treat it as a means to an end. A good conversation tests the waters and evaluates the possibility, likelihood and scope of a future bond. The goal is the friendship or relationship, to get to know the person to make as good as possible an evaluation of proceeding on the further development of the relationship, or decline to proceed.

[20]There is no dearth of books on other potential conversation starters. One such set is provided by `https://www.werenotreallystrangers.com/`

What I think is necessary that we need to be open with what genuinely doesn't interest us, and be cautious in not condemning it. We also need to be careful to separate the theme and the person[21], though this may not always be easy.

If you recall the resource content, this is really relevant. I believe the underlying problem a lot of people have is that they loose their spark, their passion. Equally it may be that they diminish their passion and loose the faith that anybody may be interested in it. Content is also determined by the capability to present it in an interesting or humouristic or whatever fashion, and this capability is developed. The value of content is also determined by those around, and it is perfectly possible that we have topics that no one around can empathise with. This can be an incredible feeling of loneliness, however this does not need to say anything about our general incapability to connect. We may be in the wrong room, however we may also need to branch out and diversify or at least maintain. Indeed one of the saddest issues of loneliness and lack of interaction, e.g. when people go into care homes, is often the deterioration of content and a self fulfilling prophecy of expecting conversational disinterest to what is left. In this case the most meaningful intervention is the provision of good content to make good conversations. On the other hand, if there is little you are currently passionate about, not all is lost. The best antidote might be to shop around and listen to passionate people. This can include children telling you about their experiences in school, playing with other kids, lego constructions and the discoveries they make in this process[22]. It can be cooks, artists, craftsment, filmmakers, scientists and engineers. It can be social workers, pastors and community builders fascinated about human connection. Passion is deeply infectious, and if you keep an interest and keep meeting people who are passionate about something, you will catch it sooner or later too. It is also good to be a bit aware of which topics are general interest (travelling, drinks, general music, general world affairs) and which are likely only to be specialist interest only (most academic sub-disciplines). The best topics are those that are niche but relateable, where people have an initial intuition and - possibility by a bit of support on base facts from you - can enter a good discussion on you. Such topics can be introductory ethics, niche food production techniques (beer brewing, wine making), horticulture and puts you in the role of the expert on something people always have wondered about trying out. While most people don't like to talk about their jobs in a private setting, it might still be interesting whether part of their daily activities encapsulates such a task which they actually enjoy and most importantly - enjoy talking to the uninitiated bystander about.

For me the general go-to topic in the past was cultural experiences made when travelling. I am passionate about languages, travels, history and cultures, but the conversation is mostly on their experiences. However similar conversations allow me to draw analogies, and thus interact with the content shared. One-upping can be a possibility I need to monitor a little bit, and it is a likely temptation on any topic where you have more experience than your conversation partner. The

[21] I am not quite sure how to describe it, but if a person touches on three topics all of which do not interest me in the least, then is is very easy to think 'X is boring' whereas the accurate sentence is that we have simply been unable to find topics or themes to connect about.

[22] I find the way kids look at the world deeply inspiring. The awe of the new, the open eyes and the wows, the naive sharpness of observation. There is nothing else quite like that and it is just so upbeat. A second thing I love is how kids are capable of finding the humorous and funny in profane daily things.

principle to aim for in a first conversation: It needs to be about your conversation partner, and yet the topic or theme needs to genuinely interest you. One item which usually is called a conversation vice, however I find it a bit of the salt in the soup[23], is interrupting. Too much is too much of course, but I sometimes wonder if not style and intent matters more. There are enhancing interruptions that expand on your story, ask a question, but even if a little detour is entered, the goal is to return to your story and stay on its track. If the other interrupting persons story is good, I might learn a new angle on my past experience, why something was precious or whether there was an additional meaning in the dish I ate in that village. In my view these exhibit possibly bad conversational technique, but that is about all I mind about them. The conversation still stays an interactive dialogue. Different are the 'capture the flag' interruptions, where the conversation partner interrupts to divert to another topic altogether. With this nature the conversation becomes more of a competitive sequence of unrelated monologues. Worst of all is the experience if the two partners have key topics they want to have discussed, and try to steer their topic always in the middle. So style matters.

Rather than a course the best training might however lie in alpha-course style random meeting rounds in small groups. Building a safe environment in small groups and keeping them together for 3-4 meetings, then giving each other feedback on style (you interrupt a lot, you wait to long and never interrupt, you think you have nothing to say yet all your comments are really interesting when you make them, ...) should do the trick. Especially after two further mixups and thus an overall three rounds of feedback most people should know where they stand, and what elements of conversational technique they might need to still pay a little attention to.

11.3 Organizations and Business

Organizations

I think if we want to increase the importance and priority of friendship in our society, then we need to follow Putnam, 2000 to set up our society and in particular our organisations, from professional working places, to sports clubs, to volunteering organisations, to schools and universities, to facilitate a better ambience for growth and maintenance of friendships in the society. Whilst most of us in principle consider friendship a private affair, this is a view that can be challenged. In the context of the 'greater good', this means supporting people to avoid being lonely when they hit retirement age. Companies can meaningfully undertake efforts to foster friendship amongst their employees. Rath, 2006, p.67 elaborates on the case of a plant manager who put friendship at a core of an employee engagement project at a manufacturing plant. The initial sentiment of hers was scepticism [24], but the subsequent effort proved her right, and on an economic level the efforts paid off, with KPIs such as customer complaints being reduced by 50%, rising en-

---

[23]Just with salt, there are some who put in a lot, and there are some who completely omit it in their life. For some people interrupting and counterinterrupting is a natural flow, some are completely thrown off course.

[24]'The last thing she wanted to do was sit down with these 'old blokes', as she called them, and talk about increasing scores on a question like 'I have a best friend at work'

gagement scores and reduction of absentee times. But even without such tangible effects on the company's KPIs[25], I believe that aside from a salary and contribution to health and pension systems, a company should have at least partially the wellbeing of its employees in mind holistically, and social connection is one of the greatest contributors to living a good life. The first step towards a friendship fostering culture is enabling good interaction and conversation. This comes down to the provision of spaces where employees can relax, sit down and simply have a chat. By this I don't mean the Google-style playgrounds for grown-ups but the old school coffee corner, with a few tables, a functioning coffee machine dispensing black liquid that at least somewhat is justified to bear the label coffee, plus access to some milk (rather than reinfused milk powder) and also some non-caffeinated alternatives (tea, soft drinks, hot chocolate, whatever). Well-functioning coffee corners also have a habit of being self-supplying with almost-out-of-date durable sweets and cookies. A friend of mine referred to the company coffee corner as the Bermuda triangle for all sweets that her children and family dog had scorned, with the remaining lifetime usually between one or three hours tops. Beyond the quick and casual coffee chat, encouraging a good networking and get-to-know culture is also key. This does not have to be done by get to know games at introduction seminars or departmental get-togethers with social matching elements (though if well done they can be really effective and fun), but enabling and encouraging habits such as a lunch-meetup culture, or the Friday 5pm pint in the pub with the colleagues. Care here must be taken to enable flexibility and non-exclusion, as certain habits may be great for some, but should not structurally exclude colleagues with children or other social duties from participating. Similarly, social and voluntary organizations can play a prominent role in connecting people. Any place is relevant where people meet because they pursue a passion, whether that is sport, church, hobbies, crafts, a place and opportunity where they can connect. The key question here is whether such organizations can become the new tribes, places that organize a warm community, where friendship develops. Rituals (and these can be institutional jokes) create a 'we'-feeling. It should not be a goal to humiliate people, but having a rite of passage that involves a mildly embarrassing element (reading a poem or doing a sketch to a new department you are joining on their Christmas celebration) provides a signal that people henceforth 'belong' and are accepted. A habit of eating and drinking together can be really simple to organise, but is highly effective to get people to mingle. One really wonderful example was the post church-service coffee get together in the parish center in St. Albans in Tokyo, and the monthly invite to the rectors lodging for a general pot luck lunch[26] with the church community was a wonderful item in the monthly social schedule building warmth and connection in the community. Warmth through hospitality is a proven concept on how to build a community that provides a fertile ground for friendships to develop.

Both companies and social organizations are a great playground for the schmoozers[27], people operating within their informal networks and bringing people together who they think fit well together because of personality, interests or humour. But it is easy to cultivate by oneself a habit of schmoozing, by being friendly, lis-

[25]key performance indicators, system of statistics to aid company steering

[26]See section on hospitality and communion 5.7.

[27]See 3.12

tening to people and also employing simply a culture and mindset of bringing people together. Hospitality is another theme, and a team-lead hosting a barbecue or encouraging the holding of one with the families is a great way to bring people together in a socially informal context. One key skill here is the bridging and integrations of generations, and by generations I mean here life stage generations (job starters, young couples, families with small children, families with elder children, mid-life employees etc.).

Depending on the size of the organization, substructures may be helpful. Whereas Dunbar puts the historical size of the social group between the boundaries of 50 to 150, I think the sweet spot is somewhere in the area of 80-100 people to bond naturally and organically over time, as small groups develop by themselves and grow to friendship circles.[28] Of course there are examples of successful social groups of 120 or 150, but for me the pinnacle and perfect example of a friendship fostering exercise is the bonding experience of undergraduates joining an Oxford and Cambridge College. A cohort is about 80-100 people strong with 120 people being the exception in the larger colleges. For two weeks' time - the infamous freshers' week and the first week when workload is still low little is planned apart from socialising. They all have their breakfasts, lunches and dinners together in their colleges, with ever changing seating arrangements, and thus get to know each other in a flurry of first, second and third impressions. Virtually every fresher at the end of those two weeks has a set of 3-10 people who basically become the key friendship candidates for the remaining years. I am not saying that other universities, say in Germany, France, India or China do not provide a decent backdrop for friendships being created, but the system cultivated in Oxford and Cambridge over the centuries of their universities existence has evolved to a class of its own in terms of effectiveness at fostering friendships. Setting aside the frequency of interaction and substantial homophily (all the students are essentially smart, excited, and driven, without getting into the debate of class/socio-economic backgrounds and access), which may not be so easily replicable, several lessons can be learned from this and emulated by other organizations. One takeaway lesson can be the establishment of cohorts as a bonding element and subtle encouragement beyond emphasising the 'freedom to self organize'. Of course most organisations deal with grown up adults, however human inertia needs to be accounted for. And whilst self responsibility is a nice slogan and cost cutting is ubiquitous, having some function in the HR department consciously thinking about how to support and foster connection in the company may be a wise investment.

Suggestions for thought:

- What are you doing to make your company, church or other organizations a welcoming and friendship fostering place?
- If someone in your company or organization proposed hosting a connection course as described in 10.7 would you participate? Would you even help organize it or serve as a table leader?

[28]The roman centuria comprised 80 soldiers separated into 10 contubernia, in the US army you have squad (4-10) - platoon (16-40) - company (60-200) - so offering significantly more variability.

The loneliness economy

Whilst it might seem problematic to profit from people's suffering, an alternative viewpoint is that if with some investment genuine solutions can be provided, that will make people less lonely, then some of those will very happily pay for it. And thus slowly something resembling a loneliness economy is making an appearance and no doubt will receive a major boost post pandemic. I am no fan of rent-a-friend or cuddle friend concepts, these just give symptom to how bad loneliness is even among those with some funds.

In a way, the paid model of Internations already points the way, however smaller scale events that spin off large events are the winning ticket. My hunch is that for a limited number the hundreds of classical event managers currently out of jobs, professional social schmoozing may become a proper business model. In Hong Kong I met one such social entrepreneur, who ran a highly successful lunch and supper club and cooking studio. With an address book or customer list of about 1000 people [29] and a truly charming personality, she repeatedly and consistently got groups of eight to twelve come together for a fun evening or cooking class. Those were not cheap, partially driven also by Hong Kong's rental market base line, yet people gladly paid up for the opportunity to meet other interesting people. This is mostly a city model where there is a sizeable group of potential customers with some free cash flow, as these events will be essentially 'going out'-costs plus organizer fees. Judging by experiences from Tokyo and Hong Kong in order for a schmoozer to have a sustainable business, they need not only know many people but be personally liked and appreciated by a sizeable subset for them to pay the event top-up fee.

The second business model will be adapting cafe's and bars to be genuinely social places. Co-working spaces might become attractive not because we can work there, but because we can go to a place with people in it and closer to home and a bit more diverse than our main employment space. However, I am more hopeful for places that style themselves as open living rooms or similar - basically cafes with plenty of space designed for people to stay and potentially interact[30]. The death of retail is a major economic problem, but in the past 20 years the main high streets have been places for processing people to maximise consumption, not to stay. Post-pandemic it might be an opportunity to reclaim the high street and sidewalks for tables with chairs for people to stay. This will only work if commercial rents decrease majorly, reducing the revenue pressure per square meter. An alternative could be for the remaining shops to subsidize social places where people like to linger in order to draw them back into the city center.

The third business model will be around social apps with a local and topic dimensions. I am not talking about Bumble BFF[31], but platforms that will get local and regional traction in focus groups, and thus can facilitate group meetings. Apps such as TubeChat [32] or digital versions of the 'friendly bench' [33] point the way. Financial feasibility should work, once a critical mass is achieved and

[29] Personal estimate

[30] See the e.g. the Klokke in Mannheim `https://www.dieklokke.de/` for such an innovative meeting space.

[31] Bumble is a popular dating website, that recently also added a platonic friendfinder function.

[32] An app designed to get Londoner's talking on the subway `https://www.tube.chat/`

[33] `https://www.thefriendlybench.co.uk/`

thus people are convinced that they will find friendship candidates via such an app. I would indeed not be surprised if Couchsurfing, almost bankrupt during the pandemic, might make a major comeback with the hangout functionality and their extensive database of vetted and vouched profiles of outgoing and friendly people.

Suggestions for thought:
Look for and give one of the connection initatives in your area a try. They depend on curious and open people to get off the ground.

11.4 General Society and Policy

Good Neighbourhood

One of the key observations of sociologists is the breakdown of neighbourhood connections in the course of time since presumably the 1970ies. Whilst neighbours were often not deep friends such as school friends or university friends, they formed a warm support network. Parents having friendly relations often was the backdrop on which their children would form the close friendship later cherished in life. The move towards city life increased anonymity. When you google 'good neighbour' most links are about avoiding noise and unpleasant odours, dealing with bad neighbours and tackling antisocial behaviour or endeavouring to clean up the neighbourhood. It basically just means 'leave me alone and do not cause any inconvenience'. None of the links hint at actually befriending the neighbour (but not as a loneliness volunteer), inviting them for a barbecue or a get to know drinks, the 'normal course of action' if you were to ask the generation born in the 40s, 50s or 60s. American houses had porches, and it was a regular pastime to just swing over to a neighbour for a beer or coffee and a chat. English houses also came equipped with a standard social corner, call it the winter garden or tea corner, equipped with comfy armchairs, a sofa, a tea-table and if you were really lucky, a fireplace. If something urgent came up, you could easily dump your kids with the neighbour or ask the neighbour to come and help. Open gardens and doors are great for kids growing up.

I have always tried to break that stereotype or newer convention by just sticking to the older custom in the new metropolitan setting and can only recommend it. It raises a few eyebrows, but the benefits in connection are absolutely worth it. When neighbours in Hong Kong changed, and I brought the new (Chinese) couple moving in a loaf of bread and a bit of salt[34] on their moving-in-day, of course it raised a few eyebrows, also from their parents assisting with the move, but it broke the ice and over the next months I got to know the young couple a bit. The sharing economy was meant to solve this, however the promises have somewhat been slow in the realisation. A UK based app called Olio allows for sharing meals with neighbours to prevent food waste. An app called Peerby allows for expensive household appliances to be shared or rented. The analogue version are the wonderful stickers of pumpipumpe.ch, which you can stick on your letterbox or next to the nameplate at your apartment or house to let other people know which

[34] Old school European custom

appliances or items you can lend to neighbours. The best apps probably are the time exchanges like giveandget.ch, where services are offered within a pool. Thus you may get credits for helping a student on his maths homework and then use them to get help with picking your cherries and apples if you cannot get up in the tree yourself anymore. Whilst they are exchanges and not the classical general pay it forward neighbourly help of our grandparents generation, they equalize value of time and person (an hour help in the garden is valued the same as an hour help with doing the taxes) offering appreciation to everyone and taking status out of the equation.

Whilst there is no need to look back on earlier decade with rose-tinted glasses, and surely there were fights and disagreements with neighbours back then just as much, a thought I sometimes wonder about is whether the conflict resolution might not have been different. The village elder or the local parish priest carried substantially more moral and societal weight, and could wade in when disputes threatened social cohesion. Disputes over apple trees overarching somebody's garden or discussions on the distribution of fruit or dealing with unpleasant odours sometimes simply [might have not been allowed] to continue.

Good neighbourhoods are also marked by social occasions such as the village festival, the open day at school, various church occasions or a local marching band club, where the members of the neighbourhood get together in regular intervals and share food and drink and are merry. Such community events are often perfectly intergenerational and highly integrating as they welcome newcomers to the community. And they are also a little crazy and creative, they encourage people to do new stuff and bring them together. Examples of such activities might be having a portable vicar [35] or a barista bike bringing around afternoon coffee and cookies to the elderly that some children made for charity or the community[36]. The key here is that good neighbourhoods do not complain about a temporary invasion of their privacy, but welcome the initiative and enthusiasm. Just as pride is antithetical to friendship, insistence on privacy is antithetical to cordial society and neighbourhoods.

Suggestions for thought:

- Are you a sociable neighbour? What do you contribute to your neighbourhood?
- How well do you know your neighbours? Do you know them well enough that either of you would be feeling comfortable dumping your kids (or care-needing parents) with the other in case either of you fell severely ill?
- How insistent are you on your privacy?

[35]Pat Allerton driving around with mega speakers on a bike to get people to sing during Covidht tps://youtu.be/OzY9Ckqs178 - what a great initiative

[36]I misplaced the link, but it was a really lovely story

Public Places

Our city centers are essentially not anymore designed to bring people together, but to extract the maximum profit. Oldenburg, 1999, p.203 coins the phrase of the hostile habitat, and this is essentially what shopping malls have become. Our buildings are designed on a weird modern sense of aesthetics (see Heine, 2003 on an interpretation of the modern residential or office blocks), but places to retreat and calm down have become far and few in between. Cafes nowadays maximise throughput, but only a few are thoughtfully designed to bring people together and facilitate good conversations. If I sit down with a friend in a cafe in a central location for a latte and sit there for an hour or two, but without consuming food, essentially the cafe is running at a substantial loss concerning our occupying the seats. And going to cafes is for those who are in jobs where disposable income post tax, rent, insurance and groceries allows for regular coffee drinking or evenings out. What is necessary is for a general strategy to make social infrastructure accessible to everyone regardless of income.

Whilst the Greek and Roman societies were anything but egalitarian, being based on the populus fed by grain from the empire's colonies and plantation, their concept of having the center of town designated as the place for meeting and public politics has been utterly forgotten. In old Rome impromptu stages allowed for theatre to occur in the street, inlays into the ground allowed for simple board games, and similar the public baths were designed for people to loiter. You were there because that is where everyone else was. It was not a see and be seen, but a hang out and actually meet (and gossip and politicise and concoct intrigues etc.). When I was travelling in Barcelona and Rome in months where temperature was not scorching hot, I also encountered this atmosphere on the sides of the parks with hundreds of elderly people convening on park benches, discussing news of the day, playing chess, reading newspapers and drinking cheap wine. The air felt alive, and it felt as if 'the city' was there. Upon returning home to Germany passing an old peoples residence home, with dozens of elderly looking out of the window onto the street on their own, the difference could not have been more contrasting.

These simple observations easily highlight that if public institutions were prioritising social wellbeing and cohesion over the profitable use of public spaces, simple measures could generate immediate benefit. A start could be to rearrange the designation of public space use towards an increase in social interaction. When concern rose over the viability of restaurants and cafes after the first lock down of the Corona pandemic, in some cities permits were given to them to capture part of the pavement or street, with some cities converting streets into pedestrian areas to repurpose this space as outdoor areas. This could give rise to a permanent improvement, if stable chairs and tables were to be installed there, however post pandemic converted into public space without the duty but opportunity to consume at the restaurant. The rent for providing the space as an opportunity to sell to some people using it could be just to keep the tables and space clean, rather than pay financial revenue to the city.

A perfect initiative would be not to just put in more park benches, but include also ensembles of two chairs and a table in the middle, where two people can sit and face each other, put down a drink, and ideally also a permanent holster where a standardised light garden umbrella could be placed, which could be rentable from a nearby coffee shop or restaurant. The UK charity 'the friendly bench' [37] points the way with an innovative concept. Of course in design and deployment one might have to consider mobility (wheelchairs, transport routes in the community,...) and quite possibly experiment at first how these places best get accepted by a genuinely broad range of the community.

Public initiatives for mutual encounter

In recent years services for befriending have come up, but these are a bit artificial. When talking to people about 'Befriending', a concept I do actually find to have great merit, some people reported being taken aback by the label, seeing it artificial. I think an emphasis on enabling more the casual first encounter could be more promising. A start could be meeting corners or meeting tables. Currently we are all struggling through the Covid crisis, and given the whole mask-wearing duty and distancing situation the thought of getting together with a random person for a chat might not be terribly appealing. But at some point this will end. And then we will be thinking on how to connect our society again. There will for sure be demand, but it will be a matter for public and private initiatives to answer this demand.

I could even see the potential for a badge to be worn like a red poppy that signals 'I am happy to talk to someone'. This could be worn and work excellently in places like the London tube during an often 1 hour commute, where just chatting with a stranger might be such a wonderful diversion to an hour of scrolling on your phone through Facebook and Instagram posts. Coming back to the publicly provided seats and tables in public spaces, these could be labelled as meeting spaces, in the sense that if you sit down on one you signal anyone to join you and chat with you. Gone would be the days of lonely lunch breaks. Apps to support this process are good in theory, but they need scale and proximity to deliver, being able to bring people together there and then. Thus if I am standing in Bishopsgate corner[38] with an hour and a half to kill (15 min probably to walk to a potential meeting place such as a pub or cafe), it would be necessary to let me know in the moment if indeed there is someone within a 5-10 min radius who is also looking for someone to spend the lunchbreak with. One such application in the making is the website 'chatty cafe'[39]. This would be like the Viennese 'two hours with a stranger' described at length in Hunt, 2018-09-03. A beautiful public initiative to reach out and be friendly to people could be designed and run in Germany around the popular folk song 'Drink doch eene mit' [40]. This song by german band Blaeck Foess is about reaching out to an elderly poor guy standing outside of a pub who wants to join the circle for a beer, but cannot afford it. When one of the circle notices him, he goes out to bring a beer to the old man and invites him to the circle. It is a true sample of the Cologne carnival spirit. The report of Thurnell-Read, 2021 points in the same direction.

---

[37] `https://www.thefriendlybench.co.uk/`

[38] Office district in London

[39] `http://thechattycafescheme.co.uk`

[40] `https://youtu.be/ONgaGWWTHNU`

Societal support and its limits

According to Aristotle it was friendship that enabled virtue and its output was the participation as a fully endowed citizen in the polis. It is through friendship that we are connected to society, and society is the right background for us to practice our friendship. An argument can be made that the restoration of our society, currently so divided and antagonistic, should at least in part be achievable through friendship. It is through good civic friendship that we can bring disconnected people back into the fold of society. Whereas Putnam, 2000 proposes the revitalisation of social infrastructure (PTAs[41], schools, neighbourhoods) as the key task, I think the step needs to go hand in hand with building direct bilateral friendships. Indeed good friendships are what will stabilize and build up this society carrying social infrastructure. And for this purpose it is worth for society, and by this I do mean also the state, to think how we can enable these integrating friendships.

There are however limits to the degree to which society can make the forming of friendships easier in it. Certainly the right framework and infrastructure can be provided and improved and like Oldenburg, 1999 I would say that many of the western capitalist societies have done a really poor job of doing so encouraging consumerism over social connection, yet friendship cannot be imposed. There is always a personal, unique, surprising and chaotic element to a friendship springing up. Whether small or substantial, a spark needs to happen and cannot be forced. Friendship, like happiness, happens while we pursue other things. All a society can do is provide a fertile ground for these spontaneous first encounters to occur and then good infrastructure both physical and social for people to follow up easily and develop their friendships. For that society will need to get people away from their TVs, out of their homes and into parks, pubs and cafes.

11.5 Legal role for friendship

As our society becomes ever more atomic with many single households, single parents and families of convenience, questions may be raised on how friends can step into support roles in a legally safe framework. This is for the US legal system examined by Leib, 2011 and previously by Rosenbury, 2007, but similarly for both British and Continental legal systems the friend's role is not clarified or defined in any meaningful way. The friend as a trustee of health decisions, economic trustee or similar kin functions is still set in front of substantial legal hurdles. Some preeminent law scholars state that 'as far as friendship and love is concerned, lawyers should not be involved/concerned' [42].

Whilst I am no legal expert, I take great interest in the fact that the issues we have with defining robustly who our friends are, translate into real-world problems for a legal definition. Leib, 2011, p.14 [43] elaborates on such difficulties of

[41] Parent Teacher Association

[42] Udo di Fabio, former member of the German Supreme Court, interview 2020, 'Bei Freundschaft und Liebe haben Juristen nichts verloren' https://www.grandios.online/bei-freundschaft-und-liebe-haben-juristen-nix-verloren

[43] '"Close personal friend" means any person 18 years of age or older who has exhibited special care and concern for the patient, and who presents an affidavit to the health care facility or to the attending or treating physician stating that he or she is a friend of the patient; is willing and able to become

institutions of finding a suitable definition. Given the difficulties of reaching a widely acceptable definition for friendship from a psychological / sociological perspective as elaborated in chapter 2, it is unlikely for this to be a promising endeavour. Given the individuality of preferences for friendship and the substantial significance of such a definition, if based on it public and civil rights and duties would be imposed on it, I think it would create too much controversy. Regardless of the criteria, and as much as I am all in for recognizing the importance of fostering friendship in society, I think most of us would instinctively feel weird with the image of an AI algorithm sponsored by some state agency downloading our list of Facebook friends, and then according to a list of fixed criteria and even the most wonderful of sophisticated models were to partition the list into 'real friends' and 'acquaintances'. It just 'feels wrong'. Leib notes Chambers, 2000 to propose a friends registry (the word used in Chambers is a registered status of 'designated friends' though half the article is about its use for romantic cohabiting relationships), and this is a great idea. There could be a fixed form, to be filled out by two friends and then deposited with a public notary, office or institutions. The role would not be so much to oblige the friend to perform certain duties, but to make a public declaration to the state that certain rights are conferred to the friend, that are family like. As in Germany we like to regulate everything, this is made possible by the instrument of the 'Generalvollmacht' (letter of authority), for which a form can be downloaded from the Ministry of justice, and through which the general areas of concern can be addressed. Depending on the choices selected, the form's signature needs to be witnessed by a public notary to take effect.

Rights could be wide ranging or narrow. In part if we consider health care, it most likely would not be symmetric or reciprocal, by sheer situation. If I have a caring family, who I believe will respect my wishes, there is no need for me to involve my friend in decisions of whether I want life-extending measures which however might inflict substantial pain on me. If I know who in my family will take care of my kids in case I have a car crash, I am covered. However, not everyone's situation is like that, and enabling a close friend to be afforded similar rights as say a sister or brother is not easy in a number of jurisdictions. Here the process could be made relatively easy, however some ethical questions remain. A substantial question is whether the state is indeed capable of defining and subsequently imposing a necessary minimum set of conditions on the quality of such a friendship, in order to prevent abuse (in particular inheritance swindling of elderly). In general there remains the whole issue of allowing to give preference to friends over family, with most jurisdictions enabling such possibilities only in the trail of the LGBTQ movement and such equalization. Indeed, when doing the research for this book I heard a few stories of bereaved elderly living together as friends registering 'civil partnerships' precisely as friends in order to be legally enabled to care for each other when push comes to shove. Rights can include visiting rights in hospital or care homes, representation on medical concerns or financial concerns, taking care of the house in absence and being allowed to access it [44], there are several cases in which a public friendship registry for such a 'civil friendship'

involved in the patient's health care; and has maintained such regular contact with the patient so as to be familiar with the patient's activities, health, and religious or moral beliefs.'

[44] The giving of a key to a neighbour is of course an implicit approval.

could really help in practical situations. Whilst during Corona the authentication standards for receiving packages were suitably lessened and neighbourly help was allowed and encouraged even to pick up prescriptions from the doctor, such practices could easily be formalised in a digital public platform administered by a responsible public office. Reasonable obligations could be to be contactable in case of death, to support the finding of addresses of other friends in case of a funeral, or to be contactable in case of emergencies and accidents. In this context, I think the ease of arranging it is crucial. Whilst the rights and obligations can be substantial in meaning, and even if deep gratitude results from it, friends will not want to talk about it too much. Lewis, 1960, p.102 [45] would predict the standard reaction of the friend to be 'Don't mention it'. It is just a precautionary risk avoidance measure for a rainy day, and the act of formalising it a hassle, albeit one necessary given our current legal system. I believe there is an opportunity here for the public and legal profession to think through and design such a service to be of low complexity both in content and process. As potential experiences of abuse also accumulate, criteria should be developed against such abuse with data and experience collected over time. At this point the question of a state approved definition of friendship may arise. This is a deeply interesting and philosophical question to ask at what point a friendship can objectively be judged true from an outside perspective. When is a friendship objectively 'good enough' to warrant appointing the friend to be a trustee on quite substantial decisions of physical and financial well-being. Indeed if there ever is such an institution, desirable or not, that would be a 'civil friendship', one could conceive of a list of fundamental questions or criteria as a questionnaire handed out for self reflection for a set time before the final act of documenting the letter of authority by the official. At the current point however, we might just take note that the issue is one worth thinking about, especially to mitigate the social problems that the atomisation of society with more and more single households and ever decreasing family bonds imply for the future.

Secondary godparenting

One great way to both honour your best friends and really make them part of your family is to designate them to be 'secondary godparents'. It is customary to assign godparentage at birth, as this also assigns guardianship in case of a fatal accident of the parents[46]. As the children develop, and some of our friends stay close whereas others draw away, it might be an idea to assign secondary godparentage around the time of the 6th - 8th birthday. At that point the child's character has developed sufficiently to see a bit of compatibility of humour and interests to a family friend, allowing the parents to choose the best one to match it. Thus you make the friend into a 'funcle' or 'faunty'. Again, whilst not granting conditional custody to them, it remains a question whether such a loose role could or should be legally formalized. This would make it easier for a secondary godparent to be called upon to cover in times of severe sickness or similar of the parents.

[45] The stereotyped "Don't mention it" here expresses what we really feel.'

[46] Whilst cheesy and stereotypical (some stereotypes of which haven't aged well), I think the movie 'Life as we know it' (2010) with Katherine Heigl and Josh Duhamel explores this theme quite well and has some funny scenes.

Suggestions for thought:

- How comfortable would you feel assuming the role of health or financial guardian for a close friend?
- What requirements or safeguards would you want to be in place?
- If you have children - have you thought about secondary godparentage? Giving them a funcle or a faunty?

11.6 Coping with Covid and future pandemics

At the point of writing the third wave of lockdowns was in full swing, and bars, pubs and restaurants had been shut for several months and a reopening was unsure at best. At the time of completion, things - at least in England- were substantially looking up. On a gut feeling, given general arguments about ongoing integration of human habitats with hitherto untouched nature, it seems safe to say that this is not the last pandemic we have seen in the coming decades. Indeed, despite vaccinations, new mutations of the virus might imply that we are looking at a repeat in the winter 2021/2022. As the Covid is not defeated yet despite existent vaccines, and other pandemics are on the horizon, the capability of societies to hunker down and reduce social flow velocity will continue to evolve. Thus, given what I put together on general friendship, I thought I would put together a couple of thoughts on this theme too.

The Covid pandemic has largely made us concentrate on our strong ties, that means family and close friends. Not everyone had those contacts available in proximity. Human contact is vital to well-being, and we must find a way of ensuring more of it in a safe way for future lock-downs. We must from a society point of view ensure that no one is left behind in terms of social needs. I have no doubt that we will get offline and meet people again. We will rediscover our appreciation for the sensation of meeting in pubs, restaurants, cafes and doing sports, seeing art and listening to live music. In the pandemic, public discussions involved terms of 'locking away the elderly/vulnerable for shielding' or 'locking away the young (to prevent super spreading)' (e.g. Golubev, AG and Sidorenko, 2020). I think we should aim to not do either.

In recent years a lot of thought has gone into intergenerational housing, with the beautiful image of grandparents or general elderly passing on their wisdom and affection to their grandchildren's generation. From a protection against an infectious disease perspective, such intergenerational households are the exact opposite of what could be desirable.[47] School closures were justified by the transmission vectors of children still interacting with parents and grandparents. The socially winning candidate could be groups of 4-8 elderly[48], coming together in

[47]It is of course an item worthy of debate whether we want to deny ourselves such wonderful concepts as intergenerational households simply on considerations of functionality under pandemics such as Covid.

[48]This number is given by requirements of board games or other social activities, allowing also for a temporary subdivision according to preferences. It is not evaluated from a scientific perspective, though the results of such an analysis would be highly interesting.

living communities. These can be materially supplied externally, but can support themselves for both their daily practical and social needs. Likewise, families with smaller children could strategically plan to form bubbles based on the children's age and compatibility for each other, ensuring continual social contact and developing social skills at all ages. And for those without strong family ties, similar measures must be undertaken. For those, the sentence 'friends are the family we choose' might become a very tangible reality.

I suppose the question boils down to how we can create village communities, or larger than atomic households in cities. Thus two houses forming an elderly bubble could be next to a house with a family bubble, with an open door policy in a non-pandemic situation and restrictions otherwise. Different concepts on how to do this can materialise, but as a society we must get our bubbles right. We must - also individually - prepare for the next pandemic in now building social groups of friends, that we can lock down with. Computational modelling research like Mizrahi, Shekhidem, and Stern, 2020 amended with insights from social networks (potentially modelling social including friendship needs) might point the way how to create pandemic resilient societies that still allow for functional social contact. We must learn **'smart bubbling'**.

Proximity in such a situation becomes a key factor. Even public transport was to be avoided to reduce infection risk. Thus a social KPI could be something like 'number of strong ties within a 10 min radius not using public transport' as a measure for social resilience for future scenarios. Alternatively, when planning for lockdowns and restrictions again with Tier systems[49] or similar, it could in future situations arise also a situation where within a low tier level we initiate the phase of moving in together into the temporary bubbles while cases are still lower in order not to spread as bubbles form.

Suggestions for thought:

- If a new lockdown came in a week, would you know the bubble you would choose?
- How are your pandemic-compatible social contacts (e.g. walking distance 10 min)?
- Have you explored moving in with friends or could you make space available in your house for a lonely friend (or family member)?

[49]The United Kingdom used a Tier system to implement different severities of restrictions per regions in line with current infection spread levels

Chapter 12

Conclusion

For casual reading only 12.4 and 12.5

12.1 Further Research

The main objective of the research project at the base of this book is to identify how friendships can be strengthened in midlife so that in later life loneliness is reduced. The theoretical construct developed here to explain friendship thus needs to be validated, even though the collected evidence gives it some plausibility. It is at this point unlikely that future investigation will unearth common themes that dominate to such a degree that a uniform theory of friendship is conceivable. Friendship is individual to a substantial degree, and friends as Rath, 2006 noticed play different roles to each other. It would be thus great to validate and quantify what needs which groups of people have both in midlife and elder life, and then to see whether there can be interventions to nudge people gently towards interacting in meaningful ways that build the friendships towards each other tailored to these needs.

For me the major insight for future friendship research is the loss of information and depth, that attempts to reduce friendship to a two, three, four or six-factor model and validate them with various survey and statistical methods incur. Friendship is a nuanced relationship, probably significantly more nuanced than romantic relationships, and needs to be treated as much. Characteristics or aspects that are crucial to one person could be negligible to the next. Reducing friendship quality to a set of one to three questions on social support, emotional sharing, discussing personal items or joint activities as is common practice in public surveys is likewise falling short of many people's diverse understanding of what friendship means to them. The need for such procedure within large scale multi-focus population surveys is of course self-evident, but for genuine research of the causes of loneliness the specific dimension in which people feel lonely (i.e. the friendship 'need') probably is a crucial ingredient of the analysis.

Before putting this to proper and practical use there is the question of how to validate the stability of the individual items further, and measure how each of the factors are influenced by age, gender, culture, etc., and impacts friendship satisfaction. This will happen as more and more texts on friendship are worked through in the above described manner, and preparing a survey study to corroborate on a larger scale the relative significance that the literature above implied.

A lot of past sociological research tried to identify general social mechanisms on the general concepts of self disclosure or support, yet used very specific questions only capturing subaspects of these themes (see Hall, 2012b for such a list of questions). It thus should be possible to recode and thus utilize a lot of past research for integration into the variable set described above. Unfortunately, open data policies only have become popular in the last five to three years, and it will be interesting what part of generated data can genuinely be salvaged from past surveys and studies for this meta study. The rewards however can potentially be significant, ideally generating insight on how to enhance and strengthen friendships on a character, gender, age or other trait configuration.

Furthermore - while romantic relationships or general family relationships are substantially and structurally different in structure than friendships, a survey could likewise be conducted on how family members score on these scales and importance, and in what aspects significant differences occur to friendships. This would also provide additional evidence to the debate of whether friendships and kinships are complementary, substitutable or to what degree they can overlap.

12.2 Topics for future research

Friendship in non WEIRD cultures
A criticism often made of western sociological studies is that they essentially only sample the WEIRD population (western educated industrial rich democratic), and within that the psychology, sociology or communications students between the age of 18-22. In this book I tried to generalise as far as possible beyond this. The expansion along the cultural dimension originally also intended to be within scope will have to wait for a future edition. There is some material discussing friendship in philosophical or religious studies oriented book of collected essays, such as Rouner, 1994 or Oliver Leaman, 1996. There are also anthropological analyses such as Desai and Killick, 2010 or Bell and Coleman, 1999. However, they are more representative of a particular school of thought rather than genuine data driven surveys of friendship preferences such as the sociological studies or book length opinion pieces such as the philosophical or qualitative sociological writings referenced in the definition section. The texts are thus not long enough to be able to apply the counting themes method robustly. Furthermore, several of the contained essays essentially are strongly influenced by a western philosophical tradition, and thus compare an image of e.g. Chinese or Islamic friendship to that of Aristotle, thus making the hypothesis plausible that the image of friendship given is as representative for the cultural sphere in question as Aristotle is for western contemporary friendship. It would be extremely helpful for international researchers to generate replication studies of Hall, 2012b and Rath, 2006. Divergences in preferences could then be compared to the literary tradition and its influence. A suggestion for a suitable standardised questionnaire is contained in the appendix and will be updated pending feedback on practicalfriendship.com.

Friendship in Ageing
Analysing what friendship is like in ageing was possible thanks to the excellent

anthropological and sociological material compiled in particular by Matthews, 1986, Adams and Blieszner, and Greif, 2009. Similarly, public surveys have rendered some insight into the matter on a general level, and in particular quantified the extent of loneliness in age. However, what is still outstanding is really survey based data on what are the concrete bottlenecks to living good friendships in age. Is it the difficulty of meeting new people? Is it financial or health obstacles to get out of the door to meet with people, new or old acquaintances alike? Are the needs really changing towards participation and affection, or are there clusters of people who want to live friendships exactly like they did when they were 15, 35 or 55 - drinking, exploring and joking? What friendship roles are needed in ageing, so that people's friendship need is fulfilled, i.e. people are not lonely? So really figuring out priorities on a broad and representative sample of elderly I think is a first necessary step before proceeding. With a view towards the sociologist view of seeing loneliness as an absence of social support, it might be necessary to separate the phenomenon of support-loneliness from enjoyment-participation loneliness and start collecting focused data on this for the ageing population.

Loneliness vs. Connectedness

Loneliness is indeed a plague, however as a hunch things are not all as bad. One major positive takeaway from Covid is that people all across society have experienced loneliness themselves in the lockdowns, and the topic is now open under discussion across society. All people now need are opportunities and tools, and as a society we are good to go. I would thus like to strike a much more optimistic line to say that there is genuine hope that we can build a more connected society. There are now a number of papers measuring loneliness and comparing figures which parts of which population are how lonely. However little is being said why they are lonely, and which measures to connect people have tried (and failed with). Research should also reflect this: it is not enough to just say 'our societies are this lonely according to that measure and that is bad'. We need more studies like the Roseto study of old, seeing what societies and communities manage to create connectedness and learn to emulate them. We need to look to alternative communes in Berlin-Mitte, to warm church communities, to Oxford colleges and nomad caravans and learn what they are doing right. Anthropology, psychology and sociology are equally required to rise to the challenge. Ideally we identify good practices and avenues to bring lonely people back into the society in general and into friendship in particular. There is no reason to follow Hertz, 2020 line of argument, pronounce doom and gloom and accept this century as the lonely century. Lets find out what we can do better to connect and then get society to do it together with us.

Social joy capital

There are by now dozens of measures of social capital around, centering on concepts of needs being met (Alkire, 2002 and Alkire and Foster, 2011), wellbeing (Diener, Emmons, et al., 1985 and Diener and Arora, 2009), and mutual social support and trust (Putnam, 2000). These are vital considerations. Having friends is great, but it does not substitute for the needs of having food, feeling empowered and developing and being supported by the wider community. Life is practical. And yet, if friendship (or using the wider term of 'close relationship') is not about survival but gives meaning to survival, we need to think about how we can look at our society with those glasses. Our care system might perfectly well prevent functional poverty and meet all our support needs, yet our society could still feel dreadfully cold, depressed and unenviable.

I think developing an operationalisation of the Max-Neef needs (see 6.11) to evaluate how we are doing on meeting of the needs to laugh, play, discuss and interact would be an excellent step to tackle joy-loneliness[1]. Administering this over time to different parts of the global population and integrating with other studies and survey could gain vital understanding of what needs are most painfully failing to be satisfied. I am not sure whether social joy capital or more elaborately Max-Neef social joy capital would be the right term for the concept of the potential of our society to experience joy through social connection, but it could be an appropriate term to begin with.

To be clear is that I do not advocate jumping to overall happiness, indeed there is a whole strand of literature devoted to this topic (e.g Demir, 2015 and Demir and Suerner, 2018). I do not want to disparage the phenomenal scholarship exemplified in trying to support people in their strife towards ultimate happiness or Eudaimonia. But what I mean at this point is to focus on the portion of happiness that is unequivocally caused through the interaction with friends measurable and determine its nature in the specific cases. Thus a person might be poor, of sick health and have deficient support, yet might find moments of happiness and joy when they are laughing together with an equally afflicted friend. This moment of bliss, laughter, connection and being understood is enough (for some) to carry them through an entire month of affliction and adversity. And as a society we should know from a human perspective, how we are doing in enabling these moments.

Once we have a clear image of a concept of social joy capital, and how to measure it robustly, we can then commence to evaluate and benchmark different loneliness interventions. While some interventions might predictably work, other quite possibly profane measures that might be simple to organize and administer might be equally effective. However, we need to move beyond the framework that evaluates friendship in the same way it does anti-depressant pills or CBT[2].

12.3 Overall state of friendship research

While this book drew on a range of sources from different schools of thought, it can be only considered an intermediate step in this line of investigation. Whilst identifying several core themes, putting it together to a framework and a process conjecture, and then showing how these insights can help us have better friendships, this needs to be subjected to scientific scrutiny, and that means testing: Testing by generating a large dataset for preferences, testing by surveying responses to proposed measures and testing by discussion with different stakeholder groups. A lot of assertions in friendship literature are well argued and feel intuitively right, but essentially are untested or uncorroborated by suitable broad sociological data. I think promising signs are on the horizon as the last years have seen a

[1] I.e. the loneliness the feeling of which is caused by the absence of social joy.
[2] Cognitive behavioural therapy

substantial rise in publications on many fronts dealing with the topic within the different schools of thoughts. With some luck the cross-fertilization will increase with philosophers picking up where their theoretical deliberations are out of tune with sociological observations on actual practices and discuss the consequences. Similarly, sociological analysis should move on from exchange based or disclosure models to considering a more holistic view of friendship closer to the intuitive understanding of lay people. I do not doubt that I will need to revisit this text in a few years as actual data and publications corroborate some hypotheses stated in this text, validating the effectiveness of some practice or thought suggestions and disprove of other hypotheses or recommendations made.

To finish with a very broad sweeping assertion: Sociologists (in extremis) are not interested in friendship, but simply in understanding how and how much social support the institution of friendship can contribute to society. To which the philosopher (in extremis) would say - that is the wrong and irrelevant question about friendship, I do friendship because it is beautiful and I love it. It would be my hope that sociologists would start gathering more philia-friendship qualitative and quantitative data in their surveys, and philosophers discuss this data meaningfully with them. Thus on this basis the two could join forces to help us all to improve our friendships both for a better supported and happier society. Once they do, I think - contrary to Blatterer, 2015, p.186 and Eve, 2002 that there is every case to be made for a 'dedicated sociology of friendship' with concrete applications and benefits to our society. Indeed I would go one step further and propose the label of **philiology** - combining philia and logos - as an apt label in its own right for the interdisciplinary study of friendship combining the methods of the disciplines of sociology, psychology, philosophy and anthropology to gain insight in this social phenomenon.

> Regardless of the debate on semantics, support is at worst the wrong (instrumental-transactional) and at best a secondary and subordinate way to think about friendship. The right measure for friendship is the contribution to quality of life experience with the facets of enjoyment, humour, personality development and meaningfulness of relationships.

Data strategy for future research

One thing I hope for the future is that a standard set of preference or role oriented questions emerges in friendship research, that could be raised every time such research is conducted and data is generated. This most likely needs to be shorter than the questionnaire attached in the appendix, but as diverse populations are sampled, over time should be designed to allow a combination of the data towards a meta study much like Hall, 2011, just more granular. It would also allow local researchers in non-core anglophone countries (US, UK) to generate datasets on friendship research that can be considered on equal terms and validity for publication.

Something that repeatedly puzzled me throughout the time of study is that whilst every psychometric or sociometric paper elaborated at great length the validity of the quantitative methods employed, little or no semantic discussion of the suitability of the questions submitted to study participants was done[3]. In several papers the actual questions used to measure concepts of openness, positivity or connection strength were even omitted. Whilst it may not need to be part of actual papers in the future, at least offline discussions or justifications why particular questions were chosen from a set of alternatives might be helpful. What kind of openness or emotional intimacy is being queried, on what level is reciprocity or acceptance defined, and what assumptions on human interactions are included might be conceptually more interesting than whether yet another statistical consistency measure is achieved to be able to apply reasonably robustly a certain sociometric factoring method.

Another great study to consider might be a mapping exercise for association of attributive sentences to friendship themes. This would take the form of stating an uncommented desirable property for friendship, such as virtue, openness or trust, and then query people which sentences most closely represented their understanding of e.g. trust in a friendship. In order to address Fisher's criticism of the disconnect between the sociologists understanding of friendship and the lay 'common' understanding, we need to look into specific aspects of friendship and how people see them, before we can build a general understanding and relative weighting. This will need to precede the development of a standardised friendship priorities questionnaire.

It would be phenomenal, both for journalism as well as anthropological research to centrally collect (anonymized) interview transcripts on friendship. Interviews are time expensive. Several books, despite beautifully written, are clearly based on the personal collection and experiences of friendships of the writer and maybe a dozen or two dozen interviews. It would be great to democratize the access to such material by generating such an interview database and potentially include searching/tagging. This would allow people who write beautifully but don't have such access to the material to write better founded books or features[4] for the general public to popularize insight into good friendship and its practices.

12.4 Implementation

I hope that some of this research will find its way into apps fostering friendship development and maintenance, and organisational programs fostering friendship in society. Whilst the Corona pandemic has put in-person close friendship development mostly on a back burner, I am absolutely certain that this will be a key focus area once the pandemic ends. Given the option to meet in person, we will appreciate this more than ever. However, the tools and practices tried and tested during the pandemic will not go away but complement our way of interacting. I hope the material collected in this text to be used in three key ways, and if this book is credited to have contributed to just one of them, then my sabbatical year will have been well spent:

[3] By this I mean the question whether e.g. going in and out of each others houses is the question to ask to measure solidarity, or whether laughing is the best question for positivity, vs. all the other alternative questions equally suitable.

[4] According to a workshop by Sirin Kale for the Guardian on 2020-04-06 a good feature includes about three case studies (=interviews) and two expert opinions.

- I hope to bring thoughts and impulses to the discussion of friendship and the broadening of themes of future self-help books on friendship that most likely will be more fluidly written and addressing a broader audience with a more entertaining writing style.

- I hope that digital tools, which develop friendships, profit from the insights and connect us in more meaningful ways.

- Finally I hope that in particular the practices of friendship maintenance among those aged 30 to 60 receive specific societal focus, and that we thus avoid the loneliness issues we are currently so painfully aware in the population of elderly in western society.

12.5 Five step program

As a final and very practical part, I hope that **you personally** will review and adopt two of the following **five steps towards better friendship** (or print and fill out the longer **pledge form** in the appendix):

1. I will at minimum match my time spent on Netflix and Co. with time spent with friends.
2. I regularly try to invite my friends for lunch, dinner or a stay over.
3. I will take more photos, give my friends gifts or write postcards and letters.
4. I will choose two friendship potentials[a] with whom I want to develop the friendship further over the next year.
5. I will try to introduce friends of mine to each other (become a platonic cupid).

[a]This can include former friends who I lost touch with however have a good feeling about.

And if it works for you, recommend this practice for other friends.

Final questions:

1. What of the multitude of various suggestions do you think you will try out?
2. Did you raise any of these topics with friends for discussions?
3. Do you have a different attitude to (some of) your friendships?

12.6 Epilogue

Clive, your partner and you ended up having a number of discussions over the coming weeks. The flow of themes and conversation triggers was constant. It did feel a bit weird when Clive brought his school copy of Aristotle's Nicomachean ethics to the pub, 'just to look things up', yet a week later that is precisely what you ended up doing when discussing reciprocity. Aside from friendship, further and wider topics in psychology and philosophy are explored in the evenings discussions.

After a few months events took another turn. The social worker Martina - teacher No 3 showed up by herself and seemingly 5 min in got messaged by the other two that they had to do emergency shifts to cover classes, and hence had to both bail on her. Not missing the opportunity, Clive approached her, and asked to buy her a beer to the confession that he had been eavesdropping on them the past weeks, and that their conversation had provided ample material for the subsequent evening conversations. Knowing Clive for a while you suspect that this beer might not have been entirely altruistic in nature. Indeed after a raised eyebrow and minor side remark, Clive admitted that the great material of the conversations had not been the only source of interest of his in the triad. Teacher No 3 was not only rather attractive, but also had been blessed with that sharp 'take no prisoners' wit which Clive cultivated as well [5].

A week later the three surprised you and Clive in the evening to join you and turn the table on you three, to hear about what their conversations had in turn triggered. Clive's humour and story telling do their share in drawing the other ones into the group in a most casual way. Your contribution on a few anecdotes from University life of how Clive regularly got himself (and you for that matter) into puddles of various degrees of severity likewise lightens up the atmosphere. At this point it turns out that teachers 1 (the classics teacher) and 2 (the sociologist) not only are colleagues, but also been married for a long time as the result of Martina's scheming and a rather cringeworthy but adorable setup.

After a joyous first evening together, the repeat invitation is just a formality. Over time the six of you bond and spend the Tuesdays evening together, not only discussing friendship but many other topics. After a years time and much teasing on behalf of the group, even Clive's novel is nearing its completion suitably called 'Morning conversations in pubs'.

> Finally, if after reading all this, you encounter a classicist or philosopher, a social scientist or psychologist, or a social worker or self-help writer, please go into a pub with them, buy them a pint and invite them to discuss the wonderful topic of friendship with you.

[5]Clive's motto always was 'you may loose a friend, but never a good joke'.

Pledges of ______________________ for the year ________

		End of year effectiveness rating					EoY
DO	**Personal Habits**	+ +	+	0	-	- -	✓ ×
	I will send a few postcards from my holidays to my friends						
	I will try to spend as much time socialising with friends as I do on Netflix and Co.						
	I will reflect of how much of my friends say I actually retain, how much I am actually listening to them rather than have them listen to me						
	I will accept the good and allow my friends to give me gifts, do me favours, help me in life even if I cannot reciprocate in the moment, that week or even this year.						
	Communication habits	+ +	+	0	-	- -	✓ ×
	When communicating with my friends, I will try to add in as many layers as possible, and try to give them my full attention						
	I will try to be more appreciative of my friends, their strengths and be grateful how they bring joy into my life						
	I will stop using the word 'busy' and 'toxic' in my communication with friends						
	I will think of who among my friends needs encouragement and a little nudging and will offer to be a caring but slightly annoying accountability buddy						
	I will be honest with my friends, and whilst not becoming judgemental, tell them if I think their behaviour is inconsistent with how I see them as a friend						
	General habits for maintenance	+ +	+	0	-	- -	✓ ×
	I will try to once a month host my friends for lunch or dinner						
	I will try the rule of six – focusing on six friends for the coming year						
	I will think about a good gift for three of my friends for this year						
	I will try out a new hobby, that a current friend enjoys and that is suitable of pursuing it together						
	I will start or continue to work on a project with a friend of mine						
	Making new friends and fostering new friendships	+ +	+	0	-	- -	✓ ×
	I will join Meetup, Internations and maybe one or two local social organisations						
	I will think of who of my friends from different circles could also become friends if introduced						
	In my organisation or local community I will think of ways how we can improve opportunities for random people to meet and get to know each other						
	I will reconnect with some old 'rust' friends from my early years						
	Thinking about friendship	+ +	+	0	-	- -	✓ ×
	I will reflect on attitudes of mine on friendship, like privacy, closeness, selflessness and see how differences in attitudes may affect current friendships						
	I will think on how streamlined and similar my friends are, in particular whether I have friends outside my social class, educational level, gender or race ?						
	I will think about three suggestions my friends made how I may change my life for the better and potentially even try them out for a while						
	I will think about what is most important to me about my friendships ? What makes them precious and why I wouldn't want to miss my friends in my life ?						
	I will think about how I share my life and how I found out most about my friends, whether by intentional and focused sharing or casual mentioning along other activities						

And at the end of this year, I will go to www.practicalfriendship.com and submit my answers anonymously. ☺☺☺

Thanks and credits

Mama & Papa for maintaining friendships - in particular to Sasa & Honza and Karin & Ralf, who have stayed friends with our family ever since you all met at RWTH Aachen in the 70ies.
Bettina & Johannes for indulging my quirkiness and keeping the familial bonds together all those years when I was abroad.
And Mama & Günter for so persistently reading through my text during the Covid lockdowns.
For friendship over the years:
David, Daniel, Johannes & Carola, Florian and Jens from early school years,
The Oxford group - Chris, Adam, Ben & Hannah, Helen, Duncan, Dan, Steve & Hayley and Andy,
BASF both as direct colleagues as well as the Nachwuchsprogramm, in particular Roland & Alex, Konstanze & Boris, Heidrun, Axel, Christine and Markus, Yasemin & Alex.
Sao Paulo, Ulm und Essen, Japan and Hong Kong, and here I would like to single out Cristina, Richard, Chris & Anja, Douglas and Fr. William, Michael & Melody and Makabe-san, Wai-Yee, Krupa and Ada.
For the support and encouragement in this book:
Jeremy Woodall for tipping the balance on me starting this book at the lunch in Cafe 8, Nick Rawlins for confirming the validity on this being a proper research proposal, Sarah Harper to accept me at the Institute of Population Ageing, and Kenneth Howse, George Leeson and Emily Schuler for critical comments along the way of the research journey in Michaelmas and Hilary Term '20/'21
I am especially indebted to Joon Nak Choi to provide continuous critical feedback and reading recommendations throughout the two years of preparation and writing.

Whilst I always felt passionate about friendship, I have had my low points, and lost friends because of breaking some of the rules set out in this book. This in some cases left me deeply sorry for years afterwards. So if you now see this book and think me a hypocrite, then a.) yes, in relation to some anecdotes you may be right, and b.) the episode probably contributed to my learning and found its way into the book in some form.
Finally I would like to name some people who have inspired me in passages of this book:
John C was one of the perfect spiders-in-the-web in my student church community introducing people; Tommy for the introduction to British humour and the proof that teachers can form friendships with former students; Sigi for good cheer (german style) and the proof that a manager can form friendships with former subordinates; Rosana for showing and implementing warmth in the workplace; Bastian and Inga for providing a great work environment in the BASF Analytics team; Jeremy, Alison and Frank as examples of how to manage good alumni networks fostering connections; the friends of my grandfather keeping my grandmother company for the better part of two decades after his passing away.

Loneliness / Friendship Need Questionnaire

Please answer on the middle section how much you agree with the statement, and pick five statement that either give you the biggest joy (left) or biggest pain (right).

	X	**I have in my life ...**	Someone				no one
			++	+	0	-	- -
1		... who listens to me					
2		... who really cares for me					
3		... with whom I can do projects and collaborate					
4		... with whom I can just spend time / hang out					
5		... who invites me for lunch or dinner					
6		... with whom I can play games (board, card, computer)					
7		... who helps me to change for the better					
8		... who loves me					
9		... who thinks my ideas are important and worthwhile					
10		... who helps with 'stuff' like baby sitting or taxes					
11		... who encourages me to attend social gatherings					
12		... with whom I can share my private thoughts					
13		... who shares his/her private thoughts with me					
14		... who makes me laugh					
15		... who expands my horizon					
16		... who is together with me part of a group of friends					
17		... who encourages or challenges me					
18		... who stands up for me					
19		... who understands me and can relate to my life					
20		... who respects or admires me					
21		... who stimulates me intellectually					
22		... who gives me advice and guidance					
23		... who teaches me and/or learns from me					
24		... who is there for me					
25		... who gives me gifts					

		I am	not constrained			constrained	
			++	+	0	-	- -
1		The free time I have at my disposal to spend with friends					
2		My current living situation					
3		By my ability to move about					
4		My financial situation					
5		My general health (hearing, seeing, remembering)					
6		'Content' in my life					

The Friendship Inventory v1.0 — Practicalfriendship.com

Welcome to the 'Friendship Inventory' of Practical Friendship. This is the companion form for the friendship personality test linked to on **http://personalitytest.practicalfriendship.com** (**for which you find the QR code in the bottom right to access with your smart phone**).

The system is still under development. It is likely that emphasis and nuances of individual properties and attributes will change over the next years. It is recommended to enter the values with a pencil after the self assessment, in order to adjust them after explicit feedback from friends, who did the survey with you as the 'study object'. The recommended sequence is as follows:

1. You take the self assessment from the aggregate view of your three closest friends. This will most likely take about 15 min as it requires a bit of thinking and asks you to imagine how your friends think about you as a friend. It is designed to give you a first glance at your key strengths, relationship attitudes and activity preferences.
   This fills the first sheet of the Friendship Inventory.
2. You take the 'for a friend' assessment repeatedly for your 5-10 best and close friends, as you see fit. After the first 'run' you will have no difficulty in completing a go in about 6-8 minutes, as you just react on impulse. You can even just allocate them initially into the form with penc without having taken the test. The test will most likely not be surprising for the main role your friends already perform. The added value of goir through the application of the test is discovering which other roles your friends also fulfil for you without you noticing and appreciating it as much as you might like to.
3. You review your 'Essentials – my company of heroes' and your 'Social circle' to see if there is any friend that is still missing.
4. For all your friends you fill in one line in the friendship plan (in pencil), guessing your role for them (i.e. how you help them most) and in the coming year making plans how you can prioritise this.
5. Not immediately, but over time you let your friends know what you appreciate about them. Practicing gratitude and appreciation is a minor but wonderfully warm practice in friendships.
6. As your friends as well take the test, you might also get feedback. Some of them in the spur in the moment might even share the test properties with you. You can use this feedback to adjust your overview of strengths, relationship attitudes and activities.

Explanations of items all to be found on the website www.practicalfriendship.com. This website will grow with recommendations for reading, activities and as resource set for this toolset.
Please feel free to reach out to me at Christian [at] practicalfriendship.com for feedback and further comments. And whilst I am not asking for money, if you feel this tool has helped you, I would like to ask you to go to https://www.givewell.org/charities/top-charities and take your pick for a donation.

Many thanks,

Christian

Personal Inventory

Strengths		Relationship Attitudes		Activity preferences	
Patience and Peace		Benevolence		Dirt time and hangout	
Positivity		Consideration and Priority		Work or pursue interest tog.	
Proactiveness		Pride in friends		Allowing Expression of Self	
Humility / Interest in Others		Trust and Confidentiality		Encouragement and Challenge	
Social Ease and Connectability		Common Memory		Expansion and Discovery	
Fun and Humour		Mutual Beliefs		Guidance / Giving Direction	
Energy and Determination		Loyalty		Practical Help	
Honesty and Integrity		Mutual Interests		Standing by / Being there	
Reliability and Consistency		Mutual Understanding		Vocal Support	
Acceptance and Tolerance		Reciprocity – Being needed		Effect change and growth	
Kindness and Warmth		Openness and Vulnerability		Generosity and Gifts	
Intelligence and Curiosity		Love, Affection and Gratitude		Teaching and Learning	
'Good Personality'/Virtue		Enjoyment		Bonding in a circle	
		Independence and Priority		Hospitality / Communion	

My key Friendship Types

(Ways in which I benefit my friends)

Type 1	Score	Type 2	Score	Type 3	Score

It is vital to be noted that these are not the only ways in which you can or do do good and meaningful things for your friends. It is just an indication what you are best at, and what your friends most value in you. There is no reason that in the right (or wrong) moment, with the right attitude and a bit of practicing other roles will come to you. Thus even if you are a clown by nature, there may be the situation when a close friend of yours is deeply sad and your clown qualities are not needed, and you just have to sit there and listen quietly like it or not.

The Friendship Inventory v1.0 Practicalfriendship.com

ese fields should likewise be filled out first with pencil according to intuition and gut feeling, but better after the dedicated age of the questionnaire on practicalfriendship.com. The benefit is the suggestion of further Friendship Types for your isting friends and showing you that both your essential and social circle are more complete than you might be imagining.

ne core group

Role	Primary	Secondary
he Best Friend		
he Coach		
he Partner in Crime		
he Clown		
he Mind opener		
he Mentor		
he Mom		
he Dad		

ly social circle

Role	Primary	Secondary
The Cheerleader		
The Rust Friend		
The Connector		
The Daredevil		
The Neighbour		
The Younger Sister/Brother		
The Saint and Idol		
The Work Pal		
The Discussant		
The Best Friends Partner		
The Single Friend		
The Running Mate		

The Friendship Plan v1.0 Practicalfriendship.com

his form is to provide an individual overview how you are good for your friends. You can generate this via the self assessment or better via direct eedback after your friends filled out the friend's assessment and tell you the roles they appreciate you most for. The link to the Friendship Personality est and Explanations of items all to be found on www.practicalfriendship.com

Name You can use Initials only	Their Roles (for you)	My Roles (for them)	Key Activities (to meet their needs)

Friendship Survey v1.0

Group	Question	BFr	Fr	Acq
A	X and I have spent lots of time hanging out with each other			
A	X and I teach and/or learn from each other			
A	X is reliable and consistent			
A	I can trust X – X treats what I tell her/him in confidence			
A	X respects my independence			
B	X and I have worked together on tasks, projects and interests			
B	X and I are part of a circle of friends which he/she actively maintains			
B	X is very accepting and tolerant of other people			
B	X and I share lots of common memories			
B	X makes our friendship a priority in his life			
C	I can express myself with X, who listens very well			
C	X is hospitable and loves to invite me over			
C	X is kind and warm with people			
C	X and I have mutual beliefs and worldview			
C	X is a very close friend			
D	X both encourages and challenges me to achieve my potential			
D	X is peaceful and patient with people			
D	X is intelligent and curious of a lot of things			
D	X and I have different beliefs and worldviews			
D	X has lots of time			
E	I can discover new interests, hobbies and topics through my interactions with X			
E	X is a very positive person			
E	X has a virtuous character			
E	X is loyal to me and our friendship			
E	X is well off – not worried about financial issues			
F	X provides me guidance in difficult situations / talks me through pros and cons			
F	X is very considerate of other people			
F	X respects my privacy			
F	X and I share interests and hobbies			
F	X is rich and has high status			

Group	Question	CFr	Fr	Acq
G	X helps me practically in my life			
G	X overall has a humble character			
G	X and I live together / do not care about our privacy towards each other			
G	X understands me on a deep level			
G	X knows a lot of people			
H	X sometimes is just there for me			
H	X is agreeable and easy to relate to			
H	X wishes me well / roots for me			
H	X both gives and takes in our relationship			
H	X is beautiful / has an attractive appearance			
I	X supports me vocally and stands up for me when I am not there			
I	X is fun and has a great humour			
I	X tries to help me however she/he can			
I	X is open and vulnerable with me			
I	X is healthy, fit and mobile			
J	I have changed in positive ways because of X			
J	X is very energetic			
J	X is proud of me and appreciates what I do			
J	X is loving and affectionate with me			
J	X knows a lot of things and has a lot to say			
K	X is generous with me			
K	X is honest and authentic			
K	X and I are equal to each other, differences in status and rank are irrelevant to us			
K	I really enjoy the company of X			
K	X lives nearby			

The recommended way to fill it out is to ask the participant to pick three people, one close or best friend, one general friend and one acquaintance. Alternatively the three closest friends can be chosen.

The questions should be answered on a Likert scale from 1-5 (1 not applicable, 5 very applicable and important), and the total within a group of five questions should be given a cap, e.g. 15 points to introduce opportunity cost.

This document can be downloaded from www.practicalfriendship.com

Appendix A

Resources for improving friendship

In this book I collected a number of suggestions on how to improve ones own friendships as well as the opportunities for friendship for the people around us. In this section I would like to provide links to tools and resources provided on the internet and elsewhere to achieve this.

A.1 Getting to know yourself

I think one of the best tests to find out what you like and in what kind of activities you are happiest (and thus most likely to make friends in) is the 240 question character strength survey [1] with the theoretical background being provided in Peterson and Seligman, 2004 and the lay version in Seligman, 2004. Similarly a simple MBTI / 16 personality test may allow you to compare yourself with the advice given in Birch, 2018b, Birch, 2018a, Birch, 2019 or Bennett, 2018, van Devender, 2020 or Cerri, 2019.

A.2 Apps

- Contact Journal is a kind of lightweight CRM that you can use to log contacts. Essentially it means that you see who you distributed your love and attention to in a given year.
- Address books: addappt has little distribution, Covve introduces more false friends than genuine additions, however this may change.
- Apps to spontaneously meet other people: Meet5 or TubeChat are great
- Apps for finding your tribe: Internations, Meetup.com, Couchsurfing ...

A.3 Reading List

In this book I have referenced a number of books on friendship and hope that you will take the opportunity to follow up on a couple of the references that piqued your interest.

- A reasonably regular of more condensed and compact content is also provided by psychologytoday.com or Medium.
- Newspapers such as Guardian, Telegraph or Atlantic can be searched for the term friendship or have channels of opinion pieces with this topic.

[1] https://www.authentichappiness.sas.upenn.edu/user/login?destination=node/434

- For advice on making new friends, I would recommend Asatryan, 2016 and Shumway, 2018 as the next books to read
- For a philosophically touched however very lucid book I would recommend Nehamas, 2016
- For books based on survey data: Delaney and Madigan, 2017 covers youth's friendships
- For books based on sociological research look at Degges-White and Borzumato-Gainey, 2011 for female friendships and Greif, 2009 for male friendships.

For friend themed literature, I would recommend

- Ronja Robbers daughter by Astrid Lindgren
- Chronicles of Narnia by C.S. Lewis

If you want to read the classics, following options

- The Loeb Editions of Aristotle, 1926 and Cicero, 1923 are still in print, in their iconic green and red covers. Any edition is good
- The Perseus Project at Tufts uses the Rackham translation of Aristotle from 1926, for which the copyright however is still held by HUP and thus could not be used for an Open Access Publication. This may change with 1st Jan 2022 when the 95 years have expired. [2]

  The Ross translation from Aristotle, 1925 is widely available, including from the MIT Classics project at http://classics.mit.edu/Aristotle/nicomachaen.html. A new slightly edited version is available in the Oxford Classics from the year 2009 and greatly recommended (ISBN 0199213615) . And the 1963 reprint of the Bywater Greek text in the OUP Clarendon series (ISBN 9780198145110) is a bibliophiles heaven.

A.4 Media List

150 Things you can do to build social capital has a lot of great general suggestions, and a number of them are great for initiating and making friends: https://www.wallawallawa.gov/home/showdocument?id=3499

A.5 Media List

Movies

Movies with a strong friendship theme I have referenced in this book include the following

- Star Trek https://www.imdb.com/title/tt0079945/ and https://www.imdb.com/title/tt0796366/ - explicit friendship commitment, chemistry of circle
- Star Wars IV-VI https://www.imdb.com/title/tt0076759/ and others - chemistry of a group
- Lord of the Rings https://www.imdb.com/title/tt0120737/ - companionship
- Ronja Robbers Daughter https://www.imdb.com/title/tt0088015/ - bonding while self sustaining, loyalty
- Pippi Longstocking https://www.imdb.com/title/tt0366905/ - adventure

[2]See https://web.law.duke.edu/cspd/publicdomainday/2021/

- Stand by me `https://www.imdb.com/title/tt0092005/` - loyalty
- Blues Brothers `https://www.imdb.com/title/tt0080455/` - circle reunion
- Things we lost in the fire `https://www.imdb.com/title/tt0469623/` - consideration, reciprocity - 'accept the good'

Foreign language movies

- Dil Chahta Hai (IN) `https://www.imdb.com/title/tt0292490/` - reconciliation, circle of friends
- Feuerzangenbowle (DE) `https://www.imdb.com/title/tt0036818/` back to school to fully participate in round of friends experientially
- Three men in the snow (DE) `https://www.imdb.com/title/tt0048014/` making friendship irrespective of background

Audio material

- Man of La Mancha (Musical) `https://youtu.be/ALWV_EA6x8I` and `https://youtu.be/G13jzheosNE?t=150`, and finally for the teary ending `https://youtu.be/sTz47QkbSgs` (watch Sanchos smiles)

Video Games

- Mass effect 1-3 and Dragon Age 1 (Bioware) - accompanying material to judge the bonding https://youtu.be/BjzXCLpgBXE

Board Games

- Therapy (Getting to know each other)
- Ludo (fun and forgiveness)
- Any card, board whatever game.

A.6 Companion website

On the companion website www.practicalfriendship.com I will keep updating links to tools, references etc. There I have also put links to preliminary version of the friendship role test, the friendship inventory, and similar resources, which I will update in the coming years as discussions progress.

A.7 Lunchroulette

On the website lunchroulette.co.uk I programmed a prototype for platonic matchmaking in groups. The goal here is to figure out which pairs in a group of say 50 people are most likely to build a friendship. Thus it optimises searching costs, helping in particular people who are introverted or generally not comfortable with making lots of acquaintances get past the long initiation and searching period. The dataset F.2 was also raised via this site as part of the Covid Support measures for students in isolation.

A.8 Other material

Various networks and charities have been named in footnotes throughout this book.

- Campaign to end loneliness (UK)
- Togetherness Hub (Germany)
- Befriending networks (UK)
- Cares Family (UK)

Appendix B

Youth

One question I struggled with was to what extent I should cover friendship in children and adolescents in this book. The argument for this obviously was that the friendships in adolescence are often termed the best and the most important in life. Being able to establish good friendships at this age pays dividends throughout the entire rest of the life. Against me covering this topic is however the even more valid argument that child and adolescent psychology is an academic discipline almost of its own merit, and in some aspects substantially distinct from the psychology of adults. There is ample literature and friendships on processes of children making friends in primary and secondary school, and while I have reasonably covered adult friendship literature, I did shy away from the adolescent literature.

The second argument why I should not cover it, is that I do not have children of my own, and thus very very little adult exposure to the troubles that avail children and adolescents. Writing how to help children make better friends would literally like a blind person teaching seeing people about art, or a deaf person teaching listening people about opera. So much for the caveat.

That having been said, based on the theory and recommendations in the book a few items of recommendations can be made on a hunch. This I will do in two sections, one as general advice to parents who might be worrying that their children are not making any friends and secondly as a set of lessons or tenets that I think would be good for an 18 year old to hold who is embarking on adult life (Things I wish I could tell my 20 year old self - adult version).

B.1 Some thoughts for parents

- Kids don't need to be taught how to build or maintain friendships. Bonding over exciting activities, silly humour and exploring the world, they are usually substantially better at it than the comparatively dulled adults.
- Joined eating is bonding. And the food needs to be tasty[1]. You do not want your kid to get the reputation 'it is great to go over there, but at the end I always have to eat this Spinachy-Healthy Stew - urgh ...'. Of course you should not indulge other kids parents with copious amounts of ice cream either, but your evangelizing veganism - unless you are an extremely gifted cook - can become a serious liability for your kid, healthy or not. [Communion and Hospitality]

[1] It is unfortunately one of life's truisms that most tasty food is unhealthy and most healthy food is undesirable, at least to a kid that hasn't been subjected to a long and effective taste adjustment education.

- Kids want to be left alone. Respect for privacy is really important, unless you managed to genuinely keep your fantasy and youthful spirit alive. Thinking back one schoolfriend of mine had parents who were serious contenders in bolstering the numbers of the AD&D hero group and genuinely fun to have around. That was cool. But in most other cases the times where we were just sitting in a room playing computer games or slaying dragons, presence of parents was unrequired. [Mutual Understanding, Privacy, Circle Bonding]
- Friendship is 100% voluntary, soft encouragement can be made, but the moment it becomes obvious the friendship becomes instrumental and worthless. I do not enter the friendship because I want to but because I comply with the request of my parents and thus hope for other benefits. I will most likely drop the 'friendship' at the first opportunity I have without giving up on the benefits of parent approval. So as much as you might want to include another kid into your sons or daughters friendship circle, whether it is for their or your child's benefit, it needs to have the full consent of your kid. [Independence]
- If you are hell bent on e.g. integrating a refugee, socially disadvantaged, fat or really shy kid, my hunch is you need to find a way to play to their strength. That means you need find out what they are really good at (e.g. catching a ball, fixing bikes, god knows). Then get your kids friends group to get a taste for that activity, and then include. As kids in principle are actually quite open, there is major potential for spark friendships, where one kid just goes - wow I had no idea you could do that, you are so cool ... and this is the effect you are gunning for. [Mutual Interest, Work together, Respect]
- If your kid is the socially disadvantaged, fat or shy kid, then my hunch would be skills are also the way out[2]. Kids in my opinion are often brutal and discriminating, but it is not genuine maliciousness but more a result of their unfiltered nature. They are 'low-self-monitors'. On the other hand the moment some status is acquired, all the past is gone and forgotten, and integration easily achieved. One tool I think that is really cool is the Character strength inventory for children [3], and that in combination with a coffee chat with a school psychologist for interpretative assistance might point to a practical path. Once respect for one status-conferring key skill is acquired, it probably spills over into other areas. [Respect, Mutual interest, Acceptance]

Please note again, that the above is little better than an unsubstantiated opinion. I don't have kids nor have I studied kids friendships. These are just thoughts for you as a parent to reflect on.

B.2 Learning goal by 18

The second part is - if I had kids or was somewhat responsible for them as a teacher or in a similar capacity - what image or idea of friendship I would want to have imparted to them by the time they hit adulthood.

- The value of friendship in life - once a deep friendship is established, it is something incredibly valuable and enriching in life. Once you have it, make sure you let your friends know your appreciation. [friendship value in life, appreciation]

[2]Here is the disclaimer - I was quite fat and hence clumsy and slow, but my saving grace was the capability to catch balls and my lego collection partnered with my fantasy.

[3]`https://www.viacharacter.org/researchers/assessments/character-strengths-inventory-for-children`

- When you are together with your friends, make sure you give them your full attention. Don't multitask, put the phone away, be there in the moment and enjoy their company and the joint activities.
- Be clear about your time management priorities. Don't use the 'b-word busy' with your core friends.
- Don't have an in kind - calculatory reciprocity[4]. Celebrate a pay it forward general benevolence[5], where you spread your blessings around your friends, and accept their blessings on you without keeping a tally. In friendship you can kill the joy of a friendship by taking its temperature.
- Actively build and maintain good memories and experiences together with your friends. When you are older, these will be the stories to bring a smile back on your face.
- Make space for hospitality in your place. Have an idea how you will cook a simple meal, have a few cans of beer or bottles of wine stashed away, know where you would put up a sleeping matrace for a friend who shows up and could stay over if it gets late. Friends staying over gets you an extra 1-2 hours of interaction time over meeting them in a pub.

[4]That means where you mentally accurately keep track of every benefit, coffee or gift you got only to repay it at the next possible moment to avoid the feeling of debt.

[5]That means you just dole out coffees and blessing without counting or keeping track

Appendix C

Friendship and Religion

Sections 1 and 2 are a lay attempt to apply the theory to a theme of Christian theology
Sections 3 and 4 are descriptions of friendship according to Judaism and Islam

I do not aim here to make a description of friendship in the bible per se, Olyan, 2017 has done that for the Old Testament, and in the literary review I commented on Cuddeback, 2010 and J.R. Miller, 1897 providing their versions on friendship according to the New Testament. I just want to lay out two thought conjectures that become a bit more rigorous to argue given the theory I put together in this book. The first is whether friendship with God is possible and how good a metaphor friendship is for describing the relationship with God. The second is, if friendship is the gift God gives to us and by which we should live as a principle, what type of friendship is actually meant.

C.1 Friendship with God - a polemic

One item of contention I frequently encountered in studying the theological material was the claim, suggestion or encouragement to have a friendship with God. Now my Christian faith is not rock stalwart, I have always more been the 50-70% Christian[1]. However I would like to take the opportunity here to make my argument that friendship is not a category to be meaningfully applied to the Christian God in the current 'now and not yet' interregnum state of post-ascension pre-return. Rather than claiming it to be 'my argument' I would classify it as an extension and elaboration of the basic concept by C. S. Lewis.

To start with the easy part - when Jesus calls his core disciples and later apostles friends, this is a perfectly understandable saying. He elevates them from disciples to friends. He acknowledges the time they spent with him. He affirms their friendship before the final scene where he knows their fear, but now giving something to counter potentially the shame of leaving him. He gives them something to encourage them and hold on to during those difficult days to come. Breaking the bread is an utmost human activity, and both by xenia and communion it is deeply entwined with friendship. When Jesus asks Peter in John 21:15 'Do you love me (as your god - agapas)', Peter responds 'you know I love you (as a friend

[1]The subsequent argument is thus open for discussion and challenge. I originally wanted to omit it, but as when discussing this book with Christian friends the topic kept coming up, I put it back in for completeness' sake. It is an argument made in the knowledge and acknowledgement that alternative arguments and sentiments exist and might be 'better'.

- philo)'. Rinse-repeat another two times[2]. This was a human-to-human philia friendship, and possibly a perfect example of it.

Another cited example is Abraham to be a friend of God. In Genesis 18:1-33 Abraham directly hosts (xenia) and haggles (over Sodom) with God. With some tongue in cheek, Abraham pleads but also morally advises and counsels God to be consistent to his teaching and spare Sodom for the existence of ten righteous men in the city. Such haggling and discussion is exactly what could be expected of a friend interceding with another friend on a personal matter and with good virtuous intentions. Despite interpretation difference on the exact meaning of the Hebrew ahav[3] and discussions in commentaries whether philos, hetairos or yet another Greek term is appropriate for the septuagint, at its foundation is still a human and a 'superhuman' directly interacting in corporal form and according to human customs and conventions. A little later on Jacob wrestles with God and despite the run in gets into his good graces. The wrestling of God with the renamed Isaac is a deeply respectful and reciprocal activity and shows a clear willingness of the OT god to interact on human terms with his flock. Characterising any relationship resulting from these interactions as a friendship is completely uncontroversial.

Arguably the Christian concept of the trinity is also that of a deep friendship - intimate knowledge, affection, dialogue. And of course there is the promise that post-return, judgement those that pass the test[4] or the church per se will join in as a fourth entity. All in all speculation based on a collection of sayings from Sunday sermons, and subject to substantial epistemic opacity.

Not wanting to go into the ethics of our relationship with AI and robotics, a first question of human-nonhuman friendship is whether to be friends with an entity we (as humans) need to encounter it in physical form. Whilst we do not 'believe' in the old Greek, Egyptian or Norse Gods anymore, an interesting thought however is to entertain their concept, as gods walking among men (like Thor in Marvel and Diana in DC Universe). Whilst disguising themselves and thus possibly breaching the 'honesty' criterion, I do think fellowship in that context could have been workable. It might be a mix between a fellowship and a friendship in a 'collaboration friendship style' of Lewis, but not a total alien concept. Thus a hypothetical Phidias could be befriended by Hephaistos noticing the love for excellence in craft. When Jesus talks to the young ruler and - noticing his zest for virtue - 'loved him' , the word agape is used, but picturing the scene it is the sort of fondness that could start a friendship between the human Jesus and the young ruler. It would be the Senior - Junior friendship, where a wise senior takes a young one under his wings and in the process builds a friendship. Thus I would not agree with Aristotle that friendship with the gods is ruled out per se. Simply debunking Aristotle's claim is neither sufficient to prove that friendship with the Christian God is possible, as Cuddeback, 2010, p.106 sets it up as his starting point: 'Can a human person have a friendship with a divine person? Aristotle gives an answer which is as crushing as it is insightful: No, human persons and God cannot be friends—because they are too different, their lives are too far apart. Now from the viewpoint of natural reason, that is, reason unaided by divine revelation, this answer makes complete sense. Indeed it is the correct answer for the human predicament without grace.' Cuddeback is however correctly interpreting Aristotle as since Plato the very humane and erring antiquity versions of Marvel Heroes had become spiritualized intellectual concepts not that far from the concept of the holy spirit as we know now.

Thus what I would like to address is the claim that friendship, in the sense that the term is commonly understood and used in normal language, is feasible and pursuable with the

[2]A sermon I think - but am not sure- I heard from Simon P hinted at an incredible potential of teasing, Jesus' humour and yet full affection for his old friend in this scene.

[3]Lover, intimate, ...

[4]I am a 99.9 % universalist, though believe in a form of purgatory and cleansing required.

Christian God[5]. Specifically, it is the Christian God that is currently represented to us by the holy spirit post ascension or some spiritualized version of Jesus who still is capable of communicating with us[6].

Putting on a semi-agnostic hat and insisting that the same criteria we would apply to a human friend would have to be likewise met by a 'friend God' or a 'friend Jesus', I will now go through the motions and discuss how this works for the relationship traits. At the foundation is that a corporal unambiguous presence is required to exercise friendship, a requirement that the Christian God does not fulfil.

- **Common memory and shared history**: whilst by assumption God knows my life, but laughing or discussing specific anecdotes of our lives for pleasure or identity development is not possible, as with a human friend. (0/1)
- **Love and affection**: We are assured of God's love, but I struggle to see how I would express or show my love for God as I would express it with a friend. I cannot hug God. I cannot prank God. (0.5/1)
- **Consideration and prioritisation**: As a good friend I want to do my friend good and meet his needs. If there is a need my friend has and expresses, I may disagree and explain to them carefully why going for a pint just before an important exam is a bad idea and that as a friend I will even prevent them from doing so. I will however not just stay silent and ignore them. Attention and showing attention among friends is a must. (0/1)
- **Loyalty**: (related to Personality trait reliability) One personality trait often associated with friends is reliability. If my car breaks down, or my girlfriend breaks up with me and I call my friend, they will directly try to help me. Moreover, they will assure me explicitly that they will do that. Even if they cannot help directly, because they are out of the country, they let me know what they can and will do. Books over books filled with stories on what to do when God stays silent[7] have been written about what to do and think when exactly that happens[8]. As the loyalty of god is a really contentious issue for Christians, I will also cite the crucifixion of Jesus himself - my God, my God, why have you forsaken me. No good friend would ever forsake his other friend. So judged by the standard set by loyalty in human friendship, God is no loyal friend[9]. Independence actually works by virtue of free will. (1/2)
- **Enjoyment**: I have heard friends say they enjoy the presence of god. (1/1)
- **Mutual understanding**: Christians are invited to get to know god through reading the scripture and arguably direct experience or revelation. The extent of getting to know god remains deeply incomplete until revelation day. One might also compare God's lecture to Job in Job 40 on the limits of human knowledge. If I want to get to know a friend, I do not want to be handed their diary (the Bible) and told to read it, I want to hear it in day-to-day interaction.(0/1)

---

[5]I would *love* to read an analogous analysis on this for the God of the Hebrew bible or the Islamic Allah, but it is completely beyond my capabilities to conduct this myself.

[6]This is my take-away from the discussions with the more evangelical-pentecostal minded.

[7]'God on Mute' by Pete Greig, or 'Where is God when it hurts' by Philip Yancey. Note that these are people at the forefront of passionate Christian evangelism acknowledging the phenomenon, not agnostic theists evaluating and describing the character of the Christian God.

[8]If even Mother Teresa writes in her diaries of years she went through undergoing doubt in god, the visibility element of the definition of standing by needs to be substantially bent.

[9]To be clear, I am not arguing that God is not loyal according to some other definition of loyalty. There might be an epistemic loyalty where everything works out in the end. There may be a hundred other issues. I am just arguing that friendship in our common meaning is a really bad metaphor

- **Reciprocity and feeling needed**: reciprocity is me feeling needed by the friend just as I need them. As C. S. Lewis observes, clearly God has no need-love for us, and only has gift-love. (0/1)
- **Trust and confidentiality**: I would say that the contents of my prayers and conversations with god stay confidential (1/1).
- **Openness and vulnerability**: This is difficult. Arguably by submitting himself to death on the cross at a human trial, the historical Jesus did embrace vulnerability. Some conversations prior to that exhibit vulnerability, too (Garden of Gethsemane). But if God is open and vulnerable with us today, directly sharing emotions and concerns, I am not sure. (0.5/1)
- **Respect, appreciation and pride and equality**: In the Old and New testament, God expressed appreciation and respect for his human counterparts. However post ascension for today's Christian I struggle to see how these terms would be meaningful in the same way I can show pride in and appreciation for a friend. The number of incidents of heavenly doves descending on baptisms has been rather small since 30 AD. (0/1)
- **Benevolence**: Aristotle claims that for friendship to exist, both parties need to publicly declare and effect their goodwill towards each other. This in a sense together with consideration and reciprocity is the biggest obstacle. In wide sight of human suffering, perceiving the declaration of gods' goodwill for us takes a substantial leap of faith. And that is the point, goodwill in friendship needs to be unambiguously declared and expressed. If we see that when we say 'you are my friend' our friend did not understand us, we repeat the message to be sure that he gets it. Arguably the story of the human bible is God again and again expressing his love for humankind and particular the people of Israel, but still there are many more that don't get the message than in human-human friendships.(0/1)
- **Mutual Interest**: Arguably possible (hymns, worship, supporting the poor) (1/1)
- **Mutual Belief**: God and humans are obviously very different, however arguably subscribing Christians have the same ideas of what constitutes a good life, what is important in life etc. (1/1).
- **Privacy** is overvalued anyway, but difficult to implement with an omniscient god. **Living together**, on the other hand, the experience of daily interactions if that is what you are after, is granted to some and not to others. (1/2)

Thus loosely judging the achievable friendship with God by human criteria, we get to roughly 7 of 16 achievable points, give or take a few depending on interpretation of doctrine. The ones that are violated, loyalty, common memory, reciprocity and consideration are also the more important aspects. I am not sure whether I want to conjecture that the sole purpose of friendship consists in **common activities**, but I would say a large part of this does, too. And these are direct interactive activities, the likes of which are rarely reported even among fully signed up Christians. Thus the activity score of rating God-human 'philia' friendship is also really low. Thousands of Gottman bids for attention and explicit positive unambiguous responses that go unanswered in our relationship with God. I would therefore argue that indeed friendship or 'philia' and the concept of the relationship with God are fundamental different categories of relationships. Think of it like an apple and a tomato, both are delicious[10], both are fruit, and yet few people would think of using one to describe the other.

By suggestion that friendship with God is possible and omitting the fine print and discussion of what kind of friendship they mean, sunday sermonists make the misleading

[10]I detest raw tomatoes, but know that is not consensus.

if not fraudulent suggestion that friendship with God would be as we would expect it with other friends, just a lot better. There is no chance of that ever materialising nor is it intended. Generating the expectation that God behaves like a friend, just an all powerful one, will in nine of ten cases lead to disillusionment or disappointment, hardly the result to be desired. Even if it is claimed that it is just meant as a metaphor, it is clearly an inadequate one at that. Note for clarity that I am not saying that the relationship with God could not be great and better, I have ample friends - though I do not consider myself among that lucky flock - to profess that. I genuinely believe them that for them their relationship with God is a key cornerstone of their life's experience, source of joy and what not. I just challenge the semantic adequacy of applying the term 'friendship' to this experienced relationship, whatever it may be. When Jesus decided to do the ascension, and remove his corporal form from the earth until revelation, he decided that the way the holy spirit was interacting with people and enabling agape was a better way than to maintain a corporal presence offering philia. This choice should be respected[11].

Lewis, 1960 provides an alternative interpretation of God's purpose for friendship. 'It is the instrument by which God reveals to each the beauties of all the others. They are no greater than the beauties of a thousand other men; by Friendship God opens our eyes to them. They are, like all beauties, derived from Him, and then, in a good Friendship, increased by Him through the Friendship itself, so that it is His instrument for creating as well as for revealing.' I would also say that by befriending people in need, be it social need of loneliness or general need such as poverty, we can give honour to this wonderful tool and use friendship in the way God intended it for us to use, to discover and love other people.

Thus I would make the claim that friendship is not the label to attach to our relationship with God if we are believers, but as a gift of God, a production sample of what life in the aftermath might be like. Desmond Tutu once said that the purpose of the human experience of life according to the Christian faith is 'to have loved, to have laughed, to have cried' (see `https://vimeo.com/63938692`). Experiencing true friendship is a possible answer to this, and what a beautiful answer and gift it is.

C.2 Christian Friendship - a suggestion

As noted in the literary section, friendship is an occasional topic in Sunday sermons. Some Sunday preachers do characterise it as god's gift to mankind, some just want to improve the social relations of their flock and give advice as part of their pastoral care. With all things biblical, the range of possible interpretations is substantial, ranging from the commune style co-living based on Jesus' group to neo-Aristotelian virtue ethics. I review the individual texts in section (E.1), what I would like to focus here are the different styles friendship could be modelled with good argument. This section is modelled on a talk I gave at Christians in Academia, an Oxford scholarly connect group, in March 2021.

- **Old Testament**: Abraham, David and John, Ruth and Naomi: Loyalty, Trust, Support in Difficult times, Hospitality, Reciprocity and Benevolence. No mention of intelligence, collaboration, fun, teaching.
- **New Testament** - Jesus and Disciples: Communion, Teaching and Learning, Affection, Consideration, Peace, Honesty, Loyalty. No mention of independence, privacy, need for change, virtue development, fun, reciprocity and collaboration in friendship.

[11] I use choice here in the same meaning as in the Lewis Trilemma (See `https://en.wikipedia.org/wiki/Lewis%27s_trilemma`) of Jesus choosing not to permit the 'Good Teacher' option as an explanation

- **Acts** - Paul and church communities: Peace, Kindness, Patience, Community building, good relationships with each other, support - also material support - within the community.
- **Neo-Aristotelian**: Friends are the means to obtain virtue, the development is the goal of the human experience on earth. 'Bad friends' therefore detract from this goal and should be shunned. No or little tolerance for vices.
- **Neo-evangelical**: Kindness, acceptance, love, joint love for god, common joy in shared activities around the church, generosity, positivity. No mention of intellectual collaboration, classical OT loyalty or privacy.
- **C.S.Lewis** (Friendship is part of 'Four Loves', a description how God's love works and how human love works, and how they differ): Independence and privacy, Collaboration, Mutual Interest, Circle Bonding (humility via Mere Christianity), no mention of self help, guidance, vulnerability, emotional involvement

So the options are ample! I am not going to state that one of them is 'the correct' one, though my hunch is that particularly hospitality, honesty and loyalty would be recurring and consistent themes. Indeed if I remember correctly, direct observations of activities in the gospels and statements of Jesus seem to have a higher pedigree and authority than reasoning-derived statements or Old Testament. However as a caveat I accept that the New-Testament-Jesus & Disciples option is also remarkably close to my personal preference, and thus I prefer to not make a preference explicit. My hunch however is that friendship of the Christian should not be conditional on the potential friends virtue, intellect or status, as Jesus surrounded himself with sinners[12], idiots[13] and poor people[14]. Thus I think the Neo-Aristotelian one as proposed by Cuddeback, 2010 has the weakest backing from a biblical point of view and feels at odds with Luke 18:11[15], but I may indeed be wrong.

As written elsewhere, I would love to include analyses on what good Chinese-Confucian or Daoist, Hindu or Buddhist friendship would put emphasis on, but there really was very little to robustly base an analysis on, and my knowledge of these faith systems was too constrained to take it on myself. For the Jewish and Muslim school of thought I did find sufficient material to compile a plausible summary.

C.3 Friendship in Jewish thought

For the Hebrew Bible faith Olyan, 2017 has done it in a very in-depth, though academic fashion, and I have extensively drawn on it. However Jewish wisdom is not constrained just the Hebrew bible, the Talmud holds substantial additional wisdom the adherents of this religion draw from. Not being Jewish myself, I reached out to a few representatives of

[12]Mary Magdalene was a prostitute, Zacchaeus a tax collector, the unknown women with the alabaster jar likely was a prostitute. Only the adulteress at the well is explicitly told to go and sin no more. It is plausible, but it is nowhere explicitly stated that they abandoned their work post conversion. This observation I attribute to a conversation with Simon P.

[13]This is not controversial, a number of acts of the apostles before they were apostles were downright idiotic and recognized to be so at the time. The miracle of Pentecost makes precisely the point that the holy spirit enabled bumbling fools to speak as eloquent and polyglot as the learned rabbi's of the pharisees. It was the recognition of 'what happened to those uneducated fishers'. This observation I attribute to a sermon of Tim M of Holy Trinity Brompton, London

[14]Parable of the poor man at the rich mans door, or the saying for the wedding 'go and grab everyone on the street', see observations of Graham Tomlin in sermons and writings.

[15]'The Pharisee stood by himself and prayed: 'God, I thank you that I am not like other people-robbers, evildoers, adulterers-or even like this tax collector.'

the faith for suitable sources describing the attitude and emphasis of mainstream Judaism[16] towards friendship. So as a caveat the following text is written by a non-Jew based on a selection of references. Specifically however for friendship, as the various of secondary sources kept coming back to a limited number of text excerpts for primary inspiration, a common ground does seem reasonably feasible. The key sources available to me are Amsel, 1994, p.77-79, the collection of content on the religious website Sefaria.org[17], the writings of Lord Sacks and Telushkin, 1994, ordered by significance of the material for the following text. It benefited additionally from substantial input and suggestions within a longer discussion with Rabbi Jeremy Gordon on 14th June.

The first common insight is that friendship is intended, pointing to Genesis 2:18: 'It is not good for man to be alone'. Whilst this refers to Adam and Eve, it is frequently drawn upon as illustration of humankinds **need for companionship**. This is elaborated by the story of Choni (Taanit 23), a prophet who miraculously slept 70 years. Upon waking up he finds that all of his companions and friends have passed away, and he pleads with God to either grant him companionship or death, the latter of which is granted. The importance of and appreciation and gratitude for friendship in Judaic thought is also emphasised in a little habit and that is the saying of a blessing or prayer of gratitude on seeing a friend again after 30 days have passed, and a prayer echoing the joy of the revival of the dead when seeing a friend again after year [18].

The theme of utility vs. end in themselves is echoed in the Mishnah (Avot 5:16) - ' Any love that is dependent on something transient: that does not last. When the thing that was the cause for that love perishes, the love will also perish. But any love that is not dependent on something transient, but rather on something lasting - for example, the love of the righteous men and the sages - never perishes. In the same way that the thing which is the cause of that love does not perish, so [too] does the love not perish.' [19] - Aristotle could not have said it more beautiful himself.

One lesson engrained in Judaic friendship is that of reciprocity and mutual generosity. It is pointed out in Avot 1:6 that the root of the word ahav - friend - is giving. Thus being friends means giving and taking, both of things and of oneself. It is a bit of a stereotype, but I think the need for genuine heartfelt generosity (and likewise the importance of hospitality) is an insight that the people of the Levant have maintained. Ahav is also the epithet given to Abraham by God, which is usually nowadays translated as friend of god. As noted before, God (in the company of two angels) was hosted and entertained by Abraham, thus satisfying the tenet that before becoming friends people needed to have eaten together.

The need for such interactive intimacy is also emphasised in two sources called Midrash Sifri Nitzavim 2 and Avot Rabbi Natan 8:3 giving a list of the elements of the befriending process: Eating together, drinking together, sleeping together [20] learning from each other and revealing secrets. Upon reflecting, it occured to me how remarkably similar it is to the general couchsurfing experience, where the guest shares a meal and drinks with the host, ends up sleeping under the same roof, and where both people by virtue of the usually very

[16] I was of course likewise cautioned on the existence of many different traditions and schools of thought within both orthodox and liberal Judaism, a sentiment most familiar from my own religion with its many denominations.

[17] The site seems to be a design tool for sermons, thus a bit of a Sermon Central with an inbuilt biblical reference and commentary system. There are dozens of articles mentioning friendship, and a few of them address it specifically.

[18] This one is a little morbid, but it could be a curious habit to imitate. I mean, just imagine the scene if you really did meet your best friend again after a year of absence, and they close quickly their eyes, fold their hands, and 30 seconds later tell you upon your questioning look with a big happy genuine grateful smile that they did just recite the blessing prayer for the revival of the dead.

[19] Quote from Bartenura on Pirkei Avot, in Kyle Zaldin in Sources of Friendship in Judaism on Sefaria.org

[20] Compare for Abraham Lincoln and Joshua Speed

engaged, open and personal conversation learn from each other and get to know fairly personal snippets from each other.

Finally the intimate knowledge and meeting of each other psychological needs is exemplified by an anecdote of Rabbi Moshe Leib (quoted from Mandel on Sefaria.org, but also found elsewhere with minor variations): 'Rabbi Moshe Leib used to tell his chassidim that he learned what it means to love a fellow Jew from two Russian peasants. Once he came to an inn, where two thoroughly drunk Russian peasants were sitting at a table, draining the last drops from a bottle of strong Ukrainian vodka. One of them, in a slurred drunken drawl yelled to his friend, 'Igor! Do you love me?' Igor, somewhat surprised by the question answered, 'Of course Ivan, of course I love you!' 'No no', insisted Ivan, 'Do you really love me, really?!' Igor, now feeling a bit cornered, assured him, 'What do you think? I don't love you? Of course I love you. You're my best friend Ivan!' 'Oh yes, yes?' countered Ivan. 'if you really loved me ... then why don't you know what hurts me and the pain I have in my heart?' (this story at times is slightly adjusted to include general needs). The point is that friendship should encompass lived out goodwill and concern for the person of the other, and knowing our friends needs is both prerequisite and consequence of this attitude.

This attitude of looking for our friends needs is taken even further by Maimonides (as singled out by Sacks commenting on generosity, tithing and community building): ' For Maimonides, the second tithe served a social purpose. It strengthened civil society. It created bonds of connectedness and friendship among the people. It encouraged visitors to share the blessings of the harvest with others. Strangers would meet and become friends. There would be an atmosphere of camaraderie among the pilgrims. There would be a sense of shared citizenship, common belonging and collective identity. Indeed Maimonides says something similar about the festivals themselves: The use of keeping festivals is plain. Man derives benefit from such assemblies: the emotions produced renew the attachment to religion; they lead to friendly and social intercourse among the people.' (Maimonides The Guide for the Perplexed III: 46). Here the meeting of needs by dedication of funds and resources precedes the friendship and builds the foundation for it.

Whilst I had these themes valued reasonably equally, subsequent discussions with a Rabbi referred to me by a friend clarified that the key of the rabbinic tradition of friendship is that of of friends cultivating both great affection as well as fierce intellectual debate. This goes in nature way beyond Heraklitus and Plutarch, who ask their friend to disagree with themselves. The thought that came to mind was of continual mutual devils advocates, testing and refining each others arguments and thoughts. Amsel, 1994, p.78 cites the story of two warring philosophical schools, that despite 'vociferously arguing on many pages of the Talmud' frequently intermarried. The arguments exchanged improve the both participants and propel them towards better insight and virtue. The Bible quote in this context is usually Proverbs 27:17 Iron sharpens Iron, which in Talmudic tradition is then interpreted also not just to include discourse but actual studying of scripture. Some authors also point to Taanit 7a, where the Rabbi quotes the three key sources of knowledge and learning as teachers, friends and students. This learning process is especially relevant to the study of scripture, see e.g 'For when they sit and engage in Torah together, and one of them makes a mistake in the law, or the division of chapters, or declares an impure thing pure, or a pure thing impure, or a forbidden thing permitted or a permitted thing forbidden, then his friend will correct him.' as per Avot 8:3 Rabbi Natan. Complementing each other both intellectually as well as generally is also a theme Sacks emphasises: ' Always seek out the friendship of those who are strong where you are weak. None of us has all the virtues. Even a Moses needed an Aaron. The work of a team, a partnership, a collaboration with others who have different gifts or different ways of looking at things, is always greater than any one individual can achieve alone.'

Most exemplary of this rabbinic discourse is the story of Yochanan and Lakish. Yohanan was already a great sage when Lakish, who was a robber or criminal encountered him. In their discussion, Yohanan convinced Lakish to let go of his ways (i.e. his weapons)[21] and come with him to study the scripture [22]. A strong and legendary friendship ensued over the years based on such discussion[23]. They were subsequently more defined as a pair of discussants in their identity. However at some point a debate erupted on the nature of the forging process regarding weapons. Then Lakish acknowledged, that the robber identity had not been forsaken, but was still part of his nature ('A robber knows his trade' referring to the weapons). Deeply wounded Yohanan dissolved the friendship[24], and despite the pleadings of his daughter, who had been married to Lakish, would not be swayed. Soon thereafter Lakish died. At this Yochanan became inconsolable, as he had realised that his treasured discussion partner had become ultimately unavailable. Searching for a new companion to take his place, none would fit the bill, as no one could challenge him to the point Lakish could. Grief stricken, Yochanan died soon after.

It is this pair friendship, that is emblemic of rabbinic friendship. Whereas western libraries are meant to be quiet, I was pointed to Torah study rooms (Yeshiva) where the seats are arranged for (!) people to discuss. It is for Jews what the Forum was to the Romans and the Agora to the Greeks, a place for interaction. Now I am unlikely to become a learned Jew in the rest of my life, but I am deeply jealous of this institution for fostering learning and mutual discussion. It is designed for pairs to engage with each other. It is designed for friends to come there to discuss and study together. For the Christian reading this, if you rethink of Jesus sending out his disciples in pairs, it is very likely that he also had partly this model of friendship in mind.

It should be noted that the discussion mode or style practised within these friendships is not the Western Socratic style of 'winning the argument'. Ever since Socrates and Aristotle, the goal of the western debate was set up to win the argument and establish truth. The Aristotelian 'A and not A cannot be true at the same time' [25] implies the existence of a single truth and hence the possibility of a winner[26]. Jewish thought is much more closer to Buddhist or Eastern philosophy accepting coexistence of conflicting theories. The 'agree to disagree' is possible, and becomes a 'having fought and debated fiercely, we have measured our opponent and gained mutual respect, and now disagree for today to reconvene tomorrow'. Thus where for Aristotle the truth and ultimate insight into virtue is the goal, and you need the friend almost as a tool to get there through debate, Jewish thought sees the debate with the friend itself as the goal. In thus it cultivates a substantially less instrumental view of friendship than Aristotle.

A final theme of Jewish tradition emphasising the building of community is the concept of the Eruv. By this I don't mean the big Eruv's of Manhattan or London, and I am not entering the fierce religious debates on how their boundaries need to be enforced and validated, but the initial concept of enlarging the private space of the house to that of a few houses, that encompass the extended family. I find it fascinating how all large religions are phenomenal in setting up rather strict rules for their followers, and then over time their learned scholars find ways how to bend those rules with a winkle in the eye to fit better to human nature and needs[27]. The restricting rule of Jewish thought is keeping the Sabbath

---

[21] [impact/effect change]

[22] [mutual interest]

[23] [collaboration, mutual identity] When I would make a Halachic pronouncement, (Rabbi Shimon) would challenge it with 24 questions, and I would answer each of them, and by that dialogue, the true understanding of the subject matter would emerge

[24] Presumably, a mutual ethical code was conditional to the friendship of Rabbis [Virtue, Acceptance]

[25] `https://en.wikipedia.org/wiki/Law_of_thought#The_law_of_non-contradiction`

[26] Maybe I am psychologically brainwashed more than others having taken a course in propositional logic back at Uni, and thus so far the existence of a single truth has always been my mantra, yet I think it is a rather universal trait in Western attitude.

[27] Catholicism - which I adhere to - in my view is the absolute master of that, and the adoption of

and staying inside for lonely people, that conflicted with Genesis 2:18. The solution here was to expand the definition of the private domain to an almost private domain encompassing the few houses of a compound, where the extended family or close friends were living too. Thus elderly people living on their own could join even during the Sabbath their neighbours for conversation and interaction, and bring food to each other without violating the 'carrying stuff outside' prohibition of the Sabbath. In essence, with the concept of the Eruv Jewish civilisation practiced 'smart bubbling'.

Takeaway
I find this idea of deeply involved friendship pairs - corresponding to the role 'partner in crime' and 'mind opener'- deeply inspiring. Indeed to put the joy of fine argument above the purpose of 'solving the problem', and just taking joy in having a worthy and understanding discussion adversary as a continual challenge.

C.4 Friendship in Islamic thought

Describing what a contemporary normative Islamic position on friendship could be was substantially harder than both for Jewish and Christian thought. Representation of friendship between people (as opposed to friendship with Allah or friendship between religions) hardly features in contemporary literature. I will try to describe what I could find and qualify my statements as an impression of an outside I compiled from the sources available to me rather than an authoritative orthodox directive.

There are two major scholarly contributions looking at friendship in (historic) Islamic thought: Lenn Goodman, 1996 and Siddiqui, 2012, where the latter does acknowledge also contemporary themes. This was accompanied by material from the website Al-islam.org of the Almadiya Muslims, which was recommended to me as being reasonably comprehensive and yet still orthodox. One other recommended text was a Q&A entry on islamqua.info[28].

The key thought seems to me that Islam acknowledges friendships to be practically useful (in the sense alliances are - Practical help) and spiritually useful (Guidance, Feedback, Change), however must be evaluated in their merit on supporting the faithful adherents pursuit of virtue and Islam (Virtue). It is thus not a good in itself to be pursued for its own worth, as the only true good is the faith in Islam and relationship with Allah, and good friendships may support in that. Siddiqui, 2012 speaks of 'rigorist conceptions in Muslim piety that Muslims should not be friends with non-Muslims, that religion alone should be the defining premise of any friendship.' There seem to be varying interpretations on this, whether only a true Muslim thus qualifies to be a friend (narrow opinion) or an unbelieving yet still righteous person can qualify too (Virtue). The text from Al Islam [29] clarifies that the instructions not to make friends with the Christians and the Jews was an instruction for the historic context, not a general command. Implied however is that the respect of the potential friend for Islam is an actual precondition on friendship (Respect).

The website also clarifies 'The Holy Qur'an tells us that Muslims should keep company and make friends with the righteous.' and vice versa 'to avoid keeping company with those who are not righteous'. It is my suspicion that a lot is contained in the specific meaning

Pagan rituals and thoughts in the first five centuries AD is breathtaking and remarkably pragmatic.

[28] `https://islamqa.info/en/answers/138390/what-are-the-characteristics-of-the-righteous-friend`

[29] `https://www.alislam.org/articles/is-it-true-that-quran-says-to-not-take-jews-christians-for-friends/`

of the Arabic words, that gets lost in translation, just like our current translations of the Hebrew and Greek Bible suffer from misunderstandings. [30] [31].

Almost as a corollary, it is consistent that Islam according to this website denies the merit of cross-sex platonic friendships. Such relationships are primarily characterised as temptations, thus their danger to the faithful to stray from the path of virtue and contemplate or even commit adultery [32]. The author notes that 'There is no doubt that a certain number of individuals can maintain a platonic friendship without committing adultery or fornication. However, Islam does not make rules for the minority. Rules are always made for the betterment of the majority.', so it is not an outright ban, more a strong recommendation accompanied by reflection on one's own capacity to withstand temptation.

Lenn Goodman, 1996 and Siddiqui, 2012 concentrate on the role of friendship in early and medieval Islam (concretely the great scholars Miskaway and al Ghazali). In the initial centuries of Islam the commitment to the faith and solidarity with the brethren is mostly emphasised. This is creating Asabiya, a feeling of belonging together necessary for the young faith community to bond and survive. Laws as tithing to support poor brethren are thus highly valued and effective. Indeed consideration for the poor and needy is a key tenet of Islam, and connection and friendships can arise on the back of this activity. It should be noted that the word here is brotherhood, so more invoking the theme of an extended family rather than a community of friends[33]. Secondly the danger of the new follower to be lead astray from his new found faith by non-following friends is emphasised, as scriptures warn against association with false friends and their deceit. [34]

Siddiqui mentions Miskaway to discuss friendship in a grand philosophical treatise, and following in the footsteps of Aristotle for most of the arguments. Lenn Goodman, 1996 agrees, crediting Miskaway with developing Islamic virtue ethics on the basis of Aristotle. Indeed it should be recalled here, that Aristotle can be interpreted to see Friends as a tool or means to the end of attaining virtue, not as a goal in themselves. Lenn Goodman, 1996 then describes Ghazali in following this tradition 'Ghazali speaks of friends as means of discovering one's own faults, either by seeking their counselor by learning from their plight'. Ghazali acknowledges the need of friends (more in the style of alliances, as also Siddiqui observes) to 'aid in time of trouble'. As according to Ghazali 'saintliness (sidq) pursues detachment, it seeks escape from the worldliness of valuing friendship for its own sake- or friends for themselves'. If I understand this correctly, the saint should thus not (!) value friendships too highly, as 'make(ing) friendship an end in itself is a secular and humanistic way of organizing one's priorities.' Ghazali according to Lenn Goodman, 1996, p.182 extols a few virtues, which arguably can provide normatives for friendship too: 'We have an obligation to our brethren, he argues, to keep silent as to their faults, their private business, and their secrets (confidentiality). We must not contradict them (respect), say anything unpleasant to them (goodwill), or criticize those whom they hold dear. If we see any fault in brethren, we must remember that we too have faults (humility) and try to excuse their failings (acceptance) and avoid suspicious or uncharitable constructions of their

[30] `https://www.alislam.org/articles/does-islam-teach-muslims-to-hate-non-believers/`

[31] As an example - 'So a believer can, therefore, have friendship, sympathy and goodwill for Christians, Jews, and Hindus and can exercise benevolence towards them, but cannot love them.' I do not understand this quote in the English translation. as friendship and goodwill would be for me synonymous with love, but here the concepts seem to be genuinely different.

[32] See 'The quest of a curious muslim' `https://www.alislam.org/book/quest-of-curious-muslim/what-does-islam-say-about-platonic-relationships/`

[33] Note that whilst Jesus ends up calling his followers his friends, Paul likewise uses the term brethren to address the early Christians, so this is not a semantic difference between religions

[34] 'O you who believe, do not take my enemies and yours as your allies, showing them friendship when they have rejected the truth you have received and have driven you and the Messenger out simply because you believe in God.' (Q 60:1) as quoted by Siddiqui, 2012

acts (trust)' [35]. Furthermore he adds (p. 186) 'Friends have a right to generosity, support, even indulgence from one another, but they should not make demands. ... Ghazali's point is simply that friends do not impose on one another.' (generosity, practical support, independence). As such friendship has a role in Islamic philosophy of religion but not a central or overly prominent one.

My question to both these scholarly references is however whether they are still practically relevant today. As written in a prior section, few contemporary Christians would turn to Augustine, Aelred and Aquinus for normative inspiration on friendship, and much rather turn e.g. to Jesus' teachings and Paul's epistles to construct 'good Christian friendship behaviour', and I would suggest that the average Imams acquaintance of Miskaway and Al Ghazali is also limited, and thus a modern practical Islamic theology of friendship would likewise move beyond them.

The website Islamqua [36] provides a collection of quotes from the Quran and religious eminences to characterise the good muslim friend. As such, the following characteristics are extolled (Items as labelled in chapters 3-6, footnotes for quotes):

- Virtue in faith beyond all other characteristics [37]
- Acceptance [38]
- Benevolence - non-harm and inspiration [39]
- Vocal Support [40]
- Kindness, generosity, peace and patience, guidance, respect [41]
- Effect change, positivity, general support, consideration [42] and again acceptance and positivity [43]
- Honesty and integrity [44]

[35] Brackets with friendship terms my addition

[36] `https://islamqa.info/en/answers/138390/what-are-the-characteristics-of-the-righteous-friend`

[37] 'The righteous friend is the righteous person who is obedient to his Lord, adheres to the teachings of his religion, is keen to please Allah, hastens on the basis of faith to do all good deeds, turns away out of fear of Allah from all evil deeds, loves the Sunnah and those who follow it, takes people as friends for the sake of Allah, opposes (the enemies of Allah) for the sake of Allah, resents sin and its people, fears Allah, is pure hearted and righteous, is not boastful, and has no rancour or envy in his heart.'

[38] 'The righteous friend is the one who does not look for or seek out the faults of his brothers; rather he seeks excuses for them.'

[39] 'You should keep company with one from whose harm you are safe, seeing him encourages you to do good, and he reminds you of your Lord'

[40] 'The righteous friend praises and speaks well of those with whom he mixes, even if he is not able to help them physically' and 'The righteous friend makes excuses for his brothers and friends; he defends them and stands up for them.'

[41] 'The characteristics of the righteous friend include his cheerful manner, gentle speech, bigheartedness, generosity, suppression of anger, and avoiding arrogant behaviour; he shows respect and expresses joy for what he is blessed with of the friendship and brotherhood of others. His heart is free of rancour, and he offers sincere advice to his brothers and accepts it from them. He is easy-going with his brothers and does not go against them in matters that are right and proper; he refrains from criticizing them.'

[42] ': Do not befriend anyone but one who, if you befriend him, will enhance you; if you are burdened with something, he will help you; if he sees a shortcoming in you, he will make it up for you; if he sees something good from you, he will keep it in mind; if you ask of him, he will give to you; if you refrain from asking of him, he will offer you (his help);'

[43] 'The righteous friend strives to conceal the faults of his brothers, to highlight their good qualities and conceal their bad qualities.'

[44] 'The righteous friend deals with his brothers honourably, honestly and sincerely.'

- Loyalty [45]
- Consideration [46]

The directive ends with the summary 'The righteous friend is the one who helps you to do all that is good, who has a good character, enjoins what is right, forbids what is wrong, and observes the rights of friendship in your absence and in your presence, paying proper attention to that in word and deed, only doing that for the sake of Allah and hoping for reward from Him.' which I think can stand on its own.

[45]'The righteous friend joins his brothers at times of difficulty as he joins them at times of ease; he does not change his manner towards them in either case.' and 'if he blames you for something, he will not desert you; and if you keep your distance from him, he will not abandon you' - note the parallel of the last sentence to the Jewish Covenant concept !

[46]'There is nothing left of the pleasure of this world except helping to meet the needs of my brothers.'

Appendix D

Discussion loneliness

The following section was originally in the introduction as a categorization of causes of loneliness and friendlessness. For brevity and fluidity sake I took it out from there, but as mentioned when discussing with someone why they have none or few friends, this should provide a good check list for potential obstacles.

1. They bought no seeds: They didn't meet people who they recognised a sufficient friendship potential with. This can be decomposed into:

   a) They did not meet any suitable people at all. They were continually in the wrong place at the wrong time[1].

   b) They did not get to know them on a first initial superficial level.

   c) They got to know them on a first superficial level, but had insufficient people knowledge to recognize the friendship potential.

2. They bought the seeds and planted them, but did not water them: They met people, got to know them and recognized the potential, but didn't develop the friendship.

   a) They did not decide to invest the time (50 hours on average - see Hall, 2018 or chapter 7 to develop the acquaintanceship into a friendship.

   b) They met up a few times and had great fun, wanted to meet up again and still had the time, but Netflix brought out a new series and they just stayed at home.

   c) Bad luck - they tried for a while to find common time but due to conflicting time schedules at work seeing each other became less and less regular until it died down. Other reasons can be a high time cost or actually financial cost[2] to see each other.

   d) They started developing the friendship, but then 'good' habits were not sufficiently strongly exercised and 'bad' habits such as selfishness, pride, not opening up or others prevented the friendship from developing its potential.

3. They planted and initially watered them, but then weed came in and suffocated the plants: They didn't maintain the friendships over time.

[1]This can be at home without the mental, physical or financial means to go out and participate in civil society.

[2]There still is substantial poverty even in 'affluent' western society, and participating in social life usually does cost money, e.g. by paying a beer and public transport to and fro on an evening out in a pub. In times of reduced social welfare, low pensions and unemployment this does(!) exclude some people from building new friendships.

a) People changed aspects of their personalities, and as this went into significantly different directions (politics), they chose to part ways.

b) People got lazy and were drained of personal energy (they discovered Netflix, Hulu or Amazon Prime).

c) Changes in situation raised the cost of maintenance: Time (kids, job), Proximity (time and finance), ill-health (mobility).

d) The benefit of 'good' habits were not sufficiently strongly exercised or appreciated and bad habits such as inattentiveness, disloyalty or insensitivity put a sudden or gradual end to the friendship.

4. Someone burned the tree down: throughout our life course people expectedly and in some cases unexpectedly die. As Bernard Shaw said: Death is the ultimate statistic, one in one dies ! You may have had good friendships and appreciate the memory of them, but they don't provide emotional and mental nourishment in the same nature ongoing active friends do.

D.1 Not meeting at all

One obvious reason for two people who could be friends do not become friends is that they do not meet each other at all. This is recognized as a substantial problem by political theorists and sociologists. Deeply entrenched socio-economic or ethnic divides can (and often will) prevent friendships by isolation parts of a population from each other. This book cannot say many things of substance about homophobia, xenophobia, aporophobia (poor) and pachyphobia(fat/overweight), racism, misogyny, tribalism, ageism and ableism[3]. Yet one key cost of theirs is that the discouraging the discriminated part of the population from participating in civil society. In some cases they are outright excluded. Either way friendships that might be beneficial and enriching to both participants are blocked. Friendship requires a desire to know the other person and where that desire is suppressed because of aversion or prejudice, friendship is not possible.

Friendship can be a powerful bridge. Through fortuitous circumstances friendship is sometimes established despite the block, e.g. by passion for art, a mutual interest in school kids football training, or situationally being placed in adjacent rooms in a care home. Then friendship (or maybe call it a calculating fear of loneliness) can provide an incentive to explore the other persons world[4]. It is in my view that friendships bridging across conflicts are possibly the only sufficiently trust building activities to sustainably 'solve' them. Racism and white privilege will only be solved, when white people can fully empathise e.g. with the fear of a black person getting searched by the police, a gay person getting discriminated at a job interview, an Asian American getting ignored by a white romantic interest. An avid Medium reader myself, I however struggle to see how these insights can be gained by clever articles and woke TED talks on Youtube[5]. Instead I suspect that an important bridge, and possibly the only one, is a proper heart-to-heart of sharing in full vulnerability enabled by the trust of a prior established friendship, that effects lasting change of mind.

---

[3]Ableism is discrimination and social prejudice against people with disabilities and/or people who are perceived to be disabled.

[4]The movie Best Exotic Marigold Hotel is one such example, where at the start the elderly lady Muriel played by Maggie Smith consistently insults each and anyone 'brown' with the most explicit racist tropes. However through exposure with the culture she grows increasingly affectionate in the end befriending her servant, the hotel owner and the other people around her.

[5]`https://www.ted.com/talks` is a website showing 15 min condensed talks on important topics by the thinkers of our time. I love them, especially items like `https://youtu.be/flqx4zjLljI`

Other issues like poverty will become increasingly difficult to resolve, as 'the ruling elite' stops interaction. Gentrification increases homophily, and one big issue on class divide is that even people in the middle middle or lower middle class don't have any more friends who are poor[6]. Of a similar situation was the Brexit vote. Practically everyone thought it was a done deal until the actual votes came in. At a subsequent panel discussion in London convened a week-ish later for remainers in mourning the speaker posed the question to the people in the auditorium how many of them actually knew people who fitted the stereotype - white, uneducated, disappointed, angry and living in the former industrial heartland of England. Not many hands went up. Similar issues arise with xenophobia, the split between Republicans and Democrats in the US, Bolsonaristas and Progressives in Brazil, Muslims and Hindus in India's north, Western oriented progressives in the middle east and their conservationist religious counterparts, the list goes on. This book will not contribute to resolve any of that in a meaningful way, but the breaking down of friendship along those tectonic faults and the barriers to friendship development across them is a societal problem, that I am unsure how it will be resolved. And finally, in order to meet people, you need to be in places where other people are and mingle. This is a full introverts nightmare, and we come to that in the next section. But the list of places where other people, whom you don't know yet, mingle usually precludes your home. Putnam, 2000 puts out the argument that we might have more leisure time than we ever had in the industrial age [7], we have placed all the gained surplus at the altar of the private entertainment industry. And as much as I am a big fan of The Witcher and Game of Thrones myself, it is not difficult to see how building conditioning and addiction is part of the business model (see Mahdawi, 2018-06-20). So enjoy the variety the channels like Amazon Prime, Netflix and Hulu offer, but don't let it prevent you from meeting new people.

D.2 Not recognising friendship potential

Recognising friendship potential needs finding out a bit about the other person, which is usually happening in conversation. There are however issues that can prevent this from happening. Shyness, absence of openness and absence of interest in the other are such issues. I have never had an issue with openness, on the contrary, I probably tend to open up to fast. But it comes out of a realisation I had a few years ago that initial dramatization of 'vulnerability' is overrated. In Game of Thrones Season 7 Sansa finally learns the following lesson from Littlefinger in an iconic payback scene: 'Sometimes when I try to understand a person's motives, I play a little game, I assume the worst'. Applied to assessing vulnerability, with the information you may be divulging in a first conversation, an analogous thought might indeed be 'If this person came to hate me, and had this information, what is the worst she/he could do with this'. And with most of it the answer is - not a lot ! And add to that the fact that generally people are not out there to pick a target and inflict maximum damage. Generally speaking, people are nice. Secondly, most likely there is already a lot of public information out there about you (you do have a Facebook profile ...). So I suppose the key insight is that the actual risk you are running of opening up a bit and giving out some private information about you, your interests and personality traits, is extremely low. The other issue is that in order to find out about the other, you need to be interested in THEM. That means listening, looking for cues, feeling how the conversation is going. For this a certain attitude and dare I say humility is required. It also requires time.

[6]This concrete challenge of whether we have a genuine friend who is actually poor I came across in a sermon 'Wealth and Poverty' by Graham Tomlin, then Director of St. Mellitus. I have not been able to find the original reference to the audio material (podcast) but the argument was repeated in written form in Walton and Swithinbank, 2019, p. x

[7]Junger, 2016 points out that in hunter-gatherer societies only 12 hours per week are spent working and the rest of the time with the family and friends in the tribe.

There are other issues why people though feeling a sympathy for each other just ignore the hunch and do not follow up, and some might be symptoms of deeper psychological issues, such as a heightened fear of rejection. Fortunately there is professional help available, but that is what is most likely required. Friendship is great, and it does remarkable things for our psychological well being. But friendship also requires trust being built up over time with an initial investment given in a leap of faith. However, it doesn't need to be a leap of faith based on nothing but your gut feeling. The book that addresses this is Asatryan, 2016 who postulates that essentially two capacities are essential - the capacity to know and the capacity to care. If this described problem is yours, i.e. you feel like you simply cannot tell whether someone should qualify for becoming your friend and you investing time in the friendship, read this book.

D.3 Not taking initiative to follow up

There might be initial sympathy, but essentially we usually develop the second impression on friendship potential after one or two conversations involving some degree of self disclosure. One of the differentiating factors e.g. of a positive work environment is a culture of following up on a sympathetic first impression. In my experience at BASF there was the Mipa culture [8] where you could and usually would follow up with a colleague who you encountered initially in a work meeting and felt a certain sympathy for. The usually one-hour lunch was effortless to organise and would give you ample time to figure out, whether the initial hunch of mutual sympathy was correct. Other institutions with a strong welcoming culture such as charismatic churches also have opportunities to follow up and meet with people again after an initial encounter as one important feature in their culture building. We will come to this aspect later, but the effort to follow up is much reduced when both people are part of an organization which provides time and space for this. It is also a function of perceived opportunity cost (getting out of the house) and the cost of time, if our lives are busy because of a demanding job and children.

D.4 Friends becoming incapable of continuing

As we get old, our health deteriorates. As we stop being able to drive and inconvenient public transport reduces our capacity to meet with people, various illnesses reduce our capacity to venture out of the house or hospital, Alzheimer reduces our capacity to remember, and death is the end of all possibilities. This is human nature. The (mostly) sad thing is that in friendship this process rarely happens suddenly and in sync. It can give rise to heartwarming scenes, a final gilding of the friendship as old friends visit each other in hospital and give comfort, warmth and joy in the final hours of their dear friend's life. But sadly, usually someone is the last one to go around, left alone on this earth.

D.5 The gap in loneliness research

Loneliness research has become ubiquitous in the past years, with a number of sociology and psychology researchers churning through public surveys and interpreting and comparing public and private statistics on which subpopulations in which countries are how lonely. The issue is that whilst large survey data is wonderful, and gets you beautiful *** p-values and correlations in models, it is also remarkable incomplete when it comes to capturing individual social circumstances. I have high hopes for the Canadian Post-Covid Social Survey organized by Kiffer Card, but apart from that looking at the general surveys

[8] Mipa is short for Mittagspause = lunchbreak

there is little to latch on to. My hunch is that it will be the anthropologists and qualitative sociologists who are best suited to investigating the theme 'cause of loneliness', swarming out to do well-designed qualitative interviews. Not labelling it 'evaluation', it would be great if they could partner up with the variety of social initiatives to support lonely people and do entry and exit interviews for the clients. Important information here would be figuring out what was the trigger that made a lonely person step forward and contact an organization, or participate in a social activity. I elsewhere write about measuring the gap in fulfilling the Max-Neef Needs in the population, and I think this is exactly the insight that research can provide that would be the highest impact to be put to good use by the various social charities. The question of quantifying loneliness is essentially settled sufficiently since Barreto et al., 2021.

Appendix E

Literature Review

This literature review was originally part of the chapter setting the scene for the definition, and in a purely academic book would have been correctly placed there. However general feedback was that background and methodology were far less interesting and illustrative as the actual meat of the main text, and thus the introduction and definition section was streamlined to lead to the framework elements without detours. As mentioned, books such as Mark Vernon, 2010 and Grayling, 2013 do a much better job of giving a epochal view of friendship, and Hojjat, Moyer, and Halpin, 2017 give an excellent overview on the current state of psycho-sociological research into friendship.

E.1 Philosophical traditions

Classical philosophers

Aristotle, 1925[1] is the first western philosopher who dedicated an entire book to friendship and a framework to think about it, after Plato's Lysis concluded rather inconclusive. The differentiation of utility, pleasure and virtue friends, the need to appreciate the friend for his sake in an almost Marxian sense, and the definition of reciprocally declared and acted out goodwill are all due to him, and many a book on friendship find some way to go through these items. However, it should also be noted (and is often less done so), that Aristotle sees friendship not so much as an end, but as a means or road to achieving virtue and the good life. What is however not appreciated outside philosophical commentaries on Aristotle (see Pangle, 2008 for the most extensive one) and contrary to common thought, is his complete disregard for privacy. In essence, he proposes for friends to live together, and questions that in the absence of such longing friendship can exist. He is also critical of wealth differences, emphasising equality among friends. Finally, while discouraging friendships that are kept solely for the purpose of utility and pleasure, he describes that friendship must encompass these elements. Thus having pleasurable times and actively doing good to each other in proportion of owned resources (both physical and personal resources) must be elements of the friendship. The key needs addressed by friendship are subsistence and protection (benefit to each other), participation (in civic life as the Greeks understood it) and identity (development of virtuous character).

Epicurus thoughts on friendship come via Laertius, 1925 citation of the basic principles and the letter to Menoeceus in the translation of Hicks to us. However, unlike with Cicero and Aristotle, who have book strength material, I turned additionally to secondary

[1] I used both Ross' (Oxford University Press, 1925) translation and Rackham's (Cambridge, Loeb classical library, 1926), citations all from Ross' translation by permission of OUP.

literature to correctly grasp Epicurus concept of friendship, concretely Mitsis, 2014 and Rist, 1980. Epicurus all importance of the avoidance of pain emphasises the benefits that friends can bring to each other, particularly in protecting each other from mishaps of life, thus enhancing pleasure. Epicurus friendship concept primarily addresses the need of subsistence and protection, and emphasises proactiveness, consideration of the friends' needs and practical help, and thus also recognises the utility of financial resources in this endeavour. Furthermore, friendships are pleasurable and thus the pursuit of friendship is justified for this reason too. However, in discussions with subject experts I was cautioned on using frequency analysis for emphasis given the dire scarcity of material of sayings attributable to Epicurus, so this classification is speculative despite the best endeavours of scholarship in the past.

Cicero, 1923[2] writes his text as a dialogue of Laelius, an accomplished general, speaking to two young family members on his deep friendship to the recently deceased Scipio Africanus. Key themes are the continual generosity of Scipio that he bestowed upon his close friends, and the virtuous character that the friendship was based on and fostered among each other, mostly flowing from Scipio to his friends. Thus friendship is of high benefit to the young who can befriend a virtuous elder (exactly the setting of the dialogue) who can guide them, admonish them, and help them grow in their identity as free citizen, it is thus very active moral development. Like Aristotle, Cicero emphasises the need to spend a lot of time together in a close setting, Laelius quoting the long military campaigns he shared with Scipio.

Contemporary philosophers

Alberoni wrote his treatise on Friendship in 1984, in English available via Alberoni, 2016 as of 2016. Alberoni proposes a friendship of the highest degree of independence and respect of each other's private affairs. Friendship is there to discover - mutual interest and the self. It is based out of affection, mutual knowledge of each other and approval and appreciation of the other's person. The difference in character or background of a friend is for him more than anyone else a boon, helpful to challenge one's own thinking. Despite his extreme focus on independence and privacy, other characteristics, behavioural attitudes and activities however all find their space. The purpose of friendship is thus a mutual deep understanding in order to build one's character, with the friendship almost taking the role of the key ingredient available.

The Princeton philosopher Alexander Nehamas, 2016 focuses on the long-term effects friendships can have on each others characters, both positive and negative. He also looks at benefits from exposure to different thinking from befriending people of different backgrounds. Despite being a philosopher, concerns for privacy and independence hardly feature in his work in line with Aristotle and Cicero and out of step with Lewis and Alberoni. Apart from that his emphasis of themes displays a high congruence with the 'consensus' friendship as per the frequency analysis. Change in friends according to his exposition comes through discussion and general exposure, not guidance and inspiration. Nehamas concept of friendship addresses needs across the board reasonably balanced.

Theological writers

There are traditions in Christian thought that do not encourage friendship, and see it as distracting both from the love of God and of the caritas-charity love of the neighbour, with names like Augustine and Kierkegaard (see e.g. Lippitt, 2013) to front the argument. What I will look at is that if a Christian chooses to be a friend what 'best practices' are

[2]Falconer translation in Loeb library, Harvard, 1923, both in hardcopy as well as Perseus Project

to be deduced from the Bible and the various Christian writers who have written about friendship.

For all the times I heard in Sunday sermons that the bible is all about friendship, scouring the Bible for statements specifically on (human) friendship, you have slim pickings. Jonathan and David, Ruth and Naomi and a few other examples in the old testament provide some input, as do proverbs. Much more illustrative is the New Testament, as Jesus is not just preaching to people, healing them or driving them from temples. A substantial amount of his time he is just sitting around with his disciples, teaching them, showing them his affection and eating with them (apparently mostly broiled fish), slowly building a trusting circle of close friends over a course of three years. And when his darkest hour approaches, he specifically requests the closest of them to stay and wake with him, a most commendable counterexample of male vulnerability in friendship. The new testament, seen through friendship-filtered glasses, really does in part become a mastercourse in how to do friendship, in a very mundane and pragmatic way without much theological theory and interpretation to it. This core activity is then continued by Paul, as the Acts and the letters show. The core friendship virtue here is also peace and patience, as also picked up upon by N. Lee and S. Lee, 2009. Furthermore, as Lewis, 1960 and Lewis, 1952 and various sermons point out, the Christian canon of virtues such as hospitality, hope, affection, consideration, acceptance and non-judgement, humility and peace make excellent characteristics to bring into a friendship. The texts are thus in the frequency analysis split into one category of specific scripture describing friendship behaviour (the Bible) and interpretative texts (aka sermons) about friendship drawing on scripture (Christianity).[3]. The key need addressed is that of mutual taking care of each other, i.e. subsistence, protection and affection.

J.R. Miller, 1897 in the 'Personal friendships of Jesus' casts the relationship of Jesus to his disciples as a friendship. For all the well-meaning of exalting the term 'Friendship' essentially however it is instructive to contrast it with C. S. Lewis 'Four Loves'. You then notice that Miller essentially characterises a pure gift love, thus re-labeling the relationship of Jesus to his disciples (and by extensions all Christians) but thus rendering the original traditional meaning obsolete. Indeed many observations of Lewis and Miller are parallel, but Lewis classifies them with the other loves, and keeps friendship a pure peer-to-peer relationship of humans with humans, choosing to keep the classical meaning of the word friendship intact. Yet given some of the virtues and habits extold it is in a way a text about friendship, albeit from a very peculiar standpoint. The key virtues of loyalty, standing by your friend, benevolence and trust are consistent with the expectations of friendship in the old testament, and friendship is characterised as primarily a relationship of affection.

The Brown Professor of Judaic Studies Olyan, 2017 carefully analyses the role of friendship in the Hebrew Bible (i.e. the Old Testament in Christian terms). Linguistically dissecting the technical terms, he shows the care that needs to be taken to translate and subsequently interpret bible passages in our time. Many passages referring to 'friendship behaviour' are thus much more statements of political allies bound by covenants or treaties, and expected to stay loyal to them, usually overriding the strong emotional image we today infer from Davids lament. Thus there are clear obligations of actions, and being friends means simply honouring the contract and thus being loyal to the friend by standing by him in crisis and supporting him.[4] The alternate view is that of inclusion in the extended family,

[3]Future versions might also incorporate Jewish as well as Islamic texts on friendship, but without guidance from a good scholarly authority on cultural and historical context I did not feel comfortable to analogously identify, select and code suitable and representative sources.

[4]Whereas in western contract thought, if one side defaults on a contract, the other party is socially and morally permitted to walk away. The framing of friendship as a covenant is thus much more binding, as even if friend A defaults on perceived obligations, friend B is still socially required to uphold his end of the bargain. This, of course, is very uncommon in our time, but it echoes through

and the strong resulting social obligation in lieu of this. Interesting here is the key characterisation of the good friend 'clinging to' his friend, impliying physical proximity, intimacy, loyalty and a lot of time spent together. The key need addressed is that of subsistence and protection, consistent with the needs of living in a harsh and unforgiving environment and society.

Cuddeback, 2010 styles his book as a Christian themed extension of Aristotle. He is uncompromising in his stance that only the virtuous[5] is capable of 'true' friendship, thus moving well beyond both the Aristotelian tradition [6] and other Christian writers such as C.S. Lewis [7]. Furthermore hardly any mention is given of the classical Christian virtues of hospitality, affection and peace. All is subjected to the joint pursue of virtue, influencing each other for better or worse on the path towards it or leading each other astray if not focused. The key needs friendship addresses in this context is that of joint development of understanding and identity.

C.S. Lewis, 1960, steeped in ancient literature both Graeco-Roman, Norsk and Christian, as well English literature in his section on Friendship in the 'Four Loves' writes about his concept of what today would be called co-creation and co-enjoyment. For him friendship exists in the circle of friends that freely came together and is focused on a specific task or mutual interest. Unlike the other libertarians, he however does not disavow duties to friends (see 4.3 (2)), but treats actual beneficence to support a friend as a mere distraction from the true purpose of the common creative and enjoyable interest. His concept is possibly the most stereotypical 'man friendship' of two friends standing side by side looking at the object of mutual interest for as long as they are interested in it, but no longer. The key needs this friendship caters to are thus creation and freedom.

E.2 Selfhelp and advice on friendship

Based on a series of interviews conducted by the Gallup Group Rath, 2006 focused on finding key roles for the core friends we have or need in our lives, ending up with the 8 roles Builder, Champion, Collaborator, Companion, Connector, Energizer, Mind Opener, Navigator. Despite seeming both to the philosopher and the sociologist a superficial and commercially or utilitarian minded book, its importance cannot be understated. The key message is that there is no such thing as the universal best or close friend, and asking for it in a survey or debating its role in a philosophical context will fail because essentially it is the wrong question. It postulates that a friend will always naturally be important in one or two ways to a person, and that the roles that two friends have towards each other thus define the nature of the friendship[8]. Despite different writing styles and audience there is a certain similarity to the Chapman, 2009 concept for romantic couples or family

---

other descriptions of loyalty required given even nowadays by friends who have been let down to still look out for an ex friend for old times sake or similar reasons.

[5]Almost merging the classical Greek virtue definition with Christian holiness in the process, given a strong emphasis on christian chastity as yardstick for virtue: 'But there must he a bottom limit, below which there is no real capability for true friendship. I would put it this way: The minimum requirement for being capable of true friendship is that a person is dedicated to the pursuit of virtue or holiness, making it the focus of life.'

[6]Aristotle despite emphasising virtuous nature still emphasised the need for pleasure and mutual utility even within the virtuous friendship

[7]Lewis, 1952 in 'Mere Christianity': 'The Christians are right: it is Pride which has been the chief cause of misery in every nation and every family since the world began. Other vices may sometimes bring people together: you may find good fellowship and jokes and friendliness among drunken people or unchaste people. But Pride always means enmity-it is enmity.'

[8]It should also be noted that these roles are substantially different to the theatrical roles of Erving Goffman. They are more like functions, love languages or ways the interaction plays to the strengths of the friend.

relationships. The key needs addressed by Rath are understanding each other and doing things together (Creation).

Friendship Formula No1 is written by psychotherapist Shumway, 2018 based on personal experience [9] with a view to help (young) people be better friends. It is full of practical advice employing different metaphors to make the topic accessible and intuitive as much as possible. The key focus of this book lies on factual teaching and learning together with a mutually humble attitude, and spending time with each other in this process, preferably over food and drink. Standing up for your friends, being emotionally available reciprocally sharing and listening is also key in this book incorporating a key lesson of 'female friendship' into the playbook. The needs catered to are balanced overall with a focus on showing affection and care for each other as well as trying together to understand each other and the world.

Friendship Formula No2 is written by a general journalist Millington, 2019 and loosely put caters to a female cosmopolitan audience in their 30ies. Despite lightly written, it is extremely dense, full of advice and very practical. It is realistic in the sense that healthy finances essentially enable a lot of the friendship activities, as well as almost as fiercely protective of privacy and independence as Alberoni, emphasising the right to walk away from a friendship. Other aspects emphasised are fun, being proud and appreciative of your friends and making sure that sufficient time is made for joint and fun activities.

Nelson, 2016 and Nelson, 2020 puts the key concept positivity, consistency and vulnerability at the key of her two books. Interestingly enough, these do register as key aspects, but in second place to other traits, which however drastically differ. Nelson, 2016 emphasizes the having and giving time to friends, peace and patience as well as reciprocity and communion. The core need addressed here is affection. Nelson, 2020 with its professional focus is much more balanced, emphasising peoples behaviour at work, and thus traits such as general kindness and being appreciative of each others positive achievements and aspects both towards as well as about each other.

Birch, author of the popular self-help book 'the love gap' supporting women maneuvering their way to the preferred contemporary quarry, in her blog also touched upon friendship, and in particular how MBTI type of friend impacts the friendship with that person. Birch, 2018b, Birch, 2018a and Birch, 2019 describe according to MBTI what strengths and weaknesses certain types have. Whilst the typology itself is most likely not backed by solid science, as a source of what is viewed as important to mention overall makes the listings into a valuable source for a relative valuation of friendship strengths, behaviours and activities, that can be sought for in friends. Thus personal energy, intelligence and the capacity to encourage, explore, give guidance and teach are emphasised. The friendship essentially caters to joint collaboration and self improvement. Being person focused, resources other than content and social connections are completely excluded from the scope.

Similar to Birch, other relationship bloggers likewise published their own friendship typologies. Cerri, 2019, van Devender, 2020 and Bennett, 2018 are currently included in here, again catering to a young and mostly female audience. Thus they emphasise fun, enjoyment, attractiveness and loyalty, focusing on the relationship itself and its leisure value.

Both the online platform Medium as well as the British Guardian have channels for opinion pieces on aspects of friendships, drawing on a variety of different authors. The Guardian as a politically left publication to no surprise emphasises the need for equality, i.e. no difference in money or power between friends, as well as eating and drinking, and the need to spend time with each other, accept and be kind to each other. Medium is more libertarian (respect of independence and privacy) and following a good relations canon, emphasising humility, peace and acceptance of each other. The sources on Youtube coded

[9] Young psychotherapist writing for a general non-academic audience rather than old achieved psychotherapist academic writing his magnum opus for posterity. Friendship maker No1: Teaching Deadlifts in the gym.

emphasize the dearth of time in our society and what it means for friendship, the need to eat and drink together to build friendships and interestingly a most emphasised desire for live-in intimacy and pulling down the walls of our society.

Several books in the self help genre are written primarily to give advice on romantic relationships, but claim relevance for platonic relationships too. Abell, 2009 provides a guided review of your attitude to your romantic and kin relationships. J. Gottman, 2001 includes a few paragraph on how to apply the theory developed to analyze and improve marriages also to friendships. Chapman, 2009 with his love languages certainly does also apply within friendships. Some contemporary Christian marriage advice books give advice on how to improve the friendship 'inside the marriage' (e.g. N. Lee and S. Lee, 2000). I included them in the review in so far as the context of their writing and recommendation would plausibly apply to strictly platonic friendships too, and not just be focused on a friendship-like trait within a romantic relationship.

E.3 Psychology, anthropology and sociology

Qualitative sociology

Rebecca Adams and Rosemary Blieszner over the course of three decades cowrote a number of publications both on adult and older age friendships. I generally subsumed them for the frequency analysis in line with their two main books Adams and Blieszner, 1989 for the Older age literature and Blieszner and Adams, 1992 for the general adult literature. Included in the analysis are also their papers Blieszner and Ogletree, 2017, Blieszner, Ogletree, and Adams, 2019, Rosemary Blieszner, 1989, Blieszner, 1995 and Adams and Torr, 1998. Given their sociological background, it comes to no surprise that the key topic studied are the impact of resources on the friendship, similarity of backgrounds as well as in particular the affective processes typical for female friendships. For younger participants they also looked at items such as attractiveness and practical help in their surveys. More to the core friendship patterns, items such as reliability, reciprocity and openness likewise feature strongly in their studies.

Matthews, 1983 also was a long-term coauthor of Adams and Blieszner, likewise mostly studying women in old age with in-depth interview based studies and emphasising the impact of financial, mobility and health constraints in old age. The full comprehensive book on the themes of friendship through the life-course Matthews, 1986 provided a treasure full of quotes and descriptions both on current and past friendships of older people. Preparing his grand sociological study of friendship structures in Britain Spencer and Pahl, 2006, Pahl, 2000 is a short readable outlook on what his take on friendship is. It is a balanced mix between the virtuous-libertarian view of Alberoni and the sociological view on friends having a strong social influence on each other as well as requiring resources to pursue friendship activities.

The book of the two counseling professors Degges-White and Borzumato-Gainey, 2011 focuses on female friendships, what role they play in women's lives and giving advice on how to improve them. It is rich in personal testimonials of female friendships. Degges-White and Borzumato-Gainey, 2011, Chapter 3, p.39 condenses the 40 rules of Argyle and Henderson, 1984 into 10 key rules, loosely mapped to the themes non-jealousy, confidentiality, practical help, openness, respect, positivity, understanding, pride about friends, acceptance, emotional support and respect of independence, items that all come out in the book again and again. In essence, it is the reference book on female friendship.[10] Whilst overall balanced on needs addressed, the key theme is participation by spending time in a circle of female friends that are also physically close.

[10] I split off Degges-White and Borzumato-Gainey, 2011, Chapter 10 on friendship in older age as a separate item to cluster with other older age literature in the frequency analysis.

The social work focussed professor Greif, 2009[11] wrote the equivalent book of Degges-White-Borzumato-Gainey for men. The book is balanced in terms of themes, with all aspects (except virtue) being touched upon. It is based on a survey with 380 participants he performed with his graduate class. Quantitative measures resulting from this survey are highly aggregated, but the testimonies of male friendship are extremely powerful. The general section emphasises proximity, mutual interest, loyalty and reliability, essentially the canon of men hanging out together. Analysing out the general adult testimonials topics such as financial and health constraints are addressed, as well as the important of social agreeableness and the need to expose oneself to friends of different backgrounds. For older adults the constraint of health becomes overarching, with partial impacts also by material constraints as well as the need to rebuild the network. Having a good time with friends especially over food and drink is the main purpose, but also here it is documented that elderly people both wish to become closer to another not being lonely and yet insist on their privacy.

Quantitative sociology

The communications professor Hall, 2012b did a study on friendship factors in 2012, building on the most preeminent friendship characteristic studies to date. Study 1 measured the strength of factors as used priorly, Study 2 surveyed 400 undergrad communications students to calibrate the measurements of the friendship dimensions. The dataset generated two main factors, and subsequently a finer subdivision (I include a discussion of the kindly provided dataset in the appendix in section F.4). Whilst the method generated great material, mapping the outcome shows the partiality of sociological research using this demographic group, with a substantial focus of the questionning on superficial resources. However focusing on attributes of friendships as input to assessing friendship quality was very much in line with the approach this book takes.

Roberts-Griffin, 2011b in his data from the Authentic Happiness Testing Website operated by Martin Seligman at UPenn evaluated mostly variables relating to personality and relationship and widely ignoring the activities. Key focus is thus on fun, loyalty, trust, being there for each other as well as the cluster intelligence, mutual interest and content, however given the open question and free text nature of the original survey this data set could be recoded to the full scope of the variables of the framework developed in this book. A number of other studies, such as Sprecher and Regan, 2002 or Oswald, Clark, and Kelly, 2004 focus on a more limited scope. Furthermore most of their developed measures were collected and tested together in the study of Hall, 2012b.

Apostolou, Keramari, et al., 2020 and Apostolou and Keramari, 2020 looks at factors for making friends and preventing the making of friends. Both are large convenience samples recruited through online media such as Facebook and focus on the initiation phase (motivation to making friends) rather than the maintenance phase (what is good about existing friends). Both studies are unconstrained like Hall, 2012b and focused on identifying factors.

E.4 Analyzing the structure of the texts

According to the method described in Appendix F.1 I created a frequency table of keywords for each of these, and from these a weights table for each of the key themes. These weights table are what were used for graphs 3.2, 4.2, 5.2 and 6.2. These n-tuples can then be

[11] I split his book three ways in the frequency analysis, 1st his general section, 2nd his section with the testimonials 20-50 and 3rd his section with the testimonials 60-90 and ex post was justified given the different emphases placed in all three.

used to calculate pairwise correlations, and the technique of multidimensional scaling [12] be used to visualize the result. Multi-dimensional scaling is a technique that brings n-tuples with a high correlation score close together on a mostly 2d map and n-tuples with low correlations at a distance. The grey lines denote items of a correlation score of higher than 0.5. A k-nearest neighbour clustering (which essentially does something similar, just with Manhattan distances rather than Euclidean distances) can produce colour clusters. Both these methods are standard methods of statistical learning to explore a multi-dimensional set. To be clear, the interpretability of this is somewhat limited. In addition to that, the method is not perfectly robust, indeed the inclusion-exclusion decision of some sources may somewhat distort the graph. Curiously whereas some elements remain close no matter what (e.g. the old age cluster of Matthews, Degges-White Old Age and Greif Old age), other elements such as Hall2012a, CS Lewis and Youtube can be quite volatile in their location on the map.

It does however confirm and question impressions of similarity. The closeness of the self-help cluster (Shumway, Nelson, Millington) is one such assurance. The utility orientation of Rath fits in well with the MBTI characterisations. There is a certain degree of partition between the theological writers (Bible, Christianity, Olyan and JR Miller) and the philosophers (Cuddeback, Alberoni, Nehamas, Aristotle and Cicero), with Cuddeback and Alberoni on the boundary. C.S. Lewis (this does not come out so well in this run, as he is close to the old age group) is a class almost completely to himself. And the quantitative sociologists (Hall2012), work on a different spectrum of questions than both the qualitative researchers as well as the philosophers. All such statements could be gained from a reasonable acquaintance with the text, but visualised this way confirms a general intuition.

[12] Mead, 1992

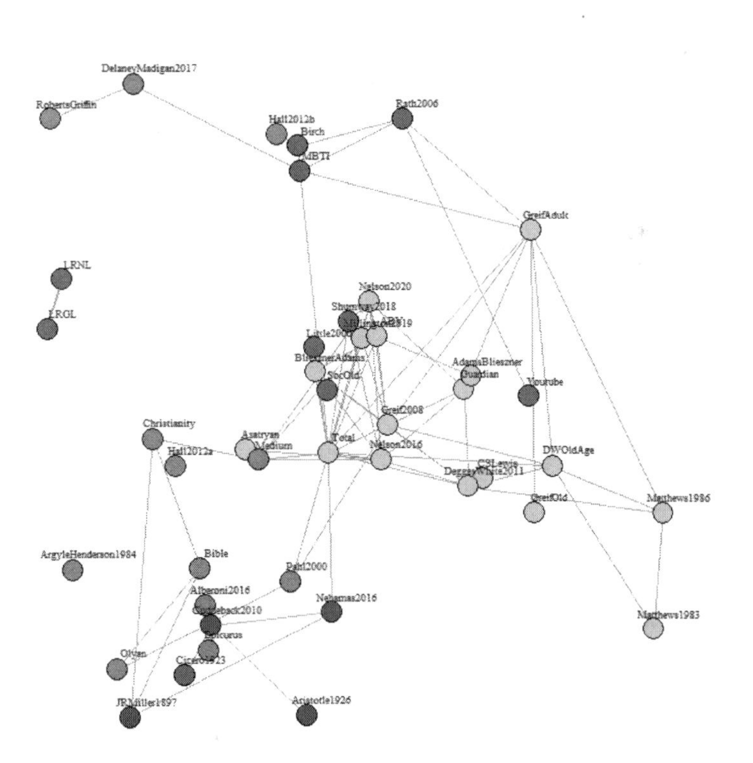

Figure E.1: Correlation structure of friendship texts

See E.4 for explanation. As print is in black & white, best turn to PDF online.

Appendix F

Datasets

F.1 Counting of keywords

Analysing the various texts on friendship and trying to generate a common structure on which to base their comparison 'objectively' I used coding techniques usually associated with the analysis of anthropological observations, diaries or conversation transcripts. Concretely I used the software Citavi to attach key words to passages. The internal datastructure is accessible through an SQLite interface, that allows for extraction of the keyword tag data into CSV, thereby allowing processing in Excel and R. As mentioned before in the end the list of total key words numbered about 300, all of which described nuances of friendship personality attributes, attitudes, needs, activities, resources and the likes. These key words would generally describe items such as 'my friend does X with or for or to me' or 'my friend is or has this desirable attribute' or 'my friend exhibits this attitude towards me'. Thus a text would have anything between 50 and 500 keywords triggered, depending on its length, topic focus and depth. Some texts (Greif, DeggesWhite) I subdivided into parts given depth and focus.Where sociological analyses such as Hall, 2012b or Roberts-Griffin, 2011b provided tables based on surveys, usually between 100 and 150 keyword tags were used to approximate the relative results and allocate it to the various keywords. In essence thus I transformed a text into a 300-keyword tuple. Using a weighting matrix of allocating the keywords to the 50 themes the individual texts were thus transformed into a weight vector of percentages.

It is clear that this is not an objective method, last but not least because the triggering of such key words is very dependent on my way of reading the text, but it is in my opinion about as objective as I could make it myself, and that was the goal. For me the purpose of the research project was getting a sense of what 'a good friendship' could be according to consensus, and to evaluate common ground and difference between texts vastly different in writing style, philosophical assumptions, convictions and methods of erudition, and employing a simple frequency table approach seemed like a robust and 'good enough' first attempt to get to grips with it. From these counts the weighting tables at the end of every 'friendship trait' subsection are generated.

Going via specific keywords and nuances was necessary to avoid misinterpretation due to inconsistent labelling. A result of the coding exercise is an appreciation for the diversity of key words and aspects also shows the need to catalogue and codify past questions used in sociological surveys. Positivity in past research could be meaning anything from affirmation to laughter, and depending on different psychological concepts or personality definitions different 'positivities' or listening styles might have very different impacts on friendship maintenance. Thus 'laughter-positivity' (fun) could be different to 'affirmation-see strengths positivity' (affirmation) to 'see positive' positivity (hope, optimism) and points to a clear cost of higher aggregation common in sociological research without clear definitions.

On scope - a reasonable cut had to be made to restrict to actual friends behaviour or expectations towards them while they are still friends. Once friends become romantic lovers or enemies this behaviour became out of scope and no keyword tags were assigned to descriptors.

Tot	10257	Total keywords	
Normative sources			
OP	517	old phil.	Aristotle, Cicero, Epicurus
CP	1319	cont. phil.	Nehamas, Alberoni, Cuddeback and Lewis
TW	1170	theol.	biblical texts, various sermons, Miller and Olyan
SH	2238	self help	Shumway, Nelson, Asatryan, Millington and Rath
CM	695	cont. media	Guardian, Medium, Atlantic and YouTube
Observational sources			
QS1	1951	qual. sociol.	Pahl, Little, Degges-White* and Greif*
QS2	631	quant. sociol.	Hall, Roberts-Griffin, Adams&Blieszner*, Argyle
OA	926	old age soc.	Adams&Blieszner*, Degges-White and Greif*
YA	809	youth age	Delaney and Madigan , MBTI types
YS	diff	youth study	Appendix F.2
Keyword triggers			

F.2 Test study of youth preferences

From about 80 students aged 18-22 their friendship preferences (what they look for in current or new friends) as well as self assessments were asked and the fifty most prominent variables from these criteria requested. On a Likert scale of 1-5 assessments were grouped into groups of 5, and a limit of 15 points could be given within each group, thus introducing opportunity costs. It was clear that this would not generate a full set for factor analysis unless a substantially higher group was recruited. A true panel to really test the validity of all the variables would probably take a panel covering different ages, ethnic and cultural groups and cover maybe 500 or 1000 people. The character strengths validation study leading to the VIA character strengths covered a multiple of that. The interest was what the inclusion of new variables hitherto not featuring in sociological analysis, i.e. the ones would do to relative dynamics, which variables would be stable in a consensus (i.e. exhibit low variance) and on which variables high differences were seen. Finally with a few texts in the keyword analysis identified as 'adolescent relevant' the question was whether this method of counting key words got a good image, and whether the authors thus captured well the sentiment of adolescent friendship, or whether there were mismatches, with the possibility of giving an outlook of what kind of statements thus could be expected. This worked well, and the differences in weights when compared to past studies such as Hall, 2012b shows that there is merit in extending the variables hitherto considered in sociological research to gain a better actual understandung of friendship.

The data was used (and this was the incentive for the participants to join) to create platonic matches. By that I mean based on essentially a correlation coefficient between someones expressed need-profile and a potential gift-profile three matches in the submitted population would be forwarded. An interesting observable was that after about 20 people were in a suitable proximity pool, about 50 % of them had at least one match above 80% quality and at 40 people in a pool about 90 % had at least one match above an 80 % quality. Furthermore it was interesting to see concentration patterns - some people had profiles that would have fitted 50 % of the population. However also more shy-individualistic 'nerd's (high scores on shyness, high focus on intellect and collaboration) did match outside the core.

F.3 Survey of Friendship Habits

At the start of this project in the period of Oct 2019 to March 2020 I conducted an online survey with convenience sampling with 182 responses, of which 157 responses were complete.[1] The participants came from a variety of backgrounds, such as friends, work colleagues, LinkedIn and Facebook contacts, or travel companions or Couchsurfing guests. The geographic split was loosely 1/3rd Germany, 1/3rd Tokyo & Hong Kong, and 1/3rd global. This surveyed friendship maintenance habits and preferences. The key focus was on time spending patterns and effectiveness of maintenance strategies. The survey was suspended in March due to the onset of the Covid crisis.

Composition of habits survey					
Age	- 30	31- 40	41,55	56-100	Total
F	9	35	29	4	77
M	12	40	37	12	101
Total	21	75	66	16	178

F.4 Available Datasets

Hall 2012

Another dataset I was kindly provided with was that of friendship expectations of Hall, 2012b. It first of all allowed me to verify my incredulity at the outcome of the two factor model on the first study. But diving into the data allowed me to really explore some issues that follow up from this research could have. One issue are some questions are fairly similar, indeed I would have classified them onto the same keyword. Yet the correlations even of in class items (e.g. items looking at humour, or ego reinforcement / praise specifically) were rather low, which to me leaves only the conclusion that peoples concept of what a good friend is may be rather vague and changing from moment to moment as they answer the questionnaire. A possible explanation, though this is mere speculation, is that the way people think about a general set of traits for a 'stereotype' friend is that they mentally cycle through a set of closest friends and when answering a single question answer it for the friend who is first on their mind.

However if the threshold for r is chosen to be 0.4, some structure does emerge. In figure F.1 I ran an MDS[2] to get the general correlational structure, having replaced the labels with appropriate keywords as I had used in the tagging analysis, as well as allocated the keywords to general categories. And thus it can be seen that there are a number of items without connection to the main fold, but loosely the needs according to Max-Neef do come out, with a separate category introduced for resources. There is a key cluster (green) of affection / empathy oriented traits. Adjacent to it is the cluster of leisure (enjoy company, fun, good conversation, orange). On the other side is the resource cluster (money, attractiveness, network - light blue) - which includes the traits agreeableness and mutual background. Interestingly two further wide areas emerge - the general personality/character cluster (virtuous character, general positive character triats, reliability - grey). Finally there is a co-creation cluster that involves mutual interests, some other parts of mutual background and similarity, as well as the resources intelligence and content and challenge. Identity improvement (guidance, honest feedback) is scattered without structure all across. What is however also interesting is that a wide range of characteristics, such as honesty show no

[1]At about 2/3 of the questionnaire a question came that was more difficult to answer at which point some people stopped the questionnaire, with 4 stopping the questionnaire before demographics at about 50 %.

[2]multidimensional scaling, see e.g. Mead, 1992

direct correlation to any other items, even in their own class. This hints at difficulties of common convention, meaning that aspects of honesty are valued substantially differently from each other in priority. This means that sociologists designing questionnaires on eliciting traits and their relative importance need to look carefully at which formulations they choose to query certain attributes reliably.

Hall, 2012a Inside the dataset were also a second set of 25 questions (or alternatively seen as one big question with 25 buckets) where the students were asked to distribute overall 100 USD between 25 traits to compose the ideal friend. This offsetting introduced opportunity costs, and thus the answers are more committed. All answers were partially double barrelled, and asked for two traits in one question which however were very closely related. So in some cases the responses to this were quoted in two traits (e.g. fitness/health and attractiveness) in statistical estimates, and in others just in one category (e.g. trust and confidentiality), where the complete content of the question was within one trait as defined here.

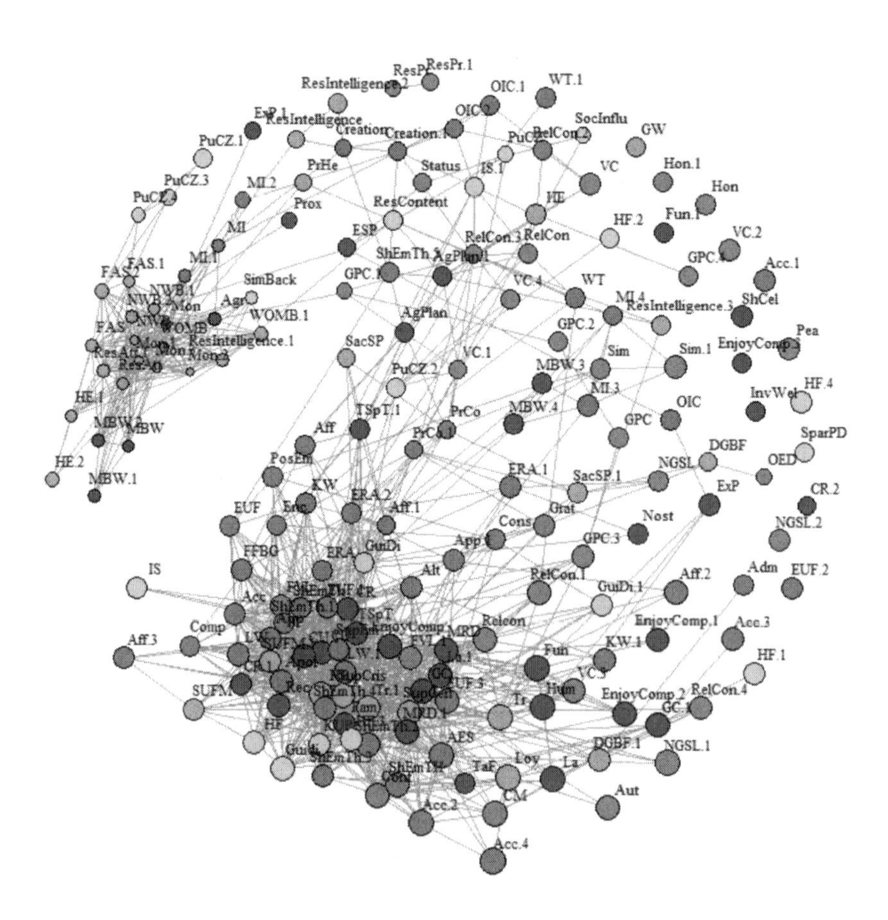

Figure F.1: Hall 2012 MDS labelled and coloured, explained in F.4

Bouwman 2020

Bouwman, 2020 published the questions used in the survey and the means, and thus classification and inclusion was possible. Her elements were all taken from Hall, 2012b and like in Hall they showed variance in weight for elements that seemingly described the same concept, such as openness, listening style or help and favours.

Apostolou 2020

The professor of sociology in Nicosia did two large surveys with Apostolou, Keramari, et al., 2020 and Apostolou and Keramari, 2020 looking at key motivators and inhibitors of friendship. The questionnaires were administered in Greek to 1316 participants (Why make friends) and 622 participants (preventing friendship) and focused of the friendship initiation phase. The two datasets were kindly provided to me and thus I managed to include the average preferences in the statistical section of this book. Contrary to the dataset of Hall, 2012b their population is mostly middle-aged adults.

Deri 2018

Deri et al., 2018 review literature to identify key relationship themes. The goal is to provide a category framework for social ties in social networks. Their focus is more general than Hall or Apostolou and this book, as they also consider romantic partners, coworkers and parents in addition to friends. The derived nine key traits are similarity, social support, trust, power, knowledge transfer, identity, status and romance. Whereas romance is out of the scope of friendship, these characteristics do losely correspond also to traits or roles identified here. Their first study could be separated out towards friends. As they kindly provided the raw dataset, I could compute rankings which I included in the statistical estimates here. The average ratings used for factor analysis were however aggregated across all groups.

Almaatouq 2016

Almaatouq et al., 2016 has a public dataset and I used it to calculate the reciprocity figures in section 9.3. The dataset queried a full MBA class of 84 students to see who they rate on a scale of 1 (hardly know) to 5 (close friend) to look at the social graph and the number of reciprocal and unreciprocated friendships.

F.5 Unavailable Datasets

Rath 2006

This is contrasted with the process taken in Rath, 2006, where respondees are asked to rate specific friends for their properties in order to generate the factor generating set. From 159 respondents from a call center it was solicited to define their closest friend at work, their closest friend away from work and an acquaintance, with a 144 survey on each of them. Iteratively using factor analysis this 144 survey is being then reduced to about 66 elements. Contrasting this with the general low internal correlations even for similar items in Hall, 2012b, the difference seems to come about by asking for specific people rather than an idealised general image.

F.6 Consequences for research on traits and roles

One consequence is that wording matters. Even as we might think that certain key words like positivity are 'obviously' meant by certain questions, question-to-trait validity might be a lot harder to establish than expected. Even then we may find that low actual correlations when high ones are expected may make it difficult to use statistical methods such as factor analysis to really decide which questions are suitable to gauge importance of particular traits or roles.

Whilst as part of this book it was originally planned to do precisely a survey based trait measuring to calibrate the roles, the review of the above datasets showed that most likely rather than producing yet another partial dataset on a conjectured set of question, the qualitative results on the traits and their nuances will probably need to enter a discursive review process, before then probably in collaboration of several research institutes or professors a diverse population can be sampled with a finalised standardised question set requesting assessments of actual friends rather than asking people to answer questions on a hypothetical ideal friend.

Thus a two step questionnaire might be used for this part: This would per trait query which of e.g. four descriptions of a trait is most representative of it, and then, choosing that representation, query its relevance to they typical best friend or just friend. Of course diverse populations are really of interest here. But if at first a test is performed with university undergraduate students, it might be highly intriguing to query different groups of students, such as psychology, sociology, economics or philosophy students and measure to what degree they adhere to a common base understanding or to what degree their convictions on friendship are impacted upon by their studies.

F.7 Mapping Factors

Trying to validate the needs as potential factors for roles, I also went through the factor generating papers of Oswald, Clark, and Kelly, 2004 and Hall, 2012b. Picking the key words from the actual questions used and mapping them to the needs in some cases gave clear and convincing allocations (such as supportiveness for Oswald or communion and enjoyment for Hall), however more often than not a rather substantial spread and thus no obvious mapping.

Part of the issue is, and this is in no way to be construed as criticism of past studies, that in the past predominantly questions regarding affection or leisure time were asked, with some practical support. Differentiated questions regarding collaboration, identity development and understanding were less in focus. Thus validating the 8/9 needs structure by reusing past datasets may prove difficult to realise. I attach the mappings of both studies for your own review.

Oswald, Clark, and Kelly, 2004					
	Total	Pos.	Support.	Open.	Interact.
Subs + Prot	3	1	1		1
Affection	16	4	9	2	1
Understanding	4	2		2	
Participation	5		2	1	2
Leisure/Idleness	6	4			2
Creation	2				2
Identity	0				
Freedom	1	1			

Hall, 2012b Study 2							
	Total	Ag	Com	Enj	Instr	Sim	Sym Rec
Subs + Prot	9	0	1	0	5	0	3
Affection	10	0	6	0	2	0	2
Understanding	2	0	0	0	0	0	2
Participation	3	0	0	1	0	2	0
Leisure/Idleness	9	0	0	7	0	0	2
Creation	2	0	0	0	0	2	0
Identity	5	1	0	1	0	2	1
Freedom	0	0	0	0	0	0	0
Resource	11	11	0	0	0	0	0

F.8 Mapping Needs

Nieboer et al., 2005 conceptualised the social production function scale with initially 58 items and then reduced it to a 15-item scale with the following items. Note that the Nieboer et al., 2005 scale emphasises in several items the superficial status aspect of identity, but ignores the social or maybe philosophical existential aspect of identity. This is the need to maybe talk with friends about meaning of life, potentially religion or other aspects. What is good is the aspect of stimulation, even though it makes no difference whether these states are achieved solitary or through company of friends or others. On the other hand, classifying comfort and stimulation as social production functions does imply a societal context. The affection category of the 58-scale does have a number of items, that also relate to other categories (empathy-understanding, reciprocity, practical support), the behavioural confirmation also looks at existential questions (right choices in life, core competency), status includes elements of independence and self-validity as person (not only justification by achievements).

To utilize this instrument in the context of loneliness research it needs to be expanded with the categories of understanding, participation as well undergo adjustments in the categories of leisure, participation and identity. Furthermore as the research of the section in resources shows, for meaningful connections the role of superficial status is almost insifignificant, whereas personal validation for values and character is much more important.

Steverink and Lindenberg, 2006 introduce the categories on p.282: 'The first need, affection, is fulfilled by relationships that give you the feeling that you are liked, loved, trusted and accepted, understood, empathized with, know that your feelings are reciprocated, feel that others are willing to help without expecting something in return, feel that your well-being is intertwined with others, and feel that others like to be either emotionally or physically close to you (e.g., to hug). Affection thus refers to the love you get for being who you are, regardless of your assets (status) or actions (behavioral confirmation). The second need, behavioral confirmation, is fulfilled by relationships that give you the feeling of doing the "right" thing in the eyes of relevant others and yourself; it includes doing good things, doing things well, being a good person, being useful, contributing to a common goal, and being part of a functional group. Behavioral confirmation thus results primarily from what you do, rather than what kind of person you are (affection) or what you have or can do (status). The third need, status, is fulfilled by relationships that give you the feeling that you are being treated with respect, are being taken seriously, are independent or autonomous, achieve more than others, have influence, realize yourself, and are known for your achievements, skills, or assets.'

Aff.	(1) Do people pay attention to you?	Aff. + Id.
Aff.	2) Do people want to help you if you have a problem?	Subs
Aff.	(3) Do you feel that people really love you?	Aff.
Behav.	(4) Do others appreciate your role in the group?	Id.
Behav.	(5) Do people find you trustworthy?	Id.
Behav.	(6) Do you feel useful to others?	Prot.
Stat.	(7) Do people think you achieve more than others?	Id.
Stat.	(8) Do people see you as someone with influence?	Id. + Prot
Stat.	(9) Do people know you for your achievements?	Id
comf.	(10) In the past months have you felt relaxed?	Leis. (?)
comf.	(11) In the past few months have you felt fit/ healthy?	General
comf.	(12) In the past few months have you felt physically comfortable?	General
stim.	(13) Are your activities challenging to you?	Leis. +Creat.
stim.	(14) Do you really enjoy your activities?	general (good).
stim.	(15) How often are you fully concentrated when doing something?	Creat.
Nieboer scale		

Appendix G

Future Research

G.1 Outstanding questions and hypotheses

As discussed in the outlook section, it is my view that a large scale comprehensive survey on friendship is going to bring substantial more insight than proceeding by one purpose limited datasets evaluating single effects. Essentially this would be a replication study of Rath, 2006 asking for traits of specific friends. Assuming the concepts conjectured in this book can be validated, here is a list of questions that further research can investigate to support addressing loneliness:

1. **General Friendship**
   - How to best estimate relative importance of traits? Budgeting 'build your friend' question?
   - How to evaluate suitability of questions for representing certain traits?
   - What is the best way to end up with a validated standardized e.g. 30 or 50 question set to characterise the key aspects of a friendship?
   - If the traits are reasonably equivalent, and the role theory proves weaker, is it possible to build an ordinal scale for friendship quality from the 25 loneliness questions or the 50 friendship quality questions?
   - Following on from that, if such a scale could be validated, to what degree can we verify and subsequently refine Dunbar's circles?
2. **Needs and loneliness**
   - Can the Max-Neef needs be validated within loneliness research?
   - To what degree are joy-leisure-participation loneliness and support-loneliness correlated? To what degree are they hurtful or harmful? How do they differ?
   - Is befriending the best way to mitigate participation loneliness or are there better ways at equal effort and cost?
3. **Roles**
   - Do roles correspond to different needs, or are there specific dialects?
   - What is the distribution of role 'availability' in the population?
   - Is part of loneliness due to structural mismatch?
4. **Society**

- Are there specific structures that evolve in groups of three, four or five? Are there certain situations that are conducive to such structures building?
- Experimental: Is it possible to imitate these mechanisms, e.g. in care homes?
- How can we identify good bridging practices, where people pull lonely people into established circles and communities?

5. **Friendship in different cultures**
   - How do the emphasis on traits change with different cultures, possibly also with political or religious backgrounds?
   - Does cultural impact friendship needs? Correspondingly, do people in different cultures experience loneliness differently?

6. **Ageing and the life course of friendship**
   - What are the friendships that lasted into old age? Why?
   - Is there a life course of friendships, where e.g. personality factors dominate in the first part, activities in the second, and relationship traits matter in the long run?
   - To what degree do which factors (resources, availability of people, bad habits) contribute to loneliness in age?

It is possible that some of these questions and hypotheses have already been answered in literature that I have not hitherto covered. In that case I would be grateful for a pointer to include it in a future edition.

G.2 A future research program

Replication studies of a variant of the Hall, 2012b and Rath, 2006 studies of '**friendship profiles**' across ages, cultures, genders and personalities I think is the most important step to expand our knowledge of what traits people mostly associate in their friends. A prototype questionnaire would be the one given in Friendship Survey 1.0, either with the combination 'best friend' - 'friend' - 'acquaintance' or the 'three closest friends'. Introducing opportunity cost is very important to avoid 5er clustering or idealisation for the 'marvelous' friend.

Whereas for most people recruiting 50 or 100 people is really hard, recruiting 15-20 people for such a questionnaire, and thus getting a dataset of 45-60 friends assessments should be within the realm of possibilities with limited effort. It could thus be an excellent standard undergraduate bachelor thesis to recruit such a sample with a reasonable homogeneity (e.g. by contacting a local care home, school, recruiting friends from University, or convincing a medium sized local company to put out such a questionnaire to its employees.). Benchmarking difference against the global total, or comparing in class (e.g. gender or age) across other classes (e.g. culture or education) can provide substantial material for comment to enable the formulation of a relatively original psychology or communication studies bachelor thesis.

Related to this would be experience of social loneliness. First the actual structure of the Max-Neef needs has to my knowledge not been validated by traditional factor methods. Given the foundational nature of the research, this is most likely not a task to be taken lightly, and thus best embraced by a research cluster with access to survey-response generating power. By this I mean it will probably need to be done not just once with a single population of students (though this could be an interesting pre-study), but probably by an institution with access to a full population panel. Aside from the psychology faculty it would be probably really valuable to include a linguist to ensure a good discussion on the ambivalence and meaning of the individual questions. Finally, while their design is intended to be interculturally valid by the author, this probably needs to be confirmed by replication studies in different culture groups.

The most important practical research is I think the one on bubbling.

Appendix H

Statistics

Personality

Honesty 3.1

Study	item	group
Roberts-Griffin, 2011a	honesty	1
Deri et al., 2018	honesty	2
Tesch and R.R. Martin, 1983	honesty	2
Hall, 2012b	'Genuineness' LaGaipa, 1977	3
Hall, 2012a	Openness	3
'A friend who is open and honest in sharing their thoughts with me'		
Bouwman, 2020	honesty	2
'Tells me the truth even if it is painful '		
Stats: Honesty		

Proposed Statements for surveys:

- X is genuine and authentic
- X has a low tolerance for dishonesty
- X is honest
- X is sincere with me

Weights per Genre:

Tot	OP	CP	TW	SH	CM	QS1	QS2	OA	YA	YS

Acceptance 3.2

The sociological and psychological studies generally do not look much into the above nuances, and the statements capturing acceptance are usually along the lines of 'X accepts me for who I am, even when others don't', 'I feel I could disclose to X things that I am ashamed of' and 'X can tolerate people of different beliefs and convictions'.

Study	item	group
Roberts-Griffin, 2011a	acceptance	3
Adams, Blieszner, and Vries, 2000	acceptance	4
Apostolou, Keramari, et al., 2020	need for acceptance	5
Hall, 2012a	genuineness	1
'A friend who likes and accepts me for who I am'		
Bouwman, 2020	acceptance	4
'Could disclose to him/her things that I am ashamed of '		
Stats: Acceptance		

Proposed Statements for surveys:

- X accepts me for who I am
- X tolerates people of different beliefs and convictions
- X will listen without making any judgement
- X forgives me

Weights per Genre:

Humility 3.3

As such, I have found no direct variable on humility in sociological studies on friendship, but conflict resolution does feature. Likewise traits are sometimes queried that express some degree of altruism and thus selflessness, which is not the same but related. Finally listening well (5.3) can be considered strongly related to humility.

Proposed Statements for surveys:

- X quietly soaks up his/her friends stories before sharing any of his/her own
- X takes a real interest in people around him
- X thrives in my accomplishement and happiness
- X is generally a humble person

Weights per Genre:

Tot	OP	CP	TW	SH	CM	QS1	QS2	OA	YA	YS

Reliability 3.4

Study	item	group
Tesch and R.R. Martin, 1983	dependability	1
Deri et al., 2018	reliability	4
Greif, 2009	dependability	2
Apostolou, Keramari, et al., 2020	someone to rely on in a time of need	4
Hall, 2012b	'conscientiousness' from Lusk, MacDonald, and Newman, 1998	4
	Stats: Reliability	

Proposed Statements for surveys:

- X is reliable
- X is dependable
- X is a rock

Weights per Genre:

Tot	OP	CP	TW	SH	CM	QS1	QS2	OA	YA	YS

Fun and Humour 3.5

Study	item	group
Roberts-Griffin, 2011a	fun	4
Roberts-Griffin, 2011a	humour	2
Deri et al., 2018	fun	1
Deri et al., 2018	humour	3
Apostolou, Keramari, et al., 2020	Someone's humor	2
Hall, 2012a	personality	1
'A friend with an outgoing, exciting personality and a great sense of humor'		
Bouwman, 2020	Humour	1
'Has a sense of humor'		
Bouwman, 2020	Fun	2
'Fun to be around'		
Bouwman, 2020	Laugh	3
'Can make me laugh '		
Stats: Fun and Humour		

Proposed Statements for surveys:

- X has a great sense of humour
- X is a clown
- X always makes people laugh
- X brings out the little kid in you

Weights per Genre:

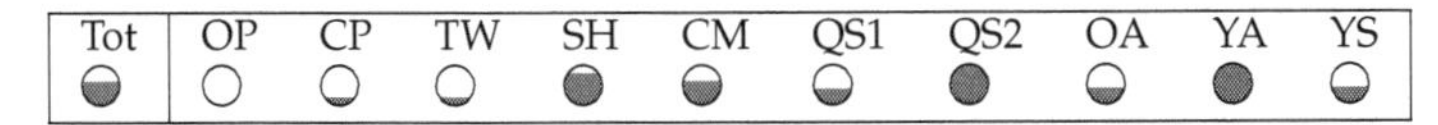

Tot	OP	CP	TW	SH	CM	QS1	QS2	OA	YA	YS

Kindness 3.6

If kindness is a key factor in making friendship, then intercultural comparisons could be an interesting how it impacts both friendship initiation and maintenance.

Study	item	group
Deri et al., 2018	kindness	5
Roberts-Griffin, 2011a	kindness	3
Hall, 2012a	warmth	5
'A friend who is a warm, kind, and affectionate person'		
Stats: kindness		

Proposed Statements for surveys:

- X has a kind personality
- X warms my heart
- X is a loving person
- X ix affectionate and loves people

Weights per Genre:

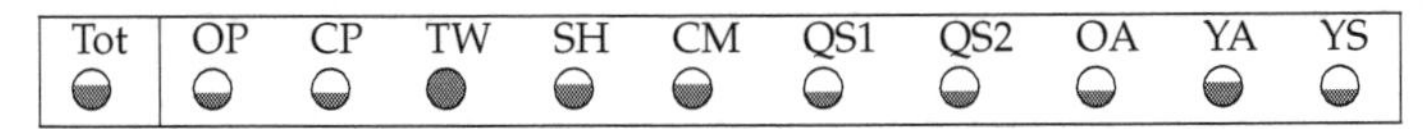

Tot	OP	CP	TW	SH	CM	QS1	QS2	OA	YA	YS

Virtue 3.7

Among the sociologists only Hall, 2012b in his study shows the centrality of good character to the nature of friendship to a significant degree. As 'virtuous' is quite an antiquated word, and 'good character' may be too vague, it is interesting to think how to phrase a good question to query this trait. I do find it a most curious and almost funny cliche fact that in Apostolou, Keramari, et al., 2020 in a survey of greek citizen on highest desirables in a friend the 'someone's character' is the highest desirable trait, true to Aristotelian tradition.

Study	item	group
Deri et al., 2018	good characteristics	1
Hall, 2012b	Good Personality Jacob M. Vigil, 2007	1
Kind, responsible, humour, personality, cooperation		
Hall, 2012b	strength of character LaGaipa, 1977	4
Hall, 2012a	citizenship	6
'A friend who has civic values, is patriotic, is concerned with making the world better'		
Apostolou, Keramari, et al., 2020	good personality	1
character 1, ethos 1, positive characteristics 1		
Stats: Good Personality		

Proposed Statements for surveys:

- X has a virtuous character
- X is a good person / has a good personality
- X has a good value system
- X inspires people to behave in a good way
- X would never ask me to do something illegal or immoral

Weights per Genre:

Tot	OP	CP	TW	SH	CM	QS1	QS2	OA	YA	YS

Intelligence and Curiosity 3.8

Study	item	group
Roberts-Griffin, 2011a	Intelligence	4
Hall, 2012b	'Academic Success' from Lusk, MacDonald, and Newman, 1998	6
Stats: Intelligence		

Proposed Statements for surveys:

- X is intelligent and smart
- X expands my horizon
- X is very curious and stimulating
- X is interested in a wide range of subjects

Weights per Genre:

Tot	OP	CP	TW	SH	CM	QS1	QS2	OA	YA	YS

Positivity 3.9

Study	item	group
Deri et al., 2018	positivity	5
Roberts-Griffin, 2011a	positivity	5
Bouwman, 2020	cheer up	2, 3
'Someone who helps keep my spirits up when things are not going my way (2) ' 'Will cheer me up when I am sad (3) '		
Oswald, Clark, and Kelly, 2004	positivity (factor)	unclear
Stats: Positivity		

Oswald, Clark, and Kelly, 2004 identify a factor 'positivity' in their study, however it encompasses a number of different items and thus cannot be used to support relevance of this item : 'Express thanks when one friend does something nice for the other?': Gratitude (Rel13), 'Try to make each other laugh?': Fun Humour (Per06), '(-) Ignore each other?' : Attention - Friendship as a priority (Rel16), 'Not return each other's messages?' : Attention and Respect (Rel04), 'Talk about each other behind friend's back?': Loyalty (Rel08), '(-) Threaten to end the friendship because of something that happened?' : Friendship Priority (Rel17) and Forgiveness (Rel13), 'Try to be upbeat and cheerful when together?' : Positivity, 'Plan specific activities to do together?': Energy and Agency (Per07), possibly mutual interest (Rel09) and dirt time (Act01), ' (-) Blame each other for bad things that happen?' : Forgiveness (Rel13), 'Reminisce about things you did together in the past?' : Nostalgia - Common Memory, '(-) Make sacrifices for each other?': This one is weird, sacrifices being negative points to non-obligation and independence of friendship, but overall in literature making sacrifices is considered a friendship enhancer, 'Become angry with each other?' : Peace and Patience (Per01). Interesting is in this context also that 'Try to make the other person 'feel good' about who they are' was classified by the factor analysis as being part of supportiveness.

Proposed Statements for surveys:

- X helps me to see a positive future
- X helps me see my strengths
- X is hopeful and optimistic

Weights per Genre:

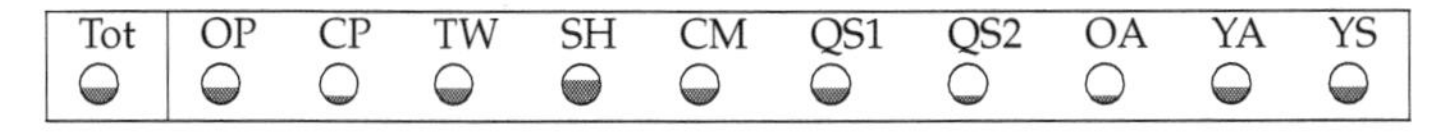

Tot	OP	CP	TW	SH	CM	QS1	QS2	OA	YA	YS

Proactiveness 3.10

The factor has not been explicitly included in any friendship traits studies, however traits are sometimes queried that express some degree of bilateral concern.

Proposed Statements for surveys:

- X knows how to help people
- X is altruistic
- X cares about others
- (-) X treats people transactionally

Weights per Genre:

Tot	OP	CP	TW	SH	CM	QS1	QS2	OA	YA	YS

Energy & Adventure 3.11

Study	item	group
Roberts-Griffin, 2011a	adventure	6
Roberts-Griffin, 2011a	presence	5
Hall, 2012b	exciting personality Sprecher and Regan, 2002	1
Hall, 2012a	ambition	5
'A friend who is competitive, active, assertive, and ambitious'		
Stats: Energy		

Proposed Statements for surveys:

- X is very adventurous
- X has an exciting life
- X makes me try new things which we otherwise would not have experienced
- X boosts your spirit

Weights per Genre:

Tot	OP	CP	TW	SH	CM	QS1	QS2	OA	YA	YS

Agreeableness 3.12

Study	item	group
Hall, 2012b	extraversion John, Naumann, and Soto, 2008	(4)
Hall, 2012a	personality	(1)
'A friend with an outgoing, exciting personality and a great sense of humor'		
Hall, 2012a	inclusion	(3)
'A friend who includes me in activities they do and in making future plans'		
Hall, 2012a	status	(6)
'A friend who comes from a good background, is popular, knows a lot of people, and is a leader'		
Apostolou, Keramari, et al., 2020	Socializing	3
'willingness to meet new people'		
Apostolou and Keramari, 2020	'introversion' factor	(3)
Apostolou and Keramari, 2020	'fear of rejection' factor	(5)
Stats: Agreeableness		

Apostolou and Keramari, 2020 Introversion: I am introverted 2 (general), I feel embarrassed when meeting new people 4 (enjoyment, social ease), I do not speak easily to people I do not know or have just met 3 (initiative, enjoyment), I am shy 3 (initiative), I expect others to take the first step 3 (initiative), I am not social 5 (social ease, network), I do not meet many new people, because I do not associate much with others 4 (social ease), I do not open up easily 1 (open), I do not feel comfortable for others to know things about me 2 (open).
Apostolou and Keramari, 2020 Fear of rejection: I fear rejection 5, I think about what others might think of me and I get anxious 5, I fear that others will judge me negatively because I do not have many friends 6 (network), I am worried that I will not be accepted 5 (acceptance), I find it difficult to communicate with others 5 (fun, humour, intelligence), I find it difficult to figure out what I need to do in order to start a friendship 6 (potentially psychological health?), I am insecure 4 (energy?), I do not think I make a good first impression 4 (status?)

Proposed Statements for surveys:

- X makes friends wherever they go
- X always encourages me to attend social gatherings
- X seems to know everyone
- Whenever I tell X of a problem, he usually has a suggestion of who might help me

Weights per Genre:

Tot	OP	CP	TW	SH	CM	QS1	QS2	OA	YA	YS

Peace & Patience 3.13

The factor has not been included in any friendship traits studies.

Proposed Statements for surveys:

- I am at peace when I am around X
- X is patient with me
- X calms me down

Weights per Genre:

Tot	OP	CP	TW	SH	CM	QS1	QS2	OA	YA	YS
◒	◒	○	◒	◒	◒	○	○	○	◒	◒

Attitudes

Common Memory 4.1

Hall, 2018 measured length of time spend together as key input variable to closeness of friendship. I discuss it in the section on 'take-time-to-grow'.

Study	item	group
Adams, Blieszner, and Vries, 2000	length of acquaintance	5
Hall, 2018	length relationship	1
The paper evaluates time spent as key variable.		
Stats: common memory		

Proposed Statements for surveys:

- X and I are good at creating memories together
- X and I share a long history
- X and I go a long way back
- X and I like to reminisce about things we did together in the past

Weights per Genre:

Tot	OP	CP	TW	SH	CM	QS1	QS2	OA	YA	YS
●	●	●	●	●	●	●	◒	●	◒	●

Love & Affection 4.2

Study	item	group
Roberts-Griffin, 2011a	love	5
Deri et al., 2018	platonic love	3
Argyle and Henderson, 1984	platonic love	5
'Should not indulge in sexual activity with the other person'		
Adams, Blieszner, and Vries, 2000	affective processes	unclear
Hall, 2012a	genuineness	1
'A friend who likes and accepts me for who I am'		
Hall, 2012a	warmth	5
'A friend who is a warm, kind, and affectionate person'		
Stats: Love and Affection		

Proposed Statements for surveys:

- It feels natural and I feel happy being hugged by X
- X shows their affection to me by sending cards or letters
- X shows their friendly affection for me openly

Weights per Genre:

Tot	OP	CP	TW	SH	CM	QS1	QS2	OA	YA	YS
◒	◒	◒	●	◒	◒	◒	◒	◒	◒	◒

Closeness 4.2

Study	item	group
Deri et al., 2018	connection strength	2
Deri et al., 2018	companionship	5
Apostolou and Keramari, 2020	'too picky' 6-factor	4
Being selective in friendship obstacle to new friendships		
Hall, 2012a	Intimacy	4
'A friend who I feel very close to, who I feel a strong connection to'		
Stats: Closeness		

Apostolou and Keramari, 2020 Too picky: I do not feel like making new friendships 3 (openness, initiative), My age - I feel I have grown old enough to start new friendships 5 (take time to grow), I do not easily give others the opportunity to become my friends 4 (initiative), I easily reject people as potential friends 3, It is difficult for me to find people with who we have common interests 2 (mutual interest), I find it difficult to find people to match 2 (mutual belief / chemistry)

Proposed Statements for surveys:

- X really loves me (platonically)
- X and I openly talk about how much our friendship means to us
- X and I have a strong/deep connection
- X and I let each other know we want our friendship to continue for a long time

Weights per Genre:

Tot	OP	CP	TW	SH	CM	QS1	QS2	OA	YA	YS
●	●	●	●	●	◒	●	◒	●	◒	●

Consideration 4.3

Study	item	group
Hall, 2012a	Support	4
'A friend who will provide me with whatever type of help or support I need'		
Oswald	'make sacrifices for each other'	neg.
	Oswald, Clark, and Kelly, 2004, Tab.1	
Bouwman, 2020	consideration	4,5
	'Goes out of his/her way to help me ' (4)	
	'Makes sacrifices for me' (5)	
Bouwman, 2020	duty	5
	'Feels a sense of duty and obligation to me'	
Stats: Consideration		

I am not sure how much weight to allocate the negative sign of 'Make sacrifices for each other' in Oswald, Clark, and Kelly, 2004, Tab.1 in this context, whether it was an outlier through composition of the sample or constituted a trend in time.

Proposed Statements for surveys:

- X makes sacrifices for me (positive)
- X would never compete with me over a potential romantic partner or job
- X goes out of their way to help me

Weights per Genre:

Tot	OP	CP	TW	SH	CM	QS1	QS2	OA	YA	YS
◒	●	◒	●	◒	◒	◒	◒	◒	◒	◒

Priority 4.3

Proposed Statements for surveys:

- X and I ensure we are attentive to each other / check in
- When X and I talk we give each other our undivided attention
- I feel X makes our friendship a priority in their life
- X values our friendship high in their life

Weights per Genre:

Tot	OP	CP	TW	SH	CM	QS1	QS2	OA	YA	YS
●	●	◕	◕	●	●	●	◒	●	◕	◕

Loyalty 4.4

Study	item	group
Roberts-Griffin, 2011a	loyalty	2
Roberts-Griffin, 2011a	commitment	6
Deri et al., 2018	loyalty	2
Argyle and Henderson, 1984	'Should be faithful to each other'	6
Hall, 2012a	commitment	2
'A friend who will always be a friend, now and into the future'		
Hall, 2012a	loyalty	2
'A friend who will stick up for me and always be on my side'		
Stats: Loyalty		

Proposed Statements for surveys:

- X would do something illegal or immoral for me
- X is faithful / loyal to me
- X will always be my friend
- X is committed to me
- With X it is us against all others

Weights per Genre:

Tot	OP	CP	TW	SH	CM	QS1	QS2	OA	YA	YS
●	◕	●	●	◒	◔	◕	●	◒	◕	◒

Independence 4.4

Study	item	group
Argyle and Henderson, 1984	non-jealousy	3
'should not be jealous or critical of other relationships'		
Stats: Independence		

Proposed Statements for surveys:

- X and I believe that friendship involves no duties to each other
- X and I believe that we are justified to walk away from the friendship without major justification, if it has run its way
- X and I are independent from each other

Weights per Genre:

Tot	OP	CP	TW	SH	CM	QS1	QS2	OA	YA	YS
◒	○	●	◔	◔	◒	◒	○	◒	○	◒

Enjoyment 4.5

Study	item	group
Roberts-Griffin, 2011a	communication	3
Deri et al., 2018	enjoyment	4
Apostolou, Keramari, et al., 2020	enjoyment	1
Good chemistry 1, need for communication 1		
Hall, 2012a	companionship	1
'A friend who is good to have around no matter what I am doing'		
Bouwman, 2020	Enjoyment	2
'We could spend an enjoyable social evening together '		
Bouwman, 2020	Enjoyment	1
'Is an enjoyable person to be around'		
Stats: Enjoyment		

Proposed Statements for surveys:

- X can make me forget the problems and worries and just have a good time
- I enjoy spending time with X / I enjoy my time with X
- X and I can talk for hours
- X makes me relax

Weights per Genre:

Tot	OP	CP	TW	SH	CM	QS1	QS2	OA	YA	YS

Mutual Understanding 4.6

Statistical estimates: Mutual Understanding

Study	item	group
Tesch and R.R. Martin, 1983	understanding	2
Roberts-Griffin, 2011a	understanding	5
Adams, Blieszner, and Vries, 2000	understanding	5
Argyle and Henderson, 1984	'should not nag the other person'	4
Argyle and Henderson, 1984	'share news'	4
'Should share news of success with the other person'		
Hall, 2012a	Empathic Understanding	3
'A friend who clearly understands me, even without me having to tell them'		
Stats: Mutual Understanding		

Proposed Statements for surveys:

- X and I understand each other on a deep level
- X just gets me, what I say and what I mean
- X knows everything about me (interests, food, personal details)
- X really understands my feelings

The understanding questions used in studies often correlate semantically with a number of other item, e.g. sharing which leads to understanding, or guidance which becomes possible or effective through understanding.

Weights per Genre:

Tot	OP	CP	TW	SH	CM	QS1	QS2	OA	YA	YS

Reciprocity 4.7

Study	item	group
Roberts-Griffin, 2011a	reciprocity	5
Hall, 2012a	reciprocity Hartmann, 1992	3
Argyle and Henderson, 1984	repay favours	4
'should seek to repay debts, favour or compliments no matter how small'		
Hall, 2012a	reciprocity	4
'A friend who will always be fair, honest, and treat me equally'		
Bouwman, 2020	fairness	1
'Will always be fair in our friendship '		
Stats: Reciprocity		

Note the substantial difference between Bouwman and Hall for this item.

Proposed Statements for surveys:

- X is fair / balanced in our friendship
- My friendship with X is both giving and taking
- I feel needed and valued through my friendship with X

Note the direction here. On one side is the reciprocity emphasis, which is bilateral. On the other hand this captures simply that there is **something / anything** how I feel useful to my friend. I give somehow. The questions how my friends gives to me or benefits to me are scattered all over the activities, usually involving elements of practical help, support or guidance.

Weights per Genre:

Tot	OP	CP	TW	SH	CM	QS1	QS2	OA	YA	YS

Trust & Confidentiality 4.8

Study	item	group
Roberts-Griffin, 2011a	trust	1
Deri et al., 2018	trust	1
Argyle and Henderson, 1984	confidentiality	1
'Should not discuss that what is said in confidence with the other person'		
Hall, 2012a	trust	1
'A friend who I can trust to come through for me, and not tell anyone else my private information'		
Apostolou and Keramari, 2020	low trust (-)	1
Low trust factor with 7 elements preventing new friendships.		
Bouwman, 2020	trust	3
'Be someone with whom I can share secrets '		
Stats: Trust		

Apostolou and Keramari, 2020 low trust: I am very selective with whom to make friendship 1 (care of choice of friends), I do not trust others easily 1 (trust, open), I am cautious 1, It is difficult for me to find people who are really interested in friendship 1 (honesty/auth), I am suspicious 2 (general), lack of trust due to bad past experiences 3 (good will, loyalty), I feel that others approach me with a purpose other than friendship 5 (hon, end in themselves).

Proposed Statements for surveys:

- X keeps my secrets
- X does not discuss what I say to them in confidence
- X is trustworthy and discrete about what they know about me
- I can trust X

Weights per Genre:

Tot	OP	CP	TW	SH	CM	QS1	QS2	OA	YA	YS
◒	○	○	◒	◒	○	○	○	○	◒	◒

Openness 4.9

Oswald, Clark, and Kelly, 2004 identify openness as one of their four factors, but given the variety of themes collected inside again this cannot support openness in the narrow sense as defined above. [1].

Study	item	group
Roberts-Griffin, 2011a	openness	4
Argyle and Henderson, 1984	openness	2
'should trust and confide with the other person'		
Argyle and Henderson, 1984	openness	5
'Should disclose to the other person one's feelings and personal problems'		
Hall, 2012b	openness Oswald, Clark, and Kelly, 2004	2
Hall, 2012a	self disclosure	4
'A friend who I can share anything with and who will share with me'		
Hall, 2012a	openness	3
'A friend who is open and honest in sharing their thoughts with me'		
Bouwman, 2020	self disclosure	4
'Could reveal my most secret hopes and ambitions '		
Bouwman, 2020	openness	2
'Could talk to this person about my personal problems '		
Stats: Openness		

Proposed Statements for surveys:

- X knows my innermost secrets (past openness)
- With X I can be completely open (capability)
- With X I am open about my current feelings (exercised openness)

Also openness is a two way street, which cannot be taken for granted. Openness is the offsetting element to trust and empathy. Me being open with a friend is something different to that friend being open with me, and survey questions likewise need to see what they want to query.

Weights per Genre:

Tot	OP	CP	TW	SH	CM	QS1	QS2	OA	YA	YS
●	◒	◒	◒	●	●	●	●	◒	◒	◒

Respect 4.10

Study	item	group
Roberts-Griffin, 2011a	respect	4
Argyle and Henderson, 1984	no public criticism	4
'should not criticise the other person publicly'		
Adams, Blieszner, and Vries, 2000	Appreciation and Respect	6
Hall, 2012b	ego reinforcement	3
LaGaipa, 1977		
Apostolou, Keramari, et al., 2020	admiration	4/6
My admiration for someone 4, someone to admire me 6		
Bouwman, 2020	appreciation	4
'Thinks my ideas are important and worthwhile'		
Stats: Respect		

[1] Openness: 'Share your private thoughts with each other?' Openness, 'Repair misunderstandings?' Conflict Resolution - Loyalty (and Humility), 'Give advice to each other?' : Guidance and Direction (Act06), 'Show signs of affection toward each other?': Affection, 'Have intellectually stimulating conversations?' Expansion and Discovery (Act05) and implied IntelligenceCuriosity (Per12)

Proposed Statements for surveys:

- X is proud of being my friend
- X has praised my work in the last month
- X admires me
- X holds me in high esteem

- X and I hold each other in high esteem
- X and I are proud to be each other's friends

What is important here is the direction. You can define it as reciprocal esteem, as well as pride/admiration towards the interviewee. Pride or admiration for the friend usually is more founded in personality traits. But this aspect questions whether there is at least something, that my friend admires / values me for. It is thus the 'personality equivalent' of the 'doing/beneficence' oriented reciprocity.

Weights per Genre:

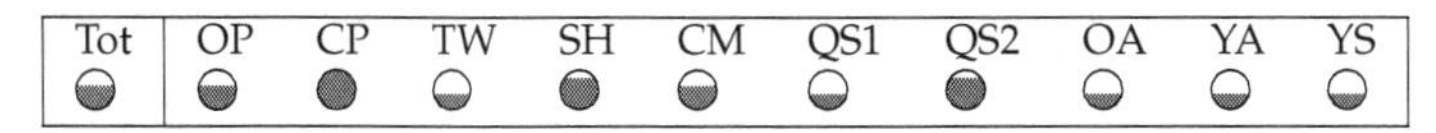

Equality 4.10

Study	item	group
Hall, 2012a	reciprocity	4
'A friend who will always be fair, honest, and treat me equally'		
Stats: Equality		

Proposed Statements for surveys:

- X and I are friends independent of our respective power or authority
- X and I feel equal to each other
- X and I treat each other as equals

Note that equality can be defined both as equality in fact (equal assets, intelligence, ...) or in esteem or value (for our friendship only our equal intellect or wit is of matter, it doesn't matter if you are a king and I am a pauper).

Weights per Genre:

Tot	OP	CP	TW	SH	CM	QS1	QS2	OA	YA	YS

Goodwill 4.11

No studies explicitly include classical good will, but Adams, Blieszner, and Vries, 2000 include the Affective Process 'Care'. It is however unclear whether the association of their definition with this theme is valid.

Study	item	group
Deri et al., 2018	care	3
Adams, Blieszner, and Vries, 2000	Affective Process 'Care'	3
Stats: Goodwill		

Proposed Statements for surveys:

- X wishes me well
- X truly wants me to succeed

- X is interested in my well being
- X cares for me

Weights per Genre:

Tot	OP	CP	TW	SH	CM	QS1	QS2	OA	YA	YS

Mutual Interest 4.12

Study	item	group
Roberts-Griffin, 2011a	shared interests	2
Adams, Blieszner, and Vries, 2000	shared interests	3
Apostolou and Keramari, 2020	element of 'too picky'	2
'It is difficult for me to find people with who we have common interests'		
Apostolou, Keramari, et al., 2020	shared interests	2
common interests with someone 2, share my interests 3		
Hall, 2012b	similarity (LaGaipa, 1977	5
includes mutual interests but is more focused on similarity and mutual belief		
Hall, 2012a	warmth	5
'A friend who likes to do the same things that I like to do'		
Stats: Mutual Interest		

Proposed Statements for surveys:

- X and I have a mutual hobby, interest or passion
- X and I have common interests / X is interested in the same things as me
- X and I talk about things we have read
- (X and I have similar goals)

Mutual interests can also be correlated to things like intellectual stimulation and collaboration.

Weights per Genre:

Tot	OP	CP	TW	SH	CM	QS1	QS2	OA	YA	YS

Mutual Belief 4.13

Study	item	group
Hall, 2012b	similarity LaGaipa, 1977	3
Adams, Blieszner, and Vries, 2000	homogeneity	6
Greif, 2009	commonality	4
Apostolou, Keramari, et al., 2020	shared opinions	3
If someone has opinions that I strongly agree with		
Hall, 2012a	similarity	5
'A friend who shares similar likes and dislikes, similar beliefs, and background'		
Bouwman, 2020	Similar views	3
'We share similar views about things that really matter in life '		
Stats: Mutual Belief		

Proposed Statements for surveys:

- X and I share opinions on many things
- X and I have a similar background, upbringing and value system
- X and I share the same political and/or religious convictions

Weights per Genre:

Tot	OP	CP	TW	SH	CM	QS1	QS2	OA	YA	YS

Different Belief 4.13

There were no statistical evaluations of this theme. Indeed generally this theme is really weak, it is just the the point is argued very strongly as part of the development-of-identity friendship theory.

Proposed Statements for surveys:

- X and I are/think very different to each other (positive)
- X and I have different political or religious convictions (positive)
- X and I live our lives in fundamentally different ways

Weights per Genre:

Tot	OP	CP	TW	SH	CM	QS1	QS2	OA	YA	YS
○	○	○	○	○	○	○	○	○	○	○

Respect of Privacy 4.14

Study	item	group
Argyle and Henderson, 1984	respect of privacy	1
Hall, 2012b	Noninterference	5
Stats: Respect of Privacy		

Proposed Statements for surveys:

- X respects my privacy
- X does not need to know everything from my life or background
- X and I share parts of our lives, but other parts I keep completely separate from the friendship
- X and I would have no intention to live together

Weights per Genre:

Tot	OP	CP	TW	SH	CM	QS1	QS2	OA	YA	YS

Living together 4.14

Study	item	group
Adams, Blieszner, and Vries, 2000	solidarity (*)	2
Stats: Living together		

Proposed Statements for surveys:

- X has or is living together with me.
- X and I are or would be perfectly happy to be living together
- X and I go in and out of each others house
- X and I maintain no privacy with each other

Weights per Genre:

Tot	OP	CP	TW	SH	CM	QS1	QS2	OA	YA	YS
○	○	○	○	○	○	○	○	◒	○	○

Activity

Dirt time 5.1

Oswald, Clark, and Kelly, 2004 fourth factor is interaction, which is reasonably close to spending time with each other, but also contains other items. [2].

Study	item	group
Hall, 2012b	Interaction* Oswald, Clark, and Kelly, 2004	4
Adams, Blieszner, and Vries, 2000	frequency of contact	4
Adams, Blieszner, and Vries, 2000	shared activities	3
Apostolou, Keramari, et al., 2020	hangout	3
companionship 3, contact with others 2, have someone to go out with 4		
Hall, 2012a	Companionship	3
'A friend who includes me in activities they do and in making future plans'		
Bouwman, 2020	Time spent	2
'Someone easy to spend time with'		
Stats: Dirt time		

Proposed Statements for surveys:

- X and I sometimes get together just to hang out
- X and I play board games together
- X and I spend lots of time together
- X and I go to social gatherings together

The key theme here is that the purpose of the reunion is the reunion, hanging out with the friend is a goal by itself.

Weights per Genre:

Tot	OP	CP	TW	SH	CM	QS1	QS2	OA	YA	YS
●	●	◕	◒	●	●	●	◕	●	◕	●

Work together 5.2

Study	item	group
Hall, 2012a	shared activities	5
'A friend who likes to do the same things that I like to do'		
Bouwman, 2020	tasks assistance	5
'Helps me complete jobs and tasks'		
Stats: work together		

Proposed Statements for surveys:

- X and I belong to the same club, NGO, sports or other association
- X and I have worked together on jobs or tasks given to us
- X and I have a joined activity, such as playing music, discussing philosophy or a joined spor
- (X and I pursue similar goals)
- X and I collaborate on stuff

[2]Interaction 'Go to social gatherings together?': Dirt time (Act01), 'Do favors for each other?': Practical Help (Act07) , 'Visit each other's homes?': Dirt time (Act01), 'Make an effort to spend time together even when you are busy?' : Friendship Priority (Rel16), 'Do new or unique activities together?': Exploration and Discovery (Act05), 'Get together just to hang-out?' Dirt time, 'Celebrate special occasions together?': Split, both Dirt time (Act01), hospitality (Act14) and friendship quality (Rel17), 'Work together on jobs or tasks?' : Work together (Act02)

The key focus of these question is that the purpose of the activity is something other than hanging out with the friend. There is a specific creative or concrete focus to the activity, such as discussing philosophy, making music. Thus if sports is just done leisurely for the fun of it, it would be classed with dirt time. But if it is sports training with the purpose of increasing the capability, also to compete in tournaments, it would be working together. The activity is successful if there is a positive output, not just if you had a good time.

Weights per Genre:

Tot	OP	CP	TW	SH	CM	QS1	QS2	OA	YA	YS
●	◒	●	○	◒	◒	●	◒	●	◒	●

Listening and Sharing 5.3

Study	item	group
Deri et al., 2018	empathy	4
Hall, 2012b	openness maintenance	2
	Oswald, Clark, and Kelly, 2004	
Hall, 2012b	empathic understanding	2
	LaGaipa, 1977	
Hall, 2012a	Emotional Support	2, 3
	'A friend who I can talk to about my fears, hopes, worries, and emotions (2)'	
	'A friend who clearly understands me, even without me having to tell them (3)'	
Hall, 2012a	Self disclosure	4
	'A friend who I can share anything with and who will share with me'	
Bouwman, 2020	Self disclosure	1,3
	'Be the kind of person I can share my private thoughts with (1)'	
	'Someone with whom I feel free to express my most inner private feelings (3)'	
Bouwman, 2020	Listening	1
	'Really listens to what I have to say'	
Bouwman, 2020	family problems	3
	'Could talk to this person about intimate family problems'	
	Stats: Listening and Sharing	

Proposed Statements for surveys:

- X makes it a point to really listen to me
- X is a great listener
- X gives me their undivided attention when I am sharing
- X and I share personal stories and emotions with each other
- X is someone with whom I express my innermost feelings
- I can talk to this problem about intimate family problems

This is a difficult one to survey, and possibly best in a double barrelled question capturing both sharing on my side and listening on the other. A second choice question is whether you want to survey one sided emotional support through this, or the reciprocal trusting sharing. The results can be potentially different.

Weights per Genre:

Tot	OP	CP	TW	SH	CM	QS1	QS2	OA	YA	YS
●	○	◒	●	●	●	●	●	●	●	●

Being There 5.4

This vague factor was also included in Oswald, Clark, and Kelly, 2004 as Supportiveness, again encompassing a whole range of activities and themes[3].

[3]Supportiveness: 'Try to make the other person "feel good" about who they are?' : Positivity, 'Let each other know you accept them for who they are?' : Acceptance, 'Support each other when

Study	item	group
Hall, 2012b	Supportiveness	2
	Oswald, Clark, and Kelly, 2004	
Roberts-Griffin, 2011a	Supportiveness	1
Argyle and Henderson, 1984	'should volunteer help in time of need'	1
Argyle and Henderson, 1984	'should look after the other person when they are ill'	5
Argyle and Henderson, 1984	'emotional support'	2
Apostolou, Keramari, et al., 2020	emotional support	3
	To have someone to discuss my problems with	
Hall, 2012a	Emotional Support	2
	'A friend who I can talk to about my fears, hopes, worries, and emotions'	
Hall, 2012a	Support	4
	'A friend who will provide me with whatever type of help or support I need'	
Bouwman, 2020	Support	2
	'Supports me when I am going through a difficult time '	
	Stats: Being there	

Proposed Statements for surveys:

- X is there for me whatever the circumstances
- X will provide me with whatever support I need
- X has shown in the past that they are there for me
- X would support me / has supported me when I am going through a difficult time
- (Is someone I can discuss my problems with)

Weights per Genre:

Tot	OP	CP	TW	SH	CM	QS1	QS2	OA	YA	YS

Practical Help 5.5

Study	item	group
Hall, 2012a	Help	2
	LaGaipa, 1977	
Hall, 2012a	Support	4
	'A friend who will provide me with whatever type of help or support I need'	
Apostolou, Keramari, et al., 2020	have someone to help me	5
Bouwman, 2020	favours	5
	'Does favors for me '	
	Stats: Practical Help	

- X helps with stuff like baby sitting, tax or homework
- X does favours for me
- X would help me move apartments

Weights per Genre:

Tot	OP	CP	TW	SH	CM	QS1	QS2	OA	YA	YS

one of you is going through a difficult time?': General Support, 'Talk about your friendship?': Friendship Quality (Rel17) and Conflict resolution, 'Apologize for something that happened?' : Humility (Per04), 'Compliment each other?': Pride and affirmation (Rel04), 'Let each other know you want the relationship to last in the future?' : Reliability and Consistency (Per09) and Loyalty (Rel08), 'Listen without making any judgment?': Acceptance (Per10), 'Provide each other with emotional support?': Split between empathic listening (Act03) and General Support (Act08), 'Phone or e-mail each other?': Affection (Rel13), 'Make compromises when you disagree about something?': Consideration (Rel03), 'Write cards or letters to each other?': Affection.

Circle Bonding 5.6

The topic has not been studied statistically.

Proposed Statements for surveys:

- X and I are part of a group of friends
- It is not just X and I, we just wouldn't be complete without Y and Z
- X is good at building a circle or group
- X and I have the most fun together in our group with Y and Z
- X loves bringing friends together for an evening

Weights per Genre:

Tot	OP	CP	TW	SH	CM	QS1	QS2	OA	YA	YS
◒	○	●	◒	◒	◒	◒	○	◒	◒	◒

Hospitality 5.7

The trait has not been studied in trait analyses.

Proposed Statements for surveys:

- X is a great host
- X and I drink, lunch or dine together
- X often has guests for lunch or dinner
- X always has a bottle of wine and some nibbles waiting for me

Weights per Genre:

Tot	OP	CP	TW	SH	CM	QS1	QS2	OA	YA	YS
◒	○	◒	◒	◒	●	◒	○	◒	◒	◒

In the context of the habits survey (see section F.3) I also raised two statistics, one regarding more the habits people employ in hosting their friends, and the other to what degree hospitality is constrained by the apartment (i.e. material wellbeing).

Hospitality habits				
	week	month	quarter	year or less
Quick Drink (Coffee/Beer/Tea/ ...)	24	55	32	51
Lunch	11	32	32	87
Dinner	9	52	43	58
Dinner and Stayover	1	12	42	107
Houseparty (more than 6 people)	0	7	37	118

Apartment suitable for receiving guests				
No space (1)	(2)	(3)	(4)	any number anytime (5)
20	50	35	48	9

Encouragement 5.8

Study	item	group
Roberts-Griffin, 2011a	kindness	3
Hall, 2012a	agency	2
'A friend who will help me become a better me, and will push me to succeed'		
Hall, 2012a	interaction	3
'A friend who is fun to go on trips with, plays sports with, or exercise with'		
Stats: Encouragement		

Proposed Statements for surveys:

- X challenges my thinking
- X helps me to see how good I am / can be
- X pushes me out of my comfort zone
- X is a great at encouraging me

Weights per Genre:

Tot	OP	CP	TW	SH	CM	QS1	QS2	OA	YA	YS

Effect Change 5.9

Study	item	group
Hall, 2012a	agency	2
'A friend who will help me become a better me, and will push me to succeed'		
Stats: Effect Change		

Proposed Statements for surveys:

- X helps me grow as a person
- My friendship with X makes me a better person
- X helps me to change in a positive way
- X challenges me to become a better person of myself
- X helps me grow in my character and virtue

Weights per Genre:

Tot	OP	CP	TW	SH	CM	QS1	QS2	OA	YA	YS

Guidance 5.10

Study	item	group
Argyle and Henderson, 1984	personal advice	3
Fischer, 1982	'Discuss personal issues'	3
Apostolou, Keramari, et al., 2020	someone to advise me	4
Bouwman, 2020	advice	1
'Someone who gives advice honestly when I ask them for it'		
Stats: Guidance		

Proposed Statements for surveys:

- X gives great advice or counsel
- X gives me honest feedback
- I can bounce thoughts and personal problems of X to improve my thinking
- X is a great sparings partner
- X helps me in my decision making

Weights per Genre:

Tot	OP	CP	TW	SH	CM	QS1	QS2	OA	YA	YS

Exploration & Discovery 5.11

The key topic of exploration and discovery not just by trips but also by conversation or play has not quite been studied.

Study	item	group
Hall, 2012b	openness to new experience John, Naumann, and Soto, 2008	5
Hall, 2012a	Interaction	3
'A friend who is fun to go on trips with, plays sports with, or exercise with'		
Stats: Exploration & Discovery		

Proposed Statements for surveys:

- I am more receptive to new ideas because of X
- My friendship with X expands my horizon / broadens my perspective
- I can discover new interests, hobbies and topics through my interactions with X
- X and I together love exploring ideas and thoughts or countries

Weights per Genre:

Tot	OP	CP	TW	SH	CM	QS1	QS2	OA	YA	YS

Teach & Learn 5.12

No statistical evaluations for this trait.

Proposed Statements for surveys:

- I learn and grow because of X I am continually learning from X
- X likes to teach me and I am trying to make their time worth it
- X provides intellectual fodder to chew on
- X and I are constantly learning from each other
- I love teaching X
- X and I love to study together

Weights per Genre:

Tot	OP	CP	TW	SH	CM	QS1	QS2	OA	YA	YS

Generosity 5.13

Study	item	group
Argyle and Henderson, 1984	giving of birthday cards and presents	6
Stats: Generosity		

Proposed Statements for surveys:

- X's gifts are a sign of their genuine affection
- X is a giving or generous person
- X gives meaningful gifts

Weights per Genre:

Tot	OP	CP	TW	SH	CM	QS1	QS2	OA	YA	YS

Vocal Support 5.14

Study	item	group
Argyle and Henderson, 1984	'Stand up for other person in their absence'	3
Hall, 2012a	loyalty	2
'A friend who will stick up for me and always be on my side'		
Bouwman, 2020	vocal support	3,4
'Stands by me through anything (3)' 'When others criticize me, stands up for me (4)'		
Stats:Vocal support		

Proposed Statements for surveys:

- X stands up for me when I am not around
- X praises my work / character in front of other people
- X would not criticise me in front of other people
- X would stand at my side when the going gets tough

Weights per Genre:

Tot	OP	CP	TW	SH	CM	QS1	QS2	OA	YA	YS
◒	○	○	◒	◒	○	◒	◒	○	○	◒

Resources

Proximity 6.2

Study	item	group
Hall, 2012a	availability	6
'A friend who lives nearby and has a lot of time to spend with me'		
Stats: Proximity		

Proposed Statements for surveys:

- X lives just round the corner / close by
- X and I can meet up really easily

Weights per Genre:

Tot	OP	CP	TW	SH	CM	QS1	QS2	OA	YA	YS
◒	◒	◒	◒	◒	◒	◒	○	●	○	◒

Content 6.3

Study	item	group
Hall, 2012a	'wealth'	6
'A friend who has money, is *highly educated*, or has high earning potential'		
Stats: Content		

Proposed Statements for surveys:

- X knows a lot of things / is well educated
- X knows everything, including the latest gossip
- X experiences a lot in his life and is thus really interesting to talk to
- X has great stories to tell

Weights per Genre:

Tot	OP	CP	TW	SH	CM	QS1	QS2	OA	YA	YS
◒	○	◒	○	◒	◒	◒	◒	◒	◒	◒

Health & Fitness 6.4

Study	item	group
Hall, 2012b	'Athletic ability'	6
Lusk, MacDonald, and Newman, 1998		
Apostolou and Keramari, 2020	Pragmatic reasons	6
Hall, 2012a	fitness	6
'A friend who is physically fit, attractive, and a good athlete'		
Bouwman, 2020	fitness	5,6,6
'Is physically fit (5), not physically handicapped (6), athletic (6) '		
Stats: Health & Fitness		

Apostolou and Keramari, 2020 Pragmatic reasons: I live in a place with few inhabitants and I do not meet new people 5 (Proximity, Network), I am in a tight-knit group of friends that prevents me from making new friends 6, I I live in country whose culture is different than my own, which makes it difficult for me to make friends 6 (mutual belief), I have psychological problems that prevent me from making friends 6 (health), I have a health problem that prevents me from socializing 6 (health), I have a disability that makes it difficult for me to socialize 6 (health). As Apostolou and Keramari, 2020 notes, the population sample is rather young, and age is positively correlated with higher health inhibition.

Proposed Statements for surveys:

- X is not limited through his health in hanging out or doing stuff with me
- X is fit and a good athlete
- More specific questions regarding psychological health probably need ethics clearance and specialist advice

There are a number of standardized scales, such as the SF-36 that are designed to query for obstacles and health impairments, that could impact loneliness. Depending on resources available, rather than consolidating it into a single question, it is probably better to resort to such instruments when the setup requires it. Getting such personal data, even if it means extra sensitivity of the data set and higher standards for ethical clearance, is probably worth it when dealing with elderly or vulnerable people, as otherwise substantial latent variable problems can distort the analysis.

Weights per Genre:

Tot	OP	CP	TW	SH	CM	QS1	QS2	OA	YA	YS

Network 6.5

Study	item	group
Apostolou, Keramari, et al., 2020	expand social circle	5
Apostolou, Keramari, et al., 2020	advance career	5
Apostolou, Keramari, et al., 2020	expand social circle for mating	2
Hall, 2012b	'business connections'	6
Hall, 2012a	status	6
'A friend who comes from a good background, is popular, knows a lot of people, and is a leader'		
Bouwman, 2020	connections	4,6
'Has social connections' (4), 'Has business connections' (6)		
Stats: Network		

Proposed Statements for surveys:

- X organizes good parties with interesting people
- X seems to know everyone
- Whenever I tell X of a problem, he usually has a suggestion who might help me
- X is great at introducing friends of his to other friends

A number of questions more emphasised the utility (for business/career/personal gain) when asking for networks, often also with Granovetters weak links in mind. However in a friend the capability to socially connect, to throw a good party might be really important. Thus the extrovert friend's network might simply be a great help and opportunity for introverts to find other friends without any business or utilitarian thoughts.

Weights per Genre:

Tot	OP	CP	TW	SH	CM	QS1	QS2	OA	YA	YS
◒	○	○	○	○	◒	◒	○	◒	◒	◒

Time 6.6

Study	item	group
Apostolou and Keramari, 2020	lack of time (-)	2
lack of time factor with 3 elements preventing new friendships.		
Hall, 2012a	availability	6
'A friend who lives nearby and has a lot of time to spend with me'		
Stats: Resource time		

Apostolou and Keramari, 2020 lack of time: Lack of time 1, I work long hours and have no time for friendships 2 (time + energy), I devote all my time to my partner and have no time for friendships 4 (priority, not time)

Proposed Statements for surveys:

- X is generous with their time
- X has lots of time
- X ensures that their friends get enough face-time with them
- X arranges their life to have time for their friends

Time is both asset and priority, the two are clearly linked.

Weights per Genre:

Tot	OP	CP	TW	SH	CM	QS1	QS2	OA	YA	YS
○	○	○	○	◒	◒	○	○	◒	○	◒

Material Wellbeing 6.7

Study	item	group
Hall, 2012b	'resources' Sprecher and Regan, 2002	5
Hall, 2012a	status	6
'A friend who comes from a *good background*, is popular, knows a lot of people, and is a leader'		
Stats: Material Wellbeing		

Proposed Statements for surveys:

- X is not rich but has no money problems
- X has a house/apartment where they can host/invite people
- X is financially unconstrained for moderate social activities

It is of course difficult to and highly subjective to ask for financial well-being. A 'more' of financial resources often does not lead to being a better friend. But severe lack of funds, e.g. because of unemployment, can substantially impair one's capability for social life. The key here is that it is enough money to fully enable social life, but less than what might attract the friends' envy and thus potentially become a liability.

Weights per Genre:

Tot	OP	CP	TW	SH	CM	QS1	QS2	OA	YA	YS
○	○	○	○	○	○	◒	◒	◒	○	◒

Money 6.8

Study	item	group
Hall, 2012a	wealth	6
'A friend who *has money*, is highly educated, or has high earning potential'		
Bouwman, 2020	Money	6,6,6
'Has money, Has high earning potential, wealthy background '		
Stats: Money		

Proposed Statements for surveys:

- X has high status
- X is rich / has a lot of money
- X has high earnings potential
- X is from a good family / aristocratic ...
- I do not know whether X is interested in me as a friend or because of my money

High earnings can be both positive but also negative because of inequality.

Weights per Genre:

Tot	OP	CP	TW	SH	CM	QS1	QS2	OA	YA	YS
○	○	○	○	○	○	○	○	○	○	○

Attractiveness 6.9

Study	item	group
Hall, 2012b	physicall attractiveness	6
Lusk, MacDonald, and Newman, 1998		
Hall, 2012a	fitness	6
'A friend who is physically fit, attractive, and a good athlete'		
Apostolou, Keramari, et al., 2020	mating (-)	5
Approach someone who interests me romantically, someone's appearance		
Bouwman, 2020	attractiveness	4,5
'Has an attractive appearance' (4), 'Is physically attractive' (5)		
Stats: Attractiveness		

Proposed Statements for surveys:

- X is beautiful
- X is very attractive
- I could be / am romantically interested in X
- I am sometimes jealous at X as they get all the attention because they are beautiful
- I do not know whether X is interested in me as a friend or romantically

Weights per Genre:

Tot	OP	CP	TW	SH	CM	QS1	QS2	OA	YA	YS
○	○	○	○	○	○	○	○	○	○	○

Index

Bibliography

Abell, S., 2009. *Authentic Relationships Inside Out*. Hodder Stoughton.

Adams, R.G. and Blieszner, R., eds, 1989. *Older adult friendship: Structure and process*. Vol. 103. SAGE Publications, Incorporated.

Adams, R.G., Blieszner, R., and Vries, B. de, 2000. Definitions of friendship in the third age: age, gender, and study location effects. *Journal of Aging Studies* [Online], 14(1), pp.117–133. Available from: https://doi.org/10.1016/S0890-4065(00)80019-5.

Adams, R.G. and Torr, R., 1998. Factors underlying the structure of older adult friendship networks. *Social Networks* [Online], 20(1), pp.51–61. Available from: https://doi.org/10.1016/S0378-8733(97)00004-X.

Aeschylus, 1926. *Oresteia. Agamemnon; Libation-bearers; Eumenides: Translation by Herbert Weir Smyth*. Vol. 2. Loeb Classical Library.

Akana, A., 2018. *4 Types of Female friends* [Online]. Available from: https://youtu.be/Z7LTlF5cntw.

Alberoni, F., 2016. *Friendship* [Online]. Vol. 20, Social and Critical Theory. Brill. Available from: https://doi.org/10.1163/9789004331303.

Albert, F., David, B., Hajdu, G., and Huszti, É., 2020. Egocentric Contact Networks of Older Adults: Featuring Quantity, Strength and Function of Ties. *The Sociological Quarterly* [Online], pp.1–20. Available from: https://doi.org/10.1080/00380253.2020.1787111.

Alcock-Ferguson, L., 2018-05-16. To beat loneliness, we must connect. Charities can show how. *Guardian*.

Alkire, S., 2002. Dimensions of human development. *World development*, 30(2), pp.181–205.

Alkire, S. and Foster, J., 2011. Counting and multidimensional poverty measurement. *Journal of public economics*, 95(7-8), pp.476–487.

Almaatouq, A., Radaelli, L., Pentland, A., and Shmueli, E., 2016. Are you your friends' friend? Poor perception of friendship ties limits the ability to promote behavioral change. *PLOS ONE*, 11(3), e0151588.

Altman, I. and Taylor, D.A., 1973. *Social penetration: The development of interpersonal relationships*. Holt, Rinehart & Winston.

Amsel, N., 1994. The Jewish encyclopedia of moral and ethical issues.

Andrews, J., 2019-12-19. Friendships Don't Exist Just To Serve Us There's cutting out toxic friends, then there's being self-absorbed. *Medium*.

Anonymous, 2018-08-10. My friend is single and lonely, but demanding. *Guardian* [Online]. Available from: https://www.theguardian.com/lifeandstyle/2018/aug/10/my-friend-is-single-and-lonely-but-demanding.

Apostolou, M. and Keramari, D., 2020. What prevents people from making friends: A taxonomy of reasons. *Personality and Individual Differences*, 163, p.110043.

Apostolou, M., Keramari, D., Kagialis, A., and Sullman, M., 2020. Why people make friends: The nature of friendship. *Personal Relationships*.

Archer, D., 2013. *Smartphone Addiction* [Online]. Available from: https://www.psychologytoday.com/us/blog/reading-between-the-headlines/201307/smartphone-addiction.

Argyle, M. and Henderson, M., 1984. The Rules of Friendship. *Journal of Social and Personal Relationships*, 1, pp.211–237.

Argyle, M., Henderson, M., and Furnham, A., 1985. The rules of social relationships. *British Journal of Social Psychology*, 24(2), pp.125–139.

Aristotle, 1925. *Nicomachean Ethics: Translation by W.D. Ross, By permission of Oxford University Press* [Online]. 1st ed. Oxford, UK: Oxford University Press. Available from: http://www.oup.com.

Aristotle, 1926. *Nicomachean Ethics: Translation by Rackham* [Online]. Loeb Classical Library, Harvard University Press, Cambridge, MA. Available from: http://data.perseus.org/citations/urn:cts:greekLit:tlg0086.tlg010.perseus-eng1:9.1.

Asatryan, K., 2016. *Stop Being Lonely*. New World Library.

Atwood, B., 2005. *The Fundamentals Of Friendship*.

Balaam, M.-.-C., 2015. A concept analysis of befriending. *Journal of Advanced Nursing*, 71(1), pp.24–34.

Baldassarri, D. and Bearman, P., 2007. Dynamics of Political Polarization. *American Sociological Review* [Online], 72(5), pp.784–811. Available from: https://doi.org/10.1177/000312240707200507.

Ball, T.B., 2020-05-23. 7 Signs Your Friendship is Toxic You've likely experienced a friendship at one point that rattled you. *Medium* [Online]. Available from: https://psiloveyou.xyz/7-signs-your-friendship-is-toxic-f2f9ace326b5.

Ball, T.B., 2020-05-18. Are You Toxic? 10 Ways to Tell (And How to Stop). *Medium* [Online]. Available from: https://psiloveyou.xyz/are-you-toxic-10-ways-to-tell-and-how-to-stop-aa5be2b857ed.

Baranski, E., Gray, J., Morse, P., and Dunlop, W., 2020. From desire to development? A multi-sample, idiographic examination of volitional personality change. *Journal of Research in Personality* [Online], 85, p.103910. Available from: https://doi.org/10.1016/j.jrp.2019.103910.

Barash, S.S., 2009. *Toxic Friends: The Antidote for Women Stuck in Complicated Friendships*. St. Martin's Press.

Barreto, M., Victor, C., Hammond, C., Eccles, A., Richins, M.T., and Qualter, P., 2021. Loneliness around the world: Age, gender, and cultural differences in loneliness. *Personality and Individual Differences* [Online], 169, p.110066. Available from: `https://doi.org/10.1016/j.paid.2020.110066`.

Bell, S. and Coleman, S., 1999. *The anthropology of friendship*. Berg Oxford.

Bennett, 2018. *The Quality That Makes You A Good Friend, According To Your Myers-Briggs Type* [Online]. Available from: `https://www.bustle.com/p/the-quality-that-makes-you-a-good-friend-according-to-your-myers-briggs-type-8629679`.

Besser, L.M., Marcus, M., and Frumkin, H., 2008. Commute time and social capital in the US. *American Journal of Preventive Medicine*, 34(3), pp.207–211.

Binder, J.F., Roberts, S.G., and Sutcliffe, A.G., 2012. Closeness, loneliness, support: Core ties and significant ties in personal communities. *Social Networks* [Online], 34(2), pp.206–214. Available from: `https://doi.org/10.1016/j.socnet.2011.12.001`.

Birch, J., 2018a. *Myers Briggs Compatibility for Friends* [Online]. Available from: `https://www.manrepeller.com/2018/03/myers-briggs-compatibility-for-friends.html` [Accessed June 27, 2020].

Birch, J., 2018b. *What you need from your friends* [Online]. Available from: `https://boldl.com/blogs/man-repeller/what-you-need-from-your-friends-according-to-your-myers-briggs`.

Birch, J., 2019. *Good Friends Are Hard to Come by—Here's What to Look for in One, According to Your MBTI Profile*.

Blatterer, H., 2015. *Everyday friendships: intimacy as freedom in a complex world*. Palgrave MacMillan.

Blease, C.R., 2015. Too Many 'Friends,' Too Few 'Likes'? Evolutionary Psychology and 'Facebook Depression'. *Review of general psychology* [Online], 19(1), pp.1–13. Available from: `https://doi.org/10.1037/gpr0000030`.

Blieszner, R., 1995. Friendship processes and well-being in the later years of life: Implications for intervention. *Journal of Geriatric Psychiatry*, 28(2), pp.165–182.

Blieszner, R. and Adams, R.G., 1992. *Adult friendship*. Vol. 3. Sage Publications.

Blieszner, R. and Adams, R.G., 1998. Problems with friends in old age. *Journal of Aging Studies*, 12(3), pp.223–238.

Blieszner, R. and Ogletree, A.M., 2017. We Get By with a Little Help from Our Friends. *Generations: Journal of the American Society on Aging* [Online], 41(2), pp.55–62. Available from: `https://doi.org/10.2307/26556284`.

Blieszner, R., Ogletree, A.M., and Adams, R.G., 2019. Friendship in Later Life: A Research Agenda. *Innovation in Aging* [Online], 3(1). Available from: `https://doi.org/10.1093/geroni/igz005`.

Bouwman, T.E., 2020. *Coping in loneliness interventions: The online Friendship Enrichment Program for people aged 50 years and older* [Online]. Doctoral thesis. VU Amsterdam. Available from: `https://research.vu.nl/en/publications/coping-in-loneliness-interventions-the-online-friendship-enrichme`.

Bouwman, T.E., Aartsen, M.J., van Tilburg, T.G., and Stevens, N.L., 2017. Does stimulating various coping strategies alleviate loneliness? Results from an online friendship enrichment program. *Journal of Social and Personal Relationships*, 34(6), pp.793–811.

Brown, C.B. and LMSW, B., 2012. *The power of vulnerability*. Sounds True Louisville, CO.

Brox, E., Luque, L.F., Evertsen, G.J., and Hernández, J.E.G., 2011. Exergames for elderly: Social exergames to persuade seniors to increase physical activity. *2011 5th International Conference on Pervasive Computing Technologies for Healthcare (PervasiveHealth) and Workshops*. Ieee, pp.546–549.

Bruggencate, T. ten, Luijkx, K.G., and Sturm, J., 2018. Social needs of older people: a systematic literature review. *Ageing and Society*, 38(9), pp.1745–1770.

Cacioppo, J.T. and Hawkley, L.C., 2009. Loneliness. *15938564*.

Cacioppo, J.T. and Patrick, W., 2008. *Loneliness: Human nature and the need for social connection*. WW Norton & Company.

Cappelli, P., 2012. *Why good people can't get jobs: The skills gap and what companies can do about it*. Wharton Digital Press.

Carley, K.M. and Krackhardt, D., 1996. Cognitive inconsistencies and non-symmetric friendship. *Social Networks*, 18(1), pp.1–27.

Carstensen, L.L., Fung, H.H., and Charles, S.T., 2003. Socioemotional selectivity theory and the regulation of emotion in the second half of life. *Motivation and emotion*, 27(2), pp.103–123.

Casagrande, L. and Castañeda, M., 2020. Conviviality after Social Platforms. *The International Journal of Illich Studies*, 7(1), pp.192–208.

Caserta, M.S., Lund, D.A., and Rice, S.J., 1999. Pathfinders: A self-care and health education program for older widows and widowers. *The Gerontologist*, 39(5), pp.615–620.

Cash, T.F. and Derlega, V.J., 1978. The Matching Hypothesis: Physical Attractiveness among Same-Sexed Friends. *Personality and Social Psychology Bulletin* [Online], 4(2), pp.240–243. Available from: `https://doi.org/10.1177/014616727800400213`.

Cattan, M., Kime, N., and Bagnall, A.-M., 2011. The use of telephone befriending in low level support for socially isolated older people – an evaluation. *Health & Social Care in the Community* [Online], 19(2), pp.198–206. Available from: `https://doi.org/10.1111/j.1365-2524.2010.00967.x`.

Cerri, 2019. *The Myers Briggs Types That Make The Best (And Worst) Friends* [Online]. Available from: `https://www.yourtango.com/2019321764/myers-briggs-types-make-best-and-worst-friends-ranked-best-worst` [Accessed June 27, 2020].

Chambers, D.L., 2000. For the Best of Friends and for Lovers of All Sorts, A Status Other than Marriage. *Notre Dame L. Rev.*, 76, p.1347.

Chapman, G., 2009. *The Five Languages Singles Edition*. Northfield.

Chopik, W.J., 2017. Associations among relational values, support, health, and well-being across the adult lifespan. *Personal Relationships* [Online], 24(2), pp.408–422. Available from: `https://doi.org/10.1111/pere.12187`.

Christensen, B., 2011. The Mandarin Moralist and the Reckless Rebel: the Improbable Literary Friendship of Du Fu and Li Bai. *Rupkatha Journal on Interdisciplinary Studies in Humanities*, 3(4), pp.417–424.

Cicero, M.T., 1923. *De Amicitia: Retrieved under CC BY-SA licence* [Online]. Loeb Classical Library, Harvard University Press, Cambridge, MA. Available from: `http://www.perseus.tufts.edu/hopper/text?doc=Perseus:text:2007.01.0052`.

Clore, G.L. and Byrne, D., 1974. A reinforcement-affect model of attraction. *Foundations of interpersonal attraction*, pp.143–170.

Cocking, D. and Kennett, J., 1998. Friendship and the Self. *Ethics*, 108(3), pp.502–527.

Cohen, T., 1992. Men's families, men's friends: A structural analysis of constraints on men's social ties. In: P. Nardi, ed. *Men's friendships*. Sage.

Coltrain, S., 2004. *Friendship* [Online]. Available from: `https://www.sermoncentral.com/sermons/friendship-scott-coltrain-sermon-on-friendship-general-71724`.

Cook, M., Pasley, J., Pellarin, E., Medow, K., Baltz, M., and Buhman-Wiggs, A., 2013. Construct validation of the five love languages. *Journal of Psychological Inquiry*, 18(2), pp.50–61.

Coplan, A., 2011. Understanding Empathy:: Its Features and Effects. *Empathy* [Online]. Oxford: Oxford University Press. Available from: `https://doi.org/10.1093/acprof:oso/9780199539956.003.0002`.

Cormie, D., 2005. *Fostering Meaningful Friendships*.

Cuddeback, J., 2010. *True Friendship: Where Virtue becomes Friendship*. Epic Publishing.

Cuddy, A., Kohut, M., and Neffinger, J., 2013. Connect, then lead. *Harvard Business Review* [Online], July-August. Available from: `https://hbr.org/2013/07/connect-then-lead`.

Deen, M.J., 2017-06-22. What if we were friends. *Youtube* [Online]. Available from: `https://www.youtube.com/watch?v=Bnm1uRc_oL0`.

Degges-White, S. and Borzumato-Gainey, C., 2011. *Friends forever: How girls and women forge lasting relationships*. Rowman & Littlefield.

Degges-White, S. and van Tieghem, J.P., 2015. *Toxic Friendships: Knowing the Rules and Dealing with the Friends who Break Them*. Rowman & Littlefield.

Delaney, T. and Madigan, T., 2017. *Friendship and happiness: And the connection between the two*. McFarland.

Demir, M., ed., 2015. *Friendship and Happiness*. Springer.

Demir, M. and Suerner, N., eds, 2018. *Close Relationships and Happiness across Cultures*. Springer.

Deri, S., Rappaz, J., Aiello, L.M., and Quercia, D., 2018. Coloring in the links: Capturing social ties as they are perceived. *Proceedings of the ACM on Human-Computer Interaction*, 2(CSCW), pp.1–18.

Desai, A. and Killick, E., 2010. *The ways of friendship: Anthropological perspectives*. Berghahn Books.

Diener, E. and Arora, R., 2009. *Assessing well-being*, Social indicators research. Social indicators research series. Dordrecht and New York: Springer.

Diener, E., Emmons, R.A., Larsen, R.J., and Griffin, S., 1985. The Satisfaction With Life Scale. *Journal of Personality Assessment*, 49(1), pp.71–75.

Diodorus, 1933. *Library of History, Volume I: Books 1-2.34: Translation by C.H. Oldfather.*

Dobelli, R., 2017. *The Art of the Good Life: 52 Surprising Shortcuts to Happiness, Wealth, and Success*. Hachette UK.

Dooley, J., 2020-02-26. The Surprising Joy of Cultivating Female Friendships in Middle Age. *Medium* [Online]. Available from: `https://humanparts.medium.com/the-surprising-joy-of-cultivating-friendships-in-middle-age-ed4399f2f271`.

Dotti Sani, G.M. and Treas, J., 2016. Educational gradients in parents' child–care time across countries, 1965–2012. *Journal of Marriage and Family*, 78(4), pp.1083–1096.

Downey, D.B. and Condron, D.J., 2004. Playing well with others in kindergarten: The benefit of siblings at home. *Journal of Marriage and Family*, 66(2), pp.333–350.

Duckworth, A.L., Peterson, C., Matthews, M.D., and Kelly, D.R., 2007. Grit: perseverance and passion for long-term goals. *Journal of personality and social psychology* [Online], 92(6), p.1087. Available from: `https://doi.org/10.1037/0022-3514.92.6.1087`.

Dufton, B., 1986. Will you be my friend? Group Psychotherapy with lonely people. In: S. Natale, ed. *Psychotherapy and the Lonely Patient*, The psychotherapy patient. New York: Haworth Press, pp.61–76.

Dumagane, C., 2018-11-26. Young people value diversity, humour and honesty in their friendships, new research. *The Conversation* [Online]. Available from: `https://theconversation.com/young-people-value-diversity-humour-and-honesty-in-their-friendships-new-research-107208`.

Dunbar, R.I., 2021. *Friends: Understanding the Power of our Most Important Relationships*. Little, Brown and Company.

Dunbar, R., 2004. Gossip in evolutionary perspective. *Review of general psychology*, 8(2), pp.100–110.

Dunbar, R., 2012. Social cognition on the Internet: testing constraints on social network size. *Philosophical Transactions: Biological Sciences* [Online], 367(1599), pp.2192–2201. Available from: `http://www.jstor.org/stable/23250496`.

Dunbar, R., 2016. Friends on Tap. *Oxford: Campaign for Real Ale.*

Egbert, N. and Polk, D., 2006. Speaking the language of relational maintenance: A validity test of Chapman's Five Love Languages. *Communication Research Reports*, 23(1), pp.19–26.

Eldredge, R., 2020-11-10. To my family who chose Trump over me: Was it worth it? *CNN* [Online]. Available from: `https://edition.cnn.com/2020/11/10/opinions/trump-tore-my-family-apart-eldredge/index.html`.

Erin M. Bryant and Jennifer Marmo, 2012. The rules of Facebook friendship. *Journal of Social and Personal Relationships*, 29(8), pp.1013–1035.

Eve, M., 2002. Is friendship a sociological topic? *European Journal of Sociology/Archives Européennes de Sociologie/Europaeisches Archiv fuer Soziologie* [Online], 43(3), pp.386–409. Available from: `http://www.jstor.org/stable/23998867`.

Fehr, B., 1996. *Friendship processes*. Vol. 12. Sage.

Feigel, 2020-07-04. Love beyond sex, money and property: a case for friendship. *Guardian* [Online]. Available from: `https://www.theguardian.com/books/2020/jul/04/love-beyond-sex-money-and-property-a-case-for-friendship`.

Feld, S.L., 1981. The Focused Organization of Social Ties. *American Journal of Sociology* [Online], 86(5), pp.1015–1035. Available from: `https://doi.org/10.1086/227352`.

Feldhahn, S. and Feldhahn, J., 2008. *For Men Only, Revised and Updated Edition: a Straightforward Guide to the Inner Lives of Women*. Multnomah.

Fischer, C.S., 1982. What do we mean by 'friend'? An inductive study. *Social Networks*, 3(4), pp.287–306.

Fletcher, A., Bonell, C., and Sorhaindo, A., 2011. You are what your friends eat: systematic review of social network analyses of young people's eating behaviours and bodyweight. *Journal of Epidemiology and Community Health (1979-)* [Online], 65(6), pp.548–555. Available from: `http://www.jstor.org/stable/23050919`.

Flowers, S., 2016. *5 People you need to be Happy: Ted Talk*.

Foa, E.B. and Foa, U.G., 1980. Resource theory. *Social exchange*. Springer, pp.77–94.

Friedkin, N.E., 1990. A Guttman scale for the strength of an interpersonal tie. *Social Networks*, 12(3), pp.239–252.

Friedman, M., 1993. *What are Friends for? Feminist Perspectives on Personal Relationships and Moral Theory*. Cornell University Press.

Fromm, E., 2000. *The art of loving: The centennial edition*. A&C Black.

Fromm, E., 2013a. *The art of listening*. Open Road Media.

Fromm, E., 2013b. *To have or to be?* A&C Black.

Gangestad, S.W. and Snyder, M., 2000. Self-monitoring: Appraisal and reappraisal. *Psychological bulletin*, 126(4), p.530.

Gardiner, C., Geldenhuys, G., and Gott, M., 2018. Interventions to reduce social isolation and loneliness among older people: an integrative review. *Health & Social Care in the Community* [Online], 26(2), pp.147–157. Available from: `https://doi.org/10.1111/hsc.12367`.

Garfield, R., 2016. *Breaking the male code*. Avery.

Gee, L.K., Jones, J.J., Fariss, C.J., Burke, M., and Fowler, J.H., 2017. The paradox of weak ties in 55 countries. *Journal of Economic Behavior & Organization*, 133, pp.362–372.

Gierveld, J.D.J. and van Tilburg, T., 2006. A 6-item scale for overall, emotional, and social loneliness: Confirmatory tests on survey data. *Research on aging*, 28(5), pp.582–598.

Gilbert, D., 2009. *Stumbling on happiness*. Vintage Canada.

Gillett, K. and Dixon, M., 2009. VitalLinks: nurturing emotional well–being in older people through one–to–one communication. *Working with Older People*.

Gilligan, C., 1982. *In a Different Voice*. Harvard University Press, Cambridge, MA.

Goffman, E., 1978. *The presentation of self in everyday life*. Harmondsworth London.

Goldhaber, M., 1997. *Attention Shoppers* [Online]. Available from: `https://www.wired.com/1997/12/es-attention/`.

Golubev, AG and Sidorenko, A.V., 2020. Theory and Practice of Aging during the COVID-19 Pandemic. *Advances in Gerontology*, 10(4), pp.303–312.

Gottman, J., 2001. *The Relationship Cure*. Harmony Books.

Gottman, J. and Silver, N., 2015. *The Seven Principles for making Marriages Work*. Harmony Books.

Gottman, J.M., 2002. *The mathematics of marriage : dynamic nonlinear models*. Cambridge, Mass. and London: MIT Press.

Gouldner, A.W., 1960. The norm of reciprocity: A preliminary statement. *American Sociological Review*, pp.161–178.

Granovetter, M., 1973. The Strength of Weak Ties. *American Journal of Sociology*, 78(6), pp.1360–1380.

Granovetter, M., 1983. The Strength of Weak Ties: A Network Theory Revisited. *Sociological Theory* [Online], 1, pp.201–233. Available from: `https://doi.org/10.2307/202051`.

Grant, A.M., 2013. *Give and take: A revolutionary approach to success*. Penguin.

Grayling, A.C., 2013. *Friendship*. Yale University Press.

Greif, G., 2009. *Buddy System - Understanding Male Friendships*. Oxford University Press.

Grosjean, F., 1982. *Life with two languages: An introduction to bilingualism*. Harvard University Press.

Hall, J.A., 2018. How many hours does it take to make a friend? *Journal of Social and Personal Relationships*.

Hall, J.A., 2011. Sex differences in friendship expectations: A meta-analysis. *Journal of Social and Personal Relationships*, 28(6), pp.723–747.

Hall, J.A., 2012a. *Friendship standards: Additional unpublished Dataset raised in connection with study, provided to and analyzed by Christian Langkamp for this book.* Unpublished.

Hall, J.A., 2012b. Friendship Standards: The dimensions of ideal expectations. *Journal of Social and Personal Relationships.*

Hartmann, L.A., 1992. Friendship development in early adolescence: Experience, expectations, and aspects of loneliness.

Hatfield, E. and Traupmann, J., 1981. Intimate relationships: A perspective from equity theory. *Personal Relationships*, 1, pp.165–178.

Hawthorne, G., 2006. Measuring social isolation in older adults: development and initial validation of the friendship scale. *Social indicators research*, 77(3), pp.521–548.

Hays, R.B., 1988. Friendship. In: S. Duck, ed. *Handbook of personal relationships: Theory, research and interventions.* New York: John Wiley & Sons, pp.391–408.

Heine, E.W., 2003. *New York liegt im Neandertal.* Diogenes.

Hertz, N., 2020. *The Lonely Century: Coming Together in a World That's Pulling Apart.* Sceptre.

Heyman, R.E. and Slep, A.M.S., 2001. The Hazards of Predicting Divorce Without Cross-validation. *Journal of Marriage and Family* [Online], 63(2), pp.473–479. Available from: `https://doi.org/10.1111/j.1741-3737.2001.00473.x`.

Hockings, K.J. and Dunbar, R., 2019. Alcohol and Humans. *Alcohol and Humans: A Long and Social Affair*, p.196.

Hodgkinson, T., 2005. *How to be Idle.* Penguin UK.

Hogan, B., Carrasco, J.A., and Wellman, B., 2007. Visualizing personal networks: Working with participant-aided sociograms. *Field methods*, 19(2), pp.116–144.

Hojjat, M., Moyer, A., and Halpin, A.M., 2017. *The psychology of friendship.* Oxford University Press.

Hunt, E., 2019-12-13. 'I thought you'd like to read this': the etiquette of gifting books. *Guardian.*

Hunt, E., 2018-09-07. 'On the bike path I feel a connection to people': your shared spaces. *Guardian* [Online]. Available from: `https://www.theguardian.com/cities/2018/sep/07/on-the-bike-path-i-feel-a-connection-to-people-your-shared-spaces`.

Hunt, E., 2018-09-03. Two hours with a stranger: can these questions open up a city? [Online]. Available from: `https://www.theguardian.com/cities/2018/sep/03/two-hours-stranger-questions-open-city-vienna`.

Huszti, É., Dávid, B., and Vajda, K., 2013. Strong tie, weak tie and in-betweens: A continuous measure of tie strength based on contact diary datasets. *Procedia-Social and Behavioral Sciences*, 79, pp.38–61.

Huxhold, O., Fiori, K.L., Webster, N.J., and Antonucci, T.C., 2020. The Strength of weaker ties: An underexplored resource for maintaining emotional well-being in later life. *The Journals of Gerontology: Series B*, 75(7), pp.1433–1442.

Jackson, J.J., Connolly, J.J., Garrison, S.M., Leveille, M.M., and Connolly, S.L., 2015. Your Friends Know How Long You Will Live: A 75-Year Study of Peer-Rated Personality Traits. *Psychological Science* [Online], 26(3), pp.335–340. Available from: `https://doi.org/10.1177/0956797614561800`.

Jacob M. Vigil, 2007. Asymmetries in the Friendship Preferences and Social Styles of Men and Women. *Human Nature*, 18, pp.143–161.

Jeske, D., 2019. *Friendship and Social Media*. Routledge, New York.

John, O.P., Naumann, L.P., and Soto, C.J., 2008. Paradigm shift to the integrative big five trait taxonomy. *Handbook of personality: Theory and research*, 3(2), pp.114–158.

June Price Tangney, 2000. Humility: Theoretical perspectives, empirical fingings and directions for future research. *Journal of Social and Clinical Psychology* [Online], 19(1), pp.70–82. Available from: `https://doi.org/10.1521/jscp.2000.19.1.70`.

Junger, S., 2016. *Tribe: On homecoming and belonging*. Twelve.

Kadushin, C., 1995. Friendship among the French financial elite. *American Sociological Review*, pp.202–221.

Kahneman, D. and Deaton, A., 2010. High income improves evaluation of life but not emotional well-being. *Proceedings of the National Academy of Sciences* [Online], 107(38), p.16489. Available from: `https://doi.org/10.1073/pnas.1011492107`.

Kale, S., 2020-02-11. The wealth gap: how changing fortunes tear close friends apart. *Guardian* [Online]. Available from: `https://www.theguardian.com/lifeandstyle/2020/feb/11/the-wealth-gap-how-changing-fortunes-tear-close-friends-apart`.

Kaplan, R.E., Obert, S.L., and van Buskirk, W.R., 1980. The Etiology of Encounter Group Casualties: "Second Facts". *Human Relations* [Online], 33(2), pp.131–148. Available from: `https://doi.org/10.1177/001872678003300204`.

Kelley, H.H. and Thibaut, J.W., 1978. *Interpersonal relations: A theory of interdependence*. John Wiley & Sons.

Kernan, S., 2020-07-12. A Crumbling Marriage Killed My Childhood Friendship. *Medium* [Online]. Available from: `https://medium.com/@seanjkernan/a-crumbling-marriage-killed-my-childhood-friendship-81455a40f69f`.

Khan, C., 2019-11-15. Our date's in the diary. Now let's see who cancels first. *Guardian*.

Kilduff, M. and Krackhardt, D., 2008. *Interpersonal networks in organizations: Cognition, personality, dynamics, and culture*. Vol. 30. Cambridge University Press.

Kilduff, M. and Lee, J.W., 2020. The integration of people and networks. *Annual Review of Organizational Psychology and Organizational Behavior*, 7, pp.155–179.

Kim, B.J.-H., 2018. *Aristotle on the value of friends*. Dphil. University of Oxford.

Krackhardt, D., 1992. The Strength of Strong Ties: The importance of Philos in Organizations. In: N. Nohria and R.G. Eccles, eds. *Networks and organizations: Structure, form, and action*. Harvard Business School Press Boston, pp.216–239.

Krackhardt, D. and Kilduff, M., 1999. Whether close or far: Social distance effects on perceived balance in friendship networks. *Journal of personality and social psychology*, 76(5), p.770.

Kübler-Ross, E., 2011. *On Death and Dying*. Simon and Schuster.

Kuegler, T., 2020-01-13. Most Of Your Friendships Will Die, I've Learned. *Medium*.

Kuehn, S., Gleich, T., Lorenz, R.C., Lindenberger, U., and Gallinat, J., 2014. Playing Super Mario induces structural brain plasticity: gray matter changes resulting from training with a commercial video game. *Molecular Psychiatry* [Online], 19(2), pp.265–271. Available from: `https://doi.org/10.1038/mp.2013.120`.

Kwon, M., Lee, J.-Y., Won, W.-Y., Park, J.-W., Min, J.-A., Hahn, C., Gu, X., Choi, J.-H., and Kim, D.-J., 2013. Development and Validation of a Smartphone Addiction Scale (SAS). *PLOS ONE* [Online], 8(2), e56936. Available from: `https://doi.org/10.1371/journal.pone.0056936`.

Laertius, D., 1925. Lives of eminent philosophers, translated by RD Hicks. *Loeb Classical Library*, 2, pp.453–455.

LaGaipa, J., 1977. Testing a multidimensional approach to friendship: Theory and practice in interpersonal attraction. In: S. Duck, ed. *Theory and practice in interpersonal attraction*. Academic Pr, pp.249–270.

Lauka, A., McCoy, J., and Firat, R.B., 2018. Mass Partisan Polarization: Measuring a Relational Concept. *American Behavioral Scientist* [Online], 62(1), pp.107–126. Available from: `https://doi.org/10.1177/0002764218759581`.

Launay, J. and Im Dunbar, R., 2015. Playing with strangers: which shared traits attract us most to new people? *PLOS ONE*, 10(6), e0129688.

Layden, E.A., Cacioppo, J.T., and Cacioppo, S., 2018. Loneliness predicts a preference for larger interpersonal distance within intimate space. *PLOS ONE* [Online], 13(9), e0203491. Available from: `https://doi.org/10.1371/journal.pone.0203491`.

Leaver, K., 2019-01-24. Can I still be friends with people who voted Brexit. *Metro* [Online]. Available from: `https://metro.co.uk/2019/01/24/lean-on-me-can-i-still-be-friends-with-people-who-voted-brexit-8378393/`.

Lee, N., 2015-07-01. The Power of Hospitality. *Youtube* [Online]. Available from: `https://youtu.be/j7vCJF0fc7Y`.

Lee, N. and Lee, S., 2000. *The Marriage Book*. Alpha International.

Lee, N. and Lee, S., 2009. *How to relate well*.

Leib, E.J., 2011. *Friend v. Friend: The Transformation of Friendship–and What the Law Has to Do with It*. Oxford University Press.

Lenn Goodman, 1996. Friendship in Aristotle, Miskawayh and al-Ghazali. In: Oliver Leaman, ed. *Friendship East and West*. Routledge, London, pp.164–191.

Lester, H., Mead, N., Gask, L., Chew-Graham, C., and Reilly, S., 2011. An exploration of the value and mechanisms of befriending for older adults in England. *Ageing and Society*, 32(2), pp.307–328.

Levine, T.R., 2014. Truth-default theory (TDT) a theory of human deception and deception detection. *Journal of Language and Social Psychology*, 33(4), pp.378–392.

Lewis, C.S., 1952. *Mere Christianity: copyright CS Lewis Pte Ltd 1942, 1943, 1944, 1952. Used with permission*. Harper Collins.

Lewis, C.S., 1960. *The Four Loves: The Four Loves by CS Lewis © copyright CS Lewis Pte Ltd 1960. Used with permission*. Geoffrey Bles.

Lewis, C.S. and Hooper, W., 1979. *They stand together: the letters of CS Lewis to Arthur Greeves (1914-1963)*. HarperCollins.

Lieberman, M.A., Yalom, I.D., and Miles, M.B., 1972. The Impact of Encounter Groups on Participants: Some Preliminary Findings. *The Journal of Applied Behavioral Science* [Online], 8(1), pp.29–50. Available from: `https://doi.org/10.1177/002188637200800102` .

Lippitt, J., 2007. Cracking the mirror: on Kierkegaard's concerns about friendship. *International Journal for Philosophy of Religion*, 61(3), pp.131–150.

Lippitt, J., 2013. Can a Christian Be a Friend? God, Friendship and Love of Neighbor. In: D. Caluori, ed. *Thinking about Friendship: Historical and Contemporary Philosophical Perspectives*. London: Palgrave Macmillan UK, pp.180–198.

Little, G., 2000. *Friendship: Being ourselves with others*. Scribe Pub.

Liu, I., 2010. Love life: Aristotle on living together with friends. *Inquiry*, 53(6), pp.579–601.

Lo, A., 2019-06-08. Heal the divide and make up with your friends. *SCMP* [Online]. Available from: `https://www.scmp.com/comment/opinion/article/3021695/heal-divide-and-make-your-friends`.

Lott, B. and Lott, A., 1960. The formation of positive attitudes toward group members. *Journal of Abnormal & Social Psychology* [Online], 61(2), pp.297–300. Available from: `https://doi.org/10.1037/h0045778`.

Lusk, J., MacDonald, K., and Newman, J.R., 1998. Resource appraisals among self, friend and leader: Implications for an evolutionary perspective on individual differences. *Personality and Individual Differences*, 24(5), pp.685–700.

MacAskill, W., 2015. *Doing good better: Effective altruism and a radical new way to make a difference*. Guardian Faber Publishing.

MacIntyre, I., Corradetti, P., Roberts, J., Browne, G., Watt, S., and Lane, A., 1999. Pilot study of a visitor volunteer programme for community elderly people receiving home health care. *Health & Social Care in the Community*, 7(3), pp.225–232.

Mahdawi, A., 2020-07-01. My friend won't physically distance – so I will have to distance from her.

Mahdawi, A., 2018-06-20. Netflix addiction is real – we are entertaining ourselves to death. *The Guardian* [Online]. Available from: https://www.theguardian.com/commentisfree/2018/jun/20/netflix-addiction-is-real-we-are-entertaining-ourselves-to-death.

Manson, M., 2018. *5 Levels of Friendship* [Online]. Available from: https://markmanson.net/5-levels-friendship.

Marcel Mauss, 1925. *The Gift*. Routledge, London.

Mark Vernon, 2010. *The Meaning of Friendship*. Palgrave MacMillan.

Marsden, P.V. and Campbell, K.E., 1984. Measuring tie strength. *Social forces*, 63(2), pp.482–501.

Martin, R.A., 2002. Is laughter the best medicine? Humor, laughter, and physical health. *Current Directions in Psychological Science*, 11(6), pp.216–220.

Martina, C.M.S. and Stevens, N.L., 2006. Breaking the cycle of loneliness? Psychological effects of a friendship enrichment program for older women. *Aging & Mental Health* [Online], 10(5), pp.467–475. Available from: https://doi.org/10.1080/13607860600637893.

Masi, C.M., Chen, H.-Y., Hawkley, L.C., and Cacioppo, J.T., 2011. A meta-analysis of interventions to reduce loneliness. *Personality and Social Psychology Review*, 15(3), pp.219–266.

Mathews, K.M., White, M.C., Long, R.G., Soper, B., and Bergen, C.W. von, 1998. Association of indicators and predictors of tie strength. *Psychological Reports*, 83(3_suppl), pp.1459–1469.

Matthews, S.H., 1983. Definitions of Friendship and their Consequences in Old Age. *Ageing and Society* [Online], 3(2), pp.141–155. Available from: https://doi.org/10.1017/S0144686X00009983.

Matthews, S.H., 1986. *Friendships through the life course: Oral biographies in old age*. Vol. 161. SAGE Publications, Incorporated.

Max-Neef, M., Elizalde, A., and Hopenhayn, M., 1992. Development and human needs. *Real-life economics: Understanding wealth creation*, 197, p.213.

McAndrew, F.T. and Milenkovic, M.A., 2002. Of tabloids and family secrets: The evolutionary psychology of gossip 1. *Journal of Applied Social Psychology*, 32(5), pp.1064–1082.

McKay, A.S., Grygiel, P., and Karwowski, M., 2017. Connected to create: A social network analysis of friendship ties and creativity. *Psychology of Aesthetics, Creativity, and the Arts*, 11(3), p.284.

McPherson, M., Smith-Lovin, L., and Cook, J.M., 2001. Birds of a feather: Homophily in social networks. *Annual review of sociology*, 27(1), pp.415–444.

Mead, A., 1992. Review of the development of multidimensional scaling methods. *Journal of the Royal Statistical Society: Series D (The Statistician)*, 41(1), pp.27–39.

Meador, K., 2001-11-16. *A Pattern Of Friendship Series.*

Mehra, A., Kilduff, M., and Brass, D.J., 1998. At the Margins: A Distinctiveness Approach to the Social Identity and Social Networks of Underrepresented Groups. *Academy of Management Journal* [Online], 41(4), pp.441–452. Available from: `https://doi.org/10.2307/257083`.

Merton, R.C., 1968. *Social theory and social structure.* Simon and Schuster.

Miller, D., Rabho, L.A., Awondo, P., Vries, M. de, Duque, M., Garvey, P., Haapio-Kirk, L., Hawkins, C., Otaegui, A., and Walton, S., 2021. *The Global Smartphone: Beyond a Youth Technology*. UCL Press.

Miller, J.R., 1897. *Personal Friendships of Jesus*. New York, US: Thomas Crowell, Company.

Miller, K., 2020. *What is positive gossip?* [Online]. Available from: `https://positivepsychology.com/positive-gossip/`.

Millington, C., 2019. *The Friendship Formula*. Croydon: Head of Zeus Ltd.

Mitsis, P., 2014. *Epicurus' ethical theory: the pleasures of invulnerability*. Cornell University Press.

Mizrahi, L., Shekhidem, H.A., and Stern, S., 2020. Age separation dramatically reduces COVID-19 mortality rate in a computational model of a large population. *Open Biology* [Online], 10(11), p.200213. Available from: `https://doi.org/10.1098/rsob.200213`.

Nakamura, J. and Csikszentmihalyi, M., 2014. The concept of flow. *Flow and the foundations of positive psychology*. Springer, pp.239–263.

Nehamas, A., 2016. *On Friendship*. Basic Books.

Nelson, S., 2016. *Frientimacy*. Seal Press.

Nelson, S., 2020. *The Business of Friendship*. Harper Collins.

Newcomb, T.M., 1961. The acquaintance process as a prototype of human interaction.

Nieboer, A., Lindenberg, S., Boomsma, A., and van Bruggen, A.C., 2005. Dimensions of well-being and their measurement: the SPF-IL scale. *Social indicators research*, 73(3), pp.313–353.

O'Meara, J.D., 1989. Cross-sex friendship: Four basic challenges of an ignored relationship. *Sex roles*, 21(7-8), pp.525–543.

Oldenburg, R., 1999. *The great good place: Cafes, coffee shops, bookstores, bars, hair salons, and other hangouts at the heart of a community*. Da Capo Press.

Oliver Leaman, ed., 1996. *Friendship East and West*. Routledge, London.

Olyan, S.M., 2017. *Friendship in the Hebrew Bible*. Yale University Press.

Oswald, D., Clark, E., and Kelly, C., 2004. Friendship Maintenance: An Analysis of individual and dyad behaviours. *Journal of Social and Clinical Psychology*.

Pahl, R., 2000. *On friendship*. Blackwell Publishing.

Paine, R., 1969. In search of friendship: an exploratory analysis in'middle-class' culture. *Man*, 4(4), pp.505–524.

Pangle, L.S., 2008. *Aristotle and the Philosophy of Friendship*. Cambridge University Press.

Peterson, C. and Seligman, M., 2004. *Character Strengths and Virtues*. Oxford University Press.

Polk, D.M. and Egbert, N., 2013. Speaking the language of love: On whether Chapman's (1992) claims stand up to empirical testing. *The Open Communication Journal*, 7(1).

Polley, M., 2017. *Making Sense of Social Prescribing*. London.

Polley, M. and Whiteside, J., 2020. *What does successful social prescribing look like? Mapping meaningful outcomes*. London.

Poscia, A., Stojanovic, J., La Milia, D.I., Duplaga, M., Grysztar, M., Moscato, U., Onder, G., Collamati, A., Ricciardi, W., and Magnavita, N., 2018. Interventions targeting loneliness and social isolation among the older people: An update systematic review. *Experimental Gerontology* [Online], 102, pp.133–144. Available from: https://doi.org/10.1016/j.exger.2017.11.017.

Putnam, R.D., 2000. *Bowling Alone*. Simon and Schuster.

Rainie, H. and Wellman, B., 2012. *Networked: The new social operating system*. Vol. 419. Mit Press Cambridge, MA.

Rath, T., 2006. *Vital Friends*. Gallup Press.

Rawlins, W.K., 2008. *The compass of friendship: Narratives, identities, and dialogues*. Sage Publications.

Rist, J.M., 1980. Epicurus on Friendship. *Classical Philology* [Online], 75(2), pp.121–129. Available from: www.jstor.org/stable/268919.

Robbins, M.L. and Karan, A., 2020. Who Gossips and How in Everyday Life? *Social Psychological and Personality Science*, 11(2), pp.185–195.

Roberto, K.A. and Kimboko, P.J., 1989. Friendships in Later Life: Definitions and Maintenance Patterns. *The International Journal of Aging and Human Development* [Online], 28(1), pp.9–19. Available from: https://doi.org/10.2190/TQ6K-MATH-8UJT-B265.

Roberts-Griffin, C.P., 2011a. What is a good friend: A qualitative analysis of desired friendship qualities. *Penn McNair Research Journal*, 3(1), p.5.

Roberts-Griffin, C.P., 2011b. What is a good friend: A qualitative analysis of desired friendship qualities. *Penn McNair Research Journal*, 3(1), p.5.

Rodin, M.J., 1978. Liking and disliking: Sketch of an alternative view. *Personality and Social Psychology Bulletin*, 4(3), pp.473–478.

Rosemary Blieszner, 1989. Developmental Processes of Friendship: Older Adult Friendship. In: R.G. Adams and R. Blieszner, eds. *Older adult friendship: Structure and process.* SAGE Publications, Incorporated, pp.108–125.

Rosenbury, L.A., 2007. Friends with benefits. *Mich. L. Rev.*, 106, p.189.

Rouner, L.S., 1994. *The changing face of friendship.* University of Notre Dame Press.

Rusbult, C.E., 1980. Satisfaction and commitment in friendships. *Representative Research in Social Psychology.*

Russell, D., Peplau, L.A., and Cutrona, C.E., 1980. The revised UCLA Loneliness Scale: concurrent and discriminant validity evidence. *Journal of personality and social psychology*, 39(3), p.472.

Russell, D., Peplau, L.A., and Ferguson, M.L., 1978. Developing a measure of loneliness. *Journal of Personality Assessment*, 42(3), pp.290–294.

Russell, D.W., 1996. UCLA Loneliness Scale (Version 3): Reliability, validity, and factor structure. *Journal of Personality Assessment*, 66(1), pp.20–40.

Schaefer, D.R. and Simpkins, S.D., 2014. Using social network analysis to clarify the role of obesity in selection of adolescent friends. *American journal of public health*, 104(7), pp.1223–1229.

Schuler, E. and Brito Dias, C.M.D.S., 2021. Legacies from Great-grandparents to Their Descendants. *Journal of Intergenerational Relationships* [Online], pp.1–18. Available from: https://doi.org/10.1080/15350770.2021.1913275.

Seligman, M., 2004. *Authentic Happiness.* Atria Books.

Seligman, M., 2009. *What You Can Change... and What You Can't*: The Complete Guide to Successful Self-Improvement.* Vintage.

Selley, A., 1986. 'I Have Been, And Ever Shall Be, Your Friend': 'Star Trek', 'The Deerslayer' and the American Romance. *Journal of Popular Culture*, 20(1), p.89.

Seneca, 1917. *Letters to Lucilius* [Online]. Loeb Classical Library, Harvard University Press, Cambridge, MA. Available from: https://en.wikisource.org/wiki/Moral_letters_to_Lucilius/Letter_9.

Shinyashiki, R., 1987. A carícia essencial: uma psicologia do afeto. 9ª edição. *São Paulo: Editora gente.*

Shumway, K., 2018. *The Friendship Formula.* Kyler Shumway.

Siddiqui, M., 2012. *The good Muslim: Reflections on classical Islamic law and theology: Chapter 7: Virtue and Limits in the Ethics of Friendship.* Cambridge University Press.

Sira M., 2020-06-14. The 7 Habits of Truly Charming People. *Medium* [Online]. Available from: https://psiloveyou.xyz/charming-5027bbf67a44.

SIRC, 2006. *Girl Talk - The new rules of female friendship and communication.*

Snyder, M., 1987. *Public appearances, Private realities: The psychology of self-monitoring.* WH Freeman/Times Books/Henry Holt & Co.

Snyder, M., Gangestad, S., and Simpson, J.A., 1983. Choosing friends as activity partners: The role of self-monitoring. *Journal of personality and social psychology*, 45(5), p.1061.

Spencer, L. and Pahl, R., 2006. *Rethinking friendship: Hidden solidarities today.* Princeton University Press.

Sprecher, S. and Regan, P.C., 2002. Liking some things (in some people) more than others: Partner preferences in romantic relationships and friendships. *Journal of Social and Personal Relationships*, 19(4), pp.463–481.

Stevens, N.L., 2001. Combating loneliness: a friendship enrichment programme for older women. *Ageing and Society* [Online], 21(2), pp.183–202. Available from: `https://doi.org/10.1017/S0144686X01008108`.

Steverink, N. and Lindenberg, S., 2006. Which social needs are important for subjective well-being? What happens to them with aging? *Psychology and Aging*, 21(2), p.281.

Stone, A.A., Schwartz, J.E., Broderick, J.E., and Deaton, A., 2010. A snapshot of the age distribution of psychological well-being in the United States. *Proceedings of the National Academy of Sciences* [Online], 107(22), p.9985. Available from: `https://doi.org/10.1073/pnas.1003744107`.

Strozier, C.B., 2016. *Your Friend Forever, A. Lincoln: The Enduring Friendship of Abraham Lincoln and Joshua Speed.* Columbia University Press.

Stutzer, A. and Frey, B.S., 2008. Stress that doesn't pay: The commuting paradox. *Scandinavian Journal of Economics*, 110(2), pp.339–366.

Surijah, E.A. and Kirana, C.T., 2020. Five Love Languages scale factor analysis. *Makara: Human Behavior Studies in Asia.*

Sutcliffe, A.G., Binder, J.F., and Arrow, H., 2012. Relationships and the social brain: Integrating psychological and evolutionary perspectives. *British Journal of Psychology*, 103, pp.149–168.

Tantrika, H., 2020-09-13. What it means to be a drama-free girlfriend. *Medium* [Online]. Available from: `https://psiloveyou.xyz/what-is-drama-free-girlfriend-8962076c391`.

Tasselli, S., Kilduff, M., and Menges, J.I., 2015. The microfoundations of organizational social networks: A review and an agenda for future research. *Journal of Management*, 41(5), pp.1361–1387.

Telushkin, J., 1994. *Jewish wisdom.* William Morrow & Company New York.

Tesch, S.A. and Martin, R.R., 1983. Friendship Concepts of Young Adults in Two Age Groups. *The Journal of Psychology* [Online], 115(1), pp.7–12. Available from: `https://doi.org/10.1080/00223980.1983.9923591`.

Theng, Y.-L., Chua, P.H., and Pham, T.P., 2012. Wii as entertainment and socialisation aids for mental and social health of the elderly. *CHI'12 Extended Abstracts on Human Factors in Computing Systems*, pp.691–702.

Thurnell-Read, T., 2021. *Open Arms: The Role of Pubs in Tackling Loneliness* [Online]. Available from: `https://hdl.handle.net/2134/13663715.v1`.

Toepoel, V., 2013. Ageing, Leisure, and Social Connectedness: How could Leisure Help Reduce Social Isolation of Older People?(Report). *Social indicators research* [Online], 113(1), p.355. Available from: `https://doi.org/10.1007/s11205-012-0097-6`.

Tomlin, G., 2010. *Wealth and Poverty: Sermon*. HTB.

Tomova, L., Wang, K.L., Thompson, T., Matthews, G.A., Takahashi, A., Tye, K.M., and Saxe, R., 2020. Acute social isolation evokes midbrain craving responses similar to hunger. *Nature Neuroscience*, 23(12), pp.1597–1605.

Turkle, S., 2017. *Alone Together*. Basic Books.

van Devender, E., 2020. *The Kind Of Friend You Are, According To Your Myers-Briggs Personality Type & Traits* [Online]. Available from: `https://www.yahoo.com/lifestyle/type-friend-according-myers-briggs-061634055.html`.

van Schaik, C. and Michel, K., 2016. *The good book of human nature: An evolutionary reading of the Bible*. Basic Books.

Vazire, S. and Carlson, E.N., 2011. Others sometimes know us better than we know ourselves. *Current Directions in Psychological Science*, 20(2), pp.104–108.

Vries, B. de, 2018. The unsung bonds of friendship—and caring—among older adults. *Generations: Journal of the American Society on Aging*, 42(3), pp.77–81.

Walton, S. and Swithinbank, H., 2019. *Poverty in the Early Church and Today: A Conversation*. Bloomsbury Academic.

Ware, B., 2012. *The top five regrets of the dying: A life transformed by the dearly departing*. Hay House, Inc.

Wellman, B. and Wortley, S., 1990. Different strokes from different folks: Community ties and social support. *American Journal of Sociology*, 96(3), pp.558–588.

Werner, C. and Parmelee, P., 1979. Similarity of activity preferences among friends: Those who play together stay together. *Social Psychology Quarterly*, pp.62–66.

Wiest, B., 2020-04-30. True Friendship Is Never a Performance. *Medium* [Online]. Available from: `https://humanparts.medium.com/true-friendship-is-never-a-performance-a68c059e4b45`.

Wiking, M., 2019. *The Art of Making Memories*. Penguin Life.

Willis, D. and Clements, B., 2017. *The Simplest Way to Change the World: Biblical Hospitality as a Way of Life*. Moody Publishers.

Xia, N. and Li, H., 2018. Loneliness, social isolation, and cardiovascular health. *Antioxidants & redox signaling*, 28(9), pp.837–851.

Yalom, I., 1975. *The theory and practice of group psychotherapy*. 2d. New York: Basic Books.

Yalom, I., 1980. *Existential Psychotherapy*. Basic Books.

Yalom, M., 2015. *The Social Sex: A History of Female Friendship*. Harper Perennial.

Zahiduzzaman, A.S., 2015. *Toxic Relationship*. AuthorHouse.

Zarbatany, L., Conley, R., and Pepper, S., 2004. Personality and gender differences in friendship needs and experiences in preadolescence and young adulthood. *International Journal of Behavioral Development*, 28(4), pp.299–310.

Zeldin, T., 2000. *Conversation: How talk can change our lives*. HiddenSpring.